# Lecture Notes in Computer Science 13869

Founding Editors

Gerhard Goos

Juris Hartmanis

## Editorial Board Members

The series Lecture Notes in Computer Science (LNCS), including its subseries Lecture Notes in Artificial Intelligence (LNAI) and Lecture Notes in Bioinformatics (LNBI), has established itself as a medium for the publication of new developments in computer science and information technology research, teaching, and education.

LNCS enjoys close cooperation with the computer science R & D community, the series counts many renowned academics among its volume editors and paper authors, and collaborates with prestigious societies. Its mission is to serve this international community by providing an invaluable service, mainly focused on the publication of conference and workshop proceedings and postproceedings. LNCS commenced publication in 1973.

Carina S. González-González ·
Baltasar Fernández-Manjón · Frederick Li ·
Francisco José García-Peñalvo ·
Filippo Sciarrone · Marc Spaniol ·
Alicia García-Holgado · Manuel Area-Moreira ·
Matthias Hemmje · Tianyong Hao
Editors

# Learning Technologies and Systems

21st International Conference on Web-Based Learning, ICWL 2022
and 7th International Symposium on Emerging Technologies for Education, SETE 2022
Tenerife, Spain, November 21–23, 2022
Revised Selected Papers

*Editors*
Carina S. González-González [iD]
Universidad de La Laguna
Tenerife, Spain

Baltasar Fernández-Manjón [iD]
Universidad Complutense de Madrid
Madrid, Spain

Frederick Li [iD]
Durham University
Durham, UK

Francisco José García-Peñalvo [iD]
Universidad de Salamanca
Salamanca, Spain

Filippo Sciarrone [iD]
Mercatorum University
Rome, Italy

Marc Spaniol [iD]
Université de Caen Normandie
Caen, France

Alicia García-Holgado [iD]
University of Salamanca
Salamanca, Spain

Manuel Area-Moreira [iD]
Universidad de La Laguna
Tenerife, Spain

Matthias Hemmje
University of Hagen
Hagen, Germany

Tianyong Hao [iD]
South China Normal University
Guangzhou, China

ISSN 0302-9743 ISSN 1611-3349 (electronic)
Lecture Notes in Computer Science
ISBN 978-3-031-33022-3 ISBN 978-3-031-33023-0 (eBook)
https://doi.org/10.1007/978-3-031-33023-0

This Springer imprint is published by the registered company Springer Nature Switzerland AG
The registered company address is: Gewerbestrasse 11, 6330 Cham, Switzerland

# Preface

This volume presents the contributions of the 21st edition of the annual International Conference on Web-based Learning (ICWL). The first edition of ICWL was held in Hong Kong in 2002. Since then, it has been held 20 more times, on three continents: Melbourne, Australia (2003); Beijing, China (2004); Hong Kong, China (2005, 2011); Penang, Malaysia (2006); Edinburgh, UK (2007); Jinhua, China (2008); Aachen, Germany (2009); Shanghai, China (2010); Sinaia, Romania (2012); Kenting, Taiwan (2013); Tallinn, Estonia (2014); Guangzhou, China (2015); Rome, Italy (2016); Cape Town, South Africa (2017); Chiang Mai, Thailand (2018); Magdeburg, Germany (2019); Ningbo, China (2020); Macao, China (2021). This year, ICWL 2022 was held on 21–23 November in San Cristobal de La Laguna, Tenerife, Spain, organized by University of La Laguna, Spain.

Furthermore, the conference continued the traditional initiative, started by ICWL 2016, of holding the 7th International Symposium on Emerging Technologies for Education (SETE) at the same location. SETE collected the traditional workshop activities managed by ICWL in the past years and additionally was organized in tracks. Workshops and tracks added new and hot topics on technology-enhanced learning, providing a better overall conference experience to the ICWL and SETE attendees.

The topics proposed in the ICWL&SETE Call for Papers included several relevant issues, ranging from Semantic Web for E-Learning, through Learning Analytics, Computer-Supported Collaborative Learning, Assessment, Pedagogical Issues, E-learning Platforms, and Tools, to Mobile Learning. Due to the impact of the COVID-19 pandemic, we decided to combine papers from ICWL 2022 and SETE 2022 into one proceedings volume this year.

We received 82 submitted contributions for ICWL&SETE 2022. All of the submitted papers were assigned to three members of the Program Committee (PC) for peer review. All reviews were checked and discussed by the PC chairs, and additional reviews or meta-reviews were elicited if necessary. Finally, we accepted 50 full and short papers for ICWL&SETE 2022 with an acceptance rate of 62.50%.

In addition to regular papers, ICWL&SETE 2022 also featured a set of special workshops and tracks:

- The 5th International Workshop on Educational Technology for Language Learning (ETLL 2022).
- The 6th International Symposium on User Modeling and Language Learning (UMLL 2022).
- Digitalization in Language and Cross-Cultural Education.
- 1st Workshop on Hardware and Software Systems as Enablers for Lifelong Learning (HASSELL).
- Immersive Web-Learning Experience Development in the Metaverse Era.

We would like to sincerely thank our keynote and invited speakers:

- Davinia Hernández Leo is a Full Professor and Serra Húnter Fellow at the Department of Information and Communication Technologies, Universitat Pompeu Fabra. She was born in Plasencia, and obtained a degree and a Ph.D. in Telecommunication Engineering at University of Valladolid, Spain. She is former associate editor for IEEE Transactions on Learning Technologies, former Vice-President of the European Association on Technology-Enhanced Learning, and is currently a member of the CSCL Committee within the International Society of the Learning Sciences, a member of the ijCSCL editorial board and of the steering committee of the European Conference on Technology-Enhanced Learning. Title: "Effective web-based collaborative teaching and learning".
- Alicia García-Holgado obtained a degree in Computer Sciences and a Ph.D. from the University of Salamanca, Spain. She is an Associate Professor in the Computer Science Department and member of the GRIAL Research Group of the University of Salamanca. She is also a member of the Women in Computing Committee of the Spanish Computing Scientific Society and sub-coordinator of the CLEI (Latin American Centre for Computer Science Studies) Community for Latin American women in computing. Title: "Gender, diversity and engineering education".
- Manuel Castro received an Industrial Engineering degree and Ph.D. in engineering from ETSII/Madrid Polytechnic University, Spain. He is currently a Professor of electronics technology and the Director of the Electrical and Computer Engineering Department at UNED. He is a member of the Board of Directors (BoD) of the IEEE, as the Division VI Director from 2019 to 2020, a member of the Administration Committee and Board of Governors (AdCOM/BoG) from 2005 to 2021. Title: "Educating online/remote Future Engineering Leaders with Practical Competences".
- Ruth Cobos is an Associate Professor in the Department of Computer Science at Universidad Autónoma de Madrid (UAM). She received her M.Sc. and Ph.D. degrees in Computer Engineering from UAM. She is the Principal Investigator from UAM of the eMadrid Research Network and of the Spanish Network of Learning Analytics – SNOLA. Title: "Learning Analytics Applications in e-Learning".

Many contributions made the conference possible and successful. First of all, we would like to thank all the authors who considered ICWL&SETE for their submission. We thank the PC members, and the additional reviewers, for their evaluations, which made the selection of the accepted papers possible.

We thank the sponsor Springer, for the enlightened and much appreciated support that helped us to dedicate the Best Paper Awards. Furthermore, we also thank the Women@Inf project (Ref. 21/1ACT/21), funded by the Institute of Women from the Spanish Ministry of Equality.

We expect that the ideas that have emerged in ICWL&SETE 2022 will result in the development of further innovations for the benefit of scientific, industrial, and social communities. We hope that the reader of this volume will be pleased by the relevance of the topics and contents of the papers, and thus be enticed to contribute to the next editions of ICWL&SETE.

Carina S. González-González
Baltasar Fernández-Manjón
Frederick Li
Francisco José García-Peñalvo
Filippo Sciarrone
Marc Spaniol
Alicia García-Holgado
Manuel Area Moreira
Matthias Hemmje
Tianyong Hao

# Organization

## ICWL 2022. International Conference on Web-based Learning

### General Conference Co-chairs

| | |
|---|---|
| Carina S. González-González | Universidad de La Laguna, Spain |
| Baltasar Fernandez Manjon | Universidad Complutense de Madrid, Spain |
| Frederick Li | Durham University, UK |

### Program Committee Co-chairs

| | |
|---|---|
| Alicia García-Holgado | Universidad de Salamanca, Spain |
| Manuel Area Moreira | Universidad de La Laguna, Spain |
| Matthias Hemmje | University of Hagen, Germany |

### Steering Committee Representatives

| | |
|---|---|
| Qing Li | Hong Kong Polytechnic University, Hong Kong SAR, China |
| Marco Temperini | Sapienza University of Rome, Italy |

### Publicity Chairs

| | |
|---|---|
| Bernardo Candela San Juan | Universidad de La Laguna, Spain |
| Carlos González Ruiz | Universidad de La Laguna, Spain |

### Local Organization Co-chairs

| | |
|---|---|
| Cándido Caballero Gil | Universidad de La Laguna, Spain |
| José Luis Sánchez de la Rosa | Universidad de La Laguna, Spain |

### Web Chair

| | |
|---|---|
| Eduardo Nacimiento García | Universidad de La Laguna, Spain |

## Finance Chairs

Pedro A. Toledo Delgado          Universidad de La Laguna, Spain
Lucía García-Holgado           Universidad de Salamanca, Spain

# SETE 2022. International Symposium on Emerging Technologies for Education

## General Conference Co-chairs

Francisco J. García Peñalvo        Universidad de Salamanca, Spain
Filippo Sciarrone            Universitas Mercatorum, Italy
Marc Spaniol             Caen-Normandy University, France
Carina S. González González       Universidad de La Laguna, Spain

## Program Committee Co-chairs

Alicia García-Holgado          Universidad de Salamanca, Spain
Tianyong Hao             South China Normal University, China

## Workshop Chair

Luigi Laura              International Telematic University Uninettuno,
                  Italy

## Steering Committee Representatives

Qing Li               Hong Kong Polytechnic University, Hong Kong
                  SAR, China
Marco Temperini            Sapienza University of Rome, Italy

## Publicity Chairs

Bernardo Candela San Juan        Universidad de La Laguna, Spain
Carlos González Ruiz          Universidad de La Laguna, Spain

## Local Organization Co-chairs

Jezabel Molina Gil                      Universidad de La Laguna, Spain
José María del Castillo-Olivares        Universidad de La Laguna, Spain

## Web Chair

Eduardo Nacimiento García              Universidad de La Laguna, Spain

## Finance Chairs

Pedro A. Toledo Delgado                 Universidad de La Laguna, Spain
Lucía García-Holgado                    Universidad de Salamanca, Spain

## Organization

**Collaborators**

Instituto Universitario de
Estudios de las Mujeres
Universidad de La Laguna

WOMEN@INF

# Designing a Game-Based Learning Environment for College Students' Campus Learning (Keynote)

Yi Hsuan Wang ⓘ

Department of Educational Technology, Tamkang University, Taipei Taiwan
annywang12345@hotmail.com

**Abstract.** The study adopted the game-based learning strategy into designing an online educational game to help college students familiarize themselves with school campus. The paper introduced the game design and discussed the game elements and principles considered during the game development. A group of students were invited to use the game and the learning performance and feedback from interview were collected for game evaluation. Overall, the findings showed that students had improved their performance after the gameplay and gave positive feedback on the game design. Future work of the study was discussed in the end of the paper.

**Keywords:** Game-based learning · Game design · Higher education

## 1 Introduction

Studies revealed that using learning technology sustains learners' motivation and learning engagement [2, 3]. The game-based way offers rich resources for situation learning [7] and thus it is also one way that attracting attention from researchers. The uses of game could be viewed as scaffolding [8] since it allows learners to do try-and-error and to achieve self-regulated learning during play. The learners set the goal and monitor the goal achievement through self-directed learning during gameplay. In a game-based learning scenario, learners can experience a wide range of ways to solve the learning tasks, and which help students to achieve better learning motivation, engagement, and adaptivity [6] as well. What make the game interesting is the processes that gamers to struggle toward the goal. Overly simple or difficult game task design will reduce gameplay experience and learning effectiveness [4, 5].

The game design is an important issue since it will affect learning results [1]. Schell [9] proposed four elements in game design which are authentic, story, mechanics, and technologies. Aesthetic is how the game looks or feels like, story is the sequence of events that support the game, mechanics is the goal of the game and what and how the learners can do and happen, and technology refers to the tools and systems used to implement or deliver the gameplay. These elements determine the goal of the game, the sequence of events that support the game, how a learner feel and experience the game, and what medium that make the game possible. Each element is important and influence each other powerfully.

**Research Purpose**

Hence, considering the benefits and potential of integrating a game-based environment for learning and the game design elements proposed by Schell (2014), this preliminary study aims to firstly explore how to design the game following the four game elements and secondly to understand college students' learning performance and perceptions of using the developed game for campus learning.

## 2  Game Design

The purpose of the game was to help college students become familiar with the campus, learn the policies and service that fresh students have to know. The game design based on Schell's four elements were described as followed and the print screen of the game was presented in Table 1.

**Story:** The game started with an animation which described a story about a monument of a university was stolen, and learners had to find out who were the possible criminals.

**Authenticity:** The game characters were created in cartoon style. The game background was designed following to the real world set up. The game map and locations of the buildings of the school were created according to the real campus environment as well.

**Technologies:** The game was developed based on Html5 website to let learners access to the game more easily. The learners can login to the game with Internet connection with their personal computers for game interaction.

**Mechanism:** The game missions and story branch were designed in the games. The learners' answers will be recorded in the game, they will experience various game scenario and get various game results according to their game scores and choose.

## 3  Game Evaluation

The game evaluation was conducted in a computer-based classroom environment. A total of 17 students in the first year of college were invited to test the game, and they had to finish the pre-test and post-test before and after the game evaluation. The items in the tests were related to the problems that students met on the campus in the game. The contents of the pre-test and post-test were the same, but the sequence was changed. The learner's interview was conducted after the post-test for collecting learners' feedback of the game.

**Table 1.** The print screen of the game with description.

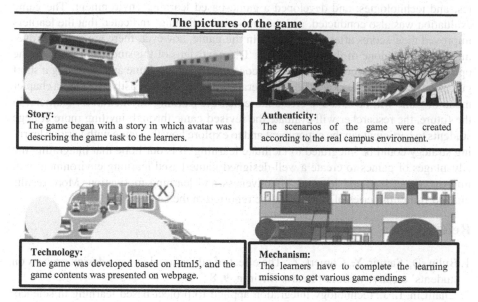

| The pictures of the game |
|---|
| **Story:** The game began with a story in which avatar was describing the game task to the learners. | **Authenticity:** The scenarios of the game were created according to the real campus environment. |
| **Technology:** The game was developed based on Html5, and the game contents was presented on webpage. | **Mechanism:** The learners have to complete the learning missions to get various game endings |

The results of the paired samples *t*-tests (Table 2) indicated that the learners showed a significant difference between the pre-test and post-test, and they improved their learning performance after the gameplay (p=0.00 < 0.05). Some valuable suggestions for revising the game were also collected from the interview section. In general, the students gave positive feedback on the game experience, but some students mentioned that the operational design could be improved. For example, the learners revealed that it is not so user-friendly to use "O" ,"Q" or "Shift" keys in the keyboard to control the game. They suggested to use "Enter" or "Space" keys for main game interaction. Besides, they also suggested to add a game menu so that they can choice different chapters of game to achieve more flexible game interaction.

**Table 2.** Paired Samples t-tests

|  | Mean | S.D | t | p |
|---|---|---|---|---|
| Pre-test | 69.41 | 11.710 | -6.452 | . 000 |
| Pos-test | 87.35 | 7.729 |  |  |

# 4   Discussion and Results

The study aims to create a game-based learning scenario to help college students exploring their school through gameplay and furthermore to become familiar with the school environment. This study referred to the four game elements, authentic, story, mechanics, and technologies, and developed a game-based learning environment. The game evaluation was also conducted, and the preliminary findings indicated that the learners improved their scores after participating in the game, however, there are still improvements could be done of the game design. The next steps of the study will improve the operational design through changing the control keys of the game and including a short guideline to help learners know how to interact with game more easily. Besides, a chapter menu of game will be added to create more flexible learning interaction for learners. In the future, the researcher will evaluate the revised game through inviting more college students to participate in the experiment and to explore how the game with various learning strategy could be integrated to facilitate learning. It is our hope that integrating the advantages of games to create a well-designed game-based learning environment will improve target learners' learning effectiveness and learning motivation. More results yielded from this series of studies will be reported in the near future.

# References

1. Bulut, D., Samur, Y., Cömert, Z.: The effect of educational ga1 me design process on students' creativity. Smart Learn. Environ. **9**, 8
2. ChanLin, L. J.:Technology integration applied to project-based learning in science. Innovations Educ. Teach. Int. **45**(1), 55–65 (2008)
3. Chen, P., McGrath, D.: Moments of joy: student engagement and conceptual learning in the design of hypermedia documents. J. Res. Technol. Educ. **35**(3), 402–22 (2003)
4. Costikyan, G.: I Have No Words & I Must Design, Toward a Critical Vocabulary for Computer Games. In F. Mäyrä (ed.) CDGC Conference Proceedings, pp. 9–33, Tampere, Tampere University Press (2002)
5. Crawford, C.: The Art of Computer Game Design. Available at: https://www.vancou ver.wsu.edu/fac/peabody/game-book/Coverpage.html (25.12.2003) (1982)
6. Plass, J.L., Homer, B.D., Kinzer, C.K.: Foundations of Game-Based Learning, Educ. Psychol. **50**(4), 258–283 (2015)
7. Piirainen-Marsh, A., Tainio, L.: Collaborative game-play as a site for participation and situated learning of a second language. Scandinavian J. Educ. Res. **53**(2), 167–183 (2009)
8. Reich, S.M., Korobkova, K.A., Black, R.W., Sumaroka, M.: Hey! Can you show me how to do this?": Digital Games Mediating Family Interactions. Children's virtual play worlds: Culture, learning and participation, Burke, A. & Marsh, J. (eds). New York, NY: Peter Lang. (2013)
9. Schell, J.: The art of game design: A book of lenses. CRC Press, 2014. ISBN-13: 978-1466598645 (2014)

# Contents

**The 5th International Workshop on Educational Technology for
Language Learning (ETLL 2022)**

**The 6th International Symposium on User Modeling and Language
Learning (UMLL 2022)**

**Digitalization in Language and Cross-Cultural Education**

# ICWL 2022. International Conference on Web-based Learning

# Digital Divide, Local and Global? Surveying Augmented Reality Educational Usage in Europe and South America

Matthias Heintz[1](✉) ⓘ, Effie L.-C. Law[2] ⓘ, Santawat Thanyadit[2] ⓘ, Hernan Nina[3],
and Pamela Andrade[1]

[1] University of Leicester, Leicester LE1 7RH, UK
{mmh21,pyas2}@leicester.ac.uk
[2] Durham University, Durham DH1 3LE, UK
{wsnv42,mdpd63}@durham.ac.uk
[3] Universidad de Lima, Santiago de Surco 15023, Peru
HNINAHA@ulima.edu.pe

**Abstract.** Augmented Reality (AR) has the potential to enhance students' learning experiences. To deploy AR as educational tool, access to the requisite infrastructure and readiness of teachers are basic conditions to be met. The lack thereof is the digital divide that can undermine the opportunity and ability to use AR educational applications (AREAs) for students and teachers. Such issues were identified in a survey with a sample of European teachers on their educational usage of AR. We aimed to study the digital divide more globally by running the same survey with teachers in South America. We collected 123 valid responses from ten South American countries. Comparing the results of the two datasets showed that the teachers sampled from both continents were facing the challenges of the digital divide to utilise AREAs. We discussed how these challenges could be addressed to allow both, teachers and students, to benefit from AR as educational tool.

**Keywords:** Augmented Reality · Educational Technology · Digital Divide

## 1 Introduction

The three basic characteristics of Augmented Reality (AR) technology - combining real and virtual content, being interactive in real-time, and registering objects in 3D [1] - make it a potentially powerful educational tool. AR is typically utilized to visualize scientific concepts, which are difficult to explain in 2D (e.g., geometric shapes [2]), in an interactive 3D environment. Deploying AR educational applications (AREAs) can enrich the learning experience, given the immersive and engaging feeling they support (e.g., [3]). Thanks to advances in mobile technology, the number of AREAs has notably increased in a range of contexts and their benefits for students and their learning have been evaluated quite extensively (e.g., [4, 5]).

Nevertheless, there exist only a handful of studies focusing on teachers' views on deploying AREAs (e.g., [6, 7]). One salient concern identified in those studies was that

---

The original version of this chapter was revised: the fourth author name of Hernan Nina was misspelled. The correction to this chapter is available at
https://doi.org/10.1007/978-3-031-33023-0_50

the teacher participants involved had limited experience in using AR applications. To understand this phenomenon better, we designed and conducted a survey to analyse the usage of AREAs from the teacher perspective. Based on the survey responses from a sample of European teachers [8, 9], we argued that one reason for the observed scale of inexperienced AR users among teachers was the lack of the requisite infrastructure, including availability of mobile devices (e.g., smartphones, tablets) and broad bandwidth for accessing web-based AR contents. This resonates with the recurrent theme of the *digital divide*, which has been exacerbated during the pandemic [10].

Indeed, the digital divide is a worldwide phenomenon [11] in the Global North (e.g., Europe) and in the Global South (e.g., South America). As the target group of our previous survey was teachers from the former [9], we were motivated to replicate the same survey with their counterparts in the latter to find out to what extent the results would be similar or different and if we could find indications for the digital divide.

Overall, the research goals of our work presented in this paper are twofold: (1) To draw comparisons between the sample of teachers from Europe with their counterparts from South America regarding their usage and experience with AREAs; (2) To identify whether the digital divide has been a significant barrier for the adoption of AREAs in the European and South American countries where the data were gathered.

## 2   Related Work

**AR in Education.**  AR has evolved from its early cumbersome frameworks in the 1960s to today's lightweight models [12]. Nevertheless, scientific publications on AREAs only emerged in the year 2000, as shown by a search in the database Scopus. Research efforts in AREAs have been stimulated by the facts that AR tools enable learners to perceive and manipulate abstract concepts in 3D (e.g., anatomical objects), which are less intuitive to understand in 2D (e.g., [13, 14]). In addition, AREAs support multisensory interactions, eliciting positive emotional experience such as fun in learners and thus contributing to positive learning effects (e.g., [3, 15]).

Despite its relative short history, several systematic literature reviews (SLRs) on AREAs have been published since 2000 (e.g., [4, 16, 17]). These SLRs drew a consistent conclusion regarding the educational efficacy of AREAs - the use of AR could result in learning gain to a moderate extent with enhanced motivation being the significant mediating variable. Nonetheless, only a few SLRs address the usability and user experience [18], despite the relevance of these qualities for the acceptance and adoption of AREAs. We were then motivated to perform an SLR with this specific focus [19]. Through the critical analysis of 48 papers, we identified common usability problems across different AREAs, including cognitive and sensory overload, frustrations caused by poor usability and other technical glitches (e.g., unstable GPS signals for location-based AREAs). Above all, considerable costs for equipment (e.g., head-mounted devices) and content development were consistently reported as barriers for the uptake of AREAs, highlighting the severity of the impact of the digital divide in this area.

**Digital Divide.**  The term was first officially used in 1999 in a governmental document in the US [20]. Accordingly, the digital divide is defined as those who have access to information and communication technologies (ICTs) as opposed to those who have not. It has been broadened to consider patterns of usage and levels of skills that enable users to enhance the quality of life through ICT [21]. Other definitions and synonyms have been put forward in the last two decades. For instance, solutions on closing the divide (e.g., by building infrastructure or improving interaction design) [22], or discipline-specific frameworks (e.g., sociological on social capitals; psychological on attitudes towards digital media) were variably used to justify how the digital divide can be defined [21]. In an increasingly digital age, those who are not engaging effectively with the digital world are at risk of being left behind. The digital divide can be examined at different levels, within and across communities, countries, or regions. The term *global digital divide* typically refers to studying how the extent of the divide differs between Global North and South (or variously known as Majority and Minority World Countries) in quantifiable measures [11]. Negative impacts of the digital divide were exacerbated during the pandemic, given the heavy reliance on online education [23]. In fact, the lack of access to equipment for utilising AR-based tools, while not yet the mainstream educational tools, might have further deprived disadvantaged learners of the learning opportunities to master complex concepts.

## 3　Methodology

Surveys are a very powerful and widely used research method for collecting a relatively large volume of data within a short period of time [24]. Based on the lessons learned from the data collection with European teachers [8, 9], e.g., missing out on data from teachers who had never used AR for teaching, we slightly adjusted the original survey by adding items for non-experienced AR teachers while leaving the core items intact to enable comparisons. All items were translated into Spanish. No time constraint was imposed on completing the survey. All participants were fully anonymous and voluntary without any compensation. Ethics approvals were obtained.

**Teacher Survey.** The survey is composed of three sections. After the Introduction page that provides the background information about the purpose of the survey and requests the participant's consent for data collection and analysis, the first section asks 6 questions on demographic and general information.

The second section asks the teachers about their general use of AR. If the participant has experience in teaching with AR, there are 10 questions asking about this experience. If the teacher has no prior experience teaching with AR, there are 7 questions about their expectations for AR.

In section three, teachers with past AR teaching experience are asked 12 questions about the most recent AR application they used for teaching to collect contextualised data about the setting and experience with reference to that particular AR application.

The survey ran from February to June 2022 with pauses in between (e.g., school holidays). Altogether 663 visits to the website were registered, 516 of which ended immediately (visit duration less than a second) while 21 browsed the survey a bit longer but for some unknown reasons they did not proceed further. Three records from Spain had to be discarded. There were 123 valid responses; 77 of which were full responses. The number of full responses from the European sample was 65.

The Spanish responses were translated into English for analysis. Details about the European results with which the South American results were compared in the following sections can be found in our previous publications covering the European survey [8, 9]. Due to the space limit, we cannot present the results of all questions or go into detail about the responses. We therefore focus on the responses that allow us to draw comparisons between the two datasets and that provide insights for addressing our research goals (Sect. 1). Specifically, we do not report on the analysis results of the additional questions about non-experienced AR participants' *expectations* for using AR in teaching. For the same reason we also do not present the detailed analysis of responses from participants who did not use AR for teaching before. However, we refer to them, where possible, to further support our findings.

## 4 Results

### 4.1 Quantitative Data Analysis

#### Section 1: Demographics

**Role.** Of the 107 responses nearly half were secondary school teachers (n = 52), about 16.8% were primary school teachers (n = 18), and nearly 7.5% were teachers at an infant/junior school (n = 8). From the 29 remaining participants who selected the answer option "other" and specified their role, the majority were a "College/University/HE professor" (n = 19, about 17.3% of all respondents).

In comparison with our European dataset, where we only had two teachers with "other" roles, which both worked in education colleges, the participants were more diverse in the South American dataset. The percentage of primary school teachers compared to secondary and infant/junior school teachers was higher within the European teacher sample. Nonetheless, as both datasets involved a range of roles, they provided representative data about the needs, expectations, and opinions of teachers.

**Gender.** The gender ratio of this sample was 69 female to 38 male. This ratio of 1.8 was slightly more balanced as compared with 2.1 of the European sample with 44 female and 21 male.

**Age.** Regarding the age distribution of our South American sample, it was similar to the European one; a difference was that the former involved teachers younger than 31 years: 21–30 (n = 8), 31–40 (n = 25), 41–50 (n = 40), 51–60 (n = 27), >60 (n = 7).

**Country of Residence.** The responses were from ten South American countries. The highest number was from Peru (n = 72) where the main contact (the fourth author) was located. Others included Colombia (n = 10), Mexico (n = 5), Ecuador (n = 4) and Brazil (n = 3). The remaining countries were represented by a single participant (n = 1): Chile, Costa Rica, Nicaragua, Tawantinsuyo, and Venezuela. One did not specify it.

This pattern matches what we already saw in the responses to our European survey: Some countries had several participants whereas some had only one (see Sect. 5.3).

**Main Teaching Subject.** Languages (n = 21), Mathematics (n = 18), and Arts & Humanities (n = 17) were the three most reported teaching subjects, followed by Computing (n = 10), Natural Sciences (n = 9), Primary levels (multiple) (n = 8), Communication (n = 8), Physical Education (n = 5), Music (n = 2), and Accounting (n = 1). Ten comments could not be classified because the subject specification was unclear.

Similar to what was reported by the European teachers, the majority of the subjects taught by their counterparts in South America were STEM.

**Teaching Experience.** The teaching experience of our participants ranges from 0 to 44 years, with an average of 17.67 (SD = 10.32). This is very similar to the experience reported by the European teachers (Mean = 17.2, SD = 7.02, Range = 4–45).

## Section 2: General Experience with AR for Teaching

**AR for Teaching.** Of the 101 respondents 39 have used AR in general whereas 62 have not used AR before at all. 56.4% of the teachers who have used AR in general did so for teaching (n = 22), the remaining 17 used it for the following non-learning activities: Entertainment (n = 6; e.g., "For entertainment, but I love the idea of using it for teaching" (T124)), Exploring AR (n = 5; e.g., "To view and review some educational material" (T77)), Research & Development (n = 3; e.g., "Software test in demonstrations" (T113)), Training (n = 2), and Shopping (n = 1). All the teachers who had not used AR for their teaching before and replied to the question of why not (n = 71), indicated that they would be interested to do so and 95.8% (n = 68) of them thought their students would benefit from learning with AR.

These questions were added for the South American survey, so we cannot compare the results with those of the European sample.

**Reason.** When asked why they had used AR in their teaching, 13 of the 20 participants chose "out of curiosity", three chose "colleagues recommending it" and another three "students recommending it". Only one chose "following the guidelines given by our Ministry of Education". Six participants had other reasons such as keeping up to date with technology (T589) and innovate learning (T478).

When comparing those answers with the responses from the European sample we found some commonalities in curiosity being the main driving force for all responding teachers, followed by recommendations by colleagues and students. However, in the European dataset, the recommendation by other teachers played a slightly bigger role (n = 12) than by students (n = 8). Whereas only one South American teacher followed official guidelines to use AR in their teaching, six did so in the European sample.

**Usage Statistics.** Regarding how long they had used AR in their teaching, six of the 20 participants said they had used it for more than 4 years (n = 6, 30%), followed by 1–2 years (n = 5, 25%) and less than a year (n = 3, 15%) as well as 3–4 years (n = 3, 15%).

These responses were in stark contrast with those of the European teachers, where most had used AR only for a short duration and the least number of participants had used it for more than four years.

Asked about how often the teachers used AR in their teaching, the majority (n = 8, 40%) was moderately active using it monthly (n = 4) or every three month (n = 4). More active were 30% who used AR weekly (n = 3) or every two weeks (n = 3). The remaining 30% were less active and only used AR every six months (n = 3), yearly (n = 2) or sporadically "in projects" (T499) (n = 1). The usage duration in one continuous period ranged from 8 min to 120 min and was on average 55.4 min (SD = 38.78).

Although most of the European teachers were also moderately active (45%), a lot less (only 17%) were considered active AR users, using AR weekly or fortnightly. More (38%) were considered less active users. Hence, our datasets suggest that South American teachers who use AR do so more actively than their European counterparts.

**(Increased) Usage.** Asked if they would like to use AR more often for their teaching all 20 respondents answered yes, whereas in the European dataset 6% each did not want to do so or were unsure.

Regarding the question what they would need to increase their usage of AR for teaching, most teachers picked that they would need to "know which AR apps are suitable" (n = 13, 65%), followed by "better access to AR hardware" (n = 10, 50%), and "more help to use AR apps" (n = 9, 45%). Only a few teachers need to "find the time" (n = 3, 15%) or expressed other needs (n = 3) such as "adaptation of curricula" (T131).

Two major differences can be seen when comparing these responses with the ones from the European teachers sampled. On the one hand, finding the time seemed not to be an issue for the South American teachers sampled, whereas it was a major problem for the European teachers. On the other hand, having better access to hardware, which was the biggest concern for the European teachers, was not the biggest problem for the South American teachers. For the latter it would be more important to learn about suitable apps (the second biggest issue for the European teachers).

**Hardware.** For the hardware used when teaching with AR, most teachers used smartphones (n = 17, 85%), followed by desktop or laptop computers with webcams (n = 11, 55%), and Tablets (n = 6, 30%). When comparing these responses it became apparent that the European teachers had more tablets to be used for AR teaching and in some cases even game consoles or VR (virtual reality) glasses to which the South American teachers did not have access for their teaching.

**School Setting.** Responses to the question on how many devices schools provided to support teaching with AR indicated that laptops with webcam were most commonly provided (mean = 31.35, SD = 91.75, range = 0–408). The other devices included tablets (mean = 12.75, SD = 24.93, range = 0–100), smartphones (mean = 10.5, SD = 29.32, range = 0–130), and desktops with cameras (mean = 7.6, SD = 12.31, range = 0–40). Two teachers reported that students used their own devices. When comparing those values with the European ones the differences were quite substantial. Desktop was the only device type where the South American schools provided more (mean = 3.0, SD = 6.7, range = 0–30, for the European sample). For all other device types the European schools provided more on average (44 laptops, 38 tablets, and 22 smartphones).

On average the South American teachers reported 26.8 students per class in their school (SD = 11.16, range = 10–60), which was slightly higher than the 23 students per class reported by the European teachers. However, that would mean that they would need even more devices if they wanted to provide one for each student in their class.

**Confidence in Using AR for Teaching.** Nine respondents reported a medium level of confidence (45%) and seven high (35%). Only a few (n = 2, 10%) teachers reported a low level of confidence, and only one respondent each (5%) was at each end of the scale with a very low or very high level of confidence.

In comparison, the European teachers showed similar confidence levels but with a slight shift towards the positive end of the scale, with fewer "medium" (36.92%), a few more "high" (36.92%), and a lot more "very high" (10.77%) responses.

### Section 3: Most Recent AR Usage for Teaching

In response to the question, "When did you last use this app?", 87.5% of the South American teachers reported they had used an AR application to teach at least once in the last year. This ratio was comparable to that of their European counterparts (81.5%).

Informatics, mathematics, biology, and physics were the most prevalent subjects covered by AR apps. It was comparable to the European results that the AR apps were predominantly on STEM. Some domains, including foreign language learning, history, art, music, physical education, and PBIS (positive behaviour intervention and support), were covered in the apps used by the European teachers sampled, but not their South American counterparts.

The participants reported that they had used AR applications with students of various ages, ranging from 17+ years old (37.5%), followed by 11–13 years old (31.3%) and 14–16 years old (25%). In contrast, for the European sample.11–13 years old (43%) was the dominant group whereas 17+ was the least (9.2%).

With regard to the usage methods, the most common one was the teacher presenting the AR app to the class (n = 9, 37.5%). The other options were students working individually with a device each (n = 7, 29.2%), students working in groups sharing a device (n = 6, 25%), and students working in groups with each of them having a device (n = 2, 8.3%). Similar patterns were observed in the European sample. These results lent further evidence to the issue of the inadequate infrastructural support provided by schools.

### 4.2 Qualitative Data Analysis

For the qualitative results collected with the South American survey, we performed thematic analysis, using the coding scheme for the European data [8, 9] as the basic framework and modifying it in the analysis process when new codes emerged.

**Needs to Increase AR Usage.** When asked about their needs to increase the usage of AR in their teaching, 19 participants elaborated. Most of them (n = 12) expressed a **need of training**. Some teachers requested to learn which apps are available and how to use them, e.g., "Training and information related to AR linked to secondary education." (T131). Others wanted to go even further and learn, how to create content themselves, e.g., "I would not only like to use AR content, but also be a content creator. Know what other platforms to use to create experiences" (T367). This corroborates the most selected quantitative answer option "know which AR apps are suitable". Some teachers (n = 4) reported **financial constraints** leading to issues, like "Lack of ICT equipment and Internet connectivity" (T374). The same number of teachers (n = 4) described the need for **quality materials**, e.g., "The applications must be adjusted to the objective of the class and the thematic field." (T327). Teachers (n = 2) also reiterated the **restrictions** as the need to "find the time", e.g., "More time to prepare classes" (T262). Surprisingly, unlike the European teachers, who sometimes asked for **technical improvements**, none of the South American teachers did so.

Compared to the European teachers, the South American teachers focused much more on expressing their need for training, which they mentioned about three times as often as financial constraints and quality materials, whereas those three issues were mentioned at similar levels by the European teachers. In contrast to the European teachers, who expressed some unique restrictions, the South American teachers only repeated and thus emphasised the time issues.

**Improvement Suggestions.** When it comes to the question of how AR applications could be changed to further improve the teachers' confidence in using AR in their teaching, the comments were coded based on the categories **access**, **training**, **content**, and **technical enhancement**. As for the question about their needs to use more AR in their teaching, again most of the teachers (n = 7) articulated a need for **training**, e.g., "Learn about more tools to create AR elements" (T478). The other responses were related to *access* (n = 4; e.g., "Enabling access from basic devices" (T495)) and *technical enhancement* (n = 4; e.g., "Looking for those that can work offline" (T374)). The least number of teachers made comments related to *content* (n = 2; e.g., "With content structured to use this technology." (T80)). Two teachers commented that no changes would be necessary.

In comparison to their European counterparts, the South American teachers emphasized training more than content (which was commented on the most in the European survey but the least in the South American one). This is in line with the pattern noticed in the quantitative responses regarding the teachers' needs to increase AR usage in teaching. While the number of comments on *technical enhancement* was more than double that on *access* in the European results (14 to 6 respectively), they are on the same level in the South American results. This again is in line with the results to the earlier questions about increasing AR usage in teaching, where no technical improvements were mentioned by the South American teachers at all.

**Rating of most Recently used AR App.** Regarding the question how the app could be improved to better support their teaching, most teachers expressed their need for **training or instructions** (n = 6; e.g., "Receive training and/or advice." (T166)). The category with the second most comments was **technical improvements** (n = 5; e.g., "updates" (T495)). This category was missing from previous similar questions but was present in the responses to this question. The difference might be explained by the fact that teachers referred to a specific application here while previous similar questions were asked in a more general way. **Flexibility to adapt apps and content** (n = 2; e.g., "Make it more adaptable" (T478)) and **scope of the apps and materials** (n = 1; "More ICT elements"), were only mentioned by very few participants. **Apps free of charge** and **more devices and hardware** were not requested in the responses to this question by the South American teachers, as opposed to the European teachers, who did so.

## 5  Discussion

### 5.1  Comparison Between Two Datasets (First Research Goal)

**Support by Educational Authorities.** One interesting difference that can be derived from our data is that in Europe, compared to South America, nearly twice as many teachers followed guidelines given by educational authorities (Ministry of Education or school board of governors) for using AR in their teaching. This shows that although using AR for teaching is pretty much a bottom-up rather than a top-down approach in both regions (as can be seen by the low number of teachers who did follow guidelines overall), European teachers seem to have more support from educational authorities. Although we did not present the results in detail here, we also noticed this as an issue expressed in the responses of teachers who have not used AR for teaching, e.g., "There is no policy of technological modernization of education in my country [Peru]" (T4).

**Increase AR Usage.** Our surveys revealed that all of the South American teachers who voiced their opinion on the topic (n = 91) would be interested to use AR (more often) in their teaching, whereas some of the European teachers (12%) had expressed reservations to do so.

**Available Hardware.** The question about available hardware for AR teaching reveals the digital divide between South America and Europe with respect to hardware access. For example, with the exception of desktop computers, which are least flexible or suitable for learning with AR, on average European schools seem providing more devices. Although not directly comparable, because this data was not collected in the European survey, the responses from teachers who have not used AR for their teaching before (n = 66) paint the same picture that on average less hardware for supporting teaching was provided by South American schools than their European counterparts.

**Confidence Levels.** The European teachers showed slightly higher confidence levels with regard to using AR in their teaching than the South American teachers. It can be argued that this difference is caused by the digital divide.

**Need for Training.** The lack of training seems to be the major barrier for using AR applications in South America, as the teachers (who used AR before as well as those who did not) identified it as the main obstacle across multiple quantitative as well as qualitative question responses. The lack of requisite skills for deploying digital technology effectively is the concern of the digital divide (Sect. 2.2).

## 5.2  Impact of the Digital Divide (Second Research Goal)

**Support by Educational Authorities.** It can be argued that teachers having to use AR out of their own curiosity or based on recommendations from colleagues and students is a barrier for the adoption of AREAs in Europe as well as South America. Ministries of Education and school boards of governors should issue guidelines and encourage teachers to use AR for teaching. This approach, together with providing teachers with necessary equipment and quality material, can address the local digital divide and lead to a stronger uptake of AR for teaching in the European and South American countries where our data were gathered. A stronger effort from the South American authorities seems needed to also address the global digital divide between Europe and South America and make sure that the South American teachers are adequately equipped to benefit from AR educational technologies as their European counterparts do.

**Increase AR Usage.** The South American teachers did not show any reservations about using AR more often for their teaching. In contrast, the European teachers had reservations, given their concerns of keeping their students' attention, their query if AR apps would be a pedagogical advancement, and their worry about low-quality AR apps. This difference in attitude between the two groups can be another sign for the digital divide. The South American teachers did not identify the potential issues as their European counterparts did (cf. "quality material" is less of a concern for South American teachers than for European ones). This suggests that the former may need to be trained on skills and knowledge to enable them to analyse the impact of AR on their teaching. The related training should not only be about benefits and use cases for AR in teaching, but also about possible issues as well as conditions under which the use of AR is not recommended. This additional support for teachers can help bridge the digital divide between South America and Europe.

**Available Hardware.** The digital divide regarding access to hardware exists between European and South American teachers. It can pose a barrier for the adoption of AREAs in South America, because inadequate hardware hinders the effective use of AR apps. For example, due to technical constraints for processing power and screen size, some apps only work on tablets and not on smartphones. Having less access to tablets (let alone even more advanced hardware like game consoles and VR glasses) can prevent South American teachers from using more advanced apps. If financial limitations could be removed, this digital divide could be addressed to a certain extent by buying better hardware for the South American teachers as well as for European teachers. This would allow for a better adoption of AREAs in teaching. Nonetheless, as the earlier initiative "one laptop per child" proved unsuccessful [25], access to hardware cannot enhance or may even harm educational opportunities unless it is supported by sound pedagogical frameworks and well-trained professionals.

**Confidence Levels.** Although the reasons for the higher confidence of the European teachers in using AR for their teaching compared to the South American teachers cannot be derived from our data, this is the digital divide that needs addressing, as teachers' confidence in their ability to deploy AR leads to their intention to use it.

**Need for Training.** The South American teachers' strong focus on training over the other possible needs such as equipment and material leads us to conclude that they may lack the related technical expertise and experience in AR to request additional changes. The European teachers expressing those needs, on the other hand, seem to have received the relevant training and gathered practical experience that allow them to do so. This shows the digital divide being caused by different training opportunities in Europe and South America. To empower South American teachers to use AR in their teaching, they need to know what is available and suitable for them. Applying this knowledge in their teaching practice will enable them to identify shortcomings in the technology and material they have access to, to get those issues addressed and resolved. Overall, more on technology training should be provided to the South America teachers to decrease the digital divide while increasing the technology adoption.

## 5.3 Limitations and Implications

Our work employed survey as the research method. We are aware of its inherent limitations such as the lack of opportunity to clarify questions or probe intriguing responses [24]. For instance, several incomprehensible responses could have been clarified if participants were interviewed. Furthermore, the generalizability of our findings is limited, given the rather low number of participants and unequal distribution over the different South American and European countries. In both cases, we relied on a central contact point to disseminate the surveys. This explained why one country had a much higher response rate. The implication is that it is necessary to recruit contact persons of individual countries to support data collection. A global research network on AR educational uses will not only address the issue of the "data divide" (i.e. the uneven distribution of data collected from different regions) but also the digital divide.

## 6 Conclusion

When comparing the experiences and needs of teachers in Europe and South America when it comes to using Augmented Reality educational applications for their teaching we found some similarities (e.g., positive attitude, low level of AR usage, desire to use it more). Regarding the digital divide, we found common issues caused by different aspects of the digital divide faced by teachers on both continents (e.g., need for training), but also some differences where issues are more concerning for the European (e.g., need for financial support for more and better equipment) or South American (e.g., support from educational authorities) teachers. These issues and thus the digital divide need to be addressed locally as well as globally, thereby enabling teachers and students to benefit from AR educational technologies and applications, which are becoming increasingly usable, pleasurable, and useful for learning and teaching.

## References

1. Azuma, R.T.: A survey of augmented reality. Presence: Teleoper. Virtual Environ. **6**(4), 355–385 (1997)

2. Thamrongrat, P., Law, E.L.-C.: Design and evaluation of an augmented reality app for learning geometric shapes in 3D. In: Lamas, D., Loizides, F., Nacke, L., Petrie, H., Winckler, M., Zaphiris, P. (eds.) Human-Computer Interaction? INTERACT 2019: 17th IFIP TC 13 International Conference, Paphos, Cyprus, September 2–6, 2019, Proceedings, Part IV, pp. 364–385. Springer, Cham (2019). https://doi.org/10.1007/978-3-030-29390-1_20

3. Huang, T.C., Chen, C.C., Chou, Y.W.: Animating eco-education: to see, feel, and discover in an augmented reality-based experiential learning environment. Comput. Educ. **96**, 72–82 (2016)

4. Ibáñez, M.B., Delgado-Kloos, C.: Augmented reality for STEM learning: a systematic review. Comput. Educ. **123**, 109–123 (2018)

5. Research report: UK The road to digital learning. https://www.birmingham.ac.uk/?Docume nts/HEFI/FUJ-Education-Report-UK.pdf. Accessed 01 July 2022

6. Tzima, S., Styliaras, G., Bassounas, A.: Augmented reality applications in education: teachers point of view. Educ. Sci. **9**(2), 99 (2019)

7. Alkhattabi, M.: Augmented reality as E-learning tool in primary schools' education: barriers to teachers' adoption. Int. J. Emerg. Technol. Learn. **12**(02), 91–100 (2017)

8. ARETE. Deliverable 4.2: Analysis of User Requirements, Needs and Visionary User Cases for ARETE. Zenodo (2021). https://doi.org/10.5281/zenodo.4724874

9. Heintz, M., Law, E.L.-C., Andrade, P.: Augmented reality as educational tool: perceptions, challenges, and requirements from teachers. In: De Laet, T., Klemke, R., Alario-Hoyos, C., Hilliger, I., Ortega-Arranz, A. (eds.) EC-TEL 2021. LNCS, vol. 12884, pp. 315–319. Springer, Cham (2021). https://doi.org/10.1007/978-3-030-86436-1_27

10. Burgess, G.: Beyond the pandemic: Tackle the digital divide (2020). https://www.cchpr.lan decon.cam.ac.uk/Research/Start-Year/2017/building_better_opportunities_new_horizons/ beyond_the_pandemic. Accessed 01 July 2022

11. Pérez-Castro, M.Á., Mohamed-Maslouhi, M., Montero-Alonso, M.Á.: The digital divide and its impact on the development of Mediterranean countries. Technol. Soc. **64**, 101452 (2021)

12. Billinghurst, M., Clark, A., Lee, G.: A survey of augmented reality. Found. Trends Human-Comput. Interact. **8**(2–3), 73–272 (2015)

13. Fleck, S., Hachet, M., Christian Bastien, J.M.: Marker-based augmented reality: instructional-design to improve children interactions with astronomical concepts. In: Proceedings of the 14th International Conference on Interaction Design and Children, pp. 21–28 (2015)

14. Layona, R., Yulianto, B., Tunardi, Y.: Web based augmented reality for human body anatomy learning. Procedia Comput. Sci. **135**, 457–464 (2018)

15. Juan, C.M., Llop, E., Abad, F., Lluch, J.: Learning words using augmented reality. In: 10th IEEE International Conference on Advanced Learning Technologies, pp. 422–426 (2010)

16. Garzón, J., Baldiris, S., Gutiérrez, J., Pavón, J.: How do pedagogical approaches affect the impact of augmented reality on education? A meta-analysis and research synthesis. Educ. Res. Rev. 100334 (2020)

17. Pellas, N., Fotaris, P., Kazanidis, I., Wells, D.: Augmenting the learning experience in primary and secondary school education: a systematic review of recent trends in augmented reality game-based learning. Virtual Reality **23**(4), 329–346 (2019)

18. ISO 9241-210: 2019 Ergonomics of human-system interaction—Part 210: Human-centred design for interactive systems

19. Law, E.L.C., Heintz, M.: Augmented reality applications for K-12 education: A systematic review from the usability and user experience perspective. Int. J. Child-Comput. Interact. **30**, 100321 (2021)

20. National Information and Telecommunications Agency: Falling Through the Net: Defining the Digital Divide (1999)

21. Van Dijk, J.A.G.M.: Digital divide: impact of access. In: The International Encyclopedia of Media Effects, pp. 1–11 (2017)

22. Hilbert, M.: The end justifies the definition: the manifold outlooks on the digital divide and their practical usefulness for policy-making. Telecommun. Policy **35**(8), 715–736 (2011)
23. UNESCO, UNICEF, The World Bank, OECD: WHAT'S NEXT? Lessons on Education Recovery. http://covid19.uis.unesco.org/wp-content/uploads/sites/11/2021/07/National-Education-Responses-to-COVID-19-Report2_v3.pdf. Accessed 01 July 2022
24. Lazar, J., Feng, J.H., Hochheiser, H.: Research Methods in Human-Computer Interaction. Morgan Kaufmann, Burlington (2017)
25. Ames, M.G.: The Charisma Machine: The Life, Death, and Legacy of One Laptop per Child. MIT Press, Canbridge (2019)

# Gamifying Experiential Learning Theory

Amani Alsaqqaf[1,2]([📧]) [iD] and Frederick W. B. Li[2]([📧]) [iD]

[1] Jamoum University College, Umm Al-Qura University, Mecca, Saudi Arabia
[2] University of Durham, Durham, UK
{amani.z.alsaqqaf,frederick.li}@durham.ac.uk

**Abstract.** Motivating student learning and enhancing student learning performance can be done by gamifying existing learning systems via adding gaming elements to the systems, or by developing dedicated games for learning purposes. However, it is both costly and challenging to develop such systems, since it requires to fill the gap in cognition and knowledge between educators and game designers before they can properly transfer learning theories to game mechanics and elements for gamification or serious game implementation. This paper proposes to gamify experiential learning theory by mapping it to the positive and negative feedback mechanisms of the internal economy of game machinations. Hence, developing serious games becomes easier, since the effort of getting mutual understanding between educators and game designers can be effectively reduced. Our study assesses the proposed model by obtaining the experts' (game designers/educators) perceptions of the model mapping, and its usefulness and usability, via an online questionnaire. A total of 23 participants answered the questionnaire by stating that our model was useful and could suitably mapped the learning theory to game design. We also present a field-based learning game as an application of our proposed model.

**Keywords:** Game-based learning · Experiential learning theory · Gamification

## 1 Introduction

Gamification is defined as using or applying game elements to a context unrelated to playing [8]. It can be applied to encourage collaboration [18], involve employees in tasks [27], or even increase customers' loyalty via stamp cards [17]. However, gamification in teaching and learning defines a systematic process rather than one task, such as collecting badges, and aims to solve a particular learning problem through increased engagement and motivation [24].

Game-based learning (GBL) is more comprehensive with regard to the game elements applied (points, badges, narrative, etc.) in addition to utilising game mechanics (physics, internal economy, progression, etc.). GBL can be seen as teaching and learning real-world knowledge and skills within a game environment, with the aim of transferring learning to real-world situations, while gamification in learning creates a gamified real-world environment for solving real-world problems. The concept of gamification is applied to learning via gamifying lessons or field trips, while it can also be utilised to gamify learning theories to design and instruct the learning process. Kolb's Experiential Learning Theory (ELT) [20] is a well-known theory considers experience to be the central source of learning and development. It consists of four stages: concrete experience (CE) involves perceiving new knowledge by experiencing the concrete through sensing real situations; reflective observation (RO) focuses on watching and reflecting on the learner's own experiences or those of others; abstract conceptualisation (AC) is about analysing, synthesising, or planning via a representative presentation; and active experiment (AE) involves doing things. These four stages have to be completed in a cycle starting from any stage, with the possibility of repeating stages as needed. The theory emphasises the importance of experience in the learning process, such as in laboratory sessions and fieldwork.

Our main contribution is gamifying ELT by mapping it to the internal economy of game machinations [3]. The main components of the internal economy mechanic (resources, internal mechanic, feedback loops) are defined for each stage of ELT, forming building blocks of experiential learning that can facilitate GBL systems development.

The remainder of the paper is structured as follows. Firstly, a review of related work regarding GBL, and modelling ELT, is presented. The next section discusses two essential concepts of modelling ELT (internal economy mechanic and game machinations). This is followed by describing the ELT model and presenting an implementation of a FBL game. Thereafter, our initial study is depicted, and the final section provides a conclusion and discusses future work.

## 2 Related Work

GBL is the procedure and practice of learning utilising games. GBL can utilise digital or non-digital games. GBL prompts learning, facilitates evaluation [29], and develops skills [7]. In games, players are actively motivated to overcome their losses and to pursue more tasks and challenges. The drive and elevated levels of motivation are what educators desire for their students to progress in the learning achievement. Any learning process that uses GBL as a tool of education benefits from engagement and motivation. However, reducing the GBL design to few game elements would limit the learning effect [21]. The limitation of GBL can be caused by a lack of theoretical foundations. Nevertheless, the literature shows the utilisation of many learning theories [12, 30] in designing GBL, such as ELT [16]. Designing GBL to provide experiential learning would produce a more effective learning experience [19]. Broadly speaking, GBL can be achieved in two ways: educators/game designers either collaborate to build games or use commercial off-the-shelf games; each way has its advantages and disadvantages. It is important to design GBL carefully to provide more than just motivation, by applying learning theories and creating a balance between learning theories on the one hand, and game elements and mechanics on the other. We propose a model to gamify ELT, in order to help game designers/educators to create a balanced GBL that increases student motivation and improves their learning performance.

Various academic disciplines employ ELT, such as chemical engineering [1], tourism [14], computer science [32], and FBL [5]. There is a tendency to apply ELT for instructing or designing GBL without following specific guidance or models [10, 11, 13, 22,

26, 28, 31]. Conceptual and theoretical models are needed to guide the process of operating and designing GBL [4]. However, there have been a few attempts to model ELT to design GBL [16, 25]. For example, the experiential gaming model [16] aims to integrate ELT with game design and flow theory. The model highlights the significance of clear goals, balancing the player's ability and the challenges provided, and delivering immediate feedback. It consists of experience and ideation loops in addition to a challenge depository. The metaphor of the heart is presented to supply challenges based on learning objectives. The model connects ELT to game design, yet it ignores two important elements of both GBL and ELT: interaction and assessment. In addition, the model does not focus on concrete guidance, but provides abstract principles. [25] presents another example of a framework for using ELT to develop GBL. The framework links each stage of the ELT cycle to one game element, such as linking Gameplay to CE, to provide engagement and linking feedback to RO and create an opportunity for reflection. The framework ignores the importance of game mechanics and is limited to a few game elements in addition to skipping guidance.

Some studies applied general models to design experiential learning in GBL [15, 23]. A final thought on gamifying ELT is presented in the literature by utilising one or two game design concepts, such as role-playing/narrative [14], and engagement [6].

## 3    Game Mechanics

Games in general build on rules of play, and digital games consider rules as mechanics that govern the relationships between gameplay components. There are five types of game mechanics: progression, physics, internal economy, tactical manoeuvring, and social interaction [2]. Usually, several game mechanics are combined with one core mechanic which has the most impact on the game's aspects. However, the internal economy is the basic mechanic and the most involved in designing digital games.

The strength of the internal economy comes from handling the flow and transaction of game elements that are considered resources (coins and lives) in quantifiable amounts. A general definition of an economy is a system that produces, consumes, and trades resources in measurable amounts; it is similar to a real-life economy. The internal economy manipulates many kinds of resources which can differ from what people are used to in real life, such as health and stars. Three components structure the internal economy, namely resources, internal mechanics, and feedback loops.

Any object that can be quantified numerically in a game is a resource, such as enemies and ammunition. Players can control things by gathering, destroying, or producing different objects which formulate resources. Some resources need to be stored in a container called an entity, such as storing collected gold in an entity (gold box). Resources flow from one entity to another according to four internal mechanics: source, drain, converter, and trader. The source mechanic produces new resources, such as creating new dots in the PacMan game. The production of the source could be based on a condition, triggered by an event or automatically based on a time interval. Also, sources have a production rate, which can be fixed or variable depending on the time or amount of another resource. The condition, automation, and changing rate are concepts that apply to all internal mechanics. The drain mechanic consumes resources, and they are removed permanently. On the other hand, the converter changes one type of resource to another, such as converting flour to bread. The trader mechanic exchanges two different resources between two different entities according to a specific rate. For example, a player can trade a shield to get a more powerful gun.

When a resource that results from a mechanic feeds back and affects the same mechanic at a later time in the game, this is called a feedback loop. For example, taking one piece of the opponent in a chess game will make it easier to take the next piece. A positive feedback loop applies when the effect of the loop becomes stronger in each loop. However, the positive feedback loop can cause deadlock when the production of two resources is mutually dependent on each. For example, when building a stonecutter's hut in Settlers III, the stonecutter's hut produces stone and at the same time the player needs the stone to build the stonecutter's hut. The game starts with some stones, but if a player uses them for other tasks before building the stonecutter's hut, then they could end up without enough stones to build the hut. A positive feedback loop helps the player to win quickly when an important difference is achieved in skill or effort. On the other hand, a negative feedback loop stabilises the production mechanism, such as in a car racing game, where the positions of players' cars appear to be attached to each other by a rubber band. No car will get too far ahead of the others or too far behind the rest. This can be balanced by powering up the slowest car with random power or increasing the difficulty of the leader car with blocks. It will increase excitement by creating chances for other players to take the lead.

The game machinations framework [3] is a tool to envision game mechanics. Our work utilises the game machinations to present the gamification of ELT aspects to an internal economy, through mapping between the ELT stages and the components of the internal economy mechanic (defining flows to form an ELT cycle as the components can be manipulated to reach the desired settings of GBL). The symbols of game machinations are a way of facilitating and supporting the modelling of the internal economy in a graphical representation. For example, entities that store resources are represented by an open circle (pool), while resources are symbolised by small, coloured circles (coins) or as numbers. Another example is the source mechanic, which is represented by a triangle pointing upwards, and a solid arrow, which represents the flow of resources from a source to a pool entity.

## 4 Gamification of Experiential Learning

The internal economy is used to gamify ELT aspects to link them to game design. For each stage of ELT, resources are defined along with a suitable internal mechanic and feedback loop when needed. These three components transfer the theory into the game's internal economy, as shown in Fig. 1. It is a model of the learner's progress in reaching different stages of the ELT cycle while performing learning tasks. By completing a stage, the knowledge/skill of player will be expanded to show progression in performance. Four resources are defined, each of which represents a different level of achievement and is associated with a specific stage of the ELT cycle. Internal mechanics (source and converter) are used to show the flow and transaction of these resources from one stage to the next. The cycle can be repeated via a feedback loop to improve performance in the next cycle by acting on the learning feedback, as shown in Fig. 2.

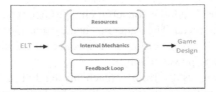

**Fig. 1.** Modelling ELT as an internal economy

The first stage is CE, and it is mapped to a simple internal mechanic where the player grasps knowledge, and it is conceptualised as the interactive source *Task* to achieve a task (Fig. 2 - (CE)). The difficulty of task is demonstrated as a gate with the player skill symbol and the probability of successfully producing *level1* as *p1*. For example, *p1* could be a fifty % chance of accomplishing the task successfully according to the ability level and making an observation resource to be stored in the *level1* pool. *Level1* is defined as observation, because in the first stage the player is expected to have a new experience and develop knowledge by observing the learning environment.

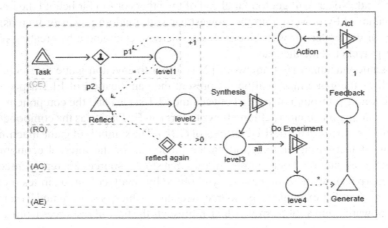

**Fig. 2.** Gamified ELT model

RO is a mental activity, which can be inspired by tasks such as encouraging conversation. In Fig. 2 - (RO), a source represents reflection, *Reflect*, it can be generated in one of two different scenarios: whether or not the player completed the task in the first stage successfully. In the first scenario, as a resource is stored in the *level1* pool, the reflection will be triggered by the trigger state connection that links *level1* to *Reflect*, as it is expected to reflect when the player has successfully accomplished the task. In the second scenario, which applies if the task could not be completed, the gate guarantees the redistribution of the player's experience to reflect by *p2*, where *p2* represents the probability of the player's ability to reflect when the task is not completed successfully, showing that he/she still learned something, even from mistakes. The player should produce resources of reflection, which are stored in the *level2* pool by the end of the second stage.

The third stage (AC) can be done via a loop of synthesising and reflecting again until the final result is formed (Fig. 2 - (AC)). The loop begins from the interactive converter *Synthesis* by transferring resources in *level2* to synthesise and plan and then save them in the *level3* pool. Storing resources in the *level3* pool will activate the interactive gate (*reflect again*) by the activator state connection and the condition specified on the label as (0 >). At this point, the player has the choice to click on the *reflect again* gate or move on to the final stage. If the player chooses to click on the gate, the source *Reflect* will be triggered to generate more resources to be stored in the *Level2* pool and these then can be synthesised again. The final stage (AE) is conceptualized with the interactive *Do Experiment* converter, which represents the action of the player undergoing a new experience based on the synthesised ideas and plan from the previous stage (*Level3*). This will result in producing new knowledge stored in the *Level4* pool after a full ELT learning cycle.

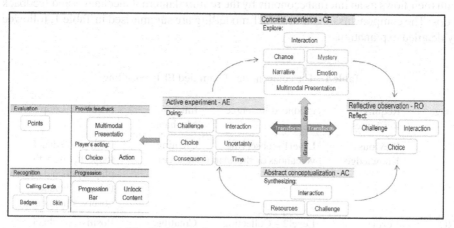

**Fig. 3.** Game elements matching scheme

Before starting a new cycle, the player is demanding feedback as a result of evaluation. The source *Generator* in Fig. 2 symbolises feedback provision, which will be triggered automatically by storing resources in *Level4*. The generated feedback will be stored in the *Feedback* pool. The player has to act on the feedback provided by clicking on the interactive converter *Act*, which will produce Action resources showing the player utilised the feedback to improve or fix something in the task performance.

Working through the whole cycle and acting on the feedback will improve the knowledge/skill of player, which will raise the probability of completing the task successfully in the following cycle. This is achieved by a label modifier with (+), where the percentage will be increased by some value as decided by the game designer/educator automatically each time resources are stored in the Action pool. Each stage of the ELT cycle forms a building block that can be facilitated in the process of designing GBL. The following step enhances the gamification process by linking the internal economy representation of stages into specific game elements, as shown in Fig. 3. Educators/game designers can utilise all the elements into the matching scheme or select what fits the learning objectives. More explanation is provided in the implementation section.

## 5  Implementation of a Field-Based Learning Game

A prototype is designed and implemented based on the gamified ELT model to provide experiential learning via a virtual field trip game (VFTG) for secondary school students. It is called Island of Volcanoes and set in Bali Island which includes three volcanoes: Mount Agung, Mount Batur, and Mount Bratan. The learning content was chosen from Key Stage 3 of the most recent National Curriculum in England for Geography - natural hazards (volcanoes) along with geographical skills (aerial view (Fig. 4 – (b)) and geographical information). It is an experience of surviving on the island by observing, collecting data, planning, and then acting. The resources of each stage are defined, along with their flows as an internal economy by the required internal mechanics and feedback loops. The components of gamified ELT modelling are summarised in Table 1, followed by detailed explanations.

**Table 1.** The components of gamified ELT modelling.

| Stage | Required Resources | Produced Resource | Internal Mechanic | Feedback Loop |
|-------|--------------------|--------------------|--------------------|----------------|
| CE | Previous Knowledge | Level1 – observing volcanoes on the island | Creating (source) | Positive feedback loop: the more the player puts out fires, the more he/she observes the island |
| RO | Level1 | Level2 – Collecting information about observed volcanoes | Creating (source) | Positive feedback loop: if the player finds one piece of information, the rest of the required data can be found easily |
| AC | Level2 | Level3 - Hypothesising and planning from observations and collected data. + Level2 | Converting (converter) | Possible negative feedback loop, where it will get harder to hypothesise and plan with the appearance of new signs of natural hazards |
| AE | Level3 | Level4 – Acting on the plan | Creating (source) | Possible negative feedback loop, where the task becomes harder for faster players |

In the CE stage, players will be motivated to explore and observe the virtual field environment (VFE) by collecting gems, a commonly found mineral in volcano lava, to fill the gun's tank with water and be able to put out the fires to save the island (Fig. 4 – (a)). The gems/fires are scattered all over the VFE, with the aim of creating level1 resource (observations of Bali). The player is expected to identify the number of volcanoes on the island as a result of observation. The design includes a positive feedback loop, where the more the player puts out the fires with the water gun, the more he/she has the chance to walk around the island and observe the environmental terrain. A second task is required in this stage, which is recalling previous knowledge (the structure of a volcano) by labelling its parts in a diagram.

In the RO stage, the player will be encouraged to reflect on the observations from the first stage, and level1 should be converted to level2 (reflecting) resource. The reflection is performed by finding geographical information about the observed environmental terrain, which is supposed to include observing volcanoes to gain further understanding of the situation on the island. The player has to collect data about a specific volcano on the island (name, country, type, status) and record them in a table inside the game (Fig. 4 – (a)). The player searches a learning resource made available for access via a button on the user interface (UI): a monitoring web page displays a volcanic map of Bali along with information. A positive feedback loop is designed so that, if the player finds one piece of information about the observed volcano, he/she can find the next required data.

In the AC stage, the player will experience one of two different scenarios: scenario1 (releasing gas earthquake) or scenario2 (releasing ash/lava and seeing some animals running). Thus, the player will be prompted to synthesise and hypothesise about the presented scenario (the natural signs) along with the observations (*level1*) and the collected data (*level2*). The result forms level3 resource by defining the situation on the island and classifying the natural signs according to two levels of danger. The feedback loop in this stage is optional and the player can choose to reflect again after synthesising until the final result is formed. A negative feedback loop could be designed to achieve a balance, whereby it becomes more difficult for the player to hypothesise and plan after forming the initial result as new signs of natural hazards emerge.

**Fig. 4.** (a) Gathering information, (b) collecting gems, putting out fires, and aerial view

In the AE stage, the player will be forced to act on the synthesised classification (*Level3*) from the third stage in connection with the resources produced by previous tasks (*Level1* and *Level2*). The player has to make a decision and act on it (doing), escaping the natural hazard by selecting the best vehicle and buying a car, or running to a safe area on the island (scenario1), or finding a boat in order to leave the island (senario2) based on the level of danger. A negative feedback loop could be designed where the task of escaping becomes more difficult for players who have completed the previous tasks in a shorter amount of time: barriers are added, impeding their route to a vehicle. CE is the most frequent entrance stage of the ELT cycle [9], so the prototype is designed to start with it. However, the model defines the building blocks of each stage, meaning that the building blocks can be rearranged to start the ELT cycle from any stage based on the player's learning style.

Some game elements were selected from Fig. 3 to enhance the gamification of the ELT stages. The interaction is utilised to design the tasks of all the ELT stages where the interaction between the player and the environment results in exploring and collecting data. For the CE stage, multimodal presentation is employed through different forms of learning materials (text and video). The narrative is introduced in the CE stage by an NPC (Red Dragon) to create an engaging context with a feeling of danger related to the volcano's eruption and the urge to survive. In the RO stage, the player is encouraged to reflect on the observation of the existent volcanoes and challenged to learn more about their status (by collecting data). The control of choice gives them the opportunity to correct any incorrect collected data. In the AC stage, interaction is applied by sending signs to the player from the environment and challenging them to understand the surroundings in order to plan an escape and survive. In the AE stage, a challenge is employed where the player has to survive the danger of a volcano within a certain amount of time. An element of choice is provided by selecting the best method (boat or car) to escape the danger. If the wrong method to escape is selected, there will be a consequence and the game will continue, with uncertainty about what will happen.

The assessment and feedback can be provided after the final stage or after each stage. The applied game elements are the awarding of points for assessment and badges for recognition. Feedback is applied according to a multimodal presentation - colour and motion. A control of choice is provided to take action to find the correct answers and is given two chances for two learning tasks (labelling the volcano's parts and collecting data). The progression step is designed as unlocking content (new tasks and materials).

The prototype was implemented via the Unity Game Engine. A heightmap of Bali was converted to a terrain. Basic elements of the environment were added, such as water, skybox, the lakes of volcanoes and the cycle of day and night. After registration and selecting an identity, the player is provided with three options: Play, Help, and Quit. The player can display the list of quests (learning tasks) by clicking a button in the top left corner of UI, as a way to interweave the learning tasks into the gameplay. A green check will appear next to each quest completed by the player. Also, some of the learning tasks and rules are hidden and introduced to the player by the Red Dragon implicitly as a part of the story, such as telling the player about the value of blue gems and the survival kit items. In addition, some learning materials intervene in the story.

Assessment and feedback are provided after completing the tasks of the CE and RO stages. A check button is provided to give the player a choice to ask and receive feedback. A flying bird appears randomly over one of the three volcanoes after the player collects at least one item of the survival kit. The player is expected to observe the flying bird and explore the area near that volcano, which leads to displaying a table to collect the geographical information. The player will gain coins for correct collected data from RO task. A timer is displayed after 30 s of classifying the level of danger to create some pressure to complete the quest within that period. The player should use coins gained from the previous task to pay for a vehicle. The purchased vehicle will appear near the seaside and the player can ride it. A gold badge is awarded when the player selects the correct vehicle based on the presented scenario. If the player selects the wrong vehicle and cannot escape the eruption by leaving the island, he/she can die from the lava or ash. However, the player may select the wrong vehicle but not die, in which case a silver badge is awarded.

## 6 Evaluation

A preliminary evaluation of the gamified ELT model was designed to seek the experts' opinions of the model. A questionnaire was designed to measure the mapping, usefulness, and usability of the gamified ELT. The questionnaire gathered data about demographic information (sex and location), and professional experience (occupation and type of learning institution). Three statements are asked about the mapping, two statements about usefulness, and ten statements are about the usability of the model, which was a modified version of the System Usability Scale (SUS). A five-point Likert scale, ranges from strongly agree = 5 to strongly disagree = 1, is applied to answer the statements. Also, three questions are asked about the overall opinion of the model and suggestions.

Twenty-three participants answered the questionnaire. The participants included 7 females (30.4%) and 16 males (69.6%), and all the participants were from the UK. There were ten educators (43.5%), seven game designers (30.4%) and six participants who defined themselves as both (23.1%). Regarding learning institution, five participants work in schools (21.1%) and 18 work at universities (78.3%). Cronbach's alpha was calculated: mapping ($\alpha = 0.824$), usefulness ($\alpha = 0.891$), and usability ($\alpha = 0.869$). The results indicate good internal consistency and reliability for the statements of each scale. All statements of the mapping scale have the same median (4) and the IQR values range from 0 to 2, which indicates that most participants expressed agreement regarding the mapping between the ELT stages and the internal economy. Regarding usefulness, the median for both statements is 4 and IQR values are 3 and 2, which reveals an agreement trend. This suggests that the participants found the model useful. The SUS scores are computed in a combined way to generate a one usability score between 0 and 100. 68.043 is he average usability score, which indicates that the usability performance is better than average.

The participants answered a question regarding the possibility of considering using the model in their future research. The highest percentage (39.13%) of participants indicated that they would definitely use it, followed by 30.43% who would probably use it, and 26.09% who would probably not use it. Only 4.35% indicated that they would definitely not use it and the common reason stated in an open-ended question is that they do not do research in this area, while one participant expressed an intention to use the model to evaluate off-shelf experimental learning games. Another open-ended question asked about any concepts missing from the model and answers included skills and more explanation about assessment and feedback.

# 7  Conclusion and Future Work

Designing GBL requires a huge effort of collaboration from educators and game designers to successfully implement the system. However, it is an expensive process, even to develop one GBL, since lots of effort is spent on identifying mutual understanding in GBL among the educators and game designers, who have a significant gap in cognition and knowledge due to the difference in their expertise. Gamifying learning theories, such as ELT, bridge the distance between the two fields and facilitate the process of design GBL. This study presented a gamified ELT model by mapping the stages of ELT into the internal economy mechanic. The mapping process defines the main components of the internal economy mechanic (resources, internal mechanic, and feedback loop) of each stage and shows the flow and transaction of resources from one stage to the next as the player progresses in reaching different stages of the ELT cycle while performing learning tasks. Future work will involve developing the model by gamifying more learning theories (social learning theories, peer assessment, high-order skills) and connecting them to ELT to enhance the design of GBL.

# References

1. Abdulwahed, M., Nagy, Z.K.: Applying Kolb's experiential learning cycle for laboratory education. J. Eng. Educ. **98**(3), 283–294 (2009)
2. Adams, E.: Fundamentals of Game Design. Pearson Education, London (2014)
3. Adams, E., Dormans, J.: Game Mechanics: Advanced Game Design. New Riders, Indianapolis (2012)
4. Alsaqqaf, A., Li, F.: Conceptual framework for virtual field trip games. In: Beck, D., et al. (eds.) iLRN 2019. CCIS, vol. 1044, pp. 43–55. Springer, Cham (2019). https://doi.org/10.1007/978-3-030-23089-0_4
5. Behrendt, M., Franklin, T.: A review of research on school field trips and their value in education. Int. J. Environ. Sci. Educ. **9**(3), 235–245 (2014)
6. Canhoto, A.I., Murphy, J.: Learning from simulation design to develop better experiential learning initiatives: an integrative approach. J. Mark. Educ. **38**(2), 98–106 (2016)
7. Carenys, J., Moya, S.: Digital game-based learning in accounting and business education. Acc. Educ. **25**(6), 598–651 (2016)
8. Deterding, S., et al.: From game design elements to gamefulness: defining "gamification". In: Proceedings of the 15th International Academic MindTrek Conference: Envisioning Future Media Environments (2011)
9. Dieleman, H., Huisingh, D.: Games by which to learn and teach about sustainable development: exploring the relevance of games and experiential learning for sustainability. J. Clean. Prod. **14**(9–11), 837–847 (2006)
10. Eckhaus, E., Klein, G., Kantor, J.: Experiential learning in management education. Bus. Manag. Econ. Eng. **15**(1), 42–56 (2017)
11. Egilmez, G., Gedik, R.: A gamification approach for experiential education of inventory control (2018)
12. Hamari, J., et al.: Challenging games help students learn: an empirical study on engagement, flow and immersion in game-based learning. Comput. Hum. Behav. **54**, 170–179 (2016)

13. Ho, S.-J., et al.: Applying game-based experiential learning to comprehensive sustainable development-based education. Sustainability **14**(3), 1172 (2022)
14. Huertas-Valdivia, I.: Role-playing a staffing process: experiential learning with undergraduate tourism students. J. Hosp. Leis. Sport Tour. Educ. **29**, 100334 (2021)
15. Kaneko, K., et al.: Does physical activity enhance learning performance?: Learning effectiveness of game-based experiential learning for university library instruction. J. Acad. Librariansh. **44**(5), 569–581 (2018)
16. Kiili, K.: Digital game-based learning: towards an experiential gaming model. Internet Higher Educ. **8**(1), 13–24 (2005)
17. Kim, S., Song, K., Lockee, B., Burton, J.: What is gamification in learning and education? In: Kim, S., Song, K., Lockee, B., Burton, J. (eds.) Gamification in Learning and Education. Advances in Game-Based Learning, pp. 25–38. Springer, Cham (2018). https://doi.org/10.1007/978-3-319-47283-6_4
18. Knutas, A., et al.: Increasing collaborative communications in a programming course with gamification: a case study. In: Proceedings of the 15th International Conference on Computer Systems and Technologies (2014)
19. Koivisto, J.-M., Niemi, H., Multisilta, J., Eriksson, E.: Nursing students' experiential learning processes using an online 3D simulation game. Educ. Inf. Technol. **22**(1), 383–398 (2015). https://doi.org/10.1007/s10639-015-9453-x
20. Kolb, D.A.: Experimental Learning: Experience as the Source of Learning and Development. Prentice Hall, Englewood Cliffs (1984)
21. Liao, C.W., Chen, C.H., Shih, S.J.: The interactivity of video and collaboration for learning achievement, intrinsic motivation, cognitive load, and behavior patterns in a digital game-based learning environment. Comput. Educ. **133**, 43–55 (2019)
22. Lőrincz, B., Iudean, B., Vescan, A.: Experience report on teaching testing through gamification. In: Proceedings of the 3rd International Workshop on Education through Advanced Software Engineering and Artificial Intelligence (2021)
23. Matsuo, M.: A framework for facilitating experiential learning. Hum. Resour. Dev. Rev. **14**(4), 442–461 (2015)
24. Nah, F.F.-H., Zeng, Q., Telaprolu, V.R., Ayyappa, A.P., Eschenbrenner, B.: Gamification of education: a review of literature. In: Nah, F.F.-H. (ed.) HCI in Business: First International Conference, HCIB 2014, Held as Part of HCI International 2014, Heraklion, Crete, Greece, June 22-27, 2014. Proceedings, pp. 401–409. Springer International Publishing, Cham (2014). https://doi.org/10.1007/978-3-319-07293-7_39
25. Odendaal, D.: A framework for using experiential learning theory to develop game-based learning. Stellenbosch University, Stellenbosch (2018)
26. Poole, S.M., et al.: Game-based learning in wine education. J. Hosp. Tour. Educ. **34**, 1–6 (2021)
27. Robson, K., et al.: Game on: engaging customers and employees through gamification. Bus. Horiz. **59**(1), 29–36 (2016)
28. Sajjadi, P., et al.: CZ investigator: Learning about critical zones through a VR serious game. In: 2020 IEEE Conference on Virtual Reality and 3D User Interfaces Abstracts and Workshops (VRW). IEEE (2020)
29. Shute, V.J., Rahimi, S.: Stealth assessment of creativity in a physics video game. Comput. Hum. Behav. **116**, 106647 (2021)
30. Spires, H.A., et al.: Problem solving and game-based learning: effects of middle grade students' hypothesis testing strategies on learning outcomes. J. Educ. Comput. Res. **44**(4), 453–472 (2011)

31. Tung, T.M.: Developing Quality Hospitality Students Through Simulation and Experiential Learning as a Guide for Hospitality Education. Reference to this paper should be referred to as follows: Tung, T.M.: Developing quality hospitality students through simulation and experiential learning as a guide for hospitality education. GATR Global J. Bus. Soc. Sci. Review 9(4), 283–292 (2021)
32. Vescan, A., Serban, C.: Facilitating model checking learning through experiential learning. In: Proceedings of the 2nd ACM SIGSOFT International Workshop on Education through Advanced Software Engineering and Artificial Intelligence (2020)

# The Learning Analytics System that Improves the Teaching-Learning Experience of MOOC Instructors and Students

Ruth Cobos(✉) [iD]

Computer Science Department, Universidad Autónoma de Madrid, Madrid, Spain
ruth.cobos@uam.es

**Abstract.** Great learning opportunities are provided through MOOCs. However, MOOCs provide a number of challenges for students. Many students find it difficult to successfully finish MOOCs due to a variety of factors, including feelings of loneliness, a lack of support, and a lack of feedback. Additionally, the instructors of these courses are highly concerned about this situation and want to reduce these difficulties for their students. Due to the large number of students registered in these courses, this is not a simple task. To help both instructors and students, we created edX-LIMS, a learning analytics (LA) system that allows MOOC instructors to monitor the progress of their students and carry out an intervention strategy in their students' learning thanks to a Web-based Instructor Dashboard. Furthermore, this LA system provides MOOC students with detailed feedback on their course performance as well as advice on how to improve it thanks to Web-based Learner Dashboards. This LA system have been used for more than two year in a MOOC at edX. During this period the Dashboards supported by the system have been improved, and as a result, MOOC students now appreciate the fact that they feel guided, engagement and motivated to complete the course, among other feelings. MOOC instructor have improved their student monitoring tasks and are better able to identify students who need assistance. Moreover thanks to the services that the intervention strategy supported by the LA system offer to them, now students and instructors feel that are connected.

**Keywords:** Learning Analytics · Massive Open Online Course · Dashboard · Engagement · Feedback · Intervention · Motivation

## 1 Introduction

Online courses have recently gained popularity, with "Massive Open Online Courses" (MOOCs) being a category of them that highlights their relevance in the Web-based Learning [1]. Since joining the edX Consortium in 2014, the Autonomous University of Madrid (UAM, Universidad Autónoma de Madrid) has made MOOCs available as a platform for student anywhere in the globe to enroll in them. The approach presented in this article was tested in a UAM course entitled "Introduction to Development of Web Applications," better known as "WebApp MOOC".

© The Author(s), under exclusive license to Springer Nature Switzerland AG 2023
C. S. González-González et al. (Eds.): ICWL 2022/SETE 2022, LNCS 13869, pp. 29–40, 2023.
https://doi.org/10.1007/978-3-031-33023-0_3

According to multiple research studies, one of the main problems with MOOCs is the lack of interaction among students and instructors, in addition, students admit to having a feeling of loneliness, lack of support and lack of feedback from teachers [2, 3]. This causes students' motivation to decline, which ultimately leads to students dropping out the course [4, 5].

In order to solve this problem in the aforementioned MOOC, edX-LIMS was developed at UAM, which is Web-based Learning Analytics System. The name of the system stands for "System for Learning Interventions and Its Monitoring for edX MOOCs" [6].

On the one hand, edX-LIMS provides MOOC student with an easy way to visualize their performance in the course on a Web-based Learner Dashboard. On the other hand, it gives MOOC instructors an easy visualization with the monitoring of the progress of their students through the Web-based Instructor Dashboard and provides instructors with a intervention strategy in their students' learning. The evolution and improvements of the services supported by this Learning Analytics system will be presented in this article.

The structure of this article is as follows: in Sect. 2, an overview of Learning Analytics in MOOCs is presented. In Sect. 3, MOOC used in the research study is presented. In Sect. 4, the development and characteristics of the Learning Analytics (LA) system and its evolution are exposed. In Sect. 5 the user satisfaction with the LA system is analyzed. Finally, the article provides conclusions and suggestions for future work.

## 2 State of the Art

Learning Analytics helps us analyze data about learning actions and contexts to understand and optimize learning and the environments in which it occurs [7, 8].

Recent reviews of the literature show that modeling student engagement and motivation, as well as analyzing retention and the learning experience, continue to be major issues in MOOC-focused research [9–11].

The LA context is increasing in relation to the vast amount of learning data now available today and the continuous research works in this area [12, 13]. This allows for drawing conclusions, in general terms, with the help of data analysis.

Furthermore, there are numerous techniques for classifying data analysis. Onah [14] offered a categorization of analytics that is one of the most well-known in the field and is based on three types of analytics: descriptive, predictive, and prescriptive.

Descriptive analytics is the basis of data processing and is based on collecting information from the past to display and prepare it for further analysis. When this analysis is applied to the area of learning analytics, it serves to transform historical learner data into organized information as different components included in dashboards [15].

Predictive analytics utilizes past and current data to predict what will happen in the future, using machine learning and data-mining techniques [14]. In applying this analysis to learning analytics, it serves to detect learners at risk for negative situations such as dropping out or failing to earn a degree or a certification, among others [16, 17].

Finally, after the other analytics, prescriptive analytics is responsible for determining possibilities and recommending actions. In LA, it is useful for recommending actions to achieve a positive impact through an intervention in the individual's learning process [14].

## 3   MOOC: Introduction to Development of Web Applications

We can find a wide range of Web-based Learning options. Being the "Massive Open Online Courses" (MOOCs) one of the most successful in recent years. Moreover, they are a suitable approach to offer potential students of both professional and academic settings lifelong learning.

Taking into account that an IT professional must have the ability to create Web Applications. The MOOC entitled "Introduction to Web Application Development" from the Autonomous University of Madrid is available on the edX platform to help gain a basic understanding of this field. This MOOC had a first run from February to March 2019. Nowadays, this MOOC is offered in self-paced mode (i.e., enrollment is free and open to anyone) from April 2019.

WebApp MOOC a five-week course. Its contents are structured in five units (one unit per week work). The students of this MOOC can learn to develop any Web Application using HTML, CSS, Python, JSON, JavaScript and Ajax.

By examining the characteristics of the World Wide Web in the first unit, the student is introduced to the context. In the second unit, HTML is explained in order to develop web pages and forms, and CSS is used to apply the proper style and format. While the third unit presents the ideas of Flask and Python to build the server-side of the Web application, the fourth unit describes the use of sessions and JSON. Finally, the fifth unit discusses both JavaScript and Ajax to develop the client-side of the Web application.

At October 2022 (three years and a half after MOOC beginning), the second run of this MOOC has 48.886 enrolled students. 1623 students of them are in the verified itinerary and are called verified students (i.e. they have paid a fee and will receive an official certificate if they pass the course). Of those, 692 have certified, that is, they passed the course because their final grade was higher than or equal 0.5 (the minimum grade is 0 and the maximum grade is 1). Only students enrolled in the verified itinerary can take evaluations (assessments) on edX, therefore only these students can be evaluated and obtain a final grade. The students that are not in the verified itinerary are audit students. An example of the student activity in the course is shown in Fig. 1 (with data from the last six months of the course. The activity of students of the verified itinerary (both verified and certified students) is higher than that of the audit students. In this graph, the number of interactions is normalized taking into account the number of student in each group.

It is estimated that from the 1613 verified student approx. 800 have dropped out of the course. To sum up, along the course, from the total of the verified students, 40% of them finish the course with a certification, 50% of them drop out and 10% of them are learning actively the course. From the beginning, instructors of this course were very concerned about the large number of verified students who did not complete the course. For this matter, they had the initiative to develop a Learning Analytic system than could help them to monitor their students' performance to have information about them that would help them to improve their learning experience.

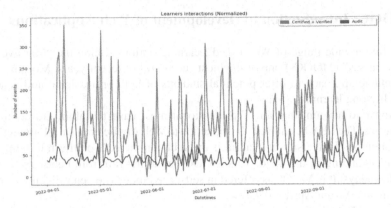

**Fig. 1.** Interactions of the students in the MOOC (in the last six months).

# 4  edX-LIMS: System for Learning Intervention and Its Monitoring for edX MOOCs

The Learning Analytics system called edX-LIMS has been evolving for two and a half years. In May 2020, the first version of edX LIMS began to be used. This one was based on findings from an earlier study that was assisted by edX-LIS tool [18]. In the next subsections the evolution of edX-LIMS is described.

## 4.1  The Initial LA System

The Learning Analytics system was developed for edX MOOCs and was created with two aims. Firstly, with the aim of providing instructors with the possibility to monitor their students and thus make it easier for them to carry out interventions in their students' learning processes. For this reason, the system was named edX-LIMS as an abbreviation for "System for Learning Interventions and Its Monitoring for edX MOOCs". Secondly, with the aim of providing feedback to MOOC students to improve their motivation, persistence and engagement in the MOOC.

The system can be used by these user roles: i) Learner (any student registered in the verified itinerary), ii) Instructor (any member of the course instructors team), and iii) Admin (any instructor who maintain and manage the course data in the system).

The functionality of the system is supported by its interconnected services, as presented below. The system provides an intervention strategy, which is activated weekly by the Admin and is made up of these steps:

1.  Extraction of Student Indicators: the Course Data Processing Service (CDPS) calculates and delivers a set of input indicators (attributes or variables) per student per day. These indicators are derived from the MOOC log tracks and serve as a daily summary of how the students interacted with the course (some examples of these input variables are the number of events in resolving assignments or viewing videos or navigating in the course, the total time in the course, the number of session in the course, among others). The indicators are stored in a MongoDB Database.

2. Generation of feedback to Students: the Learning Intervention Generation Service (LIGS) generates interactive Web-based Dashboards (one per student) based in the students' indicators. Moreover, it emails the students the relevant details they need to access these dashboards.

When students receive the email with the access to their dashboards, they can visualize them in a Web Browser thanks to the Intervention Visualization Service (IVS), which shows different graphs with information about their grades per course unit and indicators' values along the time. Moreover, all to the activity of all students on their Dashboards are recorded in the MongoDB Database.

One example of the visualizations in the Learner Dashboard is the graph with the indicators' values along the time, see Fig. 2. These measurements can be compared to the average of all students' metrics (clicking at check box 'Show course averages'). The selected metrics are displayed in the left graph, and their cumulative values are displayed in the right one. In Fig. 2, the student is visualizing his number of sessions and the time dedicated to solving evaluations (assessments) during the months he was learning in the MOOC (this student certified).

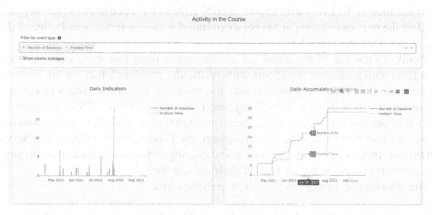

**Fig. 2.** Graphs with the daily indicators of the student.

In the case of instructors, they have access to the Instructor Dashboard where can visualize the course summary data generated by the Course Data Monitoring Service (CDMS) and the interactions of students in their Dashboards in a graph generated by the Learning Intervention Monitoring Service (LIMS), see Fig. 3. This graph is very interesting for the instructors because show the students' interests in their engagement. More in detail, in Fig. 3 we can see that the students visit their dashboards weekly (Page View line) and moreover in the last months most of them interact with their graph that show them their daily indicators (Indicator Chart line). These mentioned services extract all the needed information from the MongoDB Database to generate de Instructor Dashboard.

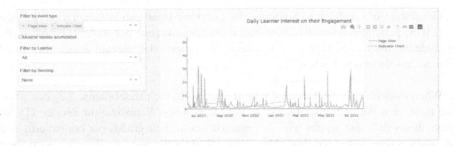

**Fig. 3.** Graph with the daily interest of all students on their engagement in the course (from July 2020 to July 2021).

edX-LIMS services are programmed in the Python language (https://www.python. org/). More details about these services are in [6]. The web interface is generated with the Dash framework (https://plotly.com/dash/), based on Flask.

### 4.2 The Improvement of the LA System

A new iteration of the LA system known as edX-LIMS+ has been in use since July 2021. Based on the previous version, it has been expanded with new services and some of their existing services were enriched.

Thanks to the use of the initial LA system we noticed that there were two types of students with problems: i) students with "difficulty problem": they are students who require more time than the usual to study the material, watch the videos or complete the evaluations ii) students with "self-regulated learning problem" ("SRL problem" for short): they are students who do not dedicate enough time to read the material, watch the videos, or finish the evaluations. For this reason, the Learner Problem Detection Service (LPDS) was incorporated, which predicts and catalogs who are the students with any of these problems based on the analysis of their indicators.

The intervention strategy was evolved in these steps:

1. Extraction of Student Indicators: the Course Data Processing Service (CDPS) continues with its calculations, in addition, it calculates for the students their time spent and attempts in different sections and elements of the course. Moreover, averages, maximums and minimums are calculated for each of the sections and elements.
2. Detection of students with problems: the LPDS predicts who has a "difficulty problem" or a "SRL problem".
3. Generation of feedback to Students: the LIGS adds a new page to the Learner Dashboard with new data. Therefore, the IVS provides students with the following in the new page: i) new graphs related to the time spent and attempts on different sections and elements and ii) the student's possible problem detected and the corresponding suggestion to manage it. Finally, the students receive an email with the relevant details to access their dashboards.

When students access their dashboards, they can visit two Web pages. The first page is the same one generated by IVS in the previous version of the system. On the second page, the Learner Feedback Service (LFS) provides the student with a section on where they have the opportunity to give feedback to the instructor whether she or he agrees or disagrees with the problem detected using a text box (the click in this text box is registered) and a text area where the student can explain the reason for her or his feedback. In addition, on this second page IVS shows the aforementioned graphs related to the time spent and attempts in different sections and elements of the course.

Now the Instructor Dashboard is extended thanks to: i) the Learner Problem Monitoring Service (LPMS) provides a table with all the data about the problems detected to the students and the data that justifies them, and ii) the Learner Feedback Monitoring Service (LFMS) provides in another table data on the feedback received from the students regarding their problems detected. That is, both the feedback of the students on whether they agree or disagree with the problem detected and as the reasons for the feedback from the students.

Figure 4 shows a summary with the flow of information and the interconnections among the services of the LA system.

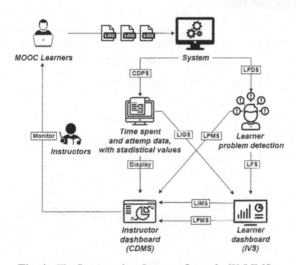

**Fig. 4.** The Intervention Strategy flow of edX-LIMS+.

On the one hand, to efficiently convey analytical information to students, Learner Dashboards have various types of charts, such as radar charts, line charts, column chats, etc. Also, most of them offer students to compare their data with peer data.

On the other hand, to efficiently convey analytical information to instructors, Instructor Dashboard provides some data in tables and some in graphs with data aggregated in box plot charts or pie charts or line charts.

## 5 User Satisfaction with the LA System

To find out how satisfied students and instructors are with the LA system, they had the opportunity to give feedback on their dashboards by filling out satisfaction questionnaires.

When students certify they receive a link to a questionnaire in the weekly email. In this questionnaire students can assess their Learner Dashboard. This questionnaire included multiple choice questions and responses on a five-point Likert-type scale as: (1) Strongly disagree; (2) Disagree; (3) Neither agree nor disagree; (4) Agree; (5) Strongly agree.

The questionnaire ask them about several aspects. For instance, they can give their satisfaction with the emails that they receive each week, they can evaluate the quality of the visualizations and they can express their perception about their motivation, engagement among other feelings, while taking the course. The questionnaire was used to this evaluation both the students who received the Learner Dashboard supported by edX-LIMS and who received it supported by edX-LIMS+.

In the case of the evaluation of the Learner Dashboard supported by edX-LIMS, in Fig. 5 we can see that students agreed that thanks to the visualizations in the dashboard, they have improved their performance, have been more motivated to study for the course, they have felt supervised and guided and "not alone" while they were learning in the course, among other feelings.

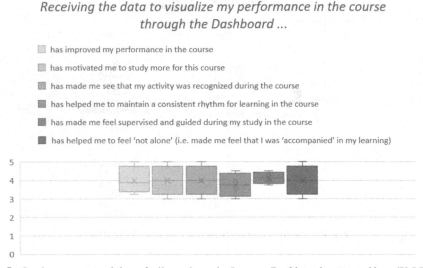

**Fig. 5.** Students expressed these feelings about the Learner Dashboard supported by edX-LIMS.

In the case of the evaluation of the Learner Dashboard supported by edX-LIMS+, in Fig. 6 we can see that students were strongly agreed that thanks to the visualizations in the dashboard, all their aforementioned feelings improved remarkably. Hence, it can be concluded that the Intervention Strategy supported by edX-LIMS+ has improved students' engagement and motivation in the course.

Finally, the Instructor Dashboard supported by edX_LIMS+ was evaluated by the MOOC instructors with another questionnaire which had textual answers (free text). It was not necessary to evaluate the initial one because it was very simple in the version supported by edX_LIMS.

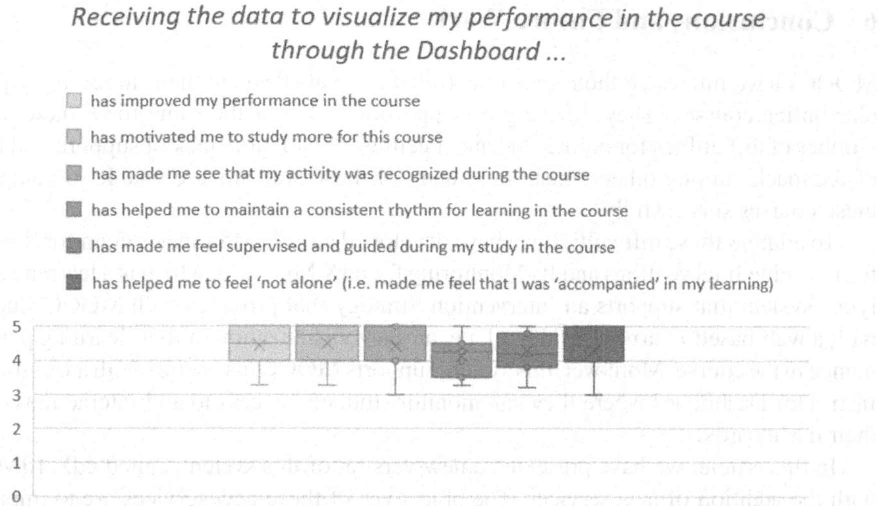

*Receiving the data to visualize my performance in the course*
*through the Dashboard ...*

☐ has improved my performance in the course

☐ has motivated me to study more for this course

■ has made me see that my activity was recognized during the course

■ has helped me to maintain a consistent rhythm for learning in the course

■ has made me feel supervised and guided during my study in the course

■ has helped me to feel 'not alone' (i.e. made me feel that I was 'accompanied' in my learning)

**Fig. 6.** Students expressed these feelings about the Learner Dashboard supported by edX-LIMS+.

They were asked *how the additional components added to the Instructor Dashboard had affected their student monitoring tasks.* They acknowledged that the visualizations of the new parts added by edX-LIMS+ helped them to better understand student progress and identify individuals who needed assistance.

Because of the newly added tables, they could make decisions to help students with problems. More specifically, they executed two extra interventions to address the needs of these students, as follows: i) the instructors sent motivational messages to the students who were making progress but seemed to lack engagement in order to motivate them to continue with the course; and ii) the instructors offered students who completed the course with a final grade close to but less than 0.5 a second opportunity to answer the assessments with poor scores to have the possibility of passing the course and earning certification.

Additionally, instructors stated that students who interacted the most with their dashboards were more receptive to being helped. They were very grateful to the instructors because they answered the emails received with either of the two additional interventions, thanking instructors for that help.

Finally, the instructors were asked *how the Intervention Strategy had improved their relationships with the students.* They recognized that, due to the student feedback on their problems detected, they felt that the communication between instructors and students was bidirectional.

To summarize, the instructors assessed that they could improve their tasks for monitoring MOOC students as a result of the new version of the Instructor Dashboard supported by edX-LIMS+.

## 6 Conclusions and Future Work

MOOCs have interested thousands of enrolled students through their increasingly popular online courses. They offer a great opportunity, but at the same time, there are a number of difficulties for online students. Feelings of isolation, lack of support, and lack of feedback, among others, mean that many of these students are unable to complete these courses successfully.

To address these difficulties, we have developed edX-LIMS (an acronym for System for Learning Interventions and Its Monitoring for edX MOOCs), which is a learning analytics system that supports an Intervention Strategy that provides each MOOC student with a web-based Learner Dashboard, i.e. an easy visualization of their learning performance in the course. Moreover, this system supports MOOC instructors with a web-based Instructor Dashboard where they can monitor students' access to and interactions with their dashboards.

In this article, we have presented a new version of this system, called edX-LIMS+, with the addition of new services. The objectives of these new services are to improve students' and instructor's dashboards. More concretely, the system has a new focus on self-regulated learning to motivate and engage students in the MOOC. In addition, the instructor dashboard receives extra data from these new services, as shown below, that help them to better monitor students and provide support.

The satisfaction of students and instructors using their dashboards were recorded using several questionnaires. This information was used to analyze how the Intervention Strategy supported by edX-LIMS+ influenced students to use the Learner Dashboard and students' engagement and motivation in the MOOC. Moreover, it aimed to determine how the Intervention Strategy influenced instructor tasks for monitoring students.

The results obtained from the analysis of these questionnaires show that the Intervention Strategy supported by edX-LIMS+ improved the perception of students and instructors of the usefulness of their dashboards. Instructors stated that the added parts in the Instructor Dashboard helped them to better understand student progress in the course and to detect students who needed assistance.

The analysis related to students' perceptions of their engagement and motivation in the MOOC revealed the following: i) they felt more motivated to learn in the course; ii) their performance was improved; iii) their activity was recognized; iv) they maintained a consistent rhythm of learning in the course; and v) they felt supervised and guided and "not alone" while they were learning in the course.

Due to the feedback received about students' detected problems, the instructors were able to conduct more effective interventions for the students who needed help, i.e. the instructors' monitoring of students improved. Specifically, each week instructors could help several students who needed motivational messages to continue to learn in the MOOC and others who needed a second chance to answer assessments with poor scores to have the possibility to pass the course and earn certification. Finally, instructors stated that the communication between students and instructors improved, and they felt closer to their students.

As future work, both the Learner Dashboard and Instructor Dashboard can be improved. For instance, new data and visualizations of the evolution of the students' problems detected could help instructors to better monitor them. Additionally, for a new version of the system, recording extra interventions by instructors and students' reactions to them could help instructors enrich these interventions.

We are currently working on developing of a Machine Learning service into the LA system which uses student activity data as input to an Artificial Intelligence model that then statistically calculates whether or not any student is likely to drop out of the course or go to pass the course (obtaining the certificate). So this new approach could warn instructors and invite them to realize interventions to students at risk of losing interest in the course and dropping out.

Finally, the system could be extended to include predictions of other types of student problems, which could be managed with machine learning techniques.

**Acknowledgments.** This work has been co-funded by the Madrid Regional Government through the e-Madrid-CM Project under Grant S2018/TCS-4307, a project which is co-funded by the European Structural Funds (FSE and FEDER). This research has been co-funded by the National Research Agency of the Spanish Ministry of Science, Innovation and Universities under project grant RED2018–102725-T (SNOLA). And, this research has been co-funded by the National Research Agency of the Spanish Ministry of Science and Innovation under project grants PID2019-105951RB-I00 (IndiGo!) and PID2021-127641OB-I00/AEI/FEDER https://doi.org/10.13039/501100011033 (BBforTAI).

# References

1. Ma, L., Lee, C.S.: Investigating the adoption of MOOCs: a technology-user-environment perspective. J. Comput. Assist. Learn. **35**(1), 89–98 (2019). https://doi.org/10.1111/jcal.12314
2. Pardo, A., Jovanovic, J., Dawson, S., Gašević, D., Mirriahi, N.: Using learning analytics to scale the provision of personalised feedback. Br. J. Educ. Technol. **50**(1), 128–138 (2019). https://doi.org/10.1111/bjet.12592
3. Iraj, H., Fudge, A., Faulkner, M., Pardo, A., Kovanović, V.: Understanding students' engagement with personalised feedback messages. In: LAK 2020 Proceedings, pp. 438–447. https://doi.org/10.1145/3375462.3375527
4. Hone, K.S., El Said, G.R.: Exploring the factors affecting MOOC retention: a survey study. Comput. Educ. **98**, 157–168 (2016). https://doi.org/10.1016/j.compedu.2016.03.016
5. Topali, P., Ortega-Arranz, A., Er, E., Martínez-Monés, A., Villagrá-Sobrino, S.L., Dimitriadis, Y.: Exploring the problems experienced by learners in a MOOC implementing active learning pedagogies. In: Calise, M., Delgado Kloos, C., Reich, J., Ruiperez-Valiente, J., Wirsing, M. (eds.) Digital Education: At the MOOC Crossroads Where the Interests of Academia and Business Converge, vol. 11475, pp. 81–90. Springer, Cham (2019). https://doi.org/10.1007/978-3-030-19875-6_10
6. Cobos, R., Soberón, J.: A proposal for monitoring the intervention strategy on the learning of MOOC learners. In: CEUR Conference Proceedings. LASI-Spain 2020. Learning Analytics Summer Institute Spain 2020: Learning Analytics. Time for Adoption? Valladolid, Spain. http://ceur-ws.org/Vol-2671/paper07.pdf
7. Lang, C., Siemens, G., Wise, A., Gasevic, D.: Handbook of Learning Analytics. Society for Learning Analytics Research (SoLAR) (2017). https://doi.org/10.18608/hla17
8. Romero, C., Ventura, S.: Educational data mining and learning analytics: an updated survey. WIREs Data Mining Knowl. Discov. **10**(3) (2020). https://doi.org/10.1002/widm.1355

9. Sa'don, N.F., Alias, R.A., Ohshima, N.: Nascent research trends in MOOCs in higher educational institutions: a systematic literature review. In: The 2014 International Conference on Web and Open Access to Learning Proceedings (ICWOAL 2014), pp. 1–4 (2014). https://doi.org/10.1109/ICWOAL.2014.7009215

10. Fauvel, S., et al.: Artificial intelligence powered MOOCs: a brief survey. In: Proceedings of the 2018 IEEE International Conference on Agents (ICA 2018), pp. 56–61 (2018). https://doi.org/10.1109/AGENTS.2018.8460059

11. Babori, A., Fassi, H.F., Zaid, A.: Research on MOOCs: current trends and taking into account of content. In: Proceedings of the 2nd ACM International Conference on Networking, Information Systems & Security (NISS 2019), art. nr. 17, pp. 1–9 (2019). https://doi.org/10.1145/3320326.3320349

12. Ferguson, R., et al.: Research evidence on the use of learning analytics - implications for education policy. In: Vuorikari, R., Castaño Muñoz, J. (eds.) European Commission's Joint Research Centre Science for Policy Report (JRC), EUR 28294 EN (2016). https://doi.org/10.2791/955210. ISBN 978-92-79-64441-2

13. Martínez Monés, A., et al.: Achievements and challenges in learning analytics in Spain: the view of SNOLA. Revista Iberoamericana de Educación a Distancia **23**(2), 187–212 (2020). https://doi.org/10.5944/RIED.23.2.26541

14. Onah, D.F.O., Pang, E.E.L., Sinclair, J.E., Uhomoibhi, J.: Learning analytics for motivating self-regulated learning and fostering the improvement of digital MOOC resources. In: Auer, M.E., Tsiatsos, T. (eds.) IMCL 2018. AISC, vol. 909, pp. 14–21. Springer, Cham (2019). https://doi.org/10.1007/978-3-030-11434-3_3

15. Verbert, K., et al.: Learning dashboards: an overview and future research opportunities. Pers. Ubiquit. Comput. **18**(6), 1499–1514 (2013). https://doi.org/10.1007/s00779-013-0751-2

16. Cobos, R., Olmos, L.: A learning analytics tool for predictive modeling of dropout and certificate acquisition on MOOCs for professional learning. In: IEEE International Conference on Industrial Engineering and Engineering Management Proceedings, vol. 2019, pp. 1533–1537 (2019). https://doi.org/10.1109/IEEM.2018.8607541

17. Moreno-Marcos, P.M., Alario-Hoyos, C., Munoz-Merino, P.J., Kloos, C.D.: Prediction in MOOCs: a review and future research directions. IEEE Trans. Learn. Technol. **12**(3), 384–401 (2019). https://doi.org/10.1109/TLT.2018.2856808

18. Cobos, R., Ruiz-Garcia, J.C.: Improving learner engagement in MOOCs using a learning intervention system: a research study in engineering education. Comput. Appl. Eng. Educ. **29**(4), 733–749 (2021). https://doi.org/10.1002/cae.22316

# Intelligent Instructional Design
# via Interactive Knowledge Graph Editing

Jerry C. K. Chan$^{(\boxtimes)}$ (ID), Yaowei Wang(ID), Qing Li(ID), George Baciu(ID),
Jiannong Cao(ID), Xiao Huang(ID), Richard Chen Li(ID), and Peter H. F. Ng(ID)

Department of Computing, Hong Kong Polytechnic University, Kowloon, Hong Kong
{ckichan,yaowei.wang,qing-prof.li,csgeorge,jiannong.cao,xiao.huang,
richard-chen.li,peter.nhf}@polyu.edu.hk

**Abstract.** The rapid emergence of knowledge graph (KG) research
opens the opportunity for revolutionary educational applications. Most
studies in this area use KGs as peripheral sources of educational materials
rather than a primary tool for Instructional Design. Considerable effort
is required to maintain the alignment between KGs and other elements
of Instructional Design practice, such as syllabus, course plans, student
learning objectives, and teaching outcome evaluation. To bridge such a
gap, we present a novel framework named *Knowledge Graph Reciprocal
Instructional Design* (KGRID), which employs KGs as an instructional
design tool to organize learning units and instructional data. Viewing
the two aspects as a unified ensemble achieves interactive and consistent
course plan editing through manipulations of KGs. The included interactive course schedule editing tool distinguishes our framework from other
timetabling approaches that only handle the initialization task. Managing instructional data in KG format is indispensable in establishing
a foundation of mass instructional data collection for KG research. We
envision a collaboration between the two disciplines. With these crucial functionalities and aspirations, KGRID outperforms the practice of
replacing Instructional Design tables with concept maps. We present the
system architecture, data flow, visualization, and algorithmic aspect of
the editing tool.

**Keywords:** Instructional design · Knowledge graphs · Course planning

## 1 Introduction

Although knowledge graphs (KGs) provides abundant and encyclopedic information, appropriate instructional design tools are necessary such that instructors
can handily leverage educational KGs. Over the decades, new approaches and
studies in Instructional Design have been proposed and conducted for addressing
challenges brought by new educational technologies or new instructional circumstances, e.g. Digital Visual Literacy [2,24] and academic library [20]. KG technology resembles these impacts, but the research of KG for educational application
is at a preliminary stage [32].

© The Author(s), under exclusive license to Springer Nature Switzerland AG 2023
C. S. González-González et al. (Eds.): ICWL 2022/SETE 2022, LNCS 13869, pp. 41–52, 2023.
https://doi.org/10.1007/978-3-031-33023-0_4

Besides the resemblance of being a challenge bring by new technology, being a representation of knowledge itself, KGs raise consistency issues in Instructional Design context. If a KG is representing a structural syllabus of a course, a course plan maps contents from the syllabus to a temporal schedule. As learning units should be "self-contained" and reusable [27], the mapping should be done in a compact way such that the schedule outlines valid learning units. As updates made on KGs might restructure the hierarchy and constituent of learning units, instructor's effort are required to restore the consistency between the syllabus and schedule (see Sect. 3.3).

We present a course plan editing tool that takes consistency management into consideration. A course plan generation process would organize and schedule course concepts from a KG into compact learning units. As the hierarchical structure of KGs has already been proven helpful in other unsupervised tasks such as learning recommendation system [19] and instructional material retrieval [26], it is plausible to apply the same strategy in the course plan generation task. Consistency between structural and temporal aspects of the course would be managed with automated consistency restoration. Such restoration process unifies different viewpoints of the design in real-time, such that interactive editing in both side is possible. Multi-view modelling approaches have been proven effective for consistency management in the field of software engineering [11]. Data visualization is also provided to support instructors design decisions.

To the best of our knowledge, there do not exist any studies that discuss course plan initialization and interactive editing through manipulating KGs. One close work from Cho et al. [10] uses concept map for collaborative Instructional Design task for a single lesson (see Sect. 2.4). As their work focuses on a scope as short as one lesson, issue such as scheduling of learning units and consistency between the schedule and the syllabus are unattended.

To provide management tools and an infrastructure for data collection as a whole, a framework, named Knowledge Graph Reciprocal Instructional Design (KGRID), is proposed. In general, we believe that a practice that integrating KGs in Instructional Design process can expedite the progress of KG technology development in a reciprocal manner.

The rest of the paper is organized as follows. The framework and the design tool would be described in Sect. 3. Brief discussion about how the proposed tool can be improved or how the instructional data collected could benefit both data science and Instructional Design discipline would be followed in Sect. 4. Backgrounds about relevant topics are given in Sect. 2.

## 2　Related Work

### 2.1　Knowledge Graphs

**Graph as Data Science Techniques.** Data science techniques, such as graph neural networks (GNNs) and knowledge graph embedding, take graph structured input and are used for prediction tasks, question answering systems and recommendation systems [13,18]. Variants of GNNs, such as Graph Convolutional

Network, learn connectivity structure of a graph and encode and representation of entities in a graph. These techniques have various applications in such as "medical, financial, cyber security, news and education" [32].

**Knowledge Graph for Education.** Educational applications of KGs are starting to gain more attention lately. Hierarchical relationships in KGs have been utilized for better personalized study recommendation service [19]. Ranawat et al. [26] utilized KGs for course material retrieval and course planning. Study about knowledge graph embedding models for educational application are conducted for theoretical purpose and benchmarking [31]. The main focus of educational KG research was said to be "basic relationship extraction" that more quality data might enable more profound educational applications [32].

## 2.2  Course Plan Generation

Research on course plan generation is to assign course concepts and timeslots considering student's maximum learning capacity. The task is an NP-complete problem that it is computationally intensive for securing an optimal solution, so heuristic approaches are often preferred [6]. Researchers have used different methods and algorithms to address this problem. For example, Betar et al. [3] use a harmony search algorithm; Lewis et al. [21] apply a grouping genetic algorithm; and Lü et al. [22] propose an adaptive tabu search algorithm. Particle swarm optimization methods is also a popular approach for the task throughout the decades [5,17,28]. The task is often formulated as a multi-objective optimization problem where instructors' or students' preferences and time budget are considered [29,30].

One recently proposed approach utilize KGs for course material retrieval [26], the sequencing however relies on minimizing the "Comprehension burden" of the course plan. Most approaches do not utilize structural information of KGs. Existing work is also decoupled with schedule editing. Interaction between user and the schedule are not handled.

## 2.3  Consistency Management

Consistency management enables users to edit multiple views of a design in a controlled manner [11]. These views, in the context of Model-Driven Engineering, separate different design concerns such that the complexity of the task is reduced [11].

Consistency "violation[s]" or "problems" is either "identif[ied]" through managerial activity undertaken by the designer [7] or "checked" by the design tool [7,23]. One violation check only identifies a particular form of inconsistency issue. Because of the incompleteness nature of formal systems, defining a rule-based system for achieving a fully consistent system or defining an objective function for consistency optimization is said to be "impossible" [16]. Given that consistency management is always an open problem, extensibility is then an important feature for design tools that support consistency management [23].

## 2.4  Instructional Design

The purpose of Instructional Design includes visualizing a systematic design process, serving as a base for project collaborations, serving as a managerial tool and providing evaluation of both Instructional Design product and theory [4, 20].

**Instructional Design Models and Tools.** To fulfill the above purposes, new Instructional Design models and tools are designed for new circumstances or challenges. Instructional Design model such as ACE (analyze, create, and evaluate), ISD (instructional system design), PAT (principles, action, and tools) [2] and the matrix model [24] were designed for Digital Visual Literacy. Systematic literature reviews are also done for academic library instruction [20]. To the best of our knowledge, research about Instructional Design models or tools for KG technology remains unexplored.

Concept maps could be conceived as a superficial resemblance of KGs without data science technology [12]. It is mostly applied as an interactive learning activity, known as collaborative concept mapping, where students' learning [12, 15, 25] in a flipped classroom configuration [12] is usually the focus.

Cho et al. [10] suggest to use concept map for visualizing lesson planning process to facilitate collaboration among colleagues. While concept map is perceived as a visual tool for design process, managerial and evaluative aspect of Instructional Design with such graph structure however is beyond the scope of their work. Research for tackling this multifold gap between Instructional Design and KG in terms of managerial, evaluative and technological aspect is vital.

**Instructional Design and Software Engineering.** The idea about sharing practice between software engineering and Instructional Design has been constantly suggested. In order to improve the Instructional Design process, practices from software engineering are suggested to be integrated [1, 8, 14]. Software engineering and Instructional Design are said to be "sister discipline" [1] (Fig. 1).

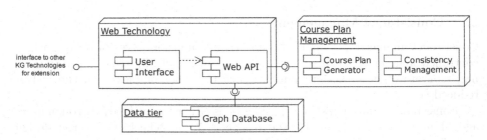

**Fig. 1.** Component diagram of KGRID.

# 3   Methodology

The input of KGRID is educational KGs that includes particular course entities, such as KG representing the syllabus of a course. KGRID consists of three steps as follows.

1. Preprocesses the course KG to produce an input that fits the downstream course plan generation process.
2. Labels entities of the course KG with a course plan generation process.
3. Supports interactive editing while maintaining the consistency of between course KG and course plan.

The algorithmic aspect of these steps will be described in the next three sections. The preprocessing component in step 1 is reused in step 3. The data flow of KGRID is described in Fig. 2. Data for any instructional element, such as course material or student assessment results, can be stored as an entity property. Network data visualization is included in the design tool.

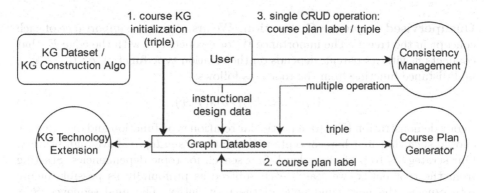

**Fig. 2.** Data flow diagram of the framework. Data flow are ordered. The third step can be repeated indefinitely as user interact with the course plan editor.

## 3.1   Knowledge Graph Preprocessing

KG is defined as a directed heterogeneous multigraph. Given a directed heterogeneous multigraph $K = (V, E, \phi, \psi)$, $\phi : V \rightarrow L_V$ and $\psi : E \rightarrow L_E$, where $L_V$ is a set of entity type labels and $L_E$ is a set of relation type labels. An unweighted homogeneous graph $G = (V, e)$ can be obtained by filtering edges according to their semantics; the mapping $\phi$ and $\psi$ is then dropped. Edges that express the semantics of subsumption (e.g., a "*sub_topic*") in an ontology or taxonomy sense would be kept. We assumed that a vertex $r \in V$ that represents the course's entity exists. A tree structure $T = (V, e')$ is then obtained using Shortest Path Tree (SPT) construction algorithm concerning the vertex $r$. The preprocessing is as follows:

---

**Procedure 1.** KG preprocessing

---

**Given:**
$K = (V, E, \phi, \psi)$; $r$; // $r \in V$
S; // a set of relation type that has a subsumption meaning
**Output:**
$e \leftarrow \{x \in E \mid \phi(x) \in S\}$
$G \leftarrow (V, e)$
$T \leftarrow SPT(G, r)$ // SPT algorithm with respect to the root
**return** $G, T$

---

### 3.2 Course Plan Generation

**Task Definition.** Given the input $T = (V, e')$ with $k$ triplets from the pre-processing process, a course plan generation task is to split concepts to $m$ course sections $H = \{h_1, h_2, ..., h_m\}$, where $h_1 \cap h_2 \cap ... \cap h_m = \emptyset$ and $h_1 \cup h_2 \cup ... \cup h_m = V$. Simultaneously, the grouping compartmentalizes the concept in $l$ weeks.

**Unsupervised Sequence Generation.** We first define the importance of each concept in the tree $T$. The importance $W_i$ of a concept $V_i$ with the edge $E_i$ that connects it with its parent, depends on the relation type function $e : L_E \to \mathbb{R}_{\geq 0}$ and distance function from the root $r$ as follows:

$$W_i = e(\psi(E_i)) \cdot dis(V_i, r). \tag{1}$$

In our demonstration (Fig. 4), a particular relation type function and distance are chosen such that first hop concepts with relation "*sub_topic*" have high priority. Our strategy is to perform a depth-first search for topic dependencies. Starting from the root entity, we search each subtree as profoundly as possible before returning to the next child node of the root entity. The final sequence $S = \{V_1, V_2, ..., V_n\}$ with $n$ concepts has the ordered information that can be used for the next stage.

**Lesson Section Generation.** The hierarchical information is utilized after sequence generation in this stage. To determine the key concepts for the course plan, we first find the candidate section concepts that concept importance is larger than threshold $\epsilon$:

$$h_i = \{V_i | W_i > \epsilon\}. \tag{2}$$

Then, we cut the concept sequence $S$ to $m$ lesson sections by the weighted subtree generation method. The approach adopts recursive search as the section sequence generation that satisfies the following:

$$V_j \in \arg\max_{h_i}(h_i - V_j)^2. \tag{3}$$

Finally, We divide the section sequence $H$ into corresponding to the weekly timestamp in a semester. We generally use the uniform distribution to classify each concept with a weekly timestamp since there is no prior for each week's schedule.

A greedy heuristic algorithm for course plan generation is outlined in Algorithm 2. The algorithm is two stages method. Firstly, we transfer the course knowledge graph to a concept sequence $S$. Secondly, we cut the concept sequence $S$ to several lesson sections, hierarchical information from the knowledge graph.

---

**Algorithm 2.** Course Plan Generation

---

**Input:** $T = (V, e')$; $\epsilon$; $l$;
**Output:** $H = \{h_1, h_2, ..., h_m\}$;
  $S = \emptyset$, $H = \emptyset$;
  **for** $V_i \in T$ **do**
    $S \leftarrow S + V_i$ with max $W_i$ based on Equation 1
    **if** $W_i > \epsilon$ **then**
      $H \leftarrow H + \{V_i\}$
    **end if**
  **end for**
  **while** $S \neq \emptyset$ **do**
    $V_j = S.pop()$
    compute $V_j$ section $h_i$ based on Equation 3
    $h_i \leftarrow h_i + V_j$
    $H \bigcup h_i$
  **end while**
  **return** $H$

---

### 3.3 Consistency Management

"Macrostructure" defined by a learning unit is said to be "self-contained " and "thematic" [27]. In KGRID, such units are represented in a nested hierarchical structure. Updates in KGs might require rescheduling of course plan to preserve such compact macrostructure.

As the course plan label is essentially an entity property, changes made in the course plan have no effect on the KG structure. The label specified by users are likely to be considered meaningful, and the interference of the rescheduling to these user-defined course plan items should be minimized. User can indicate their preference by pinning down the course plan label of specific items. When the hierarchical structure of a course KG is changed, rescheduling is done in a limited scope that includes as many items and as least pinned items as possible. Exceptionally, only descendants of a "jumping" entity would be unpinned (Fig. 3).

A KG updated is a triple $\{V_h, E_r, V_t\}$ with a "create" or "remove" command. After a KG update, the SPT algorithm is run to determine the new hierarchical structure for the course. If the direct parent of $V_t$ has changed after SPT, the entity is said to be "jumped". Entities are unpinned if any of their ancestors

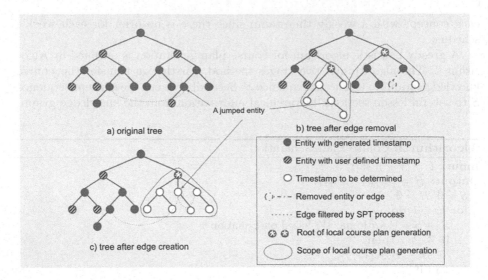

a) original tree

A jumped entity

b) tree after edge removal

c) tree after edge creation

- ● Entity with generated timestamp
- ◍ Entity with user defined timestamp
- ○ Timestamp to be determined
- ◌⊢⁻·⁻ Removed entity or edge
- ······ Edge filtered by SPT process
- ✪ ✪ Root of local course plan generation
- ⬭ Scope of local course plan generation

**Fig. 3.** Examples of consistency updates. A jumped entity with one successor is illustrated. The number of local rescheduling scope depends on whether the updated entity jumps across branches separated by pinned entity.

is "jumping". Jump has to be handled to main consistency. Given a set $U_v = \{V_h, V_t\}$ of two vertexes involved in the triple update, a set $P$ which refers to vertexes with pinned course plan label, a set $C(x)$ which refers to the descendant of a vertex $x$ and a function $H(x)$ which gives the course section of a vertex $x$, the local scope of the rescheduling is defined as follows.

$$r' = \{x \in V \mid (\exists c)[c \in C(x) \wedge c \in U_v] \wedge (\nexists c)[c \in C(x) \wedge c \in P]\}. \qquad (4)$$

$$e'' = \{\{x_1, x_2\} \in e' \mid x_1, x_2 \in C(r') \cup \{r'\}\}. \qquad (5)$$

$$T' = (C(r') \cup \{r'\}, e''). \qquad (6)$$

$$H' = \{h' \in H \mid h' \in H(C(r'))\}. \qquad (7)$$

Algorithm 2 is run with new input $T'$. The output is then mapped to $H'$, using linear interpolation and quantization.

### 3.4 Instructional Data Visualization

Graph visualization might highlight patterns of structural features of the course design. Here, graph centrality metrics are visualized for brief demonstration (Fig. 4). Similar visualization can be done on other data to facilitate Instructional Design duty. For example, visualization of the number of available course materials or student's performance of different course concepts could be included.

---

**Algorithm 3.** Consistency Maintenance

---

**Input:** $T = (V, e')$; $K$; $\{V_h, V_t\}$; $P$; $\epsilon$; $l$;

**Output:**

$T_{new} = (V, e'_{new}) \leftarrow KnowledgeGraphPreprocessing(K)$

$V_{h_{new}} \leftarrow$ an edge in $T_{new}$ where the tail entity is $V_t$

**procedure** RESCHEDULE($x$)

    $e'' \leftarrow \{\{x_1, x_2\} \in e'_{new} \mid x_1, x_2 \in descendant(V_1, T_{new}) \cup \{V_1\}\}$      ▷ Equation 5

    $T' \leftarrow (descendant(V_1, T_{new}) \cup \{V_1\}, e'')$      ▷ Equation 6

    $LessonSectionGeneration(T', \epsilon, l)$      ▷ Algorithm 2

    followed by linear interpolation and quantization

**end procedure**

$V_{h_{old}} \leftarrow$ an edge in $T$ where the tail entity is $V_t$

**if** $V_{h_{old}} \neq V_{h_{new}}$ **then**      ▷ check if $V_t$ jumped

    remove $descendant(V_t, T_{new})$ from $P$      ▷ Recursive unpinning for $V_t$

    $V_1 \leftarrow parent(V_t, T)$      ▷ Define a local scope with root $V_1$ descendant

    **while** $descendant(parent(V_1, T_{new}), T_{new}) \notin P$ **do**

        $V_1 \leftarrow descendant(parent(V_1, T_{new}), T_{new})$      ▷ Expand the scope

    **end while**

    $V_2 \leftarrow parent(V_t, T_{new})$      ▷ Define a local scope with root $V_2$

    **while** $descendant(parent(V_2, T_{new}), T_{new}) \notin P$ **do**

        $V_2 \leftarrow descendant(parent(V_2, T_{new}), T_{new})$

    **end while**

    RESCHEDULE($V_1$)

    **if** $V_1 \neq V_2$ **then**      ▷ check if $V_t$ jumped across pin-separated branches

        RESCHEDULE($V_2$)

    **end if**

**end if**

---

# 4 Future Work

## 4.1 Incorporating with Knowledge Graph Technology

While utilizing KG data visualization for Instructional Design still requires instructors' effort and experience, a data-driven approach can further lighten instructors' burden. Instructional Design in the form of KG, i.e., course contents organized in a graph structure, can be used as inputs of data science techniques. With instructional data, e.g. course plan label, instructional material or students' assessment results included as node properties, prediction of teaching performance indicators of such input can be made. Supervised learning approaches could replace the heuristics used for course plan generation in KGRID. Methodologies mentioned in Sect. 2.1 outline the technical aspect of the above application.

Data-driven approaches are promising. However, data-driven often implies data-hungry. The accuracy of the prediction depends on the amount of data that has been employed to develop the Algorithm [9]. In addition to closing

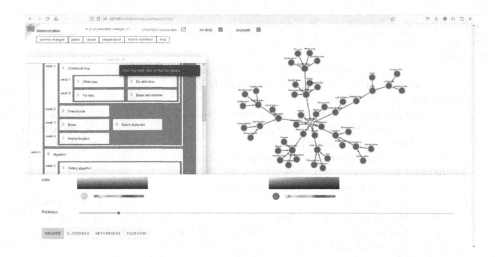

**Fig. 4.** Demonstration of graph visualization.

the gap between KG technology and Instructional Design practice, KGRID also intends to close the data gap in educational KG research.

## 4.2   Extensibility for Consistency Management

As explained in Sect. 2.3, extensibility is a crucial aspect of consistency management tools. Currently, in KGRID, only one form of consistency between the macrostructure of learning units and the course KG is considered. Extensibility issues of KGRID are left unattended. Research for developing additional consistency checks that respond to practical needs are required.

## 5   Conclusions

We have proposed KGRID for integrating KG data representation in Instructional Design. An interactive course plan editor tool with automated initialization and consistent management is described. Preliminary demonstrations of prototypes with visualization have been implemented and shown. Research directions for improvement and other related applications are briefly discussed.

To expedite the application and development of educational KG research, we believe the practices of integrating KGs in the Instructional Design process are essential.

## References

1. Adnan, N.H., Ritzhaupt, A.D.: Software engineering design principles applied to instructional design: what can we learn from our sister discipline? TechTrends **62**(1), 77–94 (2018)

2. Aisami, R.S.: Learning styles and visual literacy for learning and performance. Procedia-Soc. Behav. Sci. **176**, 538–545 (2015)
3. Al-Betar, M.A., Khader, A.T.: A harmony search algorithm for university course timetabling. Ann. Oper. Res. **194**(1), 3–31 (2012)
4. Andrews, D.H., Goodson, L.A.: A comparative analysis of models of instructional design. J. Instr. Dev. **3**(4), 2–16 (1980)
5. Ayob, M., Jaradat, G.: Hybrid ant colony systems for course timetabling problems. In: 2009 2nd Conference on Data Mining and Optimization, pp. 120–126. IEEE (2009)
6. Babaei, H., Karimpour, J., Hadidi, A.: A survey of approaches for university course timetabling problem. Comput. Ind. Eng. **86**, 43–59 (2015)
7. Bashir, R.S., Lee, S.P., Khan, S.U.R., Chang, V., Farid, S.: UML models consistency management: guidelines for software quality manager. Int. J. Inf. Manage. **36**(6), 883–899 (2016)
8. Budoya, C., Kissaka, M., Mtebe, J.: Instructional design enabled agile method using ADDIE model and feature driven development method. Int. J. Educ. Dev. ICT **15**(1) (2019)
9. Chen, P., Lu, Y., Zheng, V.W., Chen, X., Yang, B.: Knowedu: a system to construct knowledge graph for education. IEEE Access **6**, 31553–31563 (2018)
10. Cho, Y.H., Ding, N., Tawfik, A., Chávez, Ó.: Computer-supported collaborative concept mapping for learning to teach mathematics. J. Appl. Instr. Des. **4**(1), 21-x33 (2014)
11. Cicchetti, A., Ciccozzi, F., Pierantonio, A.: Multi-view approaches for software and system modelling: a systematic literature review. Softw. Syst. Model. **18**(6), 3207–3233 (2019). https://doi.org/10.1007/s10270-018-00713-w
12. Cui, J., Yu, S.: Fostering deeper learning in a flipped classroom: effects of knowledge graphs versus concept maps. Br. J. Educ. Technol. **50**(5), 2308–2328 (2019)
13. Dai, Y., Wang, S., Xiong, N.N., Guo, W.: A survey on knowledge graph embedding: approaches, applications and benchmarks. Electronics **9**(5), 750 (2020)
14. Douglas, I.: Issues in software engineering of relevance to instructional design. TechTrends **50**(5), 28–35 (2006)
15. Farrokhnia, M., Pijeira-Díaz, H.J., Noroozi, O., Hatami, J.: Computer-supported collaborative concept mapping: the effects of different instructional designs on conceptual understanding and knowledge co-construction. Comput. Educ. **142**, 103640 (2019)
16. Herzig, S.J., Qamar, A., Reichwein, Λ., Paredis, C.J.: A conceptual framework for consistency management in model-based systems engineering. In: International Design Engineering Technical Conferences and Computers and Information in Engineering Conference, vol. 54792, pp. 1329–1339 (2011)
17. Hossain, S.I., Akhand, M.A.H., Shuvo, M.I.R., Siddique, N.H., Adeli, H.: Optimization of university course scheduling problem using particle swarm optimization with selective search. Expert Syst. Appl. **127**, 9–24 (2019)
18. Ji, S., Pan, S., Cambria, E., Marttinen, P., Philip, S.Y.: A survey on knowledge graphs: representation, acquisition, and applications. IEEE Trans. Neural Netw. Learn. Syst. **33**(2), 494–514 (2021)
19. Jia, B., Huang, X., Jiao, S.: Application of semantic similarity calculation based on knowledge graph for personalized study recommendation service. Educ. Sci.: Theory Pract. **18**(6) (2018)
20. Johnson-Barlow, E.M., Lehnen, C.: A scoping review of the application of systematic instructional design and instructional design models by academic librarians. J. Acad. Librarianship **47**(5), 102382 (2021)

21. Lewis, R., Paechter, B.: Application of the grouping genetic algorithm to university course timetabling. In: Raidl, G.R., Gottlieb, J. (eds.) EvoCOP 2005. LNCS, vol. 3448, pp. 144–153. Springer, Heidelberg (2005). https://doi.org/10.1007/978-3-540-31996-2_14

22. Lü, Z., Hao, J.: Adaptive tabu search for course timetabling. Eur. J. Oper. Res. **200**(1), 235–244 (2010)

23. Lucas, F.J., Molina, F., Toval, A.: A systematic review of UML model consistency management. Inf. Softw. Technol. **51**(12), 1631–1645 (2009)

24. Martin, F.: Instructional design and the importance of instructional alignment. Commun. Coll. J. Res. Pract. **35**(12), 955–972 (2011)

25. Pinandito, A., Az-Zahra, H.M., Hirashima, T., Hayashi, Y.: User experience evaluation on computer-supported concept map authoring tool of kit-build concept map framework. In: 2019 International Conference on Sustainable Information Engineering and Technology (SIET), pp. 289–294. IEEE (2019)

26. Ranawat, R., Venkataraman, A., Subramanian, L.: Collectiveteach: a system to generate and sequence web-annotated lesson plans. In: COMPASS '21: ACM SIGCAS Conference on Computing and Sustainable Societies, Virtual Event, Australia, 28 June 2021–2 July 2021, pp. 1–13. ACM (2021)

27. Redeker, G.H.: An educational taxonomy for learning objects. In: Proceedings 3rd IEEE International Conference on Advanced Technologies, pp. 250–251. IEEE (2003)

28. Sabar, N.R., Ayob, M., Kendall, G., Qu, R.: A honey-bee mating optimization algorithm for educational timetabling problems. Eur. J. Oper. Res. **216**(3), 533–543 (2012)

29. Shakhsi-Niaei, M., Abuei-Mehrizi, H.: An optimization-based decision support system for students' personalized long-term course planning. Comput. Appl. Eng. Educ. **28**(5), 1247–1264 (2020)

30. Shiau, D.: A hybrid particle swarm optimization for a university course scheduling problem with flexible preferences. Expert Syst. Appl. **38**(1), 235–248 (2011)

31. Yao, S., Wang, R., Sun, S., Bu, D., Liu, J.: Joint embedding learning of educational knowledge graphs. In: Pinkwart, N., Liu, S. (eds.) Artificial Intelligence Supported Educational Technologies. AALT, pp. 209–224. Springer, Cham (2020). https://doi.org/10.1007/978-3-030-41099-5_12

32. Zou, X.: A survey on application of knowledge graph. J. Phys: Conf. Ser. **1487**(1), 012016 (2020)

# A Two-Step Process for Analysing Teacher's Behaviors Using a Scenario-Based Platform

Malak Kanaan and Amel Yessad[✉]

Sorbonne Université, CNRS, LIP6, Paris, France
{malak.kanaan,amel.yessad}@lip6.fr

**Abstract.** In this paper, we present research aiming to understand usage behaviors of elementary school teachers when using a scenario-based platform dedicated to the teaching of Computational Thinking concepts. In order to understand their behavior, we have defined a two-step analysis process to identify usage patterns on the platform. The first step consists of performing a clustering algorithm and the second one consists of characterizing each obtained cluster by a pattern mining algorithm. On the one hand, the k-means algorithm allows us to identify four significant clusters of teachers using the platform. On the other hand, the sequential pattern mining algorithm allows to characterize precisely the usage behaviors of each cluster. Thus, this two-step analysis process was evaluated with teachers data. We carried out an experimental study during two workshops with 29 teachers. Teachers interaction's data were collected from ScenoClasse, resulting in a dataset of 498 traces. As a result, we identify different usage behaviors for teachers while using ScenoClasse. Based on their behaviors, teachers can be adapters, explorers, viewers, or beginners.

**Keywords:** Scenario-Based-Teaching · Teaching computational thinking · Teacher's usage behavior · Traces · AI algorithms · Clustering · Pattern mining

## 1 Introduction and Background

Computational thinking (CT) is a focused approach to problem solving, incorporating thought processes that utilize abstraction, decomposition, algorithmic design, evaluation, and generalizations [14,18]. Since 2016, the teaching of CT is introduced gradually into the french elementary school curriculum [2]. This paves the way for many institutional and associative initiatives that offer learning resources in order to improve the culture and the teaching of CT. But these resources are difficult to use in class because teachers lack training to teach the CT concepts.

Sorin [16] claims that Scenario-based learning (SBL) affords learners a more active role in their learning and the opportunity to develop real life skills outside the institution, while the scenario-based teaching (SBT) allows teachers

© The Author(s), under exclusive license to Springer Nature Switzerland AG 2023
C. S. González-González et al. (Eds.): ICWL 2022/SETE 2022, LNCS 13869, pp. 53–62, 2023.
https://doi.org/10.1007/978-3-031-33023-0_5

to improve their professional practices by early identifying a number of issues (including technological and pedagogical issues, potential student difficulties) to overcome before incorporate CT activities into their classes. Moreover, previous research results revealed [1] that the academic achievement of the students was significantly influenced by the activities related to scenario-based learning method.

Thus, in order to deliver an effective learning to students, teachers have to present effective teaching [8], which is only possible when the quality of their education is good enough [11]. Here comes the main objective of scenarios, in encouraging and assisting elementary school teachers, with little training and little familiarity with CT skills, to implement such activities with their students. It could allow them to fill the gap between their prior skills and the skills targeted by the CT and better support their students. Thus, the scenario-based teaching becomes an interesting learning method for teachers as well as the scenario-based learning (SBL) is an efficient learning method for students. The teachers somehow become students themselves. Several benefits of SBL have been studied in the literature. Indeed, researchers claim that the use of scenario-based learning, is essential and necessary for students so that they can establish a connection with real life [1], it offers an effective way of engaging students and building competency mastery [15], and it is a valued and valuable means of exploring professional issues they will face in the future [10].

However, it is found that most of the studies of the literature were conducted with the aim of studying the impact of SBL on students academic results [1], and how SBL help students to solve the problems by taking the role of the performer in the scenario [17], and less the impact of SBL on prospective teachers academic achievement, knowledge, skills and attitudes within classroom applications [7].

Moreover, it is clear in the literature that the analysis of behavior helps platform managers to determine how users feel and use technology in order to obtain insights into the acceptance and adaptation of the platform [4]. Tracing behavior patterns and measuring engagement on these platforms enables the determination of user interest in certain features or content and whether these features are exploited properly for improving the participant professional practices [4].

Therefore, with this research, we aim to experiment the incorporation of the Scenario Based Teaching approach (SBT) thanks to the development of a scenario-based platform that allows teachers to create, share and adapt pedagogical resources to their preferred way.

Additionally, it is significant to point out that there is not much research in the literature that solely focus on identifying the impact of scenario based teaching on prospective teachers' behaviors. Thus, in the study presented in this paper, it is also aimed to identify the different usage behaviors of teachers while using a scenario-based platform in order to identify teacher's profiles. The objective is to support them while they create, modify and use scenarios in the platform. This will also help us to make decisions, correct unexpected uses, promote specific content, and adapt the structures of the platform to teachers.

In this paper, we focus on the two following research questions:

QR1: Is there different usage behaviors of teachers when using the scenario-based platform?

QR2: If yes, what recurring patterns to characterize these teachers' usage behaviors?

In the following sections, we will first introduce the educational context of the study we carried out as well as the scenario-based platform developed for this purpose. Then we present the methodology pursued in the research, the two-step analysis process (see Fig. 2), the primary results, the discussion and the conclusions so far.

## 2 The ScenoClasse Platform and Its Scenario Model

Initiatives like "Hour of code"[1], "Scratch junior"[2], "1,2,3 Codez"[3] offer learning activities of CT, but need to be articulated in pedagogical scenarios, since scenario-based learning helps students to go in depth the domain concepts [12].

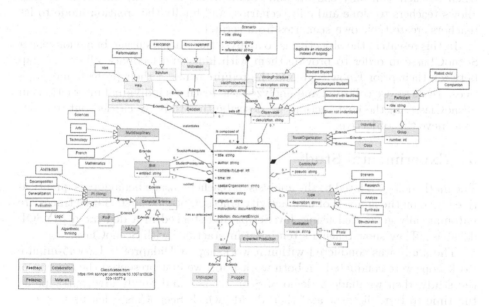

**Fig. 1.** Model of scenario description (the colored rectangles represent the descriptors of an activity and the white ones represent the possible values for these descriptors).

Therefore, in order to support elementary school teachers across teaching CT, previous research has resulted in a scenario description model (see Fig. 1) [3],

---

[1] https://hourofcode.com/fr consulted on March 20, 2022.

[2] https://www.scratchjr.org/ consulted on March 20, 2022.

[3] https://fondation-lamap.org/projet/123-codez consulted on March 20, 2022.

that was identified from a user centered design process with 22 elementary teachers [3, 13]. This model, containing a set of descriptors, allows teachers to orchestrate activities within pedagogical scenarios in order to facilitate their use and establish CT concepts with their students.

We developed a web app called ScenoClasse[4] that relies on this scenario description model. ScenoClasse supports elementary school teachers to create, adapt, share and visualize pedagogical scenarios for teaching CT. To do so, the web app was developed according to the model of scenario description Fig. 1) [3] and the classroom orchestration principle [5] that aim to help novice teachers take ownership of scenarios.

Teachers can use ScenoClasse in order to reuse and adapt activities and scenarios that have been built by others, to build their own scenarios and to share them with other teachers as well. Each teacher can give feedback and comment on each shared scenario in order to share his/her experience after using a scenario with students.

We have implemented three modes to use ScenoClasse: the consultation mode when teachers can only consult and comment scenarios, the editor mode that allows teachers to clone and edit scenarios, and finally the creation mode to let teachers create their own scenarios from scratch.

In this research, the objective is to analyse the teachers usage behaviors using ScenoCLasse in order to provide them with hints and feedback filling the gap between their prior Knowledge and the requirements of their professional practices. To do so, we collected and analyzed the teacher's individual interactions in ScenoClasse. In the next section, we describe the study we carried out in order to achieve this objective.

## 3   Experimental Study

The methodology related to the analysis of teachers' usage behaviors is quantitative based on the analysis of user activity traces in ScenoClasse. These traces are automatically generated using JavaScript and stocked in a dedicated MYSQL database. They show teacher's temporal interactions with ScenoClasse.

The study was conducted within a workshop at Didapro9[5]. Two 45-minute workshops were conducted. In both workshops, we first presented the context of the study, then we made a demo of ScenoClasse, and finally give participants the time to test, discover and then decide which ScenoClasse features to use. During the work, the participants could consult a short visual memo describing the main ScenoClasse features.

### 3.1   Participants

There were 29 participants, 11 primary school teachers, 7 trainers of primary school teachers and 12 interns school teachers. They were mixed gender (24

---

[4] https://scenoclasse.lip6.fr/.
[5] Didapro9 is a colloquium that explores themes around teaching and learning of computer science: https://www.didapro.org/9/.

female vs. 5 male), have varied experience in using digital tools with their students: Experienced (6), Moderately experienced (9), Weakly experienced (5), Not experienced (9). 23 participants reported that ScenoClasse is user friendly application and that they are able to learn to use it very quickly.

### 3.2   Traces Model

The actions performed in ScenoClasse by participants are classified into categories: actions on scenarios (create a scenario, clone a scenario, delete a scenario, print a scenario, etc.), actions on activities (create a new activity, update an activity, create a simultaneous activity, etc.), actions on activity fields (fill in the prerequisite skills, the related resources, the required materials, etc.) and finally actions that are at the platform level (create an account, search for a scenario, etc.). All these actions have been coded and are traced and stored in a dataset when performed by the user.

### 3.3   Analysis Process

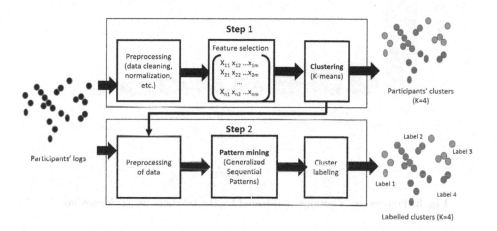

**Fig. 2.** Two-step analysis process

We have pursued a two-step analysis process (see Fig. 2). First we used clustering in order to partition our dataset in clusters, then we applied the frequent pattern mining on each cluster to label them and thus make them more readable for human. The process of clustering was based on first exporting the dataset in CSV format, normalizing the values of the attributes, selecting the relevant features, performing clustering using the k-means algorithm [9], and finally evaluating the performance of the centroid based clustering. For the pattern mining, we prepared the dataset and we used the FP-Growth operator that calculates all frequently-occurring item-sets, using the FP-tree data structure [6].

## 4   Evaluation of the Two-Step Analysis Process

The two-step analysis process was evaluated using teachers data. A dataset of 498 activity traces was obtained from teacher's temporal interactions with ScenoClasse during the workshop at Didapro9.

From the actions mentioned above, three features were selected for clustering the participants: the number of times each participant has visualized activities *#view activities*, the number of times each participant has opened the activity solutions *#consult solutions*, and the number of times each participant has cloned an existing scenario and modified it *#clone scenarios*. These features were selected after trying several other features. They allow us to obtain a good clustering performance. The traces of both evaluations were analyzed using Rapid-Miner Studio.

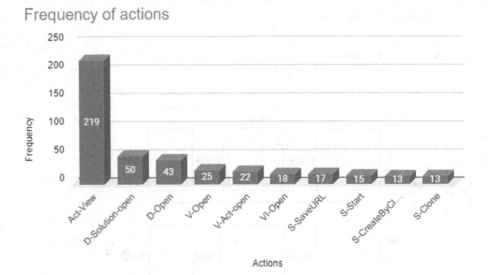

**Fig. 3.** Frequency of actions performed by the teachers using ScenoClasse

### 4.1   Clustering

As mentioned above, we decided to collect teachers' usage behaviours using ScenoClasse.

Teacher's actions were clustered with the K-means clustering approach [9] to categorise teachers with their behavior in using scenarisation platform. To maximize the average centroid distance with high interpretability of the clusters, four clusters (average centroid distance= -0.763) were selected.

In order to answer **QR2**, we analysed the following clusters that were mainly composed from 51 separate working sessions (one participant can have more than one working session)(see Fig. 4).

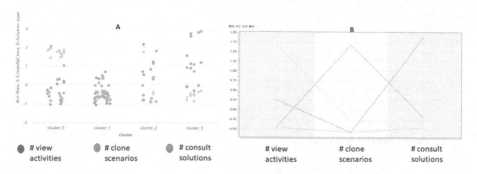

**Fig. 4.** A. The scatter plot showing Clusters B. The features that label each clusters

- **Cluster 0:** participants who were mainly interested in copying scenarios and less in consulting existing scenarios (12 working sessions).
- **Cluster 1:** participants who explore the platform, they tested different functionalities (23 working sessions).
- **Cluster 2:** participants who are interested in the activities, their descriptions and sometimes their solutions (8 working sessions).
- **Cluster 3:** participants who were mainly interested in the solutions of the activities and less in their description in terms of competences or others (8 working sessions).

## 4.2   Pattern Mining

As mentioned above, we applied the FP-Growth algorithm in order to find all frequently-occurring sequences of teachers' actions. As we can see in Fig. 3, the number of *#View activities* is highly greater than other actions -which is expected- since in the two workshops, teachers haven't much time to do several actions other than visualising activities in high frequency (frequency−219) and many more actions in less frequency. We can observe that the second frequent action after *#View activities* has a frequency of 50. So as not to distort the results, we excluded the *#View activities* from the columns of actions while performing the FP-Growth.

In fact, the amount of available data forced us to limit the features (in our case 3: *#View activities, #clone scenarios, #consult solutions*) which made the clustering result easy to read. But if we are in a context where we have a lot of interaction data (massive data), we would have the possibility to define more features and therefore we will need pattern mining to label the clusters. Thus, the preliminary pattern mining results (see Fig. 5) are consistent with what we observed on the clusters, but need to be applied on massive data to be easier to read and to be more accurate.

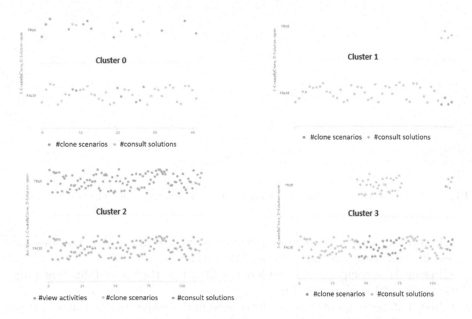

**Fig. 5.** Pattern mining on each cluster

## 4.3 Discussion

The exploratory analysis revealed many usage behavior patterns. As explained in Sect. 3.3, the process was first performing clustering, then labeling each cluster using FP-Growth.

- *Users who create scenarios by clone are less likely to visualize activities.* In fact, the blue line that represents Cluster 0 in Fig. 4 B shows that the number *#clone scenarios* is highly larger compared to the number *#View activities* and *#consult solutions* which are almost close to zero in this cluster. These results are verified while applying the FP-Growth algorithm on Cluster 0 from Fig. 5), where we can see the number *#clone scenarios* dominating the "TRUE" values of the scatter plot. Thus, we label this teachers behaviour pattern by *"Adapters"*.
- *Users who are exploring the platform, they test all of its functionalities.* This pattern is represented by the light green line of Fig. 4 B. It represents Cluster 1 and shows that the number of three features is almost equal in this cluster which means that users are doing all the actions. Thus, we can label this teachers behaviour pattern by *"Explorers"*.
- *Users who tend to learn new things, they visualize the different activities and scenarios.* This pattern is represented by the dark green line of Fig. 4 B. It represents Cluster 2 and shows that the number *#View activities* is highly larger compared to the number *#clone scenarios* and *#consult solutions* which are very low in this cluster. Moreover, the result of FP-Growth on Cluster 2 from in 5 shows the values *#View activities* dominating the "TRUE" values of

the scatter plot that verify our findings in the process of clustering. Thus, we label this teachers behaviour pattern by *"Viewers"*.

– *Users who want to be reassured about their ability to solve activities, they are mainly interested in consulting solutions of the activities.* This pattern is represented by the red line of Fig. 4 B. It represents Cluster 3 and shows that the number *#consult solutions* is highly larger compared to the number *#clone scenarios* and *#View activities*. Likewise, these results are verified while applying the FP-Growth algorithm on Cluster 3 from Fig. 5), where we can see the values *#consult solutions* dominating the "TRUE" values of the scatter plot. Thus, we label this teachers behaviour pattern by *"Beginners"*.

## 5   Conclusion and Future Work

The work presented in this paper deals with the teachers' usage behaviors using a scenario-based platform. The platform can determine how teachers use the online features available, which part of the platform has greater acceptance, and which functionalities are more useful for teachers. This knowledge allows researchers to make decisions and plan actions about the platform; these decisions and actions could cover several aspects, such as providing help to teachers, promoting interesting features to increase user engagement and engage more users, create learning scenarios adapted to users' detected needs, etc.

In conclusion, this research is a first step into investigating teacher's behaviors with a scenario-based platform. The results showed that teachers present different usage behaviors while using ScenoClasse. Depending on their behaviors, they can be adapters, explorers, viewers or beginners.

These results must be considered in light of the limitations of our methodology. For example, since teachers were in a 45-minute workshops, it was difficult to extract a stable patterns. On the other hand, having more teachers using ScenoClasse with knowing their background allows us to identify more interesting and accurate patterns.

After identifying the patterns, our future work consists of repeating the same process with a larger number of intern school teachers through two semesters, also we will go through personal interviews in order to determine the accuracy of each feature or interesting pattern. This new study will answer our next research question: What kind of support should be provided to teachers (especially novices) to help them develop a pedagogical scenario using a scenarisation platform?

**Acknowledgements.** This paper has been funded by the ANR IECARE. We thank Mathieu Muratet, Pierre Jean Lainé and Arnauld séjourné for their support.

## References

1. Aslan, S., et al.: The impact of argumentation-based teaching and scenario-based learning method on the students' academic achievement. J. Baltic Sci. Educ. **18**(2), 171–183 (2019)

2. Baron, G.L., Drot-Delange, B.: L'informatique comme objet d'enseignement à l'école primaire française? mise en perspective historique. Revue française de pédagogie. Recherches en éducation (195), 51–62 (2016)
3. Brunet, O., Yessad, A., Muratet, M., Carron, T.: Vers un modèle de scénarisation pour l'enseignement de la pensée informatique à l'école primaire. In: Didapro 8-DidaSTIC (2020)
4. Cruz-Benito, J., Therón, R., García-Peñalvo, F.J., Lucas, E.P.: Discovering usage behaviors and engagement in an educational virtual world. Comput. Hum. Behav. **47**, 18–25 (2015)
5. Dillenbourg, P., Jermann, P.: Technology for classroom orchestration. In: New Science of Learning, pp. 525–552. Springer, Cham (2010). https://doi.org/10.1007/978-1-4419-5716-0_26
6. Han, J., Pei, J., Yin, Y.: Mining frequent patterns without candidate generation. ACM Sigmod Rec. **29**(2), 1–12 (2000)
7. Hursen, C., Fasli, F.G.: Investigating the efficiency of scenario based learning and reflective learning approaches in teacher education. Eur. J. Contemp. Educ. **6**(2), 264–279 (2017)
8. Loughran, J.: Is teaching a discipline? implications for teaching and teacher education. Teachers Teach.: Theory Pract. **15**(2), 189–203 (2009)
9. MacQueen, J.: Classification and analysis of multivariate observations. In: 5th Berkeley Symposium Mathematics Statistics Probability, pp. 281–297 (1967)
10. Meldrum, K.: Preparing pre-service physical education teachers for uncertain future (s): a scenario-based learning case study from australia. Phys. Educ. Sport Pedagogy **16**(2), 133–144 (2011)
11. Özçınar, H.: Mapping teacher education domain: a document co-citation analysis from 1992 to 2012. Teach. Teacher Educ. **47**, 42–61 (2015)
12. Pal, K.: Evaluation of a scenario-based Socratic style of teaching and learning practice. In: Enhancing Teaching and Learning With Socratic Educational Strategies: Emerging Research and Opportunities, pp. 121–144. IGI Global (2022)
13. Séjourné, A., Voulgre, E., Reffay, C., Muratet, M.: Anr ie-care: Analyse d'un dispositif de formation initiale pour professeurs d'école stagiaires (pes) en informatique. communication du 13 octobre 2021 au symposium ie-care du colloque de l'université de cergy, l'école primaire au 21e siècle, france. In: L'école primaire au 21e siècle (2021)
14. Selby, C., Woollard, J.: Computational thinking: the developing definition (2013)
15. Shih, A., Schrader, P.: Scenario based learning approach in teaching statics. In: 2004 Annual Conference, pp. 9–1083 (2004)
16. Sorin, R.: Scenario-based learning: transforming tertiary teaching and learning. In: Proceedings of the 8th QS-APPLE Conference, Bali, pp. 71–81. James Cook University (2013)
17. Veznedaroğlu, M.: The effects of scenario based learning on attitudes and self efficacy beliefs of teacher candidates' towards teacher proficiency. Unpublished master's thesis). Ankara University, Ankara (2005)
18. Wing, J.M.: Computational thinking. Commun. ACM **49**(3), 33–35 (2006)

# New Digital Tools to Teach Soft Skills and Sustainability for the Labor Market: Gamification as a Tool for Competency Acquisition in Realistic Contexts

Aida López Serrano⊙, Nadia McGowan⊠⊙, Daniel Burgos⊙,
and Pablo Moreno-Ger⊙

Universidad Internacional de La Rioja, Logroño, Spain
nadia.mcgowan@unir.net

**Abstract.** This article describes the Compete! educational game, developed within the European Erasmus + framework, which aims to teach soft skills to higher education students to increase their employability. A participatory learning methodology based on a gamification tool has been used for this purpose. The game presents a series of scenarios that describe social sustainability problems and require applying of soft skills identified as key competences in a field study across different European countries. These competences are: creative problem solving, effective communication, stress management, and teamwork. On completion of each game scenario and the game itself, students receive an evaluation of both their soft skills and the strategic and operational decisions they have made. In the evaluation of these decisions, both economic and sustainability aspects of the decision are assessed. The teacher can then address the competences and sustainability issues using the different scenarios of the game, thus creating higher motivation and deeper understanding amongst the students. This hybrid learning methodology incorporates digital tools for the cross-curricular teaching-learning of sustainability and soft skills. It is therefore a methodology that promotes the SDGs.

**Keywords:** gamification · serious games · Erasmus + · sustainability · soft skills · higher education

## 1 Introduction

The modern labor market demands greater skills from its workers. These transcend academic and technical knowledge and have begun to incorporate soft skills [1]. These have progressively become a marker for increased employability [2–4]. In this context, the introduction of these skills in higher education has proven to be challenging [5]. Among these soft skills are problem-solving, stress management, effective communication, and

C. S. González-González et al. (Eds.): ICWL 2022/SETE 2022, LNCS 13869, pp. 63–73, 2023.
https://doi.org/10.1007/978-3-031-33023-0_6

teamwork, which are essential for students to find good jobs and continue updating their skills. In addition, it must be considered that technological change implies opportunities and increases productivity in a global market, where there is great competitiveness and supply of jobs that require hard or technical skills but also effectiveness and efficiency in the work, being necessary to interact with other individuals, which are achieved with soft skills [6]. Among these soft skills are problem-solving, stress management, effective communication, and teamwork.

Approaches to improving students' soft skills include the provision of learning technologies and gamification as a learning technique, which can help them succeed in a job market immersed in a global economy [7]. This has been demonstrated by previous work focused on the development of pilot courses to enhance students' intrinsic motivation for online learning during the Covid 19 pandemic [8].

*Compete!* is a serious game aimed at raising awareness among higher education students of the importance of soft skill competencies and their impact in professional and personal settings, focusing on the former. It has been developed within the European Erasmus + framework as a participatory learning methodology based on gamification. The videogame is a tool to help students critically apply soft skills and discuss their impact in classroom settings. The game design emphasized giving the students feedback on their decisions throughout the narrative it presents, in order to integrate assessment in the game design [9]. This will help improve their understanding of the impact of their decisions and how these reflect the acquisition of these skills. The goal is to help students in their final year of university improve their skills towards their incorporation into the workplace.

In this study, we present the design of this serious game, the soft skills included in it, its storyline, and a description of how they are presented to the students. This single player game (Fig. 1) can be played online through any internet browser. It can be accessed and played through the Compete! project's website[1].

**Fig. 1.** Compete! Interface.

## 2 Game Design

Educational games must strike a balance between education and entertainment [10]. While 'edutainment' generally holds negative connotations [11], games must provide a certain sense of fun to the player. In order to achieve skill acquisition while providing a fun environment, first a study of which soft skills were to be included was developed. Having selected these, a storyline was designed to maximize their impact. Finally, assessment methods were developed for the game based on soft skill competency acquisition measurements.

### 2.1 The Soft Skill Selection

The soft skill framework design for *Compete!* [12] was based on the four categories outlined by the eLene4work taxonomy [13]: social, personal, methodological, and digital skills. These categories were presented to 500 enterprises and 350 recent graduate higher education students in order to identify which skills were deemed the most relevant in the labor market [14]. The selected soft skills were creative problem-solving, effective communication, stress management, and teamwork. Each soft skill competency was divided into four basic behaviors [15]:

- Creative problem-solving: the ability to come up with unusual or clever ways to solve a problem. This competence helps solve novel, ill-defined problems in complex, real-world settings. The basic behaviors of this competency are problem definition, creative alternatives, and decision and action plan.
- Effective communication: the ability to convey a message to a person or group in an effective and efficient manner. It is the process of exchanging ideas, thoughts,

knowledge, and information in such a manner that the purpose and content of the message is fully shared and understood by the receiver. The basic behaviors of this competency are logic, empathy, and trust.

- Stress management: the ability to deal with stress-inducing situations and the subjective experience of stress, using rational arguments and tools to identify the strengths and weaknesses of alternative solutions, conclusions, or approaches to problems. It is related to the capacity to set priorities and the effective use of time and resources. The basic behaviors of this competency are resources, priorities, and timeline.
- Teamwork: the ability to work together in a group with other people, using cooperation for mutual benefit, and collaboration as a deeper communal effort toward a shared goal. Teamwork involves the capacity to count on other people's ideas and capabilities and coordinate different actions to achieve the team output. The basic behaviors of this competency are common goals, team spirit, and team organization.

## 2.2 Storyline Structure

The storyline designed for *Compete!* gamifies the approach to soft skill competency acquisition. The story revolves around sustainability and choices given to the players will have both a social and economic impact. The narrative is divided into two introductory tasks and ten challenges. The initial challenges help introduce the player to the game. Each challenge is a unique scenario where a social or environmental problem is presented.

The player takes the role of a new Project Manager on the Island of Allpa Kawsay, inspired by Ecuadorian territories. This position requires advising the local government and helping them develop the local economy sustainably while keeping the residents happy.

The initial introductory tasks present the setting, the office from where the player will work, and the gameplay.

The challenges are the following:

1. The international investor: the player is offered the chance to build a hotel on a beach that is part of a natural reserve.
2. Better fish to fry: Fish reserves are depleted in local waters.
3. High voltage: The island has a power shortage. An adequate energy source must be chosen.
4. Deep waters: Island water supplies have been polluted by the local mining industry.
5. Rubbish: The island's only landfill is full and the lack of proper on-site waste management is contributing to rising pollution levels.
6. Naturally, a disaster: Rising pollution triggers a volcanic eruption which, in turn, causes a tsunami. The player must act and help solve the crisis.
7. Poachers: An international mafia wants the locals to smuggle a rare bird for them.
8. Sea Level Rising: Water levels are at an all-time high, something must be done before the island drowns.
9. Deforestation: Forests are being consumed by farms and timber production.
10. Slave trade: The lack of local opportunities and the many crises put the inhabitants at risk of falling into human trafficking and modern slavery abroad.

## 2.3   Game Structure

The game introduction is comprised of two introductory tasks that help the player become familiar with the storyline and the gameplay. After them, he is presented with the core of the game, which are the ten challenge scenes. Each challenge follows an identical structure (Fig. 2). The structure is as follows:

1. The challenge storyline is presented.
2. The player is given a task. He must pick between two possible choices to complete it. Each choice helps measure specific soft skill competencies.
3. Counselors give their opinion of the best course of action.
4. Player decides which counselor gives him the best option. This choice will be assessed based on its sustainability and social impact.

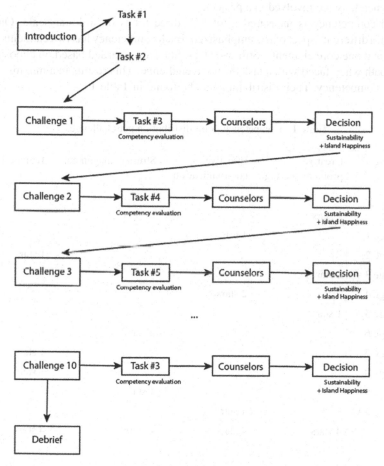

**Fig. 2.**   Game structure.

After the final challenge, the players receive feedback on their results.

## 2.4  Competency Measurement

Soft skill competencies are measured independently from social and economic impact of the decisions the player makes.

Soft skill competencies are measured in three dimensions. Each of these dimensions is measured using a binomial right or wrong (a or b) decision. Social and economic impact are measured through sustainability and island happiness. Sustainability refers to the economic impact of the decisions made by the player. Island happiness is the social impact of their decisions. Both are linked by the answer given to the competency measurement task. The correct answer will give the player access to the best option in the decision section. If the incorrect answer is chosen, the option that would have awarded the player the maximum number of points will not be available. That counselor will explain why they cannot offer advice. Giving competencies a real-life impact reflects how people who have developed their soft skills have better opportunities to achieve results when they are involved in a project.

Each competency is measured a total of three times on a 4-star scale. On each occasion, a different aspect of it is emphasized. Each competency has two elements worth one star and one core element worth two stars. Stars are awarded based on choosing the correct path when faced with a task during a challenge. This results in a maximum of 4 stars per competency. Their distribution can be found in Table 1.

**Table 1.** Competency point distribution per challenge.

| Challenge | Creative problem-solving | Effective communication | Stress management | Teambuilding |
|---|---|---|---|---|
| Puzzle 1 | | | 1 star | |
| Puzzle 2 | 2 stars | | | |
| Challenge 1 | | 1 star | | |
| Challenge 2 | | | | 1 star |
| Challenge 3 | 1 star | | | |
| Challenge 4 | | 2 stars | | |
| Challenge 5 | 1 star | | | |
| Challenge 6 | | | 2 stars | |
| Challenge 7 | | | | 1 star |
| Challenge 8 | | | | 1 star |
| Challenge 9 | | | 1 star | |
| Challenge 10 | | 1 star | | |
| Total | 4 stars | 4 stars | 4 stars | 4 stars |

Soft skill competency scores are shown in a style similar to the one presented in Fig. 3.

Creative Problem Solving

Effective Communication

Stress Management

Teamwork

**Fig. 3.** Soft skill competency scores.

Economic and social impact are measured from 0 to 15 points. In each challenge, the player must listen to his counselors and decide whose advice he will follow. These choices will impact the amount of sustainability and island happiness points. As there are five counselors, there are five possible choices (Table 2), which distribute points in the following manner:

1. 0 Sustainability, 0 Island happiness (0S + 0Ih): the choice neither develops a sustainable economy nor increases island happiness.
2. 1 Sustainability, 0 Island happiness (1S + 0Ih): the choice is good for a sustainable economy but has no positive social impact.
3. 0 Sustainability, 1 Island happiness (0S + 1Ih): the choice does not improve the local economy in a sustainable way but does have a positive local impact.
4. 1 Sustainability, 1 Island happiness (1S + 1Ih): the choice is both sustainable and will be socially positive.
5. 1.5 Sustainability, 1.5 Island happiness (1.5S + 1.5Ih): the choice is sustainable, socially positive and has the extra advantage of being a creative and well-thought-out option.

**Table 2.** Distribution of points and counselors for each challenge.

| Challenge | 0S + 0Ih | 1S + 0Ih | 0S + 1Ih | 1S + 1Ih | 1.5S + 1.5Ih |
|---|---|---|---|---|---|
| Challenge 1 | Noelia | Francesca | Martin | Yarik | Greta |
| Challenge 2 | Greta | Francesca | Martin | Yarik | Noelia |
| Challenge 3 | Noelia | Greta | Yarik | Martin | Francesca |
| Challenge 4 | Francesca | Greta | Martin | Yarik | Noelia |
| Challenge 5 | Martin | Noelia | Greta | Francesca | Yarik |
| Challenge 6 | Greta | Noelia | Francesca | Yarik | Martin |
| Challenge 7 | Martin | Yarik | Greta | Noelia | Francesca |
| Challenge 8 | Yarik | Martin | Francesca | Noelia | Greta |
| Challenge 9 | Noelia | Yarik | Greta | Francesca | Martin |
| Challenge 10 | Greta | Francesca | Martin | Noelia | Yarik |

Counselors have each distinct personalities that affect how they react to each situation the player encounters. This creates a logic behind their suggestions, although their personal views are never made explicit.

- Martin: the idealist.
- Greta: the realist.
- Francesca: money centered.
- Noelia: tourism specialist.
- Yarik: local activist.

## 2.5  Assessment

Each scene provides feedback to players regarding their choices (Fig. 4). These are divided into two sections. The first one shares the results related to social and economic impact, measured based on sustainability and island happiness of the chosen course of action. The second half is related to the soft skill competency associated with the challenge. In this case, the feedback suggests other possible courses of action or reinforces why the choice was adequate. In all cases players are encouraged to discuss the topic among their peers.

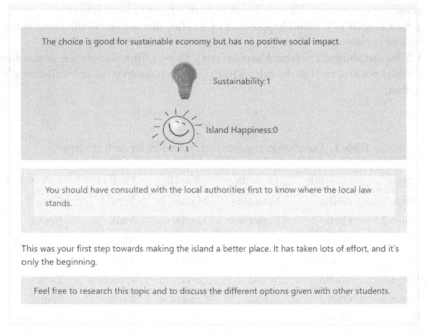

The choice is good for sustainable economy but has no positive social impact.

Sustainability:1

Island Happiness:0

You should have consulted with the local authorities first to know where the local law stands.

This was your first step towards making the island a better place. It has taken lots of effort, and it's only the beginning.

Feel free to research this topic and to discuss the different options given with other students.

**Fig. 4.** End of Challenge 1 scores.

After finalizing the tenth scenario, players access the Final Report section where their total scores are shared with them and explained. These are the accumulation of the partial scores from each scene. The aim of the design is to highlight the importance of the soft skill competencies and their critical behaviors in order to motivate the player to further develop these skills (Fig. 5).

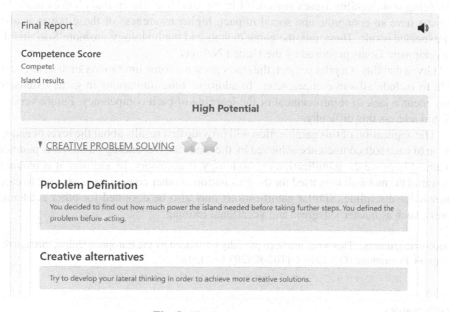

**Fig. 5.** Final report example.

External factors are measured independently during the game, from 0 to 15 points each. At the end of the game, scores are added, and results are given according to the following categories:

- Four stars (25–30 points): Expert
- Three stars (19–24 points): Professional
- Two stars (13–18 points): High potential
- One star (7–12 points): Beginner
- No stars (0–6 points): Newbie

Each soft skill competency is also awarded stars based on the results obtained in the assessment of each related behavior. The explanations related to each behavior highlight the choices the players have made and how they could have behaved differently in order to increase their competency in that soft skill area. The result is an overview of all the choices taken which can help players reflect on their overall behavior.

## 3   Conclusions

*Compete!* can be used in classroom settings as part of active teaching-learning in cross-curricular environments. The game design fosters active dialogue which can be used to increase student engagement. This is achieved through a series of scenes that introduce current topics of interest and which can create controversy regarding what would be an adequate solution for them. *Compete!* aims to increase higher education student employability by improving their soft skill competencies while also raising awareness regarding sustainability issues embedded in the storyline. Given that choices made by players have an economic and social impact, higher awareness of these issues is also an expected result. Therefore, the game design and methodology promote Sustainable Development Goals proposed by the United Nations.

Given that this is a pilot project, the study presents some limitations such as not been able to include all sub-competencies. In addition, time limitations in game extension may mean a lack of reinforcement of the learning of each competency. Future version should address this difficulty.

The application of this gamification will provide first results about the level of acquisition of each soft competence achieved by the students. Depending on this, it is planned to adjust improve the gamification methodology, if necessary. In addition, it is planned to extend the methodology used for the acquisition of other competences specific to each knowledge discipline. Similar gamifications may also be designed for other academic levels, such as master's degrees and vocational training.

**Acknowledgments.** This work has been partially co-funded by the European Union, through the Eramus+ Programme (GA 2019-1-IT02-KA203-062350).

# References

1. Andrews, J., Higson, H.: Graduate employability, 'soft skills' versus 'hard' business knowledge: a european study. High. Educ. Eur. **33**(4), 411–422 (2008). https://doi.org/10.1080/037 97720802522627
2. Remedios, R.: The role of soft skills in employability. Int. J. Manag. Res. Rev. **2**(7), 1285 (2012)
3. Succi, C., Canovi, M.: Soft skills to enhance graduate employability: comparing students and employers' perceptions. Stud. High. Educ. **45**(9), 1834–1847 (2020)
4. Yong, B.P.P., Ling, Y.L.: Skills gap: the importance of soft skills in graduate employability between the perspectives of employers and graduates. Int. J. Soc. Human. Extension (IJSHE) 10–24 (2022)
5. Tang, K.N.: Beyond employability: embedding soft skills in higher education. Turkish Online J. Educ. Technol.-TOJET **18**(2), 1–9 (2019)
6. Gómez-Gamero, M.E.: Soft Skills Competencies for the new Millennium. DIVULGARE Boletín Científico de la Escuela Superior de Actopan, 11 (2019)
7. Apandi, A.M.: Gamification meets mobile learning: soft-skills enhancement. In: Information R. Management Association: Research Anthology on Developments in Gamification and Game-Based Learning (2022). https://doi.org/10.4018/978-1-6684-3710-0.ch061
8. Takács, J.M, Pogástsnik, M., Kersánszki, T.: Improving soft skills and motivation with gamification in engineering education (2022)
9. Bellotti, F., Kapralos, B., Lee, K., Moreno-Ger, P., Berta, R.: Assessment in and of serious games: an overview. Adv. Human-Comput. Interact. **2013**(1), 1 (2013). https://doi.org/10.1155/2013/136864
10. Prensky, M.: Digital Game Based Learning. McGraw-Hill, New York (2001)

11. Moreno-Ger, P., Burgos, D., Martínez-Ortiz, I., Sierra, J.L., Fernández-Manjón, B.: Educational game design for online education. Comput. Hum. Behav. **24**(6), 2530–2540 (2008)
12. Compete! COMPetences for Effective Labour Market Entry!: Research of soft skills for employability (2020). https://competeproject.eu/wp-content/uploads/2020/06/O1_Research-on-soft-skills-for-employability.pdf
13. eLene4work. https://www.euca.eu/elene4work. Accessed 20 July 2022
14. Compete! COMPetences for Effective Labour Market Entry! Training package and game guide (2022). https://competeproject.eu/wp-content/uploads/2022/05/O4-COMPETE-Training-package-and-game-guide.pdf
15. Cardona, P., Wilkinson, H.: Creciendo como líderes Eunsa. Ediciones Universidad De Navarra, Navarra (2009)

# Pocket English Master – Language Learning with Reinforcement Learning, Augmented Reality and Artificial Intelligence

Ashini Imasha(✉), Kavindu Wimalaweera(✉), Manohari Maddumage(✉),
Dilain Gunasekara(✉), Kalpani Manathunga(✉), and Devanshi Ganegoda(✉)

Sri Lanka Institute of Information Technology, SLIIT Malabe Campus, New Kandy Road,
Malabe 10115, Sri Lanka
{it19023656,it19096476,it19023588,it18219326}@my.sliit.lk,
{kalpani.m,devanshi.g}@sliit.lk

**Abstract.** English is the most spoken language in the world. Despite this, only 1.35 billion people worldwide use English as their first or second language of communication. English is the world's main language, 83% of the world's population do not speak English. As a result, most people must spend considerable money and time to learn English. Continuous practice ensures that the language develops as often as possible. Developed, Pocket English Master (PEM) mobile app assumes the role of a full-fledged English teacher to solve the above problems. This application entails conducting an early assessment of the student's present English competence and directing him or her to the appropriate class. Using artificial intelligence, a curriculum is created that matches the knowledge level of the students. The application enables students to complete learning activities at their convenience by evaluating the student's learning style using artificial intelligence and making the student's daily activities efficient and aesthetically pleasing using reinforcement learning and algorithms. This includes an artificial intelligence component to improve students' ability to speak and read English as well as their ability to engage in natural relationships. Also, the app incorporates augmented reality, real-time handwritten text scanning, and real-time grammar and spelling error correction.

**Keywords:** Reinforcement Learning · Augmented Reality · Artificial Intelligence · English Learning · mobile

## 1 Introduction

English is the most spoken language in the world. English can also be recognized as the language of international communication. 67 different countries use English as their official language and 1.5 billion speakers can be found worldwide [1]. Additionally, English is the most often used language digitally and in commercial communication. English is the primary major language used in publishing scientific research articles, accounting for more than 85% of all research publications. It is the international language

C. S. González-González et al. (Eds.): ICWL 2022/SETE 2022, LNCS 13869, pp. 74–85, 2023.
https://doi.org/10.1007/978-3-031-33023-0_7

used for trade and commerce. In addition, international trade and business are conducted officially using English. Even in the IT sector, many software applications are written in the English language, and people connect in English with their colleagues or other software experts working around the world [2]. Under the tenets of social distance, all face-to-face lessons were halted because of the continuing COVID-19 pandemic [5]. Students started adopting e-learning platforms to finish their education as a result. Language learning has greatly benefited from e-learning. There are a ton of resources available to students online to help them learn English or other languages. Because there aren't many opportunities for pupils to engage with others, they improve their English by reading and listening to pre-recorded materials [2]. Speaking Bots will someday become the ideal English language study companion thanks to recent technological developments, enabling students to learn whenever and wherever they choose [6].

There are many different online platforms available for studying English. Although there are several web-based applications containing lessons, sample tests, and solutions, learner-specific mobile apps are still not readily available. When thinking about language learning, it is essential to have a platform that is effective and efficient, adaptable to all circumstances, and engaging with the user. Without interacting behaviours, learners cannot improve their language skills. Additionally, using that platform would be useless in the absence of adaptive behaviour. Even though there are many learning platforms, they do not engage the learner in an adaptable way since each user's level of language proficiency and learning style vary. The system does not adapt to the demands of the learner, for example, if he or she has trouble with spelling or grammar. A further comparison of the top-rated systems is detailed in the table below (Table 1).

It is important to have adaptability in English-leaning platforms when considering all the aforementioned factors. Speaking is one of the four macro skills necessary for effective communication in any language, especially when the speakers are not speaking in their native language. English speaking skills, especially in the digital age, should be taught along with other skills. Due to the significance of speech, Bailey (2005) and Goh (2007) proposed new curriculum design and teaching methods to promote speech development [3].

There are several techniques to pick from when it comes to reading handwritten writing. Hidden Markov models and integrated segmentation recognition algorithms are only a couple of examples. Adversarial Feature Enhancing Network for End-to-End Handwriting Passage Recognition is a research paper that proposed an end-to-end handwriting passage recognition system that is relatively quick called AFEN. It also introduced a module for feature extraction with a multi-scale receiver field for offline handwriting passages. It effectively manages identification-related concerns and a modified module for the Shared Feature Extractor to gather multilayer starting features [4].

One of the most efficient ways to learn English is through picture description. Describing paintings or other art pictures is something for the advanced learner of English as you also must talk about the artist's intention and the impression on the viewer. The picture description generator's main goal is to help users develop their picture description and analytical thinking skills. The picture descriptor generation component is developed

**Table 1.** Comparison of existing systems.

| | Dualingo | Speak and improve | Preply | Cambly |
|---|---|---|---|---|
| Specific to English language learning | No - Multi language learning tool | Yes | Yes | Yes |
| Consider the pre-knowledge in English | Yes | No | No | No |
| Provide Real-time conversations | No | No - It asks random questions from students | Yes - Conversations with native speakers | Yes - Conversations with native speakers |
| Detect real-time grammar and mispronunciation in speech | No | No - provides feedback but does not clarify mistakes | Yes - Real user checking | Yes - Real user checking |
| improves speaking, listening, thinking, writing, and reading skills | Yes | No - Based on speaking | No - Based on speaking | No - Based on speaking |
| Reinforcement Learning | No | No | No | No |
| Detect errors in handwritten text | No | No | No | No |
| Provide a picture description generator | No | No | No | No |
| Speech to Text | Yes | No | No | No |
| Text to Speech | Yes | No | No | No |

using machine learning, computer vision, convolutional neural networks, and image-captioning AI. All these skills work together to improve communication with native English speakers and other members of the international community. Various systems offer services for language learning. However, they have several restrictions, and their degree of accuracy is in doubt. These online resources fall short of what students need. PEM proposed mobile application can fill the above-mentioned gaps in English language learning. Mainly PEM provides students with an adaptive learning environment, conversational speaking bot, image description generator and handwritten text capture component to improve their English language skills.

## 2 Literature Review

Teaching and learning have been profoundly affected by the development of information and communication technologies (ICTs) and digital media. E-Learning is commonly used to refer to the process of acquiring knowledge through modern media technologies. Utilizing technology-enhanced learning and teaching systems, technology-enhanced learning enables students to acquire knowledge and skills with the aid of instructors, tutors, learning support tools, and technological resources [7]. Due to their capacity to assist Information technology (IT) educators in rethinking and changing their courses' learning designs to give more relevant learning experiences for their students, the value of e-learning systems has been underlined more. Students can take an active role in the learning process with these tools. According to a study, "E-Learning has grown in several ways in the fields of education, business, and training, and has varied connotations across disciplines. E-learning can assist students in completing their education with greater flexibility and convenience than traditional classroom learning" [8]. E-Learning is a dynamic educational medium and a fer-tile area for research on its influence and effectiveness on student knowledge acquisition and instructional strategy. Numerous businesses use E-Learning to educate their employees, whilst educational institutions use technology and the internet to enhance the quality of instruction [9].

The increasing prevalence of mobile phones and computers improve educational opportunities. To date, however, mobile platform learning has overcome time and place limitations and is extensively used by educators and students. As an innovative method of learning, mobile learning has garnered the attention of numerous academics both domestically and internationally, particularly in the field of foreign language acquisition [10]. Mobile learning is a form of education that can occur anywhere and at any time using mobile devices. Mobile computing devices utilized in mobile learning must be able to efficiently convey educational content and facilitate communication between teachers and students. As soon as the concept of M-learning entered the field of educational technology, it garnered a substantial number of researchers who examined it from a variety of angles. The foundation of mobile learning is digital learning, a subset of digital learning. Second, mobile learning not only shares all the characteristics of digital learning but also distinguishes itself by allowing learners to study freely, at any time and in any location, for a variety of purposes and using a variety of methods. Moreover, m-learning has connectivity, situational, convenient, personalized, and interactive learning characteristics.

## 3 Methodology

The research outcome is adaptive English language learning mobile applications which guide to improve the English skills of learners. This application consists of four core functions to enhance the learning experience. Python language was used for the development of the ML models and the mobile application was developed using the react native framework. The system architecture can be seen in Fig. 1.

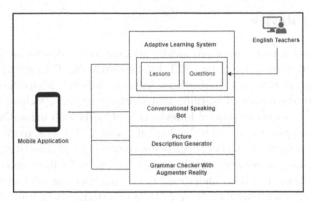

**Fig. 1.** System Architecture

### 3.1 Adaptive Learning Component

Due to the unique nature of the language learning process, we must consider the learner more than with other types of education. Consequently, the main problem is found in the absence of an adaptive learning system that provides user-specific content based on the characteristics of the users. The problem analysis made it abundantly clear that most English learners are prepared to study the language online and that they hope for a more flexible learning environment that allows them to acquire more knowledge independently. The adaptive learning component focuses primarily on providing the user with an adapted experience by assessing their prior knowledge and current learning behavior. It can offer individualized information such as homework, quizzes, exercises, and curriculum.

The main idea behind this component is to gather user information, utilize machine learning to assess it, and then provide the user with an accurate and suitable route. Prior to anything else, the following information is collected as the student interacts with the e-learning environment: user id, username, full name, email address, and birth date, learning goal. The information from the learner profile is utilized for tracking the learner, giving the necessary information, and modelling the adaptability depending on the learner profile. This will be continuously updated with data of learner characteristics. Once the user logged into the system for the first time, the learner will be taken through the English quiz to identify the learner's prior knowledge. This quiz will consist of speaking, writing, grammar, and listening activities. Then the learner will be guided through to his desired level according to the score of the quiz. After that as the user progresses through the learning process, the component will analyze learner characteristics such as learner behavior, and prior knowledge and provide resources according to the user. The foundation of the adaptivity domain, the reinforcement learning (RL) model, will employ these learner attributes as input.

Learning occurs naturally as a result of an agent's interaction with its environment in RL [11]. States and actions build up the environment. To optimize rewards delivered during the learning process, the agent interacts with the environment in a specific and strategic way. Situations are mapped into actions, Similar to other learning methods. The learner or agent determines the best course of action to pursue given the boundaries of the environment. The agent must actively perceive its surroundings and select the action that will maximize the reward function for a given state in that environment. The agent state is updated, and a new state is acquired when the appropriate path of action has been adopted.

In this research, the Q-learning algorithm is used to implement reinforcement learning. According to Balasubramanian Velusamy, The Q-learning off-policy RL technique seeks the best course of action in the context of the current circumstances [12]. Q-function returns a fixed value at the beginning of processing; as it progresses through the transition, new values are computed as agents are rewarded, thereby updating a Q-table with these new values.

Q function is denoted by,

$$Q(s_t, a_t) \leftarrow Q(s_t, a_t) + \alpha \left[ r_{t+1} + y \ \max \ Q(s_{t+1}, a) - Q(s_t, a_t) \right]$$

where,

t – Present or Current state
t + 1 – the Next state
Q (st, at) – the Q – values for the current state
R (St, at) – Reward after performing an action at in St
$\alpha$ – The rate of learning $(0 \leqslant \alpha \leqslant 1)$
$\gamma$ – Discount factor deciding the significance of the future and upcoming possible rewards $(0 \leqslant \alpha \leqslant 1)$

The RL architecture begins with the extraction of various phases of the learner's attributes. These are recorded as part of the learner logs, which are utilized for a variety of computations that inform reinforcement and, consequently, the learning path. Learners in the guided learning process will have the opportunity to attend online lessons, complete assignments, take tests, and submit when applicable. The model recognizes the learner's interactions and selects the optimal resources for the learner, based on their activities at specified moments and states. This is done for the learner to receive the maximum possible reward based on the state-action space. This process is repeated until the optimal path based on the students' combined learning attributes is identified. In the Q learning model, environment states consist of lessons, quizzes, assignments, and actions consisting of next, stay, previous. For this Considerable state action space is available. With the optimal policy generated based on learner attributes and the learner profile logs, the model will then give per-learner adaptability based on the learner's learning characteristics.

The main output of the adaptive learning component is providing the best next possible path to the user by analyzing user behavior and characteristics. Once the user logged into the system the first-time user gets to quiz and from that quiz user is categorized into levels. After, the user gets the curriculum according to level and when the learner progresses through the learning process model analyzes learner behavior. From that analysis, the model gives the next possible lesson or activity to the user.

## 3.2 Conversational Speaking Bot

The conversational speaking bot component can conduct realistic conversations with the student and the speaking bot based on a scenario (e.g., a conversation at a train station) to practice speaking English. Based on the student's answers to the questions asked by the bot, the chat detects the student's mispronunciations and grammatical errors. The speaking bot always greets the student and starts the conversation. When the student talks to the speaking Bot, the audio will be converted to text and the conversation will appear on the screen. As the student's part of the conversation appears on the screen, grammar and mispronunciation are highlighted and the correct pronunciation is suggested for students to listen to. If the student wants to listen to the bot speaking back, the displayed text is converted to audio and the student can listen to it. Also, feedback will be given based on the conversation at the end of the conversation.

Speech to Text (STT), The Facebook AI team published the Wav2vec voice encoder model in late 2019. The model has been updated since it was first created to use the Transformers architecture, and a multilingual version has had the model retrained in 12 different languages. This proposed subcomponent uses Wav2Vec 2.0 Large (LV-60) and e Libri Speech dataset contains 960 h of long audio files for the English language. The encoder network and the context network are the core two distinct networks that makeup wav2vec. Contrastive predictive coding is the concept underlying wav2vec training. Wav2vec uses a contrast loss that implicitly models the mutual information between context and future audio samples rather than actively predicting the future like a generative pretrained transformer (GPT) and specifically modelling the audio waveform. The conversational speaking bot is using LibriSpeech pre-trained dataset. The dataset has 960 h long audio samples. It used Wav2Vec 2.0. Wav2vec model is important because it is one of the most successful efforts to date to integrate self-supervised learning into the voice processing industry. For training, the LibriSpeech 960h dataset was obtained using the wave2vec model with a Word Error Rate (WER) of 1.8/3.3%. According to experimental findings, FastSpeech 2 can train users three times as quickly as Fast-Speech. Furthermore, in terms of speech quality, FastSpeech 2 and 2s beat FastSpeech, and FastSpeech 2 can even exceed automated regression models.

Text to Speech (TTS), What this component does is the speech synthesizer, which means it generates spoken language based on text input. The LJ Speech Dataset is used as the dataset for this component. This model has been trained based on the Multiple Speakers Synthesizer concept for better accuracy. Also, the Fairseq tool kit has been used for this component. The sequence modelling toolkit Fairseq(-py) enables academics and developers to train unique models for tasks including translation, summarization, language modelling, and other text production. Its core technology is PyTorch. With an accessible torch. Hub interface, it offers pre-trained models for language modelling and translation. Using the Fairseq toolkit, they implemented the FastSpeech 2 model used for this Text to Speech component. For duration prediction (to provide more information as input) and knowledge distillation (to simplify the data distribution in output), the FastSpeech model relies on an autoregressive teacher model. This can help with the one-to-many mapping problem in TTS, where multiple speech variations correspond to the same text. It generates a direct Speech waveform parallel to the text, it's a completely end-to-end return conclusion.

Chat Bot, The Facebook Blenderbot 400M Distill model is used for the chatbot component. It is a Natural Language Processing (NLP) Model implemented in the Transformer library. This model is implemented using the DistilBERT transformer variant. DistilBERT is a BERT-based Transformer model that is compact, quick, affordable, and light. Distillation is the technique adopted by DistilBERT. Once a big neural network has been trained, the idea holds that its whole output distributions may be accurately represented by a smaller network. A skilled conversationalist smoothly combines a variety of abilities necessary for a successful discussion, including offering interesting talking topics, actively listening to their companions, asking and responding to questions, and exhibiting expertise, empathy, and personality when appropriate. All of that can be achieved using the Facebook Blenderbot 400M Distill Model. The DistilBERT model preserves over 95% of BERT's performance as determined by the GLUE language comprehension benchmark while running 60% quicker and with 40% fewer parameters than Bert-base-uncased.

Detect Mispronunciation, The T5 model was used to detect mispronunciations. It compares the generated word and the vocabulary word to detect mispronunciations. A Text-to-Text format is required for that. T5 is a Transformer-based architecture that applies a text-to-text method and is also known as Text-to-Text Transformer. Every function is framed as feeding the model text as input and training it to output some goal text, including translation, question answering, and classification. This single Conversational Speaking Bot component has been tested with 20 students and the component reached 76.8% accuracy.

## 3.3 Picture Description Generator

The picture description generator provides a platform to generate picture descriptions for user-uploaded pictures. The photo description generator's main goal is to help users become more proficient in English and picture description. And here's an example (Fig. 2).

The scene in this photograph looks like it was taken from a stage play. While they are both seated, an older man is having a conversation with a younger youngster. This stage is arranged to look like the deck of a ship.
This individual is armed with a sword and is sporting a boot on his foot. It appears the young boy is paying close attention. It would appear that this stage was constructed entirely out of wood.

**Fig. 2.** Example of the picture description generator

The current existing picture caption generation systems are developed in such a way that the system is only able to develop or produce single sentences. How the 'Picture Description Generator' was developed by taking the Flickr 8K [13] as a data set and then creating a custom single caption generator. What a single caption generator does is, first it will use an InceptionV3 model to process an image. Next, the caption will be vectorized using caption vectorization, where the caption is taken as a numerical representation, which then is saved as a pickle file. There are two modules used in the process. A convolutional neural network will be used to create a dense layer while the previously given feature set is converted into a respectable output. Then, using the recurrent neural network, the encoded output will be decoded using a GRU layer and an attention layer content set will also be generated. Then, by using the above-mentioned encoder and decoder, a training model of a single sentence caption generator will be created. The weights created by the single sentence generator and the custom built 600 multi sentence datasets will be used to fine-tune the existing single sentence generating system into a multi sentence generator.

The picture description generator was tested using more than 100 image models and the system performed by providing answers or captions matching the context of the given image. To test the accuracy of the system, a standard called 'BLEU' [19] was used. 'BLEU' is an algorithm that is used to evaluate the quality of the text translated by a machine. Here, it can be used to test the quality of the machine-generated captions. The quality of the captions generated will be given within the score of 0 and 1. All the time the system was tested using the algorithm, the outputs got an average score of 0.4.

### 3.4 Augmented Reality Based Grammar Checker

The system that is being suggested is comprised of two primary subcomponents. The first component is responsible for recognizing handwritten writing and pointing out grammatical mistakes, and the second component makes use of augmented reality to provide feedback on the text that has been recognized by the first component. We were able to make it simple for the user to transition between digital and analogue media since we combined these two components into one functional component.

The grammar checking module, the text detection module, and the text recognition module make up the handwritten text recognition unit. A technique known as "character region awareness" [20] was utilized in the process of text detection. This approach was conceived with the assistance of a convolutional neural network that consists of 16 layers (VGG-16). Then, the model was trained using Supervised training in order to become more accurate. After that the transformer architecture was used for the text recognition module. And it employs both an image transformer for the extraction of features from images and a text transformer for the modelling of language. The DeiT [21] and BEiT [22] models were used to perform encoder initialization. The RoBERTa [23] and MiniLM [24] models were utilized to begin the process of initializing the decoder. LanguageTool, which is a free and open-source project, uses the recognized text from the image and loops through it to identify any grammatical or spelling errors.

After that, Google ARCore was employed to put the augmented reality component into action. This takes the output of the text detection module, which is an array of coordinates, maps it with the output of the LanguageTool, and then shows the proposed changes on the screen.

The handwritten text recognition was tested using more than 1800 images in the IAM [25] dataset and 347 images in the SROIE [26] dataset. In the IAM dataset, this model achieved a character error rate (CER) of 3.42, and for the SROIE dataset, it achieved a CER of 4.22. And this model got a word accuracy of 93.4 on the ICDAR2015 [27] dataset and an F1-score of 96.34. For the text detection model, it was able to achieve an F1-score of 84.80 on the ICDAR2015 dataset.

## 4   Results and Discussion

The proposed system, PEM, consists of four main parts. The entire system is an active RL environment that allows English learners to experience a flexible and efficient English learning environment. The RL component can identify learners' early English literacy and direct them to the right learning path. Further, the RL component suggests relevant lessons to learners based on their progress. That means PEM provides customized lesson plans to learners according to their learning style. The implemented Picture Description Generator component helps learners improve their thinking and description skills. Also, the Speaking Bot component enables learners to practice their speech without the help of anyone else. It provides conversation training sessions based on incidents encountered in daily life. The Speaking Bot component captures mispronunciations and grammatical errors in the learner's speech. Also, it provides feedback by considering the conversation. Not just speech, PEM can capture handwritten text and detect grammar and spelling errors. Various fields began to participate in the path to the future with current technology as technical findings and developments grew rapidly. The lack of adaptive e-learning systems to effectively learn English is a significant deficit in the education sector. The target of PEM is to identify learner characteristics and deliver a learning experience based on those characteristics, as well as to offer an efficient and effective learning approach. Having access to an adaptive English language learning platform that offers a personalized learning experience is a more effective means of achieving a learner's objectives. After developing the proposed application, unit tests, integration tests, and user acceptance tests were conducted. For user acceptance testing, 20 users participated and rated reading, speaking, listening, writing, grammar, pronunciation, and user-friendliness according to their user experience. Figure 3 below shows the results of the user acceptance test.

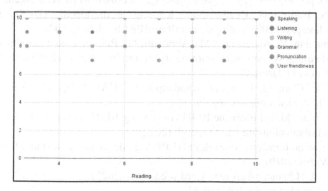

**Fig. 3.**  User acceptance test summary

## 5 Conclusion

PEM is providing unique features to the learners to enhance English language skills and practice the English language. Mainly PEM provides an adaptive learning environment to customize learners' learning environment, a Picture description generator to generate descriptions to user uploaded images, Conversational AI to practice speaking and a Realtime Grammar checker to check grammar on handwritten texts. To implement those features RL, augmented reality, and Artificial Intelligence are used.

## References

1. Myers, J.: Which languages are most widely spoken? (2015). https://www.weforum.org/
2. Ruan, S., et al.: EnglishBot: an AI-powered conversational system for second language learning (2021)
3. Boonkita, K.: Enhancing the development of speaking skills for non-native speakers of English (2010)
4. Huang, Y., Xie, Z., Jin, L., Zhu, Y., Zhang, S.: Adversarial feature enhancing network for end-to-end handwritten paragraph recognition. In: 2019 International Conference on Document Analysis and Recognition (ICDAR) (2019)
5. Agarwal, S., Kaushik, J.S.: Student's perception of online learning during COVID pandemic. Indian J. Pediatr. **87** (2021)
6. Coniam, D.F.L.: Bots for language learning now: current and future directions (2020)
7. Kabudi, T., Pappas, I., Olsen, D.H.: AI-enabled adaptive learning systems: a systematic mapping of the literature. Comput. Educ. Artif. Intell. **2**(100017), 100017 (2021)
8. Bijwe, R.P., Raut, A.B.: A survey of adaptive learning with predictive analytics to improve students learning. Bulletinmonumental.com (2022). http://www.bulletinmonumental.com/gallery/2-jan2021.pdf
9. Encarnacion, R.E., Galang, A.D., Hallar, B.A.: The impact and effectiveness of e-learning on teaching and learning. Int. J. Comput. Sci. Res. **5**(1), 383–397 (2021). https://doi.org/10.25147/ijcsr.2017.001.1.47
10. Shen, N.: A deep learning approach of English vocabulary for mobile platform. In: 2021 13th International Conference on Measuring Technology and Mechatronics Automation (ICMTMA), pp. 463–466 (2021). https://doi.org/10.1109/ICMTMA52658.2021.00106
11. Sutton, R.S., Barto, E.G.: Reinforcement learning: an introduction (2018). https://web.stanford.edu/class/psych209/Readings/SuttonBartoIPRLBook2ndEd.pdf
12. Balasubramanian, V., Anouneia, S.M., Abraham, G.: Reinforcement learning approach for adaptive e-learning systems using learning styles. Inf. Technol. J. **12**, 2306–2314 (2013)
13. adityajn. "Flickr 8k Dataset"
14. Panayotov, V., Chen, G., Povey, D., Khudanpur, S.: ICASSP. Open Speech and Language Resources. http://www.openslr.org/12/
15. Zhang, G., et al.: Mixed-phoneme BERT: improving BERT with mixed phoneme and supphoneme representations for text to speech (2022)
16. Joshi, P.: How do transformers work in NLP? A guide to the latest state-of-the-art models. Analytics Vidhya (2019)
17. Yiamwinya, T.: Character-bert-next-word-prediction (2020)
18. Microsoft. A guide to voice bots and AI
19. Shah, S.K.A., Mahmood, W.: Smart home automation using IOT and its low cost implementation. Int. J. Eng. Manuf. **10**, 28–36 (2020)

20. Arxiv.org (2022). https://arxiv.org/pdf/2012.12877.pdf
21. Bao, H., Dong, L., Piao, S., Wei, F.: Beit: BERT pre-training of Image transformers. arXiv.org (2022)
22. Liu, Y., et al.: RoBERTa: a robustly optimized BERT pretraining approach (2019)
23. Wang, W., et al.: MINILM: deep self-attention distillation for task-agnostic compression of pre-trained transformers (2020)
24. Research Group on Computer Vision and Artificial Intelligence—Computer Vision and Artificial Intelligence. Fki.tic.heia-Fr.ch, https://fki.tic.heia-fr.ch/databases/iam-handwriting-database
25. SROIE Datasetv2. https://www.kaggle.com/datasets/urbikn/sroie-datasetv2
26. Overview-Incidental Scene Text - Robust Reading Competition. (2022) Cvc.uab.es, https://rrc.cvc.uab.es/?ch=4
27. Tjandra, A.: (2020). wav2vec 2.0. Github. https://github.com/facebookresearch/fairseq/tree/main/examples/wav2vec#wav2vec-20
28. Bgn, J.: The Illustrated Wav2vec (2021). Jonathanbgn.com. https://jonathanbgn.com/2021/06/29/illustrated-wav2vec.html#:~:text=Wav2vec%20is%20a%20speech%20encoder,speech%20recognition%20or%20emotion%20recognition
29. Sus, Ł.: Wav2Vec 2.0: A Framework for Self-Supervised Learning of Speech Representations (2021). Towardsdatascience. https://towardsdatascience.com/wav2vec-2-0-a-framework-for-self-supervised-learning-of-speech-representations-7d3728688cae
30. Johnson, K.I.A.: LJ speech dataset [Data set]. In: The LJ Speech Dataset (2017). https://keithito.com/LJ-Speech-Dataset/
31. Ott, et al.: Fairseq: A Fast, Extensible Toolkit for Sequence Modeling (2019). Github. https://github.com/facebookresearch/fairseq
32. Yi, R., et al.: FastSpeech 2: fast and high-quality end-to-end text to speech (2020). https://arxiv.org/abs/2006.04558
33. Huggingface (n.d.) DistilBERT. https://huggingface.co/docs/transformers/model_doc/distilbert
34. Narsil, P.V.: Facebook/blenderbot-400M-distill (2019). https://huggingface.co/facebook/blenderbot-400M-distill?text=Hey+my+name+is+Julien%21+How+are+you%3F
35. Raffel, C., et al.: Exploring the limits of transfer learning with a unified text-to-text transformer (2019). https://arxiv.org/abs/1910.10683v3

# The Design of an Adaptive Tool Supporting Formative Assessment in Data Science Courses

Pierpaolo Vittorini[✉][ID]

University of L'Aquila, 67100 L'aquila, Italy
pierpaolo.vittorini@univaq.it

**Abstract.** The automated correction of assignments is a task that received large support from artificial intelligence. In previous research, we approached the problem of automatically providing a grade and feedback to students in solving data science exercises, that resulted in the development of the rDSA tool. In this paper, we discuss the first steps towards the development of an adaptive system – based on the rDSA tool – supporting the students' formative assessment activities. In particular, we present the context of use, the requirements – elicited through a study with a small cohort of students, the models enabling adaptation, and the user interface. Finally, we evaluated the user interface through a further study that involved both qualitative and quantitative measures.

**Keywords:** Adaptive Assessment · Automated Correction · User-Centered Design · Data Science Assignments

## 1 Introduction

The manual correction of solutions to assignments is a tedious and error-prone task, in particular when involving a large cohort of students. Artificial intelligence can be useful to support this task [8]: by automating the grading process, teachers can be assisted in making corrections, and students can receive immediate feedback and improve on their solutions before attending the exam.

In previous research [3,5,15–17], we approached the problem of the automated grading of assignments, made up of a list of commands written in R, their respective output, and comments (written in natural language). To grade them automatically and return structured feedback to students, we developed the rDSA (r Data Science Assignments) tool, within the UnivAQ Test Suite (UTS) system[1]. In this paper, we report the initial steps taken by the author to improve the rDSA system, so as to provide assignments to students in an adaptive framework. As known, adaptation in learning systems has a long tradition [6,9,14] and offers advantages over more traditional methods [2,4,7,18]. Accordingly, the main motivation of this research is to improve the efficacy of

---

[1] Available at URL https://vittorini.univaq.it/uts/.

C. S. González-González et al. (Eds.): ICWL 2022/SETE 2022, LNCS 13869, pp. 86–97, 2023.
https://doi.org/10.1007/978-3-031-33023-0_8

the rDSA tool during formative assessment, through adaptation, so to increase the students' learning performances.

In such a context, the paper initially describes the educational scenario and the impact of the rDSA tool (Sect. 2). Then, it introduces the needed background on adaptive technology (Sect. 3). Hence, following the User-centred design (UCD) methodology [12], the paper summarises the context of use, reports on a study with a small cohort of students used to elicit the system requirements, and finally delves into the design of the models supporting adaptation (Sect. 4). The paper ends with a discussion about the main results and the future work (Sect. 5).

## 2    Educational Scenario and Impact

Several courses at the University of L'Aquila (Italy) have a specific topic about executing statistical analyses in R and correctly interpreting the results into the corresponding findings. In particular, the course explains how to (i) manage datasets (i.e., import datasets from external sources, columns/rows selection, basic arithmetic operations, conversion from continuous to categorical data), (ii) carry out basic descriptive statistics (i.e., central tendency, dispersion, distribution), (iii) execute inferential statistics (i.e., confidence intervals, normality, difference - parametric and non-parametric, association), (iv) perform basic tasks of supervised learning (i.e., data preparation, classification, regression, validation), using R as the scripting language [10]. The course also proposes several exercises, used for formative assessment, related to all the aforementioned topics. For instance, the following exercise is related to the "central tendency" concept of descriptive statistics:

**Exercise:** *Let us consider the following dataset:*

| patient | before | after |
|---------|--------|-------|
| 1 | 211 | 181 |
| 2 | 200 | 210 |
| 3 | 210 | 196 |
| 4 | 203 | 200 |
| 5 | 196 | 167 |
| 6 | 191 | 161 |
| 7 | 190 | 178 |
| 8 | 177 | 180 |
| 9 | 173 | 149 |
| 10 | 170 | 119 |

*The data regards a sample of 10 hypertensive patients (variable "patient") who receive an anti-hypertensive drug. We measure the systolic blood pres-*

*sure before drug administration (variable "before") and a few hours after (variable "after").*
*Calculate the mean of the systolic blood pressure after the administration of the drug. Submit as a solution a text containing the list of R commands with the respective output.*

To solve the exercise, the student has to copy/paste the dataset into a spreadsheet, import it into R, and then execute the following command (assuming the student called the dataset "sbp"):

```
> mean(sbp$after)
[1]  174.1
```

In the educational scenario summarised above, we developed the rDSA tool [3,5,15–17]. The tool supports formative and summative assessment as follows. As for formative assessment, the tool provides students with both textual feedback and an estimated evaluation of the quality of the submitted solution [16] and enables teachers to monitor the student's progress with the assigned exercises [3]. As for summative assessment, the tool supports teachers during the manual correction of both exercises and exams. The educational benefits we measured were manifold. For students, the tool supported their understanding of the commands, the interpretation of the results, and – as a consequence – better learning outcomes [15]. For teachers, the tool reduced their workload, both in terms of correction times and errors, and in a decreased number of returning students [17].

## 3   Adaptive Learning

Adaptive learning is the set of educational and technological methods that tailor the learning activities and resources to the specific needs of each learner. It refers to the type of learning where students are given customised resources and activities to address their unique learning needs. Nevertheless, discussing all concepts behind adaptive learning and adaptive learning systems is outside the scope of the paper. Interested readers can refer to, e.g., the following papers about adaptive learning systems [6,9,14] and a few recent studies about their effectiveness [4,7,18]. On the other hand, given that the main objective of this paper is to define the different models that enable adaptation, we present them as defined in the work of Martin et al. [9]:

**Learner model** The Learner Model, also known as the student model, refers to the learner's characteristics of what a student knows and does. It includes the learner's attributes, preferences, knowledge and proficiency, as well as motivational or emotional aspects of his/her behaviour, and other characteristics useful to adapt the learning process;

**Content model** Then Content Model, also known as the domain model, refers to the content or knowledge base for the course. It involves the course's concepts and how they are related, as well as how the course content is delivered to the learner;

**Adaptive model** The Adaptive Model, also known as the instructional model, refers to the algorithm that assists in adapting the instruction, based on the content and learner model. The objective of the adaptive model is then to define what, when, and how adaptation occurs.

The definition of these models is the first task a designer has to complete before starting the actual system development. In our project, to define them, we adopted the User-centred design (UCD) methodology [12]. UCD is an iterative design process in which designers focus on the users and their needs in each phase of the design process. Usually, each iteration of the UCD requires to (i) define the context of use (i.e., the actual conditions under which the tool is used), (ii) specify the user requirements, (iii) produce the design solutions, and (iv) evaluate the design against the requirements. In the next section, we report on the results of the first UCD iteration.

## 4  Design

### 4.1  Context of Use

The context of use is almost straightforward. The users are students of data science courses, using R as the scripting language. The task implemented by the system is to support them in completing exercises preparatory for the final exam. Regarding the environment, in the current version of the system [15], students have both RStudio and the rDSA tool open in separate windows, they copy/paste the work done in RStudio into the rDSA tool, so to receive feedback and eventually submit the final solution.

### 4.2  Requirements

As discussed in the introduction, the general idea is to propose exercises using adaptive technology. To define in the detail the user requirements, we defined a structured interview, to be used with students of the "Information processing systems" course, that already used the rDSA tool in the previous academic year.

The interview was organised in terms of a discussion around the following four questions:

- The first question regards their opinion about introducing adaptivity during formative assessment, presented as the ability of the system to provide exercises that suit and stimulate the student;
- The second question is about the way in which adaptation should be provided, i.e., if adaptation should be for the course as a whole or topic-by-topic;

- The third question concerns three possible user interfaces. The first option includes (i) the learning material, (ii) the performances of the student with all exercises, (iii) the text of the exercise and (iv) the text area where to submit the solution. The second proposal does not include the learning material, while the third moves the performances of the student in the dashboard and leaves only the text of the exercise with the area to submit the solution;
- The final question is about the possibility to substitute the text area where to submit the solution, with a web-based interactive R console, so that a student can directly launch the R commands and see the output.

Six students voluntarily accepted to answer the interview. Thematic analysis showed that:

- adaptivity was unanimously considered useful, on the condition that the stimulation should not become a frustrating experience, and that the different backgrounds of students should be taken into account by the tool;
- the large majority of students preferred the topic-by-topic adaptation, seen as more gradual and soft;
- the "minimal" interface was chosen by all students, even if a summary of the performances was also considered interesting
- students were instead torn whether or not to include the web-based interactive R console: on one hand, they do not want to lose all the facilities offered by RStudio (e.g., history, environment, packages management, data import); on the other hand, switching from one window to another was considered annoying and distracting.

### 4.3   Models

According to the results of the above interviews, we hereafter report on the content, the learner and the adaptive models.

**Content Model.** The content model is based on concepts, related to each other as a tree, so to define prerequisites and a learning path that drives a student towards acquiring all the required knowledge. Each concept is modelled by a name, a short description, a set of links to the related learning material, and the possible "child" concepts. The content model also includes exercises, each referring to the related concepts. Each exercise contains a name, the text, the correct solution, and a measure of its difficulty, called $\beta$. The difficulty is a continuous value, where the higher the value, the more difficult the exercise is. A difficulty equal to zero means a "fair" difficulty, a negative difficulty means an easy exercise, and a positive difficulty means a challenging exercise. Basically, exercises are short analyses, to be executed through R commands, that solve a task related to a concept.

**Learner Model.** The learner model includes the student's characteristics (matriculation number, name, course) and his/her knowledge/proficiency. As for the latter, the learner model contains the ability a student possesses in:

– the basic computer science task (e.g., file-system management, copy/paste);
– in each of the concepts listed in the content model;
– solving the available exercises.

As already used in previous research [2], we indicate the student's ability with $\theta$, measured as a continuous value. Similarly to the difficulty value $\beta$, the higher the ability, the more proficient a student is. Moreover, an ability equal to zero is the threshold for a sufficient ability, where a negative/positive value indicates a low/high proficiency in the subject.

In addition, we store in the learner model all solutions given by a student to all exercises with the achieved grade. As discussed, exercises of this kind can be automatically corrected by the rDSA tool: even if the tool is able to return a numerical grade with structured feedback, for simplicity, we only store the grade as either a dichotomous (e.g., right/wrong) or polytomous (e.g., wrong, partially wrong, correct) result, depending on the teacher's choice.

In summary, Fig. 1 depicts the content and learner models using a Unified Modeling Language (UML) diagram.

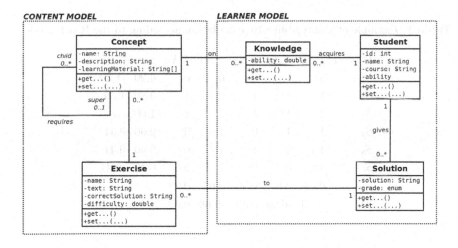

**Fig. 1.** UML diagram representing the content and learner models

**Adaptation Model.** The adaptation model has a twofold objective.

The first objective regards the difficulty of each exercise. This value can be either fixed/initialised by the teacher, or automatically calculated. Different methods exist to automatically calculate the difficulty. In our model, to estimate its value: if the exercise has a dichotomous answer, we use the Rash model [11]; if the exercise has a polytomous answer, we instead use the Rating Scale (RS) model [1]. In short, according to these models, an individual's response to a dichotomous/polytomous item is determined by the individual's ability and the item's difficulty[2]. Furthermore, such parameters can be estimated with statistical methods, given an adequate number of answers already given to the exercises.

The second objective is to provide each student with the "best" exercises. This task is performed in two steps:

- First, we select all the exercises regarding the first concept the student did not practice or showed low ability. This choice respects the requirement regarding what we called topic-by-topic adaptation;
- Then, we choose the exercise that – given the student's ability – has a higher but closest difficulty value. If more than one exercise satisfies the criteria, we randomly choose one exercise among them. If no exercise satisfies the criteria, we choose the exercise with the highest difficulty. The rationale is to respect the requirement of proposing a challenging exercise (higher difficulty), but not too much demanding and potentially frustrating (the closest difficulty).

Finally, the chosen exercise is removed from the pool of exercises available for the next iteration. To keep the difficulty and ability values comparable, also to estimate the student's ability, we use the Rasch or RS model.

**Table 1.** Example of ability/difficulty calculation according to the Rasch model

| Student | $EX_1$ | $EX_2$ | $EX_3$ | $EX_4$ | $EX_5$ | $p$ | $\theta$ |
|---|---|---|---|---|---|---|---|
| $S_1$ | 0 | 1 | 0 | 0 | 0 | 0.20 | -1.39 |
| $S_2$ | 1 | 1 | 1 | 0 | 1 | 0.80 | 1.39 |
| $S_3$ | 1 | 1 | 1 | 1 | 1 | 1.00 | $\infty$ |
| $S_4$ | 1 | 1 | 0 | 1 | 0 | 0.60 | 0.41 |
| $S_5$ | 1 | 0 | 1 | 1 | 0 | 0.60 | 0.41 |
| $S_6$ | 1 | 0 | 0 | 1 | 0 | 0.40 | -0.41 |
| $p$ | 0.83 | 0.67 | 0.50 | 0.67 | 0.33 | | |
| $\beta$ | -1.61 | -0.69 | 0.00 | -0.69 | 0.69 | | |

As a matter of example, let us take into account Table 1. The part of the table with a grey background summarises the answers given by the students ($S_1$–$S_6$) to the exercises ($EX_1$–$EX_5$). All answers are dichotomous, so a value equal to 0 means a wrong answer; a value of 1 indicates a correct answer. Furthermore, column $p$ contains the proportion of correct answers given by each student, and

---

[2] Only for the polytomous case, the RS model also includes thresholds between the different values of the answer, but this topic is outside the scope of this paper.

column $\theta$ has the estimated ability. Similarly, row $p$ contains the proportion of correct answers per exercise, and row $\beta$ shows the estimated difficulty.

To understand how the ability is estimated, let us focus on student $S_1$, that answered correctly to only one exercise (over five). So, $p_{S_1} = 1/5 = 0.20$. According to the Rasch model, the estimated ability is calculated as the natural log of the ratio of the proportion of correct answers to the proportion of incorrect answers:

$$\theta = ln\left(\frac{p}{1-p}\right)$$

Therefore, for $S_1$, we can estimate its ability $\theta_{S_1} = ln\left(\frac{0.20}{1-0.20}\right) = ln(0.25) = -1.39$. The straightforward interpretation is that the student's ability is quite low. Worth noting the case of $S_3$: the student gave all correct answers, so his/her ability is estimated to $\infty$.

A similar calculation can be followed to estimate an item's ability. Let us focus on the fifth exercise: only two students (over six) gave the correct answer. Then, $p_{EX_5} = 2/6 = 0.33$. According to the Rasch model, the item difficulty is estimated through the natural log of the ratio of the proportion of incorrect answers to the proportion of correct answers (the opposite of the ratio used for the ability):

$$\beta = ln\left(\frac{1-p}{p}\right)$$

Therefore, for the first exercise, we obtain $\beta_{S_1} = ln\left(\frac{1-0.33}{0.33}\right) = ln(2.0) = 0.69$. This value suggests that the fifth exercise is quite difficult to complete.

Given the above, let us suppose we have a student $S$ with an initial ability of $\theta_S = -0.2$. The student asks for an exercise:

- The adaptation model selects exercise $EX_3$, because it has $\beta_{EX_3} = 0.00$ and it is the exercise with a higher but closest difficulty value;
- Let us suppose that $S$ gives the right answer:
  - The proportion of correct answers is $p_S = 1.0$, then the estimated ability becomes $\theta_S = \infty$;
  - The estimated difficulty for $EX_3$ becomes $\beta_{EX_3} = -0.28$, because $p_{EX_3} = 4/7 = 0.57$;
  - $EX_3$ is removed from the pool of exercises available for the next iteration.
- The student requires another exercise: given that no exercise satisfies the criteria (all available exercises have a difficulty lower than the student's ability), the adaptation model proposes the most difficult exercise, i.e., $EX_5$;
- Let us suppose that $S$ gives the wrong answer:
  - Now, $p_S = 0.5$ and $\theta_S = 0.0$;
  - Moreover, $p_{EX_5} = 2/7 = 0.29$ and $\beta_{EX_5} = 0.92$;
  - $EX_5$ is removed from the pool of exercises available for the next iteration.

– The student asks for another exercise. Again, no exercise satisfies the criteria (all exercises have a difficulty lower than the student's ability). Among the two candidate exercises (i.e., $EX_2$ and $EX_4$, the remaining exercises with the highest difficulty level), the adaptation model randomly chooses one, say $EX_2$.
– Let us suppose that the student answers correctly:
  • $p_S = 0.67$ and $\theta_S = 0.69$;
  • $p_{EX_2} = 0.71$ and $\beta_{EX_2} = -0.92$;
  • $EX_2$ is removed from the pool of exercises available for the next iteration.

This adaptation model resembles the approach of computerised adaptive testing, which has been successfully used by the author in previous research [2]. The main differences are that (i) this model is related to a hierarchy of concepts, rather than a single pool of items; (ii) the questions are not multiple-choice-single-answers, but pieces of code that are automatically corrected by the rDSA engine.

Accordingly, the role of the rDSA engine is (i) to provide structured feedback to the student and (ii) to return either a dichotomous or polytomous evaluation of the exercise, to be used to update the exercise's difficulty, the estimated student's ability, and to suggest the next exercise as explained above.

## 4.4  Evaluation

Figure 2 depicts the current implementation of the interface to provide students with adaptive formative assessment. The interface shows (from top to bottom): (i) the concept being assessed (i.e., central tendency); (ii) the text of the exercise; (iii) the text area where to copy/paste the solution; (iv) the button to ask for the automated evaluation and feedback; (v) the currently estimated ability; (vi) the button to proceed to the next exercise and the button to exit the adaptive assessment.

It is worth pointing out that the current implementation is not complete. In UCD, it is common practice to work with mockups or partial implementations to be tested with the users, before the final system implementation. So far, the interaction is fixed, i.e., the ability, the returned feedback and the exercise do not depend on the solution entered in the text area. Anyway, it perfectly simulates the behaviour of the system. When the interface will be finalised (in agreement with the result of this study):

– the number of stars summarising the estimated ability will be deduced from $\theta$ according to the following formula:

$$N_s = \begin{cases} 0 & \text{if } \theta \leq -3 \\ 1 & \text{if } -3 < \theta \leq -1 \\ 2 & \text{if } -1 < \theta \leq 0 \\ 3 & \text{if } 0 < \theta \leq 1 \\ 4 & \text{if } 1 < \theta \leq 3 \\ 5 & \text{if } \theta > 3 \end{cases}$$

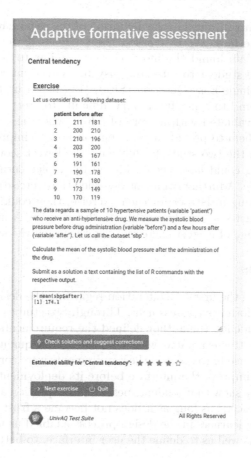

**Fig. 2.** Current implementation of the adaptive formative assessment interface

An explanation of the chosen thresholds follows. An ability $\theta = 3$ means – in the Rash model, but similar considerations can be drawn with the RS model – a ratio of correct answers $p = 0.95$; an ability $\theta = 1 \Rightarrow p = 0.73$; an ability $\theta = 0 \Rightarrow p = 0.5$; an ability $\theta = -1 \Rightarrow p = 0.27$ and an ability $\theta = -3 \Rightarrow p = 0.05$;

– when the student clicks on the button titled "Check solution and suggest corrections", the automated correction will be activated, a popup with the grade (converted in a dichotomous or polytomous outcome) and feedback will be opened, and the student's ability and exercise's difficulty will be updated;

– the area where the student can enter the solution will be a simple text area available for copy/paste of the work done in RStudio, and not the interactive web-based R console;

– when the student clicks on the button titled "Next exercise", the algorithm discussed in Sect. 4.3 is executed, and the selected exercise is displayed.

The same students involved in the definition of the requirements were invited to evaluate the interface. We first asked the students if the interface was as expected. All students found the interface very similar to their expectations. Then, we asked the student to rate how easy to use the interface was. To this aim, we used the Single-Ease Question (SEQ) [13], i.e., a usability metric that requires a rating from 1 to 7, i.e., from "very difficult" to "very easy". On average, the interface was evaluated with a score of 5.6/7, which is a very good result. Finally, we asked them to provide a comment on how to improve the interface. The comment from the two students that gave the lowest scores (i.e., 5/7) was that a better rating could have been achieved by implementing the web-based interactive R console. A further comment regarded the exercise structure: instead of requiring importing a dataset for each exercise, they could be provided e.g. via packages, so to let students focus only on the exercise. A final comment was to add the percentage of correct exercises, together with the stars.

## 5   Conclusions

The paper presented the first UCD iteration regarding the design of an adaptive system supporting formative assessment. Through two studies conducted with a small sample of students, the author defined the requirements, the models and the interface, the latter evaluated with qualitative and quantitative measures. The evaluation was useful to assess if the requirements were correctly formalised, and where/how to improve the interface before its deployment.

The main results show that students perceived adaptation as a useful support to their learning process, as long as it does not become a frustrating experience. Moreover, involving learners in the design process enabled us to elicit and refine the requirements, as well as to define the user interface, to better fit their expectations.

The next steps in the project are manifold, within a further UCD iteration. Provided that the context of use does not need updates, we will proceed to the development of a fully working version of the system, following the suggestions already given by students. Then, we will proceed with a second evaluation, with a new cohort of students, to assess the design choices (e.g., the number of stars from the estimated ability), measure its usability, the students' engagement, the efficacy of the adaptation model, and – in the long term – the learning outcomes.

## References

1. Andersen, E.B.: The Rating Scale Model. Handbook of Modern Item Response Theory, pp. 67–84 (1997). https://doi.org/10.1007/978-1-4757-2691-6_4
2. Angelone, A.M., Galassi, A., Vittorini, P.: Lessons learned about the application of adaptive testing in several first-year university courses. Int. J. Learn. Technol. 17(1), 3–26 (2022). https://doi.org/10.1504/IJLT.2022.123696
3. Bernardi, A., et al.: On the design and development of an assessment system with adaptive capabilities. In: Di Mascio, T., et al. (eds.) MIS4TEL 2018. AISC, vol. 804, pp. 190–199. Springer, Cham (2019). https://doi.org/10.1007/978-3-319-98872-6_23

4. Di Giacomo, D., et al.: The silent reading supported by adaptive learning technology: influence in the children outcomes. Comput. Hum. Behav. **55**, 1125–1130 (2016). https://doi.org/10.1016/j.chb.2014.09.053
5. Galassi, A., Vittorini, P.: Automated feedback to students in data science assignments: improved implementation and results. In: CHItaly 2021: 14th Biannual Conference of the Italian SIGCHI Chapter (CHItaly 2021). ACM, New York, NY, USA, Bolzano (2021). https://doi.org/10.1145/3464385.3464387
6. Kabudi, T., Pappas, I., Olsen, D.H.: AI-enabled adaptive learning systems: a systematic mapping of the literature. Comput. Educ.: Artif. Intell. **2**, 100017 (2021). https://doi.org/10.1016/J.CAEAI.2021.100017
7. Ling, H.C., Chiang, H.S.: Learning performance in adaptive learning systems: a case study of web programming learning recommendations. Front. Psychol. **13**, 31 (2022). https://doi.org/10.3389/FPSYG.2022.770637
8. Luckin, R., Holmes, W., Griffiths, M., Forcier, L.B.: Intelligence Unleashed: An Argument for AI in Education. Pearson, London (2016)
9. Martin, F., Chen, Y., Moore, R.L., Westine, C.D.: Systematic review of adaptive learning research designs, context, strategies, and technologies from 2009 to 2018. Educ. Technol. Res. Dev. **68**(4), 1903–1929 (2020). https://doi.org/10.1007/S11423-020-09793-2
10. R Core Team: R: A Language and Environment for Statistical Computing (2018). https://www.R-project.org/
11. Rasch, G.: Probabilistic Models for Some Intelligence and Attainment Tests. Danmarks Paedagogiske Institut (1960)
12. Still, B., Crane, K.: Fundamentals of User-Centered Design. CRC Press, Boca Raton (2017). https://doi.org/10.4324/9781315200927
13. Tullis, T., Albert, W.: Measuring the User Experience: Collecting, Analyzing, and Presenting Usability Metrics. Elsevier, Amsterdam (2013)
14. Vandewaetere, M., Desmet, P., Clarebout, G.: The contribution of learner characteristics in the development of computer-based adaptive learning environments. Comput. Hum. Behav. **27**(1), 118–130 (2011). https://doi.org/10.1016/j.chb.2010.07.038
15. Vittorini, P.: A report on the use of the rDSA tool for formative and summative assessment. In: Kubincovái, Z., Melonio, A., Durães, D., Rua Carneiro, D., Rizvi, M., Lancia, L. (eds.) Methodologies and Intelligent Systems for Technology Enhanced Learning, Workshops, 12th International Conference, MIS4TEL 2022. Lecture Notes in Networks and Systems, vol. 538, pp. 23–32. Springer, Cham (2022)
16. Vittorini, P., Galassi, A.: rDSA : an intelligent tool for data science assignments. Multimed. Tools Appl. (2022). https://doi.org/10.1007/s11042-022-14053-x
17. Vittorini, P., Menini, S., Tonelli, S.: An AI-based system for formative and summative assessment in data science courses. Int. J. Artif. Intell. Educ. **31**(2), 159–185 (2020). https://doi.org/10.1007/s40593-020-00230-2
18. Wang, S., et al.: When adaptive learning is effective learning: comparison of an adaptive learning system to teacher-led instruction. Interact. Learn. Environ. 1–11 (2020). https://doi.org/10.1080/10494820.2020.1808794

# Serious Games for Social Problems

Antonio Calvo-Morata(✉) and Baltasar Fernández-Manjón

Facultad de Informática, Complutense University of Madrid, C/ Profesor José García
Santesmases 9, 28040 Madrid, Spain
{acmorata,balta}@ucm.es

**Abstract.** Videogames have proven their usefulness in numerous fields such as education and training. This kind of videogames, usually called serious games, can also be powerful classroom tools for raising awareness about complex societal issues (e.g., gender discrimination, sex stereotypes). In this paper we describe the process followed to develop a video game to raise awareness about gender discrimination. The videogame provide students with a first-hand experience of what is feeling discrimination. With this shared experience, teachers can open a discussion on the topic in a post videogame session. We describe the first formative evaluation of the videogame with 26 users, showing some initial positive results and initial feedback to continue working to improve the videogame. Once validated the game will be accessible as open code to be freely used and even adapt and localize it to different cultures. This work will help other researchers who want to develop serious games to address social problems and also serves as an example of the usefulness of video games in addressing complex problems such as discrimination.

**Keywords:** Serious Games · Game Design · Awareness · Gender Discrimination · e-Learning

## 1 Introduction

Gender discrimination, sex discrimination or sexism refers to a set of discriminatory attitudes and behaviors focused at an individual or a group of individuals based on their gender. It is recognized not only as a serious societal problem but also as a global health issue. This type of discrimination is not only a personal belief based on individual attitudes; it is also linked to each country's culture and traditions, manifesting itself in numerous society institutions. As a result, many of these sexist behaviors have become normalized, making it a difficult problem to address [1].

This discrimination is more common in the case of women and is based on the gender roles that society has traditionally created. In many cases, it is based on sex stereotypes, where in most cultures men are more socially valued and more competent than women in a variety of activities, leaving women for secondary roles such taking care of the home and other people (e.g., kids, elderly) [1].

Sex discrimination is a complex problem prevalent across the world even if it varies greatly across continents, countries, cultures and even social environments. Many publications distinguish between hostile sexism, benevolent sexism and ambivalent sexism

C. S. González-González et al. (Eds.): ICWL 2022/SETE 2022, LNCS 13869, pp. 98–109, 2023.
https://doi.org/10.1007/978-3-031-33023-0_9

[1]. But in all cases, this discrimination has serious consequences including inequality and violence. For example, in the labor market, even in the most developed countries, is reflected in the salary gap and the glass ceiling effect [2, 3]. Sexist behaviors in personal relationships are linked to couple violence (physical and psychological) [4, 5]. In education, women can be directly banned from school or discriminated when considering some disciplines such as engineering or STEM [6]. Because of these serious consequences, sexism is a global problem that must be addressed at all ages, but we consider that is especially important to create effective tools that can be used at school to educate children breaking this vicious cycle that perpetuates the problem.

Serious games are video games with an objective that goes beyond entertainment and have proven their effectiveness in very diverse fields such as research, defense, health, business and education [7, 8]. Serious games have been used before to raise awareness about social problems such as bullying and other issues related to human rights [9, 10]. Videogames have properties that make them suitable for use as powerful educational tools. Among these educationally desirable features we can find [11, 12]:

- Videogames provide a joyful experiential learning. Videogames propose challenges and conflicts that the player must overcome to advance, making the player want to improve. They also increase in difficulty giving the player the feeling of advancing.
- Videogames' feedback loop is short, the player gets an immediate response to all his actions.
- The attention span that the player keeps on the activity increases.
- Video games show the player scenarios, personalities and events based on reality.
- The player can safely place themselves in risky scenarios and allow them to explore the consequences of hazardous behaviors.

We use the features of video games to promote reflection on sex discrimination by putting players into a situation where they will feel discriminated. However, as previously stated, sexism is a very complex phenomenon that presents itself in many contexts of society and is also influenced by each country's culture and society. It is also challenging to develop resources that effectively address the issues associated with sexism because students come in with bias and prejudices that need to be addressed. Our videogame makes players experience the discrimination that a woman may face when she enters the labor market for the first time after her STEM studies.

We believe that our work will help other researchers in: designing effective serious games to address social issues; explaining the benefits of video games; and showing the applications of games in educational context. To this purpose, Sect. 2 briefly describes other video games aimed at address violence and discrimination and the design and validation processes that are usually followed when developing them. Section 3 details the developed game as well as the process carried out for it, from its design to user testing. Section 4 describes the results obtained and finally Sect. 5 discusses the conclusions obtained from this work and its limitations.

## 2  Related Work

In the literature we can find reference to several videogames that address gender violence or gender discrimination as a main theme. However, many of these games are no longer available and usually there is no information on how they have been developed to address their objective or evidence of their effect or shortcomings [13]. This lack of information makes it difficult to take advantage of the knowledge of these developments to create more effective educational games that address the problem from the same or new perspectives. For instance, for those videogames it is very unusual to find the game design document or the experimental design of their validation in schools and let alone that the videogames are available as open code that can be reused or adapted for a different culture or situation. This lack of information about the development or access of serious games is also common on other videogames addressing societal problems [9].

There are models, frameworks and even authoring environments that can be used to simplify the design of new serious games [14, 15]. However, these are usually too generic and it is still complex to adapt them to complex problems such as raising awareness about a societal problem. While these models have characteristics in common that can help us in the development process, we must keep in mind that there are many different game genres and mechanics available that can be used to achieve the educational objective. And not all of these can be equally effective, and they imply a wide range of development costs. This is where it becomes more important the need for accessing other serious games that allow us to compare their effectiveness on the same objective as well as information on their development and design decisions.

## 3  Methods

### 3.1  Objectives

This work has different objectives:

- To design and develop a video game to address the problem of gender discrimination by teaching the topic in the classroom.
- To provide a use case of serious games with real data for the purpose of raising awareness of gender discrimination
- To exemplify the process to develop a serious narrative game with an awareness-raising objective, highlighting the issues faced. This will help other researchers improve their serious game design and development processes.

### 3.2  The Game

The title of the developed game in this work is *"La Entrevista"* ("The Interview"). This serious game is a point & click game in first person and its educational purpose is to address gender discrimination. Specifically, it focuses on discrimination against a person for being a woman as this type of discrimination is considered to encourage discrimination against women. The game is aimed at players between 18 and 25 years old (although it could be used from 16 years old). It is aimed at young people of the age to enter the working world. The video game is structured in 4 distinct sections.

- The introduction. The players are informed that they have recently completed their degree and are looking for a job. The players must answer some questions based on a CV that is provided by filling out an application to look for work.
- The exploration. The players are free to explore the scenarios within the company where they must do the interview and must interact with the characters that appear.
- The interview. The players take the interview proposed as an objective from the beginning of the game.
- The reflection. The game proposes 10 questions. The players must answer why the different situations they have experienced are uncomfortable or strange. These questions are presented as a reminder of the conversations the players have had during the game.

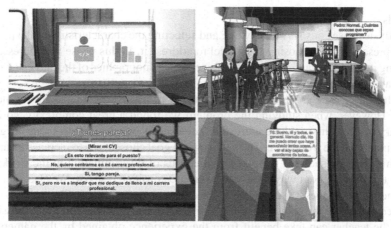

**Fig. 1.** Screenshots of the game "The Interview". At the top left the players must choose the job position for which they want to do the job interview. At the top right are the cafeteria, one of the explorable areas of the game where the players must interact with some characters. Bottom left is one of the questions asked during the job interview. Finally at the bottom right is the end of the game where it is revealed that the protagonist has been playing in the skin of a woman.

The videogame provides students with a first-hand experience of what is feeling discrimination. The players play the four parts of the game as a woman character without knowing it, the game throughout the conversations gives no information about the gender of the main character (the player). The gender of the main character will be revealed once the player completes the interview, at the end of the third part of the game. The goal of hiding that all players play as female characters during the game, this aims to make all conversations seem strange and discriminatory to the players, allowing them (specially to male players) to conclude that was because they had played as female character. Figure 1 shows the current appearance of the video game.

The game objective for players is to succeed in a job selection process. But this objective is only a way to show the player situations of discrimination. Students should use the game without knowing the educational purpose to avoid being reticent to the message or having initial biases before they experience the discriminatory situation through the game. Of course, this is not the only correct or valid way to use *"La Entrevista"* as an educational tool and the final decision always remains the teacher's.

### 3.3 Developing a Serious Game

Although there does not seem to be a specific model to follow for the design of serious games focused on social problems, in the literature we can find models and frameworks with common characteristics that can be useful to create our video game [16]. We will describe how the next 4 phases based on literature have been carried out: Analysis, Design, Development and Evaluation. It should be noted that although the details of the process are described as an iterative process, this is not really the case, and if necessary, it is possible to go back from one phase to any of the previous phases.

**Analysis**
The analysis phase consists of analyzing and selecting the characteristics of the problem to be represented and choosing the model to address it. In this phase we addressed the following items: Topic and pedagogical objective; Demographics of the players; Context of use; and Game genre.

In this case, we start from the generic topic of addressing the social problem of sexism. However, when studying the problem we found a great complexity, so it was necessary to limit the problem addressed. As a result, we decided to focus on gender discrimination in the workplace. The pedagogical goal chosen was to increase awareness about this issue by showing the players situations of discrimination in the workplace, making them think about why these situations are considered sexist. We also decided to focus the game on ages 18–25, when users can start their first job. The context of use identified was to use the game as a tool to introduce the topic of sexism in the classroom, so that the teacher can take benefit from the experience obtained by the gameplay to create a later reflection in groups.

Simulation and adventure games are the most appropriate game genres given the pedagogical objective and topic. These two game genres allow the design and use of characters that the player can relate to and perceive reality through. However, considering the cost of development, the existing tools and the knowledge of the development team, we chose the point & click adventure game genre. This choice allows us not only to show a reality but also to focus on the dialogues and reduce costs by allowing us to make a simpler game where not all the real options are represented.

**Design**
The design phase includes the choice of the characteristics that the game will have (game mechanics, the desired user experience, main events, characters, scenarios, etc.). This design was carried out taking into account the characteristics decided in the analysis phase such as the game context, the age of the players, the game genre and the pedagogical objective. In this phase, the following items were specified: Story, Scenarios and Characters; Game and Learning Mechanics; Dialogs and Graphic Design.

To adapt the videogame to the game genre and the pedagogical objective, we decided that during the game story, the player would put himself in the shoes of a person who has just finished his career and must make his first job interview, giving the player the goal of passing the interview. To choose the situations of discrimination that the game would show, we interviewed 10 people, 8 girls and 2 boys, with engineering and mathematics studies with jobs in technology companies. In these interviews these people were asked about situations of sexism they had experienced. With the events chosen to be shown in the game we identified the need for 7 different scenarios and 11 characters.

Among the mechanics to be implemented, those generic of the point & click adventure game genre were chosen, such as dialogues and exploration of the scenarios. To achieve a greater immersion of the player, we decided that the character would be in first person, being what the computer screen shows what the character sees in the game. However, as part of the learning design, the character played by the player is a girl and this is not mentioned until the end of the game. The main character uses a name that can be used by both boys and girls (Alex) and no dialogue uses adjectives that might give clues as to the gender of the character being played. With this decision we want to get the immersion of the player regardless of their gender, but also, in the case of a male player we want the situations to look weird and at the end of the game when the gender of the protagonist is discovered.

Also, at the end of the main story, we designed a section with question-answer mechanic to promote the players' thinking about the sexist situations shown in the game. In this section the player must revive some key conversations and indicate why they are weird, the player has 3 answer options of which only one is correct.

On the other hand, to avoid the monotony of the dialogues, two other mechanics were selected. One of them is the decision making, giving the player the opportunity to answer in different ways in the dialogues and having (limited) effect on them. The other mechanic is to give the main character a curriculum that the player can access during the game, in this way the player must answer the interview questions according to this curriculum trying to tell his experience as best as possible to succeed in the interview.

**Development**
The development phase consists of the creation of the video game itself, keeping in mind the game platform, the technical needs of the design, the development cost, the development time available and the experience of the developers.

For the development of this game we used the *uAdventure* authoring tool, which allows us to create simple narrative games in a fast way, providing facilities for the next phase of evaluation [17]. In addition, *uAdventure* allows us to export the game for Windows and Linux devices, in a portable version with which the games do not need to be installed. This allows us to deploy the game in most of schools.

**Evaluation**
The evaluation phase consists of performing the necessary tests on the developed game to check its adequacy with the design and the pedagogical objective. This phase is very important, since it is difficult for a first version of the game to fulfill all the requirements. There may be missing requirements in the design, the players' experience with the game may not be the expected, or some mechanics may go against the educational objective. For this reason, it is important that from the first playable prototype, tests are carried out

with experts and with users with the demographics as close as possible to those of the end users.

To carry out this evaluation, we must first define the information we want to obtain and then choose the game variables with which to obtain this information. In addition, it is necessary to define how the data will be collected and stored, paying attention to the applicable data protection regulation as well as the technological standards used to deploy the game and collect/send data.

In our case, the *uAdventure* tool integrates interaction data collection, using the xAPI format and sending data anonymized by a set of random characters by user [17]. Although the information to be obtained and the variables needed should be identified prior to testing, it is recommended that the game collect information from all interactions, whether the need for them has been identified.

In order to evaluate the game, we are interested in information about if:

- Players read the dialogues. We can obtain this information by measuring the time that runs between the time a dialog appears and disappears. Too long times may indicate that the player is distracted or bored while too short times will indicate that the player is not reading.
- Players have any difficulties with any part of the game. Repetition of the same interaction or a set of interactions may indicate that the player is having trouble making progress.
- The playing time is adequate. We can measure the time that has passed between the first interaction and the last interaction. Since the game is intended to be utilized in a classroom session, we do not want the game time to be excessively long.
- There are differences in responses to game dialogues in different groups of users (boys, girls, by age, etc.). We need to collect the age and gender of each player through an external questionnaire, so we can compare the decisions made in each dialogue according to the gender of the players and their age.
- The game succeeds in making players think. In this case we can know if the player identifies sexist events through the final questions of the game, but we will also need an external questionnaire. The goal is to verify that the game design is right and that the pedagogical objective is fulfilled.
- Education professionals see the game as an appropriate educational tool to use in their classrooms. We need an external questionnaire. As in the previous point, we must evaluate that the game is pedagogically right, regardless of the fact that professionals in the field have been involved in the design of the game.
- General opinion. We are interested to know if players like the game, and if they find it entertaining or interesting. Although the data on playing time, completion and inactivity time can give us a hint, it is recommended to carry out a questionnaire.

## 3.4 First Evaluation

To analyze the items mentioned in the previous section (gameplay time, game issues, behavior, etc.), we carried out two evaluations after the development process of the videogame. The purpose of these evaluations is to assess the game design.

On the one hand we want to check if the users find it attractive as a videogame; if the game meets the pedagogical objective, i.e. if there is any change in the player's perception of gender discrimination; and finally if the developed video game is an applicable tool in the classroom. Taking into account that the game is currently in its first stable version after an internal evaluation, we hope to get feedback with which to improve the game for its final release as a free educational tool.

The first evaluation was carried out with 22 students, between 18 and 25 years old, at the art and design school in Rubí, Barcelona. This evaluation was carried out without any researcher in the room, with the official teacher of the class in charge of deploying the game and conducting a discussion session. In addition to the remotely collected data, the teacher was interviewed for a postmortem. The second evaluation was carried out with 1 professor and 6 students from the Faculty of Education of the Complutense University of Madrid. The 6 students were in their final year of the Master's Degree in Teaching and with stable job or internship.

The structure of both evaluations was as follows:

- Pre-test. Participants are asked to fill out an initial survey which asks about: gender, age, use of video games, household activity, gender most adequate for certain activities, friendship with minorities according to their gender or sexuality, knowledge about friends who have been victims of discrimination because of their sex, and opinion on whether it is necessary to educate about sexism, sexual orientation.
- Gameplay. Participants play the videogame *"La Entrevista"*.
- Post-test. Participants are asked to fill out a second questionnaire asking again about: the gender most appropriate for some activities, friendships that have been discriminated against because of their sex and the need to educate about sexism and sexuality. Finally, they are also asked for their opinion about the video game and if it has made them reflect on any particular topic.
- Discussion session. A class debate is carried out on gender discrimination where the participants can give their opinion about their experience and/or the one lived during the game.

## 4    Results

A first analysis of the data of the evaluation shows that *"La Entrevista"* makes players reflect. Comments also show that the game can be a good educational tool to use in the classroom as a base for addressing the problem of gender discrimination. Some of the results obtained in the first evaluation with real users are shown below.

In the Ruby experiment, 22 people participated (13 girls and 9 boys, with an average age of 18.4) but 3 people did not complete the second questionnaire.

The data show a change in players' responses to common questions in pre-post questionnaires. The mean time of gameplay was 26.1 min (STD = 4.71; Min = 16.2; Max = 34.6) and only one player, who filled out the final questionnaire, did not complete the game. In the question "Who is best at... ?", there was an increase in the percentage of players who responded that it was independent of gender (Fig. 2).

In question "Do you have friends who have been discriminated against based on their gender?" 59% of people answered yes at pre-test but 74% said yes at post-test.

Regarding the players' opinion, 89% of the players made positive comments about the game, complimenting things such as: the playability, the possibility of being able to always have multiple response options and the way the game deals with the issue of sexism. 58% of the players indicated that it had made them reflect, 11% said they were already aware of the problems represented by the game and 32% answered that the game had not made them reflect. Finally, some players highlighted the need to improve some of the character animations as well as the interface, showing more clearly which character is speaking at any given moment.

During the final interview of the experience, the teacher of the school pointed out that the experience had been very interesting and enriching for the class, giving place to a later discussion about how society can discriminate against people without being aware of it.

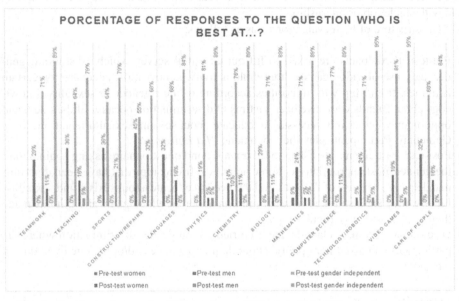

**Fig. 2.** Results to the question "Who is best at X?" where X is different types of activity.

At the second evaluation, 7 people participated, 2 men and 5 women with an average age of 32.1. The mean time of gameplay was 23.0 min (STD = 3.60; Min = 17.16; Max = 28.2). In this experiment there is no significant difference between pre-post responses. In terms of opinions, 2 of the players highlighted that the game made them feel too long and 2 others that they felt lost in the game. However, all of them positively valued the video game and highlighted the design and the way of addressing the sexism in the game. Finally, only one of the players said that the game did not make him think.

## 5 Conclusions

Videogames have proven to be an effective and powerful educational tool in different domains. Not only can they be used to teach knowledge or train skills, they can also be used to address societal problems raising awareness about these issues. But developing video games is still complex and expensive because it requires time and multidisciplinary expertise (developers, education experts, graphic designers, animators). However, we can find tools and models that facilitate its development. On the one hand, using authoring tools can allow us to work with less technical profiles or with less human resources. On the other hand, having previously proved game design models and additional in-depth case studies upon which to base our design enables us to systematize the development process, producing more effective games from the start.

We develop the video game "*La Entrevista*", which aims to address the problem of sexism. This videogame is designed as a teacher companion tool that would provide a first-hand sex discrimination common experience to all the students on which the teacher can built upon a deeper discussion with their students on this complex topic. As a result, we have obtained a 25-min video game and its first formative evaluation with 26 users. This initial data shows the usefulness as an educational tool, promising initial results on its effectiveness and has obtained positive comments from the players. From this formative evaluation we have also obtained feedback that will help us to further improve the game. And we want to continue to collect data that will allow us to better understand the effects of the game.

In this publication we also describe the steps followed for the development of "*La Entrevista*" game following a 4-phase model based on the literature. In the analysis phase, it is necessary to understand the problem to be addressed and to study which game genre is best suited to the educational objective to be achieved. In the design phase, the mechanics and other features of the game should be defined with the educational objective in mind. In the case of an awareness game where a social problem is to be addressed, it is important to represent the problem realistically. Dialogues, exploration and decision making are ideal mechanics for this type of educational objective. However, it is important to combine it with more dynamic game mechanics and/or challenges so that the player does not get bored. It is important to keep the player's attention without overwhelming him with too much text for too long. In the development phase, it is important to take into account the human resources budget and technical knowledge available. Choosing authoring tools or game editors can help reduce the cost and time of development. One option may be to create a more limited first prototype using this type of tools to make an early design validation, before to carry out with the final development. This evaluation phase is important to know the game's effectiveness. It helps us to gain insight about if the game duration is adequate to the context in which we want to use it; to know if the game keeps the players engaged during all gameplay; to know if the educational experts accept it as an educational tool they are willing to use in their classes; or to know if the game has the desired effect on the players.

However, this is still a single case study and we consider that it is important to continue studying the use of video games to address social problems. Since these problems are very complex and it is difficult to address all their characteristics with a single video game. In this work we have focused on sexism in the workplace, but there are many other areas where this problem occurs (within the couple, language, education, institutions, and law). And it is also necessary to study what types of games are most effective at different ages.

In addition, we consider that it is necessary to provide more information about serious games to improve the research and application of these games in education. For instance, making videogames free open code and publishing the design process and the game design documents will help to create better video games in a more efficient way. This type of work serves as a reference of the do's and don'ts when developing a serious game. It is also important that these games that are developed are shared openly and freely once they are finished, allowing other researchers to compare video games with the same characteristics or by replaying tests. Giving access to these video games allows other researchers to translate the game and use it in other countries to compare effectiveness according to other cultures.

As future work, we will continue to improve the game with the comments received in this first evaluation. The collection of more data will allow us to compare the effectiveness of the game in men and women, and to study if it is effective in the whole age range targeted. And once a summative evaluation has been carried out, we will proceed to publish the video game, free, on the research group's website.

**Acknowledgments.** This work has been partially funded by Regional Government of Madrid (eMadrid S2018/TCS4307, co-funded by the European Structural Funds FSE and FEDER) and by the Ministry of Education (PID2020- 119620RB-I00).

# References

1. Nelson, T.D. (ed.): Psychology Press, Hove (2015)
2. Najjar, I., et al.: Prevalence and forms of gender discrimination and sexual harassment among medical students and physicians in French- speaking Switzerland : a survey. BMJ Open **12**, 1–7 (2022)
3. Parker, K., Funk, C.: Gender discrimination comes in many forms for today's working women (2017). http://pewrsr.ch/2ytv0xx
4. Ramiro-sánchez, T., Ramiro, M.T., Bermúdez, M.P., Buela-casal, G.: Psychosocial intervention sexism in adolescent relationships : a systematic review. Psychosoc. Interv. **27**, 123–132 (2018)
5. Cristoffanini, M.T.: Gender-based violence : prevalence, sexist imaginaries, and myths among university, pp. 33–50 (2020)
6. UNESCO: UNESCO research shows women career scientists still face gender bias. https://en.unesco.org/news/unesco-research-shows-women-career-scientists-still-face-gender-bias
7. Laamarti, F., Eid, M., El Saddik, A.: An overview of serious games. Int. J. Comput. Games Technol. 2014, (2014)
8. Connolly, T.M., Boyle, E.A., Macarthur, E., Hainey, T., Boyle, J.M.: A systematic literature review of empirical evidence on computer games and serious games. Comput. Educ. **59**, 661–686 (2012)
9. Calvo-Morata, A., Alonso-Fernández, C., Freire, M., Martínez-Ortiz, I., Fernández-Manjón, B.: Serious games to prevent and detect bullying and cyberbullying: A systematic serious games and literature review. Comput. Educ. **157**, 103958 (2020)
10. Peng, W., Lee, M., Heeter, C.: The effects of a serious game on role-taking and willingness to help. J. Commun. **60**, 723–742 (2010)
11. DeKanter, N.: Gaming redefines interactivity for learning. TechTrends **49**(3), 26–31 (2004). https://doi.org/10.1007/BF02763644

12. Chen, J.: Flow in games (and everything else). Commun. ACM. **50**, 31 (2007)
13. Gloria, A., Yañez, B., Fernández, C.A.: Review of serious games to educate on gender equality. Technol. Ecosyst. Enhancing Multicult. (2020)
14. Song, M., Zhang, S.: EFM: a model for educational game design. In: Pan, Z., Zhang, X., El Rhalibi, A., Woo, W., Li, Y. (eds.) Edutainment 2008. LNCS, vol. 5093, pp. 509–517. Springer, Heidelberg (2008). https://doi.org/10.1007/978-3-540-69736-7_54
15. Ravenscroft, A., Lindstaedt, S., Kloos, C.D., Hernández-Leo, D. (eds.): LNCS, vol. 7563. Springer, Heidelberg (2012). https://doi.org/10.1007/978-3-642-33263-0
16. Ávila-pesántez, D., Rivera, L.A., Alban, M.S.: Approaches for serious game design : a systematic literature review. Comput. Educ. J. **8** (2017)
17. Perez-Colado, I., Pérez-Colado, V.M., Martinez-Ortiz, I., Freire, M., Fernandez-Manjon, B.: Simplifiying serious games authoring and validation with uAdventure and SIMVA. In: IEEE 20th International Conference on Advances Learning Technology, pp. 106–108 (2020)

# Contextual Ontology-Based Feature Selection for Teachers

Nader N. Nashed[1,2]([⊠]) [iD], Christine Lahoud[2] [iD], and Marie-Hélène Abel[1] [iD]

[1] HEUDIASYC, Université de Technologie de Compiègne, Compiègne, France
{nader.nashed,marie-helene.abel}@utc.fr
[2] Université Française d'Égypte, Cairo, Egypt
{nader.nashat,christine.lahoud}@ufe.edu.eg

**Abstract.** The context of teacher is indescribable without considering the multiple overlapping contextual situations. Teacher Context Ontology (TCO) presents a unified representation of data of these contexts. This ontology provides a relatively high number of features to consider for each context. These features result in a computational overhead during data processing in context-aware recommender systems. Therefore, the most relevant features must be favored over others without losing any potential ones using a feature selection approach. The existing approaches provide struggling results with high number of contextual features. In this paper, a new contextual ontology-based feature selection approach is introduced. This approach finds similar contexts for each insertion of new teacher using the ontology representation. Also, it selects relevant features from multiple contexts of a teacher according to their corresponding importance using a variance-based selection approach. This approach is novel in terms of representation, selection, and deriving implicit relationships for features in the multiple contexts of a teacher.

**Keywords:** ontology · feature selection · context · teacher · education · machine learning

## 1 Introduction

Education is one of the most developed fields in the past few years due to mandatory variables such as digital transformation, mindset of learners, etc. [3]. The quality of education is maintained through new technologies to help all actors in the field. The teacher is considered an essential actor in the field who needs

---

This work was funded by the French Research Agency (ANR) and by the company Vivocaz under the project France Relance - preservation of R&D employment (ANR-21-PRRD-0072-01) in collaboration with project Imhotep "Preventing teachers' psychosocial risks through contextual support of educational resources".

C. S. González-González et al. (Eds.): ICWL 2022/SETE 2022, LNCS 13869, pp. 110–121, 2023.
https://doi.org/10.1007/978-3-031-33023-0_10

the help of these new educational technologies to enhance the quality of this job. Context-aware recommender systems (CARS) is one of these technologies that provide the teacher with personalized recommendations [7]. Data representation is an essential step to achieve such objective as a teacher coexists in multiple contexts such as living context and working context. Ontology is the semantic representation of a formal domain by defining categories, properties, and relations between data. Ontology offers an extensive representation of contextual data within same context, as well as different contexts [4]. Therefore, for each teacher, two types of contexts are considered: representational contexts and interactional context. Representational context is described by social or living context and work context, while interactional context is described by sentimental state. These different types of contexts are represented by Teacher Context Ontology (TCO) [16] and its extension with Mood-Detection Ontology (MDO) and MEMORAe Core Collaboration ontology (MCC) [17]. These ontologies introduce high number of features to describe each context. The most relevant features need to be selected to reduce the computational cost of the contextual data processing.

Recently, there has been a grow in the amount of conducted research towards dimensionality reduction and feature selection to cope with the increasing amount of data in addition to favorability towards computational costs reduction. Dimensionality reduction can be achieved by one or more of these approaches: feature selection and/or feature extraction. Feature extraction approaches obtain new features from the input data, and it is widely used with the image processing applications. On the other hand, feature selection approaches get a reduced subset of the full set of existing features which directly affects the computational cost. The feature selection process enhances the computational complexity by reducing number of features and accordingly, size of data [11,12]. The elimination of irrelevant features enhances level of data personalization for each teacher. On the other hand, this complicated process has various challenges to achieve the optimal result in terms of type of data and selection criteria.

In this paper, a new ontology-based semi-hybrid feature selection approach is introduced that considers multiple contexts of a teacher and numerous features in each context. The main objective of this approach is summarized as representing the multiple contexts of a teacher with minimum number of features without neglecting relevant ones. Throughout this research, a variance-based feature selection approach is found as a suitable answer to this objective. The semantic representation of data, or ontology, provides a precise description of the multiple contexts. The proposed variance-based approach adapts with various features in different contexts. A final clustering step, using Formal Concept Analysis (FCA), is added to easily find intentions between teachers and extensions between features. The rest of this paper is assembled as follows: Sect. 2 discusses previous research related to this work in terms of feature selection trends and education-related ones. Section 3 introduces the architecture of the proposed feature selection approach and illustrates the function of ontology in it.

Section 4 presents a summary of the obtained results with additional discussion. Section 5 concludes the proposed approach and states future perspectives.

# 2   Related Work

During this section, we start with an introduction of feature selection algorithms in Sect. 2.1. Afterwards, we review the most recent approach related to our problem in general in Sect. 2.2 and education-related ones in Sect. 2.3. Finally,the reviewed papers are summarized in Sect. 2.4.

## 2.1   Feature Selection Algorithms

Feature selection algorithms are classified into supervised, semi-supervised and unsupervised approaches [11,12]. Supervised selection algorithms need labeled dataset to select the relevant features and they follow wrapper, filter, or intrinsic methodologies by using target variables. Wrapper algorithms extract highest performing features such as recursive feature elimination (RFE) while filtering algorithms use the relationship between features and target variables such as statistical and importance methods. Moreover, the intrinsic algorithms select features automatically as part of the training model such as decision trees and lasso regression. The most significant difference between supervised and semi-supervised algorithms, is the percentage of labeled data that is used throughout the algorithm. On the contrary, labelled datasets are not required for the unsupervised feature selection algorithms and these algorithms are divided into three approaches: filter, wrapper, and hybrid methods [1,5]. The filtering-based approach evaluates each feature according to the intrinsic features of the provided dataset while wrapper approach is based exclusively on a machine learning algorithm to evaluate all possible combinations according to the evaluation criterion. Wrapper approach has a high computational overhead because it uses a certain clustering method to evaluate each feature. Hybrid approaches try to compromise between both previous approaches as it tries to combine the unbiased methodology and the data over-fitting avoidance of unsupervised selection with the computational efficiency of supervised selection [22].

## 2.2   Variance-Based Feature Selection

Variance-based feature selection is considered as a filtering-based unsupervised algorithm. It eliminates features with variance less than a certain threshold across all samples. In addition, it considers the high variance as an indication to the existence of useful information. The related research to variance-based feature selection is selected using a search process using the following keywords: "education", "variance-based", "feature", and "selection". It was difficult to obtain relevant results in the educational domain. Most of the found existing research is associated with medical, textual, imaging, networking, or manufacturing applications. Therefore, the most relevant research to our proposed approach, is reviewed regardless of the domain of application. Lakshmi and Vishnuvardhan [13] apply Random Forest (RF) algorithm for feature reduction and random subset feature selection (RSFS) algorithm for feature extraction of various cancer dataset. This approach considers variance of features without setting a threshold depending on their variance which increases the computational cost. Roberts et al. [18] propose a new feature selection approach for colon and lung cancer classification. Features are selected according to differential variance of cancer subtypes classification which is computed using the ratio of variance between the cancer samples and the samples of non-cancerous tumors. Therefore, they choose not to directly use the variance across features as the selection criteria. Sadeghyan [20] combines the usage of sensitivity analysis (SA) technique with extended Fourier amplitude sensitivity test (EFAST) for a variance-based feature selection for medical and biological datasets. The variance of input features is estimated using the contribution of each feature where the threshold is selected once across each dataset without considering any other adaptable options.

The research study by Kamalov et al. [9] and extended in [8], uses an orthogonal variance-based decomposition for feature selection to identify network traffic features for intrusion detection systems (IDS). They use the uniform distribution using variance of traffic features to distinguish DDoS attacks. This approach considers variance of all features only without providing a clear explanation of the threshold setting. Veisi et al. [23] proposes a keyword extraction approach from Persian and English text documents. Keywords are selected according to token weighting depending on the corresponding variance. This research proposes a hybrid approach of variance-based feature selection with Term Frequency Inverse Document Frequency (TF-IDF). The variance of keywords acts as the selection criteria but no insightful detection of a more precise threshold. Mabkhot et al. [15] propose a variance-based manufacturing process feature selection for a decision support system. The proposed approach represents manufacturing process using ontology and introduces a set of reasoning rules to reduce the computational overhead of the algorithm execution at every new insertion. The model considers 9 features only which can be considered as a drawback to this proposition.

## 2.3 Educational-Related Feature Selection

Throughout our search operation, two important reviews are found that demonstrate the major contributions to feature selection techniques in educational data processing. The first review performed by Alyahyan and Düştegör [2] discusses the recent approaches of predicting academic success within the higher education level. The review illustrates the recent methodologies to achieve such goal for the different stages of predication including data collection and selection, data cleaning and preprocessing, feature selection, and data mining for different datasets of students. This research concludes that despite the importance of the usage of either feature selection methods (filtering or wrapper methods), it is better to use the embedded methods with the data mining tools to reduce the computational overhead. The other review introduced by Zaffar et al. [24]

presents a state of the art of trends in educational data mining (EDM) but it highlights the classification algorithms and the feature selection algorithms. This research delivers a guide to researchers planning to build an EDM with all its components. Through the feature selection section, it is observable that the wrapper methods are the most used with a percentage of 78.5% of all reviewed approaches. However, the researchers state that the wrapper methods are not the quickest when used with large datasets. All reviewed approaches target the performance of students and learners and generate useful predictions to help them as well as the educational administration.

## 2.4  Summary

From the reviewed research, we can state that the importance of using feature selection is summarized into three scenarios: decreasing computational time by selecting the most important features, the combination of feature selection with feature extraction that improves its performance significantly, and finally, the effect of feature selection on the classification accuracy. Multiple approaches follow the two-stage feature selection by applying two feature selection techniques at once. Such approach enhances the efficiency and quality of the selected features. None of these papers discusses the importance of the accurate selection of a threshold or introduces an explicit explanation of the threshold selection and the level of flexibility of this selection with other applications.

## 3  Methodology

Contexts of a teacher can form a problematic issue when it comes to feature selection methodology as well as high computational time complexity. Additionally, the lack of feature selection approaches for the context of a teacher motivates this research with a semi-hybrid feature selection approach. The proposed contextual ontology-based feature selection approach for teachers, is designed to achieve the following main functions:

i  *Map teacher data into ontology representation.* When feature selection process is performed for a new teacher, the teacher data is mapped first into the contextual ontology.
ii  *Search for similar teachers based on rules.* Semantic reasoning rules are used to search the ontology for teachers with a similar context as the new teacher.
iii  *Select features for a teacher context.* For a new teacher, features are selected based on the context using two filter-based selection methods: information gain importance, and variance-based selection.
iv  *Clustering the selected features.* Formal concept analysis is used to cluster the selected features and to construct the corresponding hierarchy for extents and intents which facilitates the future searching process for similar teachers.

The proposed approach consists of ontology representation, information grain importance calculation, variance-based feature selection, and formal concept analysis (FCA) clustering as shown in Fig. 1.

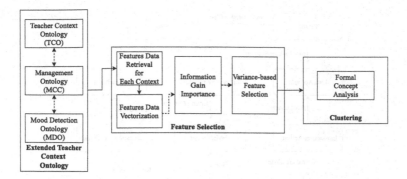

**Fig. 1.** An overview of the proposed contextual ontology-based feature selection approach for teachers.

## 3.1  Teacher Context Ontology Representation

The used ontology is based on teacher-context ontology and mood-detection ontology proposed in a previous research regarding the teacher contexts [16,17]. Protégé[1] is used as the ontology construction tool and DR2Q platform[2] is used as the relational data mapping tool. The teacher contexts representation involves four main concepts: teacher profile, living environment, working environment, and sentimental state, as shown in Fig. 2. Teacher profile involves the main information of a teacher such as name, age, experience, gender, contact details, interests, and competences. Living context is represented by personal address and type of the living area. Working context is accentuated by address and affiliation which forms the connection between the geographical location and educational level of this work environment or the educational institution. Sentimental state of a teacher is described by the mood-detection ontology through three main concepts: mood level, emotional commitment, and flow occurrence. Through this proposition, the mood level is used without considering the other two concepts for the purpose of simplification. The SWRL rule, as shown in Table 1, is applied to any new teacher entry against all saved teachers. This rule checks the similarity of the new teacher with other teachers in terms of experience, teaching style, spoken languages, living environment information, working environment information, and field of science in which a teacher is specialized. The utilization of such rule prevents the computational overhead accompanied by executing the totality of this approach for each new teacher.

## 3.2  Feature Selection Approach

The proposed feature selection approach consists of 2 filtering algorithms followed by a clustering approach as shown in Fig. 1. We start our approach by

---

[1] https://protege.stanford.edu/.
[2] http://d2rq.org/.

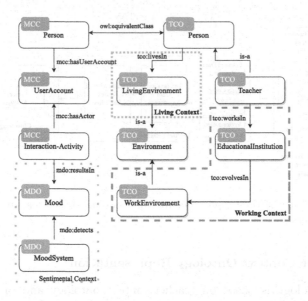

**Fig. 2.** A partial T-Box representation of the extended ontology.

**Table 1.** SWRL rule for finding a match of new teacher

| Antecedent | Consequence |
|---|---|
| tco:teacher(?t)ˆtco:teacher(?ts)ˆtco:hasYearsOfExperience(?t,?ex)ˆtco: hasYearsOfExperience(?ts,?exs)ˆswrlb:greaterThanOrEqual(?exs,? ex)ˆtco:hasTeachingStyle(?t,?tch)ˆtco:hasTeachingStyle(?ts,?tchs)ˆswrlb: stringEqualIgnoreCase(?tch,?tchs)ˆswrlb:stringEqualIgnoreCase(?tch, "MixedStyle")ˆtco:hasLanguage(?t,?lan)ˆtco:hasLanguage(?ts,?lans)ˆswrlb: contains(?lan,lans)ˆtco:livesIn(?t,?livenv)ˆtco:LivingEnvironment(? livenv)ˆtco:is-a(?livenv,?env)ˆtco:environment(?env)ˆtco:hasType(?env,? envtype)ˆtco:hasCountry(?env,?coun)ˆowl:country(?coun)ˆtco:livesIn(?ts,? livenvs)ˆtco:LivingEnvironment(?livenvs)ˆtco:is-a(?livenvs,?envs)ˆtco: environment(?envs)ˆtco:hasType(?envs,?envtypes)ˆtco:hasCountry(? envs,?couns)ˆowl:country(?couns)ˆswrlb:equal(?envtype,?envtypes)ˆswrlb: equal(?coun,?couns)ˆtco:worksIn(?t,?inst)ˆtco:EducationalInstitution(? inst)ˆtco:evolvesIn(?inst,?workenv)ˆtco:WorkingEnvironment(?worknv)ˆtco: is-a(?workenv,?wenv)ˆtco:environment(?wenv)ˆtco:hasType(?wenv,? wenvtype)ˆtco:hasEducationLevel(?inst,?edulvl)ˆdcterms:EducationLevel(? edulvl)ˆtco:worksIn(?ts,?insts)ˆtco:EducationalInstitution(?insts)ˆtco: evolvesIn(?insts,?workenvs)ˆtco:WorkingEnvironment(?worknvs)ˆtco: is-a(?workenvs,?wenvs)ˆtco:environment(?wenvs)ˆtco:hasType(? wenvs,?wenvtypes)ˆtco:hasEducationLevel(?insts,?edulvls)ˆdcterms: EducationLevel(?edulvls)ˆswrlb:equal(?envtype,?envtypes)ˆswrlb: equal(?edulvl,?edulvls)ˆtco:hasScience(?t,?sci)ˆmodsci:Science(?sci)ˆtco: hasScience(?ts,?scis)ˆmodsci:Science(?scis)ˆswrlb:equal(?sci,?scis) | sameAs(?t,?ts) |

transforming the retrieved list of features from its feature-value form to easy-to-use vectors. Binary one-hot encoding is selected for this task as it constructs one Boolean-valued feature for each possible string value of a single feature [21]. Afterwards, information gain importance is calculated to be used in the threshold calculation for the next step [10,19]. Variance-based feature selection uses the computed threshold to eliminate the less importance features [6]. Formal concept analysis (FCA) acts a clustering methodology to evaluate the selected features [14].

**Information Gain:**

Information gain utilizes the mutual information (MI) $I$ between two random features to compute the non-negative value of dependency between these two features. The calculations are based on entropy estimation used in k-nearest neighbor distance estimation as in Eq. 1. After computing the importance of all features, its mean $mean_I$ is calculated to be used as the threshold value for the variance-based feature selection.

$$I(f_1, f_2, \cdots, f_m) = \psi(k) - \frac{(m-1)}{k} + (m-1)\psi(N) - < \psi(n_{f_1}) + \psi(n_{f_2}) + \cdots + \psi(n_{f_m}) > \quad (1)$$

where $f_1, f_2, \cdots, f_m$ are the m features
$\psi$ is digamma function
$k$ is k-nearest neighbours
$N$ is set of features
$m$ is total numner of features
$n_{f_i}$ is boundry limit in which all features fall

**Variance-Based Threshold Selection:**

Variance-based threshold algorithm is baseline approach to selects features with high variances regardless of the desired output with an unsupervised approach. It eliminates all features with a variance that is less than a predetermined threshold $thr$. In our case, this threshold is calculated using the average importance $mean_I$ as shown in Eq. 2. The resulting set of features are used by the formal concept analysis to cluster the provided set of teachers.

$$thr = mean_I(1 - mean_I) \quad (2)$$

**Formal Concept Analysis:**

Formal concept analysis (FCA) delivers a model to represent a set of objects (teachers) with another set of properties (features) where each object is associated with a subset of these properties. The formal context matrix represents such relationship between teachers and features. Using this matrix, a formal ontology is constructed to describe the hierarchical representation of the relation between each sub-concept and subset of teachers using the theory of lattices.

Each formal context is represented by a set of teachers, a set of features, and incidence, or binary relation, between each teacher and feature. The pairing between a subset of teacher $T$ and a subset of features $F$ is said to be a formal concept if every teacher in $T$ has all features in $F$, and $T$ and $F$ contain only a subset of their main sets of teachers and features respectively. This formal concept is visualized into extensions and intensions using lattices as a directed acyclic graph-like representation of concepts.

## 4    Scenarios and Discussion

When we apply the proposed approach to a vectorized set of context features of a teacher as shown in Fig. 3, the correlation coefficient of all features is computed in the same manner as shown in Fig. 4. The illustrated heatmap shows that there are dependencies between features which should be eliminated by the feature selection algorithms. Afterwards, the information gain importance is calculated for all features. For example, the feature number 12 "lang1=English", represents English language as the mother tongue of a teacher, is dependent on several other features, in addition to the obtained low importance using the information gain method. Therefore, this feature can be eliminated by all feature selection methods except for the variance-based threshold method according to the used scoring algorithm. After the above data analysis, the proposed approach can be applied to any dataset of choice. For example, if a mean importance of 0.1, is computed from the information gain algorithm, a threshold of 0.09 is used for the variance-based selection. As shown from the two numbers, the threshold is slightly lower than the mean importance across all features. This threshold selection results in the avoidance of neglecting low-variance but relatively important features such as mood. This approach targets to select at least 78% of the input features without neglecting any relevant ones.

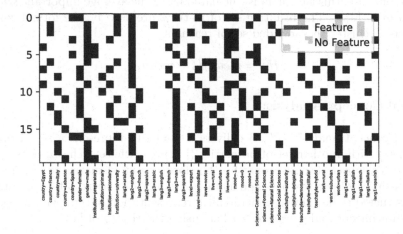

**Fig. 3.** Vectorized list of features for 20 teachers.

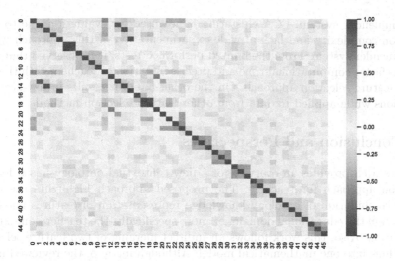

**Fig. 4.** Correlation coefficient of the selected features.

In order to validate the variance selection, we use the formal concept analysis which finds the extensions and intentions for all teachers and selected features. All teacher-feature combinations are tested to create a closed connection which indicates the correctness of the proposed algorithm. Also, it validates the completeness of connections between concepts for each subset of teachers along with the associated subset of features. The graph illustration highlights the effectiveness of the usage of the information gain importance as the threshold of the variance-based feature selection along with the ontology-based representation. Additionally, this algorithm shows a significant enhancement in the computational time when compared to other techniques due to the usage of mathematical models with low complexity.

The main importance of the used ontology can be summarized in facilitating the reasoning of the SWRL rules that are introduced in Table 1, positioning the expertise level of each teacher, and reduction of the computational overhead corresponding to repetition of the approach at each new teacher insertion into the dataset. Using the SWRL rules reasoning, the insertion of new teachers does not require re-execution of the proposed approach, as at least 10% of teachers share the same context in the used dataset. This observation directs this research to reduce the computational cost of the initial processed data. Some remarks are worthy to be highlighted concerning the selected features by this approach. Mood features are essential during this difficult period and due to the increasing importance and impact of sentimental state on the performance of teachers. The proposed approach considers mood features in the final selection regardless of its relatively moderate importance. The proposed feature selection approach keeps the main formation of all features, while on the contrary, the other methods may have dropped many important features. The usage of formal concept analysis is essential for clustering of teachers, and it can be considered as a more accurate evaluation metric during the application of this approach in a recommender system. FCA clustering is not used for evaluation due to visualization complexity and lack of wide experimentation of this approach with a recommender system. From the limited performed tests, it is observed that FCA obtains faster computational time and precise intention of teachers with the proposed feature selection approach. On the other hand, it results in low-accuracy intentions while applied to data from other feature selection methods.

## 5   Conclusion and Perspectives

This research provides an overview of a new contextual ontology-based feature selection approach for teachers. The proposed approach highlights the effect of the combination of ontology knowledge representation of features and their selection in the educational domain, or more specifically, the teacher-context representation. Also, this work follows an indirect merging of two feature selection algorithms into one mathematical model. Although many of the reviewed methods use a hybrid approach, this paper introduces a semi-hybrid approach between two filter-based feature selection without using inter-categorical hybridization. Accordingly, this paper delivers a novel work regarding the educational domain, in general, and context of teachers, specifically.

Despite the level of novelty of this work, more validation is needed to test this approach in a real-time recommender system which may enhance the resulting accuracy and shows the role of FCA clustering. We plan to test it with a dataset that represents the contexts of 100 teachers from different field of sciences, and work at different institution levels: primary education (elementary), preparatory education (middle school), secondary education (high school), and higher education (university, etc.). In this dataset, the contexts of each teacher are represented by 46 features distributed as follows: 28 features for teacher profile, 8 features for living environment context, 7 features for working environment context, and 3 for the sentimental state context. Moreover, it can be used to serve an educational resources recommender system (ERRS) to provide teachers with personalized recommendations using the full representation of their contexts, in addition to the new feature selection approach. Overall, this study is a new step towards the research in diversity of contexts in which a teacher coexists and the utilization of these contexts to enhance the information systems provided to teachers.

## References

1. Alelyani, S., Tang, J., Liu, H.: Feature selection for clustering: a review. In: Data Clustering: Algorithms and Applications, vol. 29, no. 1 (2013)
2. Alyahyan, E., Düştegör, D.: Predicting academic success in higher education: literature review and best practices. Int. J. Educ. Technol. High. Educ. 17(1), 1–21 (2020). https://doi.org/10.1186/s41239-020-0177-7
3. Cabaleiro-Cerviño, G., Vera, C.: The impact of educational technologies in higher education. GIST Educ. Learn. Res. J. 20, 155–169 (2020)
4. Chen, H., Finin, T., Joshi, A.: An ontology for context-aware pervasive computing environments. knowl. Eng. Rev. 18(3), 197–207 (2003)

5. Dong, G., Liu, H.: Feature Engineering for Machine Learning and Data Analytics. CRC Press, Boca Raton (2018)
6. Guyon, I., Elisseeff, A.: An introduction to variable and feature selection. J. Mach. Learn. Res. **3**(Mar), 1157–1182 (2003)
7. Haruna, K., et al.: Context-aware recommender system: a review of recent developmental process and future research direction. Appl. Sci. **7**(12), 1211 (2017)
8. Kamalov, F.: Orthogonal variance decomposition based feature selection. Expert Syst. Appl. **182**, 115191 (2021)
9. Kamalov, F., Moussa, S., El Khatib, Z., Mnaouer, A.B.: Orthogonal variance-based feature selection for intrusion detection systems. In: 2021 International Symposium on Networks, Computers and Communications (ISNCC), pp. 1–5. IEEE (2021)
10. Kraskov, A., Stögbauer, H., Grassberger, P.: Estimating mutual information. Phys. Rev. E **69**(6), 066138 (2004)
11. Kuhn, M., Johnson, K.: Feature Engineering and Selection: A Practical Approach for Predictive Models. CRC Press, Boca Raton (2019)
12. Kuhn, M., Johnson, K.: Applied Predictive Modeling. Springer, New York (2013). https://doi.org/10.1007/978-1-4614-6849-3
13. Lakshmi Padmaja, D., Vishnuvardhan, B.: Variance-based feature selection for enhanced classification performance. In: Satapathy, S.C., Bhateja, V., Somanah, R., Yang, X.-S., Senkerik, R. (eds.) Information Systems Design and Intelligent Applications. AISC, vol. 862, pp. 543–550. Springer, Singapore (2019). https://doi.org/10.1007/978-981-13-3329-3_51
14. Lindig, C.: Fast concept analysis. Work. Concept. Struct.-Contribut. ICCS **2000**, 152–161 (2000)
15. Mabkhot, M.M., Al-Samhan, A.M., Hidri, L.: An ontology-enabled case-based reasoning decision support system for manufacturing process selection. Adv. Mater. Sci. Eng. **2019** (2019)
16. Nashed, N.N., Lahoud, C., Abel, M.H.: TCO: a teacher context ontology. In: 2021 IEEE 24th International Conference on Computer Supported Cooperative Work in Design (CSCWD), pp. 757–762. IEEE (2021)
17. Nashed, N.N., Lahoud, C., Abel, M.H., Andrès, F., Blancan, B.: Mood detection ontology integration with teacher context. In: 2021 20th IEEE International Conference on Machine Learning and Applications (ICMLA), pp. 1710–1715. IEEE (2021)
18. Roberts, A.G., Catchpoole, D.R., Kennedy, P.J.: Variance-based feature selection for classification of cancer subtypes using gene expression data. In: 2018 International Joint Conference on Neural Networks (IJCNN), pp. 1–8. IEEE (2018)
19. Ross, B.C.: Mutual information between discrete and continuous data sets. PLoS ONE **9**(2), e87357 (2014)
20. Sadeghyan, S.: A new robust feature selection method using variance-based sensitivity analysis. arXiv preprint: arXiv:1804.05092 (2018)
21. Seger, C.: An investigation of categorical variable encoding techniques in machine learning: binary versus one-hot and feature hashing (2018)
22. Solorio-Fernández, S., Carrasco-Ochoa, J.A., Martínez-Trinidad, J.F.: A review of unsupervised feature selection methods. Artif. Intell. Rev. **53**(2), 907–948 (2020)
23. Veisi, H., Aflaki, N., Parsafard, P.: Variance-based features for keyword extraction in Persian and English text documents. Scientia Iranica **27**(3), 1301–1315 (2020)
24. Zaffar, M., Hashmani, M.A., Savita, K., Khan, S.A.: A review on feature selection methods for improving the performance of classification in educational data mining. Int. J. Inf. Technol. Manag. **20**(1–2), 110–131 (2021)

# Automated Assessment in Computer Science: A Bibliometric Analysis of the Literature

José Carlos Paiva[✉][iD], Álvaro Figueira[iD], and José Paulo Leal[iD]

CRACS - INESC TEC & DCC - FCUP, Rua do Campo Alegre, Porto, Portugal
jose.c.paiva@inesctec.pt, arfiguei@fc.up.pt, zp@dcc.fc.up.pt

**Abstract.** Over the years, several systematic literature reviews have been published reporting advances in tools and techniques for automated assessment in Computer Science. However, there is not yet a major bibliometric study that examines the relationships and influence of publications, authors, and journals to make these research trends visible. This paper presents a bibliometric study of automated assessment of programming exercises, including a descriptive analysis using various bibliometric measures and data visualizations. The data was collected from the Web of Science Core Collection. The obtained results allow us to identify the most influential authors and their affiliations, monitor the evolution of publications and citations, establish relationships between emerging themes in publications, discover research trends, and more. This paper provides a deeper knowledge of the literature and facilitates future researchers to start in this field.

**Keywords:** automated assessment · programming education · programming exercises · computer science · bibliometrics · data visualizations

## 1 Introduction

Over the years, several studies have been conducted to summarize the new developments in automated assessment for Computer Science (CS) education, at their respective times [1,12,18,23]. All of these studies focus either on comparing the features of the tools [23] or on exploring the methods and techniques for some facets of the automated assessment tools [1,12] or both [18]. These studies have been very important in understanding what has already been done in this area and what resources are available for reuse.

However, to the best of authors' knowledge, no bibliometric study has been conducted to examine the quantitative aspects of scientific publications and their relationships [2]. Such a study would contribute to a deeper knowledge of the literature and facilitate future researchers' entry into research in this field. For example, it can provide information on the authors currently worth following, an

C. S. González-González et al. (Eds.): ICWL 2022/SETE 2022, LNCS 13869, pp. 122–134, 2023.
https://doi.org/10.1007/978-3-031-33023-0_11

indication of authors' affiliations, temporal evolution of publications and citations, relationships between emerging topics in publications, co-occurrence of topics and corresponding clustering, citation networks with (and without) temporal evolution, and research trends.

In this paper we aim to present a comprehensive bibliometric study of the literature on automated assessment in programming education, considering the Web of Science Core Collection. In particular, our goal is to answer the following four groups of research questions, considering the decade 2010–2020. The first group, **RQ1**, aims to summarize the collected data, including the following questions: **RQ1-1** – "What has been the annual scientific production?"; **RQ1-2** – "What has been the average time interval for a new publication to get the first citation?"; and **RQ1-3** – "Which are the main journals/conferences to find literature in the area?". Regarding authors (**RQ2**), we want to find out **RQ2-1** – "Who are the most productive? Who is more active lately? Who has more impact?"; **RQ2-2** – "Do the most productive authors publish alone or as a group?"; and **RQ2-3** – "What are the corresponding main affiliations?". The third group (**RQ3**) has two questions about citations: **RQ3-1** – "Which are the most influential?" and **RQ3-2** – "Which are the most relevant co-citations?". Finally, the fourth group (**RQ4**) addresses the topics being discussed on publications, including: **RQ4-1** – "What are the basic, niche, motor, and emerging?"; **RQ4-2** – "How did they evolve during the past decade?"; **RQ4-3** – "What is mostly discussed?"; and **RQ4-4** – "Are there significant differences if we see their yearly frequency?". The remainder of this paper is organized as follows. Section 2 presents the methodology used to conduct this study. Section 3 presents the results of the bibliometric analysis and answers each of the research questions. Section 4 discusses the results, and compares them to recent literature review [18]. Finally, Sect. 5 summarizes the major contributions of this study.

## 2  Methodology

The data for this study has been collected from the Web of Science (WoS) Core Collection, during the third week of September 2022. To this end, a query [5] has been built to search all fields of a publication for the following combination of keywords: (automatic OR automated) AND (assessment OR evaluation OR grading OR marking) AND (programming OR computer science OR program).

The query includes a filter to limit results to those published in the decade 2010–2020. In addition to that, two refinements were needed. The first to narrow down search results to the adequate WoS categories for this area, namely: Computer Science Information Systems, Computer Science Artificial Intelligence, Computer Science Interdisciplinary Applications, Computer Science Software Engineering, Education Educational Research, Education Scientific Disciplines, Multidisciplinary Sciences, and Education Special. Even though some of these categories may still include out-of-scope publications, excluding them could result in the loss of important publications. The result was a set of 11789 publications. The full record and cited references from these publications have been retrieved. A total of twenty-four BibTeX exports were necessary to obtain the data from all the 11789 publications, due to the limitations of WoS on the number of records allowed to be exported in a single request (in these conditions, the limit is 500). Finally, the twenty-four BibTeX files obtained have been merged into a single BibTeX file. The collected set of 11789 publications was subject to a pre-processing phase, aiming to identify the relevant publications for analysis. For this phase, we have read the titles and abstracts of the papers to apply the following inclusion/exclusion criteria (as in Paiva et al. [18]). The outcome of this phase encompasses a set of 592 publications, which were selected for further analysis.

To answer the research questions that led to this study (see Subsect. 1), several graphical representations were obtained using R and bibliometrix [3] – an open-source R-tool for quantitative research in scientometrics and bibliometrics. Bibliometrix provides methods for importing bibliographic data from SCOPUS, Clarivate Analytics' WoS, PubMed, Digital Science Dimensions and Cochrane databases, and performing bibliometric analysis, including co-citation, coupling, scientific collaboration analysis and co-word analysis. Some of the research questions, however, required a more customized analysis using R and traditional packages.

## 3    Results

This section presents the results of the analysis. Each subsection answers one of the groups of research questions presented in Sect. 1, in order.

### 3.1    Data Summary

The literature on automated assessment of programming assignments demonstrates the increasing research interest in this area, reflected by a growing rate of approximately 6.57 in annual scientific production during the decade 2010–2020. However, there was a slight decrease in the number of publications in the last two years, an exceptional situation that can be associated with the COVID-19 pandemic crisis. Therefore, 2018 was the peak year with the highest number (99) of publications. Figure 1 shows a visualization of the number of publications per year, with a linear trend and the associated confidence interval responding to **RQ1-1**.

Each of the collected documents was cited by an average of 8.81 other publications, with an average rate of 1.36 per year. Thus, in response to **RQ1-2**, it takes an average of 8.82 months to receive the first citation. Figure 2 shows the average and median citations of a document per year of publication with vertical error bars representing the corresponding variability. For example, a publication of 2010 (i.e., with 10 years) has an average of 8.11 citations, while a 5-year old publication has an average of 8.49 citations.

Concerning the sources of the publications, they are distributed among 361 different sources. The top 25 publication sources (**RQ1-3**) account for more

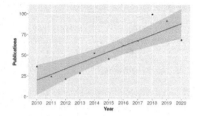

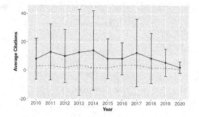

**Fig. 1.** Number of publications per year with linear trend and its confidence interval

**Fig. 2.** Average (blue line) and median (red dashed line) citations per year of publication with vertical error bars (Color figure online)

than a fourth of the total publications. The Proceedings of the 51st ACM Technical Symposium on Computer Science Education is the source with the highest number of articles collected (15), followed by ACM Special Interest Group on Programming Languages (SIGPLAN) Notices with 12 publications. Science of Computer Programming and the Proceedings of the 49th ACM Technical Symposium on Computer Science Education come up tied in third place, each with 8 publications. ACM Transactions on Software Engineering and Methodology, Computers & Education, Information and Software Technology, and the Proceedings of the ACM on Programming Languages, with 7 publications each, complete the top-5 sources.

## 3.2 Authors

There are a total of 1618 authors on the selected publications. Of these, 46 are authors of documents with only one author, while 1572 are authors of documents with multiple authors. On average, there are 3.26 authors and 3.47 co-authors per document (i.e., excluding single-author publications).

With respect to **RQ2-1**, by "most prolific authors" we mean authors who have made more publications. Figure 3 shows the top-10 authors (sorted in descending order, from top to bottom) who have made more contributions to the field, and for them the number of publications and citations per year. From this perspective, the authors who are more active recently, such as Fraser G. and Edwards S. H., and those who were more active at the beginning of the decade, such as Xie T., Queirós R., and Leal J. P., are easier to identify. Nevertheless, the most impactful works are that of Fraser G., which concentrates on software testing techniques, and Kim M., who investigates fault localization and program repairing techniques. Finally, Kim D., who works mostly in techniques for automated generation of feedback, completes the podium regarding authors' impact. This can be confirmed by measuring the authors' h-index (5, 4, and 4, respectively).

To answer **RQ2-2**, we collect all publications from the most prolific authors and construct a histogram of the number of authors per publication for each of them separately. Figure 4 illustrates the result. The only author who has worked alone is Ricardo Q. (1), while all others have no single-authored publications.

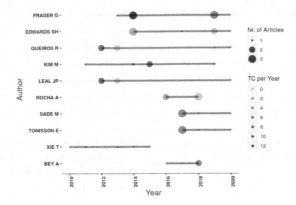

**Fig. 3.** Productivity of authors over time (TC stands for Times Cited)

Nevertheless, Edwards S. H. publishes mainly in small groups of two or three. Bey A. has only publications with two co-authors. Interestingly, Sade M. and Tonisson E. have only worked in large groups of 6 or more authors.

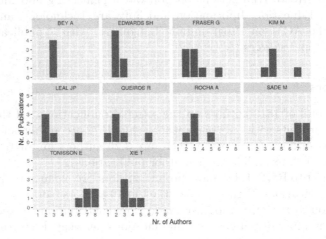

**Fig. 4.** Number of authors per publication for the most productive authors

Regarding the authors' affiliations (**RQ2-3**), there are 636 distinct identified affiliations within the collected publications. Note that a publication can count to more than one affiliation, if it involves either authors with multiple affiliations or documents with multiple authors resulting from a collaboration between different institutions. The top-20 most prolific affiliations, alone, account for more than 39% of the identified affiliations. The Carnegie Mellon University is the institution with the most publications (21), followed by the University of Porto

(17). The Nanjing University, the University of Illinois, and the University of Tartu, both appearing with 16 publications, occupy the third position.

## 3.3   Citations

In selecting the most influential publications (**RQ3-1**), it is important to have a measure that takes into account not only the number of citations but also the year of publication. For this purpose, we used the Normalized Citation Score (NCS) of a document, which is calculated by dividing the actual number of cited publications by the expected citation rate for publications of the same year. Furthermore, the answer to **RQ3-1** is twofold.

On the one hand, the local NCS (i.e., citations within the collected data) determines the most influential publications within the area. The top-5 publications under such conditions are: "A distributed system for learning programming on-line" by Verdú et al. [27]; "Marking student programs using graph similarity" by Naudé et al. [17]; "A Critical Review of Automatic Patch Generation Learned from Human-Written Patches: Essay on the Problem Statement and the Evaluation of Automatic Software Repair" by Monperrus [14]; "A system to grade computer programming skills using machine learning" by Srikant S. [26]; and "Comparing test quality measures for assessing student-written tests" by Edwards et al. [9].

On the other hand, looking at all the citations provides a global perspective on the most influential publications. The top-5 publications in this regard are: "Automated Feedback Generation for Introductory Programming from Assignments" by Singh et al. [21]; "Precise Condition Synthesis for Program Repair" by Xiong et al. [30]; "Ask the Mutants: Mutating Faulty Programs for Fault Localization" by Moon et al. [15]; "Context-Aware Patch Generation for Better Automated Program Repair" by Wen et al. [29]; and "Programming Pluralism: Using Learning Analytics to Detect Patterns in the Learning of Computer Programming" by Blikstein et al. [4].

As for **RQ3-2**, the answer is provided in the historiographic map of Fig. 5, a graph proposed by E. Garfield [11] which is a chronological network map of the most relevant co-citations from a bibliographic collection. This map identifies four separate groups corresponding to different topics, namely: **Group I (Light Blue)** encompasses works on automated feedback for CS projects [8,25]; **Group II (Purple)** captures works exploring the automated assessment of the computational thinking skills of novice programmers [7,26,28]; **Group III (Green)** includes publications on automated program repair techniques and tools [14,16]; **Group IV (Yellow)** includes automated assessment tools for assessing code and tests' quality [9,19,22,24]; **Group V (Red)** includes works integrating automated assessment tools with other e-learning tools [27,31]; **Group VI (Blue)** captures a group of works aiming to improve feedback on automated assessment [10,13,17].

**Fig. 5.** Historiographical representation of a network map of most relevant co-citations

## 3.4 Topics and Keywords

Keywords, either provided by the authors or extracted as n-grams from the title or abstract, can provide information about current issues, trends, and methods in the field. Therefore, for the group of research questions **RQ4** these are the properties that are the subject of analysis. For the first question of the group (**RQ4-1**), the answer is provided in Fig. 6, through a thematic map based on the analysis of co-word networks and clustering using the authors' keywords. This approach is similar to the proposal of Cobo et al. [6]. It identifies four types of topics (themes) based on density (i.e., degree of development) and centrality (i.e., degree of relevance), namely: emerging or declining (low centrality and low density), niche (low centrality and high density), motor (high centrality and high density), and basic (high centrality and low density) topics. Among the emerging or declining topics, a cluster involving Feedback – an important aspect of automated assessment – is notable, but so is another cluster involving Machine Learning – which unsurprisingly is also making inroads in this area – and Automated Program Repair – a technique used to automatically correct programs, which is being applied to generate feedback. Niche topics include Program Synthesis and Program Refactoring, which include techniques that can help assessing programs based on a set of constraints and/or generate accurate feedback. Motor themes focus on Static Analysis – analyzing source-code rather than its runtime behavior – while the other topics have to do with the domain itself (e.g., automated assessment, programming, and software testing). Finally, Symbolic Execution – a method of abstractly executing a program to find out what inputs cause the execution of each part of a program – is the only identified keyword that can be classified as a topic.

As for **RQ4-2**, Fig. 7 divides the decade into three sections (2010–2013, 2014–2017, and 2018–2020) and shows the thematic evolution between the three sections, based on analysis of the co-word network and the clustering of the authors' keywords [6]. Some interesting outcomes of this analysis are: the evolution of Static Analysis and its later ramifications to Testing, Tools, and Machine Learn-

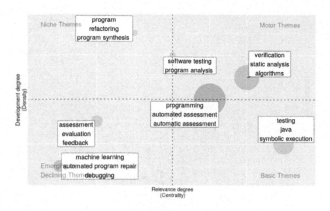

**Fig. 6.** Thematic map based on authors' keywords

ing; the rising of Machine Learning approaches that rapidly penetrate different domains and provide better results than existing techniques; and the disclosure of techniques important for feedback purposes, such as Fault Localization, Automated Test Generation, and Automated Program Repair.

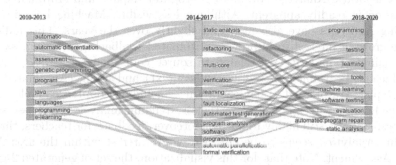

**Fig. 7.** Thematic evolution based on authors' keywords

To answer **RQ4-3**, the analysis focuses on 2-grams extracted from the abstract. To this end, Fig. 8 presents a conceptual structure map created using Multiple Correspondence Analysis (MCA) – a data analysis method to measure the association between two or more qualitative variables – and Clustering of a bipartite network of the extracted terms. Using this approach, 2-grams are divided into four clusters, which can be described as follows: **Group I (Blue)** captures terms related to automated program repair; **Group II (Green)** includes terms related to testing techniques and evaluated facets of a program; **Group III (Red)** contains 2-grams related to static analysis techniques; and **Group IV (Purple)** whose terms are more related to tools and systems.

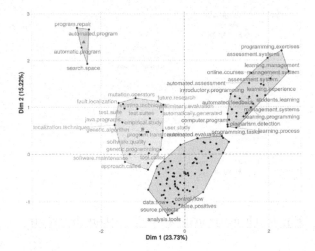

**Fig. 8.** Conceptual structure map of abstract 2-grams obtained through MCA

With respect to **RQ4-4**, Fig. 9 shows the ten most frequent abstract 2-grams by year. When looking at the frequency of these 2-grams by year, the increasing interest in Static Analysis, Automated Program Repair, and Automated Test Generation is readily apparent. Although less visible, Machine Learning and Learning Analytics have also increased slightly over the years. This indicates a large growing interest in improving automated feedback generation, as most topics gaining popularity are related to source code analysis (Static Analysis and Machine Learning – in the current context) and fixing (Automated Program Repair, Automated Test Generation – including counter-example –, and Machine Learning) techniques. Nevertheless, dynamic analysis-based assessment using test suites is still highly frequent. Moreover, feedback for teachers, through Learning Analytics, seems to be now a topic of interest within the area Automated Assessment. Note that, for this visualization, the set of generated 2-grams has been preprocessed to remove common terms (e.g., science, introductory, programming, paper, work, result, etc.) and match synonyms (e.g., apr tool and repair tool).

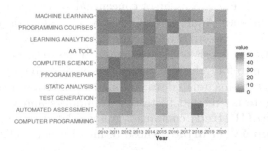

**Fig. 9.** Top-10 most frequent abstract 2-grams by year

# 4   Discussion

The results demonstrate that Automated Assessment is still an area of increasing research interest, with a significant and growing number of publications and consequently authors and citations. The only exception coincides with (and can be justified by) the COVID-19 pandemic situation, which occurred between the start of 2020 and the start of 2022. The number of citations has maintained a nearly constant rate over the years (see Fig. 2). Most of these publications appear in journals and conference proceedings, with shares of nearly 30% and 70%, respectively.

The most closely related and recent systematic literature review on automated assessment is the one by Paiva et al. [18]. This review identified a new era of automated assessment in Computer Science, the era of containerization, among other interesting findings. In particular, the growing interest in static analysis techniques to assess not only the correct functionality of a program, but also the code quality and presence of plagiarism. Furthermore, it notices the efforts towards better feedback primarily by introducing techniques from other research areas, such as automated program repair, fault localization, symbolic execution, and machine learning. Regarding automated assessment tools, more than half of the mentioned tools are open source. Finally, the increasing interest in incorporating Learning Analytics into automated assessment tools to help teachers understand student difficulties is also mentioned. A technical report by Porfirio et al. [20] presents a systematic literature mapping of the research literature on automatic source code evaluation until 2019, which also had similar findings. In particular, it (1) shows the increasing number of publications; (2) notices a few attempts to extract knowledge and visualize information about students from data produced during the automated assessment of source code (i.e., first attempts on Learning Analytics); and (3) demonstrates that functional correctness is the aspect receiving most attention.

Results from this paper concerning authors (see Subsect. 3.2) and citations (see Subsect. 3.3) are novel. The responses given in Subsect. 3.4 to research questions of group **RQ4** confirm most of the findings of previous works, namely the recent focus on static analysis approaches and the introduction of techniques from other research areas, such as automated program repair, fault localization, and machine learning. Traditional automated assessment based on running the program against a set of test cases is still the dominating strategy. Moreover, the high frequency of some keywords related to Learning Analytics corroborates the interest in integrating outcomes from this research area into automated assessment tools. Nevertheless, this research could not capture enough information to confirm the trend of containerization of automated assessment. As the conducted analysis had minimal human interference, if "docker" (or a related term) was neither a frequent keyword nor part of a frequent abstract 2-gram, then it was not identified. In contrast, in the aforementioned review [18], a number of publications were manually annotated with a predetermined set of tags after reading.

## 5   Conclusion

This paper presents a bibliometric study of publications on automatic assessment in Computer Science from the decade 2010–2020, based on the WoS Core Collection. The analysis shows that this is still a research area of growing interest, where there is still much room for improvement of current solutions, especially through static analysis and source code analysis techniques used in other research areas. Therefore, it will be worthwhile to continue pursuing this topic in the coming years. The analysis performed allowed us to answer all the research questions posed at the beginning of this study and presented in Sect. 1. In addition, part of the results are identical to a recently published systematic literature review on automated assessment in computer science.

Admittedly, this study has some limitations. In particular, the WoS Core Collection does not include publications from all sources.

**Acknowledgements.** This work is financed by National Funds through the Portuguese funding agency, FCT – Fundação para a Ciência e a Tecnologia, within project LA/P/0063/2020. J.C.P. also wishes to acknowledge the FCT for the Ph.D. Grant 2020.04430.BD.

## References

1. Ala-Mutka, K.M.: A survey of automated assessment approaches for programming assignments. Comput. Sci. Educ. **15**(2), 83–102 (2005). https://doi.org/10.1080/08993400500150747
2. Andrés, A.: Measuring Academic Research. Chandos Publishing (Oxford), Witney, England (2009)
3. Aria, M., Cuccurullo, C.: bibliometrix: an r-tool for comprehensive science mapping analysis. J. Informetrics **11**(4), 959–975 (2017). https://doi.org/10.1016/j.joi.2017.08.007
4. Blikstein, P., Worsley, M., Piech, C., Sahami, M., Cooper, S., Koller, D.: Programming pluralism: using learning analytics to detect patterns in the learning of computer programming. J. Learn. Sci. **23**(4), 561–599 (2014). https://doi.org/10.1080/10508406.2014.954750
5. Clarivate: Web of science core collection (2022). https://www.webofscience.com/wos/woscc/summary/f75398e2-c55c-4b98-b5c0-103c1ebcb3cc-53a79dff/relevance/1. Accessed 19 Sep 2022
6. Cobo, M., López-Herrera, A., Herrera-Viedma, E., Herrera, F.: An approach for detecting, quantifying, and visualizing the evolution of a research field: a practical application to the fuzzy sets theory field. J. Informetrics **5**(1), 146–166 (2011). https://doi.org/10.1016/j.joi.2010.10.002
7. da Cruz Alves, N., Wangenheim, C.G.V., Hauck, J.C.R.: Approaches to assess computational thinking competences based on code analysis in k-12 education: a systematic mapping study. Inf. Educ. **18**(1), 17–39 (2019). https://doi.org/10.15388/infedu.2019.02
8. DeNero, J., Sridhara, S., Pérez-Quiñones, M., Nayak, A., Leong, B.: Beyond autograding: advances in student feedback platforms. In: Proceedings of the 2017 ACM SIGCSE Technical Symposium on Computer Science Education. SIGCSE 2017,

Association for Computing Machinery, New York, pp. 651–652 (2017). https://doi.org/10.1145/3017680.3017686

9. Edwards, S.H., Shams, Z.: Comparing test quality measures for assessing student-written tests. In: Companion Proceedings of the 36th International Conference on Software Engineering. ICSE Companion 2014, Association for Computing Machinery, New York, pp. 354–363. (2014). https://doi.org/10.1145/2591062.2591164

10. Falkner, N., Vivian, R., Piper, D., Falkner, K.: Increasing the effectiveness of automated assessment by increasing marking granularity and feedback units. In: Proceedings of the 45th ACM Technical Symposium on Computer Science Education. SIGCSE 2014, Association for Computing Machinery, New York, pp. 9–14 (2014). https://doi.org/10.1145/2538862.2538896

11. Garfield, E.: Historiographic mapping of knowledge domains literature. J. Inf. Sci. **30**(2), 119–145 (2004). https://doi.org/10.1177/0165551504042802

12. Ihantola, P., Ahoniemi, T., Karavirta, V., Seppälä, O.: Review of recent systems for automatic assessment of programming assignments. In: Proceedings of the 10th Koli Calling International Conference on Computing Education Research - Koli Calling 2010, pp. 86–93. ACM Press, Berlin, Germany (2010). https://doi.org/10.1145/1930464.1930480

13. Insa, D., Silva, J.: Semi-automatic assessment of unrestrained java code: a library, a DSL, and a workbench to assess exams and exercises. In: Proceedings of the 2015 ACM Conference on Innovation and Technology in Computer Science Education. ITiCSE 2015, Association for Computing Machinery, New York, pp. 39–44 (2015). https://doi.org/10.1145/2729094.2742615

14. Monperrus, M.: A critical review of automatic patch generation learned from human-written patches: essay on the problem statement and the evaluation of automatic software repair. In: Proceedings of the 36th International Conference on Software Engineering. ICSE 2014, Association for Computing Machinery, New York, pp. 234–242 (2014). https://doi.org/10.1145/2568225.2568324

15. Moon, S., Kim, Y., Kim, M., Yoo, S.: Ask the mutants: mutating faulty programs for fault localization. In: 2014 IEEE Seventh International Conference on Software Testing, Verification and Validation, pp. 153–162. IEEE (2014). https://doi.org/10.1109/ICST.2014.28

16. Motwani, M., Sankaranarayanan, S., Just, R., Brun, Y.: Do automated program repair techniques repair hard and important bugs? Empirical Softw. Eng. **23**(5), 2901–2947 (2017). https://doi.org/10.1007/s10664-017-9550-0

17. Naudé, K.A., Greyling, J.H., Vogts, D.: Marking student programs using graph similarity. Comput. Educ. **54**(2), 545–561 (2010). https://doi.org/10.1016/j.compedu.2009.09.005

18. Paiva, J.C., Leal, J.P., Figueira, A.: Automated assessment in computer science education: a state-of-the-art review. ACM Trans. Comput. Educ. **22**(3) (2022). https://doi.org/10.1145/3513140

19. Pape, S., Flake, J., Beckmann, A., Jürjens, J.: Stage: a software tool for automatic grading of testing exercises: case study paper. In: Proceedings of the 38th International Conference on Software Engineering Companion. ICSE 2016, Association for Computing Machinery, New York, pp. 491–500 (2016). https://doi.org/10.1145/2889160.2889203

20. Porfirio, A., Pereira, R., Maschio, E.: Automatic source code evaluation: a systematic mapping. Technical report, Federal University of Technology, Paraná, Brazil (UTFPR) (2021). https://doi.org/10.13140/RG.2.2.36112.33287

21. Singh, R., Gulwani, S., Solar-Lezama, A.: Automated feedback generation for introductory programming assignments. In: Proceedings of the 34th ACM SIGPLAN Conference on Programming Language Design and Implementation. PLDI 2013, Association for Computing Machinery, New York, pp. 15–26 (2013). https://doi.org/10.1145/2491956.2462195

22. Smith, R., Tang, T., Warren, J., Rixner, S.: An automated system for interactively learning software testing. In: Proceedings of the 2017 ACM Conference on Innovation and Technology in Computer Science Education. ITiCSE 2017, Association for Computing Machinery, New York, pp. 98–103 (2017). https://doi.org/10.1145/3059009.3059022

23. Souza, D.M., Felizardo, K.R., Barbosa, E.F.: A systematic literature review of assessment tools for programming assignments. In: 2016 IEEE 29th International Conference on Software Engineering Education and Training (CSEET), pp. 147–156. IEEE (2016). https://doi.org/10.1109/CSEET.2016.48

24. Souza, D.M.D., Isotani, S., Barbosa, E.F.: Teaching novice programmers using progtest. Int. J. Knowl. Learn. 10(1), 60–77 (2015). https://doi.org/10.1504/IJKL.2015.071054

25. Sridhara, S., Hou, B., Lu, J., DeNero, J.: Fuzz testing projects in massive courses. In: Proceedings of the Third (2016) ACM Conference on Learning @ Scale. L@S 2016, Association for Computing Machinery, New York, pp. 361–367 (2016). https://doi.org/10.1145/2876034.2876050

26. Srikant, S., Aggarwal, V.: A system to grade computer programming skills using machine learning. In: Proceedings of the 20th ACM SIGKDD International Conference on Knowledge Discovery and Data Mining. KDD 2014, Association for Computing Machinery, New York, pp. 1887–1896 (2014). https://doi.org/10.1145/2623330.2623377

27. Verdú, E., Regueras, L.M., Verdú, M.J., Leal, J.P., de Castro, J.P., Queirós, R.: A distributed system for learning programming on-line. Comput. Educ. 58(1), 1–10 (2012). https://doi.org/10.1016/j.compedu.2011.08.015

28. von Wangenheim, C.G., et al.: Codemaster - automatic assessment and grading of app inventor and snap! programs. Inf. Educ. 17(1), 117–150 (2018). https://doi.org/10.15388/infedu.2018.08

29. Wen, M., Chen, J., Wu, R., Hao, D., Cheung, S.C.: Context-aware patch generation for better automated program repair. In: Proceedings of the 40th International Conference on Software Engineering. ICSE 2018, Association for Computing Machinery, New York, pp. 1–11 (2018). https://doi.org/10.1145/3180155.3180233

30. Xiong, Y., et al.: Precise condition synthesis for program repair. In: Proceedings of the 39th International Conference on Software Engineering. ICSE 2017, pp. 416–426. IEEE Press (2017). https://doi.org/10.1109/ICSE.2017.45

31. Yera, R., Martínez, L.: A recommendation approach for programming online judges supported by data preprocessing techniques. Appl. Intell. 47(2), 277–290 (2016). https://doi.org/10.1007/s10489-016-0892-x

# Can Educators Develop Digital Role-Playing Games?

Azhan Ahmad$^{(\boxtimes)}$ and Effie L.-C. Law

Durham University, Stockton Road, Durham DH1 3LE, UK
{cndw23,lai-chong.law}@durham.ac.uk

**Abstract.** Developing Serious Games (SG) is a complicated and expensive process, involving experts in game development and the use of specific tools. This is one of the barriers in the adoption of SGs. Few SG-specific authoring tools were proposed in the literature but lacking either in giving educators control in all aspects of the creation, or varied activities in the end product. To further reduce the process complexity and dependence on game experts, we propose an authoring tool specifically aimed for educators to create SGs themselves. This paper reports findings from a summative usability study conducted on a high-fidelity prototype of the tool with educators, who perceived the usability of the tool was high.

**Keywords:** Serious games · authoring tool · educational technology · usability

## 1 Introduction

Studies have shown that Serious Games (SG) is an effective learning tool, but adoption is still low and can be attributed to several barriers [2]. SGs can either be commercially available entertainment-based games adopted for education or games specifically designed with educational properties. These games may not entirely target different educators' teaching goals. On the other hand, creating custom SGs to meet educators' specific requirements involves a complicated and expensive process of requiring inputs from experts in game design and development. Few SG authoring tools were proposed to simplify the development phase, but educators found them complicated to use.

We propose an educator-oriented authoring tool for the creation of a Serious Role-Playing game (SRPG), aiming to improve the development of SGs by leveraging on the attributes of Role-Playing Games (RPG), by incorporating features suitable for educators. To ensure the acceptance and adoption of the tool, a usability study was conducted on a high-fidelity prototype of the proposed tool to evaluate its usability. The main aim of this paper is to present the findings of the study in order to answer two questions: 1) How do educators perceive the tool in terms of its usefulness, ease of use and learning, and satisfaction, and 2) Can educators without knowledge in game development create SRPGs? To frame the contribution of the tool, crucial works in SG authoring tools are discussed in Sect. 2. Section 3 presents a detailed description of the tool. The usability study methodology is explained in Sect. 4, followed by results of the study in Sect. 5, and discussion of the findings in Sect. 6. We conclude the paper in Sect. 7.

© The Author(s), under exclusive license to Springer Nature Switzerland AG 2023
C. S. González-González et al. (Eds.): ICWL 2022/SETE 2022, LNCS 13869, pp. 135–147, 2023.
https://doi.org/10.1007/978-3-031-33023-0_12

## 2 Related Work

While there are several game-development tools that can be used to create SGs such as Unity[1], these tools are primarily intended for game developers and do not explicitly provide features to incorporate educational components, e.g., assessments. Few existing SG-specific tools were proposed, using specific workflows and features. One such tool proposed is used to create scenario-based SGs, but requires collective effort from various users such as educators and game programmers [12]. Another tool is intended exclusively for educators and uses the concept of story-writing to program the gameplay using graph-based modelling language [9]. The graph is used to configure game components such as scenes, actors, and player actions. Educators evaluating the tool found it complicated to use. In the context of authoring tools, graph modelling systems are generally complicated for educators [11].

Block-based programming (BBP) is a visual programming approach that involves connecting blocks (i.e., a block represents a programming command) to create programs in the form of conventional text-based structure [15], and is typically used in tools intended to teach young learners the basics of programming such as Scratch[2]. Blocks can be customised in a more natural language, e.g., *"Show character"* rather than programming syntax, e.g., *"character.visible = true;"*. The concept was found easy to use by educators [5], making it a viable interface for SG authoring tools.

Another influencing factor on the usability of authoring tools is the generality of the output, where limiting what can be created improves the usability of a tool [10]. While Unity can create any form of games, it is more complicated compared to tools that produce fewer game genres [9]. RPG has the most complex gameplay that can potentially target categories and types of problem-solving in various cognitive domains [3]. RPG involves players controlling *avatars* to complete *quests* in a *virtual world*. Completing quests typically results in levelling up players' avatars through *rewards* and *experience* gained, which in turn improves avatars' *attributes* (e.g., strength) and *skills* (e.g., fighting skills). These components can essentially be incorporated within an educational context. Authentic learning is an instructional method which situates learners in a learning environment that reflects real-world situations where the learnt knowledge is expected to be used [6]. Components of authentic learning can essentially be embedded within RPG (Table 1), making RPG a very suitable genre for SGs.

## 3 ARQS Tool

ARQS (Authentic Role-playing game Quest System) Tool is a web-based authoring tool intended for educators to create SRPGs. Data from the authoring tool are formatted as JSON (Javascript Object Notation) and stored in a database. Students can run games using a web-based engine app that loads and parses game data into a runnable game. This allows quick and ad-hoc editing of games without code compilation. The tool consists of several components (Table 2) to address the various aspects of an RPG (Table 1). Most of the components use standard HTML controls (e.g., text fields, checkboxes, etc.). This section explains the other tool components that use complex interfaces.

---

[1] https://unity.com/.

[2] https://scratch.mit.edu/.

**Table 1.** Relations between Authentic Learning and RPG Components

| Authentic Learning Components [6] | | RPG Components |
|---|---|---|
| Authentic Context | Real-world environment that reflects the way knowledge will be used | Virtual World |
| Authentic Activities | Real-world tasks | Quests |
| Expert Models | Experts' thinking and modelling process | Non-Player Characters (NPCs) |
| Coach and Scaffold | Coaching by educator | NPCs |
| Reflect | Compare acquired knowledge with experts and other students | NPCs |
| Different Perspectives | Allow students to view problems from different perspectives | Player Avatars, Quests |
| Collaboration | Tasks are carried out by groups | Multiplayer |
| Articulating | Articulate students' understanding of acquired knowledge | (Out-of-game activities) |
| Integrated Assessment | Assess students' performance during performing tasks | Rewards, Player Statistics |

The *World* component is for creating the virtual world of a game, which consists of *map*(s) that contain *locations* (i.e., buildings) players can enter. A *location* consists of connected *areas* (i.e., rooms or outdoor areas) which players can explore using their avatar. Drawing editors used to create these elements employ simple operations such as selecting pre-defined images (e.g., a house, furniture, etc.) and placing it on a drawing canvas. Creating *locations* also involve creating the floorplan of a building, by drawing rectangles to define the size and placement of the areas in the building.

*Quest* is the most important component of an SRPG, where game logics and learning activities (Table 3) can be embedded. A quest consists of several components (Table 4) to define the tasks players must solve, and game logics to be executed during the quest. When a quest is first activated, the game will create the *initiator*, and starts listening for the *events* set in the first task of a quest. Events are consistently listened to as long as a quest is still active. Only event type "interacts with initiator" will be processed at this stage, which when triggered will start the quest, the first task activated, and other game-objects set in the *Initial Game-object* created. Other event types will only be processed when a quest is started. When a set event is triggered, actions for these events will be executed. If the event type requires explicit rules, checks will be made to see if players have met the set *rules* before executing the events' actions. When an "End task" action is executed, the game will deactivate the current task and checks the *sub-tasks* component. If there are any sub-tasks added to a quest, the game will activate this task. A quest will be stopped when no more tasks are found. The blocks used in the BBP editor were specifically designed to configure these components.

**Table 2.** Tool Components

| Tool Components | | Interface |
|---|---|---|
| Lesson Description | The educational objective of a game. (Shown on an introduction scene) | HTML Form controls (Fig. 1A) |
| Learning Outcomes | Learning outcomes (LO) students are expected to achieve (Shown on an introduction scene) | HTML Form Controls |
| Player Configuration | Player avatar's role, attributes and skills (related to the lesson) | HTML Form Controls |
| World | Game world | HTML Form Controls, Drawing Editor (Fig. 1B) |
| Quest | Quests (problems) players must solve in relation to the LOs | HTML Form Controls, BBP Editor (Fig. 1C) |
| Gameobjects (NPC, Enemy, Items, Props) | Game objects that are involved in the quests | HTML Form Controls, Drawing Editor (for NPC, Enemy; Fig. 1D) |

*Character game-objects* (i.e., NPC, Enemy) are actors in a quest. Drawing editor to create characters' visuals involves selecting pre-defined styles and colours for the different parts of a character (e.g., hair, shirt, etc.). This allows creating varied characters quickly. Setting visuals for *Item* and *Props* game-objects on the other hand only require users to upload image representation of these objects.

**Table 3.** Example of a learning activity on fire hazards as a quest[3]

| Lesson/LO | Quest Scenario | Player Tasks (Task Structure) |
|---|---|---|
| Lesson: In the game, students will learn the basics of fire prevention LO: Students should understand what fire hazards are | Initiator: Rose Scenario: Rose has just moved to a new house. She wants you to examine the house and ensure that there are no fire hazards | 1. Player needs to turn off the cooker (which somebody forgot to turn off) in the kitchen • When player interacts with the cooker, give them an option to "turn off" or "leave it" • If player chooses "Turn Off", give them rewards • If player chooses "Leave it", show them a message why this is not a good idea |

---

[3] https://www.london-fire.gov.uk/schools/learning-at-home/fire-safety-education-at-home/.

**Table 4.** Quest's Structure

| Quest Component | |
|---|---|
| Player Action | Common RPG player actions [4] associated with a task. Used as a supportive "help tip" for players |
| Initiator | The NPC players need to interact to start a quest |
| Initial Game-object | Game-objects that need to be created when a quest has started |
| Rules | Requirements (i.e., items that must be used, number of items/enemies that must be gathered/defeated, and time limit), if any, to complete a task |
| Events | Events (e.g., interacting with NPCs, etc.) that will be processed during a quest. When an event is triggered, actions set for the event will be executed (e.g., create dialog with NPCs, etc.) |
| Sub-Tasks | Append sub-tasks to a quest |

## 4   Usability Study of the ARQS Tool

A usability study is typically carried out when investigating how users interact with and experience a tool to evaluate their perceived effectiveness and efficiency of the tool and satisfaction with it [13]. This aligns with the basic human-centered design principle, involving target end-users from the early conception and throughout the development process of a system, thereby ensuring user acceptance and adoption of the system [7]. A formative usability study was carried out during the initial phase of the tool's development, where educators tested a low-fidelity prototype [1]. The outcome from the previous study was used to refine the design concept, which was developed into a high-fidelity prototype used in the current study, i.e., a form of summative testing normally done when a tool is at an advanced state. This section reports the methodology of the current summative usability study.

Ten university lecturers specialising in various domains were recruited for this study (Table 5). Participants were given several documents prior to the study: a participation information sheet, a consent form, a privacy notice, and a questionnaire to establish participants' general background. Each participant was required to sit for a one-hour on-site test. Each session was facilitated by the first author and took place at a designated room provided by Universiti Teknologi Brunei[4] (UTB). A computer with access to the prototype stored in a local server was provided for participants to carry out the study. The computer's screen was mirrored to another monitor located opposite the participants' computer, allowing the facilitator to constantly and unobtrusively observe participants' actions during the tests.

During the tests, participants were required to use the prototype in carrying out 13 tasks (Table 6) to create a designated game (Table 3). Documents containing the list of tasks and data for the game (e.g., how the characters and game world should look like,

---

[4] http://www.utb.edu.bn/.

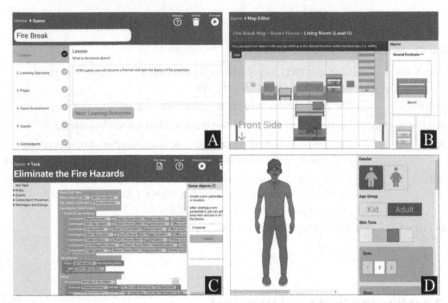

**Fig. 1.** Form control interface (A), World drawing Editor (B), BBP editor (C), and Character drawing editor (D)

etc.) were provided at the start of the test. Participants were asked to think aloud when carrying out the tasks. Audio and screen capture were recorded during each session. The safety restriction requiring the use of face masks was in place during the tests, as such recording facial expressions of participants was impossible and thus not included as one of the means in extracting user experience.

No unsolicited help was given to participants throughout the test. The only exception was during Task 13, where they were briefly explained on BBP and showed an example on carrying out one action (i.e., dragging one block from the library and adding it to the task structure). This was deemed necessary as 80% of the participants were not familiar with the concept. The time to complete each task during the tests was recorded. At the end of each task, participants were asked to rate the difficulty using a 7-point Likert scale (i.e., 1: very difficult to 7: very easy) based on the SEQ (Single Ease Question) [14]. At the end of the test, participants were asked to complete the USE (Usefulness, Satisfaction and Ease of Use) questionnaire [8], a 7-point Likert scale (i.e., 1: strongly disagree to 7: strongly agree) metrics. Both the SEQ and USE metrics are often used in usability studies. Data from the questionnaires, observation notes, transcribed audio, and screen capture recordings were used in the analysis of the study.

## 5 Results

In this section, we first present the results of the task completion rate and time (Sect. 5.1). We then continue presenting the results of the usability of the prototype tool (Sect. 5.2). Positive and negative aspects of the tool identified by participants at the end of the study are also presented (Sect. 5.3).

**Table 5.** Participants in the Usability Study

| ID | Age | Gender | Teaching (Years) | Experience in | | | | |
|----|-----|--------|------------------|---------------|--|--|--|--|
| | | | | Using SGs | Creating Games | Creating Interactive activities | Programming * | BBP |
| 1 | 25–39 | F | 9 | No | No | Yes | 1 | No |
| 2 | 25–39 | M | 10 | No | Yes | Yes | 5 | Yes |
| 3 | 25–39 | M | 12 | No | No | Yes | 3 | No |
| 4 | 40–60 | F | 17 | No | No | Yes | 4 | No |
| 5 | 40–60 | F | 23 | No | No | Yes | 3 | No |
| 6 | 40–60 | F | 17 | No | No | Yes | 2 | No |
| 7 | 40–60 | M | 25 | No | No | Yes | 3 | No |
| 8 | 40–60 | F | 27 | No | Yes | Yes | 3 | No |
| 9 | 25–39 | M | 11 | No | Yes | Yes | 4 | Yes |
| 10 | 40–60 | M | 15 | No | No | Yes | Never | No |

## 5.1 Task Completion

Table 7 shows the task completion rates for each of the participants. All participants (n = 10) were able to complete tasks 1 to 12, while only seven were able to complete Task 13. Tasks 1–4 and 8–12 were found generally "very easy", where they did not experience any difficulties in completing them since it only involved simple typing and mouse click operations using form controls.

**Table 6.** Participants' Tasks

| Tasks | | | |
|-------|--|--|--|
| 1 | Create a new Game | 8 | Create an NPC |
| 2 | Set lesson description | 9 | Create a Prop |
| 3 | Set learning outcomes | 10 | Create a quest |
| 4 | Configure player settings | 11 | Set the quest scenario |
| 5 | Create a map | 12 | Set the learning outcomes for the quest |
| 6 | Create a location | 13 | Configure the task structure for the quest |
| 7 | Create two rooms for the location | | |

*Tasks Using Drawing Editors.* Tasks 5 to 7 involved creating the game world. Difficulties experienced by participants mostly related to editing drawn objects (e.g., selecting, editing, etc.). The procedure required participant to first deselect the currently selected

**Table 7.** Participants' Tasks' Completion

| Tasks | Completion Rate | Completion Time | | | Ease of Task* | | |
|---|---|---|---|---|---|---|---|
| | | Avg | Median | Std. Dev. | Avg | Median | Std. Dev. |
| 1 | 100% | 18 s | 12 s | 0.2 | 7 | 7 | 0.3 |
| 2 | 100% | 42 s | 24 s | 0.6 | 7 | 7 | 0.3 |
| 3 | 100% | 1 min 36 s | 1 min 30 s | 0.8 | 6 | 7 | 0.9 |
| 4 | 100% | 1 min 12 s | 1 min 12 s | 0.4 | 7 | 7 | 1.0 |
| 5 | 100% | 5 min 42 s | 5 min | 2.9 | 4 | 4 | 1.6 |
| 6 | 100% | 10 min | 9 min 42 s | 5.2 | 5 | 5 | 1.5 |
| 7 | 100% | 4 min 36 s | 4 min 18 s | 2.0 | 6 | 7 | 1.2 |
| 8 | 100% | 3 min 24 s | 3 min 12 s | 1.4 | 6 | 6 | 0.9 |
| 9 | 100% | 1 min 24 s | 1 min 18 s | 0.5 | 7 | 7 | 0.5 |
| 10 | 100% | 12 s | 12 s | 0.2 | 7 | 7 | 0.3 |
| 11 | 100% | 30 s | 30 s | 0.2 | 7 | 7 | 0.3 |
| 12 | 100% | 18 s | 12 s | 0.1 | 7 | 7 | 0.4 |
| 13 | 70% | 17 min 42 s | 17 min | 6.3 | 4 | 4 | 1.7 |

drawing tool from the tools panel before selecting drawn objects to be edited, where all participants took time to figure it out. Although instructions were displayed, it took some time for them to notice the message. P6 mentioned that the instructions were positioned far from the tools panel. She suggested: *"Maybe it can be placed near the tools panel, so we easily see what is expected."*.

All participants' proficiency did improve in Task 7, showing they were able to remember and replicate the process as the task progressed. This fact was mentioned by three participants, that they just needed time to familiarise with the application. P8 said that: *"In the beginning you have to learn a new environment, but after a while it gets easier."*. Four participants did pick up the procedures quickly and was very proficient in these tasks, which they attributed to their prior experience with similar drawing tools such as Photoshop.

*Task using BBP.* Task 13 involved the BBP editor to configure the task structure of a quest. Difficulty ratings for the task were mixed, where several participants found it hard (n = 4), not difficult nor easy (n = 4), and easy (n = 2). Only 70% of the participants (n = 7) completed this task. Participants (n = 3) who did not complete the task did not set one specific field in an event block when setting the interact event for a game-object. During the observation, participants generally were able to locate the correct blocks to configure the quest structure.

## 5.2 Usability of the Tool

Table 8 shows participants' ratings on the tool for the *Usefulness, Ease of Use, Ease of Learning* and *Satisfaction* components of the USE questionnaire. The tool was rated highly on the *usefulness, ease of learning* and *satisfaction* components, while the *ease of use* scored slightly lower. This was due to the complexity of the world environment drawing tools mentioned above, and the participants' unfamiliarity with BBP.

**Table 8.** Usability of the tool

| Usefulness | Avg. Rating* |
|---|---|
| It helps me be more effective in creating educational games | 6 |
| It helps me be more productive in creating educational games | 6 |
| It is useful | 6 |
| It makes creating educational games easier to get done | 6 |
| **Ease of Use** | |
| It is easy to use | 5 |
| It is user friendly | 5 |
| It requires the fewest steps possible to accomplish what i want to do with it | 5 |
| I can use it without instructions | 3 |
| I can use it successfully every time | 5 |
| **Ease of Learning** | |
| I learned how to use it quickly | 6 |
| I easily remembered how to use it | 6 |
| It is easy to learn how to use it | 5 |
| I quickly became skillful with it | 6 |
| **Satisfaction** | |
| I am satisfied with it | 6 |
| I would recommend it to a colleague | 6 |
| It is fun to use | 6 |
| I feel I need to use it for some of my learning activities | 6 |

## 5.3 Positive and Negative Aspects of the Tool

Table 9 shows key positive and negative themes identified by participants during the study. Two participants found the general interface of the tool *familiar* and *intuitive*. P5 said that "*Some of the ways to do the tasks are repetitive and similar to other applications. Like drag and drop, and clicking.*". In terms of experience, three participants noted that the tool was *interesting* and *fun* to use. P1 was excited and felt a *sense of accomplishment* when she played the game she created. She commented while laughing: "*Yay, I made a game. In less than an hour.*" Four participants felt the authoring workflow was *easy to understand*. P6 for example commented that it was easy to master due to the *repetitive process* and *helpful component breakdown* presented in the tool. Two participants commented on the *lack of auto-save* in some of the components of the tool, where they ended up re-doing some tasks as they forgot to save their progress before navigating to another page. Five participants noted that they *needed more time to familiarise* with the process, especially the BBP editor. One negative point two participants mentioned relating to BBP is the *inconsistent block labels*. One of the events needed to be created in Task 13 (Table 6) was to "show a message", but the block required to do this was labelled "Notify Player". All participants (n = 10) kept on looking for a "Show Message" block, before asking for clarification, and confirmed by the facilitator that the blocks were the same.

**Table 9.** Positive and Negative Aspects of the tool

| Categories | Positives | Negatives |
|---|---|---|
| Experience | Interesting, Easy to learn, Easy to understand, Fun, Sense of Accomplishment | - |
| Workflow | Helpful Component Breakdown, Familiar Process, Repetitive process, BBP is understandable, | Time spent, No Auto save, Need time to familiarise, Inconsistent Block labels, Lack of Instructions |
| Object Customisation | Responsive, Quick process, Game world and object customization | Lack of Action Feedback, Unable to Zoom location, Difficult Locating Drawing Tiles, Lack of Labels on Menu/Buttons |
| Interface | Familiar, Intuitive | Not user friendly, Unclear breadcrumbs |

   In terms of creating the world environment and game-objects, four participants appreciated the *responsiveness, quick* and *easy* process of drawing the world environment and virtual characters. Three participants commented on the *inability to zoom* out the drawing canvas made it difficult to draw the floorplan of a location. P4 also commented on the *lack of labels* on the menu buttons. Menus were only presented using icons (e.g., "bin" for delete, etc.), but certain icons were not clear to participants. During Task 6, participants were asked to create a location. Once a building image on the drawing canvas was selected, they must click on the "wrench" icon on the "Edit" panel to edit and create the floorplan. All participants (n = 10) spent quite some time before actually clicking this button. When asked, all participants (n = 10) said that they were looking for a "Create a Location" button and didn't realise at first, that they could do that using the "wrench" button. *Lack of action feedback* when doing non-permissible actions was also commented by P5, as she said: "*Some hints may be useful when we do actions that can't be done, for example why we can't drop some objects on the canvas.".* *Lack of instructions* was also mentioned by three participants. Although there was a "Help" button at the top right of the screen, only three participants actually used it.

## 6 Discussion

The proposed tool was aimed to provide educators simple and quick way to create an SRPG. All participants (n = 10) agreed that the tool was generally very useful and easy to learn in this regard. All participants were also satisfied with it whereas some found it fun to use and provides a sense of accomplishment. However, participants found the world drawing editors and BBP complicated as compared to the other aspects of the tool. The complexity experienced in the world drawing editors primarily related to the user interface (UI) design and certain drawing procedures. During the world environment tasks, all the participants were looking for specific menus to perform drawing operations (e.g., select object, create location, delete, etc.). Adding clearly labelled and persistent menus on the tools panel to carry out all the necessary drawing operations can further improve the usability of the tool.

While 80% of the participants had no experience in BBP, a 70% completion rate in the BBP tasks (Task 13, Table 7) can be considered a desirable outcome. Furthermore, the participants who did not complete this task only missed to complete one field in one of the blocks. This is understandable since most were inexperienced in BBP, and had limited time to study and familiarise with the blocks. It is a big achievement for the participants to be able to develop a game from scratch within 1 h (as exemplified by P1's excitement when trying out the game she produced), considering the fact that most of them had no prior knowledge or experience in BBP and game development. Creating a similar game using typical processes would involve creating the image assets using image software such as photoshop, before importing to a game software e.g., Unity. Further tasks such as creating the game's UIs, scenes, animating characters, programming player mechanics and gameplay, would make the process longer and require more effort. Although the image assets used in the prototype tool are uniform and will result in games being similar visually, the key educational component of SRPGs is the quests. The pre-defined image library can always be expanded to include more images. A feature within the tool to allow importing custom-made assets can also be incorporated in future improvements.

Another significant feature that needs to be addressed is providing clear and obvious feedback and instructions. During Task 7 (Table 6), participants tried to add a "sofa" to a room. Some participants initially clicked on the back wall of the room, which was not permissible unless the object to be added was a "wall" ornament. They kept on clicking on the wall and wondered why it was not drawn on the canvas. An instruction was actually shown when selecting the image in the library panel, but due to its location and long wordings, was missed by these participants at first. Displaying obvious, clear and concise feedback in response to unsuccessful user actions, as well as providing visual instructions displayed at the start of carrying out each task will be helpful.

# 7  Conclusion

This paper presented the findings of a summative usability study of a high-fidelity educator-oriented SG authoring tool prototype. Ten participants who took part in the study agreed that the tool was useful, easy to learn, and was very satisfying to use. The ease-of-use of the tool, however, received a slightly lower rating. This was primarily due to certain aspects of the drawing operations in the game world drawing editor. Providing menus to perform all the necessary drawing operations as identified by participants can improve the usability of the tool.

One key component of the tool is in the creation of quests, which is the primary outlet for embedding learning activities, and thus gameplay. Block-based programming are used to configure these quests. Although 80% of the participants had no experience in BBP, 70% of them were able to configure a quest. The findings agree with the previous study on the low-fidelity prototype [1], showcasing that BBP is suitable for educators to program SGs gameplay.

Since most of the participants (n = 7) in the study had never developed games, they might not be able to appreciate the simplicity of the tool as they had no baseline to make comparisons. P2 and P9 are the only participants who had extensive knowledge and were still active in game development, as both of them were currently teaching within this field. During the study, P2 said that *"Creating the map (Game world) was quicker (than Unity)"*. In order to evaluate the extent to which this tool simplifies existing game development processes, future studies will look into a comparative analysis between the authoring process and features of the prototype and existing game development software, which will require input from experienced game developers.

One limitation of the study relates to the narrow focus on the ARQS tool. A broad study comparing the usability of various authoring tools would perhaps provide more insight into the suitability of different workflow and features. With regards to educators' experience with the ARQS tool, the usability study has demonstrated the suitability of the tool and its concept in allowing educators with no background in game development to be able to create SRPGs easily, which can bridge the gap of the low adoption in SGs. The tool can open up opportunities for educators to gamify their learning activities and present students with a more interactive and enjoyable learning experience.

**Acknowledgement.** The authors would like to thank the government of Brunei Darussalam, the sponsor for the PhD. project that the current work is part of.

# References

1. Ahmad, A., Law, E.L.-C.: Educators as Gamemasters: creating serious role playing game with "ARQS". In: Proceedings of ACM Human-Computer Interaction, vol. 5, CHI PLAY Artic. 230 September 2021 5, September (2021). https://doi.org/10.1145/3474657
2. Boyle, E.A., et al.: An update to the systematic literature review of empirical evidence of the impacts and outcomes of computer games and serious games. Comput. Educ. **94**, 178–192 (2016). https://doi.org/10.1016/j.compedu.2015.11.003

3. O'Brien, D., Lawless, K.A., Schrader, P.G.: A taxonomy of educational games. In: Gaming for Classroom-Based Learning: Digital Role Playing as a Motivator of Study, pp. 1–23. IGI Global (2010)
4. Doran, J., Parberry, I.: Towards procedural quest generation: a structural analysis of RPG quests. Department of Computer Science and Engineering, University of North Tex. Technical report, LARC-2010-02 (2010)
5. Fesakis, G., Serafeim, K.: Influence of the familiarization with "scratch" on future teachers' opinions and attitudes about programming and ICT in education. In: Proceedings of Conference on Integrating Technology into Computer Science Education. ITiCSE, pp. 258–262 (2009). https://doi.org/10.1145/1562877.1562957
6. Herrington, J., Oliver, R.: An instructional design framework for authentic learning environments. Educ. Technol. Res. Dev. **48**(3), 23–48 (2000). https://doi.org/10.1007/BF0231 9856
7. ISO 9241-210. 2019. Ergonomics of human-system interaction — Part 210: Human-centred design for interactive systems. International Standard, vol. 2, pp. 1–33. https://www.iso.org/standard/77520.html
8. Lund, A.M.: Measuring usability with the USE questionnaire12. Usability Interface **82**(2001), 3–6 (2001)
9. Marchiori, E.J., Torrente, J., Del Blanco, Á., Moreno-Ger, P., Sancho, P., Fernández-Manjón, B.: A narrative metaphor to facilitate educational game authoring. Comput. Educ. **58**(1), 590–599 (2012). https://doi.org/10.1016/j.compedu.2011.09.017
10. Murray, T.: Authoring intelligent tutoring systems: an analysis of the state of the art. Int. J. Artif. Intell. Educ. IJAIED **10**, 98–129 (1999)
11. Murray, T.: Coordinating the complexity of tools, tasks, and users: on theory-based approaches to authoring tool usability. Int. J. Artif. Intell. Educ. **26**(1), 37–71 (2015). https://doi.org/10.1007/s40593-015-0076-6
12. Nadolski, R.J., et al.: EMERGO: a methodology and toolkit for developing serious games in higher education. Simul. Gaming **39**(3), 338–352 (2008). https://doi.org/10.1177/104687810 8319278
13. (Ginny) Redish, J., Bias, R.G., Bailey, R., Molich, R., Dumas, J., Spool, J.M.: Usability in practice: formative usability evaluations - evolution and revolution. In: CHI 2002 Extended Abstracts on Human Factors in Computing Systems - CHI 2002, Minneapolis, Minnesota, USA, p. 885. ACM Press (2002). https://doi.org/10.1145/506443.506647
14. Sauro, J.: 10 Things To Know About The Single Ease Question (SEQ) – MeasuringU (2012). https://measuringu.com/seq10/. Accessed 24 May 2022
15. Weintrop, D., Wilensky, U.: To block or not to block, that is the question: students' perceptions of blocks-based programming. In: Proceedings of IDC 2015 14th International Conference on Interaction Design and Children, pp. 199–208 (2015). https://doi.org/10.1145/2771839.2771860

# Constructing Low-Redundant and High-Accuracy Knowledge Graphs for Education

Wentao Li, Huachi Zhou, Junnan Dong, Qinggang Zhang, Qing Li,
George Baciu, Jiannong Cao, and Xiao Huang(✉)

Department of Computing, Hong Kong Polytechnic University, Kowloon, Hong Kong
{wentao0406.li,huachi.zhou,hanson.dong,qinggangg.zhang}@connect.polyu.hk,
{qing-prof.li,csgeorge,jiannong.cao,xiao.huang}@polyu.edu.hk

**Abstract.** Motivated by the successful applications of commonsense knowledge graphs (KGs) and encyclopedia KGs, many KG-based applications have been developed in education, such as course content visualization and learning path/material recommendations. While KGs for education are often constructed manually, attempts have been made to leverage machine learning algorithms to extract triples from teaching materials. However, education-related KGs learned by existing algorithms contain significant amounts of redundancy and noise. It is because the entities and relations in teaching materials are often instructional, abstract, and implicit, while textbooks often contain detailed explanations, examples, and illustrations. Off-the-shelf KG construction algorithms are designed for concrete entities. To this end, we propose an effective framework to construct low-redundant and high-accuracy KGs for education. First, we design an ontology that is tailored for education. By choosing related Wikidata items, we construct an instructional entity set. We avoid using traditional methods such as named-entity recognition to extract entities from textbooks, aiming to reduce redundancy. Then, we add subtopic relations among our selected instructional entities based on the corresponding hierarchy in Wikidata, and form a backbone. Second, we design a machine reading comprehension model with pre-defined questions to extract other types of relations, such as equivalent to, applied to, and inventor of. Third, we apply active KG error detection to further refine the KG with minimal human effort. In the experiments, we take the artificial intelligence domain as an example and demonstrate the effectiveness of the proposed framework. Our KG achieves an accuracy of around 80% scored by domain experts.

**Keywords:** Educational knowledge graphs · Knowledge graph construction

## 1 Introduction

Many encyclopedia knowledge graphs (KGs) [15], commonsense KGs [5], and KGs for medical science[1] have been developed, with a wide range of applications

---

[1] https://bioportal.bioontology.org.

© The Author(s), under exclusive license to Springer Nature Switzerland AG 2023
C. S. González-González et al. (Eds.): ICWL 2022/SETE 2022, LNCS 13869, pp. 148–160, 2023.
https://doi.org/10.1007/978-3-031-33023-0_13

such as search and recommendations [26]. Motivated by this, KG-based applications have been developed in education, such as course content visualization [13,18], learning path/material recommendations [20], and university course management [3]. For example, course content KGs could illustrate concepts and knowledge in a hierarchical and systematic way [18].

While KGs for education are often constructed manually [18,20], a few attempts have been made to leverage machine learning algorithms to extract triples from teaching materials [6]. Studies on machine-learning-based KG construction for education could be divided into two classes. The former one aims to construct KGs to represent course concepts [7]. The latter targets to learn KGs to organize multimedia learning resources [11,22]. Existing studies usually employ query languages and web scrapes to construct KGs from structured data sources such as knowledge bases and HTML web pages. As for unstructured data sources like textbooks, traditional pipelines containing named entity recognition (NER) and relation extraction (RE) modules are a common solution for most KG construction tasks [2,4].

However, educational KGs developed by existing machine-learning-based algorithms often contain significant numbers of redundant relations, and erroneous triples. These issues reduce their usability in real-world teaching and learning scenarios. First, *low-accuracy*. Different from real-world or common-sense KGs, entities and relations in KGs for education are more abstract and hard to represent and extract. Even for human readers, it is difficult to distinguish the exact borders of scientific terms compared with a person's or organization's name. Inconsistent spellings in domain papers and textbooks, further interrogated the problems of entity recognition. While many existing pipelines finish this work in a sequential manner, the errors produced by the NER stage will be magnified in the RE stage, leading to noisy outputs. In addition, it is often quite difficult to infer from the text description the relationships between educational topics, such as their hierarchy. This can result in noisy or inaccurate relations in the final KGs. Second, *redundancy*. Existing methods often try to extract as many triples as possible from available data sources. While frameworks generate a large number of triples with a certain level of redundancy, the KG refinement module is often an ignored part of previous research. Without an effective way to filter the results, a large portion of the information in KGs is trivial for educational purposes. Students need to spare extra effort to distinguish valuable information when exploring the KGs. Furthermore, it remains difficult to filter out incorrect or redundant triples in KGs, given that annotations are expensive.

To solve these problems, we propose to leverage reliable resources to construct KGs for education. Starting from the initial entity set, we extend the KGs with reliable data sources like Computer Science Ontology [19] and Wikidata [24]. Then our framework takes the entities and relations from the first step as the concise backbone and then effectively expands the KG with unstructured data sources, i.e., textbooks and Wikipedia, without introducing erroneous triples into KGs. Specifically, we designed a targeted machine reading comprehension (MRC) method to extract concepts with pre-defined question patterns.

By focusing on particular relations in each step, e.g., *subtopic_of*, we automatically generate questions like 'What are subtopics of Natural Language Processing?' and extract credible answers, i.e., candidate tail concepts of the topic entity *Natural_Language_Processing* with respect to relation *subtopic_of*. We avoid employing traditional methods like NER, which will lead to noise in the final KG. After that, we filter the noisy triples by applying active error detection methods. By effectively utilizing the backbone of KG and tailored ontology, our framework achieve ideal accuracy and redundancy on the final output.

To this end, we propose a novel course KG construction framework for education guided by a standard ontology. Specifically, entity attributes and relations are well defined as criteria for computer science to avoid ambiguity. Along with the protective confines, we effectively learn from concisely structured data for building a KG backbone, as well as the abundant text corpus as unstructured data to expand it. Moreover, we apply a tailored KG error detection method with minimal human effort to further actively refine the final output by singling out suspicious triples. Extensive experiments and sufficient visualization are included in this paper to show the robustness of our constructed KG. Our contributions are summarized as follows.

- We propose an effective framework to construct low-redundant and high-accuracy KGs for education.
- To reduce the redundancy, we learn a backbone based on related Wikidata items and hierarchy, and avoid using named-entity recognition.
- To improve the accuracy, we design a machine reading comprehension task with pre-defined questions to extract relations.
- We take the artificial intelligence domain as an example and empirically evaluate the effectiveness of the proposed framework.

## 2    Methodology

Now we introduce the pipeline of the proposed framework as shown in Fig. 1, which is composed of four components. (i) The first component is ontology design, which is tailored for the education in the artificial intelligence domain. (ii) The second component aims to build the backbone of KG from reliable structured data, including hierarchical relationships. (iii) The third component designs MRC tasks and leverages the pre-trained language model to extract triples from massive real-world unstructured resources. (iv) In the fourth component, we finalize the KG by adopting an active learning based KG refinement model to remove redundant triples. In each component, we invite several AI-oriented experts to apply human inspection to the acquired triples to ensure the accuracy of the KGs for education.

### 2.1    Ontology Design

The objective of KGs construction is to extract a set of triples $(h, r, t)$, composed of a head entity $h$, a relation $r$, and a tail entity $t$ from external resources. We

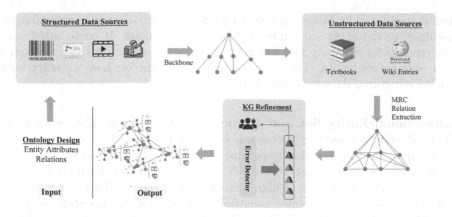

**Fig. 1.** A framework for constructing high-accuracy and low-redundancy KGs.

believe that the ontology design should be in line with the motivation facilitating the minimization of errors and redundancy in the KGs. To reduce potential errors and redundancy, we design the ontology with the capability to uniquely identify each entity. Each entity is associated with six attributes: Type, Description, Wikidata ID, Wikipedia Link, Tutorial Videos and Books. The definitions and detailed explanations of entities and relations are shown in Table 1.

**Table 1.** The definitions of entities and relations in KGs.

| Entity Attributes Definition | |
| --- | --- |
| Type | Topics or people |
| Description | Short texts explain the entity |
| Wikidata ID | Wikidata knowledge ID (if any) |
| Wikipedia Link | Link to Wikipedia (if any) |
| Tutorial Videos | Link to recommended videos (if any) |
| Tutorial Books | Link to recommended books (if any) |
| **Relation types Definition** | |
| Subtopic_of | A is a subtopic of B |
| Equivalent_to | A is an alias of B |
| Applied_to | A is applied to B |
| Invented_by | A is proposed/invented by B |

## 2.2 Backbone with Entity Set and Hierarchical Relations

After defining the entities and relations, we focus on the backbone construction of the target KG. Most real-world available knowledge could be roughly categorized into *structured* and *unstructured* forms. Empirically, structured data have been preprocessed by labor engineering while in a format directly accessible by machines, so the extracted triples are less prone to noise. It could satisfy our requirements for accuracy and low redundancy compared with those extracted from unstructured data. Therefore, we will shed light on how we start with reliable structured data to obtain initial triples first.

**Instructional Entity Set and Hierarchical Relations.** The backbone of KG establishes connections between a bunch of relevant core concepts in the specific domain, which is able to picture a concise and organized taxonomy for the domain. As we are constructing KG for abstract instructional entities, it is essential to first obtain a set of high-quality entities and relations as a backbone at the beginning to assist later construction processes. In this step, we focus on subtopic relations between the backbone entities set as an essential basis. To build the hierarchical backbone from the top, we collect high-level entities and select them from textbook glossaries, Wikidata, and the Computer Science Ontology, a large-scale ontology for taxonomy in computer science generated by the Klink-2 algorithm [16].

To add low-level entities to the backbone, we continue focusing on the pre-defined relation subtopic and refer to a large open data source Wikidata, a structured version of Wikipedia to collect instructional entities. Wikidata allows many editors to collaboratively update entries and store it in a structured manner. Therefore, the extracted knowledge has relatively higher confidence in maintaining a high-level accuracy and low-redundancy. We assign the entity name in the obtained backbone of KG as the subject of the query and use SPARQL to retrieve entities that satisfy the subtopic relation. Only the valuable triples matching the ontology design are left to conduct entity alignment and linked to the original backbone KG. The combination of extracted triples between CSO [19] and Wikidata the two reliable resources completes the backbone structure construction and the probability of introduced errors will be further reduced.

**Multimedia Entity Attributes.** We enrich the backbone by adding information to the entity's attributes, such as the video and book links. The linked e-learning resources provide comprehensive, relevant tutorial videos and teaching books for the target entity. They are beneficial for students to understand the background knowledge when exploring the KGs. The resource selection combines both domain experts' recommendations and search engine querying. For search engine querying, we define the main search keyword as the entity's name in the obtained backbone KGs. To prevent incorporating unrelated resources with the same name, we define sophisticated rules to filter erroneous resources. The ranking of candidate videos and books takes the total number of views and average ratings into consideration. Finally, we select top-1 high-quality tutorial videos and books as the target entity attributes.

## 2.3  Completing Knowledge Graph with Unstructured Data

After the KG backbone construction, we aim to extend the scale of KG by adding more relations from unstructured data such as texts and web pages. Currently, there are two mainstream methods to adopt. One is based on the open-source IE packages, and the other utilizes fine-tuned machine reading comprehension (MRC) tasks. The most popular models in IE packages are designed for specific relation extractions and often require a large amount of training corpus for a new target domain. The training data often requires expensive engineering expertise to train an applicable model. To be free of this labor, we pay attention to how we extract triples based on fine-tuned MRC tasks.

We consider two text sources: Wikipedia entries, and classical textbooks, which are relatively reliable and high-quality. The core task is to add multiple trustworthy relations, except for subtopics from different publications and open-source knowledge bases to the KG backbone.

**Table 2.** Question and answer examples used in MRC.

| Relation | Question | Answer |
| --- | --- | --- |
| Applied_to | Where is e1 applied to? | e2 |
| Subtopic_of | What is the subtopic of e3? | e4 |
| Inventor_of | Who is the inventor of e5? | e6 |

**Relation Extraction as Machine Reading Comprehension Task.** The general relation extraction procedure can be divided into two key stages: entity recognition (NER) and relation extraction (RE). In the NER stage, to push the model to identify the specialized terms in the sentences, high volume annotated data are necessary to train deep learning models while simple rule-based extraction methods have insufficient generalization capacity to extract meaningful facts. Motivated by the aforementioned problems, we propose a novel deep learning based approach by virtue of pre-trained models to identify new entities.

As many studies point out, large-scale pre-trained language models already contain a specific prerequisite knowledge about low-level semantics and factoid commonsense to produce high-quality results on many downstream tasks [17]. Pre-trained language models learn to extract generic features with unsupervised learning from large-scale unlabeled data. Therefore, we only need to fine-tune it with a few labeled data without substantial architecture modifications and training corpus. We apply it to automatically identify entities and extract relations from texts by creating MRC tasks. Given a clean text and questions with a well-defined format in advance, MRC tasks push the chosen model to retrieve answers from the texts [12].

In this way, we can transform the relation extraction task into finding the answer to a formulated question from a given text. The question input to the model is related to a particular relation and head/tail entity. Then the returned answer will be the text span of the most likely tail/head entity in the given text. The whole method consists of the following steps as shown in the Algorithm 1. First, we use several manually defined template questions tailored to extract triples for specific relations. The example questions are shown in Table 2. The placeholder will be replaced with the entity's name. Then, the long texts are segmented according to the maximum input length of the MRC model, and overlaps between segments are required to prevent splitting the possible answer span into two segments. For each text from segmented texts, we then feed each generated question in order along with text to the MRC model to get multiple candidate answers, which are sorted by the confidence scores. Last, we keep only one answer with the highest confidence scores, which represents the wanted tail entity.

---

**Algorithm 1:** MRC for Relation Extraction

---

**Input**: *inputText*; *questionTemplate*; *headEntity*;
**Output**: *tailEntity*
initialization;
*textList* ← *splitLongText*(*inputText*, *maxlength*);
*questionList* ← *generateQuestion*(*headEntity*, *questionTemplate*);
**for** *t* *in* *textList* **do**
   **for** *q* *in* *questionList* **do**
      *ans*, *ansScore* ← *MRCmodel*(*t*, *q*) ;
      **if** *ansScore* ≥ *scoreThreshold* **then**
          *ansList* = *ansList* + (*ans*, *ansScore*)

*ansList.SortbyScore*();
*tailEntity* ← *ansList.Pop*();
**return** *tailEntity*

---

Next, we improve the quality of the returned triples by excluding results with low confidence scores and those not meeting the requirements (e.g., too long word length or containing special symbols). The answer spans may consist of juxtaposed nouns, which include multiple potential entities. We further truncate this juxtaposed noun into several entities. Finally, the extracted head/tail entities and relations are linked to the KG backbone or knowledge bases obtained in the previous step.

## 2.4   Active Learning Based Knowledge Graph Refinement

In this section, we introduce a tailored KG refinement model to automatically single out suspicious and redundant triples. Early studies of KG refinement mainly rely on rule-based methods. Typically, AMIE [10] introduces a rule mining model under the Open World Assumption and uses an altered metric to measure the degree of each data instance being true, and AMIE+ [9] extends this method to large-scale KGs. Nonetheless, they are all limited by the difficulty

---

**Algorithm 2:** An Active Learning Strategy for KG Refinement

---

**Input**: a KG for pre-training $\mathcal{G}_p$ and a noisy KG for predicting $\mathcal{G}_t$
**Output**: the noisy set $\mathcal{S}_n$ and the clean set $\mathcal{S}_c$

1  $\mathcal{T}_l, \mathcal{T}_u \leftarrow \text{SPLIT}(\mathcal{G}_p, \tau)$
2  $\mathcal{S}_n \leftarrow \varnothing; \mathcal{S}_c \leftarrow \varnothing$
3  train a detector $\mathcal{D}$ based on the annotated triple set $\mathcal{T}_l$
4  $N \leftarrow$ the maximum number of iterations
5  $m \leftarrow 0$
6  **while** $m < N$ **do**
7  $\quad T \leftarrow \text{queryStrategy}(\mathcal{T}_u)$
8  $\quad$ get labels of $T$
9  $\quad \mathcal{T}_l' \leftarrow \mathcal{T}_l \cup T; \mathcal{T}_u' \leftarrow \mathcal{T}_u - T$
10  $\quad$ retrain the detector $\mathcal{D}$ based on $\mathcal{T}_l'$
11  $\quad m \leftarrow m + 1$

12  **foreach** $t \in \mathcal{G}_t$ **do**
13  $\quad \hat{l} \leftarrow$ predict the label of $t$ according to $\mathcal{D}$
14  $\quad$ **if** $\hat{l} == -1$ **then**                                        //noisy set
15  $\quad\quad \mathcal{S}_n \leftarrow$ add $t$ into $\mathcal{S}_n$
16  $\quad$ **else**                                                                    //clean set
17  $\quad\quad \mathcal{S}_c \leftarrow$ add $t$ into $\mathcal{S}_c$

18  **return** $\mathcal{S}_n$ *and* $\mathcal{S}_c$

---

of obtaining sufficient and correct rules. Given correct rules, those methods can spot erroneous triples that violate the rules, but if they are not able to detect errors that are not included in these rules, then some potential errors with complex patterns may escape detection.

Thus, we tend to leverage external labeled data to learn an effective error detector that classifies triples in KGs into *noisy* and *clean* sets. Large-scale labeled data could theoretically boost the detection ability of the proposed detector. However, gathering plenty of labeled data requires a lot of manual work. In order to decrease the number of labels while maintaining the detection model's reliability, we integrate active learning (AL) techniques into the training process.

The pseudocode of our proposed AL-based error detection method, i.e. ALED, is presented in Algorithm 2. Concretely, we first divide the pretraining KG $\mathcal{G}_p$ into a sizable unlabeled triple set $\mathcal{T}_u$ and a tiny labeled set $\mathcal{T}_l$. Then, using the labeled data $\mathcal{T}_l$, it trains a detector $\mathcal{D}$. In order to get desirable detection performance, ALED iteratively chooses a set T of data from the unlabeled pool $U$ to retrain the detector $\mathcal{D}$, using a different query method for each iteration. A well-trained detector $\mathcal{D}$ is created after $N$ iterations. Next, ALED employs the detector $\mathcal{D}$ to anticipate the label of each triple $t$ in the noisy KG $\mathcal{G}_t$. If $t$ is erroneous, it will be classified into *noisy* set, i.e. $\mathcal{S}_n$. Otherwise, it will be added into the *clean* set, i.e. $\mathcal{S}_c$.

## 3   Experiments

### 3.1   Human Evaluation and Scoring

To verify the quality of the KG, we first randomly sampled 50 triples from the KG and employed 3 experts and PhD students in the AI domain to score the results, with 0 being considered incorrect and 1 being considered correct. Our KG received a accuracy rate from the three scorers by 84%, 78%, and 82%, respectively. The Table 3 shows the comparison results for KG generated by different methods, especially rule-based methods [21] and machine learning methods [25], with the same inputs. Therefore, we can draw the conclusion that, when compared to other existing construction methods, our framework is able to produce results with higher accuracy.

**Table 3.** Evaluation Scores of KGs by different construction methods.

|  | Our KG | KG by Rules | KG by ML Models |
|---|---|---|---|
| Annotator 1 | 84% | 24% | 24% |
| Annotator 2 | 78% | 16% | 40% |
| Annotator 3 | 82% | 36% | 52% |

We then examined the coverage of domains in our KG by hiring 3 PhD students to score the taxonomic relationships and comprehensiveness based on a set of expert-annotated hierarchical relations, which contains 135 key domain relationships as a gold standard. The results show that our KG has 56 perfect matches with the expert annotated KG and 46 half matches (only matches with head entity or tail entity) within 135 key domain relationships, which guarantees satisfactory coverage in the computer science domain.

### 3.2   Visualization and Case Study

As we designed this KG with the ability to visualize connections between concepts, we then visualized a part of the results of our KG for a case study. As shown in Fig. 2, a visualization example for partial relations in KG is provided. When choosing artificial intelligence as the focused topic of the graph, our KG clearly pictures its relationship with other subtopics. It also pinpoints the relationship between the application of one topic to other domains. With the educational ontology design, the KG does not contain too much redundant information, and the visualization of the connections between entities is more intuitive. E-learning resources are included in attributes, such as recommended textbooks, which are very helpful for students to understand or learn new concepts. For clearer illustration, we further present the local structure of one subgraph in Fig. 3 centered on one subtopic.

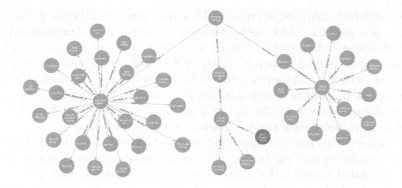

**Fig. 2.** Overall visualization of KG for certain subtopics.

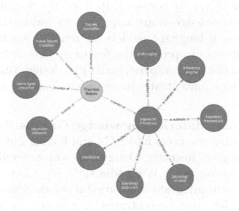

**Fig. 3.** Local structure of one subgraph.

With our KGs, students can discover potential connections between concepts through direct interaction or search queries, which is often difficult to accomplish through literal reading and traditional classroom lecturing. Compared to many large KGs, it maintains the clarity of taxonomy without providing overly complex information for beginners. It concentrates on the necessary relationships and other learning resources.

## 4   Related Work

Although high-quality KGs for education purposes often require significant amounts of effort from experts, considerable research has focused on constructing KGs with deep learning methods. We divide the previous research work into two classes as follows [1].

**Course Concept Knowledge Graphs.** This line of research aims to extract educational concepts from textbooks and other resources to represent relations between different concepts in courses. This provides visualization for abstract concepts in a domain, which helps students to have a better understanding of certain domains and establish clearer connections. Dessì et al. extracted large-scale KGs from published papers in the CS domain with relation extraction models but without emphasis on educational purposes [8]. Qin et al. studied how KGs can be used in teaching a specific subject in computer science [18]. They used web crawlers to obtain raw data from websites and then extracted entities and relations using trained machine-learning modules.

Prerequisite relations are important in teaching and learning. Prerequisite relations mining focuses on finding prerequisite relations from course descriptions and related materials for course learning. For example, which courses or knowledge should be acquired first in order to understand a new topic or take a new course. Liang et al. explored data-driven methods to recover prerequisite relations for different university courses [14]. Recently, Sun et al. proposed Con-Learn, a contextual-knowledge-aware approach to tackle this task [23]. Their work utilizes pre-trained language models to generate contextual information and graph neural networks to process the features. This mainly provides convenience for teachers to plan and prepare curriculum design. Building KGs focused on prerequisite relations concentrates more on the learning schedule and course plan.

**Multimedia Learning Material Knowledge Graphs.** Several studies focus on integrating e-learning resources into KGs and linking different concepts with relations between courses. Recently, Dang et al. constructed KGs for MOOCs with a focus on education using Wikipedia data [7]. Li et al. proposed a system named MEduKG to integrate multi-modal information into KGs for education [11]. The previous one concentrates on resource organization based on existing MOOC data into KGs. The latter one concentrates more on constructing KG from multimedia learning resources like slides, textbooks, and recordings. They used NER and RE components to construct KGs but from multi-media data resources. Aliyu et al. constructed KG for university course management based on structured data [3]. They used KGs to store and manage data for university courses, like instructors, teaching semesters, etc. It can be used to store teaching arrangement information for universities.

Errors may be accumulated during the NER process. Existing educational KGs constructed by machine learning algorithms often contain noises and redundant triples, which make these KGs impractical to some extent. Our framework employs tailored designs to learn low-redundant and high-accuracy KGs.

## 5    Conclusions and Future Work

In this paper, we proposed a framework to construct KGs for education. Unlike other KG construction methods, we aim to build a KG with high accuracy and low redundancy. Starting from the ontology to build the backbone, the framework then leverages reliable data sources with tailored methods. Moreover, we apply active KG error detection to refine the KG with minimal human effort.

Our case study and visualization demonstrate how this framework produces KG for education with high-quality and integrated learning resources, enabling the final KG to be a useful aid for education. We also designed a machine reading comprehension method to extract relations from unstructured data. This method can be applied for relation extraction in various domains without a large amount of training data. The experimental results show that it performs well for handling practical real-world data. In the future, we will focus on the following aspects: Firstly, further expanding the size of the KG by introducing more relations and entity types for education, while keeping high accuracy and low redundancy. Secondly, explore algorithms to refine the KGs more effectively and measure the quality of the outputs. Thirdly, apply the KGs to educational downstream tasks, such as question and answer systems, learning course planning, etc.

# References

1. Abu-Salih, B.: Domain-specific knowledge graphs: a survey. J. Netw. Comput. Appl. **185** (2021)
2. Agichtein, E., Gravano, L.: Snowball: extracting relations from large plain-text collections. In: Proceedings of the Fifth ACM Conference on Digital Libraries, pp. 85–94 (2000)
3. Aliyu, I., Kana, A., Aliyu, S.: Development of knowledge graph for university courses management. Int. J. Educ. Manag. Eng. **2** (2020)
4. Batista, D.S., Martins, B., Silva, M.J.: Semi-supervised bootstrapping of relationship extractors with distributional semantics. In: Proceedings of the 2015 Conference on Empirical Methods in Natural Language Processing, pp. 499–504 (2015)
5. Bosselut, A., Rashkin, H., Sap, M., Malaviya, C., Celikyilmaz, A., Choi, Y.: COMET: commonsense transformers for automatic knowledge graph construction. In: Annual Meeting of the Association for Computational Linguistics, pp. 4762–4779 (2019)
6. Chen, P., Lu, Y., Zheng, V.W., Chen, X., Yang, B.: KnowEdu: a system to construct knowledge graph for education. IEEE Access **6**, 31553–31563 (2018)
7. Dang, F.R., Tang, J.T., Pang, K.Y., Wang, T., Li, S.S., Li, X.: Constructing an educational knowledge graph with concepts linked to Wikipedia. J. Comput. Sci. Technol. **36**(5), 1200–1211 (2021)
8. Dessì, D., Osborne, F., Reforgiato Recupero, D., Buscaldi, D., Motta, E., Sack, H.: AI-KG: an automatically generated knowledge graph of artificial intelligence. In: Pan, J.Z., et al. (eds.) ISWC 2020. LNCS, vol. 12507, pp. 127–143. Springer, Cham (2020). https://doi.org/10.1007/978-3-030-62466-8_9
9. Galárraga, L., Teflioudi, C., Hose, K., Suchanek, F.M.: Fast rule mining in ontological knowledge bases with AMIE. Int. J. Very Large Data Bases **24**(6), 707–730 (2015)
10. Galárraga, L.A., Teflioudi, C., Hose, K., Suchanek, F.: AMIE: association rule mining under incomplete evidence in ontological knowledge bases. In: International World Wide Web Conference, pp. 413–422 (2013)
11. Li, N., Shen, Q., Song, R., Chi, Y., Xu, H.: MEduKG: a deep-learning-based approach for multi-modal educational knowledge graph construction. Information **13**(2) (2022)

12. Li, X., et al.: Entity-relation extraction as multi-turn question answering. In: Annual Meeting of the Association for Computational Linguistics, pp. 1340–1350 (2019)
13. Li, Y., Zhao, J., Yang, L., Zhang, Y.: Construction, visualization and application of knowledge graph of computer science major. In: International Conference on Big Data and Education, pp. 43–47 (2019)
14. Liang, C., Ye, J., Wu, Z., Pursel, B., Giles, C.L.: Recovering concept prerequisite relations from university course dependencies. In: AAAI Conference on Artificial Intelligence (2017)
15. Mahdisoltani, F., Biega, J., Suchanek, F.M.: YAGO3: a knowledge base from multilingual Wikipedias. In: Conference on Innovative Data Systems Research (2015)
16. Osborne, F., Motta, E.: Klink-2: integrating multiple web sources to generate semantic topic networks. In: Arenas, M., et al. (eds.) ISWC 2015. LNCS, vol. 9366, pp. 408–424. Springer, Cham (2015). https://doi.org/10.1007/978-3-319-25007-6_24
17. Petroni, F., et al.: Language models as knowledge bases? In: Conference on Empirical Methods in Natural Language Processing, pp. 2463–2473 (2019)
18. Qin, Y., Cao, H., Xue, L.: Research and application of knowledge graph in teaching: take the database course as an example. In: Journal of Physics: Conference Series, vol. 1607 (2020)
19. Salatino, A.A., Thanapalasingam, T., Mannocci, A., Osborne, F., Motta, E.: The computer science ontology: a large-scale taxonomy of research areas. In: Vrandečić, D., et al. (eds.) ISWC 2018. LNCS, vol. 11137, pp. 187–205. Springer, Cham (2018). https://doi.org/10.1007/978-3-030-00668-6_12
20. Shi, D., Wang, T., Xing, H., Xu, H.: A learning path recommendation model based on a multidimensional knowledge graph framework for e-learning. Knowl.-Based Syst. **195**, 105618 (2020)
21. Stewart, M., Liu, W.: Seq2kg: an end-to-end neural model for domain agnostic knowledge graph (not text graph) construction from text. In: Proceedings of the International Conference on Principles of Knowledge Representation and Reasoning, vol. 17, pp. 748–757 (2020)
22. Su, Y., Zhang, Y.: Automatic construction of subject knowledge graph based on educational big data. In: International Conference on Big Data and Education, pp. 30–36 (2020)
23. Sun, H., Li, Y., Zhang, Y.: ConLearn: contextual-knowledge-aware concept prerequisite relation learning with graph neural network. In: SIAM International Conference on Data Mining, pp. 118–126 (2022)
24. Vrandečić, D., Krötzsch, M.: Wikidata: a free collaborative knowledgebase. Commun. ACM **57**(10), 78–85 (2014)
25. Wadden, D., Wennberg, U., Luan, Y., Hajishirzi, H.: Entity, relation, and event extraction with contextualized span representations. arXiv preprint: arXiv:1909.03546 (2019)
26. Wang, H., Zhao, M., Xie, X., Li, W., Guo, M.: Knowledge graph convolutional networks for recommender systems. In: International World Wide Web Conference, pp. 3307–3313 (2019)

# Extracting the Language of the Need for Urgent Intervention in MOOCs by Analysing Text Posts

Laila Alrajhi[1,3]($\boxtimes$), Khulood Alharbi[1,4], Alexandra I. Cristea[1], and Filipe Dwan Pereira[2]

[1] Computer Science, Durham University, Durham, UK
{laila.m.alrajhi,khulood.o.alharbi,
alexandra.i.cristea}@durham.ac.uk
[2] Computer Science, Federal University of Roraima, Boa Vista, Brazil
filipe.dwan@ufrr.br
[3] Educational Technology, King Abdulaziz University, Jeddah, Saudi Arabia
[4] Computer Science, Qassim University, Qassim, Saudi Arabia

**Abstract.** Discussion forums on MOOCs are developing as a major tool for communication between learners and instructors, generating large amounts of posts, exchanged as unstructured text content. Thus, it is a major challenge for instructors to find (and respond to) urgent posts, amongst the vast amount of posts. Learners also may inadvertently pose posts that may seem more urgent than they are. However, the current literature lacks research on analysing posts from an urgency language perspective, i.e., *extracting the language used for urgent expression.* This paper explores for the first time the urgent language that learners use to express their need for immediate intervention, via an automatised approach. It describes our analysis of 5181 text posts from a course from the Stanford MOOCPosts dataset, selected for its good representation of urgent posts. We use topic modelling, here, via the widely used latent Dirichlet allocation (LDA). Moreover, we demonstrate a correlation between specific topics and urgent posts. Also, we show that most urgent posts start new threads. Additionally, constructing a visual interface for instructors or learners may support them understand the urgent language and improve intervention.

**Keywords:** Topic modeling · Latent Dirichlet allocation (LDA) · MOOCs · Urgent language · Visualisation

## 1 Introduction

With the increasing number of text posts from learners communicating in massive open online courses (MOOCs) [1] via online asynchronous 'discussion forums', instructor intervention is one solution towards reducing learner dropout. However, due to the huge number of posts and the imbalance between the number of learners and instructors, it is very challenging and time-consuming for an instructor to monitor all the available posts and detect which need urgent intervention [2]. Moreover, learners may use urgent language invertedly. Recent solutions [3–5] based on supervised machine learning (ML) reached a remarkable performance. However, whilst they have focused on identifying urgent posts, they have not extracted topics that learner used, or identified urgent language.

In this research we define the 'urgent language' as the most frequently encountered words and phrases that learners use in their posts when needing urgent attention and intervention. We argue that we need to not only detect urgent intervention, but also to establish if there is a way to make the language for the urgent intervention need explicit, by visualising it. As most people are visual, creating visual aids for instructors or learners may help the former decide *when, where and how to intervene*, and the latter to *potentially revise their language*. We formulate thus our research questions:

*RQ1. Can the language of urgency be detected from learners' posts?*
*RQ2. Can the language of urgency be visualised in a simple and intuitive way?*

The main contributions of our paper are: (1) To the best of our knowledge, this is the first work to automatically detect the language of urgency need, by modelling text posts and related them to urgent posts. (2) Showing that the majority of urgent posts for specific urgent topics start new threads. (3) Designing a visualising tool for the instructor, and suggestions for learners.

## 2   Related Work

### 2.1   Instructor Intervention in MOOCs

Instructor intervention in MOOCs is a relatively new area and an emerging hot topic, started by [6], as the first work on predicting instructor intervention in MOOCs. This work launched a body of research on finding urgent posts from discussion forums, by using text classification models, with the aim of helping instructors in deciding when to answer posts and which posts to answer to. For example, Almatrafi et al. [2] investigated different shallow ML to classify urgent posts that required urgent intervention from an instructor, using different linguistic features and metadata. A different set of works analysed new advantages introduced by deep neural networks. For instance, Guo et al. in [4] proposed hybrid neural networks based on deep learning, to identify urgent posts. In [5], Sun et al. proposed a deep learning model as an improvement of recurrent convolutional neural networks (RCNN) for the same problem. In addition, Alrajhi et al. [7] built a deep learning classification model based on text, using additional features (sentiment, confusion, urgency, opinion, question, and answer). These deep learning models outperformed shallow ML models in terms of performance. A very recent work, Khodeir [3], presented a classification model by using Bi-GRU based on BERT as a pre-trained embedding layer to classify urgent posts.

To the best of our knowledge, there is no research yet in this area that focuses on the analysis of posts and detecting the language for the urgent intervention.

### 2.2   Topic Modelling in MOOCs

With the emergence of topic modelling, there have been some researches on modelling posts from discussion forums in MOOCs by using latent Dirichlet allocation (LDA).

Attapatu and Falkner [8] used LDA to obtain the topics of the main discussion for each week in MOOCs, and labelled them to provide a framework to effectively locate and navigate the information need. Ezen-Can et al. [9] applied an unsupervised algorithm to group similar posts, then found the top topic words using LDA, to better support learners' learning. Robinson [10] used LDA to extract topics that learners used in their discussions on Cartograph. They revealed the most popular places learners talked about in class, to improve the future development of course. In fact, LDA [11] has become one of the most popular and widely used topic modelling tools.

Thus, we also use LDA here - however, to find words learners use when they need urgent intervention, as further explained in Sect. 3.3.

## 2.3 Visualisation in MOOCs

In many recent visualisation works related to MOOC discussion forums, researchers aimed at assisting instructors during their work. For example, recently, Almatrafi and Johri [12] proposed an experimental approach to improve MOOCs, based on summaries of learners' opinions about the course, extracted from discussion forums. The visual results were meant to allow both experts and non-experts understanding. Wong et al. [13] constructed a visual analytics tool (MessageLens) using different visualisation tools to assist MOOC instructors in better understanding forum discussions from three perspectives: discussion topic, learner attitude, and learner communication.

Here, we employ visualisation for instructors, to help them understand topics that learners use in their discussion on a specific course, and colour posts based on these topics to assist both instructors and learners (see Sect. 3.4).

## 3 Methods

Figure 1 shows our framework of analysis to identify urgent language and visualise it. We describe the dataset used, how we processed posts as an input to our analysis model; unsupervised approaches used to analyse and mine learners' textual posts and extract useful urgent patterns with semantic meaning. Also, we introduce a number of visualisation aids, mainly for instructors, but also for learners.

### 3.1 The Stanford MOOCPosts Data Set

We used the Stanford MOOCPost data set [14] for our research, containing anonymised learners' forum posts from 11 courses and different variables. One of them is Urgency (1–7), which describes how urgent the post is, with respect to a required response from the instructor: 1 = not urgent, 7 = very urgent. An instructor's decision if to intervene or not is a binary one, thus the 7-point scale is superfluous. Additionally, urgency data are notoriously skewed (with urgent comments being significantly fewer than non-urgent ones). Moreover, other text classification research often converted their scale to a binary one [2, 4]. Thus, we converted the above 7-point scale into a binary representation, as: $\{> 4 \rightarrow$ urgent, otherwise $\rightarrow$ non-urgent$\}$.

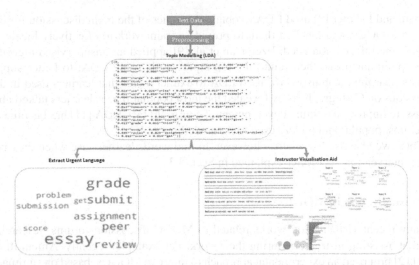

**Fig. 1.** An analysis model of urgent language and instructor visualisation aid of learners' posts.

Next, we removed unmeaningful posts, as in [7], as well as 13 posts with an empty course name in the Humanities course type. The number of posts with their percentage of urgent and non-urgent numbers of posts in each course are reported in Table 1.

Next, we chose a particular course (SciWrite) in the medical field as a case study for our analysis. The reason for selecting this course is due to the fact that it contains a large number of posts (5181), and at the same time the percentage of posts that represent urgent intervention (34.2%), as shown in Table 1, is high.

### 3.2 Data Preprocessing

To prepare the (SciWrite) course, we performed various preprocessing. This includes splitting and tokenising the sentences into a list of words, then performing cleaning, such as removing unnecessary parts, including those that may lead to identification of the learners (emails, some characters and quotes, anonymisation). Next, we converted tokens to lists. Then we built the phrase models based on bigrams (two words often appearing together in the post) and trigrams (three words appearing together), after which we applied lemmatisation and finally removed stopwords.

### 3.3 Extracting Urgent Language

To extract urgent language and answer RQ1, as a starting point for the automated language analysis 'Text-document modelling', we clustered words from forum posts into different topics, based on the unsupervised statistical model called LDA, as explained below. This is followed by associating topic lists and trending terms within urgent posts, as a potential good indicator for identifying and giving an overview of 'urgent language'. The next sub-sections explain the follow-up steps.

**Table 1.** Number of urgent and non-urgent posts for all courses on the Stanford MOOCPosts.

|  | Course | Posts # | Non-Urgent | Urgent |
|---|---|---|---|---|
| Humanities/Sciences | WomensHealth | 2141 | 1863 (87.0%) | 278 (13.0%) |
|  | StatLearning | 3029 | 2191 (72.3%) | 838 (27.7%) |
|  | Stats216 | 327 | 204 (62.4%) | 123 (37.6%) |
|  | Environmental_Physiology | 2467 | 2048 (83.0%) | 419 (17.0%) |
|  | Econ-1 | 1583 | 1249 (78.9%) | 334 (21.1%) |
|  | Econ1V | 160 | 150 (93.8%) | 10 (6.2%) |
| Medicine | Statistics_in_Medicine | 3320 | 2276 (68.6%) | 1044 (31.4%) |
|  | MedStats | 1218 | 802 (65.8%) | 416 (34.2%) |
|  | SciWrite | 5181 | 3407 (65.8%) | 1774 (34.2%) |
|  | Managing_Emergencies_What _Every_Doctor_Must_Know | 279 | 231 (82.8%) | 48 (17.2%) |
| Education | How_to_Learn_Math | 9879 | 9559 (96.8%) | 320 (3.2%) |

**Topic Modelling (LDA) Setup.** In NLP, topic modelling is an unsupervised technique commonly used for analysing a collection of documents, offering a convenient way to classify, extract, discover hidden topics associated with each topic [15] and recognise latent patterns from unstructured text [16]. The generative probabilistic topic-modelling model LDA assumes that each document is a mix of different topics; and a topic is a theme of a collection of words that frequently appear together [17]. The model processes a document term matrix, supposing each document (d) contains different topics (t), as a probability distribution $p(t|d)$. In turn, each topic (t) contains different words (w), with t a probability distribution over w $p(w|t)$. The input of this model is a bag-of-word and the output is represented by different topics, each with lists of terms (words), which are ordered from the highest relevance to the topic, to the lowest one [18]. We used Gensim to train our LDA model, written in Python. In this model, we only need to feed the model with the number of topics (k). It is a challenging task, as there is no perfect way to choose this number. A low number of topics tends to be more general; a higher number provides details [19]. Here we apply a coherence metric via one of the most used methods, c_v coherence [20], for various numbers of topics, to obtain a number close to the optimal one. Thus, we built several models with different k, starting from 2 until

20, in intervals of 1, and keep all the parameters of the models at their default values. Then, based on the coherence score, we select the best value. Next, we tune parameters (passes and iterations) to achieve the best topics; where: passes refer to the total number of passes through the corpus during training; iterations refer to controlling the maximum number of iterations through the corpus when inferring the topic distribution of a corpus. We tuned and set these two parameters to passes = 50 and iterations = 200.

**Extracting Urgent Language via LDA.** To inspect and give an overview of the terms (words and phrases), we present the top 10 terms on each topic. After that, we used t-Distributed Stochastic Neighbour Embedding (t-SNE) [21], a cutting-edge unsupervised technique for dimensionality reduction, to visualise clusters with high dimensions in 2D space. Our final aim is to reveal the key language learners use to express their need for urgent intervention. To reach this primary goal, we first find the dominant topic for every post, as every post is composed of a mixture of words, and each word is drawn from one topic. Hence, we are able to find the most representative post for each topic, as an example to understand each topic.

Finally, for each topic, we calculate the percentage of posts with predominantly urgent posts, and the same with non-urgent. We set a threshold of more than 80%, under the assumption of this ensuring that they are the most representative posts for that topic.

### 3.4 Instructor Visualisation Aid

To answer RQ2, we propose visualising aids, as mental tools to allow instructors to become aware of the topics learners use in their discussion; or learners to be aware of their own urgency language, applying three different aids: (1) Wordclouds: we visualise the top 10 terms in each topic using wordclouds. It is a visual representation of topics in a cloud shape, depicted in different sizes, based on the probability of each term (word) (instructors only). (2) pyLDAvis: is used to represent, distinguish and interpret topics (instructors). (3) coloured posts: we colour each token in the post with the topic colour, to help instructors or learners to determine urgent words.

# 4   Results and Discussion

## 4.1   Results of Topic Modelling (LDA)

As per Sect. 3.3, we estimate the best number of topics (k) based on the coherence score, see Fig. 2. Selecting 6 topics renders the highest coherence score on the y-axis.

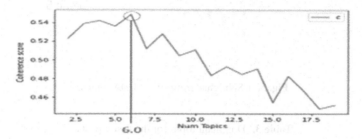

**Fig. 2.**  Selecting the optimal number of LDA topics.

## 4.2   Results of Extracting Urgent Language via LDA

The 10 most relevant terms and highest probability for every topic output as per LDA with k = 6 are presented in Table 2. We can see that some words appear in different topics, such as 'course' appears in topic 0, topic 3 and topic 4.

**Table 2.**  Most relevant terms for six topics identified by LDA.

| Topic 0 | Topic 1 | Topic 2 | Topic 3 | Topic 4 | Topic 5 |
| --- | --- | --- | --- | --- | --- |
| 0.021*course | 0.008*change | 0.023*use | 0.042*thank | 0.022*reviewer | 0.076*essay |
| 0.013*time | 0.007*risk | 0.021*write | 0.033*course | 0.021*get | 0.060*grade |
| 0.011*certificate | 0.007*use | 0.015*paper | 0.022*answer | 0.020*peer | 0.044*submit |
| 0.008*page | 0.007*com | 0.013*sentence | 0.014*question | 0.020*score | 0.037*peer |
| 0.007*hope | 0.007*think | 0.011*word | 0.013*homework | 0.020*review | 0.035*review |
| 0.007*continue | 0.006*study | 0.010*writing | 0.012*get | 0.018*course | 0.029*assignment |
| 0.007*take | 0.006*different | 0.009*think | 0.010*quiz | 0.017*comment | 0.018*submission |
| 0.006*good | 0.005*effect | 0.008*example | 0.010*post | 0.016*give | 0.017*problem |
| 0.006*hour | 0.005*mean | 0.008*scientific | 0.010*video | 0.012*grade | 0.016*score |
| 0.006*work | 0.005*include | 0.007*make | 0.009*problem | 0.011*think | 0.014*get |

Figure 3 visualises the higher dimensional data in lower dimensions, using the t-SNE algorithm. Here, the different topics are mapped onto two dimensions.

As an example of the most dominant topic, Table 3 shows the dominant topic and its percentage, with the terms for the first two posts in our corpus. For both posts, topic 3 is the dominant one, with different contributions towards it.

Table 4 shows the most representative tokens from posts for each topic, as a sample of what a topic is about. The minimum contribution is about 0.97, which shows that these tokens are representing the topic almost perfectly.

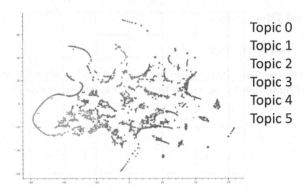

Topic 0
Topic 1
Topic 2
Topic 3
Topic 4
Topic 5

**Fig. 3.** t-SNE clustering of six LDA topics.

**Table 3.** Dominant topic for the first 2 posts.

| Dominant Topic | Topic Percentage Contribution | Keywords | Tokens of Posts |
|---|---|---|---|
| 3 | 0.53 | thank, course, answer, question, homework, get… | [hope, useful, place, discuss, related, course… |
| 3 | 0.47 | thank, course, answer, question, homework, get… | [video, unit, work, however, one, work, perfectly… |

Table 5 shows the percentage of urgent and non-urgent posts, where the dominant topics contribution is more than 80%. The total number of posts with the topic percentage contribution > 80% is 1218 posts. We found that topic 5 covers about 58% of urgent posts. That means that the most important words that learners used and expressed in texts when they need urgent intervention can be found in topic 5. These include: (essay, grade, submit, peer, review, assignment, submission, problem, score, get, …). Analysing them, these terms make sense as illustrators of urgent language, as an imminent test can provoke urgency. Also, despite topic 2 and topic 3 having many posts belonging to them, the urgent posts only cover 26% and 32%, respectively.

Then we manually inspect posts in which the dominant topics belong to topic 5, to understand why these cover 58% of the urgent comments. In discussion forums, there are two types of post: thread (the first post) and comments (reply to a specific post). Chaturvedi et.al. [6] supposed that the first post tends be a question and the reply might be an answer or comment on the question. We assume the same scenario, where the thread tends to be urgent, but the comment can be non-urgent. Therefore, we analyse urgent and non-urgent posts in topic 5, 330 posts, based on post type (thread or comment). We find that 101 posts are threads, with 96% urgent posts; and 229 are comments, with just 40% urgent posts, as per Table 6. This further explains why the language used in these non-urgent comments imitates urgent language: when replying to threads, learners used similar terms and language as that of the original thread, which may have been in urgent need of intervention; however, their reply (comment), albeit written in a similar language, did not need urgent intervention. This is important, as a 'simple' urgency ML or deep learning classifier would not be able to distinguish between the two, but having the human-in-the-loop through informed visualisation can help detect such cases.

**Table 4.** The most representative tokens of post for each topic.

| Topic Number | Topic Percentage Contribution | Keywords | Tokens of Posts |
|---|---|---|---|
| 0 | 0.97 | course, time, certificate, page, hope, continue, take, good, hour, work | [make, follow, revision, dedicated, prosthesis, allow, sprinter, run, low, metabolic_cost,... |
| 1 | 0.99 | change, risk, use, com, think, study, different, effect, mean, include | [immortality, alluring, concept, scientist, believe, possible, upload, mind, recreate,... |
| 2 | 0.99 | use, write, paper, sentence, word, writing, think, example, scientific, make | [note, necessarily, right, way, way, protective, occurrence, inhibit, reoccurrence, estimate,... |
| 3 | 0.97 | thank, course, answer, question, homework, get, quiz, post, video, problem | [subtitle, video, available, download, soon, meanwhile, view, video, course, webpage, youtube,... |
| 4 | 0.98 | reviewer, get, peer, score, review, course, comment, give, grade, think | [thank, elfatih, point, review, student, paper, helpful, receive, excellent, feedback, first,... |
| 5 | 0.99 | essay, grade, submit, peer, review, assignment, submission, problem, score, get | [dear, problem, want, post, rd, assignment, order, take, look, feedback, essay, go, section,... |

**Table 5.** The percentage of urgent and non-urgent posts for each topic where the dominant contribution is more than 80%.

| Topic Number | Posts Number | Urgent Number | Urgent % | Non-Urgent Number | Non-Urgent % |
|---|---|---|---|---|---|
| 0 | 44 | 13 | 30% | 31 | 70% |
| 1 | 55 | 11 | 20% | 44 | 80% |
| 2 | 298 | 76 | 26% | 222 | 74% |
| 3 | 320 | 102 | 32% | 218 | 68% |
| 4 | 171 | 42 | 25% | 129 | 75% |
| 5 | 330 | 190 | **58%** | 140 | 42% |

**Table 6.** The percentage of urgent and non-urgent posts for thread and comment in topic 5.

| Type of posts | Posts Number | Urgent Number | Urgent % | Non-Urgent Number | Non-Urgent % |
|---|---|---|---|---|---|
| Thread | 101 | 97 | 96% | 4 | 4% |
| Comment | 229 | 93 | 41% | 136 | 59% |

### 4.3  Results of Instructor Visualisation Aid

To enlighten the instructor and give an overview of the different topics and the probability of each term in each topic, we depict the word cloud visualisations that represent each topic in a distinct colour, and each term in a different size representing the probability of each term (word), as shown in Fig. 4.

To interpret the topics in a simple and interactive way for the instructor, we are using pyLDAvis, as shown in Fig. 5. Every topic is represented as a bubble, the size of the bubble representing the percentage of the number of posts about this topic. The largest bubble means that it contains the highest percentage of posts on this topic. The distance between the center of the bubbles indicates the similarity between the topics. The bar chart represents the top 30 terms in specific topics.

To further help both instructors and potentially learners, we additionally coloured the tokens of the posts with the topic colour, as illustrated in Fig. 6. For example, Post 1 (first post) contains different colures (red, purple and green) belonging to (topic 3, 4 and 2) respectively. Therefore, if the instructor finds a brown colour (topic 5) and it is a thread, this indicates that this post is in need of urgent intervention.

Topic 0

page
course hope
time good
hour work
take continue
certificate

Topic 1

effect
change mean
include
think use
study risk
different com

Topic 2

think writing
scientific
word example make
paper
use
write
sentence

Topic 3

thank
video get homework
answer post
course
quiz problem
question

Topic 4

give peer think
get review
grade comment
course score
reviewer

Topic 5

grade
problem get submit
submission
assignment
score peer
essay review

**Fig. 4.** Word cloud visualisation (top 10 terms) for each topic.

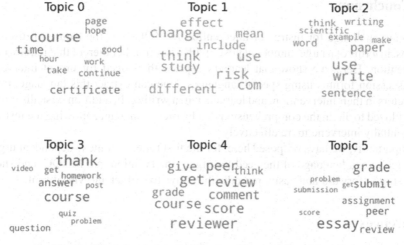

**Fig. 5.** pyLDAvis - top 30 terms for each topic.

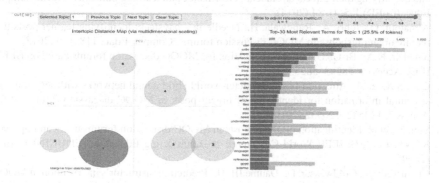

Post 1: already answer br br charitably course discuss duplicate easy follow forum guideline homework hope interpret

Post 2: work fine however issue obviously one particular perfectly unit video ...

Post 3: follow question work apply area ask button check profession radio reverse say think ...

Post 4: answer use cap correct get head letter lowercase mark match noun quiz type uppercase ...

Post 5: answer get mark contact email even ill know screen shot want ...

**Fig. 6.** Topic colouring for the first 5 posts tokens.

# 5 Conclusion

The main challenge for instructor intervention in MOOCs is the nature of discussion forums, in terms of a large number of posts, with a low number thereof that require urgent intervention. Here, we show that learners express their need for urgent intervention via discussion forums using special languages. One can extract this language, to help instructors in their intervention, and learners when writing. In addition, visualisation can be employed to aid in the comprehension of a learner's language, allowing the instructor to potentially intervene more effectively.

Importantly, we have proposed here, for the first time, a 'context-dependent urgency language', i.e. a language of the need for urgent intervention in a MOOC, and showed some straightforward and easily reproducible ways to extract and visualise it.

# References

1. Tucker, C., Pursel, B.K., Divinsky, A.: Mining student-generated textual data in MOOCs and quantifying their effects on student performance and learning outcomes. ASEE Comput. Educ. (CoED) J. **5**(4), 84 (2014)
2. Almatrafi, O., Johri, A., Rangwala, H.: Needle in a haystack: identifying learner posts that require urgent response in MOOC discussion forums. Comput. Educ. **118**, 1–9 (2018)
3. Khodeir, N.A.: Bi-GRU urgent classification for MOOC discussion forums based on BERT. IEEE Access **9**, 58243–58255 (2021)
4. Guo, S.X., et al.: Attention-based character-word hybrid neural networks with semantic and structural information for identifying of urgent posts in MOOC discussion forums. IEEE Access **7**, 120522–120532 (2019)
5. Sun, X., et al. Identification of urgent posts in MOOC discussion forums using an improved RCNN. In: 2019 IEEE World Conference on Engineering Education (EDUNINE). IEEE (2019)
6. Chaturvedi, S., Goldwasser, D., Daumé III, H.: Predicting instructor's intervention in MOOC forums. In: Proceedings of the 52nd Annual Meeting of the Association for Computational Linguistics (vol. 1: Long Papers) (2014)
7. Alrajhi, L., Alharbi, K., Cristea, A.I.: A multidimensional deep learner model of urgent instructor intervention need in MOOC forum posts. In: Kumar, V., Troussas, C. (eds.) ITS 2020. LNCS, vol. 12149, pp. 226–236. Springer, Cham (2020). https://doi.org/10.1007/978-3-030-49663-0_27
8. Atapattu, T., Falkner, K.: A framework for topic generation and labeling from MOOC discussions. In: Proceedings of the Third (2016) ACM Conference on Learning@ Scale (2016)
9. Ezen-Can, A., et al.: Unsupervised modeling for understanding MOOC discussion forums: a learning analytics approach. In: Proceedings of the Fifth International Conference on Learning Analytics and Knowledge (2015)
10. Robinson, A.C.: Exploring class discussions from a massive open online course (MOOC) on cartography. In: Brus, J., Vondrakova, A., Vozenilek, V. (eds.) Modern Trends in Cartography. LNGC, pp. 173–182. Springer, Cham (2015). https://doi.org/10.1007/978-3-319-07926-4_14
11. Blei, D.M., Ng, A.Y., Jordan, M.I.: Latent dirichlet allocation. J. Mach. Learn. Res. **3**, 993–1022 (2003)
12. Almatrafi, O., Johri, A.: Improving MOOCs using feedback/information from discussion forums: an opinion summarization and suggestion mining approach. IEEE Access (2022)

13. Wong, J.-S.: MessageLens: a visual analytics system to support multifaceted exploration of MOOC forum discussions. Vis. Inform. **2**(1), 37–49 (2018)

14. Agrawal, A., et al.: YouEDU: addressing confusion in MOOC discussion forums by recommending instructional video clips. In: The 8th International Conference on Educational Data Mining (2015)

15. Wang, X., Wen, M., Rosé, C.P.: Towards triggering higher-order thinking behaviors in MOOCs. In: Proceedings of the Sixth International Conference on Learning Analytics & Knowledge (2016)

16. Sharma, H., Sharma, A.K.: Study and analysis of topic modelling methods and tools–a survey. Am. J. Math. Comput. Model. **2**(3), 84–87 (2017)

17. Nanda, G., et al.: Analyzing large collections of open-ended feedback from MOOC learners using LDA topic modeling and qualitative analysis. IEEE Trans. Learn. Technol. (2021)

18. Wong, A.W., Wong, K., Hindle, A.: Tracing forum posts to MOOC content using topic analysis. arXiv preprint arXiv:1904.07307 (2019)

19. Asmussen, C.B., Møller, C.: Smart literature review: a practical topic modelling approach to exploratory literature review. J. Big Data **6**(1), 1–18 (2019). https://doi.org/10.1186/s40537-019-0255-7

20. Syed, S., Spruit, M.: Full-text or abstract? Examining topic coherence scores using latent dirichlet allocation. In: 2017 IEEE International Conference on Data Science and Advanced Analytics (DSAA). IEEE (2017)

21. Van der Maaten, L., Hinton, G.: Visualizing data using t-SNE. J. Mach. Learn. Res. **9**(11) (2008)

# Challenges in the Implementation of Web Based Digital Content Repository for Teachers in Bulgaria

Milena Lazarova(✉) ⓘ, Ognyan Nakov, and Daniel Djolev

Technical University of Sofia, Sofia 1000, Bulgaria
{milaz,nakov}@tu-sofia.bg

**Abstract.** Sharing of educational resources is an important aspect supporting the exchange of knowledge, skills and experience between the pedagogical specialists that be-come of vital importance with the forced distance learning during Covid-19 pandemic. The paper presents the design and development of a web based digital content repository that is used as national teachers' digital library in Bulgaria. The digital repository is aimed at publishing and sharing authored educational, didactic and methodological materials created by primary and secondary teachers. The platform allows sharing different teaching materials as presentations, video lessons, films, exercises, tests, training programs, innovative teaching methods, entertaining pedagogy as well as research and student's work. The author's materials can be used for training, self-training and testing and are stored by grades, by thematic areas and by material type. All the materials are audited for correspondence to the state educational standards and the relevant curricula. The developed web based digital content repository serves as a national digital library for e-learning materials used in primary and secondary schools in Bulgaria as well as in Bulgarian schools abroad.

**Keywords:** National digital library · Educational resource sharing · E-learning · Primary school · Secondary school

## 1 Introduction

Digitization in educational institutions is a key element of the modern school that utilizes innovations based on information and communication technologies (ICT) in order to manage and optimize the learning process and thus to increase its efficiency. The importance of access to online educational resources is widely recognized and the subject of numerous initiatives and research activities [1–3].

In recent years there has been a sustainable educational state policy in Bulgaria defined in the "Strategic framework for development of education, training and learning in the Republic of Bulgaria (2021–2030)" [4]. The importance of the school digitalization is clearly defined as strategic priority 6 "Educational innovation, digital transformation and sustainable development". The utilization of ICT in Bulgarian schools in the recent

C. S. González-González et al. (Eds.): ICWL 2022/SETE 2022, LNCS 13869, pp. 174–179, 2023.
https://doi.org/10.1007/978-3-031-33023-0_15

years has transformed the traditional educational process and improved its quality and efficiency [5, 6].

As a consequence of the government activities supporting the school digitization in Bulgaria the educational process in schools was not interrupted with the beginning of the Covid-19 pandemic and the training process successfully switched to distance learning. The relevant changes made in 2020 in the Act on Preschool and School Education in Republic of Bulgaria are aimed at regulating the distance learning in electronic environment to ensure the continuous education of children and students in different extraordinary circumstances as flu holidays, climate or other factors.

Sharing of educational resources is an important aspect supporting the exchange of knowledge, skills and experience between the pedagogical specialists that become of vital importance with the forced distance learning during Covid-19 pandemic [7–10]. The strong state policy in Bulgaria for raising the qualification and professional development of the pedagogical specialists is implemented through several national programs that support the intensive usage of ICT in the school education and the qualification of pedagogical specialists. Despite the teachers' qualification programs for usage of e-learning materials, the existence of a nationwide digital library for sharing e-learning materials became critical in March 2020.

The paper presents the design and development of a web based digital content repository that is used as a national teachers' digital library in Bulgaria. The digital repository is aimed at publishing and sharing authored educational, didactic and methodological materials created by primary and secondary teachers.

## 2 Design Methodology

The national e-library for teachers in Bulgaria is an online a web-based product designed for sharing and exchange of own learning materials between primary and secondary teachers. The general architecture of the web based digital content repository is shown on Fig. 1. The application has a three-layer architecture that comprises a front end, a backend and a database.

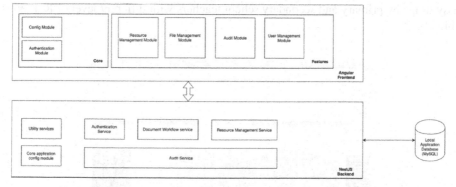

**Fig. 1.** General architecture of the web based digital content repository.

The backend server is developed using NestJS and supports several services: a utility service, an authentication service, a document workload service, a resource management service, an audit service and a core application configuration module. The backend services are implemented as REST APIs accessible by the front-end application. The frontend layer is developed using Angular framework and comprises core configuration and authentication modules as well as several modules for user access to the platform features: resource management module, file management module, audit module and user management module. The database layer of the application is a MySQL database that support storage of various heterogeneous teaching resources.

The platform supports three user roles:

- guest user has full access to the public part of the platform that allows searching for materials by selected criteria, reviewing and downloading selected teaching materials;
- user role "teacher" can create, modify and delete own learning materials;
- user role "school principal" allows access to additional functionally that allows registration of school teachers as platform users with teacher role.

In order to upload and share a learning material the registered users, either teachers or principals, should provide the following information: material title, status – draft or published, subject area, subject and grade of the material, type of the teaching material, short description as well as attached files. The materials in status "draft" are not visible to the library users. Changing the material to status "published" allows both guest and registered user to access it. All the materials are audited by the school principal user for correspondence to the state educational standards and the relevant curricula.

The platform allows sharing different teaching materials as presentations, video lessons, films, exercises, tests, training programs, innovative teaching methods, entertaining pedagogy as well as research and student's work. Thus the designed database is heterogeneous in order to allow storage and access of various resources with different file type and size. In order to support the intensive simultaneous usage of the platform by many users a software collision protection of data access is implemented.

The web based platform can be used with any browser and provides user friendly interface with a responsive design that allows its utilization on different devices and easy usage by primary and secondary school teachers with different level of ICT skills (Fig. 2).

**Fig. 2.** User interface of the digital content repository database

The author's materials can be used for training, self-training and testing and are stored by grades, by thematic areas and by material type. The categorization of the learning recourses as well the search criteria in the repository are based on the subject area, the material subject, the students' grade for which it is aimed as well as the type of the material: training, self-training or testing. All published materials are audited to ensure their compliance with the state educational standards and the relevant curricula.

## 3  Results and Analyses

A total of 2 369 state and private schools are operating on the territory of the Republic of Bulgaria. In addition, two Bulgarian public secondary schools as well as 355 Bulgarian Sunday schools are operating abroad.

The design and development of the national teachers' digital library was supported by the Ministry of Education in Bulgaria with its main goal being to assist the forced distance learning in the beginning of the Covid-19 pandemic in 2020. The repository was operational by the end of March 2020 and was intensively used by the Bulgarian teachers especially during the Covid-19 pandemic. Even if it was established due to the Covid-19 pandemic, the national digital library continues to serve as a resource repository for the teachers in primary and secondary schools in Bulgaria and abroad.

The statistics of the platform usage by June 2022 are given in Table 1. The platform has more than one hundred thousand registered users that has published and shared 7 619 training materials, downloaded totally 1 143 335 times.

The general audience overview statistics of the platform users for the period Oct 1, 2021 – Dec 15, 2021 is shown on Fig. 3. The geographic distribution of the library users for the same time period is given on Fig. 4 and Fig. 5 presents the demographic distribution of the users by age and gender.

**Table 1.** Digital e-learning library usage by June 2022.

| | |
|---|---|
| Number of registered pedagogical specialists | 109 479 |
| Number of uploaded materials (articles) | 7 619 |
| Number of uploaded files | 8 540 |
| Number of uploaded files by type/format | |
| - MS Word and text documents | 3 539 |
| - MS PowerPoint presentations | 2 846 |
| - MS Excel spreadsheets | 10 |
| - pdf documents | 1 404 |
| - images (png, jpeg, gif) | 348 |
| - audio files (mp3, mpeg) | 52 |
| - video files (mp4) | 286 |
| - binary files | 55 |
| Total number of downloads | 1 143 335 |

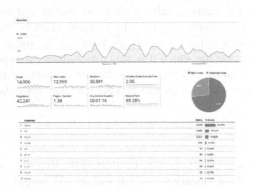

**Fig. 3.** General overview of the digital e-learning library users

**Fig. 4.** Geographic distribution of the digital e-learning library users

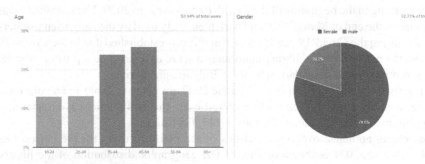

**Fig. 5.** Demographic distribution of the digital e-learning library users by age and gender

The feedback gathered through a dedicated survey among the users of the system is very positive due to the provided possibility for publishing and sharing training, didactic and methodological materials. As can be seen the platform was intensively used during the distance learning period with more than 25% of returning users. The e-learning materials are utilized by teachers in all age groups. Even if the digital library is mainly accessed by users situated in Bulgaria, the e-learning materials are also of great value to the teachers in the Bulgarian schools abroad as there are two Bulgarian state secondary schools and more than 350 Sunday schools all over the world.

## 4    Conclusion

The digital repository is aimed at publishing and sharing authored educational, didactic and methodological materials created by primary and secondary teachers. The platform allows sharing different teaching materials as presentations, video lessons, films, exercises, tests, training programs, innovative teaching methods, entertaining pedagogy as well as research and student's work. The author's materials can be used for training, self-training and testing and are stored by grades, by thematic areas and by material type. All the materials are audited for correspondence to the state educational standards and the relevant curricula. The developed web based digital content repository serves as a national digital library for e-learning materials used in primary and secondary schools in Bulgaria. The platform strongly supported the forced distance learning periods in Bulgarian schools during the Covid-19 pandemic. Furthermore, the shared educational materials are also intensively used by the teachers for face-to-face learning, for student's self-training, for teaching integrated knowledge as well as for project-based learning.

**Acknowledgements.** The research presented in the paper is funded by the European Regional Development Fund, Operational Program "Science and Education for Smart Growth" under project UNITe BG05M2OP001–1.001–0004/28.02.2018 (2018–2023).

# References

1. Mishra, S.: Open educational resources for sustainable development: guidelines for policy and capacity building. In: Jagannathan, S. (ed.). Reimagining Digital learning for Sustainable Development: How Upskilling, Data Analytics, and Educational Technologies Close the Skills Gap, 1st ed., pp. 209–219. Routledge, Milton Park (2021)
2. Iniesto, F., Tabuenca, B., Rodrigo, C., Tovar, E.: Challenges to achieving a more inclusive and sustainable open education. J. Interact. Media Educ. **2021**(1) (2021)
3. Downes, S.: A look at the future of open educational resources. Int. J. Open Educ. Resour. **1**(2), 1–17 (2019)
4. Strategic framework for development of education, training and learning in the Republic of Bulgaria. https://epale.ec.europa.eu/sites/default/files/strategicheska_ramka_za_obrazo vanieto_obuchenieto_i_ucheneto_v_republika_blgariya_2021_-_2030l.pdf
5. Paunova-Hubenova, E., Terzieva, V.: Information technologies in Bulgarian school education. In: Proceedings of the 13th International Technology, Education and Development Conference, 11–13 March 2019, Valencia, Spain, IATED, pp. 5226–5235 (2019)
6. Chikurteva, A., Spasova, N., Chikurtev, D.: E-learning: technologies, application and challenges. In: Proceedings of XXIX International Scientific Conference Electronics, pp. 1–4 (2020)
7. Otto, D.: Adoption and diffusion of open educational resources (OER) in education: a meta-analysis of 25 OER-projects. Int. Rev. Res. Open Distrib. Learn. **20**(5), 122–140 (2019)
8. Otto, D., Kerres, M.: Increasing sustainability in open learning: prospects of a distributed learning ecosystem for open educational resources. Front. Educ. **7**, 292 (2022)
9. Vrana, R.: Open educational resources (OER) as means of promotion of open education. In: Proceedings of 44th International Convention on Information, Communication and Electronic Technology, pp. 576–581 (2021)
10. National learning platforms and tools. https://en.unesco.org/covid19/educationresponse/nat ionalresponses

# Providing Meaningful Digital Competence Assessment Feedback for Supporting Teachers Professional Development

Linda Helene Sillat[1]([⊠]), Paula Joanna Sillat[1], Merlin Vares[2], and Kairit Tammets[1]

[1] Tallinn University, Narva Road 25, 10120 Tallinn, Estonia
{linda.sillat,paulajoannas,kairit.tammets}@tlu.ee
[2] Saaremaa Ühisgümnaasium, Hariduse 13, 93812 Kuressaare, Estonia
merlin.vares@hariduse.edu.ee

**Abstract.** Measuring the effectiveness of teaching is a complex and multifaceted process which requires understanding both the context and assessment goal. Based on an OECD report [7] the quality of the educational system relies heavily on the systematic assessment and development of teachers' competence while focusing on reflection. Although teachers' digital competence has been a central discussion point for the past decade, researchers are still struggling to understand what are the most effective feedback solutions to support teachers' digital competence development. The following paper gives and overview of the results of a design study which focused on understanding the digital competence self-assessment feedback loop. Based on the design study we proposed and evaluated a feedback loop prototype which supports teacher's digital competence and meaningful professional development.

**Keywords:** Teacher · Digital competence · Professional development · Feedback loop · Self-assessment

## 1 Introduction

According to the European Commission, a comprehensive digitization is underway in society and the use of technology affects all professions and fields. Taking advantage of the expanded options requires investment in skills and a thorough review of education and lifelong learning systems [1]. In 2020, the European Commission adopted a digital education action plan (Digital Education Action Plan 2021–2027). The aim is to increase the contribution of education to the European Union's recovery from the COVID-19 crisis, because amid the crisis situation the need to make the digital capabilities of schools, teaching, and learning more fit to the technological age became apparent [2].

According to the European Commission the transformation into a modern learning environment requires the creation of a strategic vision in the development plans of educational institutions with the aim of applying digital technology to teaching, learning and management activities [3]. Schools have been called upon to make joint efforts to take advantage of the opportunities offered by the digital revolution. Strategic planning

C. S. González-González et al. (Eds.): ICWL 2022/SETE 2022, LNCS 13869, pp. 180–189, 2023.
https://doi.org/10.1007/978-3-031-33023-0_16

must be linked to assessment results and the importance of digital competence frameworks and self-assessment guidelines for learners, teachers and institutions to promote digital competence acquisition and implementation of innovative teaching practices [4, 5]. This is confirmed by DigCompEdu, the digital competence framework for educators developed by the European Commission – a research-based document for directing education policy and the adoption of national and regional training programs [6]. The online self-assessment tool following the framework – Selfie for Teachers allows self-analysis to understand digital competence in the context of effective learning [2].

The OECD argues that an indicator of the quality of the education system is often based on the strong assessment system [7]. Internal evaluation supports the quality assurance system and increases the independence and self-management of the educational institutions. The main task of internal evaluation is to ensure the environment and conditions that support the development of students through the continuous development of the educational institution [2]. Measuring teaching effectiveness is a complex and multifaceted process that, but together with reflection, increases teachers' motivation and satisfaction towards their work [7, 8] and is necessary both to ensure the quality of teaching and to direct the teacher to take a closer look at their teaching practice. Furthermore, to understand their own strengths and weaknesses as a teacher and to clarify of development goals [9]. The information from the teacher evaluation process can be an important source of information and a driver for schools, teachers and other interest groups and a measure to ensure compliance with the teacher's professional requirements [7, 10, 11].

Based on the previous, the paper follows four main research questions: (1) What is the perceived connection between teachers' digital competence self-assessment and schools' digital maturity? (2) How do teachers perceive the applicability of a self-assessment instrument for digital competence assessment? (3) What is the expected digital competence assessment feedback format for teachers? And finally (4) What is the suitable feedback loop to support teachers' professional development?

## 2 Theoretical Background

As teachers are one the most important factors in achieving high-quality education, creating an appropriate self-assessment and development system and putting it into practice is a major challenge in the educational sector [12]. The complexity of analyzing and evaluating the effectiveness of learning activities includes a two-level implementation. One level is the educational institution, where based on the effectiveness of teaching, the management can implement various management decisions and changes related to learning and educational activities and personnel management. The second level is the teacher's level, which supports the teacher in teaching and educating the students. At the teacher's level, analyzing and evaluating teaching and learning activities and its effectiveness is a long-term process, in which the teacher must be ready to change their current pedagogical practice [13].

Assessment can be considered effective and can serve its purpose when it is accompanied by feedback [14]. Based on various studies, it can be argued that teachers' professional development takes place with the help of relevant and meaningful feedback

[15]. Assessment that is not purposeful, meaningful and contains only random observations without appropriate feedback are of little use. Teachers see them as mandatory procedures and not as professional evaluations aimed at increasing the effectiveness and quality of teaching and learning activities [11]. Feedback can improve teachers' performance by both recognizing teachers' strengths and addressing weaknesses in their pedagogical practice [16].

The methods and processes of teacher evaluation must be relevant and reliable, the evaluation criteria and feedback must be related to the educational requirements set by the qualification board, as they affect the effectiveness of the teacher's work and career prospects [17]. The benefits of teacher evaluation are expressed in the growth of the teacher's professional development and are the basis for aligning work results with the demands – improving learning and educational activities. Further, job satisfaction can increase through the evaluation process, especially for young teachers.

Conducting an assessment process with the aim of bringing about change in professional development, assessment tools must be relevant and reliable, providing feedback not only on their current success or failure, but should also provide information that teachers can use to improve their competence [11]. Teachers perceive the evaluation process as fair if they can participate in the selection or development of the evaluation systems. Being involved, in turn, helps to accept feedback, take responsibility and ownership of the results [18]. When presenting assessment results, it is important to keep in mind that accepting feedback and taking responsibility for further development is facilitated by a human-centered design in the entire assessment. The resulting information, which can be both explanatory and instructive, is aided by visualization presented through the respondent's dashboards in online self-assessment environments.

Based on the previous we can conclude that assessment of any competence, including digital competence is meaningful only if the assessment includes systematic feedback. Teachers are more receptive of the assessment process when they are included in the assessment planning and instrument decision phase.

## 3  Methodology

The study was conducted following design-based research methodology which focused on designing an educators' digital competence self-assessment feedback loop. Based on Edelson [19] the research was done in iterations following four phases: problem justification and reflection; design- and development process; evaluation and finally generalization.

To understand the teachers experiences and needs we used a two-stage data collection based on the design-based research methodology in two iterations. The first design session included semi-structured focus group interviews based on which the initial prototype was created. The second design session included the prototype evaluation where the teachers had to assess the suitability of the prototype, practicality and compliance with expectations. During the second design session the teachers also had the opportunity to make suggestions. Teachers evaluations were collected using a structured questionnaire survey. The questionnaire included ten statements which were evaluated using the following scale: +2 - very good; +1 – good but needs improvement; 0 – can't say;

−1 – mediocre, needs more improvement; −2 – very bad. The claims dealt with the prototype's visuals, understanding of the textual outputs, correspondence with real life teaching practices, sufficiency of options and focus towards professional development.

## 3.1 Sampling

The sample was formed based on purposive sampling principles, meaning that it was a non-probability sample and results can mainly be generalized within the sample of this study. The sample consisted of 12 educators who had prior knowledge and experience of Selfie for Teachers digital competence self-assessment tool and process. Based on the participants' profile they were divided into three homogenous groups and focus group interviews were carried out. The aim of the focus group interviews was to understand the teachers' expectations towards a digital competence computerized online self-assessment feedback loop based on their experiences with the Selfie for Teachers instrument and technological tool user experience.

## 3.2 Data Analysis

According to the design sessions two different methods were used for data analysis. For the analysis of the data collected during the focus group interviews of the first design session, qualitative content analysis was used. In the second design session, a questionnaire was used as a research instrument, during which evaluation of the prototype was carried out, i.e. collection of expert evaluations. The reliability of the results was determined in the analysis of expert judgments. A non-parametric method was used to determine the reliability of the evaluation results.

Based on the analysis of the results of the two design sessions, the prototype was modified.

# 4 Results

The goal of this study was to find out teachers' expectations towards the digital competence self-assessment feedback loops to facilitate professional development. The following chapter explores the results based on the two design sessions.

## 4.1 Connections Between Teachers' Self-assessment of Digital Competence and School's Digital Maturity

To understand and design the digital competence self-assessment feedback loop and visual design, two design sessions with teachers were conducted. The first design session focused on understanding the needs and expectations of the teachers for the feedback loop.

All teachers who participated in the group interviews had a similar understanding of the necessity of teachers' digital competence assessment which was considered important because although a teacher might have obtained the professional qualification it does not guarantee the ability to teach. When discussing the teachers' professionalism, they stated that digital competence is considered only one aspect and certainly not the most important. However, based on the experience of the last two years (Covid-19 pandemic), it was found that basic digital competence is needed.

Based on the teachers' replies, assessment, be it digital competence or other competences, was found difficult to implement and a systematical and continuous approach was expected. This was on the grounds that through systematical and continuous assessment of both skills and gaps by the school collective could be the basis for planning activities. Teachers also stated that there is a clear connection between supporting teachers' professional development and schools' strategic documents, meaning that the school development plan should clearly state the expectations for the teachers. The strategic documents should be accessible to everyone and consider transparency towards teachers. It was considered important to clarify how the school supports teachers in the development of digital competence and how the monitoring responsibilities are divided. Teachers also perceived the responsibility and the connection between their own digital competence and the digital competence of their students, which means that teachers should be role-models for students and guide students in developing digital competence. In this regard, the digital competence model was also mentioned, where before starting the self-assessment process, all teachers should familiarize themselves with both the teachers' and students' digital competence models.

The connections between self-assessment of the teacher's digital competence and the school's digital maturity was evident for all participants. They stated that the school management has a clear vision of how the school should evolve and thus the basis for implementing changes if needed, which includes the development of teachers' digital competence. Similarly, the teachers stated that it is not feasible to rely on teachers' internal motivation for digital competence self-assessment but rather that the school management should force to some extent the external motivation by systematically and regularly planning professional development activities which would hence also reflect on school's digital maturity.

### 4.2 Digital Competence Self-assessment Instrument Applicability and Feedback Expectations

All teachers who participated in the current study had previous experience with using Selfie for Teachers digital competence self-assessment instrument and tool. The participants stated that most notably the instrument was lengthy and time-consuming. The question statements were considered difficult to understand and vague, which added time to the entire self-assessment process. Teachers stated that when it came to unknown words, it was possible to use the dictionary by clicking on the words, but this was not considered a significant help, but was again associated with excessive time use. Further, it was pointed out that in some of the question statements it was necessary to further search for the definition. However, it was found that the assessment process must be thorough and well-thought-out in order for it to be able to communicate relevant information. Among the interviewed teachers there were many who found that the questionnaire answers did not give the respondent adequate information, and they did not connect with the statements.

The teachers unanimously agreed that it is important to convey personalized guidelines and information as feedback. Clear and simple guidelines and instructions were expected as feedback which describe how to move on to the next competence level. The participating teachers expressed their wish to see the feedback adapted to the national educational recommendations, not pan-European examples. They also stated that a connection with national training opportunities should be mapped which would relate to all digital competence dimensions. Based on the teacher's replies the feedback loop should additionally provide a selection of tools, examples and technological environments which can be used by the teacher to support the development of digital competence.

Teachers also had a high expectation for a more personalized approach. It was clearly desired that the evaluation of digital competence is differentiated so that the feedback received supports the planning of next steps and development goals. This could be done on school level, subject level and based on professional needs. It was believed that when teaching students of different ages and different subjects, also different digital competence is needed because the learning outcomes are different. The basic level was considered common to everyone, but from there on, the feedback received during the assessment should be based on interests and assessment results reflecting the teacher specific needs. According to the teachers, it should be possible to establish such differentiation by directing the respondents towards their subject or specification at the beginning of the questionnaire. Although expected this means that the digital competence self-assessment questionnaire considers detailed and specific nuances of each thought field which is not realistic and sustainable.

All interviewees also considered the self-assessment questionnaire an important indicator of comparability when presenting the results. It was expected that the results are comparable with other teachers in the school and also on the national level. At the same time, they stated that if the results are below average the comparison could also inhibit the motivation for digital competence and professional development.

### 4.3 Digital Competence Self-assessment Feedback Loop Prototype

The second design session focused on getting the feedback for the suitability and applicability of the feedback loop prototype that was designed based on the first design session and interviews. The second design session focused on the evaluation of the prototype and a questionnaire was used to collect feedback.

The feedback loop prototype was provided in the form of an interactive report in three sections where the first section describes the self-assessment results and the current state of digital competence. If applicable, it also provides a comparison with the last assessment results. It also provides a detailed description of all digital competence dimensions. The second section provides descriptive suggestions for digital competence development and how to move on to the next competence level. The suggestions are based on the higher competence level descriptions and other teachers' competence development experiences, meaning the prototype considers different learning and development paths. The third section focuses on personalized suggestions via additional trainings, online resources and online platforms. This considers other teachers experiences with the suggested solutions, meaning that if the teacher finds the suggestions suitable and beneficial they provide positive or negative feedback. Based on that, the system can build learning and professional development paths by mapping the connections between competence dimension, assessment result and suggestion applicability.

Teachers were asked to evaluate ten statements:

1. Visual representation;
2. Structure;
3. Volume of the information;
4. Content and understandability;
5. Clarity;
6. Adequacy of the resources;
7. Volume and adequacy of the examples;
8. Clarity of the examples and resources;
9. Connection to real life situations and teaching;
10. Practical usability of the feedback loop, examples and resources.

To ensure the reliability of the expert evaluation a non-parametric Z-value was calculated using the following formula:

$$Z = \frac{\left| f''+''-n \cdot P\{+\} \right| - 0,5}{\sqrt{n \cdot P\{+\} \cdot P\{-\}}}$$

The result is reliable if the two sides of the mean have a total of 95% or more of the number of cases. If two sides of the mean are 99% or more, then the result is particularly reliable. To explain the results (see Table 1): if $Z < 1.96$, confidence is <95%; if $Z \geq 1.96$, confidence is >95%; if $Z \geq 2.63$, the confidence is >99%.

**Table 1.** Teachers' expert evaluations

| Statement | Evaluation scores | | | | | Reduced scores | | | Z-criteria | Confidence% |
|---|---|---|---|---|---|---|---|---|---|---|
| | +2 | +1 | 0 | −1 | −2 | + | 0 | − | | |
| 1 | 7 | 5 | | | | 12 | | | 3.18 | >99% |
| 2 | 9 | 1 | 2 | | | 10 | 2 | | 2.85 | >99% |
| 3 | 5 | 5 | 1 | 1 | | 10 | 1 | 1 | 2.41 | >95% |
| 4 | 6 | 3 | 1 | 2 | | 9 | 1 | 2 | 1.81 | <95% |
| 5 | 5 | 3 | 3 | 1 | | 8 | 3 | 1 | 2 | >95% |
| 6 | 7 | 2 | 3 | | | 9 | 3 | | 2.66 | >99% |
| 7 | 5 | 4 | 3 | | | 9 | 3 | | 2.66 | >99% |
| 8 | 5 | 6 | 1 | | | 11 | 1 | | 3.01 | >99% |
| 9 | 6 | 5 | 1 | | | 11 | 1 | | 3.01 | >99% |
| 10 | 4 | 6 | 1 | 1 | | 10 | 1 | 1 | 2.41 | >95% |

The design of the prototype was rated by the teachers as very good in seven cases, and in five cases minor need for changes was noted. The prototype was considered visually attractive – using bright colors and graphics which give a clear overview of the results. The structure and articulation of the prototype were evaluated by the teachers in nine cases as very good, in two cases a minor need of improvements, and in one case it was not possible to answer. The teachers described the prototype as structured, clear and concrete.

In five cases, respondents evaluated the amount of information in the prototype as very good, in five cases a minor need for change was stated, in one case it was not possible to answer and in one case a further change were noted. It was appreciated that the prototype is not too long or dragging, does not cause confusion with unnecessary information. As a suggestion the amount of information, including appropriate augmentation through external links was added.

The content and text of the prototype were understood by the respondents in six cases as very good, in three cases minor changes were noted, in two cases as requiring a major change and in one case it was not possible to answer. Respondents rated the adequacy of the examples in seven cases very good, in three cases it was not possible to take a stand and in two cases minor changes were noted. The adequacy of the prototype resources was highly rated in five cases, in four cases minor need for change was seen and in three cases no position could be taken. In general, the number of examples was considered sufficient, but one teacher pointed out that there could be even more examples and resources.

The clarity and comprehensibility of the examples and resources included in the prototype were evaluated in five cases very good, in six cases minor need for change was needed and in one case it was not possible to evaluate. Specific recommendations and examples to get to the next level and to continue the self-assessment process were considered very good. However, it was recommended to exclude universal solutions like *YouTube*. The ability to refer to pre-mapped trainings was noted and praised on several occasions.

The connection of the prototype to real life situations and teaching was evaluated in six cases as very good, in five cases minor changes were noted as needed and in one case it was not evaluated. Practical usability of the feedback loop, examples and resources were evaluated very good in four cases and in six cases minor changes were expected. In one case there was no evaluation and one teacher saw the need for extensive changes including the result comparison and feedback applicability and granularity.

Overall the results show the proposed feedback loop is a step towards a more holistic approach on teachers' digital competence self-assessment process. Simultaneously, the results reflect that teachers need more support in understanding the assessment results and feedback to be well-informed in planning professional development activities.

# 5  Discussion and Conclusions

This paper is a continued discussion on the effectiveness of assessment instruments and systems used to support teachers' digital competence and professional development with the aim to understand what are the meaningful feedback loops in digital competence assessment. We found that due to the various alternative approaches to digital competence assessment, teachers find it difficult to understand the direct benefit and practical outlet of these assessment instruments, reports and feedback loops.

Based on the teachers' experiences the instruments are difficult to understand at times. Mainly in the way the questionnaires are designed - in complex, vague and difficult to understand language. Teachers' expectations of self-assessment questionnaires include concreteness, an individual approach, comparison possibilities with previous results or other teachers, and attractive and interactive visuals. At the same time, it is important to clarify that on the one hand the digital competence assessment instruments are developed by expert groups which rarely include in-service teachers which can explain the gap and secondly, teachers are often not well-informed in the assessment processes. Based on the findings it is important to interpret the information obtained from the self-assessment tool which requires educational technology support or in order to increase its effectiveness. It is also expected that the reflection process is connected with progress review. Additionally, it is clear that giving meaning to the selected assessment instrument and results also increases the motivation to complete it.

Based on the results we can conclude that there is a direct connection between the teachers' digital competence level and school's digital maturity. The participants expect that the school's strategic documents include a set of goals and indicators for both teacher's professional development and reaching the expected school-level benchmarks.

The feedback loop prototype proposed in this study considered the teachers' expectations and experiences with self-assessment questionnaires and professional development practices. The proposed feedback loop prototype considers the personalization of the feedback by linking the results with potential training programs, self-study opportunities and includes a detailed description of digital competence dimensions to help the teachers in understanding how it relates to their pedagogical practice.

The results of the study give way to better understand teachers' digital competence assessment processes. While self-assessment questionnaires are mainly popular due to the ease of use and resource management, it is important to focus on analyzing and making sense of the received feedback. Furthermore, it is important to increase the differentiation of these feedback loops to provide personalized feedback, for example based on the school level, subject or other specializations of teachers.

To further understand teachers' digital competence and how to support the assessment process and thus development, a longer-term impact study is needed. Future research should consider the variety of digital competence self-assessment questionnaires and focus more clearly on the practicality and applicability of different online instruments and feedback loops to support teachers' meaningful professional development.

# References

1. Euroopa Komisjon: Valge raamat: Euroopa tulevik: mõttearendusi ja tulevikustsenaariume EL 27 jaoks aastaks 2025 (2017). https://www.digar.ee/viewer/et/nlib-digar:312160/272706/page/1
2. European Commission: European Education Area European Education Area (2020). https://education.ec.europa.eu/et/digioppe-tegevuskava-2021-2027

3. European Commission: Directorate-General for Education, Youth, Sport and Culture. Opening up education: innovative teaching and learning for all through new technologies and open educational resources. Publications Office (2015). https://data.europa.eu/doi/10.2766/78746

4. Johnson, L., et al.: Horizon Report Europe: 2014 Schools Edition. Publications Office of the European Union, Luxembourg and The New Media Consortium,Austin, Texas (2014)

5. Vanari, K., Eisenschmidt, E., Põld, L., Tiisvelt, T.: Sisehindamine – tõenduspõhine koolijuhtimine (2018). https://www.hm.ee/sites/default/files/dokument.pdf

6. Redecker, C.: European framework for the digital competence of educators: DigCompEdu. Punie, Y. (toim). Publications Office of the European Union (2017). https://doi.org/10.2760/178382

7. OECD: Synergies for Better Learning: An International Perspective on Evaluation and Assessment, OECD Reviews of Evaluation and Assessment in Education. OECD Publishing, Paris (2013). https://doi.org/10.1787/9789264190658-en

8. Crehan, L.: Exploring the impact of career models on teacher motivation. UNESCO (2016). https://unesdoc.unesco.org/ark:/48223/pf0000246252

9. Taimalu, M., Uibu, K., Luik, P., Leijen, Ä., Pedaste, M.: Õpetajad ja koolijuhid väärtustatud professionaalidena. OECD rahvusvahelise õpetamise ja õppimise uuringu TALIS 2018 tulemused. 2. osa (2020). https://harno.ee/sites/default/files/documents/2021-02/TALIS2_kujund atud.pdf

10. Isoré, M.: Teacher evaluation: current practices in OECD countries and a literature review. OECD Education Working Papers, no. 23. OECD Publishing, Paris (2009). https://doi.org/10.1787/223283631428

11. Papay, J.: Refocusing the debate: assessing the purposes and tools of teacher evaluation. Harvard Educ. Rev. 2(1), 123–141 (2012). https://doi.org/10.17763/haer.82.1.v40p0833345w6384

12. Ploom, K., Irs, R.: Managing educational sector via self-evaluation policy. Haridussüsteemi juhtimine läbi sisehindamise. Estonian Discussions on Economic Policy (2010). https://doi.org/10.15157/tpep.v18i0.886

13. Eisenschmidt, E., et al.: Isehindamine Õppe - ja kasvatustegevuse analüüsimine ning hindamine. Tallinn (2011). https://www.hm.ee/sites/default/files/isehindamine.pdf

14. Murphy, R.: Testing Teachers: what works best for teacher evaluation and appraisal (2013). https://dera.ioe.ac.uk/30283/1/MURPHYTEACHEREVALUATION-FINAL-1.pdf

15. Taylor, E.S., Tyler, J.H.: The effect of evaluation on performance: evidence from longitudinal student achievement data of mid-career teachers (No. w16877). National Bureau of Economic Research (2011). https://doi.org/10.3386/w1687

16. OECD: TALIS 2018 Results (Volume II): Teachers and School Leaders as Valued Professionals. TALIS, OECD Publishing (2020). https://doi.org/10.1787/19cf08df-en

17. Looney, J.: Developing High-Quality Teachers: teacher evaluation for improvement. Eur. J. Educ. 46(4), 440–455 (2011). https://doi.org/10.1111/j.1465-3435.2011.01492.x

18. Tuytens, M., Devos, G.: How to activate teachers through teacher evaluation? Sch. Effectiveness Sch. Improv. 25(4), 509–530 (2014). https://doi.org/10.1080/09243453.2013.842601

19. Edelson, D.C.: Design research: what we learn when we engage in design. J. Learn. Sci. 11(1), 105–121 (2002). https://doi.org/10.1207/S15327809JLS1101_4

# An Intelligent Chatbot Supporting Students in Massive Open Online Courses

Alessio Calabrese[1], Alessio Rivoli[1], Filippo Sciarrone[1(✉)] (iD),
and Marco Temperini[2] (iD)

[1] Faculty of Economics, Universitas Mercatorum, Piazza Mattei, 10, Rome, Italy
filippo.sciarrone@unimercatorum.it
[2] DIAG-Department of Computer, Control and Management Engineering,
Sapienza University of Rome, Rome, Italy
marte@diag.uniroma1.it

**Abstract.** In recent years, there has been an exponential growth in the demand for distance learning. In addition, the pandemic from COVID-19 has radically changed the techniques but also the teaching/learning methodologies. In such a picture, Massive Online Open Courses (MOOCs), are increasingly emerging on the Web. Due to the big number of students, in MOOCs the traditional monitoring and instructional interventions, performed by the teacher on individual learners, are of difficult, if not impossible, application. An Artificial Intelligence approach, based on Virtual Conversational Agents or Intelligent Chatbots, can help overcoming such difficulties. In this paper we present a system, at its early stage of development and based mainly on a deep learning model, able, at different levels, to suggest didactic material to students in a query/answer modality. It is able to answer students' questions by proposing didactic material taken both from a specific knowledge domain or from Wikipedia.

We investigate the potential of such an early stage implementation, through several case studies. We also present a qualitative evaluation, based on the case studies findings, which we think is encouraging towards the development and field experimentation of a whole system.

**Keywords:** MOOCs · Intelligent Chatbot · Deep Learning · Help Systems

## 1 Introduction

The last decade has witnessed an exponential growth in the request and provision of distance learning, supported by the means of Technology Enhanced Learning (TEL). Also the continuing experience with the COVID diseases has contributed to the process. One of the results in this evolution is in that, nowadays, there is a higher and higher demand for Massive Open Online Courses (MOOCs), whose more apparent characteristics is in the great, and possibly huge, number

C. S. González-González et al. (Eds.): ICWL 2022/SETE 2022, LNCS 13869, pp. 190–201, 2023.
https://doi.org/10.1007/978-3-031-33023-0_17

of enrolled students, to be supported via distance learning. Examples of MOOCs are *Coursera*[1] and *Udemy*[2] [22]. Meanwhile, several platforms, like edX[3] have emerged to help students select MOOCs available on the network. Consequently, all the stakeholders involved in educational processes, have been forced to study and propose new solutions for these kind of courses, from both the methodological and technological points of view. As a matter of fact, the technological advancements of the last decade, and their application to distance learning, have raised the issue of having to revise and adapt the teaching and learning methodologies, in order to apply fruitfully the new tools. Such tools are coming from the innovations given in the web technology, and from the Artificial Intelligence (AI) research, whereas MOOCs are an application field of particular importance: In a MOOC, due to the high number of learners, a personalized and adaptive support for them 1) is impossible to give for the teacher [14], and 2) can be given by an automated system, provided that such system is sophisticated enough to be able to offer a support "virtually" comparable with the one that could be offered by the teacher. From a technological point of view, large institutions offering MOOCs have been equipped with powerful means for information storing and management (*cloud*), with ultra-broadband and with powerful servers, while on the teaching point of view, they have made available multimedia and interactive materials, also based on social learning, using innovative teaching methodologies [11].

Another powerful alternative, both technological and methodological, is to offer students with a *Virtual Assistant Tutor*, i.e. a *Chatbot* to support students in their learning process in a personalized way [1]. Basically, a chatbot is software that simulates and processes human conversations (written or spoken), enabling users to interact with digital devices as if they were communicating with a real person [9]. Chatbots can be implemented at different levels, from a rudimentary program, responding to a single line question, to sophisticated digital assistants, able to learn from the interactions with the human user, and so to evolve, providing increasingly better levels of personalization [13]. The interactions with humans provide training, for a chatbot, and probably such "learning through training" ability is the chatbot's most appealing and innovative aspect: Basically, the more interactions (queries) they came to process, the better their future interactions and response precision will be. Such adaptability, which is obtained through machine learning algorithms, and the related advancements of deep learning [13,16,21], makes the chatbot technology progressively more and more useful in distance learning. Chatbots are very useful in those cases where teachers cannot help students individually as in the case of MOOCs. Moreover, the use of Artificial Intelligence in education is rapidly expanding, especially by proposing deep learning models to make chatbots more adaptive.

In this paper we present an intelligent chatbot that is supposed to provide learners with services classifiable at four levels. First it can operate as a guide

---

[1] https://www.coursera.org/.
[2] https://www.udemy.com/.
[3] https://www.federica.eu/partners/edx/.

through a FAQ (Frequently Asked Questions) system: given a learner's question (in Natural Language), the learner is pointed to a relevant question stored among the FAQ. The second level of support provides an answer to the question, synthesized out of the course "context" (basically the learning material and FAQs). The third level of service that the learner can have, is made of a set of recommended links to Wikipedia, defined by a sub-system of the chatbot, based on the question. The fourth level is basically the last solution, when all the previous levels resulted unsatisfactory for the learner: the question is submitted to the teacher, and the answer (together with the question) will become part of the FAQ sub-system. The implementation of the chatbot is mainly based on a deep learning module using an enhanced version of the BERT Natural Language Processing (NLP) model [7]. The novelty of this system, with respect to the literature, is in that it uses a concept of *didactic context*, which encompasses the knowledge domain (learning material and answers to questions) as it is available in the course, and the possibility to have, as suggestions, some Wikipedia links to relevant pages for the student question. The system is at its early stage of development and here we present four case studies, one for each service level, in order to evaluate, from a qualitative point of view, its potential.

This work is organized as follows. Section 2 briefly introduces some important works on intelligent chatbots using deep learning engines or in general machine learning techniques. Section 3 shows the architecture and the workflow of the system. In Sect. 4 two case studies are discussed for a first qualitative evaluation of the system, together with the final discussion of the *RQ*. Finally, in Sect. 5, some conclusions and indications for future work are drawn.

## 2   Related Work

A chatbot is an intelligent agent capable of interacting with a user, in order to provide an appropriate response to a user's question. The literature proposes many approaches addressing chatbots fo educational purposes, and in particular for e-learning systems and MOOCs [23]. We propose an intelligent chatbot, based on 4-service levels, where, through a suitable GUI, the student can post questions concerning the knowledge domain she is learning. The chatbot, thanks to its architecture, is able to post an answer built by using different dataset and models. It is well suited for students learning in a MOOC's environment where the teacher cannot support students face to face. Here we propose some comparisons of our system with relevant studies, hightailing the main functional differences. The first proposal is *MOOCBuddy* [8], a chatbot acting as a MOOC Recommender System based on users' social media profiles and interests. It is the first educational chatbot related to MOOCs. The main aim of this chatbot is to promote the Romanian MOOCs initiatives, stored in a updated database. Moreover this chatbot can assist individual learners to find MOOCs for their personal and professional development and teachers to integrate MOOCs in their courses. Differently, the main goal of our chatbot, at least in this prototype version, is to support students in a question/answer interactive learning process and is not based on social aspects. The second proposal is that of Amarnani et al. [3]. The authors propose a complete framework consisting of a chatbot for managing the questions asked by learners in MOOC platforms, reducing in this way the workload of the instructor to answer the learners' queries manually. Their system, composed of five functional modules, uses BERT for encoding and decoding purposes. These models are pre-trained on SQUAD 2.0 dataset [17].

Our system presents some similarities with this one. Both systems aim to helping students by means of a query/answer process, using a deep learning embedding core, whereas the main difference is in the layered provision of the answer proposed in our system: in our case the FAQs (first level of answer) are initially predefined by the teacher, and then extended with new FAQs when the need arises during the learners' learning process (fourth level). In the middle, the second level is based on a tokenization of the context (learning material) through the BERT engine, and the third level produces Wikipedia suggestions.

Pererira et al. [16] present a new method for peer-to-peer MOOC essays evaluation using voice recordings. For that aim, a chatbot in Telegram IM mobile app is used to perform new voice-recording assignments. Our system does not take into account voice recording but didactic material in text format.

In [6] the authors propose a chatbot using the deep learning NMT model with Tensorflow. The system was build-up of BRNN and attention mechanism. As the chatbot knowledge base the Reddit dataset was used. The model was used to perform English to English translation. Our system uses another kind of architecture, based on four levels to respond to students' questions.

## 3   The Chatbot

This section shows the architecture and the functional modules of the system. The chatbot is intended to provide an interactive tool to help students improve their learning in MOOCs. In fact, this approach is well suited for those courses having a huge number of enrolled students, where teachers cannot check the student's learning status individually. In particular, we propose a chatbot system where four levels of service are offered to a learner, when they ask a question. The question is entered in natural language, and is supposed to regard the knowledge domain of the course. To build the chatbot and run the deep learning engine, in this prototypical version, we used the *Google Colab*[4] platform, using Python as the programming language. Colab is a free *Jupyter* notebook environment that runs entirely in the Google cloud. It supports many popular machine learning libraries, easily loaded and used for deep learning projects. Colab is quite convenient, as it does not require a setup, while the notebooks that one creates can be simultaneously shared among members of a collaborating team.

---

[4] https://colab.research.google.com/.

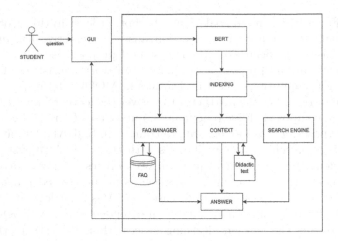

**Fig. 1.** The architecture of the system, composed of several functional blocks

## 3.1   The Architecture of the System

The overall architecture of the system is shown in Fig. 1. It consists of the following functional blocks:

- The *Student*. Students are the main actors using the system. They could be all the student of a MOOC, who need help during their learning process;
- The *Graphical User Interface* (GUI) module. It is the GUI used by the system to interact with learners. The learner can write directly the query into its appropriate section, and wait for the chatbot's response. The GUI is under development (a prototype is presented here) and has been designed to be adaptable to any computer device.
- The *BERT* engine module. BERT, *Bidirectional Encoder Representations from Transformers*, is an open source deep learning framework for NLP. It is designed to help computers understand the meaning of ambiguous language in text, by using surrounding text to establish context. The BERT framework was pre-trained using text from Wikipedia and can be fine-tuned with question/answer datasets [5]; For our chatbot's engine, we used a BERT modified version, called *DeBERTa* (Decoding-enhanced BERT with disentangled attention), a framework developed by Microsoft and based both on BERT and *RoBERTa*, which has been shown to be more efficient in text processing [7];
- The *FAQ MANAGER* module. This module is the module responsible for managing the FAQ archive, a repository of predefined questions/answers entered by the teacher and eventually extended by the users so to make it a personalized FAQ dataset;
- The *CONTEXT MANAGER* module. This module manages the context, that is a didactic dataset, containing all the subject-related data entered by the teacher and subsequently enriched by the query/answer process. This dataset

could be for example a large text containing a lesson or a generic didactic material in text format. Given the student's question, the BERT engine processes both the context and the query, producing the right answer to the student and thus providing the learner with an autonomously generated answer. The learner will be able to evaluate its correctness and validity by providing feedback to improve its performance;

– The *SEARCH ENGINE*. This module provides the student with a set of links to those Wikipedia pages deemed relevant to answering the student's question. In this way, the system's response is quick and compatible with the student's waiting time. This task is accomplished by means of the Wikipedia module which provides a set of python functions to process Wikipedia Links database;

– *TEACHER RESPONSE*. Should the student not be satisfied with the answers automatically generated by the system, then she can ask the teacher for help who can enter the answer manually. The couple (query, answer) will be added to the system FAQ dataset, i.e., to the Q/A library for future use, thus making the system constantly evolving;

– The *ANSWER* module. The task of this module is to transmit the answer generated by the system to the GUI which will display it on the user's screen, asking the learner her degree of satisfaction, to have a valuable feedback.

## 3.2 The System at Work

Here we describe a session of use of the system. The process starts when the student enters her question through the GUI.

Figure 2 shows its workflow. Given a learner's question, the system offers four distinct levels of processing, that are supposed to be performed sequentially, in such a way to perform a successive level when the previous level provided an answer that was considered unsatisfactory by the learner. In the following list we see details about the levels, and also the description of a preliminary training step.

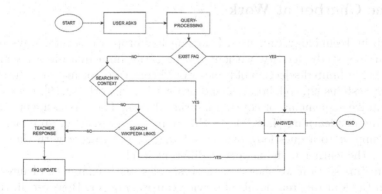

**Fig. 2.** The system at work.

- *System Initial Training.* As mentioned earlier, the system contains a deep learning module for the NLP, the CONTEXT MANAGER, which can process the didactic context, prepared by the teacher, and respond to the student appropriately. This module is implemented through a pre-trained model. It only needs to be run on the context;
- *Start.* The student inputs the question, in natural language, to the chatbot;
- *Query Processing*: the system start processing the question, by performing one of the following actions:
  1. Service level 1: processing the FAQ database. This search retrieves the FAQ most similar to the question posed by the student. In this initial version of the system, the FAQ database is predefined and fixed from the beginning by the teacher. The student can still view all of them to select the most relevant answer. If the student is not satisfied from the FAQ she can start the second level service;
  2. Service level 2: processing the context. If the question is not in the FAQ database, then the system will process the didactic context prepared by the teacher and, by means of the neural engine, build an answer that will be transmitted to the GUI module. If the user is not satisfied of the answer then can start the next service level;
  3. Service level 3: processing Wikipedia links. In this case, the system, through the Wikipedia processing module, based on the Wikipedia library, will process Wikipedia, retrieving a set of links to Wikipedia pages, relevant for the student's question. In this way the student can launch each page, improving her learning process. However, if the student is not satisfied by the answer, she can start the level 4 service;
  4. Service level 4: processing teacher's answer. Here the teacher can insert her answer manually. In this case the answer will be added to the FAQ database for future similar answers to other questions.

However, the student can activate each of the four services independently, at any stage of her learning process.

## 4   The Chatbot at Work

Research in Technology Enhanced Learning has proposed several ways to support learner's study activity, without a necessarily immediate interaction with the teacher: a limited selection of topics would comprise, for instance, Intelligent Tutoring Systems [2], collaborative and project based work [12,19], personalized and adaptive sequencing of course material [10,15], Peer Assessment, Gamification, Inquiry learning [4,18,20]. In this paper we present an approach based on the support to a question/answer exchange of the learner with the system, providing the learner with answers at different levels.

So, in this section we show four case studies, with examples of interaction in which the four different levels of service (answer) occur. However, in the real life use of the system, the student is allowed to run one of the chatbot's help levels without following any sequential order. These case studies allow for an initial qualitative analysis of the potential offered by the system, evaluated on the prototype we have presented here. To this aim a first GUI has been developed on a stand-alone client. As a learning domain or topic, for the case studies, we chose the concept of *Recursion*, for a programming language course. This is a concept that is sometimes difficult for students to understand and thus it appears well suited to illustrate the levels of help given by the system. To implement the context, we produced a text concerning the recursion concept.

## 4.1  Case Study 1: The FAQ Level of Service

This case study is the base case, where the student, in this case, submits the question: *What is recursion?* and waits for the answer as shown in Fig. 3.

question

What is recursion?

Clear                                    Submit

**Fig. 3.** The question *What is recursion?* is directly posed by the student, by first writing it in the appropriate space and then pressing the *Submit* key.

Subsequently, the system returns the nearest FAQ, retrieved by the FAQ Manager from the FAQ database and transmitted to the GUI, to be visualized to the student (see previous section for technical details). Figure 4 shows the GUI with the answer: *Recursive functions are functions that call themselves* corresponding to the retrieved FAQ.

output

Recursive functions are functions that calls itself

**Fig. 4.** An example of level 1 service. In this case the answer has been retrieved directly from the FAQ database.

## 4.2  Case Study 2: The Context Level of Service

If the student is not satisfied by the FAQ, or if the question is not present in the FAQ database, she can ask for the CONTEXT module to run. Consequently, the BERT module processes the context, i.e., the didactic unit prepared by the teacher on the particular topic (i.e. Recursion), and returns an answer to the student. In Fig. 5, the first step where the student posts her question ( the same of the previous example), while in Fig. 6 the chatbot's answer is visualized. This case study shows the use of the deep learning module, capable to process a large text in natural language. In fact, the answer is built processing the didactic unit proposed by the teacher.

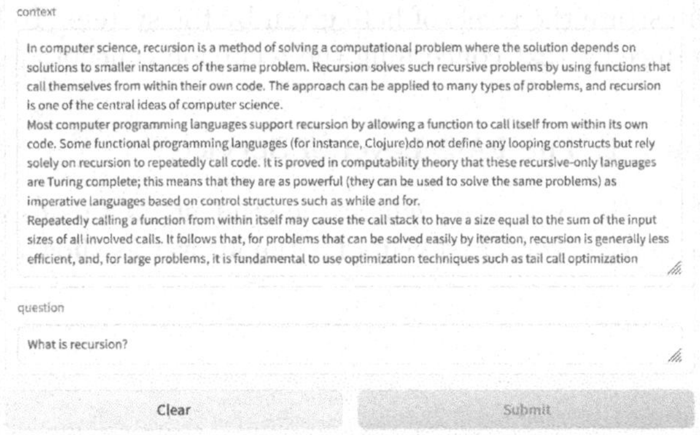

context

In computer science, recursion is a method of solving a computational problem where the solution depends on solutions to smaller instances of the same problem. Recursion solves such recursive problems by using functions that call themselves from within their own code. The approach can be applied to many types of problems, and recursion is one of the central ideas of computer science.
Most computer programming languages support recursion by allowing a function to call itself from within its own code. Some functional programming languages (for instance, Clojure)do not define any looping constructs but rely solely on recursion to repeatedly call code. It is proved in computability theory that these recursive-only languages are Turing complete; this means that they are as powerful (they can be used to solve the same problems) as imperative languages based on control structures such as while and for.
Repeatedly calling a function from within itself may cause the call stack to have a size equal to the sum of the input sizes of all involved calls. It follows that, for problems that can be solved easily by iteration, recursion is generally less efficient, and, for large problems, it is fundamental to use optimization techniques such as tail call optimization

question

What is recursion?

Clear                                    Submit

**Fig. 5.** Processing the (didactic) context: an example of level 2 sevice.

output

a method of solving a computational problem where the solution depends on solutions to smaller instances of the same problem

**Fig. 6.** The answer using a service-level 2.

## 4.3   Case Study 3: The Wikipedia Level of Service

This case study starts when the student wants to be directly connected to Wikipedia pages. To this aim she first writes her question into the GUI, in this case: *What is python recursion?*. After that, the system, through the Wikipedia Manager module, retrieves a number of links to be shown, in this case: *https: en. wikipedia. org wiki Recursion_ (computer_science)*. Consequently, the student, by clicking it, will study the topic of interest directly on the retrieved Wikipedia page, directly visualized by the system. Figure 7 shows the question, while the Fig. 8 shows the retrieved relevant Wikipedia link.

question

what is python recursion?

Clear                                    Submit

**Fig. 7.** Wikipedia search question

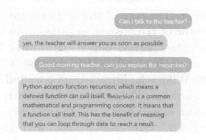

**Fig. 8.** Wikipedia search response

## 4.4    Case Study 4: The Teacher Level of Service

In this case, the teacher is asked to answer manually to the student. Figure 9 shows the question/answer process in the GUI.

**Fig. 9.** Level four of service: the teacher's answer is asynchronously edited.

## 4.5    Discussion

The four case studies allowed only a qualitative analysis about the 4-level chatbot's capabilities to support students to learn in a question/answer context.

The first case study illustrated the simplest case, that is, the case where the student finds the question (s)he wanted to ask exactly in the FAQ database.

The second case study highlighted the use of context, that is, the use of the BERT model on a didactic context, that is a didactic unit prepared manually or imported by the teacher and concerning the topic of learning. In this case, the question and answer, if deemed consistent by the student can be saved in the FAQ database for a future use.

The third case study concerns the student's possibility to use Wikipedia to study didactic material consistent with the question posed. In this case the system returns a set of links to potential relevant Wikipedia pages, ready to be learned.

The last case, concerns the student's being unsatisfied with the answers given at the previous levels: now the teacher is summoned; (s)he will receive the question and compose an answer. The teacher's answer, together with the question, is provided to the learner, and also stored in the context (in the FAQ database).

The case studies show that, although at the current state of development of the system, which is quite bare-bone and is not offering an effective interface, yet the four levels of service provide the learner with progressive ways to answer a question, that can ease the learner deepening her/his knowledge at her/his own pace and satisfaction. The system also provides the teacher with a way to extend the response capabilities of the system, by 1) solving the problem of lacking answers, 2) enriching the learning context in the process, and 3) being summoned only in a limited amount of cases.

## 5   Conclusions and Future Work

We presented an intelligent chatbot designed to help a MOOC student to learn through the query/answer model. Posted a question by the student, the chatbot provides an answer service based on 4-service levels: FAQ, CONTEXT, WIKIPEDIA, and Teacher. The core of the architecture is in the BERT encoding model, as a constructor of the answer to propose for the learner's question. In the CONTEXT case, the chatbot builds the answer based on the didactic unit prepared by the teacher. In the WIKIPEDIA case, when the previous levels result unsatisfactory, the Wikipedia library is used to find links to relevant pages related to the student's question. The system is in an early stage of development, so we could not propose an experimentation to validate it; instead we opted for the selection of a set of significant case studies, with the idea of proposing a qualitative evaluation, and show the potentialities of the system. A full implementation, with suitable graphic interface, is planned for the future work. This will make an experimentation possible, with real students.

## References

1. Adamopoulou, E., Moussiades, L.: An overview of chatbot technology. In: Maglogiannis, I., Iliadis, L., Pimenidis, E. (eds.) AIAI 2020. IAICT, vol. 584, pp. 373–383. Springer, Cham (2020). https://doi.org/10.1007/978-3-030-49186-4_31
2. Almasri, A., et al.: Intelligent tutoring systems survey for the period 2000–2018. In: Proceedings IJAER2019 (2019)
3. Amarnani, S., Bhagat, N., Ekade, H., Gupta, A., Sahu, S.: A complete chatbot based architecture for answering user's course-related queries in MOOC platforms. In: 2021 International Conference on Computing, Communication and Green Engineering (CCGE), pp. 1–7. IEEE (2021)
4. Bell, T., Urhahne, D., Schanze, S., Ploetzner, R.: Collaborative inquiry learning: models, tools, and challenges. Int. J. Sci. Educ. **32**(3), 349–377 (2010)
5. Devlin, J., Chang, M.W., Lee, K., Toutanova, K.: Bert: Pre-training of deep bidirectional transformers for language understanding. arXiv preprint arXiv:1810.04805 (2018)
6. Dhyani, M., Kumar, R.: An intelligent chatbot using deep learning with bidirectional RNN and attention model. Mater. Today: Proc. **34**, 817–824 (2021)
7. He, P., Liu, X., Gao, J., Chen, W.: DeBERTa: decoding-enhanced BERT with disentangled attention. arXiv preprint arXiv:2006.03654 (2020)
8. Holotescu, C., Holotescu, V.: MOOCBuddy: a chatbot for personalized learning with MOOCs. In: Proceedings of RoCHI (2016)

9. Hussain, S., Ameri Sianaki, O., Ababneh, N.: A survey on conversational agents/chatbots classification and design techniques. In: Barolli, L., Takizawa, M., Xhafa, F., Enokido, T. (eds.) WAINA 2019. AISC, vol. 927, pp. 946–956. Springer, Cham (2019). https://doi.org/10.1007/978-3-030-15035-8_93

10. Limongelli, C., Sciarrone, F., Temperini, M., Vaste, G.: Lecomps5: a web-based learning system for course personalization and adaptation. In: Proceedings of IADIS International Conference e-Learning, pp. 325–332 (2008)

11. N. Bezus, S., A. Abduzhalilov, K., K. Raitskaya, L.: Distance learning nowadays: the usage of didactic potential of MOOCs (on platforms coursera, edx, universarium) in higher education. In: 2020 The 4th International Conference on Education and Multimedia Technology, pp. 14–19 (2020)

12. Nelson, M., Ponciano, L.: Experiences and insights from using Github classroom to support project-based courses. In: 2021 Third International Workshop on Software Engineering Education for the Next Generation (SEENG), pp. 31–35 (2021). https://doi.org/10.1109/SEENG53126.2021.00013

13. Okonkwo, C.W., Ade-Ibijola, A.: Chatbots applications in education: a systematic review. Comput. Educ. Artif. Intell. **2**, 100033 (2021)

14. Palacios Hidalgo, F.J., Huertas Abril, C.A., Gómez Parra, M.: MOOCs: origins, concept and didactic applications: a systematic review of the literature (2012–2019). Technol. Knowl. Learn. **25**(4), 853–879 (2020)

15. Peng, H., Ma, S., Spector, J.: Personalized adaptive learning: an emerging pedagogical approach enabled by a smart learning environment. Smart Learn. Environ. **6**(9), 1–14 (2019)

16. Pereira, J., Fernández-Raga, M., Osuna-Acedo, S., Roura-Redondo, M., Almazán-López, O., Buldón-Olalla, A.: Promoting learners' voice productions using chatbots as a tool for improving the learning process in a MOOC. Technol. Knowl. Learn. **24**(4), 545–565 (2019)

17. Rajpurkar, P., Jia, R., Liang, P.: Know what you don't know: unanswerable questions for SQuAD (2018)

18. Sailer, M., Hense, J.U., Mayr, S.K., Mandl, H.: How gamification motivates: an experimental study of the effects of specific game design elements on psychological need satisfaction. Comput. Hum. Behav. **69**, 371–380 (2017)

19. Sterbini, A., Temperini, M.: Collaborative projects and self evaluation within a social reputation-based exercise-sharing system. In: Proceedings of IEEE/WIC/ACM International Joint Conference on Web Intelligence and Intelligent Agent Technology, pp. 243–246 (2009)

20. Sterbini, A., Temperini, M.: Analysis of open answers via mediated peer-assessment. In: Proceedings of 17th International Conference on System Theory, Control and Computing (ICSTCC), pp. 663–668 (2013)

21. Suta, P., Lan, X., Wu, B., Mongkolnam, P., Chan, J.: An overview of machine learning in chatbots. Int. J. Mech. Eng. Robot. Res. **9**(4), 502–510 (2020)

22. Wang, Y., Song, J.: What makes a massive open online courses (MOOCs) excellent? an investigation in business analytics courses. In: AMCIS 2021 (2021). https://aisel.aisnet.org/amcis2021/is_education/sig_education/4

23. Wong, J.S., Pursel, B., Divinsky, A., Jansen, B.J.: An analysis of cognitive learning context in mooc forum messages. In: Proceedings of the 2016 CHI Conference Extended Abstracts on Human Factors in Computing Systems, pp. 1315–1321 (2016)

# Using a MOOC to Train Teachers to Design and Deliver MOOCs

Carlos Vaz de Carvalho[1]([✉]) [iD], Diana Andone[2] [iD], Vlad Mihaescu[2] [iD],
Cengiz Hakan Aydin[3] [iD], Elif Toprak[3] [iD], Evrim Genc-Kumtepe[3], Olga Zubikova[4] [iD],
Tim Brueggemann[4], Sonja Intveen[4], Rita Butkiene[5] [iD], Daina Gudoniene[5],
and Edgaras Dambrauskas[5]

[1] Porto Polytechnic, Porto, Portugal
cmc@isep.ipp.pt
[2] Politehnica University of Timisoara, Timisoara, Romania
[3] Anadolu University, Eskisehir, Turkey
[4] Fachhochschule des Mittelstands, Bielefeld, Germany
[5] Kaunas University of Technology, Kaunas, Lithuania

**Abstract.** The open and online nature of Massive Online Open Courses (MOOC) can be a way to improve the success and efficiency of formal educational paths in Higher Education because the MOOC model provides a flexible approach that promotes different ways of learning. However, teachers must be trained and confident so that they can fully explore the methodologies, tools and resources that result from the integration of MOOCs into a formal curricula. This article reports the results of a MOOC-based training program, created and implemented in the scope of a European project, aimed at enabling teachers from Higher Education Institutions (HEIs) to develop and deliver MOOCs. The training clearly contributed to increasing the teachers' competences related to those objectives and was a relevant component for their professional development namely in terms of adopting innovating teaching practices.

**Keywords:** Massive Open Online Classes (MOOCs) · Online Education · Higher Education · Engineering Education

## 1 Introduction

The advantages of using Massive Online Open Courses (MOOCs) and educational processes based on the sharing and reuse of open resources have been established in several studies [1–4]. MOOCs promise flexibility, affordable access and fast-track completion at a low cost for learners [5].

In Higher Education, the use of MOOCs follows the need for flexible and innovative learning approaches to improve the quality of the educational offers and to promote the diversity of learners [6]. The integration of MOOC-based approaches in formal education paths offers Higher Education Institutions (HEIs) the opportunity to improve teaching, encourages them to develop distinctive missions including considerations about

C. S. González-González et al. (Eds.): ICWL 2022/SETE 2022, LNCS 13869, pp. 202–213, 2023.
https://doi.org/10.1007/978-3-031-33023-0_18

openness and access for different groups of students and "…provides them with a vehicle to think creatively and innovatively and to explore new pedagogical practices, business models and flexible learning paths in their provision" [5]. MOOCs in fact exploit the transformational benefits of digital and online technologies to enrich teaching, improve personalized learning experiences [7], therefore supporting active learning processes through technology [8]. Incorporating MOOCs in traditionally taught courses allows to: "replaying lectures, augmenting or replacing secondary materials, filling gaps in expertise, exposing students to other styles of teaching and class discussion, reinforcing key skills, and teaching students how to teach online" [9].

All these needs have become even more relevant and pressing because of the COVID-19 pandemic that forced almost (if not) all of the HEIs to move to online education. Nevertheless, most HEIs are still very reluctant in adopting MOOCs as part of their learning methodologies [10]. This might be a consequence of the natural inertia of these organizations that prevents the adoption of new educational paradigms, but it can also come from the resistance of the teachers and students to new forms of teaching and learning that requires adjustments to their established practices. The acknowledged high dropout rate in MOOCs (typically, only a very small fraction of the enrolled students, as low as 5%, completes a course) can be another factor that delays the adoption of these methodologies [11]. This dropout rate is often attributed to the specific requirements needed to be able to cope with the teaching and learning strategies used in MOOCs like having extended digital skills, possessing the adequate connected equipment, mastering self-management, self-direction and autonomous learning skills [12]. According to Onah, Sinclair, and Boyatt other reasons for this low completion rate are related to ineffective teaching strategies and learning environments that result in a feeling of isolation among learners [13]. Eriksson et al. also propose time availability as a defining factor for the high – up to 90% of the enrolled students - dropout rates [14].

Combining MOOC-based learning with formal educational processes allows to eliminate or at least minimize most of the factors leading to these high dropout rates while creating flexible and motivating environments for the students. The positive experience of incorporating MOOCs into formal education has been demonstrated by the Centre for Teaching Development and Digital Media at the Aarhus University in Denmark where the master program in ICT based Educational Design has been partly delivered as an Open Online Course for the benefit of the full-time students registered at the university and at the same time opened for students/learners outside the university [15]. This pedagogical experiment resulted in the high completion rate by both target groups. These positive results have also been demonstrated in other models that integrate MOOCs in Higher Education as the ones proposed by Bruff et al. [16], Firmin et al. [17] and Martin [18]. Wang & Zhu introduced a very interesting combination of MOOCs and flipped learning with an excellent success rate [19]. Sezgin and Cirak provide a systematic review of use of MOOCs in Engineering Education, with the different models and success rates achieved [20].

As such, the design and development of MOOCs must be carefully addressed and teachers must be prepared to do it by having a solid knowledge of open pedagogies, of MOOC design, development, and delivery techniques, of the needs of learners with different social and cultural backgrounds and of the required digital and online technologies.

MODE IT was a transnational collaboration project between HEIs in different European countries that pursued a common goal towards opening educational services to wider audiences tackling the aforementioned issues and boosting the HEI educators' awareness and skills for MOOCs design and delivery [21]. To accomplish this objective, the following results/outputs were developed:

- Self-assessment tool for HEI educators, an online tool that allows teachers to self-assess their competence to design and deliver MOOC-based teaching and determines concrete areas for skill improvement. A more complete description and evaluation of this tool is available in [22].
- A training program on MOOC design and delivery to support teachers in the redesign of existing courses into MOOCs, designing new MOOCs, integrating MOOCs into existing formal curricula, and creating personalized learning environments. The training itself adopted a MOOC approach.

The MODE IT project was expected to have a positive impact on participants in the following ways:

- HEI teachers develop their pedagogical and digital skills.
- HEIs offer innovative partly open curricula to their students, increasing their competitiveness and attracting more students. They are also able to offer training to a wider audience, including non-formal, informal and lifelong learners.
- HEI students' motivation to learn and subsequent satisfaction grows due to the innovative flexible model and the engaging learning environment.

## 2   MOOC Design and Delivery Program

As mentioned before, the MODE IT MOOC-based training program was aimed at enabling teachers from HEIs to develop and deliver MOOCs as well as to be able to integrate MOOCs into formal curricula in a didactically sound manner. By having the program itself designed as a MOOC, the delivery strategy of the program also contributed to a better practical understanding of how a MOOC could be designed and delivered. The general learning outcomes were designed to allow learners, in the end, to be able to...:

- understand and explain the foundations of open learning;
- design MOOC scenarios considering the specifics of different type of students;
- create and/or select suitable digital contents for a MOOC;
- analyze and select an appropriate platform for MOOC delivery;
- understand the principles of the integration of MOOCs and/or MOOC-based pedagogies into formal curricula.

The training consisted of 5 standalone modules, organized according to the general learning outcomes which covered different theoretical and practical aspects of MOOCs:

**Module 1: Foundations of Online Learning**

- Online learning theoretical background
- Designing online learning scenarios
- Making online learning interactive and engaging

**Module 2: MOOC Course Design**

- Introduction to MOOCs: specific theoretical considerations
- Designing online learning scenarios for large cohorts of students
- Designing learning materials for MOOCs
- Creating assessment activities for MOOCs
- Assessing quality of MOOCs

**Module 3: MOOC Content Production**

- Making good educational videos
- Producing educational videos in studio and at home
- Producing other types of materials for MOOCs (presentations with voice-overs, animated presentations, etc.)
- Locating, assessing the quality, and using Open Educational Resources

**Module 4: MOOC Delivery**

- Using major MOOC Platforms to deliver MOOCs
- Using other online education delivery tools (LMS, local servers, etc.)
- Using communication tools (conferencing, chat, social media) to establish effective and engaging interaction with and between learners
- Using analytical tools to monitor learners' activities and performance

**Module 5: MOOC in Formal Learning**

- Designing MOOCs for curriculum integration
- Setting up virtual support communities

Each module was expected to be completed in 2 weeks and required a student's workload of approximately 12 h. The contents and activities for each module consisted of several short learning videos of approximately 5–7 min, supplementary learning materials (written texts enriched with links to further sources), quizzes for self-assessment, and assignment tasks which were peer-evaluated. Detailed information about the MOOC macro and microstructure can be obtained in [21].

The piloting phase of the training began on May 24, 2021 and finished on August 1, 2021. Following the individual results of the self-assessment tool, the participants were free to select and attend the modules that concerned their specific interest and needs [22]. Therefore, it was not compulsory to complete all the 5 modules or to follow them sequentially. However, for almost all the participants, the selected option was effectively to follow sequentially the 5 modules. During the piloting phase, teachers from the MODE IT partner institutions provided organizational, pedagogical and technical support to participants.

At the end of module 5, participants completed a final project work by creating their own small-scale MOOCs, therefore proving the skills and competencies obtained from the training. They also began preparing the MOOC-based educational mode for their own teaching practices.

52 teachers registered for the training program and were active participants meaning that they viewed learning videos and materials and/or completed assessment tasks. The numbers on the completion of each module are represented in the Table 1 (numbers obtained from the MOOC delivery supporting platform).

**Table 1.** Completion of the IO2 training modules by participants (in absolute figures and in percentage, n = 52)

| Module | Completed by … persons | % |
|---|---|---|
| Module 1 | 49 | 94% |
| Module 2 | 27 | 52% |
| Module 3 | 21 | 40% |
| Module 4 | 20 | 38% |
| Module 5 | 16 | 31% |

As can be seen from Table 1, at least 16 active users (31% of the total), have completed the entire training. This is quite a good result, bearing in mind the global average MOOC completion rate, which is normally below 13% [23] or even 5% [13]. Nevertheless, it was not possible to completely prevent a negative dynamic on the module completion. The most significant dropout rate was registered after the completion of Module 1 of the training: 22 from the 49 active participants (about 45%) did not complete the following module. After that a more stable completion rate was registered.

## 3   Results

Upon completion of the training, participants were asked to share their views, opinions and their level of satisfaction with the training. An online anonymous survey was created and delivered to the participants covering the following aspects:

- Demographics
- General data about the level of the completion of the training
- Satisfaction with the training
- Knowledge and skills obtained from the training
- Impact of the training and outlook
- Reasons for the non-completion of the training/module

In addition, attendees were invited to openly share their thoughts about the training using a set of open questions. In the end, 25 persons (48% of the active participants) participated in the online survey and their feedback is presented next.

### 3.1 Demographics

The age distribution of the participants was as follows:

- under 30 years old: 2 persons (8%),
- between 31–39 years old: 12 persons (48%),
- between 40–49 years old: 6 persons (24%),
- between 50–59 years old: 3 persons (12%),
- over 60 years: 2 persons (8%).

The participants to the survey came from the 5 countries of the project partnership:

- Germany: 4 persons (16%),
- Lithuania: 9 persons (36%),
- Portugal: 5 persons (20%),
- Romania: 5 persons (20%),
- Turkey: 2 persons (8%).

Regarding gender, the majority of respondents (19) were female (76% of the total) and 6 (24%) were male. The respondents were teaching a wide range of subjects but the majority were Engineering subjects such as Chemistry, Civil Engineering, Computer Networks and Internet/Multimedia Technologies, Cyber Physical Systems, Data Structures, Informatics, Mathematics, Medical Informatics and Biostatistics, Structural Analysis, Assembly Processes and Technologies. 16% of respondents were teaching subjects related to Business and Administration, such as Business & Project Management, Accounting, Competitor Analysis, Marketing. 12% of respondents were teaching Languages (English and German) and 4% were teaching Social Sciences and Journalism and Pedagogical and Organisational Psychology.

### 3.2 Level of the Training Completion

Participants provided information on the modules they had completed, which followed a similar distribution of the numbers obtained from the platform. Nevertheless, the level of achievement reported by the participants was higher than the data recorded by the platform – this discrepancy was probably caused by the fact that the participants that replied to the questionnaire were the ones that followed the MOOC for a longer time.

As illustrated in the Fig. 1 above, 33% of the survey respondents completed all the 5 modules of the training. The completion rate constantly decreased from the previous to each subsequent module of the training. This was somehow predictable as, like mentioned previously, a certain dropout rate is quite typical for such type of courses.

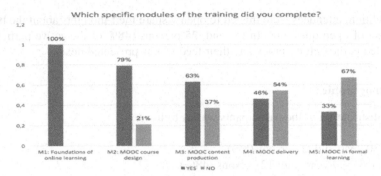

**Fig. 1.** Completion of each training module

## 3.3  Satisfaction with the Training/Module(s)

Participants were asked to indicate their level of satisfaction with different aspects of the training or of the module(s) they completed by evaluating the following eight statements:

- The structure of the training/module(s) was clear and comprehensive;
- The duration of the training/module(s) was appropriate;
- The workload of the training/module(s) was appropriate;
- The contents of the module(s) were aligned with the learning outcomes;
- Learning materials were of good quality;
- The supportive instructions of module facilitators were helpful;
- There was an appropriate mix of individual and peer learning tasks;
- The program/module(s) has met my expectations and needs.

As can be seen in Fig. 2, almost all aspects of the training achieved the threshold of 50% of positive answers, which are represented with the answer options "Rather agree" and "Strongly agree". Among the training aspects, which have received the highest scores, were:

- Clear and comprehensive structure of the training (88% of respondents),
- Alignment of the training contents with the learning outcomes (84%),
- Appropriate duration of the training (71%), closely followed by the aspects "Appropriateness of workload" and "Supportive instructions of module facilitators" (each 67%).
- The aspect relating to the appropriateness of individual and peer learning tasks received in total 46% of positive answers and at the same time the highest score of negative answers (26% composed of answer options "Rather disagree" and "Strongly disagree", each of 13%).

In addition, a few participants provided their individual open comments:

- "I missed the feedback on the assignments. I expected feedback after each module, to help me improve myself."

- "I have to express 3 main limitations, but the rest was perfect:) Some of the module videos were hard to understand due to heavy accent (especially the ones in the first module). Plus, some speakers' way of looking at the prompter was disturbing and felt a bit weird while watching. These were the issues with the materials. Next problem, some tasks were not very clear (especially the ones in the last module). What was sad was, even though some participants asked for more explanation in the forum, no one answered ☹ Lastly, I would have preferred to receive more feedback on the assignments I submitted. I only got some feedback from the second module's instructors, that's it. I submitted many assignments and many posts on the forums, yet there was no response and therefore I don't know if I did well or not... Other than these points, I learned soooo much here! Honestly, it forced me to be involved with MOOCs more than ever! Loved it, enjoyed it, and feeling grateful for all the efforts that the team put into it. Thank you for giving us this opportunity."
- "During some modules, the teachers were remarkably absent (no guidance, no interaction, no feed-back)."
- "This MOOC was clearly a good opportunity."
- "I only completed a few modules, but I intend to continue with all modules in my own pace."
- "Lovely videos in Module 2, great supporting materials. Great content on the module 1. Due to its nature, it's more theoretical, but these basics are highly needed."

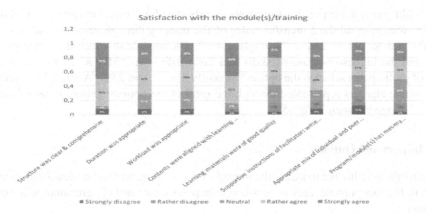

**Fig. 2.** Satisfaction of participants with different aspects of the training/training module(s)

In response to a few of the concerns mentioned in the respondents' comments, the following should be mentioned:

- To facilitate attendees' understanding of the spoken English of non-native speakers, the learning videos were supplemented with supporting subtitles, which reflected the contents of the videos and were made available to the attendees.
- In an open online training course the instructors' feedback has to be balanced with peer interaction. This is why each module included assignment task(s) aimed at receiving

feedback from peers rather than from the module facilitators. We understand that peer-support was not strong enough in this course to counterbalance some feeling of isolation from the users and that aspect should be improved.

### 3.4 Knowledge and Skills Obtained

Participants were invited to evaluate to which extent they had improved their skills and knowledge in the specific areas of the training. Each module was evaluated by different numbers of respondents depending on the completion level of the module concerned (Fig. 3).

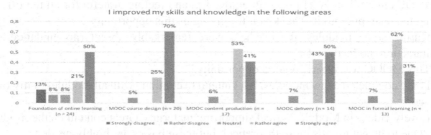

**Fig. 3.** Improvement of skills and knowledge in the modules

As illustrated in the Fig. 3, participants clearly stated the improvement of their skills and knowledge in all the 5 areas/modules of the training through selecting the answer options "Rather agree" and/or "Strongly agree". The module in which the participants indicated the highest increase of skills and knowledge was "MOOC course design": 70% of participants selected the option "Strongly agree", and 25% "Agree". In general, the positive answers represented through the total of the options "Strongly agree" and "Agree" range between 71%–95%.

### 3.5 Impact and Outlook

Participants were invited to assess the impact of the training on their professional development. For this purpose, they were asked to express their level of agreement with four statements:

- The training inspired me to innovate my teaching;
- I have concrete ideas obtained from the training towards applying new skills and knowledge in my teaching;
- The training was relevant for my professional development;

As can be seen in Fig. 4, the majority of the respondents provided positive answers regarding the impact of the training. In particular, 87% of respondents stated that they obtained concrete ideas for their teaching from the training and 66% indicated that the training provided them with some inspiration towards innovating their teaching.

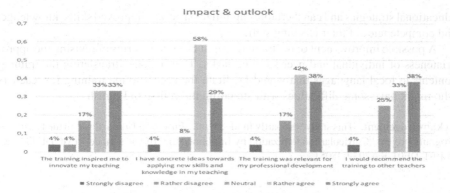

**Fig. 4.** Impact of the training on the participants

- 80% of respondents agreed that the training was relevant for their professional development and 71% of respondents would recommend the training further to their colleagues.
- 4% of respondents (1 person) constantly indicated the option "Strongly disagree" when assessing the impact of the training.

Finally, the respondents were invited to share their further ideas, recommendations and suggestions for improvements on the training/module(s). The most frequent comment related to the inclusion of more practical activities in the MOOC.

## 4  Conclusions

The detailed analysis of the feedback of the participants about the quality and impact of the open online training course on MOOC (re)design and delivery revealed a high level of satisfaction with the different aspects of the training. Among others, the respondents appreciated the clear and comprehensive structure of the MOOC, its duration and workload, the alignment of the training contents with the learning outcomes and were satisfied with the supportive instructions of module facilitators. At the same time, some participants wished more interaction with trainers.

The training has clearly contributed to increasing teachers' competences related to the design and delivery of MOOCs and their integration into formal curricula. It was considered a relevant part of teachers' professional development as well as encouraged the course participants to innovate their teaching.

Nevertheless, it was possible to observe that there were 1 or 2 participants (4%–8% of the respondents) that expressed some dissatisfaction with most aspects of the training (they selected the option "Strongly disagree"). This clearly shows that MOOC-based learning, although being clearly a positive approach to solving some of the success issues of HEI, is still not a solution for everyone and other learning and teaching preferences must still be catered for. In any case, the innovation potential provided by MOOCs was shown to be very promising for HEIs which are interested in modernizing their educational strategies and can therefore capitalize on new or improved skills, knowledge, and competencies of their teaching staff.

A possible improvement of the training might be done in terms of revising the appropriateness of individual and peer learning tasks. That includes translating the training contents to local languages that would facilitate the access to the training for teachers who might have some difficulties with attending the course in English.

**Acknowledgement.** This study was partly funded by the European Union, through the Erasmus+ program, project "Curricular modernization by implementing MOOCs model" (MODE IT), ref. 2019-1-DE01-KA203-005051.

# References

1. Vaz de Carvalho, C., Escudeiro, P., Caeiro Rodríguez, M., Llamas Nistal, M.: Sustainability strategies for open educational resources and repositories. In: Proceedings of LACLO 2016 – Latin American Conference on Learning Objects, Fortuna, Costa Rica (2016)
2. Economides, A., Perifanou, M.: MOOC affordances model. In: Proceedings of the 2018 IEEE Global Engineering Education Conference (EDUCON), pp. 605–611 (2018). https://doi.org/10.1109/EDUCON.2018.8363285
3. Heckel, U., Bach, U., Richert, A., Jeschke, S.: Massive Open Online Courses in engineering education. In: Frerich, S., et al. (eds.) Engineering Education 4.0, pp. 31–45. Springer, Cham (2016). ISBN: 978-1-7281-0930-5/20/$31.00 ©2020 IEEE Global Engineering Education Conference (EDUCON), 27–30 April 2020, Porto, Portugal, p. 1846. IEEE (2020)
4. Luan, Y.Y., He, E., Gao, D.: Discussion about the application of MOOC in engineering education. In: Proceedings International Conference on Management Science and Management Innovation (MSMI), pp. 540–543 (2015)
5. Yuan, L., Powell, S.: MOOCs and Open Education: Implications for Higher Education (2013). http://publications.cetis.ac.uk/2013/667
6. EC-DGHRS: Strategic Plan (2015). https://ec.europa.eu/info/sites/info/files/strategic-plan-2016-2020-dghr_july2016_en_0.pdf
7. EC: The Communication on Rethinking Education (2013). https://ec.europa.eu/digital-single-market/en/news/communication-rethinking-education
8. Vaz de Carvalho, C., Bauters, M.: Technology to support active learning in higher education. In: Vaz de Carvalho, C., Bauters, M. (eds.) Technology Supported Active Learning. LNET, pp. 1–11. Springer, Singapore (2021). https://doi.org/10.1007/978-981-16-2082-9_1
9. Griffiths, R., Chingos, M., Mulhern, C., Spies, R.: Interactive online learning on campus: testing MOOCs and other platforms in hybrid formats in the University System of Maryland (ITHAKA S+R Report) (2014). http://www.sr.ithaka.org/sites/default/files/reports/SR_Interactive_Online_Learning_Campus_20140716.pdf
10. Kizilcec, R.F., Piech, C., Schneider, E.: Deconstructing disengagement: analyzing learner subpopulations in massive open online courses. In: Proceedings of the Third International Conference on Learning Analytics and Knowledge, pp. 170–179 (2013)
11. EADTU: PORTO Declaration on European MOOCs (2016). http://home.eadtu.eu/images/News/Porto_Declaration_on_European_MOOCs_Final.pdf
12. Seaton, J.X., Schwier, R.: An exploratory case study of online instructors: factors associated with instructor engagement. Int. J. E-Learn. Distance Educ. **29**(1), 1–16 (2014). http://ijede.ca/index.php/jde/article/view/870/1536

13. Onah, D., Sinclair, J.: Measuring self-regulated learning in a novel e-learning platform. In: Proceedings of the 15th Koli Calling Conference on Computing Education Research, pp. 167–168 (2015). https://doi.org/10.1145/2828959.2828986
14. Eriksson, T., Adawi, T., Stöhr, C.: "Time is the bottleneck": a qualitative study exploring why learners drop out of MOOCs. J. Comput. High. Educ. **29**, 133–146 (2017). https://doi.org/10.1007/s12528-016-9127-8
15. Bang, J., Dalsgaard, C., Kjær, A., Donovan, M.M.O.: Opening up education the Danish way: considerations based on the redesign of a Master programme in ICT-based Educational Design. In: Paper Presented at EADTU Conference 2014: The Open and Flexible Higher Education Conference, Krakow, Poland (2014). http://conference.eadtu.eu/images/Proceedings/Conference_2014_-_proceedings.pdf
16. Bruff, D.O., Fisher, D.H., McEwen, K.E., Smith, B.E.: Wrapping a MOOC: student perceptions of an experiment in blended learning. J. Online Learn. Teach. **9**(2), 187–199 (2013)
17. Firmin, R., Schiorring, E., Whitmer, J., Willett, T., Collins, E.D., Sujitparapitaya, S.: Case study: using MOOCs for conventional college coursework. Distance Educ. **35**(2), 178–201 (2014)
18. Martin, F.G.: Will massive open online courses change how we teach? Commun. ACM **55**(8), 26–28 (2012)
19. Wang, K., Zhu, C.: MOOC-based flipped learning in higher education: students' participation, experience and learning performance. Int. J. Educ. Technol. High. Educ. **16**, 33 (2019). https://doi.org/10.1186/s41239-019-0163-0
20. Sezgin, S., Cirak, N.S.: The role of MOOCs in engineering education: an exploratory systematic review of peer-reviewed literature. Comput. Appl. Eng. Educ. **29**, 950–968 (2021). https://doi.org/10.1002/cae.22350
21. Vaz de Carvalho, C., Butkiene, R., Gudoniene, D., Zubikova, O., Bruegmann, T.: A MOOC-based innovative instructional approach for curriculum design. In: Proceedings of the 2020 IEEE Global Engineering Education Conference (EDUCON) (2020)
22. Mihaescu, V., et al.: Self-assessing teachers' competences for curricula modernization through MOOCs. In: Lopata, A., Gudonienė, D., Butkienė, R. (eds.) ICIST 2021. CCIS, vol. 1486, pp. 312–323. Springer, Cham (2021). https://doi.org/10.1007/978-3-030-88304-1_25
23. Onah, D., Sinclair, J.: Dropout rates of massive open online courses: behavioural patterns. In: Proceedings of the 6th International Conference on Education and New Learning Technologies (EDULEARN 2014), Barcelona, Spain (2014). https://doi.org/10.13140/RG.2.1.2402.0009

# Towards a Metaverse of Knowledge
## A Constructivist Proposition on Immersive Learning and Visual Literacy

Zackary P. T. Sin[1]([✉]) (ID), Isaac Dan Zhao[2], Astin C. H. Wu[1],
Richard Chen Li[1](ID), Peter H. F. Ng[1](ID), Xiao Huang[1](ID), George Baciu[1](ID),
Jiannong Cao[1](ID), and Qing Li[1](ID)

[1] The Hong Kong Polytechnic University, Hong Kong, Hong Kong SAR
{ptsin,chunwu,richard-chen.li,peter.nhf,xiao.huang,csgeorge,
jiannong.cao,qing-prof.li}@polyu.edu.hk
[2] Stanford University, Stanford, USA
ikezhao@stanford.edu

**Abstract.** The academic success of students can be improved by an understanding of the academic domain they are navigating. As such, they may benefit from gaining valuable perspective into the shape of their chosen field via an enhanced visual aid. We discuss K-Cube VR, a work-in-progress academic domain browser, which provides visualization of such information through knowledge graphs in virtual reality. We then present the theoretical motivations of such a project, proposing in the process new principles for learning in the metaverse. These principles are an attempt to integrate current educational trends, immersive learning, and visual literacy, within a constructivist pedagogical framework. It is hoped that the proposed principles and our implementation via K-Cube VR can inspire future metaverse learning environments.

**Keywords:** Comprehending academic domain · Constructivism · Immersive learning · Visual literacy · Metaverse learning principles

## 1 Introduction

It has been shown that almost half of the students may become confused once they enter university - and almost a third may experience confusion about their plans for course enrollment [1]. Students need to plan their courses throughout their few years in college, often before they have a top-down grasp of their disciplines of choice. Moreover, they need to plan their careers and choose course plans that support such choices. This forward planning is not a trivial thing to do, and is particularly difficult for a typical student who has yet to acquire a panoramic knowledge in the academic programme on which they have enrolled. It has been suggested in [2] that, due to the scarcity of information, students' "planning" is mainly driven by herd mentality.

© The Author(s), under exclusive license to Springer Nature Switzerland AG 2023
C. S. González-González et al. (Eds.): ICWL 2022/SETE 2022, LNCS 13869, pp. 214–225, 2023.
https://doi.org/10.1007/978-3-031-33023-0_19

Understanding an academic domain is not an easy task, even for experts. An academic domain is abstract, or rather a collection of related academic concepts, which more than often are ideas that have complex dependencies and relationships. Therefore, understanding an academic domain requires extensive experience to organise these concepts and summarise their relationships [3], which can be difficult for students. At the university level, it is common to try to inform the students about the purpose of a course by providing a programme description; this description is likely to be insufficient as it often contains a list of keywords and learning outcomes only, and the students will still have to struggle with the fact that they might not have a good understanding of those keywords and descriptions. As such, there is a need to aid students in comprehending an academic domain to benefit their studies.

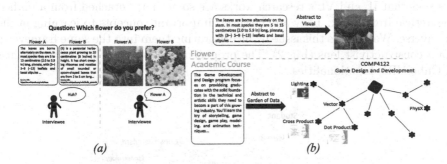

**Fig. 1.** (a) Visual representations can be more effective than textual descriptions. (b) We hypothesize abstract concepts can be converted into more intuitive representations. Some descriptive texts are from Wikipedia.

If textual description is insufficient in communicating the nature of an academic course, it may be the case that it is a medium of expression which is not optimal. To illustrate this modality issue, let us consider a hypothetical scenario where we need to decide which flower we prefer (Fig. 1a). If we were to ask a random person which flower s/he prefers, it may well be the case that s/he will be better able to answer it given images rather than textual description. To represent knowledge, it is important to consider which mode of representation is best suited for the task [4]. It is from this trail of thought that we hypothesize that there exists a more ideal and intuitive representation for an abstract entity such as an academic domain (Fig. 1b). This intuition drives us in our development of **K-Cube VR** [33]. Empowered by an interactive 3D knowledge graph (KG) in virtual reality (VR), we hope to represent the academic domain as a *garden of data* where the user can interact with academic concepts, akin to a flower in a garden.

To provide a theoretical backbone for our work, we explore several educational trends in this paper. With the advent of various extended reality (XR) technologies, *immersive learning* (IL) has become a popular topic in academia [7].

Most of the work captivates XR's ability to provide an immersive environment that can simulate realistic or reality-like scenarios for students' practices for an array of disciplines [8]. There are also discussions on learning abstract concepts with VR [9]. *Visual literacy* (VL) is referring to the person's ability to understand or communicate via visual information [5]. Educators in scientific domains may particularly concern themselves with visual literacy as visual frameworks have been shown to improve students' understanding of course materials [6]. Finally, *constructivism* is an important theory that many educators are well-versed in. It is the focus of our theoretical discussion because it is an epistemology, or a theory on the nature of knowledge. By understanding how people learn and hold knowledge in their minds, we hope to be able to develop a metaverse experience on academic knowledge that aids students' comprehension. Together, these educational ideas provide K-Cube VR with a solid theoretical backbone. Currently, it seems that IL and VL's research works are somewhat detached from a unified theoretical framework. They are, however, important concepts to learning in the metaverse. We address this issue by incorporating them into the same framework via a constructivist lens (Fig. 2). The proposed framework is utilized to discuss K-Cube VR's functionalities.

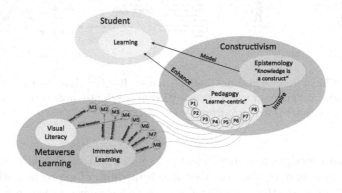

**Fig. 2.** The proposed metaverse learning principles are re-imaginations of pedagogical principles from constructivism in the context of IL and VL.

In summary, this paper aims to fill the gap in providing an effective means of presenting a more circumspect view of an academic domain to students. Our intuition is that abstraction can be expressed as a garden of data. Via a literature discussion, we show how educational trends such as IL and VL can be incorporated into constructivism. Via K-Cube VR, we also show a concrete example of how to manifest the proposed principles for metaverse learning. The paper's contributions are as follows: *(1) Incorporates immersive learning and visual literacy into constructivist pedagogy for building a metaverse learning framework; (2) Proposes eight metaverse learning principles; and (3) Demonstrates how these principles can be applied via K-Cube VR, a work-in-progress application.*

## 2    Constructivism

*Constructivism* is a term that has been adopted across a wide spectrum of disciplines, though its use in education is rooted in its place as an epistemological theory - an explanation for the nature of knowledge and how it is created. Limited by the scope of this paper, we limit ourselves to providing an overview of constructivism for enabling our theoretical discussion later.

In contrast to more classical learning theories which postulate that the world is full of static knowledge and that the process of learning is simply a matter of absorption, constructivism states that knowledge is an internal mental construction which requires learners to combine their past experiences with their present interactions with the environment where learning takes place to forge the building blocks of knowledge [12,15]. Scholars commonly attribute the origins of this brand of constructivism to developmental psychologist Jean Piaget [12]. Piaget developed his "genetic epistemology" (an early form of constructivism) in the early twentieth century. He opined that "all structures are constructed", and that with respect to the process of acquiring knowledge, "the fundamental feature is the course of this construction: Nothing is given at the start except some limiting points on which all the rest is based" [13,14].

As time passed, the theory has been extended through a myriad of branching paths over the past century [16]. There are different scholarly views on the whole picture of this epistemology; however, a so-called *mild* constructivism has core ideas that are more or less agreed upon by constructionists across the board [12]. Further, it was not until the late 70s that it was re-discovered and adopted by educational academia [12]. This transfusion from epistemology to pedagogy, may have yet again led to heterogeneous views as a theory on learning cannot be directly translated into a theory on teaching. So, there are numerous proposals for constructivist principles on teaching, but most revolves around considering how the learner will handle and internalise the learning material. In addition, constructivism's main effect within education has been in awakening the notion that learning is a process that occurs when learners grapple with new concepts, not when instructors presents them.

Here, we adopt the pedagogical principles mostly compiled from the comprehensive literature reviews on constructivist teaching by Honebein [10] and Murphy [11]. According to them, constructivist teaching embodies these principles and goals (from [10] and [11]): (P1) Provide experience with the construction of knowledge; (P2) Provide experience in and appreciation for multiple solutions; (P3) Embed learning in a realistic and authentic context; (P4) Embed relevance in learning; (P5) Encourage ownership during learning; (P6) Embed social learning; (P7) Encourage usage of multiple representations, and; (P8) Emphasize exploration to encourage students to seek knowledge independently.

## 3    Immersive Learning and Visual Literacy

*Immersive learning* (IL) has been defined previously as a set of learning activities that are performed while the user's perceived environment is modified. In recent years, this effect is achieved often through the assistance of XR technologies - an iconic example of such technologies being the VR headset and handset. The immediate question of how much immersion is required to qualify as IL has resulted in scholars concluding that immersion is a spectrum: the user's subjective sense of "presence" [24], as well as an objective sense of "immersion" [25], can be measured quantitatively and used as continuous metrics to describe the aforementioned spectrum. IL has already been applied in many educational contexts. For instance, it has enhanced and extended classroom education at all levels [26, 27], raised awareness about social issues in a viscerally engaging way [28], and simulated natural disaster protocols for increased public safety [29]. Some scholars, like Jeremy Bailenson, have come up with heuristics like the DICE criteria (i.e., Dangerous, Impossible, Counterproductive, and Expensive) to form a basis for why and when IL ought to be used [30].

It seems that constructivism and IL are sometimes considered together due to a frequently undertaken, implicit assumption that IL is interactive by nature and, frequently, also by design; as such, there are studies that discuss how users interact with the constructed learning environment and synthesise information from it [31, 32]. We further this effort by integrating the properties of IL into constructivism more concretely, showing how pedagogical principles can be adapted for metaverse learning principles. In particular, we believe IL's ability to provide social elements, simulated situations for practice [8] and engagement are some of the catalysts that are beneficial for constructivist learning.

*Visual Literacy* (VL) is an educational trend that studies how different visual media affect the quantity and quality of the user's comprehension. Different scholars have attempted to map the developments in VL, and these attempts more or less converge. For instance, Avgerinou [18,19] concludes that there are four main aspects to VL, namely "visual perception", "visual language", "visual thinking", and "visual communication"; meanwhile, Felten offers fewer categories, such as the perspective that the VL can be separated into just the two sub-domains of "visual cognition and perception" and "visual design" [5]. Regardless, they all consider users' interactions with the environment, as well as the recognition of a user's prior experience (in the form of their level of VL), which when taken together suggest that an argument could be made that these ideas - and therefore applications of VL - tend to align with the constructivist paradigm. VL has already been applied in educational settings as a "strategy for fostering creativity" in certain STEM fields [20]. Particularly interesting for our purpose is VL's ability to drive thinking and communication. We will later show how it can be part of constructivism's mental knowledge construction.

## 4    Constructivist Principles for Learning in Metaverse

From constructivism, scholars have derived pedagogical principles for educators to follow; and there are a large number of works attempting to implement a constructivist regime for students. However, according to some scholars, these regimes tend to stray from established principles of constructivism, and are limited in being mainly "learner-centric" [12].

With the advent of ever more frequent advances in XR and the metaverse, compounded by the increasing interest in their utilisation in education, we are seeing a growing tide of literature for IL. At the same time, VL gains exigency in this context as one of the strengths of XR lies in displaying visual information. Current works on IL and VL, however, do not usually anchor themselves into a greater pedagogical philosophy. Rather, they mainly investigate how their immediate methodology can assist students. We, therefore, advocate integrating IL and VL into a well-established and well-known framework such as constructivism concretely by showing how constructivist principles can manifest in the context of metaverse learning. The following are principles from Sect. 2 that are reformulated for the metaverse (Fig. 2).

(M1) **Knowledge as Visualised Construct:** One of the key ideas of constructivism is that knowledge is an internal mental construct. It is important to provide experience to students on its construction (P1). This can be addressed via a VL perspective as a visual vocabulary is believed to be able to help students think visually, and thus structurally [22].

(M2) **Immersive Simulation:** Constructivism believes that one of the main purposes of knowledge is to model reality. It is important to allow the students to look at the same problem from different angles or with multiple solutions so that they can have a robust internal model (P2). IL can provide an immersive simulation environment where the student can complete a task via different methods and thus, become more robust in their comprehension.

(M3) **Re-enact Daily Life Problem:** According to constructivism, as learners use their own experiences as building blocks for new knowledge, IL should re-enact daily life problems in an immersive simulation where the student is solving a problem they can associate with in real life (P3).

(M4) **Associate the Knowledge:** Extending upon the previous principle, for concepts that are more abstract, it is the case that learners may use their learned concepts to understand new knowledge (P4). Henceforth, the VL's visual vocabulary can show the association between concepts to help students understand how knowledge interweaves, and from there, build new understanding.

(M5) **Engage the Student in VR:** Constructivism is learner-centric; it means that students need to take ownership of their own learning (P5). IL has been shown to be able to engage students and therefore is a useful medium for students to naturally take initiative to learn [17].

(M6) **Multi-User Immersion:** Constructivism recommends that learning take place in relation with interpersonal interactions, whenever possible (P6). Meeting in a metaverse learning environment, the diverse experiences and indeed personalities of different learners, on the whole, oftentimes should offer a more dynamic and much richer set of stimuli for each learner.

(M7) **Multiple Modes of Content:** Constructivists advocate for the inclusion of multiple modes of representation to help with the mental construction of knowledge (P7). The best practice for the quantity, frequency, and presence of different types of multimedia becomes a rich ground for discourse in VR, which is more spatially adaptive to present content [34].

(M8) **Navigation of Knowledge:** Constructivism asserts that the user's exploratory interactions are important as a mechanism through which new knowledge is synthesised (P8). A good design seeks a balance of features allowing for the user's freedom to explore, as well as features designed to give guidance and structure to the user's exploration.

Not limiting ourselves to a theoretical discussion about a constructivist framework for learning in the metaverse, in the next section we provide concrete designs and implementations of how the principles can be applied.

## 5   K-Cube VR

K-Cube VR [33] is a garden of data, or a metaverse of knowledge, which aims to aid students in grasping an academic discipline via knowledge graph structure. Within this VR experience, students can visit each of the courses offered by a department and understand their content in the form of 3D graphs. Multimedia content is embedded for each course keyword to help the students understand the knowledge of the graph. A set of VR navigation functions are implemented to enable the exploration of the graph structure. Although our work uses KG that is manually annotated by experts in computer science, it is expected to be extended to a broad range of disciplines in the future. As the functionalities below show, K-Cube VR is designed based on the theoretical principles proposed in Sect. 4; hence, it demonstrates how the metaverse learning principles may manifest.

**Knowledge Graph in VR.** As presented in M1, a visual vocabulary can help the learner to understand knowledge as a construct. According to constructivism, knowledge is a mental construct that is organised. Therefore, KG is an ideal representation of knowledge. To help students better understand the discipline, we visualise KG as an immersive and interactive collection of virtual nodes which shows how academic concepts are formed and cross-related. To achieve so, there is a three-layer hierarchy formed by three levels of virtual nodes. A node, therefore, will belong to one of the three levels, disciplines (e.g. Computing), courses (e.g. Game Design and Development) and concepts (e.g. Vectors). The three-dimensional virtual space for visualisation (Fig. 3), effectively, is partitioned into a discipline space where the student can see the courses and a course space where the student can see the concepts within a course. By visually organising knowledge in such a way and showing students the connections and hierarchy of concepts, it is expected to also help students to understand new concepts by seeing how they connect with concepts they already knew (M4).

**Data Buddy.** To better engage the student (M5), we introduced a data buddy as an aide to the students during their visit to the knowledge metaverse (Fig. 4a). It basically acts as a hub of information and can be called out by the learner when needed via a button. In addition, it is expected that students are usually not familiar with KG. The data buddy, therefore, also acts as a "data storyteller" who describes the meaning of KG elements (e.g. sub-graphs) to the students which helps with students' understanding (M7).

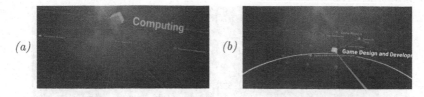

**Fig. 3.** The knowledge graph in K-Cube VR is partitioned into *(a)* a discipline space and *(b)* a course space.

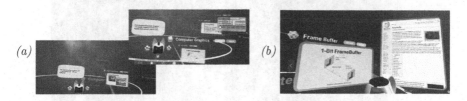

**Fig. 4.** *(a)* The data buddy is an aide to the student. It also acts as a data storyteller, describing the subgraph to the student. *(b)* The lecture notes and Wikipedia page are shown when a concept is selected.

**VR Navigation.** As discussed in (M8), it is important to provide students with the tools to freely explore the learning environment. In order to enable the student to explore the KG, several operations are provided (Fig. 5): *(a)* spatial teleportation, *(b)* node teleportation *(c)* scaling, and *(d)* translation. *Spatial teleportation* allows the user to instantly teleport themselves to a new location; they can do so by pointing at a location on the plane. There may be cases, however, where the student simply wants to "go to" a node. *Node teleportation* fulfils this need by allowing the student to point at a node and teleport in front of it. Teleportation enables travelling of large distances without incurring motion sickness, but there is an issue of causing spatial disorientation [35]. *Scaling* allows the student to rescale the size of the knowledge graph. It is a useful navigational function when the graph is too large or too small from the student's perspective. *Translation* is similar to the two teleportation methods just described, but instead of the student moving toward a location, the student grabs the entire knowledge graph and moves it around.

**Multi-source Content.** As mentioned in the beginning, students do not have a strong background in the academic domain and, therefore, may have difficulties understanding the concepts. To help them understand the concepts in the knowledge graph, multimedia content is displayed when they are viewing a concept node. The current design provides two types of multimedia content for a particular node of concept: the related lecture notes and/or the corresponding Wikipedia page (Fig. 4b). The lecture notes can be "flipped" with the directional joystick handle (left-right) and the Wikipedia page can be read freely with the handle as well (up-down). By providing this duality of view on the concept, we

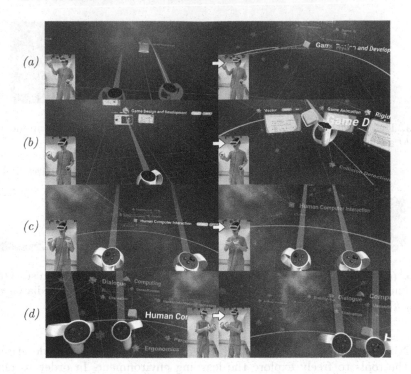

**Fig. 5.** K-Cube VR can be navigated by *(a)* spatial teleportation, *(b)* node teleportation, *(c)* scaling and *(d)* translation.

hope it can help students understand that knowledge can be expressed from different perspectives and simultaneously help with their understanding (M7). In addition, the panel can be resized for viewing by dragging (Fig. 6).

**Tags.** It is also useful to show students that there are different categories of knowledge within a certain discipline. Currently, K-Cube VR mainly focuses on computer science. We, therefore, briefly categorised the knowledge into, "concept", "algorithm", "method" and "math". The students will be able to use the tag board provided by the *data buddy* to visualise the nodes belonging to a tag (Fig. 7). It is hoped that this organisation further help students see knowledge in a clustered view (M7), and help them to locate concepts in a cluster (M8).

**Study Room.** In addition, we also provide a virtual study room for students to focus on the subgraph they are interested in (Fig. 8). The student can use a lasso to group select a collection of connected nodes. Once selected, the student will be brought to a virtual study room to help them focus on those concepts. We hope this is an engaging feature for students (M5).

K-Cube VR is a work-in-progress VR application that provides a preliminary view of a knowledge metaverse. To further complete the metaverse building, some important functionalities will be discussed in Sect. 6.

**Fig. 6.** The panel can be resized for viewing.

**Fig. 7.** Nodes are given tags such that they can be grouped and visualized.

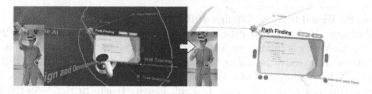

**Fig. 8.** Student can select multiple nodes at once and enter a study room.

## 6    Conclusion and Future Work

In this paper, we addressed how to aid students in their understanding of an academic domain, particularly its abstract concepts, in a metaverse environment. To provide a theoretical framework, IL and VL are introduced into a constructivist pedagogy, in which eight metaverse learning principles are formulated.

K-Cube VR is the application in which we show how to bring the metaverse learning theory to practice. To further complete our proposal for a metaverse of knowledge, however, there are some functionalities that need to be implemented as well. First, the social element is an important consideration for constructivists as they believe that learning is also driven by social interaction (M6). Therefore, an important function to implement in the future is to enable K-Cube VR to be explored by multiple students, and perhaps, with instructors in the same session. Second, we need to link the concepts with real problems that students may encounter more closely (M3). Ideally, K-Cube VR can also act as a hub that connects numerous pre-made simulations in the metaverse for learning the concepts (M2). In summary, we used K-Cube VR to show how to implement the proposed metaverse learning principles and it is hoped that these principles can inspire more metaverse learning applications in the future.

**Acknowledgement.** This work was supported in full by the Hong Kong Polytechnic University, Project of Strategic Importance (project number: P0036846). The authors thank Junnan Dong, Jerry C. K. Chan, Qinggang Zhang, Yaowei Wang, Wentao Li and Huachi Zhou for their useful discussions and feedback.

# References

1. Li, P., Zhang, Z.P., Wang, Q.Q., Yan, J.K.: College students' psychological crisis: types, factors and countermeasures. In: Proceedings of International Conference on Social Science. & Higher Education, pp. 579–581 (2018)
2. Mendez, G., Galárraga, L., Chiluiza, K.: Showing academic performance predictions during term planning: effects on students' decisions, behaviors, and preferences. In: Proceedings of CHI, vol. 22, pp. 1–17 (2021)
3. Ethel, R.G., McMeniman, M.M.: Unlocking the knowledge in action of an expert practitioner. J. Teach. Educ. **51**(2), 87–101 (2000)
4. Willingham, D.T.: Ask the cognitive scientist do visual, auditory, and kinesthetic learners need visual, auditory, and kinesthetic instruction? Am. Educ. **29**(2), 31 (2005)
5. Felten, P.: Visual literacy. Change **40**(6), 60–64 (2008)
6. Handelsman, J., et al.: Scientific teaching. Science **304**(5670), 521–522 (2004)
7. Dengel, A.: What is immersive learning?. In: Proceedings of International Conference on the Immersive Learning Research Network, pp. 1–5. IEEE (2022)
8. Akinola, Y.M., Agbonifo, O.C., Sarumi, O.A.: Virtual reality as a tool for learning: the past, present & the prospect. J. Appl. Learn. Teach. **3**(2), 51–58 (2020)
9. Dick, E.: The Promise of Immersive Learning: Augmented & Virtual Reality's Potential in Edu. Info. Tech. & Inno. Foundation (2021). https://itif.org/sites/default/files/2021-ar-vr-education.pdf. Accessed 01 Aug 2022
10. Honebein, P.C.: Seven goals for the design of constructivist learning environments. In: Wilson, B.G. (eds.) Constructivist Learning Environments: Case Studies in Instructional Design, pp. 11–24, Educational Technology (1996)
11. Murphy, E.: Constructivism: From Philosophy to Practice. ERIC (1997). https://eric.ed.gov/?id=ED444966. Accessed 01 Aug 2022
12. Sjøberg, S.: Constructivism and learning. In: Baker, E., McGaw, B., Peterson, P (eds.) International Encyclopedia of Education, 3rd Ed., pp. 485–490, Elsevier (2010)
13. Piaget, J.: Conversations Libres Avec Jean Piaget. Robert Laffont (1977)
14. Piaget, J.: Études Sociologiques. Librairie Droz (1997)
15. Von Glasersfeld, E.: Homage to Jean Piaget (1896–1982). Irish J. of Psychol. **18**(3), 293–306 (1997)
16. Derry, S.J.: Beyond symbolic processing: expanding horizons for educational psychology. J. Edu. Psychol. **84**(4), 413–418 (1992)
17. Coates, H.: The value of student engagement for higher education quality assurance. Qual. High. Educ. **11**(1), 25–36 (2005)
18. Avgerinou, M., Ericson, J.: A review of the concept of visual literacy. Br. J. Educ. Technol. **28**(4), 280–291 (1997)
19. Avgerinou, M.D., Pettersson, R.: Toward a cohesive theory of visual literacy. J. Vis. Literacy **30**(2), 1–19 (2011)
20. Martin-Erro, A., Espinosa Escudero, M.M., Domínguez Somonte, M.: Visual literacy as a strategy for fostering creativity in engineering education. In: Proceedings of International Technical Education and Development Conference (2016)

21. Lundy, A.D., Stephens, A.E.: Beyond the literal: teaching visual literacy in the $21^{st}$ cent. Classroom Procedia-Soc. Behav. Sci. **174**(2015), 1057–1060 (2015)
22. Kędra, J., Žakevičiūtė, R.: Visual literacy practices in higher education. What, why and how?. J. Vis. Literacy, **38**(1–2), 1–7 (2019)
23. Radianti, J., Majchrzak, T., Fromm J. Wohlgenannt I.: A systematic review of immersive virtual reality applications for higher education.: design elements, lessons learned, and research agenda. Comput. Educ. **147**, 103778 (2020)
24. Witmer, B.G., Singer, M.J.: Measuring presence in virtual environments.: a presence questionnaire. Presence: Teleoperators Virtual Env. **7**(3), 225–240 (1998)
25. Slater, M., Wilbur, S.: A Framework for immersive virtual environments. (FIVE). Presence Teleoperators Virtual Env. **6**(6), 603–616 (1997)
26. Piovesan, S.D., Passerino, L.M., Pereira, A.S.: Virtual reality as a tool in education. In: Proceedings of International Conference on Cognition and Exploratory Learning in Digital Age, pp. 295–298 (2012)
27. Weymuth, T., Rehler, M.: Immersive interactive quantum mechanics for teaching and learning chemistry. CHIMIA Int. J. Chem. **75**(1–2), 45–49 (2021)
28. Markowitz, D.M., Bailenson, J.N.: Virtual reality and the psychology of climate change. Current Opinion Psychol. **42**, 60–65 (2021)
29. Feng, Z., et al.: An immersive virtual reality serious game to enhance earthquake behavioral responses and post-earthquake evacuation preparedness in buildings. Adv. Eng. Inform. **45**, 101118 (2020)
30. Bailenson, J.: Experience on Demand: What Virtual Reality is, How It Works, and What It Can Do. Norton & Co (2018)
31. Aiello, P., D'elia, F., Di Tore, S., Sibilio, M.: A constructivist approach to virtual reality for experiential learning. E-Learn. Digit. Media **9**(3), 317–324 (2012)
32. Huang, H.M., Liaw, S.S.: An analysis of learners' intentions toward virtual reality learning based on constructivist and technology acceptance approaches. Int. Rev. Res. Open Distrib. Learn. 19(1), 91–115 (2018)
33. Li, Q., et al.: KCUBE: a knowledge graph uni. curriculum framework for student advising and career planning. In: Proceedings of International Conference on Blended Learning, pp. 953–958 (2022)
34. AlSada, M., Nakajima, T.: Parallel web browsing in tangible augmented reality environment In: Proceedings of CHI EA, pp. 953–958 (2015)
35. Rahimi, K., Banigan, C., Ragan, E.D.: Scene transitions and teleportation in virtual reality and the implications for spatial awareness and sickness. IEEE TVCG **26**(6), 2273–2287 (2018)

# SETE 2022. International Symposium on Emerging Technologies for Education

# Acceptance Evaluation of a Serious Game to Address Gender Stereotypes in Mexico

Alma Gloria Barrera Yañez[1]([⊠]) (ID), Cristina Alonso-Fernández[2] (ID),
and Baltasar Fernández-Manjón[1] (ID)

[1] Software Engineering and Artificial Intelligence Department, Complutense University of
Madrid, C/Profesor José García Santesmases 9, 28040 Madrid, Spain
almaba01@ucm.es, balta@fdi.ucm.es
[2] Computer Science Department, Autonomous University of Madrid, C/Francisco Tomás y
Valiente 11, 28049 Madrid, Spain
cristina.alonsof@uam.es

**Abstract.** Serious Games provide an opportunity to address social issues in an
interactive environment particularly appealing for school-aged children. Gender
stereotypes are one of the many remaining gender-related issues in current society.
Stereotypes appear at early ages and are particularly prevalent in certain cultures
and countries. This paper presents an early acceptance evaluation of Kiddo, a
serious game to address gender stereotypes in Mexico. The game has been designed
to address four of the main stereotypes still present in children in this country, and
it is intended to be used in classes by teachers to start a discussion about gender
stereotypes. The evaluation has been carried out with a prototype of the game
containing one of the game chapters and a sample including teachers and gender
experts. The goal is to verify both the usability of the game as well as its acceptance
for some of the target users that will later apply the game in their classes. Results
of both usability and acceptance questionnaires have provided a useful insight
into the strengths and areas of improvement for the game, and they are being
incorporated into the new version of Kiddo.

**Keywords:** Serious Games · Videogame · Gender Stereotypes ·
Technology-Enhanced Learning

## 1 Introduction

### 1.1 Serious Games

Serious Games (SGs) are games that have a main purpose other than entertainment,
enjoyment, or fun [1]. Among their purposes, it stands out increasing awareness, teaching
knowledge, or changing behavior. The highly interactive environment that they provide
allows many possibilities for affecting their players, including immersive learning experiences to apply their knowledge, and/or test complex scenarios in a safe environment.
Due to these characteristics, SGs have been applied in different domains with promising
results, including applications in the health field and to address social problems [2].

C. S. González-González et al. (Eds.): ICWL 2022/SETE 2022, LNCS 13869, pp. 229–240, 2023.
https://doi.org/10.1007/978-3-031-33023-0_20

To date, serious games are becoming widely used in the research community. These games are promising tools thanks to the engagement between stakeholders, the potential for interactive visualization, the capacity of developing and improving social learning and teaching decision making skills [3]. Although serious videogames are not new, their expansion has been taking place since 2010. Researchers suggest that the characteristics of serious videogames should establish clear learning objectives for students, provide continuous feedback on their progress, and their difficulty should be adapted to the learner's capabilities, as well as adding surprise elements to break the monotony of the videogame [4].

This article describes the process of creation and acceptance of Kiddo, a videogame to educate in gender equality. A pilot chapter was created and evaluated, looking for areas of opportunity before completing the videogame and launching it to the public.

## 1.2  Gender Stereotypes

One of the remaining gender-related issues in current society is the prevalence of several gender stereotypes. The United Nations' Office of the High Commissioner for Human Rights defines a gender stereotype as "a generalized view or preconception about attributes or characteristics, or the roles that are or ought to be possessed by, or performed by, women and men" [5]. These preconceptions limit individuals' development and choices and perpetuate inequalities. In certain cultures and countries, the presence of gender stereotypes is particularly striking. Such is the case of Mexico, where different reports have studied the prevalence and normalization of gender stereotypes in general society, as part of the cultural background [6], and its direct relation with sexist and gender stereotypes in primary and secondary students. Some of these reports highlight the most common stereotypes in Mexico's children [7], summarized in Table 1.

**Table 1.** Main results of questionnaire applied to a representative sample of Mexico's 6th grade primary school children (adapted from the original, in Spanish [7])

| Gender stereotype | % of boys who agree | % of girls who agree |
|---|---|---|
| Boys do need to finish school and prepare themselves to maintain their future home | 85.7 | 82.0 |
| Girls should learn to help out at home by taking care of their siblings and doing the cleaning up | 78.8 | 78.9 |
| The man is the one who should have the greatest responsibility for bringing money into the home | 77.3 | 75.2 |
| Girls should play with dolls | 75.2 | 71.7 |
| Boys should play soccer and other hard-core sports | 70.8 | 62.8 |
| The woman is the one who has to be careful not to become pregnant | 67.1 | 69.6 |

Gender stereotypes appear very early in children's development, so it is essential to address them at a young age. This happens to be especially noticeable in Latin American culture. In a study [8] aimed to determine the role and level of involvement of Latin American mothers in their children's math learning, the results showed that the mother's attention regarding their daughter's math learning, decreased overtime, especially during 5th and 6th grade, a situation paired with statements such as "math is more useful for boys". Another study [9] carried out with younger children mentions that mothers of children around 2 years of age use language related to numbers (initial mathematical approach) up to 3 times more with boys than with girls. As a result, at early school ages, the stereotype that "girls are better at reading and boys are better at mathematics" is reinforced. Although, as mentioned, this is a stereotype, it causes frustration on both sides: on the girls for "not being as good" and on the boys who have difficulties with mathematics for "not being as good as the other boys".

## 2  Related Work

Serious Games have been used to address gender issues, such as violence or abuse. Examples of this are Tsiunas [10], a game to understand essential elements for the prevention of gender-based violence and the promotion of responsible masculinities, and Jesse [11], an adventure game set in the Caribbean region that deals with domestic violence. Other examples of gender focused videogames are Berolos [12] (Spain) and Iguala-t [13] (Spain). Some of these games have academic evaluations that measure their effectiveness, most of them being successful tools that, from their approach, help to counteract gender problems. There are three main approaches that most of these games tend to use:

- Games for girls are built over gender differences and promote different concepts of femininity.
- Games for change have the approach to create awareness regarding sexism and gender stereotypes.
- Creative games are developed mostly for girls, encouraging girls to create and develop their own learning conditions and surroundings. Widely used in STEM projects focused on bringing girls closer to sciences [14].

In a review of games addressing gender-related issues [15], results showed that stereotypes were barely mentioned. Only the videogame Chuka [16], developed by The United Nations Office against Drugs and Crime (UNODC) in Mexico, included gender stereotypes as one of the topics addressed in the game.

Results also showed the limitations of the games addressing gender issues: the lack of evaluation studies to prove their effectiveness, the lack of follow-up to measure their long-term effect and the lack of participants or contrast with teachers or educators who can apply the games in their classes. Despite these limitations, serious games provide multiple advantages, one of the most relevant ones being the possibility to include analysis of player interactions. This allows to study the data collected by the game, with the objective of informing us if there are changes with respect to the perception of the problem presented to the users, before and after applying a game, videogame or simulation in which they suffer some discrimination or confrontation regarding gender stereotypes.

## 3  Kiddo

Kiddo is a narrative and decision making or "game thinking" videogame to address gender stereotypes for school-aged children (7–13 years old). Kiddo seeks to make the most common gender stereotypes visible to educate in equality. The story takes place in common scenarios in a child's development: school, home, park, etc. The main characters of the game are two twins (a boy and a girl) who will encounter situations related to gender stereotypes that they must overcome without hurting themselves or the other twin. In these scenarios, the twins Juan and María (see Fig. 1) will engage in conversations and interactions with other characters (NPC/non-playable) within the game. The game will have a mood bar, where players will be able to observe how the character feels about the decisions made.

**Fig. 1.** Screenshot of Kiddo showing the twins (left) and the scenarios of the game (right).

Players play in third-person perspective, achieving immersion in the game through elements such as narrative, character design and the use of common environments for viewers, which can help increase empathy and closeness in a player. The game contains 4 chapters (see Fig. 2) addressing different gender stereotypes:

1. Colors: "Blue is for boys and pink is for girls"
2. Educational: "Boys are better at math and girls are better at arts"
3. Physical activities: "Some sports are for girls and some are for boys"
4. House activities and responsibilities: "Domestic chores are only for girls"

Each chapter is designed to last around 5 min, so the whole game, including any pre-game and post-game interventions, can be played in a single class hour. In two of the chapters (colors and domestic chores), players will make decisions affecting Juan (the twin boy), while in the other two chapters (educational and physical activities), the choices made by the players will affect María (the twin girl).

**Fig. 2.** Screenshot of Kiddo's twins and gameplay with four available chapters. (Color figure online)

### 3.1 Design and Development

The design of Kiddo was based on the review of previous literature regarding serious games and gender stereotypes, as well as on the analysis of multiple games to address gender-related issues and other social issues. The common characteristics and mechanics of such games helped the early design of Kiddo.

The first chapter of Kiddo was subjected to two types of early testing: the first was conducted by four serious game experts of the research group, each researcher playing the game independently, and all of whom had not participated in the design and/or development of the game. Their comments and suggestions were analyzed and revised to improve several aspects of the chapter, including: the design of some items and NPCs, the dialogues in some conversations, a better description of the gender stereotypes addressed, and some other minor suggestions that were incorporated. The second test was carried out by external participants: teachers, students, parents, videogame players and non-video game players, with the purpose of contrasting the design of Kiddo, and evaluating its acceptance and usability for target users (particularly teachers) and gender experts, obtaining as many constructive comments as possible to improve Kiddo's early development.

Kiddo has been developed using uAdventure [17], a framework built on top of Unity to design educational videogames. uAdventure simplifies game development by abstracting the main narrative elements of "point and click" adventure games (e.g., scenarios, characters, conversations) into a simplified, easy-to-understand model, allowing non-expert game developers to focus on the features they need. uAdventure further incorporates default Game Learning Analytics [18] that allows to collect traces from all player-related events (e.g., interactions with game elements and NPCs; scene changes; start, ending and choices in conversations; and changes in game-state variables). This incorporated Learning Analytics will be essential in the subsequent validation of the final version of Kiddo when tested with students. Due to uAdventure multiplatform features, Kiddo's final version will be available for several platforms, currently including PC (Windows) and mobile devices (Android).

### 3.2   The First Chapter of Kiddo

The first chapter of Kiddo addresses the gender stereotype of colors attached to gender: "blue is for boys and pink is for girls" (see Fig. 3). In this chapter, players will make decisions regarding Juan (the twin boy) and the color to paint his bedrooms' walls.

The story begins with the family arriving in a new town and entering their new house. Despite being twins, Juan and María start to feel people treating them differently because of their gender. In the pilot chapter, Juan's desire is to use pink color for his room, and for the first decision crossroad, players will have to decide whether pink is a suitable color for Juan's bedroom's walls, or if a different color will be more adequate for him. During the chapter, players could decide on the color on multiple occasions, and will have to face different opinions regarding this stereotype: particularly, the twins' father will be against painting Juan's bedroom walls pink (*"men do not use pink, it is a color for girls"*) while the twins' mother will have a more open attitude towards it. In the end, however, the decision falls on the player and, after facing different opinions and comments, could change their initial opinion and decide whether they chose pink or another color.

As in the other chapters, early decisions will determine whether players achieve the "heart of courage" which will help them fight the monster that appears at the end of the chapter (see Fig. 3, right). If using the heart or final choosing to fight the stereotype, players will defeat the monster of this first chapter. In case that they still agree with the gender stereotype, they could not defeat the monster and will be directed to a short video explanation on why colors are gender neutral.

**Fig. 3.** Screenshot of Kiddo's first chapter including characters' dialogues (left) and the final monster (right). (Color figure online)

## 4   Usability and Acceptance Evaluation

### 4.1   Methods

The evaluation carried out with the first chapter of Kiddo had a twofold purpose: 1) to evaluate the usability of the game and 2) to evaluate the acceptance of the game, using its first chapter as a test pilot.

**Usability Evaluation**
The usability evaluation conduced for Kiddo is based on the usability surveys conducted

periodically by the commercial videogame company Garena, regarding its star title "Free Fire", a commercial Battle Royale videogame with millions of users across the globe. In the surveys, they ask users about their operative systems, the devices used to play the game, the devices the user has access to, etc. Those questions are highly relevant for Kiddo's usability evaluation and proved to provide highly important information. The final questionnaire used for the usability evaluation was adapted from the above-mentioned surveys [19] selecting the questions that were relevant to the content of the first chapter of Kiddo. The questionnaire started with some basic questions about the game environment (which device and operating system did they play the game in, and device they prefer to play in) and whether they had any issues installing or executing Kiddo, with an optional open text field to describe any issues encountered. After that, the usability questionnaire included 13 free-text questions (see Table 2).

**Table 2.** Questions included in Kiddo's usability questionnaire.

|    | Usability question |
|----|---------------------|
| 1  | *Were you able to talk to all the characters?* |
| 2  | *Were you able to collect all the items?* |
| 3  | *Were you able to use the objects correctly?* |
| 4  | *Were you able to interact with the map?* |
| 5  | *Were the game instructions clear?* |
| 6  | *Were the buttons easy to find?* |
| 7  | *Did you find any buttons that did not work correctly?* |
| 8  | *Did the facial expressions of the characters match the dialogue shown?* |
| 9  | *Do the scenes change correctly?* |
| 10 | *Did you ever get lost/didn't know what to do?* |
| 11 | *Was the music present throughout the game?* |
| 12 | *Did you manage to complete the game?* |
| 13 | *Did you have any problems using the game?* |

**Acceptance Evaluation**

The questionnaire to evaluate the game acceptance was based on the one used in "Campus Craft" [20]. Within the context of Kiddo's topics and by addressing questions especially designed to evaluate the pilot chapter, it contains three parts: (1) demographic information about participants, (2) acceptance of the characters of the game and (3) acceptance of the game story.

The demographic information inquired about age, gender, and profession.

The characters' acceptance questions included five questions about the opinion of game characters with 3 possible answers ("fun", "boring", and "I don't care") and two further 5-point Likert questions about the style of the characters.

The story's acceptance questions included: four 5-point Likert questions inquiring about participants' opinion about the speed of the game texts, how fun the story was, how likely they are to play new chapters of the game, and if they consider the gender equality message of the game is clearly depicted; a set of 17 tags (*Killing time; Educational; Simulation; Leisure; Social; Bored; Teamwork; Adventure; Easy to play; Understandable; Good control, comfortable to handle; Intuitive; Low demands on my computer/is light/works well on my computer; Irrelevant; Interesting; Uninteresting; Difficult*) to choose the 3 that they consider best describe Kiddo; a score (1 to 10) of how much they liked the pilot chapter; and two final free-text questions about anything that they will add/erase from the chapter and final comments/suggestions for the game.

## 4.2 Participants

The first chapter of Kiddo was played by 10 participants, between 20 and 51 years old, of different professions related to education and social studies (a social science student, two high school students, a nurse, a sociologist, a consultant, an administrative assistant, two primary education teachers, and a school supervisor) from Mexico.

## 4.3 Evaluations

The evaluations began on September 15, 2022, for 22 days ending on October 7, 2022. The evaluation was performed from the participants' homes, with their own technological devices (Laptops, PC's, smartphones, or tablets) in Mexico. A video tutorial was sent to the participants, along with the proper APK's and EXE's, to help them with the installation of the game, to avoid any issues and to ensure a clean install. However, for older users (50+) the intervention of the developer via videoconference or a phone call was needed, since they were not too familiar with the installation process. After playing the first chapter of the game, participants provided their opinion in two Google forms. Their comments are being used to modify and improve Kiddo. The changes and improvements suggested by the test users will result in the final version of the game.

# 5 Results

## 5.1 Results of Usability Evaluation

Kiddo prototype executables were created and provided for participants for both Android and Windows. Regarding participants' regular usage of videogames, two participants declare playing more than 4 h a day, three participants played between 1 and 3 h a day, two participants rarely play videogames, and the other three do not play videogames at all. In terms of their playing devices, one participant prefers to play on a console, another participant on tablet, four on smartphones and the other four prefer to play on a laptop or PC. Three participants played Kiddo on PCs, one on tablet and the other six on smartphones.

During the installation on PC/laptop, some participants experienced problems because their PCs were too slow, and/or the screen froze. During the installation on a smartphone, some participants experienced problems because they did not understand the installation instructions and were not able to install it on smartphones, so they changed to PC, where they were able to successfully install and play Kiddo. Overall, four participants successfully installed Kiddo without any issues, while three participants stated that they encountered some issues during the installation of the game. In general, participants under the age of 40 were able to install Kiddo on their devices and those over 40 required some more specific guidance to complete the installation of the executable on the desired device.

Table 3 shows the summary of the responses for the usability questions (stated in Table 2). Results show positive outcomes in game completion (question 12), scenes changes (question 9) and interactions with characters and items (questions 1 and 2). The most important errors appeared at the start of the game where participants were not sure about what they had to do (question 9), and instructions did not help them (question 5), and some issues with the game interface such as finding the buttons (question 6).

**Table 3.** Results of Kiddo's usability questionnaire.

| | Results of usability question |
|---|---|
| 1 | Most participants were able to talk to the characters; only one participant was not able to talk but only to read the dialogues |
| 2 | Most participants were able to collect the objects |
| 3 | Most participants were able to use the objects; only one participant was not able to grab the last object (the heart of courage), since it did not appear in the backpack (inventory) |
| 4 | All but one participant were able to interact with the map |
| 5 | Most participants stated that the instructions were not clear at the beginning of the videogame or that they could be improved |
| 6 | Most participants had issues finding the buttons |
| 7 | All but one participant found that buttons worked correctly |
| 8 | Most participants stated that the facial expressions matched the shown dialogue; one participant mentioned the case that when repeating the dialogues from the beginning in the living room scene, the characters' expressions do not match the dialogue |
| 9 | All participants stated that the scenes reproduce correctly |
| 10 | Most of the participants stated that they did not know what to do at the beginning of the videogame |
| 11 | All participants listened to the music throughout the videogame |
| 12 | All participants were able to finish the videogame |
| 13 | There were no other problems using the game |

## 5.2 Results of Acceptance Evaluation

Participants provided several insights in the first part of the acceptance questionnaire. About the characters María (girl) and Juan (boy), most participants think the characters are funny and they liked the style of the twins. Additionally, all participants found the twins' hair color amusing. About the parents' characters (Lucy and Roberto), most participants did not show any interest in the appearance of the parents nor were they attracted to the style of the parents. About the speed of the texts, most participants think that the speed of the texts is too slow. About new chapters, all participants said they are interested in playing a new chapter of the game. About the story, most participants think that the story is funny/interesting enough. And finally, about the message of the game, all participants stated that the message of gender equality is clear.

Regarding the list of keywords provided, in which participants selected the 3 words that they believe best describe Kiddo, main results were: all participants selected "*Educational*"; several participants selected the keywords "*Simulation*", "*Social*" "*Understandable*"; and some participants selected "*Low demands on my computer/is light/works well on my computer*", "*Good control, comfortable to handle*", "*Adventure*", "*Intuitive*", "*Easy to play*", and "*Interesting*". It is noticeable that no participant selected any of the negative keywords ("*Bored*", "*Irrelevant*", "*Uninteresting*", or "*Difficult*"). The average rating for the overall score given by participants to the first chapter (pilot) of Kiddo (in scale 1 to 10) is 7.5.

Participants provided some suggestions or areas of opportunity to improve the chapter, including possible additions to the game (e.g., more precise indications, a help button, an initial video to set up the story) and changes (e.g., shorten some of the dialogues). The final free comment section allowed for additional suggestions to improve the next chapters of Kiddo. Participants' comments included:

- "I suggest creating and fighting the stereotypical monster of fear of decision making, it would be worthwhile to add to autonomy training."
- "I liked the characters in general, but the monster is more attractive than the rest".
- "Testing with children, as an adult you may not understand a lot of things, but children are more likely to find their way around faster".
- "Add instructions and improve the style of the parent characters".
- "The hearts representing the health or the life of the character, are really confusing. I thought that those were the Hearts of Courage, but they were life indicators."
- "It is a very interesting proposal to present cases where analysis and decision making are encouraged. The design can be made more attractive and the activities and challenges of the game can be related in a more direct way."
- "I found the message of respect in terms of choice of tastes and gender interesting, but the story gets long with the dialogues, it would be good to include an introduction and instructions on how to play and at the end of the chapter a brief conclusion."

## 5.3 Summary of Evaluation Results

The results of the usability evaluation, and the acceptance evaluation of the first chapter of Kiddo are very promising. The initial evaluation carried out for its first pilot chapter has received mainly positive feedback from the participants, which lets us expect a good acceptance among the final users. The current evaluation shows that Kiddo still needs some work to be completely accessible for all users. Particularly the beginning of the game was not clear enough, and additional instructions need to be provided to players to understand the purpose of the game. The game should include a better tutorial to guide players in their initial interactions with the game and to clearly state the game goal. Although we know that there are some issues with the pilot version of Kiddo, the comments and suggestions gathered from this evaluation allow us to address these found issues and get them fixed in the final version of the game.

## 6  Conclusions

Kiddo is a videogame to address gender stereotypes in Mexico. The first prototype of the videogame has been evaluated with educators. It is important to have in mind that the pilot tests were conducted with adults for several reasons: even though kids will be the final players of the game, we needed more technical and expert opinions to be able to quickly identify the issues and bugs present in the chapter, as well as the areas for improvement that both teachers and gender experts may suggest.

The main outcome of this evaluation is that the game was very positive perceived by educators as they consider it could be a relevant content to initiate a fruitful discussion with the students based on a common experience. They consider that the game could be an effective way to address the topic of gender stereotypes at school.

However, Kiddo is still a prototype that has been formatively evaluated with a limited number of users. With all the feedback collected from educators and students we will produce the final complete version of the game. This final version will be applied in at least 2 elementary schools in Mexico (which have already agreed to apply Kiddo in their classes). In these applications, Game Learning Analytics will be collected from players' interactions with Kiddo. These collected analytics will help us to continue the summative validation of the game and measure the impact of the game on its target players.

**Acknowledgments.** This work has been partially funded by Regional Government of Madrid (eMadrid S2018/TCS4307, co-funded by the European Structural Funds FSE and FEDER) and by the Ministry of Education (PID2020-119620RB-I00) and by a student grant from Fundación Carolina.

## References

1. Michael, D.R., Chen, S.L.: Serious Games: Games That Educate, Train, and Inform. Education, pp. 1–95 (2005). https://doi.org/10.1145/2465085.2465091
2. Calvo-Morata, A., Alonso-Fernández, C., Freire, M., Martínez-Ortiz, I., Fernández-Manjón, B.: Creating awareness on bullying and cyberbullying among young people: validating the effectiveness and design of the serious game Conectado. Telematics Inform. **60**, 101568 (2021). https://doi.org/10.1016/j.tele.2021.101568

3. Aubert, A.H., Bauer, R., Lienert, J.: A review of water-related serious games to specify use in environmental Multi-Criteria Decision Analysis. Environ. Model. Softw. **105**, 64–78 (2018). https://doi.org/10.1016/j.envsoft.2018.03.023

4. Pitarch, R.C.: An approach to digital game-based learning: video-games principles and applications in foreign language learning. J. Lang. Teach. Res. **9**(6), 1147 (2018). https://doi.org/10.17507/jltr.0906.04

5. Gender stereotyping. OHCHR and women's human rights and gender equality. https://www.ohchr.org/en/women/gender-stereotyping

6. Hietanen, A.-E., Pick, S.: Gender stereotypes, sexuality, and culture in Mexico. In: Safdar, S., Kosakowska-Berezecka, N. (eds.) Psychology of Gender Through the Lens of Culture, pp. 285–305. Springer, Cham (2015). https://doi.org/10.1007/978-3-319-14005-6_14

7. Azaola, E.: Patrones, estereotipos y violencia de género en las escuelas de educación básica en México. La ventana **4**(30), 7–45 (2009). ISSN 1405-9436. https://www.scielo.org.mx/scielo.php?pid=S1405-94362009000200003&script=sci_abstract

8. Denner, J., Laursen, B., Dickson, D., Hartl, A.C.: Latino children's math confidence: the role of mothers' gender stereotypes and involvement across the transition to middle school. J. Early Adolesc. **38**(4), 513–529 (2018). https://doi.org/10.1177/0272431616675972

9. Chang, A., Sandhofer, C.M., Brown, C.S.: Gender biases in early number exposure to preschool-aged children. J. Lang. Soc. Psychol. **30**(4), 440–450 (2011). https://doi.org/10.1177/0261927X11416207

10. Tsiunas un videojuego para transformar las relaciones desiguales entre mujeres y hombres. https://colombia.unwomen.org/es/noticias-y-eventos/articulos/2018/5/tsiunas

11. Jesse – A None in Three game. http://www.noneinthree.org/barbados-and-grenada/jesse/

12. The Island Network for Gender Equality "Tenerife Violeta," "Berolos," 2020 (2020). https://www.tenerifevioleta.es/berolos/

13. Instituto Andaluz de la Mujer (Spain), "IGUALA-T," 2018 (2018). http://www.iguala-t.es/app/login

14. Kafai, Y.B.: Considering gender in digital games: implications for serious game designs in the learning sciences. In: Proceedings of the 8th International Conference on International Conference for the Learning Sciences - Volume 1 (ICLS 2008), pp. 422–429. International Society of the Learning Sciences (2008)

15. Barrera Yañez, A.G., Alonso-Fernandez, C., Fernandez Manjon, B.: Review of serious games to educate on gender equality. In: Eighth International Conference on Technological Ecosystems for Enhancing Multiculturality, pp. 662–668 (2020). https://doi.org/10.1145/3434780.3436592

16. Chuka. http://www.chukagame.com/

17. Pérez Colado, V.M., Pérez Colado, I.J., Manuel, F., Martínez-Ortiz, I., Fernández-Manjón, B.: Simplifying the creation of adventure serious games with educational-oriented features. Educ. Technol. Soc. **22**(3), 32–46 (2019). https://doi.org/10.2307/26896708

18. Freire, M., Serrano-Laguna, Á., Iglesias, B.M., Martínez-Ortiz, I., Moreno-Ger, P., Fernández-Manjón, B.: Game learning analytics: learning analytics for serious games. In: Spector, M.J., Lockee, B.B., Childress, M.D. (eds.) Learning, Design, and Technology: An International Compendium of Theory, Research, Practice, and Policy, pp. 1–29. Springer, Cham (2016). https://doi.org/10.1007/978-3-319-17727-4_21-1

19. Garena Free Fire, Usability/Satisfaction survey. https://www.surveycake.com/s/9PVwx

20. Jozkowski, K.N., Ekbia, H.R.: "Campus Craft": a game for sexual assault prevention in universities. Games Health J. **4**(2), 95–106 (2015). https://doi.org/10.1089/g4h.2014.0056

# Learning Experience Design with Maker Education

Roberto E. Araña-Suárez[1] ⓘ, Pedro M. Hernández-Castellano[1](✉) ⓘ,
María Asunción Morales-Santana[2], and Mariana Hernández-Pérez[1] ⓘ

[1] Grupo de Innovación Educativa Ingeniería de Fabricación, ULPGC, 35017 Las Palmas de
Gran Canaria, Islas Canarias, Spain
pedro.hernandez@ulpgc.es
[2] Departamento de Ingeniería Electrónica y Automática (DIEA), Facultad de Ciencias de la
Educación (FCEDU), ULPGC, 35017 Las Palmas de Gran Canaria, Islas Canarias, Spain

**Abstract.** This intervention seeks to improve the teaching of the Technology
subject in the 1st and 2nd courses of secondary education, introducing in the
classroom aspects related to the Maker Movement in education through Maker
Education, a learning approach that focuses on practical learning through projects
and is related to STEAM education. The main objective of this work has been
to generate a significant experience in students that helps them to awake interest
in scientific-technological areas. This has been worked through a project based
on Maker Education in which the students, in groups, have developed a Chained
Effect project, working on skills such as creativity, problem solving, teamwork
and collaboration, and having the opportunity to put into practice the knowledge
acquired. During this experience, a visit to a Makerspace Las Cocinas belonging
to the School of Industrial and Civil Engineering of University of Las Palmas de
Gran Canaria was also made, aiming at including new spaces in the teaching-
learning process. This space was used to teach them the process of designing and
manufacturing of customized parts for each student, bringing students closer to
the world of engineering, design and manufacturing through meaningful learning,
with the goal of impacting favourably on them.

**Keywords:** Maker Education · Project Based Learning · STEAM Education

## 1 Introduction

The rapid advance of technology has meant that society has had to constantly adapt to
a field that does not stop evolving, where everything is constantly being replaced. This
constant change is reflected in society, in this sense the European Parliament approved
the concept of the Third Industrial Revolution in 2007 [1] and in 2016 authors such as
Schwab [2] were already beginning the Fourth Industrial Revolution, currently known as
the Digital Revolution or Industry 4.0, which is based on pillars such as robotics, artificial
intelligence, the Internet of Things (IOT), additive manufacturing and Big Data, among
others [3].

C. S. González-González et al. (Eds.): ICWL 2022/SETE 2022, LNCS 13869, pp. 241–252, 2023.
https://doi.org/10.1007/978-3-031-33023-0_21

Recently, knowledge related to computational thinking, digital competence, STEAM (Science, Technology, Engineering, the Arts and Mathematics) competence, and the use of Learning and Knowledge Technologies (LKT) are being incorporated into educational curricula. Some innovative experiences that have arisen outside the school to respond to this are *The Intel Computer Clubhouse Network* and the *Maker Movement.* Experiences that aim to carry out significant learning while creating a sense of community, offering students and adults the opportunity to get involved in activities related to the STEAM field [4].

In an attempt to introduce these aspects in the school, this paper propose to implant the Maker Culture in the students through Maker Education. With the aim that through actions as playing, experimenting, expressing, building, and connecting, students are able to learn in an active and participatory way, becoming the builder of their own learning. At the same time that they cooperate with their colleagues working on the mentioned pillars and updating the methodology to the technological moment we live in, in the context of Industry 4.0 (Fourth Industrial Revolution).

This proposal also seeks to awaken scientific-technological vocations in students, since, although a future marked by scientific-technological professions is in sight, the number of students who currently choose to study this scientific-technological branch is being reduced, thereby anticipating a significant lack of these professionals [5].

Currently, a large amount of data can be found that supports the lack of scientific-technological vocations among students who finish their high school studies, to give an example, at the University of Las Palmas de Gran Canaria (ULPGC) in Spain we find that among 2013 and 2017, all degrees related to engineering or architecture have presented a decrease in the number of enrollments of up to 32% [6]. Similar numbers occur in all careers in the STEM field around the world, such is the case that UNESCO has carried out projects to promote these scientific-technological vocations, emphasizing girls and adolescents because they present a lower percentage of participation in this field, reaching situations like the one we can observe in Colombia, where only 26% of professionals belonging to STEM careers are women [7].

This document aims to provide literature that supports the use and benefits of this approach, presenting the results obtained in a pilot experience that decided to introduce Maker Education in high schools, aiming at promoting the aforementioned values, awakening STEAM vocations and at the same time reducing the gender gap in the scientific-technological field. This work is included within the *co-edu* research project, that is developing in School of Industrial and Civil Engineering (EIIC) titled *Competencias transversales desde la EIIC para su ecosistema social* (2020EDU20).

## 2   Maker Education

The Maker movement is a social movement made up of people of different profiles who are known as Maker, with the term Maker we include fans, thinkers, engineers, designers, and artists who share the same goal: the design and construction of artifacts [8].

This has been the evolution of the Do It Yourself (DIY) movement and is closely related to learning by doing, promoting teamwork and the generation of knowledge in community [9].

Hatch [10] in his book The Maker Manifesto compiles a series of actions that define the Maker movement, which are: Make, create, give, learn, share, play, change, participate and support [11]. Based on these actions, other authors group some actions and claim that the values of the movement are: design, create, learn, share and improve [12].

Halverson and Sheridan [13] in an article published for the Harvard Educational Review indicated that the Maker movement could not only help the way in which students acquire knowledge and skills, but that this movement could create opportunities to engage the student, generating a connection with the scientific-technological field.

An investigation carried out by the Harvard Project Zero research center establishes three characteristics of learning that are improved from the use of educational experiences centered on the Maker movement [14]. First, it establishes that this experience creates a community based on collaboration and the exchange of information, knowledge and ideas. Second, it claims that aspects such as problem solving, student flexibility, experiential learning and student curiosity are worked on through Making. Finally, this research speaks of the fact that, through the use of this movement, students can access new places of creation with tools that are not usually available in classrooms. This refers to the Makerspace, open spaces that allow anyone to use them, always encouraging participants to share what they do and to learn from others [12].

Although creativity and innovation are fundamental in engineering, there are not many open design experiences that are carried out in university environments [15], this prevents students from outside the university from being able to get involved in activities of this type. However, through the use of the Makerspace as a connector, a link in which students from different educational stages meet and share experiences can be created, since, as Neumeyer and Santos [16] said, the Makerspaces have gone from being spaces of work to places where to achieve a connection between students, users and tools. Davidson and Price [17] claim that involving students in a project in the Makerspace favors self-directed experiential learning, which ends up resulting in improved risk tolerance and increased persistence in complex problem solving for students, skills that are increasingly important in the 21st century citizen.

The Maker movement has been developed in areas outside education and mainly adults were involved in these activities. However, in recent years, efforts have been made to incorporate this movement in lower education, generating the opportunity for students to participate in design and engineering practices, thereby promoting STEAM practice at an earlier age [18], resulting in the concept of Maker Education.

There is no generally accepted definition for the concept of Maker Education, Maaia [19] establishes a relationship between Maker Education and the pedagogy behind problem-based learning. Martinez and Stager [20] established hands-on learning, Problem-Based Learning, and arts-based initiatives as the foundations of this movement, while linking this movement to constructionism and constructivism.

Other authors such as Jurkowski [14] establish that Maker Education encompasses aspects such as the DIY movement, STEM and STEAM education, the increase in technological resources, Project-Based Learning and the need for students to be interested in STEM vocations.

West-Puckett defines this movement as an approach based on the Maker movement that brings the work of manufacture to the front, and through aspects such as design, experimentation, retouching, production and interpretation, the student is able to learn theory and practice [21]. Everything under the premise that through manipulating materials, ideas and objects the student carries out significant learning and is able to better assimilate the contents.

The goal of Maker Education is that students can apply design principles while developing ideas and building prototypes, having access to a variety of design and manufacturing equipment [16], creating opportunities for young people to develop confidence, creativity and interest in the STEAM field through creation [19]. While fostering academic learning through teamwork, experimentation, and problem solving [21, 22].

The use of active methodologies such as those used by Maker Education encourages "Learning by doing", a pedagogy that puts practice as the foundations of any learning process, and that ensures that the student is always thinking and doing, two situations that greatly favor the learning process [23].

In a study published in 2014, Halverson & Sheridan [13] argued that Making was about to have a huge impact in schools. Harlow & Hansen years later also affirmed that this movement was about to transform education, changing the typical focus of schools and giving an emphasis to creation and creativity [24].

However, as Maaia [19] indicates in her thesis *The keys of Maker Education: A Longitudinal Ethnographic Study of a STEM-to-STEAM Curriculum-in-the-Making*, there is currently a great lack of qualitative research in classrooms using the Maker Education, thus generating a lack of literature that supports the use and benefits of using this approach.

## 3   Methodology

The experience we have developed has consisted of the design and manufacture of a chained effect applying the values of Maker Education. It was used for 1st and 2nd course of students of compulsory secondary education (ESO) to get in touch with the technology and tools that we had in the workshop, learning to work collaboratively in a new space for them and following the principles of the Maker movement, as it was the first project carried out in the workshop this should be a easy project in which they could apply the principles of the methodology. A Chained Effect is an automatic machine in which the effects that occur in it take place by themselves from an initial effect.

This experience is divided into four different stages, which encompass the different phases of a technological project: Definition and analysis of the problem, search for information, design, planning, manufacturing, evaluation, and disclosure.

In the first stage, the project is explained to the students, and teams are formed, indicating the requirements and how it will be evaluated. The students also have to carry out a search for information on chained effects, identifying what it is and extracting ideas from other similar projects previously carried out in other schools.

In the second stage, design and planning, each team is in charge of designing the chained effect that will try to build throughout the development of the experience, from that design they look for the way to carry out a construction using recycled or reused materials or elements.

The students are also asked to design a piece that they will have to integrate into the chained effect, this piece will later be built using the machines that the university Makerspace have and that will be visited by the students. Applying sketching and 2D design strategies using CAD software and 3D design using Tinkercad.

During the third stage, the students develop the proposal in the center's workshop classroom. A visit to the Makerspace is also made so that the students can see how the pieces they have designed themselves are manufactured, seeking to generate a positive impact by seeing what they have proposed "theoretically" becomes a reality, at the same time as they share space with university students. Generating with this a learning in diverse fields. This work focuses on this visit.

In the last stage, the students share and promulgate their project with the rest of the class, explaining the decisions they made and what they thought about the experience.

**Experience in *Las Cocinas* Makerspace**

Due to the planning of the academic year and the few class sessions that are available at the time of proposing this experience, an adaptation to the original approach of the proposal had to be made, modifying the part of the experience in which the students designed the pieces that were later going to be generated in the Makerspace because we did not have the necessary time to teach them how to use the necessary tools for this. This is why the piece that is manufactured in the Makerspace was previously designed by the teacher, once they visit the space they can see how this piece is manufactured and, at that moment, they are given the opportunity to customize it, making each unique piece and involving the student in the final design of it, even if it is only in the aesthetic aspect and not in the functional one.

The Makerspace used for this experience is known as *Taller Las Cocinas*. It belongs to the EIIC and has collaborative workstations, 3D printing machines, a $CO_2$ laser cutting machine, computers with CAD software installed and manual tools.

This visit was carried out on two different days by two groups of 1st ESO, made up of 48 students, one day for each group, during the visit the students were divided into three groups that rotated between different activities related to modeling, 3D printing and laser cutting.

In the modeling activity, a student of the Engineering Degree in Industrial Design and Product Development gave them a practical experience in which they used several computer-aided design (CAD) programs. He showed the students how the parts that were going to be manufactured that day were designed, in addition to show the design of other types of objects, allowing them to participate actively through questions about aspects they wanted to modify in pieces that were shown on the screen. In addition, the virtual and physical model of some pieces that were in the Makerspace were also shown, making them see that what was done in the CAD could be brought to reality (Fig. 1).

The 3D printing activity was guided by a PhD student in the QUIMEFA doctoral program from ULPGC. In this activity they were given a short introduction to 3D printing, focusing key aspects but at a very basic level, with the intention that they could easily understand it. The explanation was carried out in a practical way using the printers that the space has. At the end of the explanation, the students could take the piece they had seen being made, one for each student. Also, some other pieces manufactured with 3D printing were shown, showing them with this the variety of pieces that can be made. A

**Fig. 1.** 3D printing activity during the visit.

greater interest was observed by the girls who participated in this activity, they were more active and participative asking questions to the PhD student who was in charge of the activity, it could be assumed that this was due to female students feels more comfortable when is also a female who guides the activity (Fig. 2).

**Fig. 2.** Laser cutting activity during the visit.

The laser cutting was guided by a student of the Master's Degree in Teacher Training for Secondary School with previous experience in engineering, who was developing his internship in the visiting educational center and carrying out this educational innovation experience as his master's thesis, in this activity the students saw how the pieces that were going to have to integrate in the Chained Effect were manufactured. As with 3D printing, the explanation given to them was done in a practical way, with simple concepts and at a level that they could understand. In addition, as had been proposed, they were allowed to customize their pieces, teaching through this how modifications could be made to the design through the CAD program and on the machine itself. During the activity they were also allowed to get involved in the preparations for the manufacture of the piece, interacting directly with the machine in the process.

# 4  Results

A total of 89 students participated in the experience, divided into 48 students from 1st ESO and 41 students from 2nd ESO, with 43 female students and 46 male students. It should be noted that for management reasons at the center where the experience took place, the 2nd ESO students were unable to visit the Makerspace. Even so, these students also received a customized part that they would include in the chained effect.

To evaluate the impact that the intervention has had on the students, two questionnaires were administered, both adapted to the specific situation of the experience. These questionnaires use a quantitative evaluation, using the Likert scale, in addition, they include a question that allows evaluating qualitative aspects of the experience.

The first questionnaire is based on the instrument for evaluating the quality of teaching Course Experience Questionnaire [25]. This sought to evaluate the impact that the trip to the Makerspace had. It was given to the 1st ESO students a few days after the visit. Of the 48 students who participated in the visit, 39 answered the questionnaire.

The second questionnaire, based on the one used in the experience presented in the Engaging High School Girls in Interdisciplinary STEAM article [26], evaluated the general experience of the intervention, this was given to all the students who participated in the intervention experience. 62 out of 89 students answered this questionnaire.

## 4.1  Makerspace Visit Questionnaire

Analyzing the answers obtained in this questionnaire that seeks to evaluate the student's learning experience, it can be seen that of the 21 sections, only one obtained a score between 3 and 3.5; seven received a score between 3.5 and 4; ten received a score between 4 and 4.5, and three received a score between 4.5 and 5. This gives a total average of 4.083, which is approximately 8 out of 10, which is considered a very good score for a first experience of this type even though we consider that it has different aspects to improve.

It can be seen that the activity was interesting for them and that most of them consider that it was worth doing it, in addition, they believe that it broadened their vision of technology. None of the students seems to have felt left out of the group and they feel that it was a stimulating learning experience. However, the scores obtained in the sections corresponding to interest in the field of study and motivation seem to be lower than the rest. Since these sections are very relevant in the appearance of STEAM vocations, an individual analysis will be carried out on the answers obtained for questions 11 and 12, corresponding to "The activity has stimulated my interest in the field of study" and "The activity has been motivating for me" with the intention of identifying if there was any problem related to these aspects.

In question 11, which reports on the interest that this activity generated in the field of study, 13 out of the 39 students gave a neutral answer, 21 considered that they agreed or strongly agreed with this question and only 5 disagreed or strongly disagreed. Although the final average mark was 3.56, through the individual analysis of the answers it can be seen that it has influenced 21 students in a positive way.

Observing the individual responses in question 12, referred to whether the activity had been motivating for them, the average was 3.72, but only 7 students disagreed with this statement, 9 gave a neutral score and 23 agreed or strongly agreed (Fig. 3).

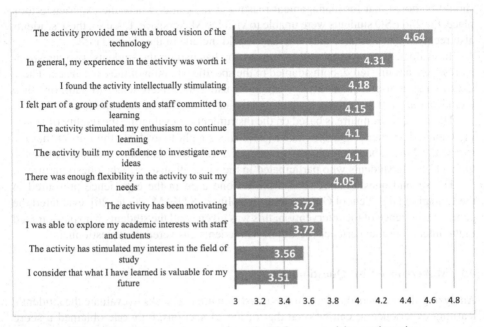

**Fig. 3.** Most relevant responses from the Makerspace visit questionnaire.

Since the percentage of female students who participated and answered the survey is lower, there were also fewer who received a good impact. However, the results of the impact that it has on them is worrying because the activity was raised to avoid gender differences. Even with this, only 30% of the female students considered that the activity stimulated their interest in technology, compared to 65% of male students who did consider it stimulating. Regarding motivation, only 38% of the girls considered the activity as motivating, while 62% of the boys did consider it to be so, although the sample is relatively small, this difference between boys and girls is very relevant.

If we complement this quantitative data with the qualitative answers given by some students, we can see that the 34 students who answered generally stated that they found the activity interesting, that they had fun, they had learned a lot and that they liked it.

We want to highlight the message left by a student who says "I liked it a lot. They treated us very well and I learned a lot", because there are several students who made a comment like this one, although with slight variations. Regarding the rest of the comments, we will highlight one student who said "I feel like dedicating myself to it" and another who said "I did not like it very much because I do not like this subject, but it seemed interesting to me", representing with this a student for whom this activity seemed to have had a very positive impact and another who, even though he did not like technology, considered the activity interesting.

### 4.2  Classroom Experience Questionnaire

To carry out the analysis of the answers given by the 62 students, an individual study of the different categories in which the questions that make up the questionnaire can be grouped, which can be divided into: Work by projects, preferences of learning, perception of impact and vocations. Below are some of the most interesting.

Starting with the opinion of the students about carrying out projects in class, it can be seen in the graph of Fig. 4 that the results obtained are very good, with all the items achieving a score equal to or greater than 4 and obtaining an average of 4.23.

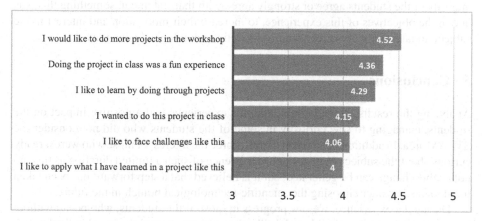

**Fig. 4.** Answers of the sections about your opinion about working by projects.

As can be seen in Fig. 4, the students liked the activity very much and would like to carry out more projects of this style, they also consider that the experience is fun and at the same time they learned. This can be complemented with some of the comments made, a sample of which we list below:

– Student 15: "I really liked the work I'm doing. I have learned to handle tools."
– Student 30: "I like doing technology classes of this type much more, they are much more fun, and I learn more than supposedly paying attention in class. PLEASE DO NOT CHANGE IT"
– Student 50: "I had a lot of fun, do it again"
– Student 53: "I liked working in the workshop and it has taught me many things"

Analyzing the part corresponding to learning preferences, it is observed that most of the students prefer to work in a group rather than individually, in addition, they generally believe that they can contribute a lot when they work as a team, although not many feel identified with the role of group leader.

Within the answers obtained, it can also be seen that the majority of the students agree that they usually apply what they know to solve the problems they face.

In general, through the answers obtained, it is observed that the experience had a very good impact on some self-perception factors of the students, including the ability to use tools, teamwork, and the ability to design and create things.

The section with the lowest average score is the one corresponding to "It helped me develop strategies to solve problems", although this section is above 3 and, therefore, a part of the class agrees or strongly agrees with it. We were surprised that he presented such a low score since through systematic observation it has been possible to see the influence that the activity has had on their abilities to solve problems, which we believe have been improved.

Another of the scores obtained and that reaffirms the correctness of the intervention is "It made me more interested in technology" and "It increased my motivation in the subject of technology", since both sections received a 4 or higher score, that is, that the majority of the students agree or strongly agree with that statement, something that was one of the objectives of this experience, to increase their motivation and interest in the subject, to later think about awakening scientific-technological vocations.

## 5   Conclusions

Analyzing the results, it can be seen that this experience had a positive impact on the students, managing to sow curiosity in some of the students who did not consider the STEAM area. In addition, it has served to reinforce the interest of those who were already curious about the subject. With a single experience of such a limited duration as this, no noticeable change can be generated, but it is believed that a step forward has been taken for students consider choosing the scientific-technological branch in the future.

During the experience, we saw progress in most of the students, who began without being able to use tools or build models like the ones we showed them and in final weeks they demonstrated that they were capable of using these tools with ease, also showing a security at work that they did not show before. However, when asked through the questionnaire, the marks received do not fully correspond with this perception.

It has also been identified that their ability to provide solutions to the problems that appeared was increased during the experience, although they did not perceive it in the questionnaires. This could be observed through the change that they presented between the first and the last sessions. In the first sessions they constantly asked the teachers how they could solve the problems that appeared, while in the last ones they were the ones who, autonomously, looked for a solution.

All the improvement perceived in the students during the experience is very difficult to reveal through standardized questionnaires or questions asked to the students, since they are not usually able to notice their own improvement. However, the teacher is able to see such improvement. This has reminded us of the contribution made by Maaia [19] in her thesis mentioned before in which she said that it was very difficult to find qualitative research in the classroom using Maker Education, with this intervention it has been seen that this lack of literature is believed to be due to the difficulty of capturing these data of a subjective and individual nature.

In addition, it is considered that the results of this intervention show that it is necessary to design activities specifically aimed at girls to try to overcome prejudices and stereotypes that better attract their attention and to be able to motivate them to open new learning opportunities in this area. This result is coincidental with much of the available literature on the gender gap. For future experiences, it has been considered convenient that most of the training activities could be taught by female engineering students so that they could be a more direct reference for the participating female students.

**Acknowledgments.** This work was partially funded by the The Next Generation EU (NGEU) fund under "Real Decreto 641/2021, de 27 de julio, por el que se regula la concesión directa de subvenciones a universidades públicas españolas para la modernización y digitalización del sistema universitario español en el marco del plan de recuperación, transformación y resiliencia (UNIDIGITAL) - Proyectos de Innovación Educativa para la Formación Interdisciplinar (PIEFI) - Línea 3. Contenidos y programas de formación" in the scope of the Teaching Innovation Project "Aplicando Ingeniería para el Aprendizaje en la EIIC (PIE2021-10)".

We also want to thank Antonio Ramírez, who tutored during internship and the Colegio Sagrado Corazón de Tafira for give us the opportunity to make this activity.

# References

1. Lastra Lastra, J.M.: Rifkin, Jeremy, La Tercera Revolución Industrial. Bol. Mex. Derecho Comp. **50**, 1457–1462 (2017)
2. Schwab, K.: La cuarta revolución industrial. Debate (2016)
3. Basco, A.I., Beliz, G., Coatz, D., Garnero, P.: Industria 4.0: fabricando el futuro. Inter-American Development Bank (2018)
4. Berrocoso, J.V., Sánchez, M.R.F., del Carmen Garrido Arroyo, M.: El pensamiento computacional y las nuevas ecologías del aprendizaje. Rev. Educ. Distancia RED **46**, 1–18 (2015)
5. Rubio, I.: Las matriculaciones en carreras técnicas bajan pese a la demanda laboral. El País (2019)
6. ULPGC - Número de Matriculados. https://www2.ulpgc.es/index.php?pagina=transpare ncia&ver=matriculados
7. Cajiao, M.C.R., Herrera, A., Álvarez, M.M.M.: Ingenieros sin fronteras e ingeniosas: estrategias para la educación en ingeniería. Encuentro Internacional de Educación en Ingeniería (2021)
8. Kwon, B.-R., Lee, J.: What makes a maker: the motivation for the maker movement in ICT. Inf. Technol. Dev. **23**, 318–335 (2017). https://doi.org/10.1080/02681102.2016.1238816
9. Cardona Liberado, N., Mileida Rodríguez, B., Páez Fajardo, E.: Una experiencia pedagógica significativa basada en los principios del Movimiento "Maker" enfocada al fortalecimiento de las competencias tecnológicas y la integración de las TIC (2019)
10. Hatch, M.: The Maker Movement Manifesto: Rules for Innovation in the New World of Crafters, Hackers, and Tinkerers. McGraw Hill Professional, New York (2014)
11. Domínguez, F., Antequera, J.G.: El movimiento Maker como ecología de aprendizaje: estudio del caso Gumiparty. In: CIAIQ 2017, vol. 1 (2017)
12. Dougherty, D.: Free to Make: How the Maker Movement is Changing Our Schools, Our Jobs, and Our Minds. North Atlantic Books, Berkeley (2016)
13. Halverson, E.R., Sheridan, K.: The maker movement in education. Harv. Educ. Rev. **84**, 495–504 (2014)
14. Jurkowski, K.G.: Teachers' Experiences with Learning through Making (2019)
15. Forest, C.R., et al.: The invention studio: a university maker space and culture. Adv. Eng. Educ. **4**, n2 (2014)
16. Neumeyer, X., Santos, S.C.: Makerspaces as learning sites at the intersection of engineering and entrepreneurship education. Int. J. Eng. Educ. **36**, 1295–1301 (2020)

17. Davidson, A.-L., Price, D.W.: Does your school have the maker fever? An experiential learning approach to developing maker competencies. Learn. Landsc. **11**, 103–120 (2017)
18. Martin, L.: The promise of the maker movement for education. J. Pre-Coll. Eng. Educ. Res. J-PEER **5**, 4 (2015)
19. Maaia, L.C.: The Keys to Maker Education: A Longitudinal Ethnographic Study of a STEM-to-STEAM Curriculum-in-the-Making (2018)
20. Martinez, S.L., Stager, G.: Invent to learn. In: Making, Tinkering, and Engineering in the Classroom. Constructing Modern Knowledge, Torrance, Canada (2013)
21. West-Puckett, S.J.: Materializing makerspaces: queerly composing space, time, and (what) matters (2017)
22. Herold, B.: The Maker Movement in K-12 Education: A Guide to Emerging Research (2016). https://www.edweek.org/teaching-learning/the-maker-movement-in-k-12-education-a-guide-to-emerging-research/2016/04
23. Bevan, B., Gutwill, J.P., Petrich, M., Wilkinson, K.: Learning through STEM-rich tinkering: findings from a jointly negotiated research project taken up in practice. Sci. Educ. **99**, 98–120 (2015)
24. Harlow, D., Hansen, A.: School maker faires: this event blends next generation science standards goals with the concepts of the maker movement. Sci. Child. **55**, 30–37 (2018)
25. Wilson, K.L., Lizzio, A., Ramsden, P.: The development, validation and application of the Course Experience Questionnaire. Stud. High. Educ. **22**(1), 33–53 (1997). https://doi.org/10.1080/03075079712331381121
26. Kennedy, T.J., Odell, M.R.L.: Engaging students in STEM education. Sci. Educ. Int. **25**(3), 3 (2014)

# Mobile English Learning: A Meta-analysis

Juan Garzón[1](✉) (iD), Georgios Lampropoulos[2] (iD), and Daniel Burgos[3] (iD)

[1] Universidad Católica de Oriente, 054040 Rionegro, Antioquia, Colombia
fgarzon@uco.edu.co
[2] International Hellenic University, 57001 Thessaloniki, Nea Moudania, Greece
[3] Universidad Internacional de la Rioja, La Rioja, 26006 Logroño, Spain

**Abstract.** The advantages of mobile learning (m-learning) in English education have been widely described in previous research; however, there is little evidence of its effects on student outcomes. To fill this research gap, we conducted a meta-analysis of 54 empirical studies to measure its impact on student achievement. In addition, we estimated the moderating effects of the pedagogical approach, the learning environment, the education level, the control treatment, and the mobile device. The results indicate that m-learning has a large impact ($g = 0.94$) on students' achievement. This effect is influenced by the pedagogical approach, the education level, and the control treatment, but not by the learning environment or the mobile device. Finally, we explain the nature of these results in light of learning theories.

**Keywords:** English Learning · ESL · Meta-Analysis · Mobile Learning

## 1 Introduction

Mobile learning (m-learning) has experienced rapid growth since 2013. That year, UNESCO released its policy guidelines for mobile learning [1], setting a milestone in the field of educational technology. According to UNESCO [2], m-learning expands and enriches education for all types of learners. Therefore, this organization has encouraged research into this approach as a strategy to eliminate space and time barriers in education, thus increasing the number of people who access educational content.

### 1.1 M-Learning in English Education

Learning English as a Second Language (ESL) has become necessary to meet 21st-century demands. This language is used for business, entertainment, education, and research. Hence, teachers and researchers are encouraged to do their best to provide students with the right pedagogical tools to help them succeed in learning English.

Learning a language involves four primary skills: reading, writing, listening, and speaking [3]. Therefore, English education must include different strategies to help students acquire these abilities. Previous studies have noted that an effective way to promote multiple abilities when learning a second language is to use active learning techniques

C. S. González-González et al. (Eds.): ICWL 2022/SETE 2022, LNCS 13869, pp. 253–264, 2023.
https://doi.org/10.1007/978-3-031-33023-0_22

that allow students to participate in the construction of knowledge [4, 5]. Mobile devices have proven to help present information in multiple formats [6]. That is, mobile devices allow students to actively construct knowledge using multiple means in ways hardly possible with other pedagogic alternatives. However, although mobile devices provide multiple possibilities, it is not the technical tools that guarantee academic success, but the pedagogical strategies underpinning educational interventions [7]. We, therefore, propose that using mobile devices as part of a well-structured academic intervention enhances students' chances of mastering ESL.

## 1.2 Related Works

To estimate the impact of m-learning on education, the meta-analysis technique has been widely used. A meta-analysis establishes the general characteristics of an experimental treatment by analyzing the results of individual studies that have investigated it [8]. Some comprehensive meta-analyses have measured the impact of m-learning on students' outcomes [9, 10]. Other meta-analytical studies have focused on education levels [11], mobile devices [12], or pedagogical approaches [13]. Additionally, other studies have analyzed the impact of m-learning on language learning [14, 15] or have focused on specific English skills, such as vocabulary acquisition [16].

To the best of our knowledge, only one meta-analysis has estimated the impact of m-learning on English learning [17]. This study analyzed 29 studies published in gray literature and peer-reviewed journals between 2008 and 2019. It found an effect of $g = 0.89$ on student learning. Furthermore, the study found that this effect is influenced by the education level and mobile device, but not by the learning environment or the intervention duration. However, this work had some research gaps. First, the inclusion of non-peer-reviewed papers did not allow the authors to guarantee the quality of the meta-analysis [18]. Second, the reduced number of analyzed studies risked biasing the conclusions of the meta-analysis [19]. Third, the study did not analyze the educational theory underpinning each intervention, ignoring the importance of the pedagogical approach in guaranteeing academic success [20]. Fourth, the study failed to analyze the pedagogical strategies included in the control treatment to determine the amount of knowledge that could be explicitly attributed to m-learning [13].

## 1.3 Purpose of the Study

Based on the previous background, the current study presents a comprehensive meta-analysis to measure the impact of m-learning on student achievement in English education. Furthermore, the study estimates the moderating effect of the pedagogical approach, the learning environment, the education level, the control treatment, and the mobile device. Specifically, the study answers the following research questions (RQ):

RQ1: What is the impact of m-learning on student learning in English education?

RQ2: What factors moderate the impact of m-learning on student learning in English education?

# 2 Methods

To identify the impact of m-learning on student learning, we conducted a meta-analysis. A meta-analysis entails the analysis of the results of a group of empirical studies to integrate their findings [21]. The primary purpose of a meta-analysis is to estimate the effect size that represents the magnitude of the effect of an experimental treatment, transformed into a standardized mean difference [22]. We followed a four-step procedure to conduct the meta-analysis [23]: study selection, data coding, effect size calculation, and moderating effect analysis.

## 2.1 Study Selection

This meta-analysis followed the PRISMA principles [24]. The search for relevant studies was performed on the Web of Science, Scopus, Science Direct, and IEEE Xplore. These databases were chosen as they address the field of educational technology and include high-quality journals and conference proceedings. The search included the terms "mobile," "English," and "education." In addition, we used alternative search terms to produce a more comprehensive collection of studies. Alternative search terms for "mobile" were "handheld" and "ubiquitous," alternative search terms for "English" were "ESL" and "EFL," and alternative search terms for "education" were "teaching," "instruction," and "learning." The last search was performed on June 30, 2022. After removing duplicates, we identified 227 potential studies.

We limited the search to studies published from 2013 onward to align with the UNESCO policy guidelines for mobile learning [1]. In addition, we considered only studies from peer-reviewed journals or conference proceedings to ensure the strength and quality of the analysis [18]. Table 1 presents the inclusion/exclusion criteria.

**Table 1.** Inclusion/exclusion criteria.

| Include if all the following criteria are met | Exclude if any of the following criteria is met |
|---|---|
| Empirical research | Secondary data analysis |
| Includes a mobile device | Work in progress |
| Relates to English education | Thesis, editorial, or book reviews |
| Measures students' learning gains | Uses laptops or stationary game consoles as the learning device |
| Includes a control condition | Data are obtained through a self-assessment |
| Applies a true experimental design or a quasi-experimental design | Does not provide sufficient information to estimate the effect size |

Two authors performed the initial screening based on title, abstract, and keywords. This process reduced the number of studies to 165. The same authors then reviewed the methods section of each study in light of the inclusion/exclusion criteria. This process yielded 54 studies relevant to the research questions. At all stages of the process, occasional disagreements were resolved through consensus.

## 2.2 Data Coding

We designed a data extraction form to collect the data. It included the year of publication, type of research design, pedagogical approach, learning environment, education level, control treatment, mobile device, sample size, mean values, and standard deviations. The first and third authors extracted the information from each paper using the content analysis technique [25]. Inter-coder reliability was calculated according to Cohen's kappa. This value was found to be 89%, indicating a high degree of agreement [26]. As in the study selection process, occasional disagreements were resolved through consensus.

## 2.3 Effect Size Calculation

To measure the impact of m-learning on student learning, we calculated the effect size of each study based on Hedges' $g$ [27]. We followed the procedure recommended by Borenstein et al. [8], which consists of three steps: 1) calculate the effect size of each study based on Cohen's $d$, 2) convert this value into the Hedges' $g$ value, and 3) combine the effect sizes to estimate the weighted average effect size.

To calculate the effect size of each study, we used the formula proposed by Borenstein et al. [8]. We then transformed each effect into the Hedges' $g$ using the Hedges' correction [11, p. 27]. Finally, to estimate the weighted average effect size, we combined the effects based on the random effects model [11, p. 69]. This model was chosen because the study samples were drawn from populations with varying effect sizes [27]. As recommended, each study contributed a single effect size [8].

Finally, to rule out Hawthorne effects [22], we did not consider studies that did not involve a control condition. Consequently, we included pretest-posttest with control (PPC) and posttest only with control (POWC) research design studies [22]. The guidelines to interpret the effect sizes were as follow: $-0.15 < g < 0.15$ negligible; $0.15 \leq g < 0.40$ small; $0.40 \leq g < 0.75$ medium; $0.75 \leq g < 1.10$ large, $1.10 \leq g < 1.45$ very large; and $1.45 \leq g$ huge [28].

## 2.4 Moderating Effect Analysis

This analysis was performed to evaluate whether the impact of m-learning on student achievement varied according to the specific characteristics of the studies. We tested the homogeneity of effect sizes across studies using the $Q$, $I^2$, and $p$ statistics [27]. The values of these statistics (see Table 2) indicated heterogeneity in effect sizes, suggesting the possibility of moderator variables. We conducted a preplanned analysis to identify whether the pedagogical approach, the learning environment, the education level, the control treatment, or the mobile device influenced the overall effect size.

**Pedagogical Approach.** This analysis helped identify which learning theories best support each specific situation. This data can be used to inform researchers about what strategies to implement in m-learning interventions. We classified the studies according to categories proposed in previous research [20, 29]: game-based learning (GBL), cognitive theory of multimedia learning (CTML), situated learning (SL), collaborative learning (CL), project-based learning (PBL), and inquiry-based learning (IBL). If a study included elements of different approaches, we coded it according to the more influential approach in the intervention [20]. Similarly, if a study did not explicitly mention a pedagogical approach, we identified the underlying approach by analyzing the characteristics of the intervention [30].

**Learning Environment.** This analysis was important in identifying which contexts favor students' achievement and enable them to make the most of the advantages of using mobile devices. We classified the learning environment in each study, following suggestions in previous research [30]: formal settings (FS) (classrooms and laboratories), semi-formal settings (SS) (field trips, outdoor activities, museums, and homes), informal settings (IS) (means of transportation, parks, and recreational places), and multiple settings (MS) (more than two settings simultaneously).

**Education Level.** This analysis revealed which levels of education benefit the most from m-learning, allowing us to establish under what conditions it is advantageous or not to use mobile devices in education. We coded the education level in each study according to the UNESCO classification [31]: early childhood education (ECE), primary education (PE), lower secondary education (LSE), upper secondary education (USE), post-secondary non-tertiary education (PNTE), short-cycle tertiary education (SCTE), bachelor's level (BL), master's level (ML), and doctoral level (DL).

**Control Treatment.** This analysis was crucial as it allowed us to identify the learning that can be explicitly attributed to m-learning. We coded the control treatment in each study following the categories recommended in previous research [32]: multimedia (M) (other multimedia non-mobile resources), traditional pedagogical tools (TPT) (non-technological educational resources), and traditional lectures (TL) (lectures and curriculum-based teaching methods).

**Mobile Device.** This analysis helped identify which mobile devices should or should not be used according to the students' characteristics. Additionally, it provided an idea of what type of device investments should be directed towards. We classified the mobile devices used in each study according to the different devices that have been used in education in the last decade: smartphone (S), tablet (T), personal digital assistant (PDA), game-consoles (GC), smartwatches (SW), and smartglasses (SG).

# 3 Results and Discussion

All the effect sizes were found to be positive. According to the guidelines, there were 2 negligible effects, 4 small effects, 22 medium effects, 8 large effects, 6 very large effects, and 12 huge effects. There was one unusually huge effect size of $g = 7.16$ [33]. This study was excluded as its effect could bias the results [34]. We used the random effects model to calculate the weighted mean effect of the remaining studies.

## 3.1 Descriptive Data of the Studies

Fifty-four studies published between 2013 and 2022 were included in the meta-analysis. The participants ($N = 4,403$) were randomly assigned to the m-learning condition ($N = 2,252$) or the control condition ($N = 2,151$). Two studies were published in 2013, one in 2014, seven in 2015, four in 2016, six in 2017, four in 2018, nine in 2019, six in 2020, eight in 2021, and seven in 2022. The studies were conducted in 17 different countries on all inhabited continents, which supports the idea that m-learning has attracted interest worldwide. They were published in 36 peer-reviewed journals and conference proceedings. As usual in English education, *Computer Assisted Language Learning* published the largest number of studies ($N = 8$).

## 3.2 Impact of M-Learning on Student Achievement

The overall weighted effect size was $g = 0.94$, with a 95% confidence interval [0.79 − 1.10] and $p < .001$, indicating that m-learning positively impacts student achievement in English education (see Table 2). That is, using mobile devices in English education can improve knowledge scores by 0.94 standard deviations, which can be classified as a large effect according to the proposed guidelines [28]. Furthermore, the standard score indicated significant statistical differences in achievement between the experimental and control groups ($z = 11.91, p < .001$).

**Table 2.** Effect size path coefficients.

| Variable | Value |
|---|---|
| Number of samples ($K$) | 53 |
| Total sample size ($N$) | 4,320 |
| Effect size ($g$) | 0.94 |
| Confidence interval (95%) | [0.79–1.10] |
| Standard score ($Z$) | 11.91 |
| Probability value ($p$) | $< .001$ |
| Heterogeneity test ($Q$) | 291.77 |
| Heterogeneity test ($I^2$) | 82.18 |

These positive results can be explained by the multimedia nature of mobile devices, which allow multiple senses to be stimulated to develop skills such as reading, writing, listening, and speaking [3]. In addition, mobile devices work as pedagogical tools that students can use to construct learning actively [5]. These tools can extend learning environments to outdoor spaces, thus eliminating space and time constraints. Finally, mobile devices' usability allows students to feel more confident in the learning process [5], which translates into better academic achievement [15].

**Heterogeneity Test.** As depicted in Table 2, the studies included in the meta-analysis had heterogeneous effects on the evaluated population, suggesting that the variance among the studies was unlikely to be due to sampling errors [8]. The $Q$ value was higher than the critical value ($Q = 291.77 > 69.93, df = 52$) at a 95% significance level from the Chi-square distribution table. Similarly, the $I^2$ index was measured to identify the level of true heterogeneity. This value indicated that 83.40% of the total variance reflected real differences in effect sizes [35]. Finally, the $p - value$ lower than .05 also indicated heterogeneity. These three values support the assumption of the random effects model and imply the possibility of moderating variables.

**Publication Bias.** Publication bias was evaluated using three methods, namely, a trim-and-fill plot [36], Egger's regression test [37], and the classic fail-safe N [38]. As depicted in Fig. 1, the studies are symmetrically plotted according to their combined effect size. Most of the studies appear in the upper part of the graph, suggesting the absence of publication bias [36]. This visual inspection was confirmed through Egger's regression ($t[52] = 5.10, p < .001$). Additionally, the classic fail-safe N for this meta-analysis was found to be 8,926. This value indicates that it would be necessary to include 8,926 "null" studies to nullify the effect. This analysis indicates that the meta-analysis results are reliable and unlikely to suffer publication bias.

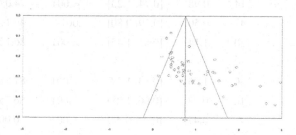

**Fig. 1.** Funnel Plot of Standard Error by Hedges' $g$.

### 3.3 Moderator Analysis

Table 3 summarizes the moderator analysis. We evaluated the between-group homogeneity ($Q_B$) using the mixed method approach to identify group differences. This value allowed us to determine whether a variable moderates the impact of m-learning on student achievement or not.

**Pedagogical Approach.** The between-groups analysis indicated that the effect of m-learning on student achievement differs significantly according to the pedagogical approach used ($Q_B = 12.70, p < .05$). The effect was found to be huge on CL ($g = 1.50, p < .001$), large on SL ($g = 0.95, p < .001$) and GBL ($g = 0.83, p < .001$), and medium on CTML ($g = 0.70, p < .001$). No studies included PBL or IBL, perhaps because these approaches are more common in engineering (PBL) or science (IBL) related fields [9].

**Table 3.** Summary of the moderating analysis.

| Moderator variable | N | g | 95%CI | p | $I^2$ | $Q_B$ |
|---|---|---|---|---|---|---|
| Pedagogical approach | | | | | | 12.70* |
| GBL | 9 | 0.83 | [0.52, 1.14] | <.001 | 71.91 | |
| CTML | 6 | 0.70 | [0.60, 0.80] | <.001 | 19.10 | |
| SL | 8 | 0.95 | [0.51, 1.39] | <.001 | 79.28 | |
| CL | 6 | 1.50 | [0.86, 2.15] | <.001 | 86.50 | |
| Learning environment | | | | | | 3.692 |
| FS | 35 | 0.81 | [0.66, 0.97] | <.001 | 76.42 | |
| SS | 15 | 1.11 | [0.76, 1.46] | <.001 | 83.13 | |
| MS | 3 | 1.59 | [0.37, 2.82] | .011 | 91.55 | |
| Education level | | | | | | 17.33* |
| ECE | 2 | 0.51 | [0.19, 0.82] | .001 | 0.00 | |
| PE | 8 | 1.01 | [0.45, 1.58] | <.001 | 87.44 | |
| LSE | 5 | 0.56 | [0.31, 0.81] | <.001 | 26.62 | |
| USE | 14 | 0.98 | [0.74, 1.23] | <.001 | 74.07 | |
| SCTE | 4 | 0.50 | [0.19, 0.80] | .001 | 49.11 | |
| BL | 20 | 1.14 | [0.82, 1.45] | <.001 | 86.12 | |
| Control treatment | | | | | | 18.95* |
| TL | 30 | 1.05 | [0.83, 1.27] | <.001 | 81.82 | |
| TPT | 16 | 0.97 | [0.66, 1.28] | <.001 | 86.75 | |
| M | 7 | 0.47 | [0.30, 0.64] | <.001 | 0.00 | |
| Mobile device | | | | | | 5.83 |
| S | 42 | 0.98 | [0.3, 1.01] | <.001 | 84.19 | |
| T | 9 | 0.70 | [0.55, 0.86] | <.001 | 0.00 | |
| PDA | 2 | 1.58 | [0.18, 3.34] | .078 | 94.58 | |

Note: *$p < .05$.

The most positive results from interventions adopting the CL approach can be attributed to its ability to increase students' confidence [15] and reduce their cognitive load and cognitive anxiety [14]. Additionally, the results in interventions adopting the SL or the GBL approaches were significantly positive. The SL approach helps immerse students in real English learning contests [7], while the GBL approach increases students' motivation, which is vital to succeeding in any learning process [20].

**Learning Environment.** The between-groups analysis indicated that the learning environment does not moderate m-learning's effect on student achievement ($Q_B = 3.69, p = .16$). The effect was found to be very large on SS ($g = 1.11, p < .001$) and large on FS ($g = 0.81, p < .001$). On the other hand, the effect on MS was found to be huge ($g = 1.59, p = .011$); however, the small sample size did not permit establishing a reliable conclusion regarding this result.

Results showed no significant differences regarding the learning environment, indicating that similar positive results may be produced in all types of environments. This fact is in line with the results of Chen [17] and further validates the flexibility and versatility that m-learning brings to traditional learning activities by taking education outside traditional classrooms [2].

**Education Level.** The between-groups analysis indicates that the education level moderates m-learning's effect on student achievement ($Q_B = 17.33, p < .05$). The effect was very large on BL ($g = 1.14, p < .001$), large on PE ($g = 1.01, p < .001$) and USE ($g = 0.98, p < .001$), and medium on LSE ($g = 0.56, p = .001$). The effect was also medium on ECE ($g = 0.51, p = .001$) and SCTE ($g = 0.50, p = .001$). However, the small sample size does not allow establishing reliable conclusions regarding those education levels.

The positive results at all educational levels indicate that using mobile devices is an effective strategy to help all students learn English, regardless of their age. In BL and secondary education (USE and LSE), institutions tend to exploit the Bring Your Own Device (BYOD) concept to lower the costs related to purchasing devices [39]. This fact positively affects the students' confidence, yielding better academic results. However, the BYOD concept is better applied to a mature population, as the risk of distraction and usability issues is lower [10]. This may explain why LSE students' results are not as good as those of students at the USE and BL levels, and perhaps indicate that these students are not ready to use smartphones as a learning tool.

## 4 Control Treatment

The between-groups analysis indicated differences in the effect of m-learning on student achievement according to the control treatment ($Q_B = 18.95, p < .05$). The effect was found to be very large when compared with TL ($g = 1.05, p < .001$), large when compared with TPT ($g = 0.97, p < .001$), and medium when compared with M ($g = 0.47, p < .001$).

These results were expected as previous research has established that English language learning is more effective when active learning techniques are employed [4, 5]. Consequently, the effects of m-learning are more evident when compared with traditional passive lectures, which do not motivate the students to learn the academic content. In the same line, the positive effects of m-learning are less evident when compared with those of other multimedia resources, as those strategies also represent active learning techniques.

**Mobile Device.** The between-groups analysis indicated that the mobile device used does not moderate the effect of m-learning on student achievement ($Q_B = 5.83, p = .05$). The effect was found to be large when using S ($g = 0.98, p < .001$) and medium when using T ($g = 0.70, p < .001$). The effect on PDA was found to be huge ($g = 1.58, p = .08$); however, the small sample size did not allow us to establish reliable conclusions.

These results indicate that similar positive effects can be obtained regardless of the device. Our results contradict the study by Chen [17], as that study found a negative impact when PDA or smartphone applications were used. However, it is important to note that the mentioned study included gray literature papers; therefore, the results may have been confounding.

## 5  Conclusion

This study aimed to assess the impact of m-learning on student achievement in English education and to identify the factors that moderate the impact. To fulfill this, a meta-analysis of 54 empirical studies published from 2013 to 2022 was carried out. As language learning is a significant aspect of one's life, no educational level was excluded. Based on the results, it can be inferred that m-learning has a large impact on student achievement. The pedagogical approach, the education level, and the control treatment significantly moderate that impact, while the learning environment and the type of mobile device do not. Furthermore, even though m-learning's flexibility and versatility, along with its availability in time and space, are some of its main advantages, most studies have taken place in semi-informal or formal settings. As most favorable outcomes were observed in multiple settings and semi-informal settings, future research should focus on exploring outer environments to reap the benefits of m-learning and reach its full potential. Given that modern students grow up surrounded by digital devices and technological applications, they are more accustomed to handling mobile devices even from a young age. This fact can justify the positive impact of integrating m-learning in English education at all educational levels. Additionally, it seems evident that the positive outcomes are due to using mobile devices and not the intervention, as better learning results were observed in m-learning interventions compared to traditional approaches and other multimedia resources. The results of this study can be invaluable for researchers and teachers, providing insights to help them design and develop compelling learning experiences, materials, and activities. This study highlights the potential benefits of m-learning in English education and answers UNESCO's call to investigate this matter. It can be concluded that m-learning is a flexible and versatile pedagogical approach that can be integrated into all education levels, enrich and support existing educational practices, and be implemented in diverse contexts while providing high-quality education for everyone.

## References

1. West, M., Vosloo, S.: Policy Guidelines for Mobile Learning. UNESCO, UNESCO Publishing, Paris (2013)
2. UNESCO: Global Education Coalition. https://en.unesco.org/covid19/educationresponse/globalcoalition
3. Thomas, N., Bowen, N.E.J.A., Reynolds, B.L., Osment, C., Pun, J.K.H., Mikolajewska, A.: A systematic review of the core components of language learning strategy research in Taiwan. English Teach. Learn. 45, 355–374 (2021). https://doi.org/10.1007/s42321-021-00095-1

4. Qiu, J.: A preliminary study of english mobile learning model based on constructivism. Theory Pract. Lang. Stud. **9**, 1167–1172 (2019)
5. Orak, S.D., Al-Khresheh, M.H.: In between 21st century skills and constructivism in ELT: designing a model derived from a narrative literature review. World J. English Lang. **11**, 166–176 (2021)
6. Klimova, B.: Evaluating impact of mobile applications on EFL university learners' vocabulary learning - a review study. Procedia Comput. Sci. **184**, 859–864 (2021)
7. Santos, J., Figueiredo, A.S., Vieira, M.: Innovative pedagogical practices in higher education: an integrative literature review. Nurse Educ. Today **72**, 12–17 (2019)
8. Borenstein, M., Hedges, L.V., Higgins, J.P.T., Rothstein, H.R.: Introduction to Meta-Analysis. Wiley, Hoboken (2009)
9. Talan, T.: The effect of mobile learning on learning performance: a meta-analysis study. Educ. Sci. Theory Pract. **20**, 79–103 (2020). https://doi.org/10.12738/jestp.2020.1.006
10. Güler, M., Bütüner, S.Ö., Danişman, Ş, Gürsoy, K.: A meta-analysis of the impact of mobile learning on mathematics achievement. Educ. Inf. Technol. **27**, 1725–1745 (2021)
11. Burden, K., Kearney, M., Schuck, S., Hall, T.: Investigating the use of innovative mobile pedagogies for school-aged students: a systematic literature review. Comput. Educ. **138**, 83–100 (2019)
12. Kim, J.H., Park, H.: Effects of smartphone-based mobile learning in nursing education: a systematic review and meta-analysis. Asian Nurs. Res. (Korean. Soc. Nurs. Sci). **13**, 20–29 (2019)
13. Sung, Y.T., Yang, J.M., Lee, H.Y.: The effects of mobile-computer-supported collaborative learning: meta-analysis and critical synthesis. Rev. Educ. Res. **87**, 768–805 (2017)
14. Cho, K., Lee, S., Joo, M.H., Becker, B.J.: The effects of using mobile devices on student achievement in language learning: a meta-analysis. Educ. Sci. **8**, 13–15 (2018)
15. Chen, Z., Chen, W., Jia, J., An, H.: The effects of using mobile devices on language learning: a meta-analysis. Educ. Tech. Res. Dev. **68**(4), 1769–1789 (2020). https://doi.org/10.1007/s11 423-020-09801-5
16. Lin, J.J., Lin, H.: Mobile-assisted ESL/EFL vocabulary learning: a systematic review and meta-analysis. Comput. Assist. Lang. Learn. **32**, 878–919 (2019)
17. Chen, M.L.: The impact of mobile learning on the effectiveness of english teaching and learning - a meta-analysis. IEEE Access. **10**, 38324–38334 (2022)
18. Gurevitch, J., Koricheva, J., Nakagawa, S., Stewart, G.: Meta-analysis and the science of research synthesis. Nature **555**, 175–182 (2018)
19. Pigott, T.D., Polanin, J.R.: Methodological guidance paper: high-quality meta-analysis in a systematic review. Rev. Educ. Res. **90**, 24–46 (2020)
20. Garzón, J., Kinshuk, Baldiris, S., Gutiérrez, J., Pavón, J.: How do pedagogical approaches affect the impact of augmented reality on education? A meta-analysis and research synthesis. Educ. Res. Rev. **31**, 1–19 (2020)
21. Glass, G.V.: Primary, secondary, and meta-analysis of research. Educ. Res. **5**, 3–8 (1976)
22. Morris, S.B.: Estimating effect sizes from pretest-posttest-control group designs. Organ. Res. Methods. **11**, 364–386 (2008). https://doi.org/10.1177/1094428106291059
23. Glass, G.V., Smith, M.L., McGaw, B.: Meta-Analysis in Social Research. Sage Publications, Thousand Oaks (1981)
24. Page, M.J., et al.: The PRISMA 2020 statement: an updated guideline for reporting systematic reviews. Syst. Rev. **10**, 1–11 (2021)
25. Krippendorff, K.: Content Analysis: An Introduction to its Methodology. Sage publications, Thousand Oaks (2018)
26. Cohen, L., Manion, L., Morrison, K.: Research Methods in Education. Routledge, London (2002)

27. Hedges, L.V., Olkin, I.: Statistical Methods for Meta-Analysis. Academic Press, New York (1985)
28. Thalheimer, W., Cook, S.: How to calculate effect sizes from published research: a simplified methodology. Work. Res. 1–9 (2002). https://doi.org/10.1113/jphysiol.2004.078915
29. Hainey, T., Connolly, T.M., Boyle, E.A., Wilson, A., Razak, A.: A systematic literature review of games-based learning empirical evidence in primary education. Comput. Educ. **102**, 202–223 (2016)
30. Bano, M., Zowghi, D., Kearney, M., Schuck, S., Aubusson, P.: Mobile learning for science and mathematics school education: a systematic review of empirical evidence. Comput. Educ. **121**, 30–58 (2018)
31. UNESCO: International Standard Classification of Education: ISCED 2011. UNESCO Institute for Statistics, Montreal (2012)
32. Garzón, J., Acevedo, J.: Meta-analysis of the impact of augmented reality on students' learning effectiveness. Educ. Res. Rev. **27**, 244–260 (2019)
33. Zakian, M., Xodabande, I., Valizadeh, M., Yousefvand, M.: Out-of-the-classroom learning of English vocabulary by EFL learners: investigating the effectiveness of mobile assisted learning with digital flashcards. Asian-Pac. J. Second Foreign Lang. Educ. **7**, 1–16 (2022)
34. Lipsey, M.W., Wilson, D.B.: Practical Meta-Analysis. Sage publications, Thousand Oaks (2001)
35. Huedo-Medina, T.B., Sánchez-Meca, J., Marín-Martínez, F., Botella, J.: Assessing heterogeneity in meta-analysis: Q statistic or I2 index? Psychol. Methods. **11**, 193–206 (2006)
36. Duval, S., Tweedie, R.: Trim and fill: a simple funnel-plot-based method of testing and adjusting for publication bias in meta-analysis. Biometrics **56**, 455–463 (2000)
37. Egger, M., Smith, G.D., Schneider, M., Minder, C.: Bias in metaanalysis detected by a simple, graphical test. BMJ **315**, 629–634 (1997)
38. Rosenthal, R.: Parametric measures of effect size. In: Cooper, H. and Hedges, L. (eds.) The Handbook of Research Synthesis, pp. 231–244 (1994)
39. Afreen, R.: Bring your own device (BYOD) in higher education: opportunities and challenges. Int. J. Emerg. Trends Technol. Comput. Sci. **3**, 233–236 (2014)

# 360° Tour as an Interactive Tool for Virtual Laboratories: A Proposal

Felipe Hernández-Rodríguez[1]([✉]) [iD] and Nicia Guillén-Yparrea[2] [iD]

[1] School of Engineering and Science, Tecnologico de Monterrey, Saltillo, Mexico
`felipe.hdz@tec.mx`
[2] School of Engineering and Science, Tecnologico de Monterrey, Monterrey, Mexico
`nicia.gy@tec.mx`

**Abstract.** This study proposes the use of virtual tours as an interactive tool in engineering laboratories in order to increase the student's motivation and academic performance. The experimentation space corresponds to the integrated manufacturing systems laboratory on campus, which has specialized machinery, such as CNC equipment, industrial robots, and material handling and storage systems. In the first stage, students will not only be able to visit the laboratory remotely but also learn about the components of a manufacturing system. In this way, they will be able to identify the elements and their interaction while learning about specific equipment features. As part of the *Industry 4.0* strategy, the virtualization of systems and analysis tools is a global trend. Through this project, students are expected to interact with cutting-edge technology and face real situations that will allow them to develop disciplinary and transversal competencies.

**Keywords:** Virtual Laboratories · Educational Innovation · Higher education · Virtual Environments · Industry 4.0 · Engineering education

## 1 Introduction

In recent years, due to the increase in the offer of online courses in our institution, such as FITC (Flexible, Interactive and Technological Courses), Regional Courses and FDM (Flexible Digital Model), and recently due to the contingency, there is a deficit in the student's experiential experience in courses that involve the use of laboratories. We believe that the use of virtual tours can help to solve this problem. Virtual learning environments are required to guarantee the experiential experience of the student in those courses that involve laboratory equipment.

There are different categories of this technology: 360° Tours, Virtual, Augmented, and Mixed Reality.

360° videos can be used in education to showcase complex scenarios difficult to explain with images, words, or even conventional video. One basic advantage using 360° video is that the instructor can be on screen and narrate the video, creating teacher presence without actually being physically there, unveiling the opportunity to record observations more accurately. Also, using observational techniques for studying group

C. S. González-González et al. (Eds.): ICWL 2022/SETE 2022, LNCS 13869, pp. 265–269, 2023.
https://doi.org/10.1007/978-3-031-33023-0_23

collaboration and participation, the 360° video offers a unique opportunity for data collection [1].

The ability to implement 360° virtual laboratory tours to build student confidence prior to a laboratory session, or to build their laboratory skills, or even to replace traditional laboratory classes, can be available to anyone [2].

The implementation of this new technology in teaching and learning increases student motivation [3]. Other benefits of incorporating this technology into educational experiences include improved student engagement and attention, and the opportunity for students to experience and remember what they have learned [4]. Bridging the gap between the real world and the digital world makes the environment more flexible, more adaptable, yet requires greater skill from users [5].

Campbell proposes the need to create and have virtual spaces in the future for education. He emphasizes that virtual reality as a tool for education does not seek to displace current methods of education [6].

The main purpose of this study is to create virtual spaces to ensure students' remote access to campus learning spaces, with the aim of developing competencies and skills for the use of existing equipment in the engineering laboratories.

## 2  Approach

This proposal offers virtual interaction in engineering laboratories for students to learn about the equipment present in these laboratories. It begins with the creation of virtual tours in manufacturing laboratories, where there is specialized machinery, such as CNC lathes and milling machines, industrial robots, collaborative robots, material handling systems, among others. These virtual tours show students the distribution of devices and their main features.

The virtual tour can be accessed using high-end mixed reality devices such as Microsoft's Hololens, or more affordable devices such as cardboard viewers, but with the restriction of no interaction with objects.

Additionally, virtual tours have the possibility to interact with machines, from which it is possible to obtain descriptions of elements or operational instructions, which allows the implementation of training without the physical presence of an instructor. During the virtual tour, it is possible to insert AR elements, such as images, links to instructional videos, or visual elements overlapping the machines as a tool to point out their components.

In the first stage, students will have the opportunity to visit the laboratory remotely, learning about the components of a manufacturing system. In this way, they will be able to identify the elements and their interaction, at the same time that they learn about specific characteristics of the equipment.

The variables of interest for this project are academic performance and student motivation. For the registration and measurement of academic performance, standardized tests will be used to show the student's learning accomplishment with the use of technology in engineering laboratories. On the other hand, motivation will be analyzed through the evaluation instrument called "Self-Efficacy", which measures the motivation that an individual can show to produce specific performance achievements [7].

# 3  Actual or Anticipated Outcomes

Analyzing the impact of learning in the use of tools within a virtual laboratory through Virtual Tours, Augmented Reality, and Mixed Reality activities linked to laboratory practices to generate a training report that meets the evidence of technical competencies and transversal competencies.

By the use of a 360 camera and specialized software such as UNITY, an image study was carried out for the creation of a virtual tour, which allows students to have access to the campus manufacturing laboratory remotely.

The procedure is not complicated, 360 captures are taken at different points of the space of interest, taking into account the occlusions and overlaps in the views of the images, so that, when processed in the selected software, a complete view of the elements available in the laboratory is obtained.

We named the technique used: "Spatial distribution of 360° objects for navigation". Figure 1 shows an example of this proposal outline, where the 360° elements are distributed in spheres over the layout of the laboratory, emphasizing the points where the information is located to be displayed. The interaction with the machines will be developed through links to external tools of the virtual tour.

**Fig. 1.** Spatial distribution of 360 objects for navigation.

Figure 2 shows some of the screenshots taken for the creation of the virtual tour of the manufacturing laboratory, through panoramic images that can be spherically observed that are essential for the creation of the strategy proposed, and Fig. 3 shows a distant view of the virtually generated laboratory (generated with matterport software).

Students would be working through this platform to do different kinds of practice tasks, in which they will be able to identify the elements inside the laboratories, as well as learn about the functions they perform individually and what is their role within an automated manufacturing system. With remote access, students can also self-manage their learning and progress at their own pace without the direct supervision of an instructor. This strategy reinforces disciplinary and transversal competencies that help the integral development of the student. Academic reinforcement and motivation are two essential factors for the development of the competencies proposed in the TEC21 model.

Besides the academic purposes, there is the possibility of generating distance collaboration links with other educational institutions, providing the opportunity not only to bring students and professors who do not have physical spaces like these closer together

**Fig. 2.** Sample images for 360 view of the manufacturing laboratory

**Fig. 3.** Distant view of the virtual laboratory (generated with matterport software)

but also to promote the development of more complete and feasible solutions through the exchange and ease of cooperation offered by virtual spaces.

The instruments used for the evaluation of the success of the strategy will be focused on checklists and surveys that show the level of acceptance by users, giving us to know the motivation generated by the use of the tool for student learning. In the same way, quick tests will be conducted to measure the level of knowledge that is being generated individually, being able to implement a personalized strategy for each student.

## 4  Conclusions

This project is aligned with the strategy of the TEC21 educational model of Tecnologico de Monterrey, developing tools related to the Industry 4.0 trend, and providing students with competitive advantages at a professional level.

The strategy will be of relevance for the educational and industrial sectors, and for those researchers interested in finding effective methods with the use of technology to promote the development of skills and knowledge in students of any discipline. This plan gives rise to the generation of innovative resources to reinforce learning and encourage motivation toward self-learning. In addition to being a versatile tool for teachers in charge of training in collaborative spaces.

As part of the expected results of the implementation, is the increase in motivation and academic performance of students. Through virtual environments, such as engineering laboratories, the transversal competence related to digital learning is reinforced under the conditions of distance education models.

**Acknowledgement.** The authors acknowledge the financial support of the Novus Grant with PEP No. PHHT009-20ZZNV001, TecLabs, Tecnologico de Monterrey, Mexico, in the production of this work.

The authors wish to acknowledge the financial support of Writing Lab, Institute for the Future of Education, Tecnologico de Monterrey, Mexico, in the production of this work.

## References

1. Reyna, J.: The potential of 360-degree videos for teaching, learning, and research. In: INTED2018 Proceedings, pp. 1448–1454 (2018)
2. Levonis, S., Tauber, A., Schweiker, S.: 360° virtual laboratory tour with embedded skills videos. J. Chem. Educ. **98**(2), 651–654 (2021). https://doi.org/10.1021/acs.jchemed.0c00622
3. Kirkley, S.E., Kirkley, J.R.: Creating next generation blended learning environments using mixed reality, video games and simulations. TechTrends **49**(3), 42–53 (2005)
4. Hanson, K., Shelton, B.E.: Design and development of virtual reality: analysis of challenges faced by educators. Educ. Technol. Soc. **11**(1), 118–131 (2008)
5. Tang, Ym., Ho, G.T., Wu, C.H.: Engineering Education with Mixed Reality (MR) (2019)
6. Quint, F., Sebastian, K., Gorecky, D.: A mixed-reality learning environment. Proc. Comput. Sci. **75**, 43–48 (2015)
7. Mamaril, N.: Measuring undergraduate students' engineering self-efficacy: a validation study. J. Eng. Educ. **105**, 366–395 (2016)

# Wearable Devices for Smart Education Based on Sensing Data: Methods and Applications

Qian Dong[1]($\boxtimes$) and Rong Miao[2]

[1] Department of Education, Beijing Normal University, Beijing, China
`st16625m@gse.pku.edu.cn`
[2] Department of Educational Technology, Graduate School of Education, Peking University, Beijing, China
`miao@gse.pku.edu.cn`

**Abstract.** Data is an important prerequisite for research on smart education. The development of sensing technology and flexible wearable devices have greatly improved the ability of data collection, data analysis, and data application. In this review, based on the analysis of the features and functions of sensing technology, and the history of wearable devices, we analyze the trajectory of sensing data approaches to flexible wearable devices for smart education. Likewise, we summarize recent advances in wearable devices in different educational situations, with particular emphasis on the methods and applications of wearable devices in smart education based on sensing data. The challenges and opportunities relating to wearable devices based on sensing data for smart education are also discussed.

**Keywords:** Wearable devices · Sensing data · Smart education · Wearable technology · Affordance

## 1 Introduction

The application of wearable devices has significantly reshaped many practices in the field of educational informatization, while continuous improvement based on sensing data on smart education of their iterative products might dictate our educational future. In recent years, wearable devices have been an explosion in the range of smart education, including more than hundreds of wearable devices available to teachers and students across a range of teaching and learning sectors, such as Google Glass, Fitbit, Oculus Rift, and Brain link. For instance, wearable technology can support record tracking of the surgical videos in training of novice orthopedic OR nurses [1], help collect motor action and heart rate data in physical education, [2] and enhance students' motivation in running class. [3] Wearable devices are defined as "portable, flexible, and smart electronic devices in various forms" [4] that are used to collect, analyze, and present data in real teaching circumstances.

With the flourishing wearable markets, there has been considerable growth in the research into the application and affordances of wearable devices in education [5, 6]

C. S. González-González et al. (Eds.): ICWL 2022/SETE 2022, LNCS 13869, pp. 270–281, 2023.
https://doi.org/10.1007/978-3-031-33023-0_24

over the past several decades and there is evidence that technology as a research discipline is now maturing.[7] During this process, the amount of data that can be collected continues to expand, and the types of data are becoming more diversified, which makes it possible for the teaching paradigm to move from experience to data-driven. Yet, the application of wearable technologies in smart education from the perspective of sensing data remains limited. Without an understanding based on sensing data, educators cannot fully comprehend the affordances of wearable devices in smart education, and hence struggle to bring into full play wearable devices, thereby affecting the effectiveness of teachers' teaching and students' learning.

This paper analysis the features and functions of sensing technology and sensing data, and the history of wearable devices to examine and recount the methods and application of wearable devices in different educational environments from an angle of sensing data. From this perspective, we understood and interpreted the related methods and application documents, which may help find and address the challenges and opportunities of wearable devices in smart education and thus guide us in the quest for future smart education.

## 2 Sensing Technology and Sensing Data

### 2.1 Sensing Technology

Sensing technology is a high-accuracy, high-efficiency, and high-reliability technology for collecting, recording, and transmitting various data, which is partly like an extension of the human senses. Basic sensors consist of not only light sensors(eyes), taste sensors(tongue), touch sensors(hands), hearing sensors(ears), and chemical sensors(nose), but also motion sensors, temperature sensors, humidity sensors, position sensors and other variables [8].

Under the context of the Internet of Things, sensing technology has become smaller, smarter, and more integrated with each passing day. First, the volume and mass of the sensing element are becoming smaller and smaller, and have been developed to be portable and miniaturized [9]. Some sensors are often combined with daily accessories, such as wristwatches, glass, and smartphones, which are easy to carry and use. Secondly, sensors can not only expand human biological organs to sense vision, hearing, tactile sensation, temperature, and so on but also be more sensitive and efficient than human senses. Meanwhile, with the support of Internet technology, sensors have essentially dominated the efforts to collect data automatically and preprocess the data, store data and compute data, which are known as "smart sensors" or "intelligent sensors". Thirdly, multiple sensing elements can be integrated on one platform or embedded into smart terminals, like smartphones, and tablet PC to collect data in real-time and realize multi-functional integration by analyzing data and presenting results. In particular, the ingenious combination of micro miniaturization, intellectualization, and integration renders sensors or sensing technology with such unique qualities that are nearly impossible for other elements or technologies to rival.

## 2.2 Sensors and Sensing Data

Sensors are defined as "devices that transform physical quantities into output signals that serve as inputs for control systems." [10] Sensors can be divided into a variety of categories according to different classification methods. According to the operating principles, sensors are classified into resistance sensors, capacitance sensors, inductance sensors, photoelectric sensors, grating sensors, thermoelectric sensors, piezoelectric sensors, infrared sensors, optical fiber sensors, infrared sensors, and laser sensors. Based on application scenarios, it can be used in various fields such as agriculture, business, sports, entertainment, education, and other fields. Regardless of classification used, it is possible to classify: motion sensors, biosensors, and environmental sensors according to functional differences. [11] According to this sensor classification method, its specific sensor type and corresponding measurable sensor data can be further subdivided (Table 1).

**Table 1.** Types of Sensors and their measurable sensing data.

|  | Sensor Type | Sensing Data |
|---|---|---|
| Motion sensors | Acceleration sensor | Acceleration |
|  | Rotation sensor | Rotation angle |
|  | Gyroscope sensor | Palstance |
|  | Force sensor | Tension, pressure, gravity |
| Biosensors | EEG/ERP | Brain waves |
|  | EKG | Heart rate, blood pressure, oxygen saturation of blood, respiratory rhythm |
|  | EDA/SCR | Skin conductance |
|  | Glucose sensor | Plasma glucose concentration |
|  | Eye-tracking | Eye movements, eye blink rate |
|  | Emotion sensor | Facial expression, gesture, heart rate, blood pressure |
| Environmental sensors | Position sensor | Position |
|  | Humidity sensor | Humidity |
|  | Pressure sensor(barometers) | Pressure |
|  | Temperature sensor | Temperature |
|  | Light sensor | Strength of illumination |
|  | Air quality sensor | Concentrations of $CO_2$, $SO_2$, PM2.5 |

The motion sensor is a tiny element placed in various parts of the human body to recognize human activities(HAR), including sensing data like acceleration, rotation angle, palstance, gravity, etc. [12, 13] Motion sensors, which can be used to monitor joint and muscle motion with the aim of sensing posture, movement, and even breathing. Thus, motion sensors had been frequently used as medical and nursing monitoring instruments, sports training aids, and sports teaching evaluation tools. Biosensors can measure the physiological characteristics of the human body without feelings and perception, whose data list includes brain waves, heart rate, skin conductance, eye movement, facial expression, etc., and realize continuous monitoring through real-time data transmission. With this supremacy, biosensors have essentially dominated the efforts to monitor health and diagnose diseases in the medical field, record visual tracks, recognize expressions, and measure attention changes in psychology, seek regular patterns of brain activity in neuroscience. Environmental sensors can capture information of the human living environment, for instance, using GPS to get location data, using a thermometer to monitor ambient temperature, and collect pressure data from barometers. The sensors of the environment concept would lead to a smart home design. The integration of multiple sensors to build a sensing unit could provide users with more robust and comprehensive information. [14] Sensing data as part of data becomes a popular term and key phenomenon in the information society nowadays in the promotion of the Internet and wearable devices [15], which captured intense attention from worldwide education researchers.

## 3 Wearable Devices

The history of wearable devices has gone through four stages: the origin stage, the initial stage, the development stage, and the exploration stage.

### 3.1 The Origin Stage (the 1960s—early 1970s)

In the 1960s, the rudiment of wearable devices started with mathematicians' research on the probability of casino games. In the 16th century, Girolamo Cardano was the first to systematically calculate the probability. Subsequently, the probability theory has been developing continuously. Many mathematicians began to study and practice casino games and explored whether they could fight against opportunities through scientific computing. Among them, Edward O. Thorp, a math professor at MIT came up with the idea of wearable computers to improve the success rate of roulette gambling in casinos. [16] He and his cooperative partner Claude E. Shannon seemed to succeed when they applied the equipment to a roulette game test in the underground laboratory and increased the winning rate by 44% in 1961. However, Keith Taft invented George, a wearable computer operated by big toes, but lost 4000 dollars in a weekend in 1972. The quest that led to wearable devices has been bittersweet with accumulated contributions from numerous dedicated mathematicians.

### 3.2 The Initial Stage (the 1970s—early 1990s)

Since the 1970s, Steve Mann, an electronic maniac, has been using wearable computers to help improve his vision. In that seminal work, he installed a display screen on his right eye and connected the computer and the Internet through the device. This can be called the first wearable glasses. It was not until 1975, the world's first calculator watch, Pulsar, was officially released, with a price of 3750 dollars, triggering a fashion trend.

Therefore, the appearance of this watch makes wearable devices get rid of gambling and enter people's daily life.

One well-known work that must be emphasized was conducted by Professor Alex Pentland, the director of the Human Dynamics Laboratory at MIT. He established the "wearable computing" project in the era before the development of wireless networks and mobile technology in the 1980s. Thanks to the project, the wearable devices with "social measurement signs" that can measure movement, capture sound, detect Bluetooth and communicate face-to-face had attracted much attention. Since then, Alex had become one of the most cited scientists in the field of wearable computing and human behavior analysis, and is known as the "father of wearable devices". Nevertheless, he had cultivated such outstanding talents as Steve Mann, the electronic maniac, and Thad Starner, the development director of Google Glasses, for the wearable device field. Armed with the knowledge of wearable devices and the guidance of Alex, Steve Mann designed the backpack computer whose display was a camera viewfinder connected to the helmet in 1981. He connected an Apple II 6502 computer to the backpack with a steel frame to control the photography equipment. He also developed a wearable wireless camera to record life and began to upload images to the network in 1994. Such pioneering work offered the second camera to appear on the network, and can be viewed as "the first person to record life". Although several wearable devices had been developed under the guidelines, there had been failure cases. The first digital hearing aid resulted failure due to its large size and endurance in 1987.

## 3.3 The Development Stage (the Late 1990s—early 20th Century)

With the development of computer hardware and Internet technology, universities and other research institutions have promoted the first wave of wearable devices. Massachusetts Institute of Technology, University of Toronto, Columbia University, Xerox Europe Laboratory, and other scientific research institutions began the prototype development of wearable computers. The Massachusetts Institute of Technology, Carnegie Mellon University, and Georgia Institute of Technology jointly sponsored the first International Symposium on Wearable Computers (ISWC) in 1997. The convening of the seminar not only caused a sensation in the academic community but also attracted extensive attention from the industry. American academia and defense departments started to research wearable technology from 1998 to 1999. For example, the National Science Foundation of the United States continues to fund research projects in the field of wearable computing in the people-centered program. In addition, military forces, such as the U.S. Department of Defense and the National Aeronautics and Space Administration, are also important funders of wearable computing. Professor Chen Dongyi of the University of Electronic Science and Technology of China developed the first wearable computer prototype in China in 1999. The European Commission launched the wearable computing research project wearIT@work in 2004, which was the largest single civil project in the world. After that, research institutions in Japan, South Korea, Russia, France, the United Kingdom, and other countries also set up special wearable-related laboratories or research groups.

### 3.4 The Exploration Stage (20th Century to Present)

The sluggish progress and sharp decrease in wearable devices were due to the emergence of the Internet bubble at the end of the 20th century. Blessed by the development of technology, wearable devices were booming, gradually improving in form and function, and expanding in application fields in the 21st century. In the field of fitness, Nike and Apple jointly launched Nike + iPod in 2006. The device allows users to synchronize their personal sports data to the iPod Sport Kit. James Park and Eric Friedman jointly established Fitbit in San Francisco, the United States in 2007, and launched Fitbit Tracker in 2009, which could record user's step data through the device.

Since then, the functions of wearable devices had been gradually expanded, showing application potential in many fields. The pebble smart watch appeared in 2012. Users could view communication messages (such as SMS, incoming calls, email, social media, etc.), browse the web, and receive real-time email alerts through the watch. Google released Google Glass in April of the same year. Wearing glasses, people could complete a variety of practical operations, such as direction recognition, video calling, voice control photography, processing text messages, and e-mail.

After the preliminary exploration in 2013, the products on the market were constantly emerging. China Wearable Computer Promotion Alliance was established in Chengdu and discussed the blowout growth market of China's wearable technology at the meeting in November 2013. Amazon established its wearable technology store, which was also known as the "Wearable Year" in 2014.[17]. The 2015 OFweek China Wearable Device Summit Forum was held in Shenzhen, where the industry and academia jointly discussed the construction of the wearable ecosystem in April 2015. Subsequently, the Baidu Gudong bracelet, Intel launched "responsive clothing", INDEMIND mixed reality head display MELLO, Samsung wearable smart belt, and other products, and wearable devices continued to upgrade in appearance design, interaction mode, data collection, and other aspects, covering sports, medical, entertainment, games and other fields.

In retrospect, the late 1980s witnessed the first wave of enthusiasm for wearable devices, mainly driven by American national defense, enterprises, and universities in various countries, hence, it established a technique reserve for wearable technology entering the industry. The work of Google launching Google Glass inspired a wave of efforts in designing and developing more wearable devices for the public, which had given rise to the 'quantified self' phenomenon [18].

## 4 Wearable Devices for Smart Education Based on Sensing Data

Wearable devices can not only simulate people as an extension of human senses but also help people through interaction between wearable devices and humans, which set the foundation for the potential application of wearable devices for smart education.

### 4.1 Research History of Wearable Devices for Smart Education

The waves of wearable devices in other fields cover a sequence of key discoveries and technical achievements that eventually led to the birth of wearable devices in education.

Based on literature analysis on the Web of Science and CNKI, Nakasugi developed a wearable computer system to help individuals understand history in 2002, which was the starting point of wearable devices applied in education. [19] After decades of sporadic attempts [20], the accumulated experience provided a sufficient technology reserve for the researchers attempting to integrate these wearable devices. There were more than 10 studies on wearable devices in educational applications every year since 2015.

When evaluated in terms of studying period, colleges and universities were listed as the no.1 among the over 100 researches that used wearable devices for smart education from 2002 till now, and primary and secondary schools followed closely. Besides, wearable devices were widely used in physical education, medicine, psychology, science and engineering, literature and history, economics and management, as well as interdisciplinary school activity competitions, STEM/maker education, etc. Among them, it had the most application in physical education, followed by medical and psychological applications.

With further development of wearable devices, Christine Kern summarized seven kinds of products of wearable devices in education, including Autographers camera, Key gloves, Muse headband, VR ant vision wearable helmet, Smart Watches, GoPro camera, and Google glass. [21] All seven kinds of devices can be the foundation for learning or teaching tools because these technologies help to cultivate students' abilities of team cooperation, problem-solving, and independent learning.

### 4.2    Method and Application of Wearable Devices for Smart Education

When considering smart education, multi-wearable devices ideally should be able to partly assume the role of human beings. For instance, use motion sensors to collect position, displacement, and acceleration sensing data to improve students' running performance, use biosensors to shed light on physiological changes in the learning process by measuring students' heart rate and skin electrical sensing data to help teachers adjust the instructional design, and use environmental sensors to monitor temperature or light changes for creating a better learning environment to provide evidence-based decision-making reference for education administrators. [22] For smart education, scholars use sensor data collected by wearable devices to establish a connection with learning state indicators in the learning process.

In physical education, the application of wearable technology can collect students' heart rate, steps, breathing, position, and other sensing data, not only to evaluate exercise load, and reduce sports accident injuries [23, 24], but also to integrate the game-based teaching method and help students improve their sports enthusiasm with the interactive function of wearable devices. For example, Lindberg R et al. [2] developed a sports game called Running Othello 2(RO2) which were used in physical education class of third-grade students in Korean primary schools. It found that students who used RO2 showed higher heart rates and class participation. Another example is the work reported by Chaloupsky et al. [25], who designed a fitness tracker and conducted a two-year experimental study on 133 college students. The results showed that the number of students in the experimental group (wearing wearable devices and helping students know their own position and heart rate data) who passed the running course standard increased, besides, the students' enthusiasm for running also improved.

Despite the application in physical education, wearable devices with biosensors that can collect brain waves, and facial expression sensing data were widely used in understanding students' mental states in learning activities. At a preschool stage, there are both SH09 wearable devices for children aged 3–6, which continuously collect children's emotional development data through face recognition, emotion recognition, and behavior recognition sensors [26], and emotional perception monitoring devices for autistic children to improve their participation in learning activities [27]. In primary and secondary schools, the Brainlink headband can collect students' EEG sensing data to understand whether students are concentrated or relaxed. In the field of colleges and universities, laboratories in the United States, Germany, and the United Kingdom are also constantly designing, developing, and testing wearable devices to understand students' learning status and brain changes. For example, Woolf's team at the University of Massachusetts Amherst in the United States developed an intelligent tutoring system based on real-time computing agents from 2007 to 2011. The system determined the emotional state of students at any point in time and provided adaptive support. Research showed that long-term use could improve students' learning [28].

As one of the typical patterns of an online education communication system, smart education also consists of five components: student(S), teacher(T), instructional resources(I), educational communication tools(C), and teaching activities(A) [29]. Students and teachers are the subjects of teaching behavior. Instructional resources reflect the role of technology in knowledge expression and presentation. Communication tools reflect the intermediary role of technology. Teaching activities are the core of driving the operation of other elements of the model. Among all applications of wearable devices in smart education, the most complex process of wearable technology in the dynamic interaction of various elements was T-C-I-C-S-C-T. For example, when the University of California, Irvine School of Medicine [30] practiced in anatomy and hospitals, teachers (T) presented the specific operating procedures of anatomy and other courses (I) through Google Glasses (C), and made voice calls with students (S) through Google Glasses (C). They can also record and play students' video-sensing data through Google Glasses (C), and transmit it to teachers (T). In this process, the interaction flow between elements was T-C-I-C-S-C-T. Wearable devices not only establish a connection for the transmission of teaching content between students and teachers but also serve as an interactive bridge for communication between teachers and students. They also helped teachers collect and record student data, and then conducted targeted feedback.

Wearable technology is the extension of human function, and can create new teaching interaction modes, and expand the learning environment [31] based on sensing data.

## 5   Conclusion and Discussion

This paper demonstrates the features and functions of sensing technology and sensing data, and the trajectory of sensing data approaches to flexible wearable devices for smart education. It can be concluded that the application of wearable devices for smart education based on sensing data is in adolescence. An increase in the number of published papers related to the affordances of wearable devices is to be expected, as well as more papers related to technology compatibility, and data security of wearable devices based on sensing data. All this research effort is in order to achieve fully smart education in the near future.

## 5.1 Adolescence of Application

Brian Arthur, a well-known economist proposed that common technologies will gather into clusters, which form a "domain" to share the phenomenon group and the common goal or share the same theory in the book The Essence of Technology. The life cycle of the domain includes four distinct stages: (1) the birth stage: solving specific problems in the parent domain, solidifying and developing in understanding and practice; (2) adolescence: solving obstacles in development, generating feasible technologies, and applying them to the market; (3) maturity stage: the market moves from fanaticism to calmness, and the new domain deeply affects the economy in its own way, entering a stable growth stage; (4) old stage: few important ideas are produced, some domains will be replaced, but most of them can still exist and serve mankind [32].

According to Arthur's life cycle division of domains, the application of wearable devices for smart education based on sensing data is in adolescence. Combined with the development history of wearable technology, it can be found that wearable technology was first used in casinos, and entered daily life after the 1970s. In 2014, various devices continued to emerge, and new technologies were constantly generated in medicine, sports, fitness, games, communications, and other fields and applied to the market. At present, the market is relatively stable. However, the application of wearable technology in education is later than that in the fields of communication, fitness, medical care, entertainment, etc., but appears in the booming period when the number of wearable devices increases and the technology is relatively mature. From the perspective of an application function, the educational application of wearable devices based on sensing data mainly focuses on the migration of more mature technologies in other fields, such as physiological indicator monitoring in the medical and fitness fields. In terms of applied subjects, wearable technology is also widely used in physical education to collect heart rate data, and in other courses to monitor students' mental state data. At present, the application of wearable devices for smart education based on sensing data is still solving the problems and obstacles of technology in education, exploring feasible new technologies, designing and developing new devices, and testing their application in teaching practice. Therefore, wearable devices as a whole are in the middle period of transition from adolescence to maturity, and their application in smart education based on sensing data is in adolescence.

## 5.2 Challenges and Opportunities

Although the rapid advances in the Internet and wearable technology over the years have been driving the explosive growth of wearable devices in smart education based on sensing data, the shadow of challenges of technology compatibility, and data security still long existed. According to Bower [33], wearable devices can provide affordances in education as follows: pedagogical uses (in situ contextual information, recording, simulation, communication, first-person view, in situ guidance, feedback, distribution, gamification), educational quality (engagement, efficiency, presence), logistical and other implications (hands-free access, free up spaces). Meanwhile, Bower also provided a summary of issues of wearable technologies, grouped into the two emergent themes of educational quality (distraction, cheating, overreliance on wearable technology, technology before pedagogy, familiarization with interface, small interfaces) and logistical and other implications issues (privacy, cost, technical problems, technical support, legal issues, development of software, processing power). Accordingly, the affordance of wearable devices in smart education based on sensing data needs to be expanded and improved.

Wearable technology, like Pandora's box, has two sides, but it is our responsibility to use it responsibly. [34] As Kirschner said, education has always been a unique combination of technology, society, educational background, and affordances. [35] In practice, on the one hand, in line with the current education problems and needs, and on the basis of the education theory, we need to do a good job in top-level design, define the purpose, connect indicators representing learning process and wearable devices that can collect corresponding sensing data, and then carry out technology development to achieve the organic integration of technology and education; on the other hand, it is necessary to conduct long-term in-depth analysis and research on the impact of wearable devices on smart education quality.

# References

1. Zhao, X., Cong, L.: Effect of problem and scripting-based learning combining wearable technology on orthopedic operating room nurses' learning outcomes. Nurse Educ. Today **73**, 13–16 (2019)
2. Lindberg, R., Seo, J., Laine, T.H.: Enhancing physical education with exergames and wearable technology. IEEE Trans. Learn. Technol. **9**(4), 328–341 (2016)
3. Chaloupsky, D., Hrusova, D., Chaloupská, P.: Use of fitness trackers in fitness running classes to enhance students' motivation. In: Blended Learning, pp. 303–315 (2019)
4. Sharma, K., Pappas, I.O., Papavlasupoulou, S., Giannakos, M.N.: Towards automatic and pervasive physiological sensing of collaborative learning. In: 13th International Conference of Computer-Supported Collaborative Learning, pp. 684–687 (2019)
5. Havard, B., Podsiad, M.: A meta-analysis of wearables research in educational settings published 2016–2019. Educ. Tech. Res. Dev. **68**(4), 1829–1854 (2020). https://doi.org/10.1007/s11423-020-09789-y
6. Bower, M., Sturman, D.: What are the educational affordances of wearable technologies? Comput. Educ. **88**, 343–353 (2015)
7. Conole, G., Dyke, M., Oliver, M., Seale, J.: Mapping pedagogy and tools for effective learning design. Comput. Educ. **43**, 17–33 (2004)
8. Swan, M.: Sensor mania! The Internet of Things, wearable computing, objective metrics, and the quantified self 2.0. J. Sens. Actuat. Netw. **1**(3), 217–253 (2012)
9. Sun, X., et al.: Wearable near-field communication sensors for healthcare: materials, fabrication and application. Micromachines. **13**(5), 784 (2022)
10. Norton, H.: Transducer Fundamentals in Handbook of Transducers, ch. 2. Prentice Hall, Englewood Cliffs (1989)
11. Thüs, H., Chatti, M.A., Yalcin, E., et al.: Mobile learning in context. Int. J. Technol. Enhanced Learn. **4**(5/6), 332–344 (2012)

12. Liu, Y., Feng, S., Zhao, Z., et al.: Highly efficient human action recognition with quantum genetic algorithm optimized support vector machine (2017). arXiv:1711.09511

13. Boland, C.S., Khan, U., Backes, C., et al.: Sensitive, high-strain, high-rate bodily motion sensors based on graphene-rubber composites. ACS Nano **8**(9), 8819–8830 (2014)

14. Lee, Y.C., Hsieh, M.L., Lin, P.S., et al.: CMOS-MEMS technologies for the applications of environment sensors and environment sensing hubs. J. Micromech. Microeng. **31**(7), 074004(41pp) (2021)

15. Rodrigues, M.V., Gonzalez, M.E.Q.: Semiotic information in data-driven societies: where are we heading to? Educ. Inf. **34**(3), 199–214 (2018)

16. Brillinger, D.R.: Beat the dealer: a winning strategy for the game of twenty-one by Edward O. Thorp. Am. Math. Monthly **72**(4), 438:99–100 (1965)

17. Max Knoblauch. The History of Wearable Tech, From the Casino to the Consumer [EB/OL]. https://mashable.com/2014/05/13/wearable-technology-history/,2014-05-13

18. Swan, M.: The quantified self: fundamental disruption in big data science and biological discovery. Big Data **1**(2), 85–99 (2013)

19. Nakasugi, H., Yamauchi, Y.: International Conference on Computers in Education - Auckland, New Zealand, 3–6 December, 2002. Proceedings. Past Viewer: Development of Wearable Learning System for History Education, vol. 1, pp. 1311–1312. IEEE Computer Society (2002)

20. Borthwick, A.C., Anderson, C.L., Fineness, E.S., et al.: Special article personal wearable technologies in education: value or villain? J. Digit. Learn. Teach. Educ. **31**(3), 85–92 (2015)

21. Christine, K.: Are Wearables the Next Big Innovation in Classroom Tools? [EB/OL]. https://www.varinsights.com/doc/are-wearables-the-next-big-innovation-in-classroom-tools-0001,2014-06

22. Barfield, W, Caudell, T.: Basic concepts in wearable computers and augmented reality. In: Fundamentals of Wearable Computers and Augmented Reality, pp. 3–26 (2001)

23. Miao, R., Dong, Q., Weng, W.Y., et al.: The application model of wearable devices in physical education. Blend. Learn. Enhanc. Learn. Success, pp. 311–322 (2018)

24. Dong, Q., Qu, X., Miao, R.: Data analysis model of wearable devices in physical education. Blend. Learn. 225–238 (2019)

25. Chaloupsky, D., Hrusova, D., Chaloupská, P.: Use of fitness trackers in fitness running classes to enhance students' motivation. Blend. Learn. 303–315 (2019)

26. Yongqing, Y., Wei, L.: Research on individualized education scheme for children aged 3–6 based on intelligent wearable device environment-taking Xiaoao SH09 wearable device as an example. Electron. World **04**, 42–43 (2019)

27. Boulton, H., Brown, D., Standen, P., et al.: Multi-modalities in classroom learning environments. In: 12th International Technology, Education and Development Conference, pp. 1–8 (2018)

28. Woolf, B.P., Burleson, W., Arroyo, I., et al.: Affect -aware tutors: recognizing and responding to student affect. Int. J. Learn. Technol. **4**(3/4), 129–164 (2009)

29. Wenge, G.: The classification of online course model: from the perspective of online education communication system. J. Dist. Educ. **32**(05), 41–46 (2014)

30. Johnson, L., Becker, S.A., Estrada, V., et al.: Horizon report of new media alliance (2015 Higher Education Edition). J. Beij. Radio Telev. Univ. **2015**(S1), 1–18 (2015)

31. Cai, W.: Review on the Frontier of educational application research of wearable technology. Overseas Chin. Educ. **05**, 697–707 (2016)

32. Arthur, B.: The Essence of Technology: What is Technology and How It Evolves, pp. 73–76. Zhejiang People's Publishing Press, Zhejiang (2014)

33. Bower, M., Sturman, D.: What are the educational affordances of wearable technologies?. Comput. Educ. **88**(C), 343–353 (2015)

34. Norman, D.A.: The paradox of wearable technologies: Can devices like Google Glass aug-
ment our activities without-distracting us from the physical world? MIT Technology Review
[EB/OL]. https://www.technologyreview.com/s/517346/the-paradox-of-wearable-technolog
ies/. Accessed 24 July 2013
35. Kirschner, P., Strijbos, J.W., Kreijns, K., et al.: Designing electronic collaborative learning
environments. Educ. Tech. Res. Dev. 52(3), 47 (2004)

# The Use of Verbs in International Chinese Language Education

Shan Wang(✉)

Department of Chinese and Literature, Faculty of Arts and Humanities, University of Macau, Macau SAR, China
shanwang@um.edu.mo

**Abstract.** Verbs are not only the core of sentences, but also the focus of vocabulary research and teaching. This paper takes a commonly used verb *xiàn* 'trap' as an example to explore the use of verbs. This word is listed in *The Chinese Proficiency Grading Standards for International Chinese Language Education*, which has been newly implemented worldwide since 2021. This study has analyzed the syntactic use of *xiàn* 'trap' from the aspects of syntactic functions and intensity of syntactic collocations, as well as the semantic use of *xiàn* 'trap' from the aspect of its semantic roles. It combines quantitative statistics and qualitative analysis to explore the syntactic and semantic use, which not only deepens the linguistic research of verbs, but also provides reference for verb teaching in language education and the compilation of Chinese learners' dictionaries.

**Keywords:** Verbs · Syntax · Semantics · International Chinese Language Education

## 1 Introduction

Verbs, occupying a dominant position in languages, are the focus of linguistic research and teaching. *The Grammatical Knowledge-base of Contemporary Chinese—A Complete Specification* [1] established a part-of-speech system according to the principle of grammatical function distribution and classified more than 73,000 words; the verb database in this *Knowledge-base* shows verbs' grammatical properties. Yang and Shi [2] explored the internal mechanism of quasi-valence verb acquisition from three perspectives: the construction of box-type consciousness, unconventional form-meaning relationships, and special interface features. They pointed out that the acquisition of quasi-valence verbs is characterized by many sources of errors, acquisition difficulty, and a long acquisition cycle. The research of Hao, Wang and Liu [3] showed that learners experience a comprehensive acquisition of verb valence ability of verbs, but the acquisition of most of the valence functions has not reached a native level of target language proficiency. Specifically, there is an insufficient use of adverbs, objects, compound sentence relationships, adjuncts of tenses and an excessive use of subject and conjunction relations; affected by the mother tongue, the development of verb valence of second language learners is more complex than that of Chinese children; the development of verb valence of learners is a continuous, gradual, and changeable process. Also, it is a process

© The Author(s), under exclusive license to Springer Nature Switzerland AG 2023
C. S. González-González et al. (Eds.): ICWL 2022/SETE 2022, LNCS 13869, pp. 282–289, 2023.
https://doi.org/10.1007/978-3-031-33023-0_25

where learners' understand verb's main valences first and then understand and perfect its secondary valences gradually. Although there are many studies on Chinese verbs, the research of their syntactic and semantic features based on large-scale corpora is quite limited; existing dictionaries do not have enough syntactic and semantic information about verbs either. A corpus is an indispensable and powerful helper for lexicography [4]. The system constructed by Fu, Wu, Zhang and Li [5] aims to manage lexicography workflow through human-computer interaction. It includes establishing new dictionary projects, setting entry structure, selecting words and establishing projects, editing, revising, approving, retaining entries and retrospective editing and reviewing process, as well as auxiliary dictionary writing, etc. At the same time, it also integrates multiple corpora, existing dictionaries, and word lists, which serves as a reference for dictionary editors.

Dependency grammar is featured with conciseness of form and simplicity of annotation and application [6, 7]. From the perspective of natural language processing, the analysis of syntactic and semantic categories of languages according to dependency grammar is of great significance [8]. Liu and Feng [9] proposed a Probabilistic Valency Pattern (PVP) for natural language processing. This pattern not only helps to explain the process of language understanding and generation from a probabilistic point of view, but also plays a certain role in the search for better statistical-based natural language processing algorithms. Liu [10] proposed a methodology for constructing syntactic networks based on a syntactic theory and summarized some statistical properties of Chinese syntactic dependency networks based on two different types of Chinese treebanks. In addition, there are also many Chinese linguistic studies based on dependency grammar. Liu, Niu and Liu [11] found that the proportion of parts of speech serving the same syntactic functions in different language styles (oral and written) is quite different. It is reflected in the fact that most subjects in written language are nouns while most subjects in spoken language are pronouns; the correspondence between attributes and parts-of-speech is relatively scattered, and nouns dominantly serve as attributes in written language, etc. Li and Liu [8] constructed a corpus of Chinese children's three-word sentences based on dependency grammar and quantitatively analyzed syntactic properties including dependency types, dependency relations, and average dependency distance. Combining the characteristics of Chinese imperative sentence dependency grammar, Tu and Zhu [12] proposed a classification method of imperative sentences based on the meaning of core words. It used dependency grammar to extract core words with semantic features in imperative sentences and then used Word2Vec to represent words in a distributed manner.

*The Chinese Proficiency Grading Standards for International Chinese Language Education* [13] was published by the Ministry of Education of the People's Republic of China and the State Language Commission on March 24, 2021. It was implemented on July 1 of the same year, which is the latest standard of teaching Chinese as a second language. It stipulates the level of language proficiency for learners to communicate in life, study, work, and other fields, which it is an important standard for the teaching, testing, and evaluation of international Chinese education. This paper has selected the advanced-level verb *xiàn* 'trap' to analyze its syntactic and semantic use based on dependency grammar. This study can not only enrich the research on Chinese verbs, but also meet the needs of Chinese language education.

## 2  Research Methods

This study collected sentences of *xiàn* 'trap' using the following procedures [14, 15]. First, downloaded all the passages that contain *xiàn* 'trap' from the following corpora: Sogou Lab [16], BCC, CCL, People's Daily, Reference News, Chinese Gigaword (used through Chinese Word Sketch) [17, 18], and Tencent News. Among them, the two sub-corpora of BCC, literature and newspapers, were selected, since their language use is more canonical than other sub-corpora like micro-blogs. The limit for downloading BCC sentences is set at 10,000 sentences per sub-corpus, and all sentences of *xiàn* 'trap' in other corpora were fully downloaded. Second, split the downloaded paragraphs with end-of-sentence punctuations, kept the sentences containing *xiàn* 'trap', and deleted the incomplete sentences in the right window.

As the syntactic function of a word is embodied in a clause, this study screened out the single sentences and excluded complex sentences with two or more clauses.

To achieve this, the following steps were performed. First, the sentences containing Chinese commas (,) and Chinese semicolons (;) were excluded, and complex sentences are excluded to obtain a single sentence set A. Second, excluded single sentences containing non-Chinese characters and non-Chinese punctuation marks; only the sentences whose punctuations conform to Chinese norms were retained, and thus single sentence set B is obtained. Third, performed word segmentation and part-of-speech tagging on the single-sentence set B. This study further excluded single sentences with *xiàn* 'trap' with a non-verbal part-of-speech and *xiàn* 'trap' as a morpheme; it also excluded single sentences with two or more *xiàn* 'trap' and single sentences which exceeds 20 words. After deduplication, a single sentence set C is obtained, with a total of 436 single sentences. Given the complexity of syntactic and semantic annotation, this paper randomly selected a total of 257 sentences for annotation, which accounts for 58.94%. Finally, after collecting single sentences of *xiàn* 'trap', this paper used the annotation tool [14, 15] to perform the annotation based on dependency grammar through the API interface of the Language Technology Platform [19].

## 3  The Use of *Xiàn* 'Trap'

According to dependency grammar, if a word modifies another word in a sentence, then the modifier is called a subordinate word or a dependent word, while the modified word is called a dominant word or a core word [20]. The syntactic functions of *xiàn* 'trap' mentioned in this section are the cases when *xiàn* 'trap' is a subordinate word; the semantic roles refer to the words that are dominated by *xiàn* 'trap'.

### 3.1  The Syntactic Use of *Xiàn* 'Trap'

This section explores the syntactic use of *xiàn* 'trap' from the perspectives of syntactic functions and the intensity of syntactic collocations of *xiàn* 'trap'.

**Syntactic Functions of Xiàn 'Trap'**
When a verb is syntactically subordinate, the type of syntactic dependency arc pointing

to the verb can determine the syntactic function that the verb fulfills. The syntactic dependency labelling of single sentences reveals that the syntactic functions that *xiàn* 'trap' can function in single sentences are head (HED, that is, a predicate), verb-object (VOB), attribute (ATT), coordinate (COO), subject (SBV) and preposition-object (POB), with the percentages of 56.03%, 18.68%, 13.62%, 10.12%, 1.17%, and 0.39% respectively, as shown in Table 1. The common function of verbs is to serve as a predicate, which takes up over half of the sentences.

**Table 1.** The syntactic function distribution of *xiàn* 'trap'

| Category | Number | Percentage | Examples |
|---|---|---|---|
| HED | 144 | 56.03% | Wǒmen bùyào zài *xiàn* jìn zhè zhǒng jiǒngjìng lǐ qù le<br>we_don't_again_trap_enter_this_kind_awkward situation_inside_go_ASP<br>'Let's not be trapped in this awkward situation any more.' |
| VOB | 48 | 18.68% | Wǒmen bùnéng ràng zhème duō de rén niánjì qīngqīng jiù *xiàn* zài shīyè de nítán lǐ<br>we_can't_let_so_many_DE_people_age_young_(adverb)_trap_in_<br>unemployment_DE_quagmire_inside<br>'We can't let so many people get stuck in the quagmire of unemployment at a young age.' |
| ATT | 35 | 13.62% | Wǒmen yǐ bǎituō guòqù zhè ge xiàtiān shēn *xiàn* de kùnjìng<br>we_already_get rid of_past_this_CL_summer_deep_trap_DE_dilemma<br>'We've come out of the dilemma that we've been stuck in this past summer.' |
| COO | 26 | 10.12% | Fángzhǐ xīn cún jiǎoxìng, *xiàn* de tài shēn, zǒu dào bùkějiùyào de dìbù<br>avoid_heart_exist_lucky, trap_DE_too_deep, walk_reach_hopeless_DE_situation<br>'Avoid taking chances and getting too deep into the hopeless situation.' |
| SBV | 3 | 1.17% | *Xiàn* chē shì jiācháng biànfàn<br>trap_car_be_common occurence<br>'Cars getting stuck are common occurrences.' |
| POB | 1 | 0.39% | Ruògān jūnguān céng duì méngguó zì *xiàn* Yīlākè de nízhǎo sīxià biǎoshì guānqiè<br>some_military-officer_once_to_allied country_self_trap_Iraq_DE_quagmire_<br>privately_express_concern<br>'Several military officers have privately expressed concerns about the allied countries trapping in the quagmire of Iraq.' |
| Total | 257 | 100.00% | / |

## The Intensity of Syntactic Collocations of Xiàn 'Trap'

This part calculates the syntactic dependency dominated by *xiàn* 'trap' to obtain the syntactic collocation intensity of this verb. The calculation formula [21] is as follows:

$$D_{\text{intensity of syntactic collocations}} =$$
$$\left(A_{\text{number of syntactic dependencies directly dominated by the verb}} - B_{\text{number of WP}}\right)$$
$$\div S_{\text{number of single sentences containing the verb}} \tag{1}$$

In this formula, A represents the number of syntactic dependencies directly dominated by the verb. According to the labeling specification of dependency grammar, the syntactic dependencies directly dominated by verbs contain punctuation marks, but they have nothing to do with the syntactic functions of a verb. Therefore, when calculating the syntactic collocation intensity of the verb D, it is necessary to subtract the number of WP (punctuation marks). The result is shown in Table 2.

**Table 2.** The intensity of syntactic collocations of *xiàn* 'trap'

| Type | Number |
|---|---|
| A number of syntactic dependencies directly dominated by the verb | 946 |
| B number of WP | 145 |
| A-B | 801 |
| S number of single sentences of the verb | 257 |
| D intensity of syntactic collocations | 3.12 |

The greater the number of syntactic dependencies dominated by a verb, the stronger its syntactic collocational ability is. It can be seen from Table 2 that the overall intensity of syntactic collocations of *xiàn* 'trap' is 3.12. That it, it usually has about three dependencies in a single sentence.

### 3.2   The Semantic Use of *Xiàn* 'Trap'

This section analyzes the semantic use of *xiàn* 'trap' from the perspectives of its semantic roles. Agent-like roles and patient-like roles are two most important semantic roles of a verb. The statistical results of the semantic roles of *xiàn* 'trap' are shown in Table 3. Among the agent-like roles of *xiàn* 'trap', Experiencer (78.72%) far exceeds Agent (12.34%), which shows that trapping emphasizes more on things which have no subjective initiative. Among the patient-like roles of *xiàn* 'trap', Content (5.53%) slightly exceeds Patient (3.40%).

**Table 3.**  Agent-like roles and patient-like roles of *xiàn* 'trap'

| Semantic Roles | | Number | Percentage | Example |
|---|---|---|---|---|
| agent-like roles | Agent | 29 | 12.34% | Rìběn qīnlüèzhě zài nínǎo zhōng yuè *xiàn* yuè shēn<br>Japan_aggressor_exist_quagmire_in_gradually_trap_gradually_deep<br>'The Japanese invaders fell deeper and deeper into the mire.' |
| | Experiencer | 185 | 78.72% | Měiguó de nóngyè yě shēn shēn de *xiàn* zài wéijī zhōng<br>America_DE_agriculture_also_deep_deep_DE_trap_exist_crisis_in<br>'American agriculture is also deeply in crisis.' |
| | Total | 214 | 91.06% | / |
| patient-like roles | Patient | 8 | 3.40% | Jǐ liàng kǎchē hé sǎo xuě jī bèi *xiàn* jìn le xuěduī<br>several_CL_truck_and_sweep_snow_machine_PV_trap_in_ASP_snowdrifts<br>'Several trucks and snowplows got stuck in the snowdrifts.' |
| | Content | 13 | 5.53% | Dálìsāngdéluó zhuǎnhuì zài *xiàn* yíyún<br>Dalisandro_transfer_again_trap_doubt<br>'Dalisandro's transfer is again in doubt.' |
| | Total | 21 | 8.94% | / |

The statistics of the situational roles of *xiàn* 'trap' is shown in Table 4. The most frequently collocated situational role of *xiàn* 'trap' is Location (LOC), accounting for 72.87%; followed by Manner (8.91%), State (6.98%), Time (5.43%), Feature (4.65%), Measure (0.78%), Scope (0.39%). In contrast, Tool, Material, and Reason generally do not act as situational roles of *xiàn* 'trap'.

**Table 4.** Situational roles of *xiàn* 'trap'

| Situational Roles | Number | Percentage | Example |
|---|---|---|---|
| Location | 188 | 72.87% | Rénmen wàngjì le *xiàn* jìn bīng kū de wéixiǎn<br>people_forget_ASP_trap_enter_ice_cave_DE_danger<br>'People forget about the dangers of falling into ice caves.' |
| Manner | 23 | 8.91% | Níhèlǔ bùxī yī cì yòu yī cì de *xiàn* zài zìxiāngmáodùn de nítán zhōng<br>Nehru_not<br>stint_one_CL_again_one_CL_DE_trap_exist_self-contradiction_DE_mire_inside<br>'Nehru did not hesitate to fall into the mire of self-contradiction again and again.' |
| State | 18 | 6.98% | Tóngchuān méikuàng *xiàn* tānhuàn zhuàngtài<br>Tongchuan_coal mine_trap_paralysis_state<br>'Tongchuan Coal Mine is in a state of collapse.' |
| Time | 14 | 5.43% | *Xiàn*zài suǒyǒu de jūmín lóu dōu *xiàn* zài hēi'àn lǐ<br>now_all_DE_resident_building_all_trap_exist_dark_inside<br>'All residential buildings are now in darkness.' |
| Feature | 12 | 4.65% | Chē *xiàn* de zuìshēn shí lián jiàshǐshì de mén dōu dǎ bù kāi<br>car_trap_DE_deepest_when_even_driver's cab_DE_door_even_do_no_open<br>'Even the cab door cannot be opened when the car sank the deepest.' |
| Measure | 2 | 0.78% | Nántóu *xiàn* zhúshān zhèn mínzhái réng *xiàn* zài tǔ shí duī zhōng<br>Nantou_county_Zhushan_township_ civilian house_still_trap_exist_earth_stone_mound<br>'Some civilian houses in Zhushan Township, Nantou County are still trapped in the mound of earth and rock.' |
| Scope | 1 | 0.39% | Zhè jiàn shì nǐ hé wǒ *xiàn* de yīyàng shēn<br>this_CL_thing_you_and_I_trap_DE_same_deep<br>'You are as deeply involved as me in this matter.' |
| Total | 258 | 100.00% | / |

# 4 Conclusion

A verb has complex syntactic and semantic relationships in a sentence, which has been the focus of linguistic research and language teaching. This paper has selected a commonly used verb *xiàn* 'trap' as an example to explore the use of verbs. It is a word listed in *The Chinese Proficiency Grading Standards for International Chinese Language Education*, which has been promulgated and implemented around the world since 2021. This study screened out 257 single sentences from various Chinese corpora and further analyzed the use of *xiàn* 'trap'. This study found that, in terms of the syntactic use, the three most commonly used syntactic functions of *xiàn* 'trap' are Head (56.03%), Verb-Object (18.68%), and Attribute (13.62%). In terms of the semantic use, it often collocates with

Experiencer, up to 78.72%, indicating that an unconscious subject often appears in the sentences. The situational role of *xiàn* 'trap' most commonly appears as a Location, accounting for as much as 72.87% of its usage, which indicates that the spatial aspect of the action frequently appears in sentences. The quantitative and qualitative analysis of the syntactic and semantic features of *xiàn* 'trap' in this study not only deepens the linguistic research of verbs, but also provides reference for the application fields of Chinese learners' dictionary compilation and verb teaching.

**Acknowledgement.** This research is supported by the University of Macau (MYRG2022–00191-FAH; MYRG2019–00013-FAH).

# References

1. Yu, S., et al.: The Grammatical Knowledge-Base of Contemporary Chinese—A Complete Specification (xiàndài hànyǔ yǔfǎ xìnxī cídiǎn xiángjiě), 2nd edn. Tsinghua University Press, Beijing (2003)
2. Yang, Z., Shi, C.: Acquisition of Chinese quasi-divalent verbs and its built-in mechanism in CSL (hànyǔ zhǔnjià dòngcí de èryǔ xídé biǎoxiàn jíqí nèizài jīzhì). Chinese Teaching in the World (shìjiè hànyǔ jiàoxué) **27**, 558–573 (2013)
3. Hao, Y., Wang, X., Liu, H.: Development of Chinese interlanguage's verbal valence based on syntactically-annotated corpus (jīyú jùfǎ biāozhù yǔliàokù de hànyǔ zhōngjièyǔ dòngcí pèijià fāzhǎn jìliàng yánjiū). Applied Linguistics (yǔyán wénzì yìngyòng) 29–41 (2021)
4. Bergenholtz, H., Nielsen, J.S.: What is a lexicographical database? Lexikos **23**, 77–87 (2013)
5. Fu, A., Wu, J., Zhang, H., Li, Y.: On the human-machine interactive Chinese dictionary compilation system (rénjī jiāohùshì de hànyǔ císhū biānzuǎn xìtǒng). Lexicographical Studies (císhū yánjiū) 1–12+93 (2013)
6. Li, Z.: Research on key technologies of Chinese dependency parsing (hànyǔ yīcún jùfǎ fēnxī guānjiàn jìshù yánjiū). Harbin Institute of Technology, Harbin (2013)
7. Niu, R., Osborne, T.: Chunks are components: a dependency grammar approach to the syntactic structure of Mandarin. Lingua **224**, 60–83 (2019)
8. Li, H., Liu, H.: A study of Chinese children's acquisition of three-word sentences based on an annotated corpus (jīyú jùfǎ biāozhù yǔliàokù de hànyǔ értóng sāncíjù xídé yánjiū). Applied Linguistics (yǔyán wénzì yìngyòng) 107–116 (2017)
9. Liu, H., Feng, Z.: probabilistic valency pattern theory for natural language processing (zìrán yǔyán chǔlǐ de gàilù pèijià móshì lǐlùn). Linguistic Sciences (yǔyán kēxué), pp. 32–41 (2007)
10. Liu, H.: The complexity of Chinese syntactic dependency networks. Phys. A: Stat. Mech. Appl. **387**, 3048–3058 (2008)
11. Liu, B., Niu, Y., Liu, H.: Word class, syntactic function and style: a comparative study based on annotated corpora (jīyú yīcún jùfǎ biāozhù shùkù de hànyǔ yǔtǐ chāyì yánjiū). Appl. Linguist. (yǔyán wénzì yìngyòng) 134–142 (2012)
12. Tu, J., Zhu, M.: imperative sentence classification based on dependency parsing (jīyú yīcún yǔfǎ de qíshǐjù fēnlèi yánjiū). Comput. Appl. Softw. (jìsuànjī yìngyòng yǔ ruǎnjiàn) **36**, 279–283+322 (2019)
13. Ministry of Education of the People's Republic of China & National Language Commission: The Chinese proficiency standards for international Chinese education (guójì zhōngwén jiàoyù zhōngwén shuǐpíng děngjí biāozhǔn). Language Specification (yǔyán wénzì guīfàn), vol. GF0025-2021, Beijing (2021)

14. Wang, S., Liu, X., Zhou, J.: Developing a syntactic and semantic annotation tool for research on Chinese vocabulary. In: Dong, M., Gu, Y., Hong, J.-F. (eds.) Chinese Lexical Semantics, pp. 272–294. Springer, Cham (2022)
15. Wang, S.: Investigating verbs of confession through a syntactic and semantic annotation tool. In: Dong, M., Gu, Y., Hong, J.-F. (eds.) Chinese Lexical Semantics, pp. 198–211. Springer, Cham (2022)
16. Liu, Y., et al.: Identifying web spam with the wisdom of the crowds. ACM Trans. Web **6**, 1–30 (2012)
17. Kilgarriff, A., Huang, C.-R., Rychlý, P., Smith, S., Tugwell, D.: Chinese Word Sketches. ASIALEX 2005: Words in Asian Cultural Context, Singapore (2005)
18. Lexical Data Consortium, University of Pennsylvania. http://www.ldc.upenn.edu/Catalog/cat alogEntry.jsp?catalogId=LDC2009T14
19. Che, W., Li, Z., Liu, T.: LTP: A Chinese language technology platform. In: Liu, T., Liu, Y. (eds.) Coling 2010: Demonstrations, pp. 13–16 (2010)
20. Feng, Z.: Tesnière and dependency grammer-commemorating the 60th anniversary of Tesnière's death (tàinf'āi yǔ yīcún yǔfǎ——jì'niàn tàinf'āi shìshì 60 zhōunián). Modern Chinese (xiàndài yǔwén) (language research edition) (yǔyán yánjiū bǎn), pp. 4–9 (2014)
21. Wang, S., Zhou, J.: Syntax and Semantics of Chinese learner's dictionary--Taking Verbs of Complaining as an Example (hànyǔ xuéxí cídiǎn de jùfǎ yǔyì xìnxī——yǐ bàoyuàn lèi dòngcí wéi lì). The 12th Annual Conference of the Educational Linguistics Professional Committee of Association for Comparative Studies of English and Chinese of China (Zhōngguó yīnghànyǔ bǐjiào yánjiū huì jiàoyù yǔyán xué zhuānyè wěiyuánhuì dì 12 jiè niánhuì), Shanghai Jiao Tong University (2021)

# A Tangible Learning Application from the 3D Printer for the Practical Teaching of Meat Cutting in Inclusive Vocational Education

Victoria Batz[✉] [ID], Fabian Kühne, Kristin Hasak, Frederik Pufe, Matthias Morfeld, and Michael A. Herzog [ID]

Magdeburg-Stendal UAS, Breitscheidstr. 2, 30114 Magdeburg, Germany
victoria.batz@h2.de

**Abstract.** Vocational education and training in Germany are distinguished by the separation of training groups of different learning levels. In chef training, theoretical teaching content is mainly conveyed using lectures and textbooks. The abstract presentations and texts are not suitable for inclusive education. By pursuing a design science research process, a digital-analog learning application was developed for trainees with and without mental impairment. The tangible prototype for teaching meat cutting from pork was evaluated using 7 participants (trainee chef, trainee kitchen assistants and employees in the kitchen of a sheltered workshop) in an inclusive teaching setting with a mixed-method approach. The usability was evaluated with a User Experience Questionnaire, the results of which were positive. The learning outcomes using the 3D model were surveyed by means of a qualitative questionnaire and showed a high level of potential among all target groups. Two unstructured classroom observations documented the social interaction of the trainees. The learning application facilitates learning and promotes collaborative work.

**Keywords:** Inclusive Vocational Education · Interactive Learning · Game-based Learning · Serious Games · 3D Printing · Rapid Prototyping

## 1 Introduction

With the ratification of the UN Convention on the Rights of Persons with Disabilities in 2009, Germany committed to implementing equal opportunities and participation at all levels for people with disabilities and to preventing discrimination [1]. Article 24 calls on States Parties to ensure an "inclusive education system at all levels and lifelong learning" [2]. Article 27 focuses on the "equal right to work of persons with disabilities" [2]. Both the German Vocational Training Act (BBiG) and the Handicrafts Code (HwO) require that people with disabilities be trained in the general dual system, which features a direct connection between vocational schools and training companies as learning locations [3]. The practical implementation, however, features substantial deficits [4]. The legal foundation contrasts with the often-rigid structures of the education system, which is characterized by segregated learning of trainees and people with learning disabilities to

C. S. González-González et al. (Eds.): ICWL 2022/SETE 2022, LNCS 13869, pp. 290–301, 2023.
https://doi.org/10.1007/978-3-031-33023-0_26

the point of the clear separation of people with intellectual disabilities (PWD) [5]. More than 90% of the students with mental impairment start working in sheltered workshops (SW) after leaving school, and these do not offer qualifications for access to the general labor market [6]. The employment rate from SW to the general labor market is less than one percent [7]. According to §66 of the Vocational Training Act, people with learning disabilities are offered less theoretical training to become kitchen assistants [8]. "Inclusive vocational training could be broadly described as the right of PWD to participate in vocational education in a recognized training occupation, to be provided in shared learning facilities with people without disabilities." [9].

This study examines how theoretical learning content can be conveyed in a practical and inclusive way with the help of learning technologies using the example of training to become a chef. New teaching formats, methods and inclusive teaching materials are needed to bring together the three training groups of trainee cooks, kitchen assistants and kitchen staff in sheltered workshops to implement inclusive vocational education [10]. Digital technologies offer great potential for improving equal participation and reducing barriers to access [10]. The development and design of digital learning applications for PWD usually focus on specific groups, e.g. blind or deaf people. People with intellectual and mental impairments, on the other hand, are given little consideration in current research [11]. Serious Games in particular are usually developed for people without impairments instead of following a "design for all" approach. Using Serious Games in the classroom can help to convey theoretical knowledge in a playful way while addressing different cognitive abilities and impairments [11]. Using a design science research process, a haptic, digital-analog learning application was developed for trainees with and without intellectual disabilities [12] (Fig. 1).

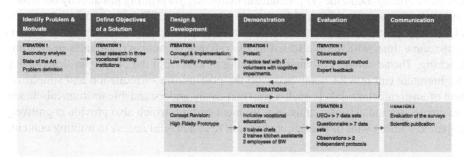

**Fig. 1.** Design science research process according to Pfeffers et al. [12].

In order to analyze requirements, user research was conducted in three institutions of vocational education (Oberstufenzentrum Prignitz, BBZ Berufsbildungszentrum Prignitz GmbH and Lebenshilfe e.V. Prignitz). In the first iteration, a low-fidelity prototype was created, which was evaluated by employees of the SW. The results provided the basis for the conceptual development of a functional high-fidelity prototype. The digital-analog learning application was then evaluated with 7 participants (chef trainees, kitchen assistants and employees of an SW) in an inclusive classroom setting using a mixed-method approach consisting of qualitative and quantitative methods [13]. The standardized User Experience Questionnaire (UEQ) was used to assess usability aspects of the learning application [14]. Additionally, a qualitative questionnaire was used to collect data on learning success and increased motivation through the use of the prototype. Two independent, unstructured, and non-participatory observations in class documented the social interaction and cooperation of the trainees as well as the development of solution strategies. The aim was to use gamified and hands-on concepts to teach theory in a sustainable way, to include all learners by differentiating the teaching content and to increase the interaction between trainees in inclusive lessons.

## 2 State of the Art

A literature review was aligned with the propositional inventory method [15, 16]. For searching in Google Scholar, IEEEXplore and dblp.org, the keywords selected were 3D printing, vocational training or vocational education, and disabilities or impairments. The search was conducted including synonyms and related terms in German and English. The review of the articles describing concrete applications shows that to date only assistive projects in the field of physical disabilities (16 publications) have been published in the analyzed field, and in particular on severe visual impairments (9 publications). 3D printing now plays a major role in the context of prosthetic prototyping for physical deficits such as amputations, which originated, for example, in the co-creation of developers and PWD in inclusive makerspaces [17]. No publications were identified that used haptic learning or 3D printing for PWD in inclusive learning scenarios. However, upon expanding the search to other educational domains, numerous papers were found that used 3D printed objects to better communicate knowledge and save resources, for example, in veterinary medicine [18]. In human medicine, 3D printing has already been used and researched as a learning tool for around 10 years [19]. 3D printing offers the option of fast reproduction from current or historical 3D data (e.g. MRI, CT) for many learners at the same time, which has also led to less reliance on human plastinates in anatomy teaching. The advantages of tangible learning objects from the 3D printer described in the literature can now be combined with the possibilities of reduction and simplification of anatomical models in such a way that easily understandable anatomical objects are created for inclusive teaching, e.g. for meat cutting, which also provide cognitively impaired trainees with intuitive, communicative and playful access to training content.

## 3 Prototype

### 3.1 Learning Objectives

The learning objectives of the meat cutting topic are an integral part of chef training. Currently, vocational school teaching content is predominantly taught using theoretical methods (lecturing) and abstract graphics from the textbook, "The Young Chef" [20]. The lack of time, resources and raw materials means that real butchered animals are seldom cut. The aim of the learning application is to help trainees to name the parts of the pig correctly, to identify them according to shape and position and to describe how they are cooked.

The constructivist learning culture describes the learning process not in terms of knowledge transfer, but as the independent acquisition of knowledge by learners. Only through one's own experience can practical knowledge be taught in a sustainable way. Three basic principles for student-centered teaching have been identified: (1) a variety of methods with a focus on action orientation, (2) the awareness of the increasing heterogeneity of learners and their individual support through differentiation of the teaching content, and (3) the strengthening of the learners' responsibility for their own actions through opportunities to participate in the design of the learning environment [21]. Instructional content is learned more effectively through independent exploration using the "research-based learning" method [22]. When experimenting in the context of research-based learning, the teacher can support the learning process to various degrees [23]. For this purpose, the teacher's role changes from imparting knowledge to providing support through a gradual reduction of instruction to moderation, which allows learners a steadily increasing degree of autonomy in the learning process [23]. The degree of independence must be adjusted to the needs of the class or, in an inclusive setting, to the needs of the individual learner [23].

First, the learning objectives for the three test groups were defined and elaborated together with trainers and a special educator from the vocational training kitchen at the SW. The "à la Carte" module of regular chef training covers the topics of texture, processing and the cutting up of meat from different slaughtered animals [24]. These animals include mainly cattle, pigs, and sheep. The sub-area of "pork" was selected for inclusive teaching because it is most frequently prepared in German kitchens. The individual learning objectives differ in the amount of knowledge acquired and are determined by the students themselves. Learning objective 1 covers the rough cutting of the pig and the naming of the cuts. For learning objective 2, trainees should also be able to locate and name the offcuts from the fine cutting process, as well as identify pieces of meat by their shape, size, muscles and bones. In addition, they are familiar with the use and appropriate cooking methods for the various cuts of meat. Learning objective 3 is an independent identification of the position and naming of all cuts including alternative terms (c.g. pointed leg = trotter).

## 3.2  Concept

For the concept of an inclusive learning application, knowledge should be written in simple language and the amount of information should be adaptable [11]. Users with heterogeneous learning levels must not be deterred by the abundance of information [11]. Categorizing information and teaching in several stages with increasing information density is suited to this purpose. To promote interaction and collaboration among learners with different educational backgrounds, different levels of teaching content should not be processed separately. For this purpose, the content is transformed into practical scenarios. The application can be used both for group collaboration and alone for practice purposes. The differentiation of learning requirements is not about developing a separate concept for each of the three target groups (trainee chefs, kitchen assistants and SW kitchen employees), but rather an inclusive teaching experience that is shared by all trainees as a common path. For different learning requirements, needs, and abilities, learning applications should provide infinite levels of difficulty to avoid clustering within the classroom [11] (Fig. 2).

**Fig. 2.** 3D printed pig in the 5 colors of rough cutting

The learning application includes a 3D printed model of half a pig, a poster and 16 cards to go with it. The poster shows the 5 rough cutting parts on the front and the 16 fine cutting parts on the back. The 3D model consists of a total of 16 parts (fine cutting). There is one card from the set for each part of the pig. The cards contain all the additional information: professional terms, appearance and position of the cut. The back has detailed information about the texture of the meat, alternative names, methods of preparation and possible dishes. On the edges of the poster are colored markers for each piece of pork. The corresponding playing cards are placed on the correct piece on the poster. Then the 3D pieces of the pig are assigned to the corresponding card. If the solution is correct, the colors of the poster, card and 3D part match.

### 3.3  Implementation

A 3D veterinary anatomical model of a pig was used as the basis for the professional implementation. To extract the meat cuts, the model was adapted in Cinema 4D, Maya and Rhinoceros and, among other things, superfluous organs and textures were removed. The 3D print-out was created using the FDM (Fused Deposition Modeling) rapid prototyping method, as it both conserves resources and is time-efficient. Three Prusa MK3S printers were used for this purpose. To prevent the risk of injury, improve the touch and feel and minimize wear, a flexible thermoplastic elastomer was used as the printing material. Fiberflex filament can be printed at temperatures of 200–220 °C and requires a heating bed temperature of 50–70 °C. To enable the printed meat cuts to be easily assembled, small neodymium magnets were embedded in the prints. Organs and bone structures were embodied by a supporting base plate made of birch plywood. The volume was represented by the layering of wooden slices created with a laser cutter. In addition, the names and outlines of the meat cuts were engraved on the model. The slices are glued together and painted with wood stain.

## 4  Evaluation

### 4.1  Test Setting

The test was conducted in inclusive vocational school lessons at the Oberstufenzentrum Prignitz. Two teachers led the lesson working as a team; a special needs teacher assisted the participants from the SW, and two vocational schoolteachers supported the lesson as inactive audience. A rehabilitation psychologist and an interaction designer conducted unstructured, non-participant observations during testing. Three trainee chefs, two trainee kitchen assistants and two employees of the SW took part in the lessons (n = 7). The class was divided into 3 heterogeneous groups of 2–3 people. First, the basics of the topic of butchery were taught. This was followed by more in-depth information on rough and fine cutting. For using the prototypical learning application, all 3 groups received a task sheet. The cuts of meat, their uses and cooking methods had to be collected and filled in a table with 3 columns. The missing information had to be completed with the help of the learning application. Working groups that were able to solve all tasks were given additional tasks with more difficult questions to be answered with the help of the study cards (Fig. 3).

**Fig. 3.** Testing the learning application in inclusive education; color-coded card set

## 4.2  UEQ+

The usability of the interactive learning application was evaluated using the UEQ + standardized test procedure [14]. To evaluate the accomplishment of the objectives, 9 out of 20 available evaluation categories were selected: Perspicuity, Stimulation, Novelty, Haptics, Usefulness, Value, Visual Aesthetics, Intuitive Use and Quality of Content. Each dimension included 4 items consisting of two terms with contrasting meanings (e.g., efficient and inefficient). On a 7-point Likert scale, participants rated the usability aspect very negatively (−3), neutrally (0) or positively (+3). An opening sentence described the context of the respective dimension [25]. There was an additional item with which the participants indicated the relevance of the respective UX dimension for the overall impression of the product.

The mean values of all items surveyed are in the positive range above 0 (between 1.29 and 2.71). The best rating was achieved by the item's clarity of teaching content (M = 2.71; SD = 0.45), preparation of the teaching content (M = 2.71; SD = 0.70), intuitive use of the learning application (M = 2.71; SD = 0.45) and value of the product (M = 2.71; SD = 0.45). The lowest scores were given to the item's learning application innovation (M = 1.29; SD = 1.48), ease of handling (M = 1.57; SD = 1.99), excitement during the game (M = 1.71; SD = 0.70), and visual aesthetics of the prototype (M = 1.71; SD = 0.88) (Table 1).

**Table 1.** Means for all 36 UEQ + items (n = 7).

| UX Dimension | Left item | Right item | M | SD |
|---|---|---|---|---|
| Perspicuity | not understandable | understandable | 1.86 | 1.64 |
| | difficult to learn | easy to learn | 2.29 | 0.70 |
| | complicated | easy | 2.43 | 0.73 |
| | confusing | clear | 2.29 | 1.03 |
| Stimulation | not interesting | interesting | 2.29 | 0.70 |
| | boring | exiting | 1.71 | 0.70 |
| | inferior | valuable | 2.29 | 0.88 |
| | demotivating | motivating | 2.43 | 0.49 |
| Novelty | dull | creative | 2.57 | 0.49 |
| | conventional | inventive | 2.14 | 0.35 |
| | commonplace | leading edge | 2.14 | 0.83 |
| | conservative | innovative | 1.29 | 1.48 |
| Haptics | unstable | stable | 1.86 | 0.64 |
| | unpleasant to touch | pleasant to touch | 2.43 | 0.73 |
| | rough | smooth | 2.43 | 0.49 |
| | slippery | slip-resistant | 2.14 | 0.64 |
| Usefulness | useless | useful | 2.14 | 0.35 |
| | not helpful | helpful | 2.43 | 0.49 |
| | not beneficial | beneficial | 2.00 | 0.76 |
| | not rewarding | rewarding | 2.29 | 0.45 |
| Value | inferior | valuable | 1.86 | 0.64 |
| | not presentable | presentable | 2.71 | 0.45 |
| | tasteless | tasteful | 1.86 | 1.12 |
| | not elegant | elegant | 1.86 | 0.83 |
| Visual Aesthetics | ugly | beautiful | 2.14 | 0.64 |
| | lacking style | stylish | 2.00 | 0.93 |
| | unappealing | appealing | 2.00 | 0.53 |
| | unpleasant | pleasant | 1.71 | 0.88 |
| Intuitive Use | difficult | easy | 1.57 | 1.99 |
| | illogical | logical | 2.57 | 0.73 |
| | not plausible | plausible | 2.71 | 0.45 |
| | inconclusive | conclusive | 2.57 | 0.73 |
| Quality of Content | obsolete | up-to-date | 2.14 | 0.99 |
| | not interesting | interesting | 2.29 | 0.70 |
| | poorly prepared | well prepared | 2.71 | 0.70 |
| | incomprehensible | comprehensible | 2.,71 | 0.45 |

It is assumed that the item "demanding - effortless" was not correctly understood by all participants. This pair of terms is an exception in the dimension "Intuitive use". This is also indicated by a strikingly high variance value of 4.62. On average, the dimensions "Quality of content" (M = 2.46; SD = 0.78) and "Intuitive use" (M = 2.36; SD = 1.23) received the highest mean values for their four associated items. The dimensions "Visual aesthetics" (M = 1.96; SD = 0.78) and "Novelty" (M = 2.04; SD = 1.02) received the lowest overall scores for their associated items.

When assessing the relevance of usability criteria, the dimensions "Perspicuity" (M = 2.29; SD = 0.70), "Intuitive use" (M = 2.14; SD = 0.83), and "Quality of Content" (M = 2.14; SD = 0.83) were rated on average as most important for the evaluation of the SG. The dimensions "Haptics" (M = 1.71; SD = 0.88), "Visual aesthetics" (M = 1.96; SD = 1.12) and "Novelty" (M = 2.04; SD = 0.83) received the lowest mean values. Overall, the evaluation of all 9 scales is in the positive range (>0.8) and are considered important aspects for the quality of the learning application by the test subjects.

### 4.3 Survey

All 7 trainees in inclusive education participated in the qualitative survey. With 17 items, the trainees assessed their personal learning successes using the prototype and the acceptance of the inclusive training setting. On a 6-point Likert scale, participants indicated whether they strongly disagreed or agreed with the given statement (1 = strongly disagree; 6 = strongly agree) (Fig. 4).

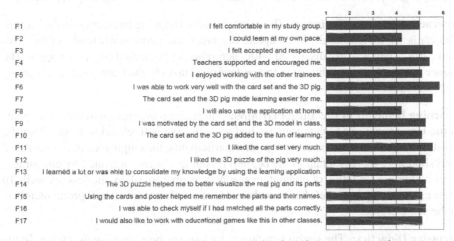

**Fig. 4.** Results of qualitative survey; 17 items assessing learning successes and acceptance of inclusive training setting.

The mean values of all 17 items were above 4 out of a maximum of 6. Accordingly, the majority of participants tended to agree with every statement. The statements F6 "I got along well with the set of cards and the 3D model" (M = 5.86; SD = 0.38), F3 "I felt accepted and respected" (M = 5.57; SD = 0.79), F7 "The cards and the 3D pig made learning easier for me" (M = 5.57; SD = 0.53), and F11 "I liked the card set very much" (M = 5.57; SD = 0.53) received the highest agreement. Items F2 "I was able to learn at my own pace" (M = 4.29; SD = 1.11) and F8 "I will use the cards at home" (M = 4.29; SD = 1.11) received the lowest level of agreement.

Two further items ask for personal opinions on the realization of the learning application with open answer options. The question "What did you like best about the card set or 3D model of the pig?" was answered by six out of seven respondents as follows: "You had something in your hand and didn't just have to imagine it.", "The vividness of the pictures.", "The 3D pig and the explanations on the cards. ", "You can learn well with it.", "The concepts were easily understood, and the explanations are good.", "It was very nice to look at all of cards and the poster; visually appealing, super prepared, a lot of knowledge in a relatively compact form.".

Learning material that you can work with very well. "There was one answer to the second question", "What did you not like and what would you change about the learning set or the 3D model?", which was, "The magnets in the 3D model are a little weak."

### 4.4 Observation

Two researchers conducted unstructured, non-participatory observations. One observation focused on the collaboration of a group of three while using the learning application. The second observation followed all of the classroom activities. The observation time covered the entire lesson of $3 \times 45$ min. To evaluate the findings, the observations were divided into four categories: (1) interaction between trainees, (2) learning behavior of the target groups, (3) inclusive didactics, and (4) handling of the learning application.

**Interaction Between Trainees:** The game prompted ongoing interaction in the groups. The cards were distributed. To complete the tasks, the participants read out the relevant cards. They actively discussed with each other and searched for the answers. The trainee chef took on a guiding role and pedagogical tasks in the team, such as assigning responsibilities.

**Learning Behavior of the Target Groups:** The active participation of the participants in the lessons increased when trainees had enough time beforehand to think about the questions and tasks. Compared to the other participants, the employees of the sheltered workshop were more hesitant in the beginning, but they were motivated by encouragement and praise. In terms of content, everyone was able to follow the lessons well. To some extent, the trainee chefs had to make more of an effort to involve all group members to the same degree.

**Inclusive Didactics:** The lesson was taught by two teachers working as a team. In the beginning, the trainees found it difficult to follow the lessons due to the frequent swapping between teachers. In the second half of the lesson, each teacher took over the presentation role for longer periods, which made the lessons more structured. It was helpful if the second teacher was available to advise the groups. However, the teachers should only provide support when needed. It is noticeable that the trainee chefs were addressed more frequently by the teachers. Inclusive teaching requires a high degree of relationship work without prejudices and special treatment. The two vocational schoolteachers commented very positively on the structure, process and content of the learning application.

**Handling of the Learning Application:** The teacher used the 3D model to explain rough and fine cutting. Card matching was easy even without reading ability and with increasing complexity. When working on different worksheets, trainees became confused about the order of tasks to be solved. Therefore, structured instructions for handling the application during the lesson are needed. If no differentiated work assignments were given, trainees with higher support needs were unable to follow.

## 5 Discussion

The analysis of the theoretical foundations in Sect. 3 indicates that in vocational education and training too (1) a variety of methods with a focus on action orientation, (2) the perception of the increasing heterogeneity of learners and their individual support through differentiation of the teaching content, and (3) the strengthening of learners' responsibility for their own actions through opportunities to co-design the learning environment are successful. Given this theoretical background, the present study was designed with the aim of promoting the development and research of gamified and hands-on approaches to inclusive, vocational education and training, as well as the sustainable delivery of instructional content in chef training. The differentiation of the teaching content is intended to integrate learners with and without intellectual disabilities and to promote interaction between trainees in inclusive teaching. The overall perception of the learning application was positive across the whole class. In particular, the participants rated the "preparation and quality of the content" and "intuitive use" of the learning application very positively. They confirmed that they "got along well" with the learning application. Despite the fact that the set was developed digitally, once in front of the learners it was not perceived by them to be "technological". In terms of post-digitization [26], the avoidance of a screen-based user interface contributed to the low-barrier nature of the learning application. The qualitative survey made clear that the prototype facilitates inclusive learning, so that new knowledge is acquired and consolidated, and the imagination is improved. The evaluation confirms noticeable learning success from the participant's point of view.

The Serious Game promoted inclusive group work, which increased interaction between trainees, so all participants felt respected and accepted. Two factors need to come together for successful inclusive learning of practical teaching content: good material and qualified teachers for inclusive vocational training. Team teaching proved to be an important motivating factor, with one teacher leading and the other being available to provide individual support. While groups work on tasks and do not actively ask for help, teachers do not need to offer guidance. The social nature of communication between teachers and learners makes learning easier in inclusive classroom settings [27].

The participants agreed least with the statements that they could "learn at their own pace" with the learning application, as well as "would also use the learning application at home". For individual use, the game became effective especially with a concrete work instruction like questions about the information on the cards or placing the cuts of meat. Co-teaching of different educational groups would be more successful if there were differentiation of learning objectives and certified qualifications, as well as suitable applications for acquiring the learning content. A game manual for different purposes with differentiated formulations of tasks could support the promotion of personal strengths in the team (e.g., through role assignment, integration of automated feedback).

Three separate educational systems present a significant challenge in coordinating an inclusive instructional setting in terms of time and space. The trial could only be conducted with a small number of participants, due to logistical reasons as well as pandemic contact restrictions. From the results of the cross-sectional study conducted here, tendencies can be inferred but no cause-and-effect conclusions can be drawn. In addition, it was not possible to identify any accessible, standardized survey methods for evaluating the usability of learning applications and successful learning outcomes in vocational training for people with cognitive impairments. There is substantial potential for future research into and development of inclusive survey tools.

The application supports teachers in inclusive vocational education and can be easily integrated into the curriculum. The analog handling reduces the need for preparation and training of digital competencies, allowing trainees with higher support needs to be involved more quickly. Digital creation enables sharing and adaptation of the learning materials as Open Education Resources (OER). The potential for further development of the learning set can be increased through the simplification of 3D printing hardware and software. Furthermore, the game principle of the 3D application is applicable to virtual space. A virtual reality (VR) learning application holds additional possibilities in vocational education. The use of VR could make a significant contribution to equal participation for special educational requirements in the target group of PWD. However, to date, accessibility, and the perspective of PWD have barely been considered in the creation of VR applications and have not yet been systematically researched [28].

# References

1. Amirpur, D.: Migrationsbedingt behindert? Eine intersektionale Perspektive. transcript Verlag, Bielefeld, Familien im Hilfesystem (2016)
2. UN-Behindertenrechtskonvention: Übereinkommen über die Rechte von Menschen mit Behinderungen, pp. 21–25. https://www.institut-fuer-menschenrechte.de. Accessed 01 Nov 2018
3. Enggruber, R., Rützel, J.: Berufsausbildung junger Menschen mit Behinderungen. Eine repräsentative Befragung von Betrieben. 1st edn. Bertelsmann, Gütersloh (2014)
4. UNESCO: Inklusion: Leitlinien für die Bildungspolitik. 3rd edn. Dt. UNESCO-Kommission e.V., Bonn (2014)
5. Euler, D.: Inklusion in der Berufsausbildung. In: Inklusion in der Berufsbildung: Befunde, Konzepte, Diskussionen. BiBB, Bielefeld, pp. 27–42 (2016)
6. Baethge, M.: Berufsbildung für Menschen mit Behinderungen. Perspektiven des nationalen Bildungsberichts 2014. In: Inklusion in der Berufsbildung: Befunde – Konzepte – Diskussionen. Bertelsmann, Bielefeld, pp. 43–58 (2016)
7. Stöppler, R., Schuck, H.: Berufliche Bildung bei Menschen mit geistiger Behinderung. Auf dem Weg zur beruflichen Integration/Inklusion!? In: bwp@ Spezial 5 – Hochschultage Berufliche Bildung, Fachtagung 02 (2011)
8. Bundeszentrale für politische Bildung: Die drei Sektoren der beruflichen Bildung –Duales System. https://www.bpb.de. Accessed 03 May 2021
9. Euler, D., Severing, E.: Inklusion in der Berufsbildung. In: Zeitschrift für Berufs-und Wirtschaftspädagogik (ZBW) 110(1), 29 (2014)
10. Batz, V., et al.: The digital competence of vocational education teachers and of learners with and without cognitive disabilities. In: Conference Proceedings SETE 2021 – Sixth Annual International Symposium on Emerging Technologies for Education (2021)

11. Batz, V., Lipowski, I., Morfeld, M., Hansen, C., Herzog, M. A.: Accessible design of serious games for people with intellectual disabilities in inclusive vocational education. In: Conference Proceedings DiGRA Digital Library (2022)
12. Peffers, K., Tuunanen, T., Rothenberger, M. A., Chatterjee, S.: A design science research methodology for information systems research. J. Manag. Inf. Syst. **24**(3), 45–77 (2007)
13. Stahl, N., Lampi, J., King, J. R.: Expanding approaches for research: Mixed methods. J. Dev. Educ. **42**(2), 28–30 (2019)
14. Schrepp, M., Hinderks, A., Thomaschewski, J.: Design and evaluation of a short version of the user experience questionnaire (UEQ-S). Int. J. Interact. Multimed. Artif. Intell. **4**(6), 103–108 (2017)
15. Bonfadelli, H., Meier, W.: Meta-Forschung in der Publizistikwissenschaft. Zur Problematik der Synthese von empirischer Forschung. In: Rundfunk und Fernsehen 32. Jg. H. 4, pp. 537–550 (1984)
16. Lueginger, E., Renger, R.: Das weite Feld der Metaanalyse. Sekundär-, literatur- und metaanalytische Verfahren im Vergleich. In: kommunikation.medien, no. 2, pp. 1–31 (2013)
17. Bosse, I.K., Pelka, B.: Peer production by persons with disabilities–opening 3D printing aids to everybody in an inclusive MakerSpace. J. Enabling Technol. **14**(1), 41–53 (2020)
18. Assis Di Donato, B., et al.: Three-dimensional digitalized and printed tongue models of the cow, dog, pig, and horse for undergraduate veterinary education. Int. J. Morphol. **39**(2) (2021)
19. McMenamin, P.G., Quayle, M.R., McHenry, C.R., Adams, J.W.: The production of anatomical teaching resources using three-dimensional (3D) printing technology. Anatom. Sci. Educ. **7**(6), 479–486 (2014)
20. Lipowski, I., Batz, V.: Hospitationsbericht 1 des Projektes "IKKE- Bildungs- und Barrierefreiheit durch Digitalisierungsinstrumente in der beruflichen Ausbildung". https://inklusive-kueche.h2.de/veroeffentlichungen/. Accessed 2019/03/25
21. Jank, W., Meyer, H.: Didaktische Modelle. 14th edn. Cornelsen-Scriptor (2002)
22. Schmidkunz, H., Lindemann, H.: Das forschend-entwickelnde Unterrichtsverfahren: Problemlösen im naturwissenschaftlichen Unterricht. Westarp-Wiss (1992)
23. Mayer, J., Ziemek, H. P.: Offenes Experimentieren: Forschendes Lernen im Biologieunterricht. Unterricht Biologie **20**, 4–12 (2006)
24. Grüner, H., Metz, R., Hummel, M.: Der junge Koch, die junge Köchin. Pfannberg (1999)
25. Schrepp, M., Sandkühler, H., Thomaschewski, J.: How to create short forms of UEQ+ based questionnaires? In: Mensch und Computer 2021 – Workshopband (2021)
26. Jandrić, P., Knox, J., Besley, T., Ryberg, T., Suoranta, J., Hayes, S.: Postdigital science and education. Educ. Philos. Theory **50**(10), 893–899 (2018)
27. Scheer, J.P.D.D., Laubenstein, D.: Auswirkungen der Corona-Schulschließungen auf Schüler* innen mit und ohne Förderbedarf der emotionalen und sozialen Entwicklung (COFESE). Projektskizze. Pädagogische Hochschule Heidelberg & Universität Paderborn. https://osf.io/rg2zy/. Accessed 01 Nov 2020
28. Goertz, L.: Virtual Reality zum Lernen – für Menschen mit Handicap noch nicht ausgereift. https://www.mmb-institut.de/blog/. Accessed 01 July 2020

# A New World of Open Space: Reflections and Perspectives of Chinese Scholars on the Digital Transformation of Education and Future Education Research

Qin Qin[1]([✉]) [ID] and Li Ao[2] [ID]

[1] Institute for Advanced Study of Education Development in Guangdong-Hong-Kong-Macao Greater Bay Area, South China Normal University, Guangzhou, China
prettyqin99@126.com
[2] School of Education Science, South China Normal University, Guangzhou, China

**Abstract.** There is an urgent need to advance theoretical research and broaden academic conversation in relevant domains in order to undertake strategic initiatives for the digitalization of education. The topics of metaverse and educational ecological reconstruction, artificial intelligence (AI) and future educational development, big data and educational governance, and future educational research paradigm change are thoroughly discussed through interviews with 16 experts in the field of educational information technology. The study found that: (1) 'Metaverse' should be substituted to the development of education, it brings new problems to education, and also put forward new requirements for modern education; (2) Artificial intelligence is an all-round challenge to education, which has a significant impact on talent training, both in teaching and learning, as well as the restructuring of the entire education system; (3) Under the background of artificial intelligence, the future education will mainly lead to changes in educational values and objectives, and changes in the means of educational scenarios will also lead to changes in traditional educational forms; (4) The duplexing empowerment between education research and new technology; (5) In the context of new technologies, such as AI and the Metaverse, science fiction could be used as a new method for educational research..

**Keywords:** Artificial Intelligence · Virtual Reality · Digital Transformation · Big Data · Educational Restructuring

## 1 Introduction

At present, the new technological revolution represented by artificial intelligence (AI), virtual reality (VR), cloud computing and big data is booming, and the human society has entered the era of intelligence. Education is the core driving force of the current AI technology revolution, and it is also the most important application scenario and development direction of AI. Education technology can improve the effectiveness of decision-making and work efficiency of educational subjects, realize personalized teaching and break through the barriers of time and space to traditional education models. This has come to the fore in the global educational response to the COVID-19, and has pushed the global digital transformation of education to a new wave. The use of information technology to drive educational change has become an international consensus and has been incorporated into the education-related policies of various countries, such as the National Education Technology Plan of the United States and the Mast Plan of Singapore, all of which have plans on how to use technology to promote innovation and ecological restructuring in education. It can be said that, education as a core area of technology use and reform and innovation, has also become a sector that has not been reshaped by technology so far. The issues of 'how artificial intelligence technology will reshape the future education ecosystem' and 'how new technologies can contribute to the future development of education' have become the focus of discussion in education and society as a whole.

The general assertion that 'technology is transforming education' is indisputable, but in the face of this 'dark horse' artificial intelligence technology, especially as several schools to realize the great potential of smart technology and began to introduce, relying too much on emotional alienation resulting from smart technology, knowledge of cocoon, the digital divide, gender discrimination, as well as to the issues of education fairness concerns are increasingly apparent. The uncertainty brought by the new technological revolution to education, especially the increased risk of technology abuse, has brought different degrees of anxiety and worry to all stakeholders in the field of education.[1] Then, what new ideas, technologies and challenges will the digital transformation of education bring to the field of education? What new opportunities and new space will there be for education and research in the field of education in the future?

In order to answer these questions, the research team conducted in-depth interviews with 16 experts from the field of educational information technology on topics such as 'metaverse and future education' Artificial intelligence and machine learning' 'The development of computational social science' and 'Prospects for future education research'. Specific topics of discussion and main progress were as follows: (1) Whether 'metaverse' is a concept that must be incorporated to characterize the new impact of new technologies on education, or a novel but transient concept. If the concept of 'metaverse' is incorporated into the field of educational research, what will be the impact on educational research, and how can we cope with it; (2) Starting from the large-scale education reform caused by artificial intelligence, we deeply analyzed the problems of how to carry out teaching and learning under the technological conditions created by artificial intelligence, and how to feed back the development of artificial intelligence technology in education; (3) From the perspective of the systematic reform of education in the era of artificial intelligence, we discussed the general picture and trend of the future education system and education form; (4) With the influence of artificial intelligence and metaverse on educational research methods and paradigms, how science fiction can be used as a future educational research paradigm and how to realize it. For the discussion of these issues, we can share the research contents of talent strategy and theoretical frontier in the intelligent era, intelligent application scenarios and educational governance, intelligent learning and teaching innovation, and the reshaping of educational ecology driven by artificial intelligence, so as to outline the future picture of educational ecology.

## 2  Digital Transformation of Education in China

At present, China is in an important stage of digital transformation and upgrading of traditional industries, and the driving force for the development of digital trade is strong. In October 2021, Iresearch (a data research institute) published the "global digital trade white Paper" pointed out that in 2020, the scale of China's digital economy reached 39.2 trillion yuan, accounting for 38.6% of GDP, ranked the world's second, with a year-on-year growth of 2.4% points, the world's first growth rate [2].

In recent years, China has developed the education informationization as a strategic high ground, take the initiative to meet and adapt to the change of information technology, technology education to promote education reform, improve the efficiency of education, reshape the education ecology, especially the outbreak of COVID-19 in 2020, makes the rapid development of online education, accelerated the pace of education informatization. According to the 2022 China Internet Statistics Report released by the China Internet Network Center, the country's Internet penetration rate has reached 74.4%, and this figure is also reached 58.8%in rural areas [3]. According to the statistics of Foresight Industrial Research Institute, the number of online education users in China reached 342 million in 2020 [4]. The popularization of the internet is the basic guarantee for the development of online education, which makes education informatization continue to advance, the digital construction of educational resources become more abundant, and promotes the flow of high-quality resources among different regions, which is conducive to promoting educational equity and improving educational efficiency.

The strategic action to digitise education has been included in the priorities of the Ministry of Education in 2022. Officially launched in March 2022, the platform provides basic education, vocational education and higher education such as high-quality digital education resources and university students' employment service, to serve the students' all-round development, teachers' teaching, service all-round social progress as the basic criterion, the digital education in talents cultivation, the whole process of teaching reform, education management and social service. Adhering to the principles of demand-oriented, application is king, service is Paramount, economy and efficiency, it has gathered 34,000 basic education course resources, 6,628 high-quality online vocational education courses, and 27,000 high-quality higher education courses. According to data released by the Ministry of Education, 111 live courses of "Internet plus career guidance" have been launched on the platform, with 310 million viewers.[5].

While promoting the digital transformation of education, the Chinese government has issued a series of regulations and policies to guide and regulate this process.Since 2018, the Chinese government issued a series of related documents of the key of the education informationization, on one hand, attention and encourage the development of the education of information technology, at the other hand, strengthen the management on the use of the information technology education and guidance, establish and improve the mechanism of sustainable development of education informationization, construction of network, digital, intelligent, personalized, the lifelong education system. Table1 lists several key documents and main contents (Table 1).

At present, the integration of artificial intelligence, 5G, big data and education is accelerating, promoting the rapid evolution of education informatization into education digitalization. The smart education industry has been developing during the epidemic.

**Table 1.** China's Policy on Education Informatization (2018–2022)

| File | Date | Main Point about Education Informationization |
|---|---|---|
| Education Information Technology2.0 Action Plan | Apr.13, 2018 | Internet + Education: deep integration of information technology and education teaching |
| China Education Modernization 2035 | Feb.23, 2019 | Build an intelligent campus |
| Opinions on Deepening Educational Teaching Reform to Comprehensively Improve theQuality of Compulsory Education | Jun.23, 2019 | Promote the integration of information technology and education teaching applications. Accelerate the construction of digital campus and actively explore Internet-based teaching |
| Promoting the Healthy Development of Online Education | Sep.25, 2019 | Provide online education services, increase the effective supply of educational resources |
| Strengthening the application of the "three classrooms" | Mar.5, 2020 | Support the construction of a new ecology of 'Internet + education |
| Strengthening Information Technology in Education Management in the New Era | Mar.15, 2021 | Coordination of education management informatization; improve education data management and infrastructure support capability |
| Specifications for the Construction of Digital Campus of Higher Education Institutions | Mar.16, 2021 | Systematic construction of network security, intelligent connection of information resources, digital transformation of campus environment |
| Highlights of the Department of Higher Education of the Ministry of Education for 2022 | Feb.23, 2022 | Comprehensively promote the digitalization of higher education teaching |
| Access Management Specification for National Public Service Platform for Intelligent Education | Jul.28, 2022 | management of platforms at all levels that access the National Public Service Platform for Smart Education |

The Chinese government has realized that smart education is of great help to China's sustainable development strategy and policy, and the application of smart technology in education still has great potential, but at the same time, the uncertainty brought by the new technological revolution to education also brings different degrees of anxiety to people. Based on the current situation of educational digital transformation in China, how should we understand the impact of technological change on education in the future? In section one, we have stated the purpose and intention of this research. Next, we will elaborate the research proposal.

# 3 Data Collection and Analysis

## 3.1 Interviews

Interviews are the main source of material for analysis in descriptive analysis of phenomena in order to clarify the structure of participants' conceptions of particular phenomena. This interview was conducted in a semi-open-ended questioning session with the aim of obtaining information on: (1) the understanding of and attitudes towards 'metaverse'; (2) the new problems and challenges that new technologies bring to education; (3) what new requirements AI poses for modern education; (4) how education feeds into the development of AI technology; (5) future trends in education in the context of AI; (6) the impact of AI on educational research methods. The interviews were conducted in the form of face-to-face talks, which lasted from 20 to 40 min, with an average length of 30 min.

The interviewees included 16 faculty members from universities in Beijing, Shanghai and Guangzhou, working in 12 different universities. The interviewee have not only been engaged in teaching and research in universities for more than ten years, but some of them also hold administrative positions (e.g. dean of teaching, department head, etc.). They are involved in teaching, research or management of information technology in education, and have a broad theoretical knowledge and practical experience of information technology-assisted teaching. Participation in this study was voluntary and after consulting the respondents, whose real names are not presented in the text (replaced by codings), the basic information of the respondents is listed in Table 2.

## 3.2 Data Analysis

To ensure the authenticity of the data, the interviews were recorded throughout. After the interviews were completed, the researcher transcribed the audio recordings into text and analyzed them. First, the researcher repeatedly read the narratives of the speakers to ensure that the information and details provided by each participant had not been missed. The researcher then sorted through the participants' statements and categorized them. In this process, the focus was on the respondents' perceptions of the digital transformation of education and their vision of the future of education in this context.

At the same time, an analysis of relevant literature, including Chinese government policy documents and articles published by scholars on education digital transformation strategies, was used to sort out the government strategies on education digital transformation in China. Data from respondents and documents were analyzed through the development and application of codes, and the researchers categorized all new ideas relevant to the study into themes. For example, the Opinions on Promoting the Development of 'Internet + Education' at the end of 2021, and the Ministry of Education included the digital transformation of education as a key task in 2022, reflecting the high importance attached to this change at the national level. Combining the above two aspects of textual analysis, the conclusions of this paper are drawn.

**Table 2.** Basic Information About the Interviewees

| Serial number | Coding | Gender | Identity | Title | Interview time |
|---|---|---|---|---|---|
| 01 | M01 | Male | Director of MIS/educational researcher | Professor | 40 min |
| 02 | M02 | Male | dean/educational researcher | Professor | 20min |
| 03 | M03 | Male | dean/educational researcher | Professor | 30min |
| 04 | M04 | Male | educational researcher | Professor | 20min |
| 05 | M05 | Male | educational researcher | Professor | 40min |
| 06 | W01 | Female | educational researcher | Professor | 25min |
| 07 | M06 | Male | educational researcher | Professor | 30min |
| 08 | M07 | Male | Dean/educational researcher | Professor | 20min |
| 09 | M08 | Male | dean/educational researcher | Professor | 30min |
| 10 | M09 | Male | educational researcher | Professor | 30min |
| 11 | M10 | Male | educational researcher | Professor | 30min |
| 12 | M11 | Male | educational researcher | Professor | 20min |
| 13 | M12 | Male | dean/educational researcher | Professor | 30min |
| 14 | M13 | Male | educational researcher | Professor | 30min |
| 15 | M14 | Male | educational researcher | Researcher | 40min |
| 16 | M15 | Male | educational researcher | Researcher | 35min |

# 4  Findings

## 4.1  Understanding and Attitudes Towards of Metaverse

'Metaverse' is one of the major emerging global buzzwords in 2021. The Oxford English Dictionary defined it as 'a virtual reality space in which users can interact with computergenerated environments and other people'. Wikipedia defined 'a Metaverse as a physical reality that is convergent and physically persistent through virtual reality, a 3D virtual space based on the future Internet with connectivity perception and sharing characteristics'. Semantically, Metaverse refers to the creation of an immersive, virtual, invisible, immense, permanent, evolving, 24-hour-a-day online artificial electronic space that enables a virtual mapped version of the human real world - one in which people in the real world can break the boundaries of space and time and live in a variety of digital avatars. in which people in the real world can break the boundaries of time and space and live in a variety of digital forms, thus achieving a perfectly immersive experience that transcends reality [6–7]. In reality, it is hoped that the "metaverse" can be created as an artificial online virtual world (space) that is unconnected, parallel to and independent of the real world through a variety of high-tech, internet, mobile communication and specialized devices.

For educational researchers and practitioners, is the 'metaverse' a fleeting concept, or is it a concept that has new implications for education? Scholars have different understandings. From the results of the interviews, respondents' attitudes can be broadly divided into two parts: one is positive towards the new concept and practice of 'metaverse', believing that 'metaverse' develops along with educational theory. Still, there is a cautious attitude towards this new concept, believing that the use of the term 'metaverse' is inappropriate in terms of doctrine, that virtual space is not the main direction for the future development of education and educational technology, and that the gap between the virtual and the real is too wide and not fully interoperable. Here are some of the responses from the participants, explaining briefly how they understand the concept of 'metaverse' and their attitude towards this new concept'.

*'Our attitude should be to unleash our imagination while embracing reality'.*He also added that, *'metaverse is an ultimate goal of digital transformation in education, and the changes it brings are to facilitate the reorganization of the entire educational ecology.'* *(M01).*

*'The vision of education is to create another virtual space, or a world that is a combination of the real and the imaginary, touchable, recognizable and understandable.'* *(M04).*

There are also some scholars who believe that metaverse can be judged as a typical research question, without drawing definite conclusions for the time being, and are generally optimistic about moving forward.

*'Metaverse integrates the real world with the future world in depth, and modern technology is moving so fast that as educational researchers we should take the initiative to take up the challenges of new technologies in education.'* *(M03).*

In addition, a few scholars are still cautious about the concept of 'metaverse'. It is believed that the use of metaverse is theoretically inappropriate, as the original meaning of metaverse refers to the virtual reality, while the current human knowledge of the universe is very limited, and it is impossible for humans to virtually predict and transcend what they do not yet know, and it is impossible to transcend the universe. Therefore, we should treat this thing seriously and calmly.

## 4.2 New Issues and Challenges in the Field of Education Brought About by the Metaverse

There is a consensus that AI and Metaverse will deeply extend the space of human life, expand human perception and enrich the human existence experience [8]. However, the digital or virtual existence of human beings cannot replace modern existence, and the Metaverse must also follow the legal and ethical bottom line. Is the Metaverse a technological utopia, or is it the inevitable result of the development of information technology? Researcher conducted in-depth interviews with the interviewees on the theme of 'What challenges does the Metaverse bring to education', focusing on the following questions.

Firstly, what are the effects of the Metaverse as a new technology and a new way of practice on education nowadays? On a technological level, through the reshaping of the economy and society to create a new world that approaches the infinite openness of space. At the level of pedagogy, it can empower teaching methods in pedagogical practice, help teachers and students engage in deep dialogue, and improve audiovisual effects and provide students with the opportunity to subvert the experience [9].

Secondly, what new issues might Metaverse bring to education? As a technology, the development of Metaverse is still facing the following challenges: (1) Technology risk, The technology related to Metaverse is still in its infancy, and technical limitations are the biggest bottleneck for development; (2) market risk, the current software and hardware ecology in the Metaverse track is not yet mature, whether the scenario application has real market demand is still unknown; (3) policy risk, the free trading and decentralization of the Metaverse (e.g. digital system, NFT trading, games), which faces risks in terms of policy regulation.

Thirdly, what new issues does the Metaverse pose in the context of the educational arena? One is the overlap between 'digital identity' and 'value systems'. Digital identity is the condensation of real identity information into a digital code, forming a public secret key that can be queried and identified through the Internet and related devices, while the value system is the superposition of the Metaverse own value system and the real value system.

Forthly, there was the issue of addictiveness. Some interviewees felt that the problem of addictiveness is more prominent in 3D immersion experiences as young students.The last was the issue of humanistic interactivity. While educational technology opens up possibilities for pedagogical innovation, it may also face the challenges, such as:

*'terminal friendliness, transmission capacity and computing power, modelling speed for the cost of developing massive amounts of content, and security and corroboration.'* (M02).

### 4.3  AI Poses New Requirements for Modern Education

AI is an all-round challenge for education, with a significant impact on talent training, teachers' teaching and students' learning, as well as the reconfiguration of the entire education system.

Firstly, AI + education places higher demands on talent development goals.

*'The judgment of a person's knowledge is not about being talented or rich in learning, but that talents in the AI era place more emphasis on creativity, communication skills, cooperation skills, and the ability to empathize with society.' (M06).*

Secondly, AI is changing the teaching. AI + education places new demands on teacher literacy. Rather than purely technological applications, AI + education uses technological intelligence to make teaching a truly nurturing art. Teachers should not only improve their ability to apply technology, but more importantly, innovate their pedagogy and develop an awareness, philosophy and ability to match AI education.

*'The most important thing is that through big data analysis, using smart classrooms and machine translation, to the right teacher, it also allows the teacher to match the right student.' (M07).*

Thirdly, AI is transforming students' learning. Human learning has to learn from machine learning, but more importantly, it has to go beyond machine learning. It is important to break away from rote learning and 'fill the classroom' approaches in teaching and learning, and to engage students in hands-on participation and experience, moving from 'learning to use' to 'using to learn'.

### 4.4  Duplexing Empowerment Between Education (Research) and AI, Big Data Technology

AI and big data technology will lead to the paradigm change of educational research. Firstly, the technology of big data provides full sample data for educational research. Secondly, big data technology provides polymorphism data for educational research. Thirdly, big data technology provides theoretical basis for educational reform and implementation of practical activities. Fourthly, AI and computer simulation provide a lot of support for complex educational experiment research.

AI technology is a huge boost to education. In turn, can education feed into AI technology and drive the development of the technology? How does education feed back the development of AI technology? Firstly, human learning mechanisms and skills in the education process would be a huge boost to AI machine learning. Human learning is not about the simplistic, mechanistic parameters of making models for a single category, but has a plethora of mechanisms that inspire association. Secondly, the application of human recognition mechanisms to machine learning systems would greatly reduce energy consumption.

*'Most human target recognition originates from the human visual system. The human visual system has only a very short consumption relative to a computer to enable the construction of a computer system as a whole.' (M10).*

### 4.5 Future Trends in Education in the Context of AI

In the context of AI, the future of education will mainly undergo relatively large changes and transformations in two aspects: on the one hand, a large number of heavy and mechanical human tasks will be replaced by machines, which will lead to changes in educational values and goals; on the other hand, the means of educational scenarios, which will lead to changes in the traditional form of education. Specifically, the future of education is likely to see the following development trends.

Firstly, education will change from serving the known to serving the unknown. The rapid development of network technology and AI, the rapid turnover of old and new fields and industries, the future development has a strong uncertainty [10].

Secondly, the school form will transform from a temporal and spatial homogeneity to a scattered step-by-step transformation. In the future, technologies such as big data, AI and the Internet will break the existing temporal and spatial limitations of education, make the analysis of educational content, data resource construction and individual learning data more three-dimensional and precise. Virtual simulation technology and multimodal interactive technology will further compress space and time, making educational situations more realistic and effective.

Thirdly, teaching and learning will shift from a predominantly manual to a collaborative human-machine approach. In future education, not all those engaged in teaching will be teachers, and not necessarily full-time teachers, but there will be human-computer collaboration and a fine division of labour. As an interviewees said:

*'I think that teachers as learning guides mainly carry out guidance on learning methods, cultivate excellence and strengthen home-school communication, etc.' (M07).*

Finally, AI and Metaverse may change the research methods and paradigms in education. Some researchers have suggested that, 'science fiction can be used as a method and tool for studying the future, pulling thinking about the future into the present, thinking about reality based on a vision of the future, and thus developing non-deterministic ideas or theories about the possibilities of the future and the present.[11].

*'science fiction can be used as a method and tool for studying the future, drawing on the narrative method of science fiction to intersect the two temporalities of the future and the present, pulling thinking about the future into the present, thinking about reality based on a vision of the future, and thus developing non-deterministic ideas or theories about the possibilities of the future and the present.' (M13).*

### 4.6 How AI Will Drive the Future of Education

In the future, education will be gradually moving from an industrialized education system to an intelligent education system. How can artificial intelligence drive the future of education? It can be summarized by three key words: personalization, diversification, and human-computer cooperation. First of all, the future of education should realize the organic combination of large-scale education and personalized training. Diversity includes not only the education model, the content of education, but also the interaction of teaching and learning, especially the revolutionary restructuring of educational thinking. Secondly, in terms of the evaluation system of education, a more flexible and diversified teaching and evaluation integration system should be constructed. Thirdly, in the teaching process, human-machine cooperation means that machines and teachers collaborate with each other to achieve a more efficient way of learning.For example, three interviewees made the following statement:

*'What will the future of education be like? Different students learning different content at different times and places to reach the highest level he can reach.' (M06).*

*'Education combined with artificial intelligence, in terms of the evaluation system of education, should be a process of teaching and learning, a process in which the learning ability and nature of each person is fully developed, without using a uniform evaluation scale to evaluate it, but rather a process of teaching people to fish.' (M11).*

*'The class is a virtual reality class where students are brought in to wear a headset, and the virtual human classroom allows all students who take the class to break the space barrier, hundreds of people in a new, virtual, interactive environment have an immersive experience.' (M14).*

## 5 Conclusions

The implementation of strategic initiatives on the digitization of education urgently requires deepening theoretical research and increasing academic dialogue in related fields. Through interviews with 16 experts from the field of educational information technology, this paper has conducted in-depth discussions on topics such as Metaverse and education ecological reconstruction, AI and future education development, big data and education governance, and future education research paradigm change. These topics involve research on issues that create a holistic, strategic and forward-looking future education development, and are important for dissecting education reform and innovation and serving national education decision-making. The research results show that Most of the scholars treat the Metaverse as research question to be explored, but do not draw any definite conclusions for the time being, and generally take an optimistic attitude to move forward.

The 'Metaverse' brings new problems to the development of education, and put forward new requirements for modern education. It will extend the space of human life, expand human perception and enrich the experience of human existence. However, the digital or virtual survival of human beings cannot replace modern survival. This is because the metaverse also has to follow the legal bottom line and the human ethical bottom line.

AI is an all-round challenge for education, with major implications for talent development, teachers' teaching and students' learning, and the reconfiguration of the entire education system.In turn, education can feed into AI technology.

In the context of AI, the future of education will mainly change in two aspects: Firstly, a large number of heavy mechanical human work is replaced by machines, so that the value and objectives of education will change; Secondly, the means of educational scenarios, so that the traditional form of education will change.

The duplexing empowerment between education research and new technology: the rapid development of data science and AI technology have become the main object of educational research and utilization. In turn, education feed into AI technology and drive the development of the technology.

Overall, the digitalisation strategy for higher education has become an important part of China's national development strategy. There is an urgent need to build an interdisciplinary research framework, analyse the impact of AI on learning, knowledge innovation and teachers according to the demands of society on education in the era of AI, study the role of AI in reconstructing the education ecosystem, and ultimately outline the blueprint of future education reshaped by AI as a whole, so as to provide a basis for national policy formulation in the areas of AI, ethics and education regulations. The study will provide a basis for the formulation of national policies on AI, ethics and education regulations.

**Acknowledgements.** This work was supported by The National Social Science Foundation "14th Five-Year Plan" of 2021 education general project (No.BIA0191), the 68th batch of China Postdoctoral Science Foundation (2020M682743).

# References

1. Chen T., Han Q.: The formation mechanism of technology anxiety in educational field and its management direction-based on the epochal interpretation of Marx's thought of 'man and machine'. Chongqing Higher Education Research, pp.48–61 (2022)
2. iResearch: White Paper on Global Digital Trade 2021 (2022). https://www.thepaper.cn/newsDetail_forward_16768232
3. Ministry of Education of the People's Republic of China: Notice of the General Office of the Ministry of Education on the issuance of the Nation Smart Education Public Service Platform Access Management Standards (2022). http://m.moe.gov.cn/srcsite/A16/s3342/202208/t20220819_653868.html. Accessed 1 Oct 2022
4. Ministry of Education of the People's Republic of China website: To introduce the progress of the construction and application of the national smart education platform (2022). http://www.moe.gov.cn/fbh/live/2022/54324/. Accessed 1 Oct 2022
5. China Internet Network Information Center: The 50th Statistical Report on the Development of Internet in China (2022). http://www.cnnic.net.cn/n4/2022/0914/c88-10226.html
6. Ray Schroeder: Is the Metaverse Finally Emerging? (2022). https://www.insidehighered.com/digital-learning/blogs/online-trending-now/metaverse-finally-emerging
7. Ray Schroeder: Tech Trends in Higher Ed: e, NFT and DAO (2022). https://www.insidehighered.com/digital-learning/blogs/online-trending-now/tech-trends-higher-ed-metaverse-nft-and-dao
8. Elkordy, A., Iovinelli, J.: Competencies, culture, and change: a model for digital transformation in K-12 educational contexts. In: Ifenthaler, D., Hofhues, S., Egloffstein, M., Helbig, C. (eds.) Digital Transformation of Learning Organizations, pp. 203–218. Springer, Cham (2021). https://doi.org/10.1007/978-3-030-55878-9_12
9. Davis, N., Eickelmann, B., Zaka, P.: Restructuring of educational systems in the digital age from a co-evolutionary perspective. J. Comput. Assist. Learn. 438–450(2013)
10. Wayne, H., Ilkka, T.: State of the art and practice in AI in education. Eur. J. Educ. 1–29 (2022). https://doi.org/10.1111/ejed.12533
11. Gu, X., Cai, H.: Predicting the future of artificial intelligence and its educational impact: a thought experiment based on social science fiction. Educ. Res. 137–147 (2021)

# Game-Based Co-creation for Children and Adolescents with Complex Health Conditions

Sarah Muñoz-Violant[3] ⓘ, Carina S. González-González[2(✉)] ⓘ, M. Paula Céspedes[4], and Verónica Violant-Holz[1] ⓘ

[1] Department of Psychiatry, Faculty of Medicine, The University of British Columbia, Vancouver, BC V6T 1Z4, Canada
[2] Department of Computer Engineering and Systems, Women Studies Institute, Universidad de La Laguna, San Cristóbal de La Laguna, Spain
cjgonza@ull.edu.es
[3] Department Od Didactic and Educational Organization, Hospital Pedagogy in Neonatology and Pediatrics-Research Group and International Observatory in Hospital Pedagogy, Universitat de Barcelona, Barcelona, Spain
sarah.munozviolant@ubc.ca
[4] Hospital Pedagogy Social Program at Fundación Cardioinfantil, Bogotá, Colombia

**Abstract.** Children and adolescents with special health care needs require specialized pediatric care and, possibly some period of hospitalization in a tertiary care center with high complexity. This work aims to help the treatment of this children identifying well-being factors during the hospitalization and home care convalescence through game-based co-creation methods. The explorative study follows the qualitative and multimethod approach. In this paper, it is described the co-creation procedure and the methodological proposal for children and adolescents.

**Keywords:** Children studies · Game-based learning · Co-creation · Complex Health Conditions

## 1 Introduction

The term Adolescent Children with Special Health Care Needs (NANAS) was first defined in the United States as "all those who have or are at risk of presenting a chronic physical, developmental, behavioral, emotional illness and who also require increased utilization of health services" [1]. Studies in developed countries show a prevalence of NANAS between 13% and 19% [2–4]. This has meant an increase in the number of children with chronic pathology, sometimes with lifelong disabilities, with increased frailty and medical complexity [5, 6].

Among NANAS there is a small group characterized by the presence of severe and widespread conditions that are defined as Complex Health Conditions (CHC) [7]. CHCs are defined as children and adolescents with a duration of symptoms that can be expected to exceed 12 months (barring death), involving different systems, but large enough

C. S. González-González et al. (Eds.): ICWL 2022/SETE 2022, LNCS 13869, pp. 314–320, 2023.
https://doi.org/10.1007/978-3-031-33023-0_28

to require specialized pediatric care and, possibly some period of hospitalization in a tertiary care center [7, 8]. Examples include infants and adolescents with congenital or acquired diseases, severe neurological conditions with significant functional impairment, or cancer patients or cancer survivors with ongoing disability [9].

The prevalence of CHC continues to increase due to reduced infant mortality, access to new technologies, and improved social and health markers [10, 11]. Thirty years ago, children with this condition did not survive. Today, however, they can be treated and survived with fragile medical profiles and special care needs [9]. In the specific case of cancer, 80% of affected European children survive to adulthood, but many of them need ongoing medical follow-up to treat associated complications [12].

Although children with CHC represent less than 1%, their care needs are significant and substantial [13, 14], representing a significant proportion of hospital disease [3]. This is related mainly to the fact that there are many hospitalizations, a higher rate of admission to intensive care units (ICU), more extended stays, a greater need for technological assistance, and a greater need for services with a higher level of specialization [13, 15–17]. In the study conducted by Climent et al. [18], it was possible to identify that the mean hospitalization of children admitted with CSC is usually 25 days. Besides, this is a group of patients more susceptible to diseases such as infections, respiratory deterioration, nutritional problems, and complications derived from technological support, which, together with the possibility of exacerbation of their underlying disease, can lead to frequent readmissions [13, 18, 19].

Child hospitalization is defined as a situation that places infants and adolescents in a crisis' situation [20]. During this process, they must face a new reality, in which they depend on third persons who are strangers, lose their autonomy and privacy, experiencing a possible dependence on health professionals, accepting special rules, as well as our living habits for their feeding and of are [21]. In this sense, the experience of suffering from non-nominal malingering is governed by the somatic manifestations kicked by children and adolescents, however, social, cultural, and relational experiences [22].

Pediatric patients and suffering physical discomfort due to all that their discase implies, the hospitalization process implies a loss of references about their daily life; it can become a traumatic experience [23]. It implies a high rate of mental health problems, as is the case of anxiety and depression [24, 25]. Specifically, depression may accompany hospitalization because this situation requires the patient to face conflicts of dependence and separation from family and friends [26]. Also, the pediatric patient must adapt to health personnel and other patients, people who may be seen as intruders.

Feelings of anxiety and depression, pores and fears that often characterize child-hood hospitalization, can cause significant behavioral alterations such as oppositional behaviors, aggressiveness, lack of adherence to medication, sleep disorders, avoidance responses, mutism, and attention deficits [26]. In general, the presence of mental health problems, especially in children and adolescents hospitalized for medical or surgical problems, as is the case of HCC, is associated with more admissions and worse therapeutic outcomes [26] and leads to worse pain management [25]. On the other hand, the psychological state of the child and adolescent, determined by their habits, beliefs, and behaviors, can condition the immune response and lead to the disease's evolution.

The increase of children and adolescents with CHC [18] demands a change of mentality in pediatric care planning programs, which must be focused on providing comprehensive, multidisciplinary, and coordinated care [18]. Health professionals must be aware of the problems and uncertainties typical of the infant-juvenile hospitalization process and their family environment to be able to offer and optimize global care of the pediatric patient, thus promoting, in this way, excellence in infant-juvenile hospital care [27].

Hospitalized children and adolescents need their family, play, extracurricular activities, guidance, and individualized attention for all their care to avoid developmental delay and, as far as possible, to ensure an everyday life appropriate to their stage of development [28, 29]. Adverse experiences during childhood are related to some painful health outcomes in adulthood [30]. These circumstances justify the need to develop and implement specific interventions to reduce the adverse effects of hospitalization, aimed at promoting physical activity during their free time, providing emotional recovery, reducing school deficiencies, cultivating children's joy and their social relationships, attending to the formation of the child's character and will, achieving adaptation to hospitalization and the situation of discomfort, reducing the adverse effects as a consequence of hospitalization and in general, improving the quality of life of the hospitalized child and adolescent [31, 32]. In this sense, play-based activities take on relevance. For this reason, in this work, we aim to identify through game-based co-creation methods factors of well-being during hospitalization and home convalescence in children and adolescents with CHC. The aim of this study is to identify factors of well-being during hospitalization and home convalescence in children and adolescents with Complex Health Conditions.

## 2 Research Methods

The following qualitative study was designed with an exploratory and multi-method approach: observational - co-creation spaces with pedagogical materials designed ad hoc and selective - use of standardized tests. The sample included children and adolescents with Complex Health Conditions, their families, and professionals participating in their care. The sample included participants from multiple rural and urban provinces of Catalonia, hospitalized or receiving convalescence care. The data was collected through the organization of co-creation spaces with pedagogical materials designed for each group on an ad hoc basis. Participants also completed standardized tests adapted to their age on "Resilience", "Psychological Well-being", and "Positive Mental Health" before each co-creation space. Analysis: Qualitative data was analyzed using the Diamond Technique and MAXQDA program and quantitative data was analyzed using the non-parametric Mann Whitney U test, establishing a type I error of 0.05 and the R Statistical Program.

## 3 Game Based Co-creation Proposal

Co-creation allows us "to offer the group an X-ray, as rigorous as possible, of its problems, but it also has to make all its members feel identified with them, that is, as a consequence of the imitation of the results of the whole process [...] it also involves a recurrent and organized reflection, which allows people to clarify their needs" [33].

Co-creation is organized in three phases.

1. In the first phase: situations are identified that generate benefits for the participants (from the imagination of the future but considering their experiences) (Fig. 1).
2. In the second phase: the relationships among them are established (group categorization)
3. In the third and last phase: the diamond strategy is used [34] (Fig. 2).

The procedure followed in co-creation is as follows: the session begins by presenting an initial stimulating situation through the game, representing the first phase of co-creation and how the conversation will be activated. Once the children have connected with the activity, the session continues with the two remaining phases of co-creation: establishing relationships and reflecting with the community. The sessions are conducted virtually with hospitalized and convalescent children (co-creation and questionnaire) and their families (questionnaire).

The types of games are designed according to age, with symbolic play being chosen for the age ranges 3 to 5 years and 6 to 8 years. The rules game is applied to the age range of 9 to 12 years and the simulation games in the age range of 13 to 18 (adolescents).

**Fig. 1.** Games used in the first phase of co-creation.

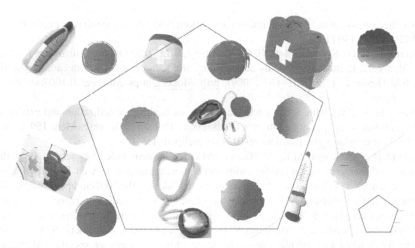

**Fig. 2.** Diamond technique used in the third phase of co-creation with 3–5-year-old

All participants in the co-creation spaces answer a test of resilience or positive health-emotional state. The purpose is to be able to co-relate the results of the test with different personal variables: age, gender, type of illness, context (hospital - home), being a participant in a situation of illness or being a family member; and at the same time to co-relate them with the results of the co-creation space (well-being factors). The co-creation results are extracted with the diamond technique, and the results are analyzed with the qualitative analysis program (MaxQDA). An interpretative analysis is also performed to obtain the analytical evidence and factor orientation about the frequency and concurrence of well-being factors (the concepts at the voltage of each factor - relational maps/numbers) and their interpretation and triangulation. Besides, standardized tests are performed to analyze the relationship between categorical quantitative variables and discrete and continuous quantitative variables.

## 4   Conclusion

The experience of hospitalization and home convalescence is decisive in the adequate evolution of patients and their family environment, and in the appearance of sequelae. Hence, it is necessary to explore the perspective of these patients and their families to identify indicators of well-being that can be utilized as reference to optimize the process of hospitalization and home convalescence. This project presents the opportunity to achieve bolder empowerment of health, growth, and development.

**Acknowledgement.** The authors gratefully acknowledge the support of Barça Foundation and Foundation Bosch i Gimpera. Grand support FBG 14749 (2020–2021).

## References

1. McPherson, M., et al.: A new definition of children with special health care needs. Pediatrics **102**(1), 137–140 (1998)
2. Bramlett, M.D., Read, D., Bethell, C., Blumberg, S.J.: Differentiating subgroups of children with special health care needs by health status and complexity of health care needs. Mater. Child Health J. **13**(2), 151–163 (2009). http://doi.org/https://doi.org/10.1007/s10995-008-0339-z
3. Newacheck, P.W., Kim, S.E.. A national profile of health care utilization and expenditures for children with special health care needs. Arch. Pediatrics Adolesc. Med. **159**(1), 10–17 (2005). http://doi.org/https://doi.org/10.1001/archpedi.159.1.10
4. Van Dyck, P.C., Kogan, M.D., McPherson, M.G., Weissman, G.R., Newacheck, P.W.: Prevalence and characteristics of children with special health care needs. Arch. Pediatrics Adolesc. Med. **158**(9), 884–890 (2004). http://doi.org/https://doi.org/10.1001/archpedi.158.9.884
5. Burke, R.T., Alverson, M.D.: Impact of children with medically complex conditions. Pediatrics **126**(4), 789–790 (2010). http://doi.org/https://doi.org/10.1542/peds.2010.1885
6. Miller, A.R., Condin, C.J., McKellin, W.H., Shaw, N., Klassen, A.F., Sheps, S.: Continuity of care for children with complex chronic health conditions: parents' perspectives. BMC Health Serv. Res. **9**, 242 (2009). http://https://doi.org/10.1186/1472-6963-9-242

7. Pinto, M., Gomes, R., Tanabe, R.F., da Costa, A.C.C., Moreira, M.C.N.: Analysis of the cost of care for children and adolescents with medical complex chronic conditions. Ciencia E Saude Coletiva **24**(11), 4043–4052 (2019). http://doi.org/https://doi.org/10.1590/1413-812320182 411.08912018

8. Feudtner, C, Hays, R.M., Haynes, G., Russell, J., Neff, J.M., Koepsell, T.D.: Deaths attributed to pediatric complex chronic conditions: national trends and implications for supportive care services. Pediatrics **107**, e.99 (2001). http://doi.org/https://doi.org/10.1542/peds.107.6e99

9. Cohen, E., et al.: Children with medical complexity: an emerging population for clinical and research initiatives. Pediatrics **127**(3), 529–538 (2011). https://doi.org/10.1542/peds.2010-0910

10. Burns, K.H., Casey, P.H., Lyle, R.E., Bird, T.M., Fussell, J.J., Robbins, J.M.: Increasing prevalence of medically complex children in US hospitals. Pediatrics **126**(4), 638–646 (2010). http://doi.org/https://doi.org/10.1542/peds.2009-1658

11. Vieira, M.A., de Lima, R.A.G.: Crianças e adolescentes com doença crônica: convivendo com mudanças. Rev. Lat. Am. Enfermagem **10**(4), 552–560 (2002). https://doi.org/10.1590/s0104-11692002000400013

12. Berg Kelly, K.: Sustainable transition process for young people with chronic conditions: A narrative summary on achieved cooperation between paediatric and adult medical teams. Child: Care Health Dev. **37**(6), 800–805 (2011). http://doi.org/https://doi.org/10.1111/j.1365-2214.2011.01330.x

13. Berry, J.G., Hall, M., Cohen, E., O'Neill, M., Feudtner, C.: Ways to identify children with medical complexity and the importance of why. J. Pediatrics **167**(2), 229–237 (2015). http://doi.org/https://doi.org/10.1016/j.jpeds.2015.04.068

14. Dewan, T., Cohen, E.: Children with medical complexity in Canada. Paediatrics and Child Health (Canada) **18**(10), 518–522 (2013). http://doi.org/https://doi.org/10.1093/pch/18.10.518

15. Nunes, M.C., Albernaz, L.V., Ribeiro, M., Fernandes, R., Falcao, R.: Recomendações para uma linha de cuidados para crianças e adolescentes com condições crônicas complexas de saúde. Cadernos de Saude Publica **33**(11) (2017). http://doi.org/https://doi.org/10.1590/0102-311X00189516

16. Srivastava, R., Murphy, N.: Hospitalist care of the medically complex child. Pediatric Clín. North Am. **52**(4), 1165–1187 (2005). http://doi.org/https://doi.org/10.1016/j.pcl.2005.03.007

17. Typpo, K., Petersen, N., Petersen, L., Mariscalco, M.: Children with chronic illness return to their baseline functional status after organ dysfunction on the first day of admission in the pediatric intensive care unit. J. Pediatrics **157**(1), 108–113 (2010). http://doi.org/https://doi.org/10.1016/j.jpeds.2009.12.029

18. Climent, F.J., García, M., Escosa, L., Rodriguez, A., Albajara, L.: Unidad de niños con patología crónica compleja. Un modelo necesario en nuestros hospitales. Anales de Pediatria, **88**(1), 12–18 (2017)http://doi.org/https://doi.org/10.1016/j.anpedi.2017.04.002

19. Jerrell, J., Osborne, C., Tripathi, A. Blanck, G., Mark, Y.: Long-term neurodevelopmental outcomes in children and adolescent with congenital heart disease. Prim. Care Comp. **17**(5), 1–5 (2015). http://doi.org/https://doi.org/10.4088/PCC.15m01843

20. Violant, V.: Enfermedad y hospitalización en el niño. Guía para padres y profesionales de la salud y la educación. Ciudad de Mexico: Trillas (2017)

21. Silva, G.. Las vivencias de los niños hospitalizados. IEP, Perú (2012)

22. Skrzypek, M.: The social origin of the illness experience - an outline of problems. Annals Agric. Environ. Med. **21**(3), 654–660 (2014). http://doi.org/https://doi.org/10.5604/12321966.1120619

23. Alfaro, A.K., Atria, R.P.: Factores ambientales y su incidencia en la experiencia emocional del niño hospitalizado. Revista Pediatría Electrónica **6**(1), 36–54 (2019)

24. Doupnik, S.K., et al.: Mental health conditions and symptoms in pediatric hospitalizations: a single-center point prevalence study. Acad. Pediatrics **17**(2), 184–190 (2017). http://doi.org/https://doi.org/10.1016/j.acap.2016.08.009
25. Myrvik, M., Burks, L., Hoffman, R., Dasgupta, M., Panepinto, J.: Mental health disorders influence admission rates for pain in children with sickle cell disease. Pediatr. Blood Cancer **50**, 1018–1025 (2012). https://doi.org/10.1002/pbc.24394
26. Lizasoáin, O.: Educando al niño enfermo. Ediciones Eunate: España (2000)
27. Myrvik, M., Campbell, A., Davis, M., Butcher, J.: Impact of psychiatric diagnoses on hospital length of stay in children with sickle cell anemia. Pediatric Blood Cancer **58**, 239–243 (2012). http://doi.org/https://doi.org/10.1002/pbc
28. Butragueño, L., et al.: Percepción de los adolescentes sobre el ingreso hospitalario. Importancia de la humanización de los hospitales infantiles. Revista Chilena de Pediatria **87**(5), 373–379 (2016). http://doi.org/https://doi.org/10.1016/j.rchipe.2016.04.003
29. Lizasoáin, O., Ochoa, B.: Repercusiones de la hospitalización pediátrica en el niño enfermo. Osasunaz **5**, 75–85 (2003)
30. González-González, C.S., Holz, V.V., Moro, A.I., García, L.C., Franco, M.D.G.: Robótica educativa en contextos inclusivos: el caso de las aulas hospitalarias. Educación XX1, 24(1) (2021)
31. González-González, C., Toledo-Delgado, P., Collazos-Ordoñez, C., González-Sánchez, J.L.: Design and analysis of collaborative interactions in social educational videogames. Comput. Hum. Behav. **31**, 602–611 (2014)
32. González, C. S., Toledo, P., Padrón, M., Santos, E., & Cairos, M. TANGO: H: creating active educational games for hospitalized children. In Management Intelligent Systems (pp. 135–142). Springer, Heidelberg. (2013)
33. Shonkoff, J. P., Garner, A. S., Siegel, B. S., Dobbins, M. I., Earls, M. F., McGuinn, L., … Wegner, L. M. The lifelong effects of early childhood adversity and toxic stress. Pediatrics, 129(1). http://doi.org/https://doi.org/10.1542/peds.2011-2663. (2012)
34. Reid, K., Hopkins, D., Holly, P.: Towards the effective schools. Blackwell, Oxford (1987)

# A Deep Learning System to Help Students Build Concept Maps

Francesco Pes[1], Filippo Sciarrone[1(✉)] [iD], and Marco Temperini[2] [iD]

[1] Faculty of Economics, Universitas Mercatorum, Piazza Mattei, 10, Rome, Italy
`filippo.sciarrone@unimercatorum.it`
[2] Diag-Dipartimento di Ingegneria Informatica Automatica e Gestionale, Sapienza University of Rome, Via Ariosto, 25, Rome, Italy
`marte@diag.uniroma1.it`

**Abstract.** Nowadays, overwhelmed as people are by the amount of information available, it becomes more and more difficult to build an adequate cognitive process of knowledge building and discovery, on any one knowledge domain. Therefore, having knowledge-building tools at disposition, especially in the age of schooling, is of great importance. Knowledge building occurs by linking new concepts to already learned ones, thus connecting concepts together by means of semantic links representing their relationship. To accomplish this task, most of learners use Concept Maps, that is graphic tools, particularly suitable, to organize, represent and share knowledge. In fact, a Concept Map can explicitly express the knowledge of a person or group, about a given domain of interest: from primary school to university, and to professional/vocational training, Concept Maps can stimulate and unveil the occurrence of the so-called *meaningful learning*, according to the Ausubel's learning theory. In this paper we investigate the use of a deep learning-based architecture, called TransH, designed for Knowledge Graph Embedding, to support the process of Concept Maps building. This approach has not been yet investigated for this particular educational task. Some preliminary case studies are discussed, confirming the potential of this approach.

**Keywords:** Knowledge Graph Embedding · Concept Maps · Meaningful Learning

## 1 Introduction

In recent years, digital innovation has undergone a very strong acceleration, due both to the Covid-19 pandemic, and to the ever increasing amount of knowledge available through the Network. The development of digital technologies is at the basis of advancements in many fields of human activities and in particular in Education [1, 6, 11, 12, 19]: using tools that allow to represent, build and share knowledge is of fundamental importance in training and education fields. To this aim, Concept Maps (CMs) are very powerful tools for representing and sharing

C. S. González-González et al. (Eds.): ICWL 2022/SETE 2022, LNCS 13869, pp. 321–332, 2023.
https://doi.org/10.1007/978-3-031-33023-0_29

one's vision about a knowledge domain [21,23]. Consequently, CMs are widely used and recommended in the educational field both for students and teachers. On the one hand most of students use CMs at school to better represent and share their learning process, while, on the other hand, teachers exploit the potential of CMs to evaluate students' skills. To learn meaningfully, individuals must be able to connect the new information to relevant concepts and propositions they already possess: knowledge occurs through meaning processing. In *rote learning*, on the other hand, the content is already defined in its meaning and the learner has to imprint it in the mind only. In fact, graphical representations can help both teachers and learners: teachers can access/visualize the learner's state of knowledge, while learners can show her knowledge, as well as being helped learning about a domain of which a knowledge representation is given [2,21,22]. Consequently, concept mapping, i.e., the activity of drawing and updating a CM, allows experts and non-experts to express, clarify and establish their own understanding of how the knowledge is structured in a given Knowledge Domain (KD). From a structural point of view, a CM can be considered a Directed Acyclic Graph (DAG), where nodes depict concepts, and relationships between couples of concepts are represented by edges (arcs) with their semantic labels [9,10,18,25]. Moreover, a CM shows a hierarchical structure involving all the elements of a KD: the key and secondary concepts, the links between them, giving the possibility to follow and reconstruct the unfolding of reasoning: this typical structure makes a CM a *Knowledge Graph* (KG), that is a useful and valuable tool to support meaningful learning. In fact, KGs have emerged as an effective way to integrate disparate data sources and model underlying relationships for applications such as search and knowledge discovering and building. A KG, also known as a semantic network, represents a network of real-world entities, i.e., objects, events, situations, or concepts and shows the relationships between them. This information is usually stored in a graph database and visualized as a graph structure [14,15]. So, CMs are special kinds of KGs, based on a DAG topological structure. In order to be automatically processed, CMs need to be represented in such a way to be easily managed, and *Knowledge Graph Embedding* (KGE) is that area of Deep Learning that deals with representing KGs, such as CMs, through embeddings i.e., through vectors of real numbers in an n-dimensional space [8]. In this paper we present an engine based on KGE, designed and implemented to help students build knowledge, that is, connect concepts to each other, as in the case of the CM building activity. Our main goal is to investigate the feasibility of using a KGE engine to build a system to help students build CMs. In practice, we use the deep learning TransH KGE architecture by [17] training a deep neural network in a supervised way: at runtime, given two concepts, the system suggests a semantic relationship between them. This approach could be useful to develop help systems for students with special needs, where the phase of connecting concepts could be a hard process [4]. So, the research question of this paper is the following:

*RQ: Is the KGE-based engine able to help students in their CM building activity?*

To verify the $RQ$, we propose two case studies, for a first system qualitative evaluation.

This work is organized as follows. Section 2 briefly introduces some important works on Knowledge Building systems and CMs. Section 3 shows the architecture and the workflow of the system. In Sect. 4 two case studies are discussed for a first qualitative evaluation of the system, together with the final discussion of the $RQ$. In Sect. 5, some conclusions are drawn.

## 2 Related Work

In this section we give a brief background both on CMs and on KGE.

### 2.1 Concept Maps

CMs were first theorized by Novak [21,23,24] and later developed with Gowin and Johansen [23], as a novel strategy to help students learn and represent the meanings of scientific concepts. In particular, CMs are based on some important pedagogical theories such as *Cognitive Constructivism, Meaningful Learning*, on the role of *Prior Knowledge* [3], on *Learning by Experience, Scaffolding* [7]. In Fig. 1, an example of a CM is shown, where the KD is *Water*: the main concept is represented in the highest node while the relationships between couples of concepts can be represented both by lines (reading from the top to the bottom) or by arrows (as in the case of cross-links). Moreover, each semantic connection is labelled with the type of the corresponding relationship. The basic unit of a generic CM is the triple $T \equiv \{head, link, tail\}$, where *head* is the starting concept, *link* is the semantic relationship, and *tail* is the second concept.

The literature proposes many cloud-based web platforms that allow people to build and share CMs by visual *drag and drop* techniques.

The *Graphed* system, proposed by Ionas and Geana [16] allows users to build CMs through a visual environment on the web. The characteristic of this platform is to have the availability of a set of standard relationships between concepts the user can choose from to build her own CM. Moreover, a CM can be shared among multiple users[1]. This standard set of relationships is used by our system as a links dictionary (explained in detail in the next section).

Another web and also stand-alone platform is *Cmaptools* [9]. It is a web platform which helps users build, navigate, share and criticize knowledge models represented as CMs. This platform allows users to build CMs in their local machine, share them on servers anywhere on the Net. Moreover, users can link their CMs to other CMs stored on distributed servers and automatically create web pages showing their CMs. Finally, users can search in the web for information relevant to a CM[2].

---

[1] https://graphed.igiresearch.com.
[2] https://cmap.ihmc.us/cmaptools/.

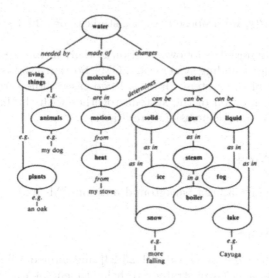

**Fig. 1.** A CM representing the *Water* KD.

## 2.2  Knowledge Graph Embedding

By means of KGE, a KG is embedded into a low-dimensional continuous vector space while certain properties of it are preserved [5]. In recent years, many knowledge embedding methods have been developed, usually including the following three approaches: *KGE* models with only symbolic triplets, Embedding with Textual Information models, and Embedding with Category Information models [13]. In our context the first approach only is used, because in the CMs context, we use a limited set of relationships between concepts. However, at our knowledge, the use of KGE for CMs has not been proposed yet. Here we present some similar approaches based on deep learning and in particular on graph embedding applied to KGs.

In [20], the authors propose a system based on a deep learning approach for measuring CMs similarity. They use two sentence embedding technique: *Infersent* and *Universal*. All the two CMs triples $T$, are first embedded by the sentence embedding engine and after compared among them to compute a similarity measure. This approach has been validated by a group of teachers with positive results. Our system uses a deep learning approach as well, but for helping students build their own CMs.

In [13], the authors propose a Knowledge Graph Embedding with Concepts model that embeds entities and concepts of entities jointly into a semantic space. Their embedding model performs concept space projection for KGE, where the loss vector of a triplet $T$ is projected onto a concept subspace as a hyperplane that represents the concept relevance between entities. They evaluate with positive results their approach on several benchmark datasets, showing the goodness of their choices. Differently from us, they add other information to the triplets, such as textual and concepts information. Our approach takes into account the triplets only, in order to help students: no other information is needed, because our set of relationships is limited to the one proposed by the graphed system.

## 3    The System

Currently, the system is in its early stage of development and we experimented its engine only. However, we designed its architecture with its general modes of operation. The main goal of the system is to help students build their knowledge on a particular KD, according to the Ausubel's learning theory.

### 3.1    The Architecture

The system consists of two main layers: The Graphic User Interface (GUI) and the Engine, as shown in Fig. 2.

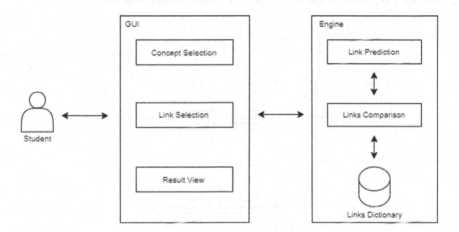

**Fig. 2.** The architecture of the system.

The *GUI* is the module by which the user, i.e., the student, interacts with the system. By this module, she can select two concepts, from the CM she has to build, and proposes a semantic link between them choosing the link $l_u$ or from a predefined list of suggested links or directly input by her. Then she can compare her choice with the one proposed by the system.

The *Engine* is activated by the GUI. It receives in input the student triple $T_u$. After that, the *Link Prediction* module processes the couple $(h_u, t_u)$ producing the correct link $l_s$. The *Links Comparison* module compares $l_u$ with $l_s$, communicating the difference to the GUI.

The *Link Dictionary* is a collection of predefined semantic links taken by the *graphcd* platform (see Sect. 2) [16], where a set of standard predefined semantic connections are proposed. In our system, the dictionary can be enriched by adding new relationships by the student or by the teacher, to be used for future sessions.

## 3.2   The System at Work

The overall system's workflow is depicted in Fig. 3.   A student has to build a new CM on a specific KD and has some problems to connect the concepts $A$ and $D$, as shown in Fig. 4a).

So, through the GUI, the student selects the two concepts $(A, D)$ to be connected and proposes the semantic connection or link $R_u$, selected from the Links Dictionary or inserted as a new one. The *Result View* module sends the triple $T_u \equiv \{A, R_u, D\}$ to the *Link Prediction* Module which processes the triple $T_u$ through its neural engine. Consequently it produces the suggested semantic connection $R_s$.

Finally, the *Links Comparison* module compares the user link $R_u$ Vs. the system link $R_s$, evaluating their difference and acting as follows:

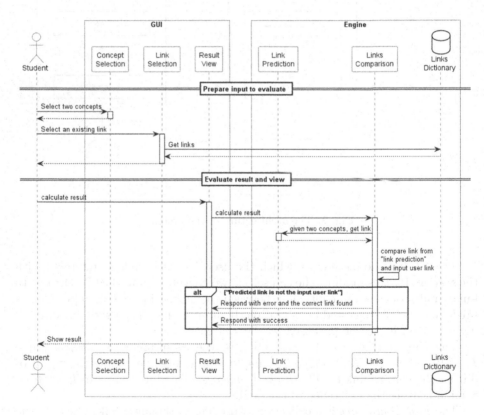

**Fig. 3.** The UML sequence diagram of the system workflow.

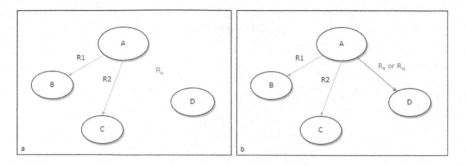

**Fig. 4.** Abstract CM with missing link between A and D (a) and with link (b)

- if $R_s = R_u$ => the engine will communicate to the GUI a *success* message;
- if $R_s \neq R_u$ => the engine will communicate to the GUI an *error* message together with the right connection.

The result is showed in Fig. 4b.

If the user is not satisfied by the system suggestion can add her own link, enriching in this way the Link Dictionary.

## 4   Case Studies

In this section we show two case studies. As the KD we use the *Natural Science* domain and in particular the *Solar System*. The first case study shows a simple suggestion to connect two given concepts. The second case study shows an example on how the system can help for meaningful learning.

### 4.1   First Case Study

The student is asked to complete the CM shown in Fig. 5. Following the workflow shown in the previous section, we have:

1. *CM preparation.* In this step, the teacher prepares a set of those concepts composing the CM, that is: $CM \equiv \{C_1, C_2 \ldots C_n\}$;
2. *TransH model training*: for this first experiment we prepared a dataset composed of 137 training records in the form of the triples $T \equiv \{h, l, t\}$. However it can be extended later;
3. *Input.* Here the user is asked to select, through the system GUI, for each couple of concepts, the right relationship;
4. *The System Answer.* The system will suggest its relationship between the two concepts;
5. *Links Library Updating.* In the case of a new relationship, the student or the teacher can update the Links Dictionary by adding it. Consequently, the TransH model will be updated.

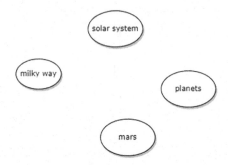

**Fig. 5.** The CM with two entities and without a link between them.

As shown in Fig. 5, the student has to accomplish the task to choose the right relationship between the two concepts *solar system* and *milky way*. The system shows the list of the pre-defined links, stored in the links dictionary, allowing the student for selecting one of them. Meanwhile the two concepts are given in input to the neural model, obtaining in output the ranked list shown in Tab. 1. The student has two possibilities: to propose the right relationship without taking into account the suggested ranked list or to choose the relationship directly from the ranked suggested list. In the first case, her choice is compared to those ones proposed by the system. If the student is not satisfied by the system suggestion, she can add her relationship into the Links Dictionary.

**Table 1.** The ranked list proposed by the system to connect the two concepts (Solar System) and (Milky Way).

| head | relation | tail | score result | link direction | link type |
|------|----------|------|--------------|----------------|-----------|
| solar system | is included in | milky way | 8.555538 | −1 | inclusion |
| solar system | generates | milky way | 0.823429 | 1 | action |
| solar system | has type | milky way | 0.820323 | 1 | characteristic |
| solar system | composed of | milky way | 0.389552 | 1 | inclusion |

As shown in Table 1, the system suggests not only the relationship but also its direction:

- link direction = "1" means that the relation has direction from head to tail (parent to child);
- link direction = "0" means that the relation is bi-directional (sibling to sibling);
- link direction = "−1" means that the relation has direction from tail to head (child to parent).

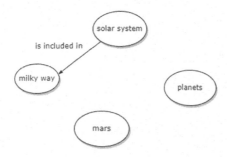

**Fig. 6.** The $CM$ completed with the suggested relationship.

In this case, the suggested link direction is $d = -1$, that is a link from the tail (Milky Way) to the head (Solar System). So, from the empty CM of Fig. 5 we have the one shown in Fig. 6.

### 4.2   Second Case Study

This case study is useful to better highlight the power of the help system to enhance meaningful learning. Let us suppose that the student inserts the two concepts Solar System and Mars as the input couple of concepts. Then, the system will respond with the ranked relationships shown in Table 2.

**Table 2.** The ranked list prompted by the system as the answer to the Solar System and Mars concepts.

| head | relation | tail | score result | link direction | link type |
|------|----------|------|--------------|----------------|-----------|
| solar system | includes | mars | 8.25749 | 1 | inclusion |
| solar system | generates | mars | 0.823429 | 1 | action |
| solar system | composed of | mars | 0.383369 | 1 | inclusion |
| solar system | is included in | mars | 0.334567 | 1 | characteristic |
| solar system | has type | mars | 0.219367 | $-1$ | characteristic |

We notice how the model finds out a relation between the two given concepts, generalizing in such a way what learned during the training step where this relationships did not belong to the training dataset, as shown in Fig. 7. This case allows us to conclude that the system, is able to suggest new and unexpected links between concepts having the same semantic relationship (in this case <includes>), but not present in the initial Links Dictionary. It is worth of noting that this relationship has not been inserted directly into the Links Dictionary but it is the result of the neural engine inference. This result reinforces the meaningful learning process since it helps students for the connection of new knowledge to prior knowledge, according to Ausubel's theory.

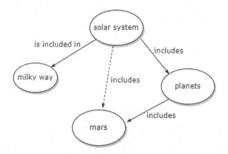

**Fig. 7.** The *CM* completed with the connection (in dashed line) between Solar System and Mars, a link not belonging to the initial Links Dictionary but inferred by the neural model.

## 4.3   Discussion

The system has not been implemented in all its parts, but we verified its effectiveness simulating two important case studies. The first one showed that a student can be helped through the hints provided by the system, at the time when he or she should have some difficulty to find out the right link. In the second case study, the simulation showed the capability of the system of supporting meaningful learning: new relationships can be suggested between concepts that were not expected when training the neural model. We can conclude, from this qualitative evaluation, that our *RQ* is satisfied: the system has a good potential to support the CM building process.

## 5   Conclusions and Future Work

In this paper we have presented a system, in its initial stage of development, to help students construct concept maps. The system is based on a deep learning architecture called TransH which is used to perform the Knowledge Graph Embedding operation. This makes it much easier to process computationally and semantically organized knowledge bases such as concept maps. Through two case studies we have illustrated the potential of this approach which is able to suggest connections between concepts and new connections to the student thereby enhancing meaningful learning. As a future development we plan to implement all functional blocks and carry out a strong experimentation with students and teachers.

## References

1. Albino, V., Berardi, U., Dangelico, R.: Smart cities: definitions, dimensions, performance, and initiatives. J. Urban Technol. **22**(1), 3–21 (2015)
2. Ausubel, D.: The Psychology of Meaningful Verbal Learning. Grane and Stratton, New York (1960)

3. Ausubel, D., Novak, J., Hanesian, H.: Educational Psychology: A Cognitive View, 2nd edn. Holt, Rinehart and Winston (1978)

4. Baldoni, M., Berionni, A.: Concept maps and learning disorders. In: Proceedings of the Fifth Internationa Conference on Concept Mapping (2012)

5. Bordes, A., Weston, J., Collobert, R., Bengio, Y.: Learning structured embeddings of knowledge bases. In: Twenty-Fifth AAAI Conference on Artificial Intelligence (2011)

6. Botticelli, M., Gasparetti, F., Sciarrone, F., Temperini, M.: Deep learning to monitor massive open online courses dynamics. In: De la Prieta, F., et al. (eds.) MIS4TEL 2021. LNNS, vol. 326, pp. 114–123. Springer, Cham (2022). https://doi.org/10.1007/978-3-030-86618-1_12

7. Brusilowsky, P., Vassileva, J.: Course sequencing techniques for large-scale web-based education. Int. J. Continuing Eng. Educ. Life-long Learn. **13**, 75–94 (2003)

8. Cai, H., Zheng, V.W., Chang, K.C.C.: A comprehensive survey of graph embedding: Problems, techniques and applications. Comput. Sci. 15 (2018)

9. Cañas, A.J., Valerio, A., Lalinde-Pulido, J., Carvalho, M., Arguedas, M.: Using wordnet for word sense disambiguation to support concept map construction. In: Nascimento, M.A., de Moura, E.S., Oliveira, A.L. (eds.) SPIRE 2003. LNCS, vol. 2857, pp. 350–359. Springer, Heidelberg (2003). https://doi.org/10.1007/978-3-540-39984-1_27

10. Elsayed, O., Limongelli, C., Sciarrone, F., Lombardi, M., Marani, A., Temperini, M.: An on-line framework for experimenting with concept maps. In: 2019 18th International Conference on Information Technology Based Higher Education and Training (ITHET), pp. 1–8 (2019). https://doi.org/10.1109/ITHET46829.2019.8937376

11. Gasparetti, F., Sciarrone, F., Temperini, M.: Using graph embedding to monitor communities of learners. In: Cristea, A.I., Troussas, C. (eds.) ITS 2021. LNCS, vol. 12677, pp. 350–356. Springer, Cham (2021). https://doi.org/10.1007/978-3-030-80421-3_38

12. Gomede, E., Gaffo, F., Briganó, G., De Barros, R., De Souza Mendes, L.: Application of computational intelligence to improve education in smart cities. Sensors **18**(1), 267 (2018)

13. Guan, N., Song, D., Liao, L.: Knowledge graph embedding with concepts. Knowl.-Based Syst. **164**, 38–44 (2019)

14. Gutierrez, C., Sequeda, J.F.: Knowledge graphs. Commun. ACM **64**(3), 96–104 (2021)

15. Hogan, A., et al.: Knowledge graphs. ACM Comput. Surv. **54**(4), 1–37 (2021)

16. Ionas, I.G., Geana, M.V.: A web-based concept mapping application for instruction and research. In: The Seventh International Conference on Higher Education Advances, pp. 563–570 (2021)

17. Ji, G., He, S., Xu, L., Liu, K., Zhao, J.: Knowledge graph embedding via dynamic mapping matrix. In: Proceedings of the 53rd Annual Meeting of the Association for Computational Linguistics and the 7th International Joint Conference on Natural Language Processing, vol. 1: Long papers, pp. 687–696 (2015)

18. Limongelli, C., Marani, A., Sciarrone, F., Temperini, M.: Measuring the similarity of concept maps according to pedagogical criteria. IEEE Access **10**, 27655–27669 (2022)

19. Liu, D., Huang, R., Wosinski, M.: Development of smart cities: educational perspective. In: Smart Learning in Smart Cities. LNET, pp. 3–14. Springer, Singapore (2017). https://doi.org/10.1007/978-981-10-4343-7_1

20. Montanaro, A., Sciarrone, F., Temperini, M.: A deep learning approach to concept maps similarity. In: The 26rd International Conference Information Visualisation (IV), p. In Press (2022)
21. Novak, J.: The importance of conceptual schemes for teaching science. Sci. Teach. **31**(6), 10–13 (1964)
22. Novak, J.: Meaningful learning: The essential factor for conceptual change in limited or inappropriate propositional hierarchies leading to empowerment of learners. Sci. Educ. **5**(86), 548–571 (2002)
23. Novak, J., Gowin, D., Johansen, G.: Meaningful learning: the essential factor for conceptual change in limited or inappropriate propositional hierarchies leading to empowerment of learners. Sci. Educ. **5**(67), 625–645 (1983)
24. Novak, J.D.: Learning How to Learn. Cambridge University Press, Cambridge (1984)
25. Sciarrone, F.: Machine learning and learning analytics: Integrating data with learning. In: 2018 17th International Conference on Information Technology Based Higher Education and Training (ITHET), pp. 1–5 (2018). https://doi.org/10.1109/ITHET.2018.8424780

# Flexible Heuristics for Supporting Recommendations Within an AI Platform Aimed at Non-expert Users

Andrea Vázquez-Ingelmo[1]([✉]) [iD], Alicia García-Holgado[1] [iD],
Francisco José García-Peñalvo[1] [iD], Esther Andrés-Fraile[1], Pablo Pérez-Sánchez[2] [iD],
Pablo Antúnez-Muiños[3] [iD], Antonio Sánchez-Puente[4] [iD], Víctor Vicente-Palacios[5] [iD],
Pedro Ignacio Dorado-Díaz[2] [iD], Ignacio Cruz-González[3] [iD], and Pedro Luis Sánchez[3]

[1] GRIAL Research Group, Computer Science Department, Universidad de Salamanca,
Salamanca, Spain
{andreavazquez,aliciagh,esther.andres}@usal.es
[2] Biomedical Research Institute of Salamanca (IBSAL), Salamanca, Spain
[3] University Hospital of Salamanca, CIBERCV and Biomedical Research Institute of
Salamanca (IBSAL), Salamanca, Spain
pedrolsanchez@me.com
[4] University Hospital of Salamanca and CIBERCV, Salamanca, Spain
[5] Philips Ibérica, Madrid, Spain

**Abstract.** The use of Machine Learning (ML) to resolve complex tasks has become popular in several contexts. While these approaches are very effective and have many related benefits, they are still very tricky for the general audience. In this sense, expert knowledge is crucial to apply ML algorithms properly and to avoid potential issues. However, in some situations, it is not possible to rely on experts to guide the development of ML pipelines. To tackle this issue, we present an approach to provide customized heuristics and recommendations through a graphical platform to build ML pipelines, namely KoopaML, focused on the medical domain. With this approach, we aim not only at providing an easy way to apply ML for non-expert users, but also at providing a learning experience for them to understand how these methods work.

**Keywords:** Information system · Medical data management · Medical imaging management · Artificial Intelligence · Health platform · HCI

## 1 Introduction

Machine Learning (ML) has become a powerful method to tackle complex problems in different contexts. These algorithms ease the analysis of great quantities of data to discover hidden patterns, reach new insights, and even predict events.

Some data-intensive contexts, like the health domain, benefit from developing ML pipelines for their data, to support time- and resource- consuming tasks, such as diagnoses, disease detection, segmentation, assessment of organ functions, etc. [1–3].

C. S. González-González et al. (Eds.): ICWL 2022/SETE 2022, LNCS 13869, pp. 333–338, 2023.
https://doi.org/10.1007/978-3-031-33023-0_30

However, applying these algorithms is not straightforward. There are some algorithms that work better under some specific circumstances, or with datasets that have certain characteristics [4–8]. Otherwise, if ML algorithms are applied without understanding the process, the outputs of the trained models could lead to wrong conclusions, discrimination, and other hazardous issues [9–11].

While health professionals have a deep understanding of the input data, they could lack skills related to theoretical and practical foundations of ML. In this context, it is necessary to provide novice, lay, and non-expert users with tools that alleviate the learning curve of ML. This way, non-expert users can benefit from the application of ML without risking the quality of their models.

In this work, we present an approach to customize heuristics and recommendations for assisting novice users in the development of ML pipelines. This approach is integrated in a graphical platform (KoopaML) [12] that allow the instantiation and design of ML pipelines through visual means.

The goal of integrating the management of heuristics in KoopaML is to assist users in the development of their pipelines while providing a learning experience related to the suitability of certain algorithms given the input data, or the problem to solve.

The rest of this paper is structured as follows. Section 2 provides an overview of KoopaML's architecture. Section 3 describes the heuristics management module. Finally, Sect. 4 discusses the approach and presents the conclusions of this work.

## 2  Architecture

Due to the constant improvement and evolution of ML approaches, it is necessary to rely on a flexible architecture. For this reason, KoopaML is based on different modules that communicate with each other through data streams [12].

These modules include the user management, the pipelines management, the tasks management, and the heuristics management.

Particularly, the heuristics management module is in charge of providing an interface for designing heuristics in the form of decision trees. These heuristics sets are stored persistently and can be interchanged to apply different sets of heuristics depending on the problem.

The defined heuristics are then used by the pipelines management module to yield recommendations given the current state of the workspace, as will be detailed in the next section.

## 3  Heuristics Management

As introduced in the previous section, the heuristics management module of KoopaML provides functionality to create, modify, delete, and apply different rules to obtain useful recommendations for novice users while designing ML pipelines.

Figure 1 shows the main interface for this module, where a list of the available heuristics of the system is displayed. Each available set of heuristics can be modified and deleted at any time, as well as marked as default (so it is applied to every new pipeline).

**Fig. 1.** Available heuristics interface. Contents in Spanish.

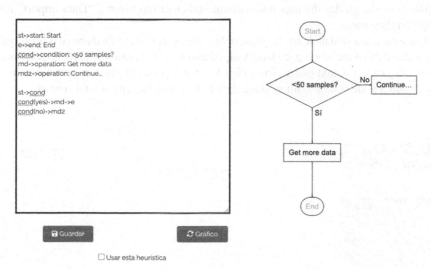

**Fig. 2.** Definition of a new heuristic. The interface is composed by a text field in which the heuristics are codified (left) and a canvas that shows the generated tree from the DSL (right).

The Domain Specific Language (DSL) provided by the flowchart.js (https://github.com/adrai/flowchart.js) library is then employed to define the rules and conditions of the heuristic's decision tree (Fig. 2). This library allows textual and graphical representation of flow charts, which provides a fine-grained manipulation of heuristics and rule-based recommendation.

The heuristics are then processed in the backend to restructure them as a nested dictionary that can be easily traversed programmatically. This dictionary is stored and finally employed by the workspace to yield the recommendations.

After defining the heuristics and starting a new project, the process carried out in the workspace is as follows:

**1.** Every time the workspace is initialized or modified, a request is sent to the backend containing the current state of the workspace (number and type of the nodes, dataset characteristics, etc.)
**2.** The backend retrieves the default heuristic and goes through the dictionary using the current state. In this step, each condition is read and applied using the available data from the workspace.
**3.** Whenever a condition reaches a leaf node, the process is stopped, and the recommendation is sent back to the client.
**4.** The interface shows the text obtained after applying the rules of the heuristic.

This process is displayed in Figs. 4 and 5. In Fig. 4, the workspace is empty, so a non-expert user could have some difficulties knowing where to start. In this case, the default heuristic guides the user and recommends them to insert a "Data import" node to upload their data.

Once the requested node has been included, the process described above is fired again, but, as the state of the workspace has changed and now it includes a "Data import" node, the recommendation text differs from Fig. 3. At this point, the system recommends the user to add a node to deal with missing data before training any model (Fig. 4).

**Fig. 3.** Recommendation yielded in an empty workspace: "Insert the first node «Data import» and select the data file that you want to use". Contents in Spanish.

**Fig. 4.** Recommendation yielded after including a "Data import" node: "Insert the node «Fill missing values»". Contents in Spanish.

## 4 Discussion and Conclusions

This work presents a flexible approach based on heuristics for guiding non-expert users in the development of ML pipelines without the necessity of having programming skills.

The heuristics can be dynamically defined through a graphical interface using a DSL, which enables the possibility of evolving the rules based on new evidence, or even applying different sets of rules depending on the type of user.

Using tangible heuristics has been pointed out in previous works. Some authors, for example, have noticed that heuristics can lead to greater insights and greater engagement of the users in the process of applying ML [13, 14]. In addition, some works remark the importance of using human-readable rules when selecting AI algorithms in certain contexts [15].

Another potential benefit of using these kinds of recommendations in KoopaML is the educational experience offered to the users, which can learn from the heuristics and trace the explanations related to the recommendations yielded by the system, providing more transparency to the recommendation process.

Future research will involve the evaluation of the heuristics management module and their usefulness with non-expert users.

**Acknowledgements.** This research was partially funded by Ministry of Science and Innovation through the AVisSA project grant number (PID2020-118345RB-I00). This work was also supported by national (PI14/00695, PIE14/00066, PI17/00145, DTS19/00098, PI19/00658, PI19/00656 Institute of Health Carlos III, Spanish Ministry of Economy and Competitiveness and co-funded by ERDF/ESF, "Investing in your future") and community (GRS 2033/A/19, GRS 2030/A/19, GRS 2031/A/19, GRS 2032/A/19, SACYL, Junta Castilla y León) competitive grants.

# References

1. Litjens, G., et al.: A survey on deep learning in medical image analysis. Med. Image Anal. **42**, 60–88 (2017)
2. González Izard, S., Sánchez Torres, R., Alonso Plaza, Ó., Juanes Méndez, J.A., García-Peñalvo, F.J.: Nextmed: Automatic Imaging Segmentation, 3D Reconstruction, and 3D Model Visualization Platform Using Augmented and Virtual Reality. Sensors (Basel) **20**, 2962 (2020)
3. Izard, S.G., Juanes, J.A., García Peñalvo, F.J., Estella, J.M.G., Ledesma, M.J.S., Ruisoto, P.: Virtual reality as an educational and training tool for medicine. J. Med. Syst. **42**(3), 1–5 (2018). https://doi.org/10.1007/s10916-018-0900-2
4. Rivolli, A., Garcia, L.P.F., Soares, C., Vanschoren, J., de Carvalho, A.C.P.L.F.: Meta-features for meta-learning. Knowledge-Based Systems **240**, 108101 (2022)
5. Vanschoren, J.: Meta-learning. Automated machine learning, pp. 35–61. Springer, Cham (2019)
6. Taratukhin, O., Muravyov, S.: Meta-learning based feature selection for clustering. In: IDEAL 2021: Intelligent Data Engineering and Automated Learning – IDEAL 2021, pp. 548-559. Springer International Publishing (Year)
7. Nayak, A., Božić, B., Longo, L.: An ontological approach for recommending a feature selection algorithm. In: ICWE 2022: Web Engineering, pp. 300–314. Springer International Publishing (Year)
8. Vilalta, R., Drissi, Y.: A perspective view and survey of meta-learning. Artif. Intell. Rev. **18**, 77–95 (2002)
9. Weyerer, J.C., Langer, P.F.: Garbage in, garbage out: The vicious cycle of ai-based discrimination in the public sector. In: Proceedings of the 20th Annual International Conference on Digital Government Research, pp. 509–511 (Year)
10. Ferrer, X., van Nuenen, T., Such, J.M., Coté, M., Criado, N.: Bias and discrimination in AI: a cross-disciplinary perspective. IEEE Technol. Soc. Mag. **40**, 72–80 (2021)
11. Hoffman, S.: The emerging hazard of ai-related health care discrimination. Hastings Cent. Rep. **51**, 8–9 (2021)
12. García-Peñalvo, F.J., et al.: KoopaML: a graphical platform for building machine learning pipelines adapted to health professionals. Int. J. Interactive Multimedia and Artificial Intelligence (In Press)
13. Reilly, D., Taylor, M., Fergus, P., Chalmers, C., Thompson, S.: The categorical data conundrum: heuristics for classification problems—a case study on domestic fire injuries. IEEE Access **10**, 70113–70125 (2022)
14. Lu, Z., Yin, M.: Human reliance on machine learning models when performance feedback is limited: heuristics and risks. In: Proceedings of the 2021 CHI Conference on Human Factors in Computing Systems, pp. Article 78. Association for Computing Machinery, Yokohama, Japan (2021)
15. Golshanrad, P., Rahmani, H., Karimian, B., Karimkhani, F., Weiss, G.: MEGA: Predicting the best classifier combination using meta-learning and a genetic algorithm. Intelligent Data Analysis **25**, 1547–1563 (2021)

# The 5th International Workshop on Educational Technology for Language Learning (ETLL 2022)

# Grammatical Strategies for Clause Combining and the Acquisition by Chinese EFL Learners

Xiaoping Lin[1] and Shili Ge[1,2](✉)

[1] Center for Linguistics and Applied Linguistics, Guangdong University of Foreign Studies, Guangzhou 510420, China
geshili@gdufs.edu.cn
[2] Laboratory of Language and Artificial Intelligence, Guangdong University of Foreign Studies, Guangzhou 510420, China

**Abstract.** Grammar instruction has long been an important task in foreign language teaching to foster students' grammatical competence. However, in terms of sentence grammar, the current grammar instruction gives preference to teaching the usage of certain syntactic patterns, while ignoring the clause-complex-level grammar that governs clause combing. As a result, students may encounter difficulties when organizing several clauses into a clause complex, and thus fail to produce long sentence of high quality. To unveil the issue, this study proposed a classification system for grammatical clause-combining strategies under the Clause Complex Theory, and explored how Chinese EFL learners master four subtypes of grammatical strategies based on the CLEC corpus. The error analysis reveals that unfamiliarity of the strategies and the negative transfer of mother language are two main reasons for the misuses of grammatical clause-combining strategies. Hence, a systematic grammar instruction on the clause complex level is called for, so as to improve Chinese EFL learners' ability to write structurally-correct clause complexes.

**Keywords:** Grammatical strategies · Clause complex · Chinese EFL Learners

## 1 Introduction

Clause complex, a notion first introduced by Halliday, is defined to be a grammatical construction consisting of two or more clauses. As for how the clauses are related to each other, Halliday proposed that two basic systems play a role: the taxis system describes the interdependency between clauses and the logico-semantic system describes the logico-semantic relations between them [1]. Such a proposal, however, roots in the functional nature of Halliday's theory, and thus gives few insights into the formal or structural aspects of clause combining.

Unlike Halliday, Song takes a formal and structural perspective and put forward the Clause Complex Theory [2]. Under the theory, three mechanisms contribute to clause combining, including component sharing, lexical reference and logic-semantic relationship. Being the focus of the theory, the component sharing mechanism are carefully investigated in both Chinese and English corpus. It is found that although Chinese and English share common component-sharing patterns, they have different pattern distributions and may adopt different grammatical strategies to realize each pattern.

The findings under the Clause Complex Theory give a new insight for the grammar instruction in second language acquisition. By far, most grammar instruction takes a traditional grammar perspective and focus on teaching certain syntactic patterns, such as relative clauses, expletive constructions, conditional clauses, etc. [3]. Although grammar instruction of this kind does help students produce correct sentences with no more than two clauses, they may perform poorly in constructing longer sentences made up of several clauses.

This paper proposed grammar instruction on clause complex level. A classification system for grammatical clause-combining strategies is put forward. Meanwhile, Chinese EFL students' mastery of these strategies will be investigated with error analysis on the CLEC corpus. The results are expected to reveal the importance of grammar instruction of clause-combing strategies for Chinese EFL students.

## 2 Clause Complex Theory

Clause Complex Theory defines a clause complex to be a combination of NT clauses through component sharing, lexical reference and logic-semantic relationship [2]. In terms of NT clause, it refers to a clause composed of a naming and a telling, with the naming defined as a referential component occupying a position at the beginning of a clause and the telling as the component that predicates or explains the naming. A clause complex may apply three mechanisms simultaneously to combine clauses, or may use just one of the mechanisms. Example 1 presents a clause complex that applies all the three mechanisms. It should be noted that all the examples in Sect. 2 and Sect. 3 are chosen from the Wall Street Journal corpus of the Penn Treebank.

> **Example 1:**
> She gives *the Artist* a sense of purpose,
>     but also alerts *him* to the serious inadequacy of *his* vagrant life.

The clause complex in Example 1 consists of two clauses. Firstly, the clause complex utilizes the component sharing mechanism by combining the two clauses with the shared pronoun "She". Secondly, the noun "the Artist" is reproduced as "him" and "his" in the second clause, which is a mechanism to combine the clauses by referential relationship. Thirdly, the conjunction "but also" connects the two clauses that hold progressive relationship.

## 3 A Classification of Grammatical Strategies for Clause Combining

Among the three mechanisms mentioned above, the component sharing mechanism and the lexical reference mechanism rely on the structural or formal connections between clauses, while the logic-semantic relationship relies more on semantic relations. This paper is concerned with the former two mechanisms and refer to both of them as grammatical mechanisms. Meanwhile, based on the previous corpus annotation [4], specific strategies under each grammatical mechanism could be summarized, and they are classified and shown in Fig. 1.

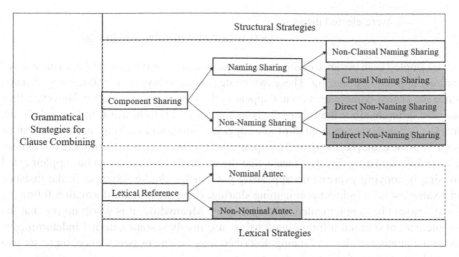

**Fig. 1.** A classification system for grammatical strategies for clause combining.

From Fig. 1, it can be seen that there are two major grammatical strategies for clause combining. Strategies under the component sharing mechanism fall into the category of structural strategies, while those under the lexical reference mechanism fall into the category of lexical strategies. Based on the position of the shared component, the structural strategies can be classified into naming sharing, whose shared component is at the beginning of a clause, and non-naming sharing, whose shared component is in the middle or final position. Example 1 presents an instance of naming sharing, since the shared component "She" locates at the beginning of a clause. Meanwhile, as the naming "She" is nominal in syntactic nature, this instance is an example of non-clausal naming sharing. The following examples show other types of structural strategies.

Example 2 is an instance of clausal naming sharing, which is adopted when a telling shares a clause or a series of clauses as its naming. In this example, the last line of the clause complex is a non-finite clause and a telling for the clausal naming; the clausal naming is a combination of three constituents, namely "Leon J. Level", "F. Warren McFarlan" and "were elected directors". Apart from non-finite clauses, relative clauses introduced by the relative word "which" or an appositive could also take a clausal naming.

**Example 2: Clausal Naming Sharing**
[Leon J. Level,
                    vice president of this computer services concern,
and F. Warren McFarlan,
    |                        a professor at Harvard University,]  ─┐
                                                                   │
  └─► were elected directors,
                    increasing board membership to nine.

Example 3 is an instance of direct non-naming sharing and Example 4 is an instance of indirect non-naming sharing. These two strategies are subtypes of non-naming sharing, since the shared components do not appear at the beginning of a clause. However, they are also different since they share the components in different ways. In Example 3, the marks " +" in the second and third line suggest a direct non-naming sharing. As can be seen from the example, the shared component of this instance is in the middle of a clause. Meanwhile, by being direct, it means that the omitted constituent can be supplemented by simply copying expressions appearing previously. Unlike Example 3, the instance in Example 4 is an indirect non-naming sharing, since the elided information following "why" cannot be supplemented by simple copy. Meanwhile, it is worth noting that the supplement of omitted information for this case involves some internal indeterminacy, since the number of the book being described may be one or two. Hence, there are two possible resolutions for the wh-clause.

**Example 3: Direct Non-Naming Sharing**
Delivery of the first aircraft is set for early November,
++++++++ a second+++++++++ for December
and++++++++ two     ++++++++++ for April 1990.

**Example 4: Indirect Non-Naming Sharing**
Briefly describe one or two books
            |                        that you have read in the last year
            |                        that have most affected you
and explain why <the book/books has/have most affected you>.

As for the lexical strategies, there are two subtypes, including nominal-antecedent anaphora and non-nominal-antecedent anaphora. The distinction is made based on the syntactic nature of antecedents; the former represents an anaphoric strategy which takes a noun phrase as its antecedent while the latter represents an anaphoric strategy which takes an antecedent of clausal nature. Examples of lexical strategies are shown as follows.

**Example 5: Nominal Antecedent Anaphora**
There are **many successful schools** scattered throughout this nation,
some of **them** in the poorest of ghettos,
and **they** are all sending us the same message.

**Example 6: Non-Nominal Antecedent Anaphora**

I told him **to make Mitchell reach for everything,**
and **that's** what we did.

In Example 5, the pronouns in both the second and third line of refer to the noun phrase "many successful schools" on the first line. In Example 6, the pronoun "that" on the second line is also referential, while it refers to a clausal antecedent in the first line, namely "to make Mitchell reach for everything".

# 4 Chinese EFL Learners' Misuses of Grammatical Strategies for Clause Combing

Ideally, Chinese EFL learners should be instructed to apply the above-mentioned strategies to produce English clause complexes in appropriate ways. However, the truth is that a systematic instruction of clause-complex-level grammar has long been ignored in foreign language teaching. As a result, students will undoubtedly make mistakes when producing clause complexes, for example, choosing wrong grammatical strategies or using certain grammatical strategies in improper ways. This section will present and analyze Chinese EFL learners' misuses of these clause-complex-level grammatical strategies, with an aim to gain more attention for the issue.

A case study method is adopted for analyzing Chinese EFL learners' misuses of four infrequently-discussed grammatical strategies, including three subtypes of component sharing strategies and one subtype of lexical reference strategies. All the error cases are withdrawn from the Chinese Learner English Corpus (CLEC corpus) [5]. The CLEC corpus has a scale of over one million words and cover essays of Chinese EFL learners of different levels, including middle school students, non-English-major students and English-major students. Each essay is tagged with various kinds of linguistic errors, but no special tags arc designed for the clause-complex-level errors. Hence, the software AntConc is used for the effective searching of targeted error cases. It should be mentioned that the error tags in the CLEC corpus will be deleted in all the examples shown below.

## 4.1 Misuses of Clausal Naming Sharing

This section chooses cases of sentential relative clauses, one of the grammatical constructions taking clausal namings, for error analysis.

Based on the traditional grammar, a sentential relative clause is a kind of relative clause whose antecedent is a clause, a sentence or even a series of sentences [6]. This kind of relative clause is most frequently introduced by the relative word "which", and a comma should be used to separate the main clause and the sentential relative clause. According to Quirk, sentential relative clauses undertake functions similar to those of comment clauses, for example, to deny or affirm propositions in previous clauses, or to state the effectives of the events expressed in previous clauses. By observing data from the CLEC corpus, it is found that some Chinese students do not fully understand the functions of this strategy, and would use it improperly. Example 7 is an instance of misuse of sentential relative clauses.

**Example 7:** Some working mothers make a success in their career, <u>which</u> does give them pride and self-confidence, but also makes them "guilty" towards their children.

Semantically, the relative word "which" should refer to the state of achieving success in their career. However, under such a grammatical construction, the word "which" can only refer to the previous clause as a whole, whose proposition is not as required. A better choice is to replace "which" with the phrase "this kind of success". Meanwhile, another mistake exists in this example, that is, the second and third clauses should not be connected with the conjunction "but also". This is because the two clauses are in concession relation, while the conjunction suggests a progressive relation.

## 4.2 Misuses of Direct Non-naming Sharing

Direct non-naming sharing is a strategy to combine two clauses by sharing components in the middle or at the end of a clause. This strategy usually appears in parallel constructions, and the components shared could be verb phrase or head nouns of noun phrases, etc.

**Example 8:** The first step is the basis, and the second step is based on it, and <u>the third step is based on the second</u>, and so on.

In Example 8, the second and the third clauses are in parallel construction, and hence the direct non-naming share strategy could have been applied to make the expression more concise. Specifically, the third clause could share the verb phrase "is based" in the second clause, and be changed into "and the third step on the second one". To adopt a more concise expression, even the head noun "step" could be omitted, and hence the third clause could be further changed into "and the third on the second".

## 4.3 Misuses of Indirect Non-naming Sharing

Indirect non-naming sharing is a special strategy for component sharing. Clauses combined through this strategy do not share the exact component, since some adjustments should be made before the "shared" component is supplemented for certain clauses. This kind of strategy is applied in one type of ellipsis, that is, sluicing, which elides everything from a question sentence except for the question word.

**Example 9:** Some of the phenomena are so common that we all take them for granted, but Gelileo asked <u>why</u> and tried to find the answers.

In Example 9, the use of "why" is an instance of indirect non-naming sharing. Yet, it is not used in appropriate ways. There may be two reasons accounting for the misuse. One reason is the literal translation of the Chinese expression "(Gelileo总是)问为什么", which is used to embody the curiosity of a person. The literal translation misinterprets the meaning of the Chinese expression. Another reason is that the student did not master the non-naming sharing usage of "why". Under such a construction, the word "why" is used to question some propositions expressed in previous clauses, and this is obviously not what the student tried to express. The student is not aware of the function of "why" under this construction, and hence does not realize the mistake in this clause complex.

### 4.4 Misuses of Non-nominal Antecedent Anaphora

For non-nominal-antecedent anaphora, two typical pronouns are "this" and "that", which are revealed to be distributed differently in terms of the attentional state and the intentional structure of discourse [7]. In terms of the attentional state, "this" is used for establishing the referent cognitively within the addresser's discourse sphere as well as for signaling persistence of the same topic, while "that" signals the intended referent is not cognitively or subjectively within the addresser's discourse sphere. In terms of the intentional structures, "this" usually "falls into discourse units that elaborate a topic through explanation, interpretation and result relations", while "that" usually falls into those elaborating a topic through contrast, condition and topic-comment relations.

**Example 10:** Once you are well off, <u>that</u> means you have spare money besides the expense affording the daily life.

In Example 10, the pronoun underlined in the main clause is used to refer to the proposition expressed in the subordinate clause. While the clause complex is correct in terms of syntax, it is strange from the perspective of pragmatics. Two reasons account for this strangeness. Firstly, the pronoun "that" falls into a discourse unit whose relation with the previous one is atypical in English. In Example 10, the conjunction "once" suggests that the two clauses hold the circumstance relation, with the first clause being a time adverbial. However, the pronoun "that" is generally not used under this context. Secondly, the misuse of "that" in this example is also related to the negative transfer of Chinese construction "一旦…，就意味着…"。In this Chinese construction, the proposition in the first clause is referred to in the second clause with zero anaphor. Hence, the Chinese student simply used this construction to organize and express ideas in English, and adds the pronoun "that" as a subject to satisfy the syntactic demand, while ignoring the pragmatic constraints of using "that" as discourse deixis marker.

## 5  Conclusion

This study proposed a classification system for grammatical strategies for clause combining under the Clause Complex Theory. The classification system divides the strategies into component sharing strategies and lexical reference strategies, each of which are further divided into subtypes. Meanwhile, a case study method is adopted for error analysis of four less-frequently discussed grammatical strategies with instances withdrawn from the CLEC corpus. It is revealed that some students fail to utilize these grammatical strategies in correct ways. There are two reasons behind this situation: 1) they do not have systematic knowledge of these strategies, and therefore fail to choose appropriate strategies under different situations, and may ignore usage constraints for each strategy; 2) the way of clause-combining in Chinese is negatively transferred into English clause combination. The result shows that the instruction of certain syntactic patterns is far from being enough, and that that a systematic instruction of clause-combing is needed to help Chinese students get rid of the negative transfer effects of mother language and write clause complexes with multiple clauses in an appropriate way.

**Acknowledgements.** This work is financially supported by the scientific research and innovation project for postgraduates titled "A Computation-Oriented Study of Clause-Complex-Level Abstract Anaphora on English Written Discourse" (NO. 22GWCXXM-071) of Guangdong University of Foreign Studies.

# References

1. Halliday, M.A.K., Matthiessen, C.: An introduction to functional grammar, 3rd edn. Hodder Arnold, London (2014)
2. Song, R.: Grammatical Structure of Clause Complex, 1st edn. The Commercial Press, Beijing (2022)
3. Zhang, Z.: A new English grammar coursebook, 6th edn. Shanghai Foreign Language Education Press, Shanghai (2017)
4. Ge, S., Lin, X., Song, R.: The Annotation Scheme of English-Chinese Clause Alignment Corpus. In: Sun, M., Li, S., Zhang, Y., Liu, Y., He, S., Rao, G. (eds.) CCL 2020. LNCS (LNAI), vol. 12522, pp. 287–299. Springer, Cham (2020). https://doi.org/10.1007/978-3-030-63031-7_21
5. Gui, S., Yang, H.: Chinese Learner English Corpus, 1st edn. Shanghai Foreign Language Education Press, Shanghai (2003)
6. Quirk, R., Greenbaum, S., Leech, G., Svartvik, J.: A comprehensive grammar of the English language, 1st edn. Longman, London and New York (1985)
7. Çokal, D.: Discourse deixis and anaphora in L2 writing. Dilbilim Araştırmaları Dergisi **30**(2), 241–271 (2019)

# Corpus-Based Sociolinguistic Study of Undergraduate English Writing and Its Implications for Business English Teaching

Xiaoxiao Chen[1,2(✉)]

[1] School of English for International Business, Guangdong University of Foreign Studies, Guangzhou 510420, China
201410043@oamail.gdufs.edu.cn
[2] Laboratory of Language and Artificial Intelligence, Guangdong University of Foreign Studies, Guangzhou 510420, China

**Abstract.** Business English (BE) is widely taught around the world, especially in China. In order to improve the teaching of BE in China, the fundamental lexical and syntactical features of BE writing by undergraduate students are investigated under the theoretical framework of sociolinguistics. First, students BE writing was collected to construct a writing corpus. Then, the corpus was quantitatively analyzed with self-coded Python programs. At last, the lexical and syntactical features were also manually examined to ensure the accuracy of the research. The results of this study find that the linguistic features of BE writing by Chinese undergraduate students are in concordance with sociolinguistic theories, especially from a developing perspective. This finding may be helpful in BE writing teaching and curricula design in China.

**Keywords:** Corpus-Based Study · Sociolinguistic Study · Business English Teaching · Chinese Undergraduate English Writing

## 1 Introduction

Business English (BE), as a variety of ESP (English for Specific Purposes) [1], is widely taught around the world, especially in China. According to official data, by the beginning of 2019, BE major is taught in totally 393 colleges and universities with about 100,000 undergraduate students engaged in learning [2]. BE is a variety used in business world and variety is, in fact, a sociolinguistic perspective of seeing a language. Theoretically, sociolinguistics can be a framework for BE study, but there are only a few studies from this perspective, such as [3, 4]. BE, beside the features of sociolinguistic variety, also occupies an important niche in second language acquisition (SLA) studies, especially in the field of BE writing. Second language writing itself is a central topic in SLA research and practice. BE writing, with more complicated features and requirements, draws a lot of attention in teaching practice. However, the sociolinguistic features of undergraduate BE writing are still waiting for discovery, especially the development of those features along students' learning of BE in colleges and universities.

C. S. González-González et al. (Eds.): ICWL 2022/SETE 2022, LNCS 13869, pp. 349–355, 2023.
https://doi.org/10.1007/978-3-031-33023-0_32

## 2   Related Works

### 2.1   Sociolinguistic Study of Second Language Acquisition

Second language acquisition, which is also known as second language learning, is mainly about the process of learning a new or foreign language. Many people believe that second language learners should focus primarily on communicating messages to meet immediate needs rather than paying any attention to sociolinguistic variation of the learning language. However, Geeslin argues for the importance of sociolinguistic awareness in the context of SLA and emphasizes that "failure to understand the social norms for communication may lead to difficulties in social interactions as well as commercial and academic ones" [5].

A central theme in SLA research is interlanguage [6]. This theory indicates that the language that learners learn and use is not a static result of differences between their native languages they already know and the target language that they are learning, but "a complete language system in its own right", with its own systematic rules. This interlanguage is a continuum from a blank sheet to near native proficiency of the target language, which gradually develops as learners are exposed to the targeted language. The development covers every dimension of the language, including phonology, lexicon, syntax and pragmatics and so on [7].

The development of interlanguage depends on the exposure of learners to the target language context, which is also a key research field in sociolinguistics known as language contact. Language contact occurs when speakers of different languages or varieties interact and influence each other. The possible outcomes of language contact can be put into three categories: language maintenance, language shift, and language creation [8]. Among the three categories, language shift is closely related to SLA. As indicated by Bayley [9], sociolinguistic study of SLA from variationist perspective makes four potential contributions: (1) a clear way to study the effects of language transfer, which focuses on the speakers' first language; (2) how the target language function in language transfer and language acquisition, which focus on the learners' target language, especially the non-standard input of the target language; (3) a means of testing SLA process in the transfer; and (4) the examination of the acquisition patterns that learners may move (or fail to move) beyond the formal style of classroom instruction. These four contributions are all about language shift or transfer, which clearly shows the advantage of studying SLA from the perspective of sociolinguistics.

### 2.2   Business English Learning as SLA

SLA, as an important branch of applied linguistics, mainly studies people's second language learning process and its result, which can facilitate the formation of people's learning process and help people learn a second language better [10]. BE learning, as part of SLA, including the acquisition of the same four fundamental language skills of listening, speaking, reading, and writing, only that they are usually performed in certain business situations or tasks [11]. Researchers and teachers carried out BE learning in all the four skills area, such as listening [12], speaking [13], reading [14], and writing

[15]. Certainly, there are some studies focusing on the combination of BE teaching as a whole set [16], and some about BE evaluation [11, 17].

The research methods adopted in BE studies and especially in BE teaching studies are all the same as in SLA studies or language teaching studies. One thing should be emphasized is that the corpus application in BE teaching, such as [4, 13, 17], represents impressive achievement.

## 2.3 Business English Writing and Corpus Study

BE writing includes writings of different types and genres for different business situations and tasks. The categorization of BE writing is a complicated issue [1].

BE writing can be briefly defined as the creation of written discourse in a business context with English as the medium [17]. With the expansion of international trade, the demand of the society for the number and quality of BE talents has also increased, and the scope of BE writing has gradually expanded. Researchers based on the review of BE writing textbooks in the past 30 years in China, summed up three stages of the development of BE writing textbooks: (1) the stage of writing foreign trade letters and telegrams, which mainly focuses on letters, telegrams, telexes and other genres, and the teaching content mainly focuses on the application of commonly used terms and sentence patterns in business activities; (2) at the stage of BE practical writing, in such textbooks, common genres in international business and trade appeared in the textbooks to cope with various writing demands in the workplace, and the teaching content also extended to economics, law and finance; (3) at the stage of business communication focused textbooks, these textbooks are influenced by foreign business English textbooks, covering social culture, work scenes and business events at large [18]. The teaching content of BE writing is not limited to discourse level discussion, but also goes deep into social customs, culture and professional knowledge behind the discourse. It can be inferred from this review that in the past decades, the teaching of BE writing in China has gradually expanded in both breadth and depth.

As previous studies indicate that lexical items, including BE terms, are one specific feature for the evaluation of BE writing quality [17]. Clear communication with short and logical sentences is also an essential requirement in business situations [1]. Therefore, this study is going to investigate the progress of undergraduate students in their BE writing learning across three semesters (one and a half years) regarding these features with corpus-based method.

# 3  Research Design

## 3.1  Learner BE Writing Corpus

In order to observe the development of students' BE writing, a learner BE writing corpus was compiled. The corpus consists of 901 pieces of writing from 53 undergraduate BE majors. Since the students started their BE writing class at the beginning of their first year in university, they were required to finish and hand in one piece of BE writing every two or three weeks for three semesters (one and a half years). The writings were collected in MicroSoft Word format. Every piece of writing was corrected and evaluated by the BE writing instructor. All the original writings were transformed into.txt format and saved as one corpus file with tags of messages, such as title, writer, time, and score, etc. The description of the corpus is shown in Table 1.

**Table 1.** A description of the learner BE writing corpus.

| Corpus section | No. of files | No. of tokens | No. of word types | Topic areas |
|---|---|---|---|---|
| 1<sup>st</sup> semester | 371 | 49708 | 1198 | Narration, Description, Exemplification, Analysis by Division, Process Analysis, Cause and Effect, Classification, Comparison and Contrast |
| 2<sup>nd</sup> semester | 318 | 47165 | 1241 | Memo, E-mail, Application Letter, Letter of Congratulation, Apology Letter, Invitation Letter |
| 3<sup>rd</sup> semester | 212 | 80495 | 2296 | Business Report, Business Contract, Company Profile, Business Proposal |

After the collection of all 901 pieces of writing, all tables, references, figures and charts were removed from the texts so as to prepare them for analysis.

## 3.2 Procedures of Analysis

The purpose of this study is to examine the development of BE writing by undergraduate students in the learner BE writing corpus under the theoretical framework of sociolinguistics. To achieve this purpose, quantitative analysis was first conducted to investigate the lexical items, including BE terms, to identify the developing trend of BE learners' ability to write different types of BE articles in different stages. Then, the sentence length in the three subsections BE writing corpus was analyzed. Along with quantitative study of the lexical items and sentence length, the writing content, including lexical and syntactical features were also examined through manually reading and evaluation of the course instructor.

Self-coded Python programs are adopted to analyze the lexical features and sentence length of the corpus.

# 4 Results and Discussion

## 4.1 Overall Developing Trend

During the three semesters in one and a half years, BE major students are required to write paragraphs in the first semester, short essays in the second and long articles in the third. The topics range from short narrations and descriptions to long reports and proposals. Table 2 presents the overall development of BE writing.

**Table 2.** The overall development of undergraduate BE writing.

| Corpus section | Ave. Length | Standard deviation | Min. Length | Max. Length |
|---|---|---|---|---|
| 1st semester | 133.98 | 19.83 | 78 | 179 |
| 2nd semester | 148.32 | 23.54 | 75 | 222 |
| 3rd semester | 379.69 | 26.58 | 213 | 471 |

From Table 2 we can see that the average length of students' BE writing is growing in every semester. One reason is certainly the development of students' writing competence and the other is the difference of writing topics. Paragraph writing in the first semester is the shortest; memo, email and letter writing in the second semester goes in between; and report and proposal writing in the third semester is the longest, which present a clear communicative purpose of different writing prompts and topics. The variation of writing length is quite consistent, with a minor increase in different semesters, which also reflects the features of different topics. Through manual reading, it can be found that the differences also originate from students' progress of writing capability.

## 4.2 Lexical Items

As reviewed in Sect. 2.1, lexical items used in BE writing are worth investigating from the perspective of sociolinguistics. One feature that widely adopted in lexical studies is type-token ratio (TTR), which can represent the lexical complexity of a piece of writing. There are actually many different ways of calculating the feature of lexical complexity [19]. Since the writing texts collected are written by college students of same or similar English proficiency and the length in each subsection of the corpus is similar, the simple formula is adopted:

$$type - token\ ratio = (number\ of\ types/number\ of\ tokens) * 100 \qquad (1)$$

The calculated TTR for students' BE writing in the three semesters are 2.41, 2.63, and 2.85 respectively, which shows that students are making use of more and more new words in their writing along with their learning of BE. Yet, through manual evaluation of students' writing, it is found that the progress of lexical complexity is not obvious since students are more tending to use short and simple words, which is also a salient feature of BE.

### 4.3  Sentence Length

Sentence length is often adopted in writing quality evaluation as a predictive feature [17, 19]. BE writing is usually "based on a core of the most useful and basic structures" [1]. That means that sentence length should be limited in BE writing. The calculated sentence length is listed in Table 3 with titles, openings and closings of writings excluded.

Table 3.  Sentence length of undergraduate BE writing.

| Corpus section | Ave. Length | Standard deviation | Min. Length | Max. Length |
|---|---|---|---|---|
| 1st semester | 16.32 | 7.62 | 3 | 39 |
| 2nd semester | 14.51 | 6.59 | 3 | 32 |
| 3rd semester | 19.72 | 10.08 | 5 | 52 |

From Table 2 we can see that the average length of students' BE writing is not growing as lexical complexity in every semester. The second semester writing is relatively shorter than the writing in the first semester. The reason is obviously the sociolinguistic feature of BE that business English expressions, idioms or business terms used in emails and letter are succinct, concise and suitable to express writers' opinions. Certainly, business reports and proposals have much longer sentences, which is also within expectation as they are more formal writing than those in the first two semesters.

## 5  Conclusion and Implication

Through computerized and manual investigation of Chinese undergraduate students' BE writing, fundamental lexical and syntactical features are uncovered. It is hoped that the findings of this study could complement BE writing research on Chinese undergraduate students and thus inform BE writing teaching in BE classroom and contribute to BE writing curricula design.

## References

1. Ellis, M., Johnson, C.: Teaching Business English. Oxford University Press, Oxford New York (1994)
2. Wang, L., Ai, B.: Forty years of reform and opening-up: revisiting and rethinking the historical development of business english education. J. Beijing Int. Stud. Univ. 1, 3–19 (2019)
3. Wang, J., Guo, J.: The language study of business english in sociolinguistics perspective. J. Jilin Nor. Univ. (Humanities & Social Science Edition) 2, 54–56 (2010)
4. Chen, X., Ge, S.: Corpus-Based Sociolinguistic Study of Corporate Emails and the Implication for Business English Teaching. In: Pang, C., et al. (eds.) SETE/ICWL -2020. LNCS, vol. 12511, pp. 393–400. Springer, Cham (2021). https://doi.org/10.1007/978-3-030-66906-5_37
5. Geeslin, K.L.: Variable Structures and Sociolinguistic Variation. In: Malovrh, P.A., Benati, A.G. (eds.) The Handbook of Advanced Proficiency in Second Language Acquisition, 1st edn., pp. 547–565. John Wiley & Sons Inc, Hoboken (2018)

6. Selinker, L.: Interlanguage. International Review of Applied Linguistics in Language Teaching **10**(3), 209–231 (1972)
7. Yang, L.: Multidimensional Intermediary Language Linguistics Research. Foreign Language Teaching and Research Press, Beijing (2015)
8. Thomason, S.G., Kaufman, G.: Language contact, Creolization, and Genetic Linguistics. University of California Press, California (1991)
9. Bayley, R.: Second language acquisition: a variationist perspective. In: Bayley, R., Lucas, C. (eds.) Sociolinguistic Variation: Theories, Methods, and Applications, pp. 133–144. Cambridge University Press, Cambridge (2007)
10. Ellis, R.: SLA Research and Language Teaching. Oxford University Press, New York (2008)
11. O'Sullivan, B.: Issues in Testing Business English: The Revision of The Cambridge Business English Certificates. Cambridge University Press, New York (2006)
12. Hu, L.: The implication of Krashen's second language acquisition theory on Cambridge business English listening teaching. China Electric Power Education **2**, 197–198 (2011)
13. Curado Fuentes, A.: The use of corpora and IT in a comparative evaluation approach to oral business English. ReCALL **15**(2), 189–201 (2003)
14. Xu, X.: The construction and application of microlecture mode on business English reading course. J. Mudanjiang Univ. **28**(5), 139–141 (2019)
15. Li, X.: Thoughts on the Construction of Communicative Situation in the Teaching of L2 Writing Based on the Practice of Business English Writing. Foreign Language and Literature **27**(3), 133–136 (2011)
16. Wang, L., Cui, C.: Implementing the Teaching Guide for Undergraduate Business English Major and improving business English talent education. Foreign Language World **3**, 5–11 (2020)
17. Ge, S.: The Automated Evaluation of Business English Writing. China Science Publishing & Media Ltd., Beijing (2021)
18. Zhou, W., Wang, R., Shi, L.: The Review of Business English Writing Textbook and Problems Analysis in China. J. Qiqihar Univ. (Philosophy & Social Science Edition) **2**, 172–175 (2014)
19. Ge, S.: A Research on General Computerized Composition Scoring and Feed-Back for College English Teaching in China. Shanghai Foreign Language Education Press, Shanghai (2015)

# Learner Portrait in Blended College English Listening and Speaking Instruction

Ting Xie, Jingnan Li, Isabelle C. Chou[✉], and Jiehui Hu

University of Electronic Science and Technology of China, 611731 Chengdu,
Sichuan, People's Republic of China
isabellecchou@uestc.edu.cn

**Abstract.** Learner portrait is a term derived from "user portrait" in business marketing. Many educational apps try to model a portrait for individual users, so that targeted course recommendations can be provided for each learner. With the wide adoption of blended learning, learning apps has become an indispensable part of college education. Scholars have been working on more accurate portrait constructing, so that more personalized learning plans and better content recommendations can be achieved. Compared to studies on portrait modeling, much less research has been done in the role learner portrait plays for learners and teachers—the two key possible users of learner portrait. Even less literature can be found in the use of portraits for intermediate and advanced language teaching and learning, which is more skill-based and less easy to provide a clear knowledge map. This research focuses on the impact of portrait feedback provided by a listening and speaking app used in a blended college level English as a Foreign Language (EFL) course. The app generates group portraits for teachers, which divide learners into 9 categories based on a profile of learners' time on app and academic performance. Individual portraits that summarize their performance in the app are also provided for individual learners. Through platform data analysis, questionnaire surveys and in-depth interviews, the study finds that: 1) Teachers' interventional guidance based on group portraits effectively promotes student learning; 2) Students adjust learning plans based on portrait feedbacks; 3) Students hope that the platform can provide more refined portraits with more detailed analysis of learning behavior data.

**Keywords:** Learner Portrait · Blended Learning · College English

## 1 Introduction

The concept of "learner portrait" originated from the term "user persona" proposed by Alan Cooper, who used the term to present a range of users sharing some same natural or social traits. Based on the profile of a user's attributes, preferences, and behaviors, computer algorithms can extract the user's traits, and sketch a highly generalized portrait of the user, which highlights the user's traits and makes the user easier to understand. User portrait has been widely applied in marketing, especially in the field of product recommendation.

© The Author(s), under exclusive license to Springer Nature Switzerland AG 2023
C. S. González-González et al. (Eds.): ICWL 2022/SETE 2022, LNCS 13869, pp. 356–362, 2023.
https://doi.org/10.1007/978-3-031-33023-0_33

In the educational field, learners are often viewed as users of services, and a learner portrait can be viewed as an objective summary and specific description of learner features [1]. Efforts have been made on more targeted and detailed description to students [2]. For example, now most language learning applications recommend courses based on the interest tags users choose and clicks users make in the app [3]. However, a learner portrait is more than tags and clicks, and its role should not be limited to recommendations. Xiao et al. [4] proposes that learner portrait can be used to support targeted learning design, and thus improve learner participation in online courses. Sun and Dong [5] propose to collect learners' online learning behavior data and build learning style models, so that we can assess online learners' risk of academic failure, and recommend resources, design activities, and adjust teaching methods accordingly. Zhao et al. [6] design a learner portrait model based on knowledge mapping, and applied it in a high school physics course. The result shows that the model helped with the learner's knowledge construction and ability development. Chen et al. [7] develop a personalized portrait model with tags for an online computer programing course and found that the portraits constructed can express the learner traits, and contribute to personalized learning.

Most learner portrait applications are designed for courses of business, science and technology [8]. Courses in these fields usually have a clear knowledge map. Little literature can be found in language teaching and learning for intermediate and advanced learners, which is more skill-based and less easy to provide a clear knowledge map. Language learners at this level usually benefit more from personalized teaching and learning. With wide adoption of blended learning, learning apps has become an indispensable part of College English courses [9]. A portrait based on the analysis of a learner's learning behaviors in the app has great value both for the learner and the teacher. The current study focuses on the impact of the learner portraits generated by a listening and speaking app used for a blended college level English as a Foreign Language (EFL) course, and tries to answer the following questions:

1) What impact do learner portraits have on learning?
2) What are the learners' attitudes towards the portrait constructed?
3) How refined do learners want the portrait to be?

## 2    Learner Portrait Modeling and Application

A portrait construction undergoes five steps—Objective setting, data collection, model building, portrait output, portrait application [10]. A learning app generates learner portraits to encourage better learning, so both summary and specific description of learner features are included. Two groups of data are usually collected—static data, like the basic information about the learners, and dynamic data reflecting the online study behaviors, including the starting and ending time of each task, repeating times of each task, answers for each question, scores for the tasks, etc. The collected data is then cleaned, mined, and modeled, with features extracted and tagged. Then a learner portrait is established and visualized for output. A learner can adjust his/her learning behavior according to the portrait generated, while a teacher can intervene when necessary. The five steps are shown in Fig. 1.

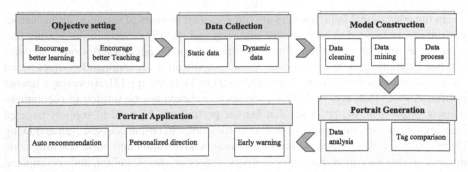

**Fig. 1.** Five steps of learning portrait building and application

This study is based on a listening and speaking training app adopted in a college EFL blended course. Altogether 4138 students signed up for the course. The online training part consists of six units, each about a specific topic, like sports, health, etc. All the six units have parallel structures, including video lectures, listening comprehension tasks, and a listen-and-repeat practice. For each unit, students first finish the online learning tasks, and then go to the classroom for oral activities like discussion, debate, or presentation. Each unit provides a portrait for individual users, and a group portrait for the teacher.

## 3   Learner Portrait for Teachers

A nine-category group portrait is generated for teachers. In Fig. 2, the horizontal axis shows the time a learner spends on the materials and tasks in the unit. The vertical axis represents the score a learner gets for the unit. This group portrait guides teachers in decision making on intervention. For example, learners tagged with A1 have the below-average study time, and achieved less than 60% correct answers. For learners with this tag, teachers should intervene in time to figure out if they are real low achievers with low motivation, or if they were just hindered by technology problems. Different actions should follow for different situations. Learners tagged with B1 and C1 spend average and above average time on learning, but with very low achievements. Interventions can help them to find out what adjustment they need to make to their study plans. As is shown in Fig. 2, different interventions are suggested for different learner groups. Special attention is suggested for A1, B1 and C1 students, while encouragement and specific helps are recommended for other groups. Details for each learner are available with some clicks, so that teachers can make more informed decisions based on individual learner portraits.

Figure 3 and Fig. 4 show the average score of the six units and the average time spent on each unit. The effect of the portrait-based personalized intervention is shown by the steady increase of the average score for each unit, and the continuous decrease of the time spent on each unit.

Figure 5 shows the number of students with different tags in the group portrait. The three lines on top shows the number of high achievers with a unit score of over 80%, where most of the students belong. We can see that the number of efficient high achievers

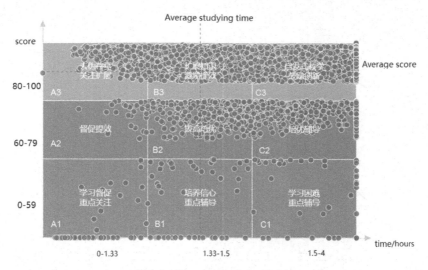

**Fig. 2.** Group portrait for Unit 1

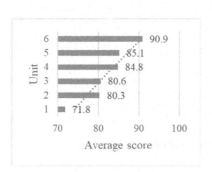

**Fig. 3.** Average scores

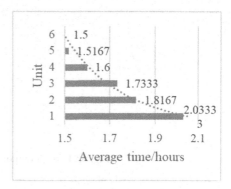

**Fig. 4.** Average time

with reasonably low study time, labeled as A3, are on a steady rise, from 293 in Unit 1 to 1322 in Unit 6. Low efficient high achievers (C3) with comparatively long study time decreased from 1854 to 1240. Interventions with these two groups achieves the best result.

## 4  Learner Portrait for Students

The portrait for individual learners summarizes the learning behaviors in general, with a comparison to the average performance of the whole class. It also includes a detailed description of the oral performance from three perspectives—accuracy, fluency, and complexity (Fig. 6).

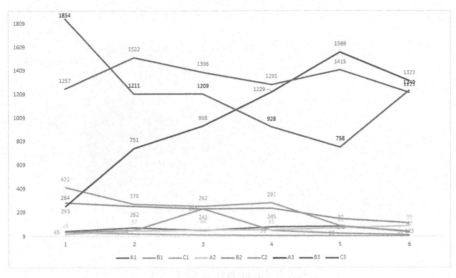

**Fig. 5.** Numbers of students with different tags for six units

**Fig. 6.** Portrait output for individual learners

The result of a 5-point Likert questionnaire after the course show students' positive attitude towards the portrait. Almost all students say that they check their portrait generated by the app regularly, especially the scores for the practices, and adjust learning plans based on the feedbacks. As for the ranks of students in class or among all the learners of this course, which most apps include in learner portrait, the students in the survey did not show that much interest. They care more about their own performance. Figure 7 shows that except for a summary report of the behaviors and scores, students want to see their performance record together with the labels indicating the purpose of each practice task—which knowledge points it covers, whether this is a critical point, and what skill this task tries to develop. This need for a more refined portrait, especially a more detailed description of the language ability they have displayed during the practice, is not satisfied by the learner portrait currently available.

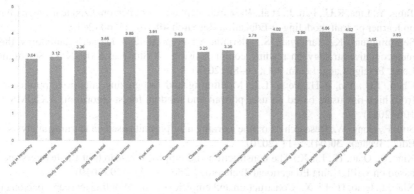

**Fig. 7.** Survey results for student feedback needs on a 5-point Likert scale (n = 186, Cronbach α = 0.965)

## 5   Conclusion

Learning applications now can generate learner portraits for both teachers and students. The current study based on a listening and speaking app adopted by a blended learning College English course finds that.

1) Group portraits help teachers to make informed decisions and offer appropriate interventions in time to achieve better results;
2) Students adjust learning plans based on portrait feedbacks;
3) Portraits for individual learners summarize their performance in general, but the current available portraits cannot provide more detailed feedbacks learners want.

It is obvious that the purpose and usage of user portrait and learner portrait remain of significant difference. A user portrait is generated for producers or service providers rather than for a real user. On the contrary, a learner portrait can serve for all the parties involved—app providers, school administrators, teachers, and most importantly, learners. So in the design of learner portrait modeling, app developers should take different end users into consideration, extract different data, and sketch portraits of different styles of the same user to meet different needs. More studies should be done in what portrait style learners and teachers need, and how to use these portraits in everyday teaching and learning.

**Grant Information.**   This project is supported by the National Social Science Fund of China (20BYY115).

## References

1. Chen, H., Dai, Y., Han, D., et al.: Learner's portrait and individualized teaching in open education. Open Education Research **23**(03), 105–112 (2017)
2. Zhang, Z.B.: Construction and Empirical Study of Learner Portrait in Online General Education Course. Discrete Dynamics in Nature and Society 2022 (2022)

3. Tang, Y., Lina, R.U., Fan, J., et al.: Research on planning of personalized learning path based on learner portrait modeling. e-Education Research **40**(10), 53–60 (2019)
4. Septiningrum, K., Tarwiyah, S., Mariam, S.: A portrait of learner's autonomy through metacognitive strategy on reading comprehension (A Study at SMP N 32 Semarang). J. Lang. Foreign Lang. Learn. **7**(1), 66–82 (2018)
5. Chen, T.G., Yin, X.H., Peng, L.J.: Monitoring and recognizing enterprise public opinion from high-risk users based on user portrait and random forest algorithm. AXIOMS **10**(2), 106 (2021)
6. Sun, F., Dong, W.: Research on online learning user portrait based on learning analysis. Mod. Educ. Technol. **30**(04), 5–11 (2020)
7. Xiao, J., Qiao, H., Li, X.: The construction and empirical research of the learners' persona based on xAPI. China Educational Technology **25**(01), 123–129 (2019)
8. Xiao, J., Qiao, H., Li, X.: Construction and empirical study of online learners' persona in the big data environment. Open Education Research **25**(04), 111–120 (2019)
9. Zhao, L., Fan, J., Zhao, Y., Tang, Y., Zhong, S.: The design and application of the learners' portrait model based on knowledge mapping. Mod. Educ. Technol. **31**(02), 95–101 (2021)
10. Porter, W.W., Graham, C.R., Spring, K.A., et al.: Blended learning in higher education: Institutional adoption and implementation. Comput. Educ. **75**, 185–195 (2014)

# Turning the Class into a Boardgame: Conceptualizing a Gamified Flipped Model for ESL Classes

Keming Peng[✉] and Xiaowan Qin

Guangdong University of Foreign Studies, Guangzhou 510420, China
pengkeming@gdufs.edu.cn

**Abstract.** Motivation, both intrinsic and extrinsic, are fundamental in language learning. This study aims to conceptualize and construct a gamified flipped model for English as Second Language (ESL) classes for secondary schoolers to explore whether they can be motivated to learn English, and to examine participants' attitudes toward the model. The gamified flipped model, which is a dynamic combination of the flipped classroom with game elements, is to foster ubiquitous learning by students both in and out of class. The author reviewed relevant literature on ESL, gamification, and flipped classrooms, and designed a model to turn the traditional ESL class into a real-person boardgame. Preliminary feedback shows that participants are motivated to increase their out-of-class learning thanks to the new model. The study can shed light on the pedagogy of ESL.

**Keywords:** Gamification · Flipped Class · English as Second Language (ESL) · Motivation

## 1 Introduction

Because of modern technology, people have begun to "take high-intensity engagement and active participation for granted" (Mcgonigal, 2011, p. 91). Schools today face significant problems motivating students and keeping them engaged in the learning process (Lee & Hammer, 2011). A major reason is that traditional schooling is perceived as ineffective and boring by many students (Dicheva et al., 2015).

Recently, much has been written about whether gamification or gamified elements (for example, points, badges, and leaderboards) can promote learning, and how. The purpose of gamification is to equip non-game activities with game mechanics (such as progress, rewards, and competitions) to increase student engagement in learning activities (Kapp, 2013). First used in business settings (Robson et al., 2015), gamification has proved helpful in teaching and reinforcing learning behaviors and supporting important skills such as problem-solving, collaboration, and communication. As a result, gamification is regarded as a potential means of engaging and motivating learners in educational settings (Dicheva et al., 2015; de-Marcos et al., 2014).

C. S. González-González et al. (Eds.): ICWL 2022/SETE 2022, LNCS 13869, pp. 363–374, 2023.
https://doi.org/10.1007/978-3-031-33023-0_34

However, most of the previous studies on gamified learning focused only on learning in the classroom, omitting the out-of-class self-learning of students. Out-of-class experiences are indispensable, for they provide rich contexts for learning, allowing young students to take part in learning activities that are personally meaningful and engaging (Bell et al., 2013; Crowley et al., 2015). For ESL learners, out-of-class learning constitutes an important context of language learning because it affords authentic language exposure and use and plays essential roles in maintaining student motivation in learning (Benson, 2011; Richards, 2015).

Research on ESL has primarily been conducted in instructional situations, and not enough attention has been paid to out-of-class contexts (Lai, Hu, & Lyu, 2018). As a result, the earlier studies do not form connections between classroom performance and out-of-class learning experiences. How can learners' out-of-class experiences be integrated into the class? Some scholars have designed out-of-class platforms to motivate student learning, such as the Reading Battle (Chu, 2016). Another possible solution is the flipped classroom, the literature of which has focused on multimedia lectures that are provided for students to watch out of class and at their own pace (O'Flaherty and Phillips, 2015). To some extent, the flipped classroom model can serve as a complement to gamified learning. Borrowing the concept of gamification and flipped classroom, this section aims to construct a model combining gamified elements and flipped concepts to devise new ways to engage learners both in and out of class.

# 2   Literature Review

## 2.1   Gamification in Educational Scenarios

Gamification is the use of game elements and game-design techniques in non-game contexts (Werbach and Hunter, 2015) to promote desired behaviors and drive corporate learning outcomes (Zainuddin et al., 2020). With game elements, gamified settings can be used in any environment, including the workplace and the classroom (Table 1).

**Table 1.**  Common game elements and explanations (from Werbach and Hunter, 2015)

| Game Elements | Explanation |
| --- | --- |
| Points | Numeric accumulation based on certain activities |
| Badges | Visual representation of achievements for the use shown online |
| Leaderboard | How the players are ranked based on success |
| Progress | Shows the status of a player |
| Levels | A section or part of the game |
| Avatar | Visual representation of a player or alter ego |
| Social Elements | Relationships with other users during the game |
| Rewards | System for motivating players who complete a task |
| Achievements | The goals achieved |

Gamification has been the subject of research, discussion, and application in second-language (L2) learning and second-language acquisition (SLA). Despite the differences in methods, the core of language teaching and learning lies in intensive training. Given that language training in most cases consists of repetition and reinforcement, language learners need to be motivated, and gamification opens the door for L2 learners to enhance their language-learning experiences, acquiring at the same time the skills needed to solve any language task or challenge both inside and outside the classroom, and meet instructional goals (De-Marcos et al., 2014). Berns, Gonzalez-Pardo, and Camacho (2013) constructed a 3-D virtual environment to explore students' motivation to learn German. Students were given language training in a virtual world, and their learning behaviors were recorded. The researchers report that the games resulted in easier and faster learning, providing real-time feedback that helped players succeed in the various game activities. The immersive game environment and the fact that vocabulary was presented in context made it easier for students to understand and learn, the researchers conclude. Hwang et al. (2017) developed a problem-based English listening game and analyzed the progress and learning anxiety of 77 ninth-graders. It was found that the gamified approach benefited the learning achievement and motivation of the students.

Most of the studies concluded that gamification has a positive influence on language learning. Yet, there are a few studies that indicate contradictory effects. For example, Hanus and Fox (2015) conducted a comparative study and found that students in a gamified course demonstrated less motivation, satisfaction, and empowerment over time than those in the non-gamified class, and that the test scores of the gamified class were also lower. Berkling and Thomas (2013) reported the negative influence of gamification elements on student learning motivations when students view gamification as an unnecessary hindrance in studying for exams. Overall, research on gamification and its relevance to second-language education is far from sufficient and systematic, and there is much to be explored.

## 2.2 The Flipped Classroom

The flipped-classroom movement was inspired in part by the work of Salman Khan, who created the "Khan Academy," a library of free online tutoring videos spanning a variety of academic subjects. Khan reported that his motivation was to eliminate the "dreary process that sometimes went on in classrooms -- rote memorization and plug-in formulas aimed at nothing more lasting or meaningful than a good grade on the next exam" (2012, p. 7). The term "flipping" comes from the idea of swapping homework for classwork. Students typically are assigned a video to watch as homework, thereby freeing up class time that was formerly devoted to lectures in favor of hands-on activities (Ash, 2012). The motivation behind flipping is that students can receive more one-on-one attention from the classroom teacher if they actively work on an assignment in class. Proponents claim that the flipping approach leads to a better understanding of a given lesson (Davies, Dean, & Ball, 2013). Abeysekera and Dawson (2015) define the flipped classroom as a type of blended learning, integrating online learning and the classroom experience. However, certain differences are apparent. First of all, the students vary in how they are oriented to take the course. Unlike the traditional online course, a flipped class provides students with short and to-the-point videos designed to enable them to familiarize themselves with the course. The second feature is its individualization. Rather than following the progress of the whole class or the teachers, or the syllabus, students can learn at their own pace with the help of short videos. In this way, they are more engaged and motivated.

### 2.3 The Definition of the Gamified Flipped Model

Previous studies have demonstrated the effectiveness of gamified elements and the flipped model in teaching and learning. Still, there are obvious research gaps.

First, the gamified approach to learning mostly disregards the out-of-class self-learning by students. Out-of-class learning is often seen as "a mechanism to help explain achievement differences among students and as a means to improve achievement" (Schunk & Zimmerman, 2012, p. vii). It is thus necessary to examine whether and how gamification can motivate students' self-learning after class. Second, the flipped classroom model relies heavily on the students' self-regulation rather than on their motivation. The flipped classroom can largely help bridge the gap between class learning and self-learning, but only when students are strongly motivated to finish the preview and review the material after class.

In this section, game-thinking and game mechanics are used to engage users and solve problems (Zichermann & Cunningham, 2011). The flipped classroom refers to pedagogical approaches that move most information-transmission teaching out of the classroom, thus freeing up class time for learning activities that are active and social, and that require students to complete pre- and/or post-class activities (Abeysekera & Dawson, 2015). Combining the features of gamification and the flipped classroom, the author intends to construct a gamified flipped pedagogical method that adopts game elements to engage learners both in and out of class, in which students learn basic linguistic knowledge outside the classroom via the flipped method and finish a boardgame quest inside the class. This model aims to facilitate ubiquitous learning for English-language instruction. The model proposes that gameplay be utilized during class hours, that students be directed to preview and review course content and homework outside class, and that the out-of-class performance of students be transferred as enhancements for class gameplay.

## 3  Extrinsic and Intrinsic Motivations: Theoretical Foundations of the Gamified Flipped Learning Model

Scholars tend to believe that many of our behaviors have purposes and are directed toward specific goals (Watts & Swanson, 2002), which can be described as motivation. Deci & Ryan (1985) proposed the Self-Determination Theory (SDT), which distinguished between different types of motivation based on the different reasons or goals that give rise to an action. The most basic distinction is between intrinsic motivation, which refers to doing something because it is inherently interesting or enjoyable, and extrinsic motivation, which refers to doing something because it leads to a separable outcome (Ryan & Deci, 2000). While both motivations are important, researchers have

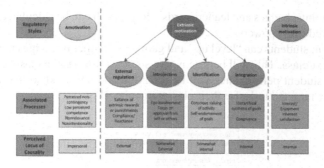

**Fig. 1.** A taxonomy of human motivation (Ryan and Deci, 2000)

found that intrinsic and extrinsic motivations can have different effects on behaviors and how people pursue goals (Fig. 1).

Individuals need the satisfaction of three basic psychological needs, innate and universal, to be motivated. These needs are autonomy (a personal endorsement of one's action deriving from self), competence (self-confidence in the ability to complete activities), and relatedness (positive interpersonal relationships with others). When these needs are satisfied by the individual's social milieu, the individual becomes more motivated to act and shows greater positive outcomes in the education setting (Deci & Ryan, 1985, 2002).

Language learning motivation is often perceived as important by teachers and students alike and has a very significant role in explaining failure and success in language learning contexts (Dörnyei, 2001; Dörnyei and Csizér, 1998). Second language learning requires much repetition, and thus heavily relies upon the learner's motivation. We can thus ground the gamified flipped classroom in the motivations theory.

# 4 The Classroom Boardgame: A Gamified Flipped Class

## 4.1 The Formation of a Gamified Flipped Class

A typical Gamified Flipped Class is divided into three parts that are closely linked to each other. The first is Before Class, in which students preview the knowledge points to be taught and learned. Secondly, in the Class Hours session, students will experience gamified teaching and learning-based Quests. Thirdly, in the After Class session, students finish more quests to improve their proficiency.

Following the course design of Hew et al. (2016), the gamified courses is set in a real-person board game, in which students will form groups and finish each goal by answering questions. The course content is taken from students' textbooks offering the language points for a certain daily communication setting.

In the model, there are several highlights. First, there is a link between before-class preview, in-class gameplay, and out-of-class review. By integrating game elements in the overall process, students will be motivated to learn during regular class hours and in out-of-class self-learning and practice sessions. Second, the use of game elements will not be isolated. Students' out-of-class learning and practice will also be gamified with elements of points, badges and leaderboards, all of which can be calculated together and then transferred into "powers."

Simply put, students can "level up" and gain new competitive edges in the gameplay during the next class. This will better involve students not only in class, but also out of class. Third, student performance will be recorded and analyzed so that teachers may provide better-targeted tasks for their class gameplay (Fig. 2).

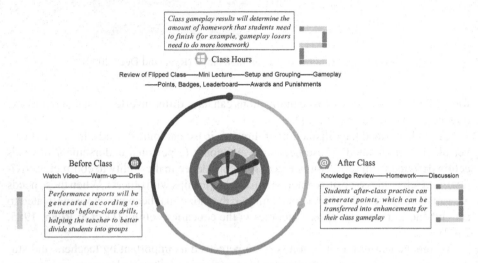

**Fig. 2.** The Gamified Flipped Model

## 4.2 Integration of Game Elements

The class hours are set into a real-person board game, in which students form groups and finish the goal by answering textbook-related language questions (Fig. 3).

**Fig. 3.** Real-person boardgame layout (taken by the author)

Winning State: In a group competition setting, the group that first finishes the board will be declared the winner. In an individual competition setting, the student who finishes the board with the most number of correct answers will be the winner.

Points: In an ordinary block, one point will be given for a correct answer, and in the joker's block, three points will be given. Students with the highest points will be given badges.

Badges: There are four badges in the game that are given to individual students, namely, the achiever, the socializer, the explorer, and the killer. The criteria for each badge are in the following Table 2.

**Table 2.** Samples of Badges.

| Badges | Criteria |
|---|---|
| Killer | The student who has the most number of correct answers |
| Achiever | The student who answers most questions |
| Socializer | The student who offers the most help in answering questions |
| Explorer | The student who gives the mostnumber of correct answers to open questions |

Leaderboard: The rankings are determined by the total badge number for either individual students or groups. All students can access the leaderboard to see their ranking and badge accumulations compared to all other students. Each will be required to create an anonymous avatar to view his/her achievements without direct comparison (Table 3).

**Table 3.** Samples of Leaderboard.

| Rank | Group Name or Student Name | Badges Won |
|---|---|---|
| 1 | Zeus X | Killer Achiever Socializer |
| 2 | Guns 'n Roses | Killer Achiever Socializer |
| 3 | Hobbit | Achiever |

## 5  Participants' Acceptance of the Model

A pilot study was carried out with 14 learners of ESL, who participated in a 7-day English learning Winter Camp. They followed the course requirements as per the gamified flipped model. After the one-week session, they are asked to return a questionnaire, the fundamental questions of which are listed in the following Table 4:

**Table 4.**  Major questions in the questionnaire.

| Category | NO | Questions | Response Options |
|---|---|---|---|
| General | 1 | What did you like best in the real-person boardgame? | Empty field to write a comment |
|  | 2 | What suggestions do you have for its improvement? | Empty field to write a comment |
| Playing the Game | 4 | Did you learn more words/grammar/sentences with the boardgame? | Yes, Neutral or No |
|  | 5 | Compared to a traditional teaching class, would you prefer a boardgame class? | Yes, Neutral or No |
|  | 6 | Would you like to play the boardgame again? | Yes, Neutral or No |
|  | 7 | To win in the boardgame, how much time are you willing to spend after the class? | Empty field to fill in a number |
|  | 8 | Did you win badges? | Yes, Neutral or No |
|  | 9 | Were your team on the leaderboard? | Yes or No |
|  | 10 | Will winning badges or being on the leaderboard be exciting? | Yes, Neutral or No |
|  | 11 | Are the game rules clear? | Yes, Neutral or No |
|  | 12 | Did you have fun playing the game? | Yes, Neutral or No |
|  | 13 | Will you do more exercise after class to win the game in the class? | Yes, Neutral or No |
| Game Design | 14 | Is the question level appropriate for the learning content? | Yes, Neutral or No |
|  | 15 | Is the number of questions appropriate for the boardgame? | Yes, Neutral or No |

The participants came from an English learning Winter Camp, consisting of junior and senior school students. Their consent were acquired before implementing the Gamified Flipped Model, and they agreed to take the questionnaire voluntarily after the 7-day session. These participants received traditional lecture-based classes at school and were exposed to the new model for a week, so they can compare the differences of the two teaching methods. The demographic information of the participants is as follows (Table 5):

**Table 5.** Demographic information of the participants.

| Gender | Grade | Years of English Learning |
|---|---|---|
| Male: 8 | Junior Grade One: 1 | 1–3 Years: 3 |
| | Junior Grade Two: 7 | 4–5 Years: 7 |
| Female: 6 | Senior Grade One: 4 | ≥5 Years: 4 |
| | Senior Grade Two: 2 | |
| Total: 14 | | |

Analyzing the responses revealed the following trends. In the first part, the answers to the first two open questions indicate participants' overall satisfaction with the real-person model. A majority of the students like the gamified class because it is fun, active, and competitive. Also intriguing to them was the social element, because they can form teams and "battle" with each other. These elements, they reported, were not in their former English classes. Most of their suggestions, however, did not pertain to the Gamified Flipped Model, but rather to whether they could design their own avatars or badges.

In the second part, more than half of the participants reported that they had learned more language points with the boardgame, and an overwhelming majority of participants preferred the gamified approach to traditional English classes, and reported that they would like to play with the boardgame again (Fig. 4).

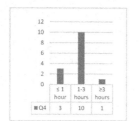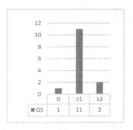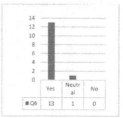

**Fig. 4.** Participants' reply on Q4–6

Regarding question 7, two-thirds of the students replied they are willing to spend more than one hour with the course material before the class, in order to win on the boardgame. Almost 80% of participants won at least one badge in the 7-day session, and 50% were on the leaderboard more than once (Fig. 5).

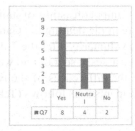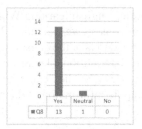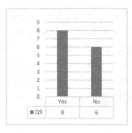

**Fig. 5.** Participants' reply on Q7–9

When asked whether they were excited about winning (badges or being on the leaderboard), almost everyone replied yes. Also, 3/4 of the participants considered the rules clear. Most of them (75%) were having fun when playing with the boardgame during the class (Fig. 6).

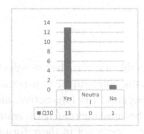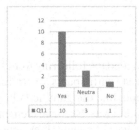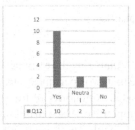

**Fig. 6.** Participants' reply on Q10–12

More than 80% of the participants reported that they would do more exercise after the class. However, given that participants came from different grades, only one-third of them thought the language content was suitable for their language proficiency. About half of them considered the number of questions appropriate for the game (Fig. 7).

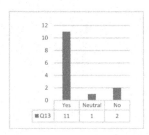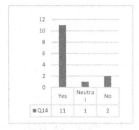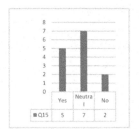

**Fig. 7.** Participants' reply on Q13–15

# 6 Conclusion and Future Research

In the Metaverse era, learning has become more immersive. Traditional language teaching methods, though proved to be applicable, should be complemented by more methods to raise students' learning motivation and engagement. The author conceptualized a gamified flipped model to turn a language learning class into a real-person boardgame and examined students' attitudes towards such a model. A pilot study and preliminary results show that the gamification + flipped approach can be an instrument for the ESL teacher's toolbox when applying a blended learning concept. The initial feedback we collected indicates that the model is appropriate to tackle the requirements identified for the intended use. Above all, participants confirmed the effect of raising learning motivation and fun in the context of language-loaded content. Of course, more evaluation is necessary to gain sound findings. Future research can focus on the implementation of more game elements, and evaluate the effects of different elements on students' EAL learning motivation. Also, more could be studied regarding the age groups suitable for such a gamified flipped model. The conceptualization and construction of such a model enriched ESL teachers' toolbox of language teaching.

# References

Abeysekera, L., Dawson, P.: Motivation and cognitive load in the flipped classroom: definition, rationale and a call for research. High. Educ. Res. Dev. **34**, 1–14 (2015). https://doi.org/10.1080/07294360.2014.934336

Ash, K.: Educators evaluate flipped classrooms. Educ. Week **32**, s6–s8 (2012)

Bell, P., Bricker, L., Reeve, S., Zimmerman, H.T., Tzou, C.: Discovering and supporting successful learning pathways of youth in and out of school: accounting for the development of everyday expertise across settings. In: Bevan, B., Bell, P., Stevens, R., Razfar, A. (eds.) LOST Opportunities: Learning in Out-of-School Time, pp. 119–140. Springer Netherlands, Dordrecht (2013). https://doi.org/10.1007/978-94-007-4304-5_9

Benson, P.: Language learning and teaching beyond the classroom: an introduction to the field. In: Benson, P., Reinders, H. (eds.) Beyond the Language Classroom, pp. 7–16. Palgrave Macmillan UK, London (2011). https://doi.org/10.1057/9780230306790_2

Berkling, K., Thomas, C.: Gamification of a Software Engineering course and a detailed analysis of the factors that lead to it's failure. In: 2013 International Conference on Interactive Collaborative Learning (ICL), pp. 525–530. IEEE (2013). https://doi.org/10.1109/ICL.2013.6644642

Berns, A., Gonzalez-Pardo, A., Camacho, D.: Game-like language learning in 3-D virtual environments. Comput. Educ. **60**, 210–220 (2013). https://doi.org/10.1016/j.compedu.2012.07.001

Crowley, K., Barron, B., Knutson, K., Martin, C.K.: Interest and the development of pathways to science. In: Ann Renninger, K., Nieswandt, M., Hidi, S. (eds.) Interest in Mathematics and Science Learning, pp. 297–313. American Educational Research Association (2015). https://doi.org/10.3102/978-0-935302-42-4_17

Davies, R.S., Dean, D.L., Ball, N.: Flipping the classroom and instructional technology integration in a college-level information systems spreadsheet course. Educ. Tech. Res. Dev. **61**, 563–580 (2013). https://doi.org/10.1007/s11423-013-9305-6

Deci, E.L., Ryan, R.M.: Handbook of Self-Determination Research. University Rochester Press (2004)

Deci, E.L., Ryan, R.M.: Intrinsic motivation and self-determination in human behavior. Springer Science & Business Media (2013)

De-Marcos, L., Domínguez, A., Saenz-de-Navarrete, J., Pagés, C.: An empirical study comparing gamification and social networking on e-learning. Comput. Educ. **75**, 82–91 (2014). https://doi.org/10.1016/j.compedu.2014.01.012

Dicheva, D., Dichev, C., Agre, G., Angelova, G.: Gamification in education: a systematic mapping study. J. Educ. Technol. Soc. **18**, 75–88 (2015)

Dörnyei, Z., Csizér, K.: Ten commandments for motivating language learners: results of an empirical study. Lang. Teach. Res. **2**(3), 203–229 (1998)

Dörnyei, Z.: New themes and approaches in second language motivation research. Annu. Rev. Appl. Linguist. **21**, 43–59 (2001). https://doi.org/10.1017/S0267190501000034

Gallistel, R., Pashler, H.E., Pashler, H.: Stevens' Handbook of Experimental Psychology: Learning, Motivation, and Emotion. John Wiley & Sons, Incorporated (2004)

Hanus, M.D., Fox, J.: Assessing the effects of gamification in the classroom: a longitudinal study on intrinsic motivation, social comparison, satisfaction, effort, and academic performance. Comput. Educ. **80**, 152–161 (2015). https://doi.org/10.1016/j.compedu.2014.08.019

Hew, K.F., Huang, B., Chu, K.W.S., Chiu, D.K.: Engaging Asian students through game mechanics: findings from two experiment studies. Comput. Educ. **92**, 221–236 (2016). https://doi.org/10.1016/j.compedu.2015.10.010

Hsu, T.-C.: Learning English with augmented reality: do learning styles matter? Comput. Educ. **106**, 137–149 (2017). https://doi.org/10.1016/j.compedu.2016.12.007

Hwang, G.-J., Hsu, T.-C., Lai, C.-L., Hsueh, C.-J.: Interaction of problem-based gaming and learning anxiety in language students' English listening performance and progressive behavioral patterns. Comput. Educ. **106**, 26–42 (2017). https://doi.org/10.1016/j.compedu.2016.11.010

Kapp, K.M.: The Gamification of Learning and Instruction Fieldbook: Ideas into Practice. John Wiley & Sons (2013)

Khan, S.: The One World Schoolhouse: Education Reimagined. Twelve (2012)

Lai, C., Hu, X., Lyu, B.: Understanding the nature of learners' out-of-class language learning experience with technology. Comput. Assist. Lang. Learn. **31**, 114–143 (2018). https://doi.org/10.1080/09588221.2017.1391293

McGonigal, J.: Reality is Broken: Why Games Make us Better and How They can Change the World. Penguin (2011)

O'Flaherty, J., Phillips, C.: The use of flipped classrooms in higher education: a scoping review. The Internet High. Educ. **25**, 85–95 (2015). https://doi.org/10.1016/j.iheduc.2015.02.002

Richards, J.C.: The changing face of language learning: learning beyond the classroom. RELC J. **46**, 5–22 (2015)

Robson, K., Plangger, K., Kietzmann, J.H., McCarthy, I., Pitt, L.: Is it all a game? understanding the principles of gamification. Bus. Horiz. **58**, 411–420 (2015). https://doi.org/10.1016/j.bushor.2015.03.006

Ryan, R.M., Deci, E.L.: Intrinsic and extrinsic motivations: Classic definitions and new directions. Contemp. Educ. Psychol. **25**, 54–67 (2000). https://doi.org/10.1006/ceps.1999.1020

Schunk, D.H., Zimmerman, B.J. (eds.): Motivation and self-regulated learning. Routledge (2012). https://doi.org/10.4324/9780203831076

Stories of Seven 300s – Enhance students' reading comprehension skills with Reading Battle (RB) research findings - All News - Media – HKU. https://www.hku.hk/press/news_detail_14836.html. Last accessed 7 Nov 2022

Werbach, K., Hunter, D.: The Gamification Toolkit: Dynamics, Mechanics, and Components for the Win. University of Pennsylvania Press (2015)

# Using Video Dubbing to Foster EFL College Students' English News Broadcasting Ability

Meng-lian Liu(✉)

Laboratory of Language and Artificial Intelligence, Guangdong University of Foreign Studies,
Guangzhou 510420, China
Lmenglian@gdufs.edu.cn

**Abstract.** While previous studies have focused on the outcomes of using dubbing apps to foster learner's development of English news broadcasting ability, this study, grounded in cognitive apprenticeship (CA), is an investigation of the learning processes, which included modeling, coaching, scaffolding, articulation, reflection, and exploration, involved in the use of a dubbing approach. Participants included 216 college students at a university in the mainland China. Data included deep speaking pre-and post-test scores, initial and final dubbing videos, learning logs, and reflective essays. The results showed that after engaging in video dubbing the students improved their English-speaking and English news broadcasting ability, in terms of accuracy and fluency. Coaching and modeling were ranked as the two most useful processes which supported students as they improved their English-news broadcasting ability through repeatedly listening, echoing, and imitating. Implications and limitations of the study are discussed.

**Keywords:** Video dubbing · EFL · English News-broadcasting ability ·
cognitive apprenticeship

## 1 Introduction

Speaking is the most demanding skills among the main language skills because it is commonly equated with knowing a language [1]. Many researchers have claimed that speaking is considered to be the most crucial skill among the four language competences of every language [2]. English speaking, however, may be a challenging for English as a Foreign Language (EFL) learners [3] as it involves combining knowledge of vocabulary, grammar, semantic rules et al. with communication skills. EFL learners have to spend much time on speaking training in order to improve English speaking skills.

Teaching the spoken language has long been a challenge for EFL teachers because of many factors (e.g. Limited hours, heavy learning burdens). To find a solution to EFL learners' needs for ample speaking practice in authentic contexts, different types of rehearsed speaking activities (such as shadowing, repetition, mirroring, and elicited imitation) are alternative ways of practicing spoken English [4]. Meanwhile, some new mediated ways, such as video creation [5] and video dubbing [6] are also integrated into the language learning contexts to facilitate students' speaking ability. These activities

C. S. González-González et al. (Eds.): ICWL 2022/SETE 2022, LNCS 13869, pp. 375–382, 2023.
https://doi.org/10.1007/978-3-031-33023-0_35

are proved to be successful as they can provide authentic language use opportunities for learners to go through constant meaningful language input and output practices [7].

This paper focuses on effect analysis of English video news based dubbing activities in Chinese EFL undergraduates' course learning which is *A Critical Approach to English News*. By using cognitive apprenticeship(CA) as the theoretical framework, this research wants to explore whether the students can enhance English news broadcasting capability after the experiment. The following research questions guided the study:

a. What is the impact of English video news dubbing on EFL students' English news broadcasting ability?
b. To what extent does CA-supported process in the video dubbing process affect EFL students' English news broadcasting ability?

## 2  Literature Review

### 2.1  Cognitive Apprenticeship

Cognitive apprenticeship(CA) is a theoretical framework that allows learners to learn from an experienced person by cognitively internalizing knowledge while engaging in an activity in which they are interested [8]. It is a method of teaching aimed primarily at teaching the processes that experts use to handle complex tasks. The focus of this learning-through-guided-experience is on cognitive and metacognitive skills, rather than on the physical skills and processes of traditional apprenticeships.

There are six processes for cognitive apprenticeship which are modelling, coaching, scaffolding, articulation, reflection, and exploration. Modeling means a strand of behavioral modelling whereby learning occurs through observation, and then the leaner will reciprocate the behavior (such as imitating it) without any comment or reinforcement of the behaviors. Coaching means the skilled master teach or guide the novice how to do through a wide range of activities. Scaffolding is the support the master gives apprentices in carrying out a task. This can range from doing almost the entire task for them to giving occasional hints as to what to do next. Articulation is discussing one's thought process with others with the aim of making thinking visible. Reflection allows students to "compare their own problem-solving processes with those of an expert, another student, and ultimately, an internal cognitive model of expertise" [9]. A technique for reflection could be to examine the past performances of both expert and novice and to highlight similarities and differences. The goal of reflection is for students to look back and analyze their performances with a desire for understanding and improvement towards the behavior of an expert. Exploration involves giving students room to problem solve on their own and teaching students exploration strategies.

To summarize, cognitive apprenticeship has been widely used as the theoretical framework to support effective learning in different areas. The study chooses CA as the theoretical framework, while modeling and reflection will be mainly discussed in it.

### 2.2  Video Dubbing and EFL Speaking Training

Originally, dubbing means a way of translating and dubbing films, cartoons and TV shows when the original language is replaced and the other is completely superimposed on the video. Dubbing is a particularly powerful didactic tool because it involves "not only the construction of more or less parallel texts, but also a process of reception and production of linguistically and culturally complex objects, enriched with extra-verbal elements" [10] It can be a compelling language learning tool if students participate in the dubbing process themselves.

Video dubbing, also known as lip-synchronized dubbing, enables learners to substitute the speech of characters in videos with their own voices [11]. It offers learners a chance to approximate the intonation, pronunciation, and speed of native English speakers by imitating them so that it has been accepted into language classroom to support learners' English-speaking development [12].

There are some studies which use video dubbing to help EFL students' speaking skills. Mandasari [13] and Martinsen [14] reported that video dubbing could improve learners' English-speaking performances such as vocabulary enhancement, phonology comprehension and phoneme perception. Burston [15] found that learners selected the videos they are interested and monitored autonomously to improve their oral performance by re-dubbing as often as needed to get the best possible results. Other studies which revealed that video dubbing mobile apps have positive effects on learners' English-speaking skills development in terms of pronunciation [16], phonetics [17] and oral performances [18]. Huang [19] found accomplishing video-dubbing tasks could enhance English speaking proficiency, reduce foreign language anxiety and increase group cohesion. The research result of Jao et al. [20] showed that after engaging in video dubbing the students improved their English-speaking ability, in terms of accuracy and fluency. The study also used cognitive apprenticeship theory and discovered that coaching and modeling were ranked as the two most useful processes which supported students as they improved their English-speaking ability through repeatedly listening, echoing, and imitating.

In summary, the previous studies mainly focused on the effects of video dubbing approach on EFL learners' speaking performances, less have seen on the improvement of their oral English news broadcasting ability by application of video dubbing from the perspective of language teaching and learning. Therefore, as mentioned above, this study is an exploration of the impact of the processes of a video dubbing approach with CA theory on EFL college students' development of English news broadcasting ability in a college English course in China.

## 3   Method

### 3.1   Participants

A group of 62 Chinese EFL college students who are sophomore participated in this study. 32 students served as the experimental group (Class A) and another 30 as the control group (Class B). They are all less commonly taught language (LCTL) students. The majors of Class A are Turkish, Persian and Hebrew and those of Class B are Arabic, Urdu, Hindi.

## 3.2   Research Design

**This Study Involved an 8-Week Video English News Listening and Exercise Doing activity.** One piece of English news is distributed every week to both Class A and B on the self-learning website, and all students are required to listen to the news and do exercises according to the news content. It last 8 weeks.

**Simulated English News Broadcast Self-Training and News Watching Together with Exercise Doing.** During the 8 weeks, the students of Class A are asked to do the following tasks: a) Watch the English news and write down some information such as the features of the reporter's pronunciation and intonation, the tone, the speed and the body language. Watch how the reporter does with those noted parts. b) Do simulated English news broadcast self-training, and think carefully the noted parts, try to do just like the news reporter do. The Class B are asked to listen to the distributed news and finish the exercises attached and meanwhile to summarize the news by recording their speaking and upload to the website. They are also asked to explore some extra news connected with the given topic to have an Extensive listening.

**Video Dubbing Activity.** Dubbing based on English news videos was carried out for Class A every two weeks. They will use a dubbing app to do this and save their dubbing work through the app. They will also do live dubbing about the same news in class. And Class B are asked to summarize the news, record their speaking summary and upload it to the website at the same week time.

**Speaking and Broadcasting Assessment Criteria.** The study chooses China's Standards of English language Ability- oral expression rubric as the speaking assessment criteria. In order to be easily controlled, the study chooses the following four major criteria for each dubbing: pronunciation, accuracy, fluency, communication capability and matching degree with the original reporter.

**Questionnaire Design.** Design a questionnaire to obtain the students' attitude as well as effect after the experiment. It concludes 10 questions, in which 4 are open.

## 3.3   Procedures and Data Collection

This study is undertaken in three phases and the procedures are like the followings.

**Do Speaking Achievement Pre-test.** Carry out English speaking achievement pre-test to both Class A and B. Class A meanwhile will do a short English news dubbing pre-test. Save all the scores of pre-test which gives the beginning level of all the students.

**8-Week Video English News Listening, Watching and Dubbing Activity.** Both Class A and B are asked to listen to the distributed news and finish the exercises attached it. Then Class A do the dubbing self-training and live dubbing activities while Class B do summary speaking and extensive news watching activities.

**Do Speaking Achievement Post-test.** Carry out speaking achievement post-test to both Class A and B. Class A also will do a short English news dubbing post-test. Save the post-test scores which give the end level of all the students.

**Questionnaire.** Distributed 32 questionnaires and received 32 valid ones. The questionnaire return rate was 100%.

# 4  Results

## 4.1  The Impact of English Video News Dubbing on EFL Students' English News Broad-Casting Ability

**The Comparison of the Two Classes in Pre- and Post-test in Terms of Being Pertinent to the Topic of the Effect of English Video News Dubbing on EFL Students' English News Broadcasting Ability, That Class A do Better than Class B.** The result of the pre-test shows that there are 19 students in Class A (experimental group) whose English spoken language are regarded as good, while in Class B, there are also 19 students. The percentage in different class is 59.4% and 63.3% respectively. It shows, in terms of being pertinent to the topic who are better while speaking English as well as English news reporting, the students in both classes are almost at the same level. In the post-test, the number of good students in Class A is 29, while in Class B is 25, with the percentage 90.6% and 83.3% respectively. The number as well as the percentage in Class A is higher than that in Class B, which shows that the students in Class A do better than Class B after the experiment. It just answers the first research question that English video news dubbing is effective in improving EFL learners' English new broadcast ability. Table 1 shows the comparison of the good student's number and percentage of two classes in pre-test and post-test in terms of the effect of English video news dubbing on EFL students' English news broad-casting ability.

**Table 1.  Effect of English video news dubbing**

| number and percentage of the good students | | |
|---|---|---|
| | pre-test | post-test |
| Class A | 19 (59.4%) | 29 (90.6%) |
| Class B | 19 (63.3%) | 25 (83.3%) |

The final exam results comparison in the semester also shows this point. The following Table 2 reflects the comparison of the final exam scores of the courses learning between the experiment Class A and control group of Class B. The proportion of achievements in Class A is 100%, Class B is 93%. The results show that the scores of the students in Class A are generally higher than that of Class B.

**Table 2.** Final exam comparison

Proportion of achievements (%)

| Class | Rate | Excellent | Good | General | Pass | Failed |
|-------|------|-----------|------|---------|------|--------|
| A | 100 | 4 | 23 | 3 | 1 | 0 |
| B | 93 | 2 | 20 | 5 | 2 | 2 |

**Within-group Comparison of Pre-test and Post-test in Experimental Group.** There are great changes within-group comparison of pre-test and post-test in the experimental class. By using the four major assessment criteria for each dubbing: pronunciation (P), accuracy (A), fluency (F), communication capability (C) and matching degree with the original reporter (M), we can get the kinds of scores. Table 3 shows the difference at the same group comparison. It shows after the video news dubbing, the pronunciation, accuracy, fluency, communication capability and match degree with the original news of the experimental Class all increase. The match degree grows abrupt, which means the student have an excellent result for this item after English video news dubbing. Then are the fluency and communication capability, both of them rise greatly. All of these point to the result that English video news dubbing can greatly improve EFL students' English news broadcasting ability.

**Table 3.** Within-group comparison

Mean and growth rate of the pre- and post-test with Class A

| | Pronunciation | Accuracy | Fluency | Communication capability | Match degree |
|---|---------------|----------|---------|--------------------------|--------------|
| pre-test | 82 | 65 | 63 | 61 | 45 |
| post-test | 90 | 88 | 90 | 87 | 80 |
| rate | 9.80% | 35.38% | 42.86% | 42.62% | 77.80% |

## 4.2 Modeling Plays the Strongest Role in Improving English News Learners' Speaking Tone, Body Language and Communication Capability

One of the result the questionnaire shows is that modeling plays the strongest role in enhancing EFL learners' speaking tone, speed and communication capability, especially in English new broadcasting capability construction. News broadcast ability is a professional skill that requires hard training, so as English speaking skills. Modeling just has the function of letting expert showing how a task is completed. The new learners or the novice can just observe the experts both how to do by showing both skills and attributes. English news broadcast is different from general English speaking. How to report in a suitable and energetic tone with a not too slowly or too fast speed, how to report with a neutral accent and how to use communication capabilities like eye contact and other body language skillfully? All of these are behavioral performance and language learners can get these experience and dealing methods by watching and imitating how the experts do. And video dubbing is just the suitable way to satisfy the requirements of English news learning and broadcasting in EFL context.

### 4.3 Reflection Plays an Important Role in Improving English News Learners' Pronunciation, Intonation, Accents and Dialects

Another result the questionnaire shows is that reflection plays an important role in enhancing EFL learners' pronunciation and intonation while reporting English news. English news broadcast is different from general English speaking. For pronunciation and intonation, the reporters always enunciate each word carefully by pronouncing each word fully and correctly with a not too slowly or too fast speed. They also use a neutral accent, avoid slang and colloquialism and stay away from filler words like "um" and "uh". All of these are behavioral performance and language learners can get these experience and dealing methods by watching, imitating and reflecting how the experts do. By reflection, learners can compare the experienced performance with his own and adjust their methods so as to gain the effective to go on training.

## 5   Conclusion and Discussion

The present study set out to explore the effect of employing video dubbing as a cognitive apprenticeship strategy on Chines EFL students to foster their English news broadcasting ability. A quasiexperiment is carried out, research data are collected and analyzed. It can be concluded that the approach of English video news dubbing is efficient in enhancing Chinese EFL students' English news broadcasting ability. While Modeling plays the strongest role in improving English news learners' speaking tone, body language and communication capability, reflection is more powerful in improving English news learners' pronunciation, intonation, accents and dialects.

There are still some questions to be discussed for the future study such as enhancing the accuracy of pre-test and post-test result. Much work should be done to improve the test. For specific function analysis of more tools of Cognitive apprenticeship for Chinese EFL learners, it need to study deeply. The study sample also needs to be expanded.

## References

1. Dincer, A., Dariyemez, T.: Proficient speakers of English as a foreign language: a focus-group study. IAFOR J. Educ. **8**(1), 83–99 (2020)
2. Chien, S.Y., Hwang, G.J., Jong, M.S.Y.: Effects of peer assessment within the context of spherical video-based virtual reality on EFL students' English-Speaking performance and learning perceptions. Comput. Educ. **146**, 103751 (2020)
3. Amoah, S., Yeboah, J.: The speaking difficulties of Chinese EFL learners and their motivation towards speaking the English language. J. Lang. Linguist. Stud. **17**(1), 56–69 (2021)
4. Li, X.: Teaching EFL learners shadowing for listening: Developing learners' bottom-up skills. Yo Hamada, vol. 32, pp. 185–186. Porta Linguarum (2017)

5. Chen, K.T.C.: The effects of technology-mediated TBLT on enhancing the speaking abilities of university students in a collaborative EFL learning environment. Appl. Linguist. Rev. **12**(2), 331–352 (2019)
6. Pamungkas, F.D.: How video dubbing can improve students' speaking pronunciation. ETERNAL (Engl., Teach. Learn. Res. J.) **5**(1), 41 (2019). https://doi.org/10.24252/Eternal.V51.2019.A4
7. Li, X.: Teaching EFL learners shadowing for listening: Developing learners' bottom-up skills. Porta Linguarum Revista Interuniversitaria De Didáctica De Las Lenguas Extranjeras **32**, 185–186 (2019)
8. Collins, A., Brown, J.S., Holum, A.: Cognitive apprenticeship: Making thinking visible. Am. Educ. **15**(3), 6–11 (1991)
9. Collins, A., Brown, J.S., Newman, S.E.: Cognitive apprenticeship: Teaching the craft of reading, writing and mathematics (Technical Report No. 403). BBN Laboratories, Cambridge, MA. Centre for the Study of Reading, University of Illinois, Jan, 1987
10. Heiss, C.: La traduzione filmica come pratica didattica. In: Bollettieri Bosinelli, R.M., Heiss, C., Soffritti, M., Bernardini, S. (eds.) La traduzione multimediale. Quale traduzione per quale testo? pp. 183–196. CLUEB, Bologna (2000)
11. Lertola, J.: Audiovisual Translation in the Foreign Language Classroom: Applications in the Teaching of English and Other Foreign Languages. Research-publishing.net (2019)
12. Burston, J.: Video dubbing projects in the foreign language curriculum. CALICO J. **23**(1), 79–92 (2005)
13. Mandasari, Z., Rochsantiningsih, D., Sarosa, T.: Improving students' speaking skill through video dubbing. Engl. Educ. J. **5**(3), 7–35 (2017)
14. Martinsen, R., Montgomery, C., Willardson, V.: The effectiveness of videobased shadowing and tracking pronunciation exercises for foreign language learners. Foreign Lang. Ann. **50**(4), 661–680 (2017)
15. Burston, J.: Video dubbing projects in the foreign language curriculum. CALICO J. **23**(1), 79–92 (2005)
16. Lv, S.: A flipped design of college english speaking class in the perspective wisdom teaching. In: 2nd International Conference on Judicial, Administrative and Humanitarian Problems of State Structures and Economic Subjects (JAHP 2017), Atlantis Press (2017)
17. Wu, H., Ekstam, J.: Beyond parroting: using English fun dubbing to improve English oral performance. Chin. J. Appl. Linguist. **44**(2), 203–218 (2021). https://doi.org/10.1515/CJAL-2021-0012
18. Zhang, S.: Mobile English learning: an empirical study on an APP, English fun dubbing. Int. J. Emerg. Technol. Learn. (IJET) **11**, 4–8 (2016). https://doi.org/10.3991/ijet.v11i12.6314
19. Huang, H.-T.D.: Investigating the influence of video-dubbing tasks on EFL learning. Lang. Learn. Technol. **26**(1), 1–20 (2022)
20. Jao, C.Y., Yeh, H.C., Huang, W.R., Chen, N.S.: Using video dubbing to foster college students' English-speaking ability. Comput. Assist. Lang. Learn. (2022) https://doi.org/10.1080/09588221.2022.2049824

# The 6th International Symposium on User Modeling and Language Learning (UMLL 2022)

# Exploring Learning Engagement of Higher Vocational College Students in MALL

Jie Ou[✉] [iD]

Guangdong Industry Polytechnic, Guangzhou 510300, Guangdong, China
2004107039@gdip.edu.cn

**Abstract.** Even though computers and mobile devices are widely applied to language teaching and learning, few attempts have been made to explore the learning engagement of higher vocational college students in MALL environment. This study set out to investigate learning engagement of higher vocational college students in MALL by using validated learning engagement scale. A total of 339 students were enrolled in the investigation. The data were analyzed from three dimensions: behavioral engagement, emotional engagement and cognitive engagement. The results reveal that higher vocational college students' learning engagement in MALL environment is at a moderately high level. Additionally we found that there is no significant difference between male and female college students in English learning engagement. And there is no significant profession difference on emotional and cognitive engagement, but a significant profession difference exists on behavioral engagement in MALL environment.

**Keywords:** Learning Engagement · Higher Vocational College Students · Mobile-assisted Language Learning (MALL) · Investigation

## 1 Introduction

With the rapid development of Internet and information technology, mobile devices are widely used among college students. Mobile learning becomes a new way of online learning. Smart phone becomes an important tool for college students to get information and for entertainment. Because of the flexibility and ease of access, mobile learning has been integrated with language learning and teaching. Mobile-assisted language learning(MALL) mode has emerged as a widespread learning mode for EFL learners. More recent attention has focused on the provision of using smartphone in language learning [1, 2].

Learning engagement refers to the positive, fulfilling, learning-related state of mind that a learner puts into the learning process [3]. Learning engagement has been considered as an effective indicator that reflects the quality of online school education [3, 4]. However, a major problem in language learning is low level of engagement. Low levels of engagement have been found in quite a few studies on MALL [5, 6]. Therefore, it is of great practical significance to explore the factors that may influence student engagement in mobile learning. While some research about learning engagement has been carried out in China, there have been few empirical investigations into higher vocational college students. The aim of this essay is to investigate the overall situation on student engagement in higher vocational college and seek to obtain data which will help to strengthen students' engagement in MALL, and ultimately improve their independent learning ability.

In the literature, student engagement can be defined as a meta-construct that includes behavioral, emotional and cognitive engagement [7]. The three dimensions of engagement are closely interrelated. Behavioral engagement is relating to positive conduct in class and at school, involvement at academic tasks, and participation in school activities [7, 8]. Behaviors include engaging in class event, attending classes, following the rules and performing tasks. Emotional engagement relates to the extent of positive (and negative) reactions to teachers, classmates, academics or school [9]. Emotional engagement includes students' affective reactions such as happiness, sadness, boredom, anxiety, and interest [7, 8]. Cognitive engagement is concerned with psychological investment in learning and strategic learning [8, 9].

Mobile technology provides various resources and tools for language learning that encourage learners to be more motivated, autonomous, and socially interactive [1]. But students may not maintain constant high level of learning engagement in MALL, especially higher vocational college students. In compared with undergraduate students, most higher vocational college students are enrolled because of lower scores. Therefore, their academic achievement and English proficiency is not very high. According to some research, their learning motivation is insufficient, and some of them lack effective learning methods and self-control [10, 11]. On the other hand, it is found that higher vocational college students' learning values tend to be more practical and they hope to learn practical technology and practical skills [12].

Gender variation exists in school students' motivation levels, engagement and interaction behaviour to learn English when using mobile apps [13]. Among the personal factors, gender is identified to be a predictor to explain the differences in students' attitudes toward MALL [14]. However, there is a dearth of studies on gender-based engagement for MALL involving higher vocational college students.

Most studies in the field of student engagement have only focused on undergraduates. In the study, we set out to answer the following questions:

(1) What is the overall situation of higher vocational college students' learning engagement in MALL?
(2) Is there any gender or profession difference of higher vocational college students' learning engagement in MALL?

## 2  Method

### 2.1  Participants

The participants in this study are college students from a higher vocational college in Guangzhou, China. A total of 424 questionnaires were sent out, 424 were returned and 339 were valid, with effective recovery of 80%.

The data of 339 students were analyzed in the survey. All the participants have one or two-year experience of using mobile devices in English classes. The data can be seen in Table 1.

**Table 1.** Frequency and percentage of the participants by gender and major

| Items | Categories | N | Percent (%) |
|---|---|---|---|
| Gender | Female | 219 | 64.60 |
| | Male | 120 | 35.40 |
| Major | English major | 41 | 12.09 |
| | liberal arts | 89 | 26.25 |
| | science and engineering | 165 | 48.67 |
| | art | 44 | 12.98 |
| Total | | 339 | 100.0 |

## 2.2 Instrument

Many researchers have utilised validated self-reported scales to measure learning engagement [2, 15–17]. Interviews and observations are also common methods for assessing students engagement [9, 19].

The instrument of the study was adapted from existing validated scales. The original scales of online learning engagement can be used in MALL learning environment. Thereby, we only modified the items based on MALL learning environment. The scale used a 5-point Likert rating (5 = strongly agree, 4 = agree, 3 = neither agree nor disagree, 2 = disagree, 1 = strongly disagree). The learning engagement scale was adopted and modified from Dixson (2015) [15], Shuang Li &Chen Yu (2015) [16] and Kuo, *et al.* (2021) [17]. The 23-item scale is designed to measure three types of learning engagement in terms of behavioral engagement, emotional engagement and cognitive engagement.

All analyses were carried out using online statistical analysis software SPSSAU [18]. First we evaluate the validity and reliability of the scale. Next we explore the overall situations of learning engagement through descriptive analysis, independent *t* test, one way ANOVA analysis of variance.

# 3 Results and Discussion

## 3.1 Reliability and Validity Test Analysis

The learning engagement scale contains three dimensions: behavioral engagement (6 items), emotional engagement (7 items) and cognitive engagement (6 items).

As can be seen from Table 2: the reliability coefficient value are 0.909, 0.917, 0.867 respectively, which are all above 0.8, thus indicating a high quality of reliability of the study data.

**Table 2.** Reliability Statistics

Cronbach Alpha

|  | N of Items | n | Cronbach α |
|---|---|---|---|
| behavioral engagement | 6 | 339 | 0.909 |
| emotional engagement | 7 | 339 | 0.917 |
| cognitive engagement | 6 | 339 | 0.867 |

The validity was verified using KMO and Bartlett's test. The KMO value was 0.950, with a KMO value greater than 0.8, indicating a good validity.

### 3.2 Overall Situation of Higher Vocational College Students' Learning Engagement

The basic principles followed in this study are: the higher the score, the higher level of engagement; the lower the score, the lower the level of engagement. The scores of 1–5 indicate respectively "strongly disagree" to "strongly agree". Theoretically, the average value is 3 points. Higher than the theoretical average means that students have a better learning engagement.

Table 3 shows that students maintain a moderately high level of engagement in MALL environment. The scores of cognitive engagement, behavioral engagement, and emotional engagement are all above 3. This indicates that students have a better learning engagement. From the perspective of each dimension, emotional engagement has the highest average mean value(M = 4.001), which indicates that students have positive attitudes to teachers, classmates and course contents in MALL environment. The lowest is the average mean value (M = 3.901) of cognitive engagement, which reflects that students' learning strategies in MALL environment needs improvement. The average mean value of behavioral engagement is 3.970, which aims at exploring students' learning activities and performance in class.

**Table 3.** Descriptive statistics of overall learning engagement

| Items | N | Min | Max | Mean | Std. Deviation |
|---|---|---|---|---|---|
| behavioral engagement | 339 | 2.000 | 5.000 | 3.970 | 0.678 |
| emotional engagement | 339 | 1.143 | 5.000 | 4.001 | 0.636 |
| cognitive engagement | 339 | 1.000 | 5.000 | 3.901 | 0.594 |

### 3.3 Descriptive Analysis of Behavioral Engagement

The study investigated the current situations of higher vocational college students' behavioral engagement in the scale (item B1–B6), including participation, interaction and absorption in MALL. As shown in Table 4, item B4 "I am actively involved in chatting, discussing, or making comments in online English discussion forums, or communicating with teachers and other students via email." has the lowest average value (M = 3.844), showing a lack of interaction activities for students in class. The English proficiency of higher vocational college students is generally not high. Most students are shy to communicate with teachers and their peers. The highest average value is item B1 (M = 4.127) "I follow and keep up with the progress of the online class.", showing that students get involved in class when using mobile devices. The average value of item B5 "I always listen carefully and take good notes when using mobile devices in class." is 3.914, indicating that students are not focused enough in class when using smartphones.

The rest of average value are as follows: item B2 "I complete the online videos and exercises on time" (M = 4.097), item B3 "I listen and read the English material delivered carefully."(M = 3.971), item B6 "If I have a problem, I do something to figure it out" (M = 3.864).

Table 4. Descriptive statistics of behavioral engagement

| Items | N of samples | Min | Max | Mean | Std. Deviation |
|---|---|---|---|---|---|
| B1 | 339 | 2.000 | 5.000 | 4.127 | 0.802 |
| B2 | 339 | 2.000 | 5.000 | 4.097 | 0.795 |
| B3 | 339 | 1.000 | 5.000 | 3.971 | 0.849 |
| B4 | 339 | 2.000 | 5.000 | 3.844 | 0.861 |
| B5 | 339 | 1.000 | 5.000 | 3.914 | 0.778 |
| B6 | 339 | 1.000 | 5.000 | 3.864 | 0.819 |

### 3.4 Descriptive Analysis of Emotional Engagement

In terms of emotional engagement, the scale includes 7 items (E1-E7), covering desire, interest, attitudes and values in MALL. As can be seen in Table 5, item E1 "I am willing to use mobile devices to assist English learning." has the highest average value (M = 4.118), suggesting that students have a strong desire to use mobile devices in class. The lowest average value is item E5 (M = 3.912) "I like using mobile devices to complete English exercises.", showing that students are not interested in using mobile devices to do exercises or submit an assignment. Item E6 (M=3.976) "My experience in MALL class has had a significant impact on my academic and professional development." and item E7(M=4.003) "What I learned in MALL class is very important to me." were designed to measure students' values. The results of item E6 and E7 reflect that students are aware of the significance of learning experience and technique.

The rest of average value are as follows: item E2 "I feel that using mobile devices to assist in English learning is convenient and fun." (M = 4.074), item E3 "I like to use mobile devices in English language learning process."(M = 3.979), item E4 " I am interested in the course content on my mobile device." (M = 3.944).

**Table 5.** Descriptive statistics of emotional engagement

| Items | N of samples | Min | Max | Mean | Std. Deviation |
|---|---|---|---|---|---|
| E1 | 339 | 1.000 | 5.000 | 4.118 | 0.744 |
| E2 | 339 | 1.000 | 5.000 | 4.074 | 0.787 |
| E3 | 339 | 1.000 | 5.000 | 3.979 | 0.794 |
| E4 | 339 | 1.000 | 5.000 | 3.944 | 0.777 |
| E5 | 339 | 1.000 | 5.000 | 3.912 | 0.849 |
| E6 | 339 | 1.000 | 5.000 | 3.976 | 0.737 |
| E7 | 339 | 1.000 | 5.000 | 4.003 | 0.760 |

## 3.5 Descriptive Analysis of Cognitive Engagement

In three dimensions, cognitive engagement has the lowest average value. The result is not consistent with the research conclusions of Zhen-zhen, Chen (2019) [2]. Zhen-zhen finds that cognitive engagement is higher than behavioral engagement among undergraduates [2].

In the investigation, item C1-C6 were designed to measure students' learning strategies in MALL. As shown in Table 6, item C1 "Even without the weekly quizzes, I still use mobile device to assist English learning" has the lowest average value (M = 3.805), which indicates a lack of self-motivation in language learning. Item C6 "When encountering setbacks in studies, I will find some ways to strengthen and regain confidence."(M = 3.959) had the highest average value, showing that students can use emotion management strategies to adjust emotions. The average value are: item C3 "Before using mobile devices for English tests, I will plan how to review." (M = 3.867), C5 "I can organize study time when using mobile devices to assist English learning" (M = 3.897). The results of item C3 and C5 indicates insufficient self-directed learning abilities of higher vocational students.

The rest of average value are: item C2 "I try to look for some course-related information on other resources such as videos, articles, and news, etc." (M = 3.929), item C4 "I will search for relevant materials and ask for help when meeting problems." (M = 3.947)

**Table 6.** Descriptive statistics of cognitive engagement

| Items | N of samples | Min | Max | Mean | Std. Deviation |
|---|---|---|---|---|---|
| C1 | 339 | 1.000 | 5.000 | 3.805 | 0.859 |
| C2 | 339 | 1.000 | 5.000 | 3.929 | 0.774 |
| C3 | 339 | 1.000 | 5.000 | 3.867 | 0.756 |
| C4 | 339 | 1.000 | 5.000 | 3.947 | 0.716 |
| C5 | 339 | 1.000 | 5.000 | 3.897 | 0.772 |
| C6 | 339 | 1.000 | 5.000 | 3.959 | 0.716 |

## 3.6 Comparison of Gender Differences in Learning Engagement

In this study, independent $t$ test was used to investigate gender differences of higher vocational college students' three dimensions of learning engagement. As Table 7 shows, the p-values of the variance between male and female students on behavioral, emotional and cognitive engagement are all above 0.05 (p > 0.05). It means that there is no significant difference between male and female students on their English learning engagement in MALL environment.

However, due to the large number gap between male and female students and the limited data available in the study, the result of "no significant difference" is only the result in this study. It does not represent the gender difference in students' learning engagement in a broader scope.

**Table 7.** Statistics of independent $t$ test on gender differences

|  | Gender (Mean ± Std. Deviation) | | t | p |
|---|---|---|---|---|
|  | Female (n = 219) | Male (n = 120) | | |
| behavioral engagement | 3.96 ± 0.67 | 3.99 ± 0.70 | −0.445 | 0.657 |
| emotional engagement | 4.02 ± 0.58 | 3.97 ± 0.73 | 0.708 | 0.480 |
| cognitive engagement | 3.90 ± 0.54 | 3.89 ± 0.68 | 0.164 | 0.870 |

* p < 0.05 ** p < 0.01

## 3.7 Comparison of Profession Differences in Learning Engagement

This study used one-way ANOVA to investigate profession differences of higher vocational college students' three dimensions of learning engagement. As can be seen in Table 8, the p-values of the variance of majors on emotional and cognitive engagement are all above 0.05 (p > 0.05). It means that there is no significant profession difference on emotional and cognitive engagement in MALL environment.

What is surprising is that p-value of the variance of majors on behavioral engagement presents a 0.05 level of significance (F = 2.995, p = 0.031). This finding was unexpected and suggests that there is a significant profession difference on behavioral engagement in MALL environment. The results show that art students and science and engineering students are significantly higher than English major students in terms of behavioral engagement.

**Table 8.** Statistics of one-way ANOVA on major differences

| | (Mean ± Std. Deviation) | | | | F | p |
|---|---|---|---|---|---|---|
| | English major (n = 41) | Liberal arts (n = 89) | Science and engineering (n = 165) | Art (n = 44) | | |
| behavioral engagement | 3.73 ± 0.56 | 3.91 ± 0.67 | 4.03 ± 0.69 | 4.10 ± 0.70 | 2.995 | 0.031* |
| emotional engagement | 3.95 ± 0.55 | 3.98 ± 0.58 | 3.98 ± 0.70 | 4.16 ± 0.58 | 1.023 | 0.383 |
| cognitive engagement | 3.82 ± 0.56 | 3.85 ± 0.56 | 3.91 ± 0.63 | 4.04 ± 0.54 | 1.311 | 0.271 |

* $p < 0.05$ ** $p < 0.01$

## 4 Conclusion

This study investigates the overall situation of higher vocational college students' learning engagement in MALL environment. First of all, the descriptive statistics reveal that higher vocational college students' learning engagement in MALL environment is not at a low level. The mean values of the three dimensions are ranging from 3.901 to 4.001. Emotional engagement performs best, with a mean score of 4.001, while cognitive engagement shows the lowest level (M = 3.901). The results indicate that higher vocational college students show positive engagement in learning, but students' learning strategies needs further improving.

Second, the findings show that there is no significant gender difference between male and female students on learning engagement in MALL environment. Third, the investigation shows that there is no significant profession difference on emotional and cognitive engagement, but a significant profession difference exists on behavioral engagement in MALL environment. The results show that art students and science and engineering students have a higher level of behavioral engagement than English major students. Limited data and scope may be one important factor for this result. The data was collected from one or several classes in one vocational college, not in a large scope. Another important reason is that learning engagement is influenced by a variety of factors. Individual and environmental elements should be considered [19]. Thus, the results may be influenced by the class learning atmosphere, environment, teaching method, interaction with peers or teachers. It is equally possible that students who have good academic results may be disengaged from learning tasks and school activities [20].

## 5 Limitations and Future Research

Derived from the theory of learning engagement and based on the results of the former research, this study investigated the overall situation of higher vocational college students' learning engagement in MALL environment. Our findings may not reflect all the phenomena in MALL environment. The main weakness of this study is the small sample size and limited scope. The investigation was conducted in one higher vocational college. Another limitation of this study is that the measurement of learning engagement has been conducted only via survey items and questionnaire.

In spite of its limitations, this study certainly adds to our understanding of the higher vocational college students' learning engagement in MALL environment. Further investigations, using a broader range of samples, could shed more light on students' learning engagement. Future studies could employ more rigorous data collection methods, such as teacher self-report and observation, student self-report observation, or stratified sampling to improve the data quality.

**Acknowledgement.** This work was financially supported by 1) 2021 Foreign Language Education Teaching Reform Project of Foreign Language Teaching Steering Committee of Vocational Colleges, Ministry of Education, "Research on the Construction of College English Learning Community in Educational Informatization" (Project number: WYJZW-2021-2059).

2) 2022 Education and Teaching Reform Project of Guangdong Industry Polytechnic (Project number: JG202212)

# References

1. Kim, H., Kwon, Y.: Exploring smartphone applications for effective mobile-assisted language learning. Multimed.-Assist. Lang. Learn. **15**(1), 31–57 (2012)
2. Chen, Z.-Z.: Student engagement in smartphone-assisted foreign language classroom. Technol. Enhanced Foreign Lang. Educ. **3**, 49–54 (2019)
3. Jung, Y., Lee, J.: Learning engagement and persistence in massive open online courses (MOOCS). Comput. Educ. **122**, 9–22 (2018)
4. Soffer, T., Cohen, A.: Students' engagement characteristics predict success and completion of online courses. J. Comput. Assist. Learn., **35**(3), 378–389 (2019)
5. García Botero, G., Questier, F., Zhu, C.: Self-directed language learning in a mobile-assisted, out-of-class context: do students walk the talk? Comput. Assist. Lang. Learn. **32**(1–2), 71–97 (2019)
6. Hanson, A.E.S., Brown, C.M.: Enhancing L2 learning through a mobile assisted spaced-repetition tool: an effective but bitter pill? Comput. Assist. Lang. Learn. **33**(1–2), 133–155 (2020)
7. Fredricks, J.A., Blumenfeld, P.C., Paris, A.H.: School engagement: potential of the concept, state of the evidence. Rev. Educ. Res. **74**(1), 59–109 (2004)
8. Zhang, Z.V., Hyland, K.: Student engagement with teacher and automated feedback on L2 writing. Assessing Writ. **36**, 90–102 (2018)
9. Fredricks, J.A., McColskey, W.: The measurement of student engagement: a comparative analysis of various methods and student self-report instruments. In: Handbook of Research on Student Engagement, pp. 763–782. Springer, Boston, MA.(2012)
10. Zhang, Y.: Study characteristics and countermeasures of students in higher vocational colleges. Educ. Modernization **5**(42), 316–317 (2018)
11. Chen, Q., Guo, L., Wang, J., Zhang, C.: Intelligence structure characteristics and learning ability improvement strategies of students in higher vocational colleges. Chin. Vocat. Tech. Educ. **35**, 95–97 (2013)
12. Wen, J.: Research and practice of higher vocational education countermeasure based on students' learning characteristics. Educ. Vocat. **5**, 173–174 (2014)

13. Rajendran, R., et al.: Impact of gender on motivation, engagement and interaction behavior in mobile assisted learning of English. In: 2020 IEEE 20th International Conference on Advanced Learning Technologies (ICALT). IEEE (2020)

14. Viberg, O., Grönlund, Åke.: Cross-cultural analysis of users' attitudes toward the use of mobile devices in second and foreign language learning in higher education: a case from Sweden and China. Comput. Educ. **69**, 169–180 (2013)

15. Dixson, M.: Measuring student engagement in the online course: the online student engagement scale (OSE). Online Learn. **19**(4), n4 (2015)

16. Li, S., Yu, C.: Development and implementation of distance student engagement scale. Open Educ. Res. **21**(6), 62–70 (2015)

17. Kuo, T.M., Tsai, C.C., Wang, J.C.: Linking web-based learning self-efficacy and learning engagement in MOOCs: the role of online academic hardiness. The Internet High. Educ. **51**, 100819 (2021)

18. The SPSSAU project: SPSSAU. (Version 22.0) [Online Application Software]. https://www.spssau.com (2022). Last accessed 1 Oct 2022

19. Yan, L., Chun, L.: A university based case study: the research on the overall situation and influencing factors of non-english major postgraduates' learning engagement. Sci. Soc. Res. **4**(1), 33–39 (2022)

20. Willms, J.D.: Student engagement at school: A sense of belonging and participation: Results from PISA 2000. Oecd (2003)

# Flipped Data Science Classrooms with Peer Instruction and Just-In-Time Teaching: Students' Perceptions and Learning Experiences

Haoran Xie[1] (iD), Xinyi Huang[2] (iD), Gary Cheng[2] (iD), Fu Lee Wang[3](✉) (iD),
and James Chit Ming Chong[1]

[1] Lingnan University, 8 Castle Peak Road, Tuen Mun, Hong Kong
hrxie@ieee.org, jameschong@ln.edu.hk
[2] The Education University of Hong Kong, 10 Lo Ping Road, Tai Po, New Territories, Hong Kong
{hxinyi,chengks}@eduhk.hk
[3] Hong Kong Metropolitan University, Homantin, Kowloon, Hong Kong
pwang@hkmu.edu.hk

**Abstract.** This paper focused on students' learning experiences in a flipped data science class integrated with peer instruction and just-in-time teaching. University students in Hong Kong participated in the research during the pandemic. Students' perceptions of the flipped learning mode were investigated by a 5-point Likert scale questionnaire. According to the results, most students felt they enjoyed learning with the flipped mode since it allowed them to learn flexibly and independently. The course materials (i.e., instructional videos, lecture notes, and in-class exercises) were well-designed, and students perceived the materials were useful and user-friendly. As suggested by the students, more time should be given to the pre-class learning activities. Based on the suggestions, the researchers provide practical implications on improving teaching in the flipped science class. This study demonstrates how to flip a data science class and proves its value on students' learning, providing implications for using flipped learning during the pandemic period.

**Keywords:** Flipped Learning · Peer Instruction · Just-in-time teaching

## 1 Introduction

Flipped classroom are commonly used in different educational fields. It refers to an instructional model that makes learning activities conducted in the classroom become home activities, whereas the homework to be finished after classes become classroom activities [1]. In this learning mode, students access learning via videos or other media at home and conduct hands-on activities during class [2]. However, face-to-face teaching cannot be achieved due to the pandemic issue. The flipped classroom is integrated with other online learning tools to support teaching and learning. Zoom, a web-based a video conferencing tool that allowed users to communicate synchronously, was chosen as

C. S. González-González et al. (Eds.): ICWL 2022/SETE 2022, LNCS 13869, pp. 395–402, 2023.
https://doi.org/10.1007/978-3-031-33023-0_37

an educational tool in higher education during the pandemic period [3]. With Zoom, online lectures, meetings, and webinars can be held. Beason-Abmayr et al. [4] flipped a physiology class with Zoom; similarly, Roy et al. [5] flipped a medical lesson with Zoom.

Computer science is one of the major educational field that adopted flipped learning [6]. It emphasized computational thinking and problem-solving abilities, while the current pedagogical approaches have failed to achieve these purposes [7]. In addition, teachers were difficult to adjust individual needs due to the student-center nature of computer science work [8]. It was challenging for instructors to conduct one-on-one class time. Therefore, this study aims to flip a data science class with peer instruction (PI) and just-in-time teaching (JiTT), which were the approaches based around problem-solving and collaborative learning [9]. Students' learning experiences and perceptions of flipped learning will be investigated. It helps practitioners understand students' attitudes towards the class and provides implications for conducting flipped learning during the pandemic period. The following questions guides the present research:

(1) What were students' attitudes towards a flipped classroom?
(2) How to further improved the flipped data science classroom?

## 2  Literature Review

### 2.1  Flipped Classroom

Flipped classrooms enhanced learning outcomes, enabled students to learn flexibly, and improved high-order thinking skills [1, 10], making researchers frequently adopt this method in higher education. For example, Awidi and Paynter [11] flipped an undergraduate biology course in their study. Results indicated that students were satisfied with the flipped approach. They reported that pre-class learning helped them construct knowledge because they could easily access information and resources, and clearly understand the assessment criteria. Zou et al. [12] integrated Wikipedia with flipped learning. It was found that students had a better learning outcome in a flipped mode outperformed comparing with the traditional mode. The flipped learning approach enabled students to have richer collaborative opportunities during class; therefore, they paid more effort to improve their wiki entries. Similarly, Hsieh et al. [13] flipped an English class and revealed that flipped classrooms motivated students to learn, enhanced students' academic performances, and engaged students in the learning tasks. Students tended to pay more effort in learning since they needed to plan their after-class time reasonably, resulting in self-regulated learning.

Studies also revealed several challenges of conducting flipped learning. Akçayır and Akçayır [1] reported that challenges of the flipped classroom from a pedagogical perspective included the inability to receive help while out of class, the inability of instructors to know students' learning progress, and inadequate guidelines for students to learn at home. Zou et al. [10] had similar findings that teachers could not guaranteed that students finished the pre-class learning tasks. From students' perspectives, they reported that flipped learning required additional time and effort at school and home [1,

13]. Students in Awidi and Paynter [11] were also unsatisfied with the design of the in-class learning activities. They claimed the activities were ineffective and the group size of discussion was too big. To address the issues above, additional learning approaches should be adopted.

## 2.2 Just-In-Time Teaching and Peer Instruction

Peer instruction (PI) is a teaching method developed in physics but successfully applied in computing [14]. It supported student-center learning by allowing students to construct knowledge based on a question-based approach with discussion [15]. In a PI class, the instructors posed a ConceptTest (a multiple-choice question), and students were required to answer them individually in the first place. Next, the learners discussed the same question and might revise their answers. The instructor facilitated the whole class discussion and provided further explanation [14, 16]. Both PI and computer science emphasized student-center learning, and hence, PI was frequently used in computer science education [14, 15].

Just-in-time teaching (JiTT) is a set of online pre-instruction assignments that prepare students before class, which extends classroom instruction via the Web [17]. It might include watching videos, completing tasks, and reporting learning difficulties regarding the assignments [9]. JiTT was regarded as a complement of PI as it provided feedback on students' learning progress at home [9, 17]. These two approaches were widely adopted in various education fields, and their significance was well recognized [e.g., 17–19]. Researchers also proved that integrating PI and JiTT in the flipped classroom helped enhance students learning since these approaches provide students to conduct individual and collaborative learning [9, 19]. As flipped learning and peer instruction were frequently adopted in computer science, it was essential to understand students' perceptions of these approaches. Furthermore, current studies mostly focus on either one of these approaches rather than combing PI and JiTT in a flipped computer science class, which requires further exploration of the usefulness of the combined approaches. To fill these gaps, this research was conducted to investigate students' learning experiences in a PI and JiTT-supported flipped data science class.

## 3 Methodology

This study was conducted in a semester-long computer science class (i.e., Data Structure and Object-oriented Programming) at a university in Hong Kong. The instructors would upload instructional videos and online exercises to the learning platform a few days before the class. Students needed to watch the videos and complete relevant exercises that promote critical thinking skills before coming to class. In this way, students have some basic understanding of the learning content. Due to the pandemic issue, the in-class learning activities would be conducted via Zoom. The instructor would quickly review the videos and deliver the key concepts to students in the first place. Next, students needed to finish the exercises by themselves without discussion. Examples and guidance would also be provided for guiding students. After that, students discussed the exercises with their groupmates. At the end of the lesson, the instructor reviewed all the answers and summed up the lesson. Questions that students had could also be raised at this stage.

After completing the class, students filled in an online questionnaire about their learning experiences in the flipped classroom. The first part of the questionnaire consists 3 questions that focus on students' experiences with the flipped model. 7 questions were included to investigate students' attitudes toward the course materials in the second part of the questionnaire. An open-ended question on how to improve the flipped classroom was also included in the questionnaire. The participants reported with reported their attitudes with a five-point Likert scale, ranging from 1 strongly disagree and 5 strongly agree. In total, 14 responses were received.

## 4  Results

As shown in Fig. 1, 50% of the participants felt that they enjoyed the flexibility of the flipped classroom, and 35.7% of the participants had a stronger sense of feelings. However, 14.3% of the participants had a neutral attitude toward this statement.

1. I like the flexibility of the flipped classroom because I could study the online materials anywhere and anytime.
14 responses

**Fig. 1.** Attitudes towards the flexibility of the flipped classroom

Participants also felt they had greater independence and control over learning, with 71.4% of participants sharing this opinion (Fig. 2). 21.4% of the students were neutral towards this opinion, and only 7.1% did not think they were more independent during flipped learning.

Regarding the perceptions towards JiTT and PI instruction activities, 50% of students had neutral attitudes towards them. Figure 3 also showed that 28.6% of the participants felt they enjoyed the activities, and 14.3% of the students strongly agreed with the statement. Some students did not enjoy those activities, with 7.1% of the total participants.

From the perspective of students' perceptions of the course materials, we divided them into pre-class learning activities, lecture notes, in-class reviews, and in-class exercises. Overall, most students had positive attitudes toward the pre-class learning activities, with 92.9% feeling the materials were useful, leaving and 7.1% of the participants being neutral about them. Similarly, 92.9% of students agreed that the lecture notes

2. I feel I have greater independence and control over my learning.
14 responses

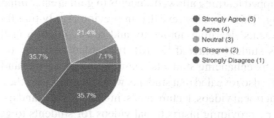

- ● Strongly Agree (5)
- ● Agree (4)
- ● Neutral (3)
- ● Disagree (2)
- ● Strongly Disagree (1)

**Fig. 2.** Interdependence and control over flipped learning

3. I enjoy the just-in-time-teaching and peer instruction activities (i.e., group discussion about in-class exercises).
14 responses

- ● Strongly Agree (5)
- ● Agree (4)
- ● Neutral (3)
- ● Disagree (2)
- ● Strongly Disagree (1)

**Fig. 3.** Students' perceptions of JiTT and PI instruction activities

were well-designed, and 7.1% held a neutral attitude. For the in-class review section, 50% of the participants felt it was helpful to consolidate their knowledge, and 42.9% of students strongly agreed with it. In addition, students agreed that the in-class exercises were useful and interesting, which accounted for 57.1%. Moreover, 35.7% of students strongly agree with the statement.

42.9% of the participants felt the learning materials increased their motivation, and 35.7% strongly agreed; 57.1% regarded the learning materials as user-friendly, and 21.4% agreed. Furthermore, it was showed that 64.3% of the participants agreed that the overall design was good, and 28.5^% strongly agreed with it, leaving 7.1% of participants to hold a neutral attitude.

Students also gave some suggestions to improve the flipped course. The common suggestion they provided was that more time should be given for the pre-class learning tasks and in-class exercises. Some students also suggested that the key concepts could be taught at the beginning of the semester since they were unfamiliar with them.

## 5 Discussion

The results showed that the participants had positive attitude of the flipped learning model. They enjoyed learning with this model since it allowed them to learn flexibly and independently. It was in consistent with the previous study that flipped classroom benefited students in allowing students to learn flexibly [1, 2]. It might be because that flipped classroom allowed students to learn anywhere and anytime. Our research also found that flipped learning allowed students to gain greater impendence and control over their learning. This was also revealed in previous study that flipped classrooms helped cultivate students' learning autonomy and self-regulation [10]. The nature of flipped learning was student-centered [2, 10]. It enabled students to pause and re-watch the videos, thereby enhancing students' learning independence and autonomy.

Our study also revealed that students were satisfied with the course materials, including the instructional videos, lecture notes, in-class review, and in-class exercises. We integrated JiTT by providing instructional videos for students to get a basic understanding of the concept before class so that students were well prepared for the in-class activities. It gave students a sense of ownership since the activities were tailored for their specific understandings of the topics [19]. Students were also asked to complete the in-class exercises and discuss with their peers, which was used to demonstrate PI. It was different from the traditional flipped approach in that students only received instructors' feedback without attempting to find out solutions [9]. Students were highly engaged in discussions to solve related issues and learned from each other [19]. Higher-order thinking and problem-solving abilities were developed during this process [1, 9], which was essential for computer science education. It showed that integrating PI and JiTT into flipped learning model enabled collaborative learning and provided adequate practice of critical thinking [9, 19], which helped overcome the common challenges identified in data science classrooms [8].

Students suggested that more time should be given to the pre-class learning activities. Akçayır and Akçayır [1], Karabulut-llgu et al. [2], and Zou et al. [10] also revealed a similar problem that students reported the workload of pre-class learning was heavy, which required more time for it. Therefore, we suggested that the practitioners upload the learning materials earlier to give students more time to complete them. Students in this study also reported that they were not engaged during group discussion since they were weak in coding. It was hard to engage all students in learning was another common problem in the flipped classroom [2]. In this case, a teacher-led class-wide discussion was needed. It provided students with more detailed and in-depth explanations, which was essential for students with lower learning abilities [14]. Therefore, the practitioner needs to further explain the learning content by conducting a whole-class discussion.

# 6  Conclusion

This study investigated students' learning experiences in a flipped data science classroom that integrated with PI and JiTT. It was found that students enjoyed the flipped learning model since it allowed them to learn flexibly. They held positive attitudes toward the learning materials (i.e., instructional videos, in-class exercises, and lecture notes) since they were useful and user-friendly. Further improvement of the flipped model included more time should be given to the pre-class learning activities, and more elaboration should be given on the key concepts.

However, our study had its limitations. First of all, the sample size was small. Future research could apply this model to a larger sample to get a generalizable result. In addition, we only adopted the quantitative method in investigating students' learning experiences. Future research might consider conducting an interview to get more in-depth analysis. Our research demonstrated how to flip a data science class with PI and JiTT. It helped solve common challenges in data science classes and could be adopted in practical classroom settings.

**Acknowledgement.** The research reported in this paper has been supported by the Teaching Development Grant (102489) from Lingnan University.

# References

1. Akçayır, G., Akçayır, M.: The flipped classroom: a review of its advantages and challenges. Comput. Educ. **126**, 334–345 (2018)
2. Karabulut-Ilgu, A., Jaramillo Cherrez, N., Jahren, C.T.: A systematic review of research on the flipped learning method in engineering education: flipped learning in engineering education. Br. J. Educ. Technol. **49**(3), 398–411 (2018). https://doi.org/10.1111/bjet.12548
3. Serhan, D.: Transitioning from face-to-face to remote learning: students' attitudes and perceptions of using zoom during COVID-19 pandemic. IJTES **4**, 335–342 (2020)
4. Beason-Abmayr, B., Caprette, D.R., Gopalan, C.: Flipped teaching eased the transition from face-to-face teaching to online instruction during the COVID-19 pandemic. Adv. Physiol. Educ. **45**, 384–389 (2021)
5. Roy, H., Ray, K., Saha, S., Ghosal, A.K.: A study on students' perceptions for online zoom-app based flipped class sessions on anatomy organised during the lockdown period of COVID-19 epoch. JCDR **14**(6), 1–4 (2020)
6. Hwang, G.-J., Yin, C., Chu, H.-C.: The era of flipped learning: promoting active learning and higher order thinking with innovative flipped learning strategies and supporting systems. Interact. Learn. Environ. **27**, 991–994 (2019)
7. Pirker, J., Riffnaller-Schiefer, M., Gütl, C.: Motivational active learning: engaging university students in computer science education. In: Proceedings of the Proceedings of the 2014 conference on Innovation & technology in computer science education – ITiCSE'14, pp. 297–302. ACM Press: Uppsala, Sweden (2014)
8. Yadav, A., Gretter, S., Hambrusch, S., Sands, P.: Expanding computer science education in schools: understanding teacher experiences and challenges. Comput. Sci. Educ. **26**, 235–254 (2016)
9. Zou, D., Xie, H.: Flipping an English writing class with technology-enhanced just-in-time teaching and peer instruction. Interact. Learn. Environ. **27**, 1127–1142 (2019)
10. Zou, D., Luo, S., Xie, H., Hwang, G.-J.: A systematic review of research on flipped language classrooms: theoretical foundations, learning activities, tools, research topics and findings. Comput. Assist. Lang. Learn. **35**, 1811–1837 (2020)
11. Awidi, I.T., Paynter, M.: The impact of a flipped classroom approach on student learning experience. Comput. Educ. **128**, 269–283 (2019)
12. Zou, D., Xie, H., Wang, F.L., Kwan, R.: Flipped learning with wikipedia in higher education. Stud. High. Educ. **45**, 1026–1045 (2020)
13. Hsieh, J.S., Wu, W.-C.V., Marek, M.W.: Using the flipped classroom to enhance EFL learning. Comput. Assist. Lang. Learn. **30**, 1–21 (2017)
14. Zingaro, D., Porter, L.: Peer instruction in computing: the value of instructor intervention. Comput. Educ. **71**, 87–96 (2014)

15. Porter, L., Lee, C.B., Simon, B.: Halving fail rates using peer instruction: a study of four computer science courses. In: Proceedings of the Proceeding of the 44th ACM technical symposium on Computer science education, pp.177–182. Association of Computing Machinery, New York (2013)
16. Zhang, Z.V., Hyland, K.: student engagement with teacher and automated feedback on l2 writing. Assessing Writ. **36**, 90–102 (2018)
17. Novak, G.M.: Just-in-time teaching. New Dir. Teach. Learn. **2011**(128), 63–73 (2011)
18. Sayer, R., Marshman, E., Singh, C.: Case study evaluating just-in-time teaching and peer instruction using clickers in a quantum mechanics course. Phys. Rev. Phys. Educ. Res. **12**, 020133 (2016)
19. Rowley, N., Green, J.: Just-in-time teaching and peer instruction in the flipped classroom to enhance student learning. Educ. Pract. **2**, 14–17 (2015)
20. Kitch, W.: Evaluation of effectiveness of just-in-time teaching and peer instruction methods in civil engineering courses. In: Proceedings of the 2011 ASEE Annual Conference & Exposition Proceedings, pp. 22.651.1–22.651.11. ASEE Conferences, Vancouver (2011)

# Using Vicarious Learning Feedback Videos as Self-directed Learning Resources in a LMOOC Context

Huiwan Zhang[1] and Wei Wei[2(✉)]

[1] Macau University of Science and Technology, Macao SAR, China
[2] Macao Polytechnic University, Macao SAR, China
weiweitesting@hotmail.com

**Abstract.** Providing feedback in a LMOOC context is challenging. Video feedback has the potential to serve online language learners on a large scale, as they can download, study, revise these feedback videos repeatedly and hopefully transfer their learning to complete future tasks. Vicarious learning feedback videos have not been investigated extensively, as most previous studies focused on the extent to which feedback receivers can learn from their own mistakes and feedback directly addressed to their work. The opportunities to learn from others' mistakes and feedback on others' work have more significant potential to serve an extensive online learning community. This study filled the gap by investigating and comparing learners' preferences and the use of two types of vicarious learning feedback videos as self-directed learning resources in LMOOCs, i.e., teacher and peer feedback videos.

This study collected both quantitative and qualitative data from 16 s language learners. Quantitative data mainly came from the dashboard of a learning management system, including frequency (the frequency of each video being played) and engagement level (the proportion of each feedback video being watched). Qualitative data referred to participants' reflections on their learning experiences with these videos. The results suggested that 1) teacher feedback videos were watched more frequently than others as learners regarded them as their desired performance and ultimate learning goals. They preferred teachers' explanations of the expected learning outcomes and elaborations of marking rubrics in the videos; and 2) the online learners watched a much higher percentage of the content in peer feedback videos, which indicated a higher engagement level with the peer feedback videos than teacher feedback videos. Interview data suggested that it was in the peer feedback videos that online students carried out more peer evaluation, self-reflection, and assessment practices.

**Keywords:** Video Feedback · Technology-mediated Feedback · Teaching Chinese as a Foreign Language

## 1 Introduction

LMOOCs (Language Massive Open Online Courses) are faced with the challenge of providing feedback at a large scale since it is difficult to track and offer interactions for

C. S. González-González et al. (Eds.): ICWL 2022/SETE 2022, LNCS 13869, pp. 403–411, 2023.
https://doi.org/10.1007/978-3-031-33023-0_38

thousands of registered online learners all over the world [1]. Additionally, developing learning resources for LMOOCs is challenging as it needs to promote greater use of self-directed learning strategies in a virtual environment with a low level of supervision. After all, some empirical studies suggested online learners' disengagement to perceive LMOOCs as information resources rather than a communicative space with opportunities for productive knowledge [2, 3]. To deal with these challenges, learning from others' mistakes and feedback experiences has excellent potential to serve a massive number of online language learners and create an active learning community for them to increase their engagement level. Therefore, developing teacher and peer video feedback as instructional materials for online learners is believed to promote greater use of self-directed learning strategies, and lead to better learning outcomes in online courses for second language learning.

## 2 Literature Review

### 2.1 Two Models of Feedback Practices

There are two popular language teaching and learning models when discussing the effectiveness of various feedback practices or the relationship between learners and teachers, i.e., the information-transmission model and the shared-responsibility model. Teacher video feedback refers to the first one, which is based on cognitivism and puts more emphasis on feedback providers. In contrast, the peer vicarious learning feedback videos are proposed based on socio-constructivism, which stress more learning autonomy from a student perspective [4]. In other words, the peer feedback video emphasizes feedback receivers' initiatives and capabilities in learning from the feedback given to other peers' work, comparing their own work with those identified mistakes and feedback, and using the feedback to revise their performance in future tasks.

As a conventional and widely accepted practice, the studies based on the information-transmission model identified the key features and characteristics of feedback practice or feedback givers, linking them with learners' improved learning outcomes. In other words, it largely neglected feedback receivers' initiatives and roles in seeking, digesting and acting upon the received information. It was assumed that as long as the proper feedback was given to students at the right time and under suitable conditions, they should learn and react without exercising personalized control or understanding [5, 6].

The shared-responsibility model, however, focused on the other side of the feedback practice, which highlighted the value of self-regulation, learners' engagement, and further revisions. In other words, it put feedback receivers at the center and considered them "proactive recipiences" rather than passive listeners [7, 8]. Learners' participation from the beginning of feedback sessions was considered vital, such as feedback seeking and identifying potential feedback givers. A meta-review of feedback research conducted by Van de Kleij and others [9] also confirmed that the two models produced different conceptualized student roles, including transmission, information processing, communication, and dialogical categories. It suggested that the studies in recent years had evolved to student-centered perspectives, and there was increased recognition of students' interaction and engagement in their learning processes.

## 2.2 Synchronous, Asynchronous and Vicarious Video Feedback

The frequent use of learning technologies in second language education led to video-based feedback, which stimulated interest, conveyed more information and provided permanent learning records [10]. There are three types of video feedback based on its relevance to the reviewers. The first type referred to synchronous video-mediated feedback in a communicative approach, in which learners received personalized feedback from their teachers or peers and interacted in video format. This mode made up for traditional feedback's deficiencies by increasing visual elements and the sense of interpersonal connections, and students reported this dialogical feedback to be more supportive [11, 12]. The second type was asynchronous recorded video-mediated feedback, in which online learners watched their own performance recorded by videos, and then they received feedback from their instructors, peers or themselves [13]. In this way, teachers provided verbal explanations with the help of recorded videos to give students specific feedback and point out the weaknesses or achievements for students to better understand directly and visually [14, 15].

The third type, which had not received sufficient attention, referred to learners studying the video feedback to others vicariously. In other words, the video feedback did not directly address the viewers' work, but others' work. The reviewers were expected to take advantage of the openness of feedback, observe video comments on others' work, and transfer what they learned from others' mistakes and suggestions into further revisions of their work. Therefore, this type of feedback video has great potential to serve online learners at a much larger scale and create a learning community. This idea was mentioned by Mayes [16], who proposed vicarious learning as the learning process of observing others in multimedia recorded versions of tutorial dialogues. Regretfully, limited studies have focused on the use of vicarious feedback videos. This study fills in this gap by focusing on this category of video feedback to investigate LMOOCs learners' preferences for two types of vicarious video feedback and the reasons behind their choices. Two research questions are being raised:

1) What are the online language learners' preferences of learning teacher and peer vicarious feedback videos in LMOOCs?
2) What are the underlying reasons behind learners' choices?

## 3 Method

This study collected data from an established online one-and-one language program provided by a well-known teacher training university in the Greater Bay area, China. The 15-week program aimed to provide free Chinese language courses for overseas students whose first language was not Chinese. Each online course lasted 1.5 h per week during a semester between one teacher and one student. Invitation letters were sent to all enrolled learners in the program, and finally sixteen adult participants agreed to participate in the study. They were lower-intermediate participants in HSK levels 2–3, with an average age of 22 and a similar number of males and females. Most participants had bachelor's degrees in fields ranging from linguistics, international trade, sports education to literature. Their main nationalities were Canada, Italy, Thailand, Vietnam, Kenya and South Africa.

After consulting experienced language teachers in this program, two rounds of data collection (four videos of teacher and peer feedback) were developed as online learning materials to examine students' preferences and justifications (Table 1). The teacher and peer feedback videos were recorded based on the same textbook unit. The first round targeted the vocabulary knowledge of relevant topic *dressing*, and the second round focused on the vocabulary knowledge about *time*. The content of teacher feedback videos included: 1) demonstrating expected vocabulary learning outcomes, 2) presenting common mistakes and problems based on their previous teaching experience, and 3) giving feedback and solutions to these common mistakes without explicitly addressing any individual student. The content of peer feedback videos consisted of three aspects: 1) the performance of some language points in Chinese by one language learner, 2) the provision of peer feedback by the other learner, and 3) the discussion of these language points or the mistakes made from the two learners to better improve personal understandings. In total, four videos were recorded on two different topics, and consent forms from teachers and learners in these video recordings were obtained before these materials

**Table 1.** Video materials

| Feedback Name | Content |
| --- | --- |
| Video 1 | Teacher-to-all feedback on the vocabulary knowledge with the topic of *dressing* |
| Video 2 | Peer feedback on the vocabulary knowledge with the topic of *dressing* |
| Video 3 | Teacher-to-all feedback on the vocabulary knowledge with the topic of *time* |
| Video 4 | Peer feedback on the vocabulary knowledge with the topic of *time* |

These teacher-to-all and peer feedback videos were uploaded to a learning management system, and participants were reminded to study these videos online and encouraged to play those videos or use navigation functions such as pausing, rewinding or fast-forward to learn from the teacher or peer feedback videos as they prefer, or even comment to share their ideas.

The quantitative data were obtained from the dashboard of the online learning management system to collect and generate watchers' analytics automatically, including frequency (the frequency of each video being played) and engagement level (the proportion of each feedback video being watched). The qualitative data regarding the reasons for their choices were collected through the transcripts of semi-structured interviews, then analyzed thematically. The initial coding system came from the critical components in the self-directed learning strategies, including goal settings, motivation maintenance, self-evaluation and feedback seeking [17, 18].

## 3.1 Quantitative Results

In response to the first research question, descriptive data (Table 2) revealed that the teacher feedback videos in the two rounds were played 41 and 36 times respectively, more frequently by the participants, while the peer feedback videos were only played 21 and 29 times. It suggests that the learners played the teacher videos more often than the peer feedback videos. However, playing the videos many times did not mean that these learners had studied most parts of them. In terms of the proportion of each video being watched, the data suggested that a much higher percentage of the peer feedback videos had been viewed (91.3% and 62.5%) in both rounds, compared with the two teacher feedback videos (45.3% and 48.0%). These results can be interpreted as online language learners' higher preference level in engaging with the content in the two peer feedback videos. Overall, the descriptive data indicated that in comparison with peer feedback videos, the participants played the teacher feedback more often, while watching only a relatively small part of them.

**Table 2.** Descriptive data about learners' choices.

| Feedback videos | View frequency | Percentage viewed |
| --- | --- | --- |
| Teacher-to-all (first round) | 41 | 45.3% |
| Peer (first round) | 21 | 91.3% |
| Teacher-to-all (second round) | 36 | 48.0% |
| Peer (second round) | 29 | 62.5% |

## 3.2 Quantitative Results

The interview transcripts offered more insights into the preference for teacher feedback videos and the engagement of peer discussion videos. Participants watched the teacher videos more frequently, and they reported two reasons, including 1) their perceptions to consider teacher videos as their desired performance and ultimate learning goals, because teachers provided exemplars for students to follow, and in this way, they gained improvement from experts' versions of expected learning outcomes; and 2) they preferred learning teachers' elaborations of vocabulary knowledge and feedback towards students' performance in the videos, with experts' annotations or explanations of marking rubrics to reduce them misinterpretations and improve their assessment understanding. For example, two interviewees reflected,

> I listened to teacher's all the time because she definitely knows a lot of Chinese than I... I must listen to her all the time, and I compare my knowledge with her. If I were wrong, I would correct myself.

> I prefer the first one, the longest teacher's video...I liked how the teacher taught, and I also like the way she explains the languages...I just like how the technical things are used.

Moreover, these second language online learners watched a much higher percentage of the content in peer feedback videos, which indicated a higher engagement level and students' interest in these videos. Interview data found that these participants had carried out more peer evaluation and self-reflection practices when studying the peer feedback videos. In other words, they used what they learned from the teacher feedback videos to evaluate the two peers' work in the peer feedback videos, identify their own mistakes by comparing peer performance with their own work, and then self-generated feedback with those in the videos. As two participants reported,

> You can also hear how much more fluent Adam (note: the high-level student in the video) speaks than Sean (note: the low-level one). I think that's how I judge…I just look at their fluidity and I compare their pronunciation to the native-speaking teacher.

> Because you know they doubt themselves…he is not very sure, and so I avoid repeating what he is saying, so that I don't fall into the same mistakes.

Last, four online learners subscribed to the channel of uploaded feedback videos on this learning management system, demonstrating these participants' increased level of interest and commitment to using these materials further. Moreover, two students posted positive comments *Awesome* and *excellent work* to show their satisfaction with these feedback videos.

## 4   Discussion

The research results suggested that teacher feedback videos were watched more frequently than others as learners regarded them as their desired performance and ultimate learning goals. They preferred teachers' explanations of the expected learning outcomes and elaborations of marking rubrics in the videos. The possible reason may be that students regarded teachers' explanations and feedback as the best learning examples to follow in their daily study. It echoes previous studies that revealed students' authority-dependent intention. Learners in academic English courses reported their preference for teachers' evaluative feedback and their willingness to act on it, rather than proactively seeking feedback themselves [19]. Compared with self-and peer-assessment, some undergraduates reported their concerns about lecturer feedback because of the structured content and its usefulness in guiding students to realize their levels to achieve deep learning [20].

The results also suggested that online learners watched a much higher percentage of the content in peer feedback videos, which indicated a higher engagement level with the peer feedback videos than in teacher feedback videos. Interview data suggested that it was in the peer feedback videos that online students carried out more peer evaluation, self-reflection and assessment practices. It can be interpreted as students' increased sense of belonging in an active learning community to improve their engagement level when watching peer feedback videos. Therefore, their learning autonomy is believed to be promoted with improved motivation and greater use of self-directed learning strategies. As some studies revealed [21, 22], online feedback encouraged students' deeper cognitive processing of target language knowledge and their practice, which motivated them to revise their work and achieve self-reflection and knowledge transfer. Lee & Mori [23] also suggested similar findings, in which students reported the reinforced value of receiving peer feedback as a learning resource and its diagnostic function for their personalized learning needs to improve their self-directed learning competencies. These students also indicated their preferences for teacher feedback which backs up this research's findings.

# 5 Conclusion

In conclusion, this study focused on vicarious learning feedback videos, which have not been investigated extensively by previous research. It filled the gap by examining learners' preferences and engagement of two types of vicarious learning feedback videos, i.e., teacher-to-all and peer feedback videos, as self-directed learning resources in LMOOCs. Employed mixed research methods, this study suggested two perspectives from second language learners. Firstly, teacher-to-all feedback videos were watched more frequently than peer feedback videos, as learners regarded them as their expected performance and ultimate learning goals. They preferred teachers' explanations of the desired learning outcomes and teachers' elaborations of marking rubrics in the videos. Secondly, these online learners watched a much higher percentage of the content in peer feedback videos, which indicated their higher engagement level with the peer feedback videos than teacher-to-all feedback videos. They performed more peer evaluation and self-reflection, with the help of the obtained knowledge from teacher-to-all feedback videos, to assess the two peers' performance and identify the mistakes of their individual work. Eventually, they achieved self-generated feedback in an active online learning community.

Some limitations should also be addressed. This study only used the dashboard of an online learning management system and semi-structured interviews to collect data. It would be better to triangulate the findings with user analytics retrieved from servers as second language learners' actual online video watching behaviors, to determine if their self-reported watching preferences and feedback video engagement were consistent with their actual online learning processes. Also, only 16 participants watched the two types of vicarious feedback videos, which could have caused bias of the findings.

Further research on vicarious learning feedback videos should employ a longitudinal design to explore the learning mechanisms of second language students. When they are offered these feedback videos in LMOOCs in the long-term, their subsequent revisions of their own work and second language performance are recommended to be investigated, together with their perceptions of vicarious learning feedback videos. This investigation would provide a comprehensive picture of how second language learners realize the potential benefits of these self-directed learning resources in an online community-based environment.

**Funding.** This research was supported by the Education Fund of the Macao Special Administrative Region [Grant Number: HSS-MUST-2021-06].

# References

1. Lundqvist, K., Liyanagunawardena, T., Starkey, L.: Evaluation of student feedback within a MOOC using sentiment analysis and target groups. Int. Rev. Res. Open Distrib. Learn. **21**(3), 140–156 (2020)
2. Mac Lochlainn, C., Mhichíl, M.N.G., Beirne, E.: Clicking, but connecting? L2 learning engagement on an ab initio Irish language LMOOC. ReCALL **33**(2), 111–127 (2021)
3. Zeng, S., Zhang, J., Gao, M., Xu, K.M., Zhang, J.: Using learning analytics to understand collective attention in language MOOCs. Comput. Assist. Lang. Learn. **35**(7), 1594–1619 (2022)
4. Winstone, N., Pitt, E., Nash, R.: Educators' perceptions of responsibility-sharing in feedback processes. Assess. Eval. High. Educ. **46**(1), 118–131 (2021)
5. Boud, D.: Reframing assessment as if learning were important. In: Boud, D., Falchikov, N. (eds.) Rethinking Assessment in Higher Education, pp. 24–36. Routledge, London (2007)
6. Nicol, D.: From monologue to dialogue: improving written feedback processes in mass higher education. Assess. Eval. High. Educ. **35**(5), 501–517 (2010)
7. Boud, D., Molloy, E.: Rethinking models of feedback for learning: the challenge of design. Assess. Eval. High. Educ. **38**(6), 698–712 (2013)
8. Winstone, N.E., Nash, R.A., Parker, M., Rowntree, J.: Supporting learners' agentic engagement with feedback: a systematic review and a taxonomy of recipience processes. Educ. Psychol. **52**(1), 17–37 (2017)
9. Van der Kleij, F.M., Adie, L.E., Cumming, J.J.: A meta-review of the student role in feedback. Int. J. Educ. Res. **98**, 303–323 (2019)
10. Ge, Z.G.: Exploring the effect of video feedback from unknown peers on e-learners' English-Chinese translation performance. Comput. Assist. Lang. Learn. **35**(1–2), 169–189 (2022). https://doi.org/10.1080/09588221.2019.1677721
11. Cunningham, K.J., Link, S.: Video and text feedback on ESL writing: understanding attitude and negotiating relationships. J. Second. Lang. Writ. **52**, 100797 (2021)
12. Ryan, T., Henderson, M., Phillips, M.: Digitally recorded assessment feedback in a secondary school context: student engagement, perception and impact. Technol. Pedagog. Educ. **29**(3), 311–325 (2020)
13. Rombouts, E., Meuris, K., Maes, B., De Meyer, A.M., Zink, I.: Video feedback in key word signing training for preservice direct support staff. J. Speech Lang. Hear. Res. **59**(2), 342–348 (2016)
14. Murphy Odo, D.: An action research investigation of the impact of using online feedback videos to promote self-reflection on the microteaching of preservice EFL teachers. Syst. Pract. Action Res. **35**, 1–17 (2021)
15. Potdevin, F., Huchez, V., Davids, K., Schnitzler, C.: How can video feedback be used in physical education to support novice learning in gymnastics? Effects on motor learning, self-assessment and motivation. Phys. Educ. Sport Pedagog. **23**(6), 559–574 (2018)
16. Mayes, J.T.: Still to learn from vicarious learning. E-Learning Digit. Media **12**(3), 361–371 (2015)
17. Beckers, J., Dolmans, D., van Merriënboer, J.: Student, direct thyself! Facilitating self-directed learning skills and motivation with an electronic development portfolio. J. Res. Technol. Educ. **54**(4), 617–634 (2021)
18. Pan, X.: Technology acceptance, technological self-efficacy, and attitude toward technology-based self-directed learning: learning motivation as a mediator. Front. Psychol. **11**, 564294 (2020)
19. Gan, Z., Hu, G., Wang, W., Nang, H., An, Z.: Feedback behavior and preference in university academic english courses: associations with english language self-efficacy. Assess. Eval. High. Educ. **46**(5), 740–755 (2021)

20. Lynch, R., McNamara, P.M., Seery, N.: Promoting deep learning in a teacher education programme through self-and peer-assessment and feedback. Eur. J. Teach. Educ. **35**(2), 179–197 (2012)

21. Chen, W., Gao, J.: Creating an online community of inquiry: learner practice and perceptions of community-based feedback giving in academic writing. Comput. Assist. Lang. Learn. 1–28 (2022)

22. Wei, W., Yi, Y., Ge, G.: Investigating learners' changing expectations on learning experience in a MOOC of professional translation and interpreting training. SAGE Open, October-December, 1–11 (2022). https://doi.org/10.1177/21582440221134577

23. Lee, H., Mori, C.: Reflective practices and self-directed learning competencies in second language university classes. Asia Pac. J. Educ. **41**(1), 130–151 (2021)

# Blended Learning Approach in English Teaching: Effectiveness and Challenges

Zhang Xueshan[✉]

Hongkong Polytechnic University, Hongkong, China
zhxs19872016@163.com

**Abstract.** This paper provides a review of empirical studies on the adoption of a blended learning approach in teaching English as a second/foreign languages since 2021. The review contributed to the topic by documenting and synthesizing latest empirical evidence. To select articles, two international education databases were included: SCOPUS and Web of Science. After excluding theoretical paper, literature review and commentaries, 9 articles remained. The in-depth analysis revealed that the current main topics of these studies included the student perception, teacher perception, enhancing learners' specific language skills as well as students' language learning autonomy. In addition, the blended learning designs in these studies were various, combining different instructional methods, multiple delivery media, and pedagogical approaches. It can be concluded that with the significant effectiveness of blended learning approach in English study, numerous context-specific challenges were existed. In addition, there is a need for more related studies to focus on the K-12 setting as well as the long-term influence of blended learning approach in learners' English proficiency and abilities.

**Keywords:** Blended learning approach · Teaching English as a second/foreign language · Effectiveness · Challenges

## 1 Introduction

In the last few decades, educationists have advocated a modern approach to the teaching and learning process, named a "blended learning approach". According to Driscoll (2002), the connotation of blended learning is highly flexible as it denotes the mixture of different things, such as different instruction methods, diverse teaching pedagogies, and a combination of physical and virtual classroom study. Driscoll (2002) stressed that as the blended learning possesses the "untapped potential" (p. 1) it means different things to different people. Similarly, Singh (2021) emphasized that the use of a blend of learning approaches enables organizations to provide "the right content in the right format to the right people at the right time" (p. 16).

When describing the blended learning, Graham (2006) pointed out that the blended learning combines face-to-face instruction with computer-mediated instruction (p. 5). In another definition, Garrison and Kanuka (2004) defined the blended learning approach as "the thoughtful integration of face-to-face learning experience with online learning experience" (P.96). Garrison and Kanuka emphasized the quality dimension of the

C. S. González-González et al. (Eds.): ICWL 2022/SETE 2022, LNCS 13869, pp. 412–417, 2023.
https://doi.org/10.1007/978-3-031-33023-0_39

blended learning approach: the thoughtful plan of combination. According to Staker and Horn (2012), this kind of curriculum could be implemented flexibly through mixtures of online instruction and face-to-face activities, such as collaborative project design, private tutoring, small group discussions, and peer-review activities. In other words, the blended learning is regarded as a scalable and flexible way of teaching and learning, which provides students more opportunities to engage in learning activities in and out of classrooms (Senffner and Kepler, 2015).

## 2  Blended Learning Approach in English Teaching and Learning

According to Osguthorpe and Graham (2003), educators who are in favor of blended learning approach hold the belief that there are inherent benefits of online methods and traditional methods. The combination of them aims to "achieve a harmonious balance between the easy access to online knowledge and face-to-face human interaction" (p. 228). With the influence of the blended learning approach in mainstream education, researchers of second/foreign language education have paid more attention to the adoption of the blended learning approach in English teaching and learning.

The present study focused on related empirical research to document what latest data-driven research has been conducted since 2021 and to identify gaps of understandings of benefits and challenges of employing blended learning approach in English teaching and learning. Due to the space limit of this paper, empirical studies included were selected from two international education databases: SCOPUS and Web of Science. The search term was "blended learning in English teaching and learning". The initial research yielded 92 articles. After reading article titles, abstracts and full text versions, when necessary, studies were excluded if they were theoretical papers, commentaries and literature reviews. The final selection yielded 9 studies.

Among the 9 studies, five of them focused on stakeholders' perceptions of adoption of the blended learning approach in English teaching and learning; three of them discussed the effectiveness of blended learning approach in improving learners' specific language skill; the final one examined how to enhance learners' study autonomy by adopting the blended learning mode.

For the studies related to English lecturers' and students' perceptions of the blended learning approach, two of them adopted a holistic view to examine both teachers and students' perception; another two of them solely focused on teachers' perception; one of them only focused on students' perception. One common theme recurred in these studies was both teachers' and students' favorable attitude towards the blended learning in English teaching and learning, such as the flexibility, high efficiency and convenience. According to Watanapokakul (2022), most of teachers and students from a Thailand University in the study agreed that blended on-line learning (a mixture of the live virtual classroom and asynchronous online learning platform LMS) for the course of foundation English was beneficial in improving students' overall language proficiency. Students thought that the synchronous online learning mode saved their time and money as they did not need to travel to the university. Meanwhile they valued the asynchronous online learning because of the easy access to the learning materials at any time anywhere. However, it seemed that students' positive perception (i.e., suitable and convenient) of this blended on-line learning mode was related directly to the social distancing caused by the pandemic. Unlike the blended on-line learning mode in Watanapokakul's (2022) study, the design of a mixture of face-to-face learning and the online learning platform MOOC was adopted in the study of Wu and Luo (2022). Participants in this study were university students and lecturers in China. Learners expressed that they had a better understanding of the learning content, and a richer learning experience, a higher motivation as well as a higher level of interaction. The instructors also identified the positive impact of the blended learning mode. Although both of these two studies focused on the tertiary education context, they focused on different courses with different blended learning design in different countries. Therefore, they reported distinct challenges encountered by students and teachers. While the biggest challenge of the course of Watanapokakul's (2022) study was that it was less effective in improving students' oral and writing skills of English due to the lack of immediate feedbacks on students' assignment, participants in the study of Wu and Luo (2022) reported that their normal face-to-face instruction time was not less and the on-line learning was additional. Hence, students reported that they were overwhelmed by the on-line tasks. Unlike the mixed research method adopted by these two studies, another study by Bezliudna et al. (2021) mainly used the quantitative data and reported the favorable perception of master students from a Ukraine university perception of the blended learning (a mixture of online and offline learning) for the course of English for Specific Purposes. Different to challenges mention by the previous two studies, Bezliudna et al. (2021) identified the inequality of technological support facilities and infrastructures as the biggest challenge in this study. Therefore, it can be concluded that learners and lecturers' challenges were susceptible to the specific local context. It is necessary for educators and school managers to raise their awareness for identifying concrete difficulties encountered by in-service teachers and students.

Another two studies of Le et al. (2022) and Mulyono et al. (2021) did not targeted teachers' perception of blended learning approach for one particular course but their general attitude towards the innovative pedagogy. One contrasting feature of these two studies was that Le et al. (2022) adopted a qualitative design while Mulyono et al. (2021) employed a quantitative design. It may because that Mulyono et al. (2021) focused on the similarities and differences of Indonesian foreign language (EFL) teachers' perceptions of blended learning in reference to their gender and teaching levels (i.e., lower secondary school, upper secondary school, university, informal education and other levels). Differently, Le et al. (2022) aimed to gain an in-depth understanding of the barriers and drawbacks encountered by 30 English teachers in Vietnamese university when they implemented blended teaching. Le et al. (2022)'s study found that teachers' challenges included their lack of related knowledge, skills, experience and insufficient time, which were partially congruent with findings of Mulyono et al. (2021). Mulyono et al. (2021) reported that compared with teachers of other teaching level, university English teachers had a better understanding of the context of blended learning. For all English teacher of various teaching levels, the primary challenge was the insufficient training and supports on blended learning. Therefore, although blended learning in English teaching and learning has received considerable attention during the past two decades, there is still a large space for its improvement as in-service teachers still possess insufficient knowledge and training for its design and implement.

For studies examining the effectiveness of blended learning approach in improving learners' specific language skill, while one of them focused on learners' writing skills, another two examined learners' oral and reading skill respectively. It is worth mentioning that the study by Akbari et al. (2021) was different from others in terms of comparing three learning approaches: the traditional approach, the blended learning approach (a mixture of on-line and off-line mode), and the virtual teaching approach based on web-based technologies. Hence, students' participants in Iranian universities in this study were divided into three groups accordingly to examine the effect of different teaching mode on improving reading comprehension. Findings indicated that the group of virtual teaching approach made the most significant progress in comparison with the other two groups. It might because that virtual learning environment led to learners' better confidence in reading comprehension. As Akbari et al.'s (2021) study adopted the quantitative approach, they failed to provide in-depth explanation for the advantages of the virtual learning environment in enhancing learners' confidence compared with the blended learning approach. Different to the study of Akbari et al.'s (2021), there were two compared groups of participants in the study of Teng and Zeng (2022). They reported that the blended learning method had remarkable effect on the improvement of learners' oral accuracy and fluency, but not complexity in a Chinese middle school. The significant improvement of accuracy might be because of teachers' feedback on students' oral tasks and the easy access to correct pronunciation audio files. Meanwhile, because of the flexibility of on-line learning, learners' anxiety for their oral practice reduced and their oral influence was improved. However, due to their concern about making mistakes, they tended to avoid use complex sentences and words, and their complexity of oral English was not changed obviously. However, it is doubted that whether the students' oral competence development could last over a longer period of time.

Similar to the study of Teng and Zeng (2022), another study by Florence and Kolski (2021) also focused on the K-12 setting. Unlike Teng and Zeng (2022), Florence and Kolski (2021) examined the effect of a specific blended teaching and learning approach: the flipped classroom model on high school students' writing quality without a compared group by a mixed-method. Findings indicated that the flipped classroom model helped students improve their writing skills as well as their engagement in learning. It might because that the flipped classroom model enabled the students to gain deeper and meaningful learning by watching vivid videos, finishing on-line tasks with promote feedback, completing collaborative tasks with peers and obtaining individualized instruction. It can be included that these empirical studies provided evidence for the effectiveness of the innovative pedagogy. However, as their aims, designs and contexts were distinctive, it is quite difficult to make comparison between them. In addition, none of them focused on the long-term impact of the blended learning mode on learners' language skills.

Unlike previous studies, Wang and Zhang (2022) developed an optimized SPOC-based blended learning mode by combing on-line and offline teaching in English to stimulate Chinese university students' learning motivation and cultivate their autonomous learning ability. Learners were required to finish the learning tasks before class with the technical support, and rich resources of E-learning and the knowledge extension activities after the situational communication and interactive discussion in face-to face class. One prominent feature of this study was that it continually collected stakeholders' perception of the design of the blended learning mode to optimize its function. By emphasizing students' individuality and providing students personalized learning experience, it was helpful in turning learners' inefficient passive learning into effective active learning. However, similar to previous discuss, the long-term impact of the blended learning mode on learners' autonomous learning ability still needs to be testified.

## 3 Conclusion

To conclude, while most of empirical studies acknowledged the positive impact of and favorable attitudes of students and teachers toward the blended learning mode in English teaching and learning, there were still numerous challenges reported by different studies. It can be concluded that the challenges were susceptible to specific and concrete contexts. Therefore, it is necessary for school managers and teacher educators to raise their awareness to notice local challenges, to focus on students and in-service teachers' perception of the blended learning mode continuously, and provide appropriate external support. In addition, more studies are needed to examine the long-term impact of blended learning approach on improvement of students' language skill or learning ability. Finally, most of the current empirical studies focused on university students and lecturers, more attention is needed to be paid to the K-12 setting.

## References

Akbari, J., Tabrizi, H.H., Chalak, A.: Effectiveness of virtual Vs. non-virtual teaching in improving reading comprehension of Iranian undergraduate EFL students. Turk. Online J. Distance Educ. **22**(2), 272–283 (2021)

Bezliudna, V., Shcherban, I., Kolomiyets, O., Mykolaiko, V., Bezliudnyi, R.: Master students' perceptions of blended learning in the process of studying english during covid 19 pandemic in Ukraine. Rupkatha J. Interdisc. Stud. Humanit. **13**(4), 1–14 (2021)

Driscoll, M.: Blended learning: Let's get beyond the hype. e-Learning **1**(4), 1–4 (2002)

Florence, E.A., Kolski, T.: Investigating the flipped classroom model in a high school writing course: action research to impact student writing achievement and engagement. TechTrends **65**(6), 1042–1052 (2021)

Garrison, D.R., Kanuka, H.: Blended learning: uncovering its transformative potential in higher education. Internet High. Educ. **7**, 95–105 (2004)

Graham, C.R.: Blended learning systems: Definition, current trends and future directions. In: Bonk, C.J., Graham, C.R. (eds.) The Handbook of Blended Learning: Global Perspectives, Local Designs, pp. 3–21. Pfeiffer, San Francisco (2006)

Le, T.N., Allen, B., Johnson, N.F.: Blended learning: barriers and drawbacks for english language lecturers at vietnamese universities. E-Learning and Digital Media **19**(2), 225–239 (2022)

Mulyono, H., Ismayama, D., Liestyana, A.R., Komara, C.: EFL teachers' perceptions of Indonesia blended learning course across gender and teaching levels. Teach. English Technol. **21**(1), 60–74 (2021)

Osguthorpe, R.T., Graham, C.R.: Blended learning environments: definitions and directions. Q. Rev. Dist. Learn. **4**(3), 227–233 (2003)

Senffner, D., Kepler, L.G.: Blended learning that works. Association for Talent Development, Alexandria, VA (2015)

Staker, H., Horn, M.B.: Classifying K-12 blended learning. Innosight Institute (2012)

Singh, H.: Building effective blended learning programs. In: Khan, B.H., Affouneh, S., Hussein Salha, S., Najee Khlaif, Z. (eds.) Challenges and Opportunities for the Global Implementation of E-Learning Frameworks, pp. 15–23. IGI Global (2021)

Teng, X., Zeng, Y.: The effects of blended learning on foreign language learners' oral english competence. Theor. Pract. Lang. Stud. **12**(2), 281–291 (2022)

Watanapokakul, S.: Blended online learning: perceptions and experiences of EFL university students and teachers. Reflections **29**(1), 60–87 (2022)

Wang, X., Zhang, W.: Improvement of students' autonomous learning behavior by optimizing foreign language blended learning mode. SAGE Open **12**(1), 215824402110711 (2022)

Wu, H., Luo, S.: Integrating MOOCs in an undergraduate english course: students' and teachers' perceptions of blended learning. SAGE Open **12**(2), 1–15 (2022)

**Digitalization in Language
and Cross-Cultural Education**

# The Structure of Motivation in Online Translation Learning and the Role of L2 Motivation Self System

Yukai Hu[1], Xuange Ma[1](✉), Yike Gao[1], and Qi Wang[2]

[1] School of Humanities and Social Sciences, University of Science and Technology of China, Hefei, China
Maxuange@mail.ustc.edu.cn
[2] West Anhui Health Vocational College, Lu'an, China

**Abstract.** With the advancement of online learning technologies, translation learning, teaching, and learning motivation have been influenced and even reshaped. So, there is a need for empirical investigations on the motivation in learning translation online. Under the framework of the L2 Motivation Self System, this study uses exploratory factor analysis and structural equation model to analyze 150 college students' motivation for online translation learning and identifies six motivation factors: IL2S Factor, Escape/Stimulation Factor, Social Contact Factor, Social Service Factor, L2LE Factor, and OL2S Factor. The research findings show that motivation in online translation learning is not instrumental, and the Ideal L2 Self is the most significant and dominant motivation in online translation learning.

**Keywords:** Online Translation Learning · L2 Motivation Self System · Structure of Motivation

## 1 Introduction

In contrast to motivation studies in language learning, the motivation underlying translation learning, an essential component of language learning, has been far less studied. Translation learning and language learning are similar but not the same. Considerable researches have previously established the significance of motivation, which is an essential factor determining academic performance, in language learning [1–4]. But in translation learning, the structure and influence of motivation has not been well revealed. Besides, the advancement of technology has always been closely linked with learning and teaching a second language [5]. Technology cannot significantly advance foreign language learning if pertinent theories are not incorporated into foreign language learning. With the advancement of online learning technologies, translation learning, teaching and learning motivation have been influenced and even reshaped. So there is a need for empirical investigations on the motivation in learning translation online.

C. S. González-González et al. (Eds.): ICWL 2022/SETE 2022, LNCS 13869, pp. 421–432, 2023.
https://doi.org/10.1007/978-3-031-33023-0_40

The growing interest in studying translation education has been observed in recent years [6–9]. But few researches have touched on the topic of motivation in online translation learning. The research attempts to model the structure of motivation in online translation learning by exploratory factor analysis and structural equation model (SEM). Considering the role of motivation in L2 learning, this research will investigate the relationship between online translation learning motivation and L2 Motivation Self System (L2MSS), which is a powerful analytical framework for reconceptualizing L2 learner motivation [10].

## 2   Literature Review

### 2.1   L2 Motivation Self System

To interpret individual variations in motivation for language acquisition, Dörnyei introduced the L2 Motivational Self System (L2MSS) in 2005. Several theories have an impact on the L2MSS, most notably the socio-educational model [11–13], the self-discrepancy theory, and the possible self's theory [14]. A central assumption of the L2MSS is that learners may be motivated to close perceived gaps and achieve the desired end-state when they see a difference between their present state and their future self-guide (i.e., ideal or ought). The first anthology putting this theory to the test was published in 2009, presenting a series of empirical studies that, in the words of Dörnyei, provided substantial confirmation for the proposed self-system [15].

The Ideal L2 Self, the Ought-to L2 Self, and the L2 Learning Experience are the three parts of the L2 Motivational Self System (L2MSS) theory. Due to the desire to narrow the gap between one's actual and ideal selves, the concept of the 'Ideal L2 Self' (IL2S) or 'L2-specific facet of one's ideal self' serves as a powerful motivation for learning the L2 (e.g., traditional integrative and internalized instrumental motives). Ought-to L2 Self (OL2S) concerns are the attributes one thinks one should have to live up to expectations and prevent undesirable results. This component relates to ought self and, as a result it relates to more external instrumental motives. L2 learning experiences include situated and executive motivations specific to the current learning environment and experience (such as the school environment, the teacher-student interaction, and the success/failure experience).

Numerous studies have confirmed L2MSS and its various components. Recent research on the L2MSS revealed that the ideal L2 self is still arguably the biggest motivator for language learners [16–19]. To a significant extent, learners' intentional effort or motivated conduct in L2 learning is mostly impacted by the ideal L2 self-compared to ought-to L2 self and L2 Learning Experience [20]. In several investigations, the impact of the ought-to L2 self on effort is negligible [21], negative [22] or positive but not very strong [1]. The ideal L2 self shows a more explanatory power in learners' motivation than integrativeness, according to Liu's research of Chinese EFL learners [3]. Yu's study of 190 Chinese college students found that most students have a high ideal L2 self and a positive L2 learning experience. This study also finds that the ideal L2 self explained more variation in students' motivation. The ideal L2 self of English majors was higher than those of non-English majors, despite the lack of a significant difference in their ought-to L2 self [23].

More research on L2MSS is required in light of the diversity of learners, complexity of SL/FL learning and motivation, and rapidly accelerating globalization [24, 25], even though numerous studies conducted within the framework of L2MSS have produced interesting findings.

According to previous studies, IL2S as a part of L2MSS is the biggest motivator for L2 learners, but there are few studies having tested the influence of IL2S on translation learning motivations. There is a need to combine L2MSS theory with online translation learning study to better comprehend student's translation learning motivation.

## 2.2 Motivation in Translation Learning

To investigate motivation in translation learning, Liu (2019) used a Master student's diaries reflecting on daily translation training and semi-structured interviews to investigate factors influencing students' translation learning motivation. The findings also show how the ideal self, the ought self, the actual self, and the feared self-interact dynamically with one another in the dynamic setting [26]. This study indicates that L2MSS could help to explain motivation in translation learning. The conclusions of this study, however, need to be tested further because it only looks at one case. Jabu (2021) investigated Indonesian students' motivation to translation training and found that students' portrayals of their future selves serve as their primary sources of motivation for taking the translation course [27]. Obviously, it can be regarded the same as IL2S. In terms of technology and translation learning motivation, Kassem (2021) found that employing computer-aided translation has a significant positive impact on students' motivation and translation [28]. This suggests that technology may affect the motivation to learn translation. In order to determine whether there is a difference, it is necessary to investigate the motive for online translation learning. Besides, many other studies focus on motivation to do translating instead of motivation in translation learning or training. Studies on motivation in translation learning is not abundant.

## 2.3 Online Learning and Non-constraint Learning

With the popularization of the concept of lifelong learning and the rapid development of network communication technology, adult online learning and autonomous learning will become a new normal. Online learning, based on lifelong learning, is active and non-academic, referred to in this paper as unconstrained learning. Exploring the motivation assessment scale for learning in this free state allows for the analysis and observation of the original composition of motivation for learning. The assessment scale of this study is developed by the type of non-constraint learning or adult learning because the online learning in this study belongs to non-constraint learning. The factors of online translation learning are very similar to this assessment scale.

Wu Feng (2015) investigated the assessment scale of motivation for adult online learning. Based on previous research and substantial data, his new assessment scale was created using eight exploratory factor analysis and reliability and validity tests. His scale has a total of 43 items and comprises six dimensions: cognitive interest, professional advancement, interpersonal relations, getting out of routine, external influence, and community service [29]. This scale's most significant distinction from earlier research is that it considers the characteristics of online learning.

Under the premise of lifelong learning, students place more value on active learning, heightening the cognitive interest factor. According to its range of applications, this evaluation scale with non-constraint is appropriate for all kinds of adult online learning scenarios.

In studies about online learning motivations, Kim (2011) found that when starting self-directed online learning, people are more likely to be motivated if they believe the learning objectives to be more pertinent and have more excellent technological proficiency [30]. Besides, strong inner motivation (ideal self) and external motivation (ought-to self) positively influence students' perceptions of online classes. The more driven students learn English, the more open-minded they are to the online courses [31]. Previous researches on motivation in online learning suggests that IL2S and OL2S could be just as helpful as normal and that academic success online is still significantly influenced by motivation.

The following are the study's research questions:

1. What is the motivation structure of online translation learning?
2. .How do OL2S, L2LE, and IL2S fit into the motivation structure? Is IL2S still the primary motivation for those learning translation online?
3. What factors influence IL2S or are influenced by IL2S?

## 3  Methodology

### 3.1  Survey Design and Data Collection

First, a questionnaire for this study was created on the basis of the assessment scale for adult online learning indicated above because it considers the characteristics of online learning. The questionnaire, which has a 5-point Likert scale, has six dimensions: cognitive interest, professional advancement, interpersonal relations, getting out of routine, external influence, and community. The questionnaire has a total of 22 questions selected from 43 items of the former scale, and each question represents a factor of online translation learning (Table 1).

The online poll was completed by 156 college students (150 valid) from 69 different universities who have learned translation online. They included 78% of participants who have been using online translation learning platforms for more than a month, 30% who have been using them for more than six months, and 17.3% who have been using them for more than a year. Among the respondents, 64% are majoring in a foreign language now or have previously done so, compared to 36% who have not.

### 3.2  Exploratory Factor Analysis

Next, the team looked at the validity and reliability of the survey data (Table 2).

The Cronbach's alpha coefficient is 0.942, indicating that the questionnaire's reliability is very high; the KMO coefficient is 0.896; and the Bartlett Test of Sphericity

**Table 1.** Dimensions and Factors

| Dimension | Factors | Code |
| --- | --- | --- |
| Cognitive Preference | Thirst for knowledge | A1 |
| | Profession Preference | A2 |
| | Make up for Shortcomings | A3 |
| | Accomplishment | A4 |
| Career and Academic Development | Qualification | B1 |
| | Career Preparation | B2 |
| | Academic Achievement | B3 |
| | General Skills | B4 |
| | Further Study | B5 |
| Interpersonal Communication | Expand socially | C1 |
| | Integrate into the group | C2 |
| | Improve relationships | C3 |
| | Earn Respect | C4 |
| Out of the Box | Passing Time | D1 |
| | Break the routine | D2 |
| | Spiritual support | D3 |
| | Diversion | D4 |
| External influence | Influenced by others | E1 |
| | Recommended by experts | E2 |
| | Influenced by COVID-19 | E3 |
| Social Services | Help others | F1 |
| | Serve Society | F2 |

**Table 2.** Validity and Reliability

| Cronbach's α | KMO | Bartlett Test of Sphericity |
| --- | --- | --- |
| 0.942 | 0.896 | P=0.000*** |

shows that the significance p-value is 0.000***(p<0.01), indicating that the variables are correlated and the data is appropriate for factor analysis.

After testing validity and reliability of data collected from the survey, the authors attempt to find out new public factors by exploratory factor analysis. For psychological assessments such as motivation assessments, internal structure-based validity evidence is crucial, and factor analysis helps assess this internal structure [32] (Table 3).

**Table 3.** Factor loading (Rotated)

| Code | Factor Loading (Rotated) | | | | | | Community |
|------|---------|---------|---------|---------|---------|---------|-----------|
|      | Factor1 | Factor2 | Factor3 | Factor4 | Factor5 | Factor6 |           |
| A1   | 0.835   | 0.175   | −0.021  | 0.091   | 0.119   | 0.035   | 0.751     |
| A2   | 0.801   | 0.157   | 0.104   | 0.071   | −0.016  | 0.066   | 0.686     |
| A3   | 0.637   | 0.082   | 0.106   | 0.093   | 0.267   | 0.357   | 0.631     |
| A4   | 0.716   | −0.078  | 0.179   | 0.21    | 0.279   | 0.018   | 0.673     |
| B1   | 0.482   | 0.171   | 0.473   | −0.02   | 0.291   | 0.146   | 0.591     |
| B2   | 0.456   | 0.084   | 0.456   | 0.297   | 0.296   | 0.158   | 0.624     |
| B3   | 0.504   | 0.149   | 0.183   | 0.004   | 0.27    | 0.59    | 0.731     |
| B4   | 0.59    | 0.225   | 0.125   | 0.338   | 0.113   | 0.344   | 0.661     |
| B5   | 0.597   | 0.159   | 0.344   | 0.312   | −0.069  | 0.038   | 0.604     |
| C1   | 0.208   | 0.494   | 0.681   | 0.173   | 0.14    | 0.157   | 0.825     |
| C2   | 0.121   | 0.2     | 0.755   | 0.275   | 0.164   | 0.155   | 0.751     |
| C4   | 0.216   | 0.247   | 0.454   | 0.455   | −0.09   | 0.494   | 0.774     |
| D1   | 0.185   | 0.772   | 0.208   | 0.235   | 0.157   | 0.064   | 0.758     |
| C3   | 0.087   | 0.373   | 0.754   | 0.129   | 0.138   | 0.192   | 0.788     |
| D2   | 0.056   | 0.448   | 0.214   | 0.537   | 0.15    | 0.407   | 0.725     |
| D3   | 0.11    | 0.803   | 0.238   | 0.177   | 0.203   | 0.087   | 0.794     |
| D4   | 0.133   | 0.792   | 0.243   | 0.142   | 0.153   | 0.142   | 0.767     |
| E1   | 0.186   | 0.3     | 0.121   | 0.156   | 0.817   | −0.04   | 0.833     |
| E3   | 0.204   | 0.418   | 0.351   | 0.024   | 0.518   | 0.186   | 0.642     |
| E2   | 0.174   | 0.15    | 0.183   | 0.349   | 0.608   | 0.314   | 0.677     |
| F1   | 0.391   | 0.353   | 0.194   | 0.647   | 0.24    | 0.094   | 0.8       |
| F2   | 0.279   | 0.229   | 0.239   | 0.713   | 0.24    | 0.081   | 0.76      |

The next step is to give them new names. High factor loadings for factor 1 are found in A1 (0.835), A2 (0.801), A4 (0.714), and A3 (0.637). It demonstrates that all Cognitive Preference components have high loadings for Factor 1, yet Factor 1 also has significant loadings for other items like B5(0.597) and B4 (0.59). Therefore, the combination of cognitive preference and academic and career development constitutes Factor 1. What if we changed a perspective?

The survey question of A1, on which Factor 1 has the highest loading, is "I am eager to learn many new things and want to satisfy my desire for knowledge." The question of A3 is "I want to make up for my shortcomings in translation studies." A4 is "Mastering a lot of new knowledge will give me a greater sense of accomplishment." B5 is "I hope to study translation in depth to prepare for further study in translation studies (graduate school, Ph.D.) in the future." The phrase IL2S describes the positive self-image of oneself that learners have for their future L2 acquisition and usage [33], and the ideal L2 self serves as a potent motivator if one is aware of the mismatch between their actual L2 competency and the intended future self-image. According to the narratives of the above questions, Factor 1 can proportionally name as "IL2S Factor". Besides, the "IL2S Factor" has the highest explained variance among the 6 extracted new factors, so IL2S is still the primary motivation in learning translation online.

Factor 2 is highly loaded in the dimension of "Out of the Box". The survey questions in this dimension are as follows, D1: I hope to pass the time and fill the emptiness in my life through online translation learning; D3: I hope to find spiritual and mental support through online translation learning, and D4: I hope to be able to divert my attention from other difficulties and problems through online translation learning. Because of this, Factor 2 may be titled as "Escape/Stimulation Factor",

Interpersonal communication factors with high loadings in Factor 3 include C1: I hope to expand my social circle and make new friends through the online translation learning platform; C2: I hope to become more integrated into my current circle and take part in more group activities; and C3: I hope to strengthen my bonds with my classmates, friends, and even family through the online translation learning platform. Factor 3 can thus be titled as "Social Contact Factor".

Factor 4 might be referred to as the "Social Service Factor" because it strongly suggests that social services are one of its features.

The high factor loadings of Factor 5 exist in Dimension E, "External Influence". The external influence in this case is particularly connected to translation learning or L2 learning. The survey question of E1 reads, "I was influenced by my classmates, friends, and teachers before I started to use the online translation learning platform." E2: "Excellent learners and experts on the Internet or around me recommend using online translation learning platforms." E3, "I started to use the online translation learning platform because I was affected by the epidemic and could not or did not want to participate in offline translation learning." L2 learning experiences include situated and executive motivations specific to the current learning environment and experience (such as the school environment, the teacher-student interaction, and the success/failure experience). So, this factor is reasonably named as "L2LE Factor".

The two future self-guides representing possible (ideal and ought-to) selves have traditionally received more theoretical attention within the L2 Motivational Self System, leaving the third key feature of the construct, the L2 Learning Experience, somewhat under-theorized. However, empirical research that repeatedly shows that the L2 Learning Experience is not only a significant predictor of numerous criterion measures but is frequently the most potent predictor of motivated behavior shows that this third component is not minor in significance [34].

Factor 6 is a little bit different. It has high factor loadings across different dimensions as the "IL2S Factor". The high loadings of Factor 6 exist on B3 (0.59) and C4 (0.494). B3 is classified as "Academic Achievement" and its survey question reads: "I would like to learn through the online translation platform and achieve good grades in my school courses." C4 is tagged as "Earn Respect", and its narrative is "I want to learn and enhance my translation skills through online translation to gain recognition and respect from others." A good box to B3 and C4 is OL2S. The properties one believes one should possess to live up to expectations and avoid negative outcomes are known as ought-to L2 Self (OL2S) concerns. This element has to do with one's obligation, therefore it also has to do with more external instrumental motives. In the narratives of B3 and E2, "learning translation online" is compared to a tool or equipment that one can use to get good marks and win respect. So, Factor 6 is the "OL2S Factor".

### 3.3 Structural Equation Model

To better investigate the structure of the six factors, the authors attempted to develop a structural equation model. The structural equation model was used to investigate the motivation for video-synchronous speaking practice, asynchronous collaborative writing practice, course satisfaction, and the mediating role of course satisfaction on behavioral intentions to use language learning technology in the context of a fully online foreign language English course. Chen (2022) investigated the motivation to utilize the digital game-based learning software CHEN-slate among Taiwanese undergraduate EFL students studying English-to-Chinese translation. According to the study's findings, the most common motivations for Taiwanese students to pursue translation studies are improving their self-image and having a positive translation learning experience [35]. It suggests the primary role of IL2S in translation learning. But in terms of online translation learning, what factors influence IL2S or are influenced by IL2S? In other words, what's the relationship between the six factors extracted from survey data?

In order to answer the question, the authors employed a structural equation model (SEM). Then, the author investigated how IL2S influences the other five motivations.

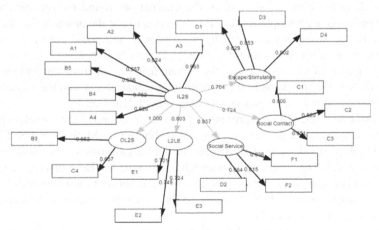

**Fig. 1.** How does IL2S influence other Factors in SEM of Online Translation Learning Motivation

Figure 1 shows the paths connecting IL2S and the other 4 major motivations, and all of the four path coefficients indicate that IL2S has a positive influence on OL2S, L2LE, Social Service, Social Contract, and Escape/Stimulation. In previous studies, Zhao (2022) found that for English majors in China, the ideal L2 self positively predicts

**Table 4.** Estimates and significance of each path in the SEM

| Path | Estimate | Standard Error | P |
|---|---|---|---|
| IL2S→Escape/Stimulation | 0.704 | 0.154 | 0.000*** |
| IL2S→Social Contact | 0.724 | 0.162 | 0.000*** |
| IL2S→Social Service | 0.857 | 0.145 | 0.000*** |
| IL2S→L2LE | 0.803 | 0.152 | 0.000*** |
| IL2S→OL2S | 1 | 0.149 | 0.000*** |

the L2 learning experience [10]. According to the statistics on Fig. 1, the conclusion is valid in online translation learning.

According to Table 4, the other five motives and IL2S have direct positive linear correlations, and the p-values for all of the paths were all less than 0.01, indicating the significance of these linear correlations (Fig. 2).

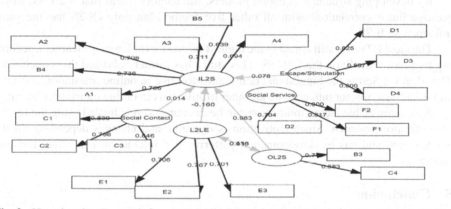

**Fig. 2.** How do other Factors influence IL2S in SEM of Online Translation Learning Motivation

The strong direct positive linear correlations are not present along the path towards IL2S. The high association is only visible along one line from OL2S to IL2S. No other factor has as much of an impact as IL2S. The estimates of other paths are quite small and their p-values are all bigger than 0.5, so other correlations are not significant.

## 4   Results and Discussion

To develop the motivation model for online translation learning, the authors conducted an exploratory factor analysis. IL2S is the main driving force for online translation learning, followed by "Escape/Stimulation," "Social Service," and "L2 Learning Experience," all of which have comparable factor weights. Out of the six motivations, OL2S comes in last. This study's empirical findings support those of earlier studies: IL2S is arguably the strongest motivator for language learners, while OL2S may be positive but isn't a very strong motivator for online translation learning. It further demonstrates that motivation is not instrumental motivation when studying translation online (Table 5).

**Table 5.** Factor Weight

| Component | Variance Rotated (%) | Accumulative Variance Rotated (%) | Weight (%) |
|---|---|---|---|
| IL2S Factor | 18.961 | 18.961 | 26.325 |
| Escape/Stimulation Factor | 14.635 | 33.597 | 20.319 |
| Social Contact Factor | 13.332 | 46.928 | 18.509 |
| Social Service Factor | 9.835 | 56.764 | 13.655 |
| L2LE Factor | 9.24 | 66.004 | 12.829 |
| OL2S Factor | 6.024 | 72.028 | 8.363 |

By developing structural equation models, the authors found that IL2S has direct positive linear correlations with all other five factors, but only OL2S has the same influence on IL2S.

The ideal L2 self is still arguably the biggest motivator for language learners, according to a recent study on the L2MSS. This study has further validated this conclusion. The Ideal L2 Self is the biggest and dominant incentive in online translation learning, and it has a significant influence on all other motivations in online translation learning.

As a controllable factor, motivation can be encouraged or adjusted using the results of motivation research. Since motivation is dynamic and changes depending on the environment and has its developmental patterns, this interaction can affect learning outcomes.

## 5  Conclusion

This study investigates 150 college students' motivation in online translation learning and then uses exploratory factor analysis and structural equation model (SEM) two methods to model the structure of motivation in online translation learning and explores the relationship between the motivation structure and L2 motivation self-system.

This research finds six types of major motivations in online translation learning: IL2S Factor, Escape/Stimulation Factor, Social Contact Factor, Social Service Factor, L2LE Factor, and OL2S Factor. Among the motivations, IL2S is the strongest motivator for language learners, while OL2S may be positive but isn't a very strong one. It further demonstrates that motivation in online translation learning is not instrumental. Besides, IL2S has direct positive linear correlations with all other five factors, but only OL2S has the same influence on IL2S in response.

**Acknowledgements.** The work was supported by 2021 Provincial Quality Engineering Project of colleges and universities, project name: Research on the application of micro-lesson in Ideological and Political Teaching of College English Course (Project No.2021jyxm1646).

# References

1. Csizér, K., Kormos, J.: Learning experiences, selves and motivated learning behaviour: a comparative analysis of structural models for Hungarian secondary and university learners of English. In: Motivation, Language Identity and the L2 Self, vol. 36, pp. 98–119 (2009)
2. Papi, M., Abdollahzadeh, E.: Teacher motivational practice, student motivation, and possible L2 selves: an examination in the Iranian EFL context. Lang. Learn. **62**(2), 571–594 (2012)
3. Liu, F.: A study on Chinese EFL learners' motivation from the perspective of L2MSS. Ph.D dissertation, Shanghai International Studies University, China (2010)
4. Alshahrani, A.A.S.: L2 motivational self system among Arab EFL learners: Saudi prespective. Int. J. Appl. Linguist. Eng. Lit. **5**(5), 145–152 (2016)
5. Salaberry, M.R.: The use of technology for second language learning and teaching: a retrospective. Mod. Lang. J. **85**(1), 39–56 (2001)
6. Davitti, E., Pasquandrea, S.: Enhancing research-led interpreter education: an exploratory study in applied conversation analysis. Interpret. Transl. Train. **8**(3), 374–398 (2014)
7. Jääskeläinen, R., Kujamäki, P., Mäkisalo, J.: Towards professionalism—or against it? Dealing with the changing world in translation research and translator education. Across Lang. Cult. **12**(2), 143–156 (2011)
8. Li, X.: Self-assessment as 'assessment as learning' in translator and interpreter education: validity and washback. Interpret. Transl. Train. **12**(1), 48–67 (2018)
9. Washbourne, K.: The self-directed learner: intentionality in translator training and education. Perspectives **22**(3), 373–387 (2014)
10. Zhao, X., Xiao, W., Zhang, J.: L2 motivational self system, international posture and the sustainable development of L2 proficiency in the COVID-19 era: a case of English majors in China. Sustainability **14**(13), 8087 (2022)
11. Gardner, R.C.: Social psychological aspects of second language acquisition. In: Giles, H., St. Clair, R. (eds.) Language and Social Psychology. Basil Blackwell, Oxford (1979)
12. Gardner, R.C., Lalonde, R.N., Moorcroft, R.: The role of attitudes and motivation in second language learning: correlational and experimental considerations. Lang. Learn. **35**(2), 207–227 (1985)
13. Gardner, R.C.: Motivation and Second Language Acquisition: The Socio-educational Model, vol. 10. Peter Lang, New York (2010)
14. Markus, H., Nurius, P.: Possible selves. Am. Psychologist **41**(9), 954 (1986)
15. Dörnyei, Z.: The L2 motivational self system. In: Motivation, Language Identity and the L2 Self, vol. 36, no. 3, 9–11 (2009)
16. Lukács, G.: The comparative analysis of motivation, attitudes and selves: the case of English and German in Hungary. System **38**(1), 1–13 (2010)
17. Taguchi, T., Magid, M., Papi, M.: The L2 motivational self system among Japanese, Chinese and Iranian learners of English: a comparative study. In: Motivation, Language Identity and the L2 Self, vol. 36, pp. 66–97 (2009)
18. Teimouri, Y.: L2 selves, emotions, and motivated behaviors. Stud. Second. Lang. Acquis. **39**(4), 681–709 (2017)
19. You, C., Dörnyei, Z., Csizér, K.: Motivation, vision, and gender: a survey of learners of English in China. Lang. Learn. **66**(1), 94–123 (2016)
20. Xie, Y.: L2 self of beginning-level heritage and nonheritage postsecondary learners of Chinese. Foreign Lang. Ann. **47**(1), 189–203 (2014)
21. Kormos, J., Kiddle, T., Csizer, K.: Systems of goals, attitudes, and self-related beliefs in second-language-learning motivation. Appl. Linguist. **32**(5), 495–516 (2011)
22. Lee, Y., Ahn, K.: English learning motivation and English academic achievement of Korean elementary school students: the effects of L2 selves, international posture, and family encouragement. Modern English Educ. **14**(1), 127–152 (2013)

23. Yu, X.: College students' L2MSS. MA thesis, Jiangxi Normal University, China (2015)
24. Boo, Z., Dörnyei, Z., Ryan, S.: L2 motivation research 2005–2014: understanding a publication surge and a changing landscape. System **55**, 145–157 (2015)
25. Dörnyei, Z.: Researching complex dynamic systems:'Retrodictive qualitative modelling'in the language classroom. Lang. Teach. **47**(1), 80–91 (2014)
26. Liu, C., Yu, C.: Understanding students' motivation in translation learning: a case study from the self-concept perspective. Asian-Pacific J. Second Foreign Lang. Educ. **4**(1), 1–19(2019)
27. Jabu, B., Abduh, A.: Motivation and challenges of trainee translators participating in translation training. Int. J. Lang. Educ. **5**(1), 490–500 (2021)
28. Kassem, M.A.M.: The effect of utilizing CAT technology on English majors' translation and motivation. Asian EFL J. **28**(2.3), 135–155 (2021)
29. Wu, F., Wang, C., Li, J.: An assessment scale to measure adult learners' motivation in online learning environment with non-constraint. Modern Dist. Educ. Res. [现代远程教育研究] **4**, 60–65 (2015)
30. Kim, K.J., Frick, T.W.: Changes in student motivation during online learning. J. Educ. Comput. Res. **44**(1), 1–23 (2011)
31. Fang, X.:The impact of online teaching on the English learning motivation of Chinese students during COVID-19. In: Proceedings of the International Symposium on Education, Culture and Social Sciences, pp. 15–16. BCP, Xi'an, China (2020)
32. Natalya, L., Purwanto, C.V.: Exploratory and confirmatory factor analysis of the academic motivation scale (AMS)–Bahasa Indonesia. Makara Hum. Behav. Stud. Asia **22**(1), 29–42 (2018)
33. Kim, T.-Y., Kim, Y.-K.: A structural model for perceptual learning styles, the ideal L2 self, motivated behavior, and English proficiency. System **46**, 14–27 (2014)
34. Dörnyei, Z.: Towards a better understanding of the L2 learning experience, the Cinderella of the L2 motivational self system. stud. Second Lang. Learn. Teach. 9.1 (2019)
35. Chen, Y.: Using a game-based translation learning app and google apps to enhance translation skills: amplification and omission. Int. J. Hum.–Comput. Interact. 1–15 (2022)

# Transediting of Children's Literature in the Age of Technology

Xinyu Hu and Lu Tian[✉]

School of Interpreting and Translation Studies, Guangdong University of Foreign Studies,
Guangzhou, China
ivytianlu@gdufs.edu.cn

**Abstract.** Translation for children inevitably involves editing to the text as children have their own cognitive characteristics and restrictions. In this regard, this study takes translation of children's literature as a kind of transediting and probes into the principles and methods of transediting children's literary works. Taking the classic children's literature *The Wizard of Oz* and its Bookworm bilingual version as a case for analysis, this study finds that transediting of children's literature involves considerations from three dimensions—narrative, language, and culture. To tailor to children's cognitive characteristics, transeditors usually make adaptions to the original text. Such measures include deleting branching plots and extracting the main storyline, using basic vocabulary and simple sentence structures, and transforming foreign cultural elements into familiar ones. The study also points out that technology-empowered children's literary books have shown their advantages in enhancing children's reading experience and in giving full play to the educational significance.

**Keywords:** Transediting · Children's literature · Technology · Education

## 1 Introduction

Children's literature is one of the earliest forms of discourse that individuals have access to in their growth, having an important influence on and guidance in the enhancement of language competence, the development of cognitive ability, and the formation of values. Therefore, children's literature is an integral part of children's education. An excellent children's literary work will resonate with children in emotion and bring them spiritual pleasure, and in this way cultivate their sentiment and help with their aesthetics and ability to create.

In order to expose children to a more diverse culture context and improve their cognitive ability, the introduction and translation of children's literary works from other countries has become a usual complement to readings originally created in their own mother language and culture context. As children's literature is often created and translated by adult professionals, during the creation and translation process, they have to always bear children in their mind, taking account of the necessary background information to facilitate comprehension, the potential language difficulties and barriers, as well as the cognitive characteristics of children. Otherwise, it will inevitably bring trouble to children's understanding of the text, thus failing to achieve the expected educational effect.

Due to the above concerns including the differences in cultural contexts and the characteristics of children's cognition, translation of children's literature often involves adaptation and reconstruction of the original text, so it is more precisely a kind of "transediting", a phenomenon that editing is involved in the translation process. In transediting, the translator may change the content and the form of the original text to a certain extent in order to suit the need of the target readers (e.g., children) or to meet a particular purpose of the translation [1]. At the same time, to bring children's literature into full play in cultivating children's literacy and fulfilling its educational significance, application of various technologies, such as the use of talking pens and multimodal display of information, has become commonplace for children's literary works. Taking *The Wizard of Oz* from the Oxford Bookworm bilingual series as an example, this study explores the editing and translation strategies adopted in the transediting of children's literature in the age of technology.

## 2   Studies on the Translation of Children's Literature

Since the 1980s, research on children's literature has become increasingly popular around the world (e.g. [2, 3]). Accordingly, studies of children's literature in translation have also flourished with abundant research monographs published (e.g. [4–6]). Some representative ones include Coillie and Verschueren's [7] collected volume on translation of children's literature and Lathey's [8, 9] two books *The Translation of Children's Literature: A Reader* and *The Role of Translators in Children's Literature: Invisible Storytellers* published in 2006 and 2010 respectively. These studies cover a wide range of topics including polysystem theory, country-specific studies, translation history, ideology and censorship.

Translation activities of children's literature in China began in the late Qing Dynasty [10]. Although earlier litterateurs and writers, such as Lin Shu, Zhou Zuoren and Lu Xun, translated foreign children's literary works into Chinese, few relevant studies were conducted at that time. With the deepening of globalization and the large-scale introduction of foreign children's literature to China in the new millennium, studies on the translation of children's literature have received more attention (e.g. [11–13]). In the past decade in particular, relevant studies have shown an increasing trend. Zhao Juanli [14] combed through studies on translation of children's literature in China in the past 30 years and categorized previous studies into eight aspects, viz. Translation standards, translation methods and strategies, retranslation studies, descriptive studies, translator subjectivity, translation history, translator studies, and translation criticism. It is pointed out that the main problems of relevant research lie in a lack of depth and width and that the overall research in China lagged behind that of the international circle. Based on analysis of the current situation of the translation and spread of Chinese children's literature to other countries, Zhao Jirong [15] found that there were not enough translation practitioners and researchers in the field and a systematic model with effective paths for the translation and spread of Chinese children's literature overseas has not yet been established.

## 3 Transediting for Children

Transediting is a form and method of translation. It happens when a text is not only translated into another language but also edited to a certain degree as need be. Therefore, transeditors have to possess both abilities of translating and editing. Apart from language competence, relevant professional knowledge and translation skills, the abilities to analyze, synthesize, and restructure information are also indispensable [16]. Through transediting it may help create the same effects in the target text readers what the original author expects to have on the source text readers. According to Zhang Meifang [1], the term "transediting" itself implies the meaning of "change". Transeditors make changes to the content and sometimes the form of the original text to suit the need of the target reader. At present, transediting has been widely explored in journalistic translation [17–19], and its application to studies of children's literature is still limited.

Translation of children's literature is in many cases a kind of transediting as it often involves adaptation and adjustment of the text to suit the different readership, the altered discourse environment, as well as the cultural and ideological requirements. Such transediting often involves rearrangement of the structure, narration, perspective and focus of the original text to ensure the coherence and acceptance of the translated text. When a children's literary work is translated, the text is inevitably rewritten and recreated by the transeditor from a target-oriented perspective and their mediation may reflect a certain degree of ideological manipulation. Translation, therefore, becomes a form of rewriting and adaptation. This is particularly true in the spread of children's literature as many stories and fairytales have become welcomed and enjoyed worldwide through translation [20].

In this technology era, children are exposed to not only paper books but also various technology-facilitated readings such as audio books. These technology-enhanced children's literary works have contributed to the cultivation of children's literacy and cognitive ability. In this regard, this study takes transediting of children's literature in a broad sense. Against the backdrop of the new era, transediting of children's literature involves not only changes to the discourse, but also alterations to the form of children's literary works in conveying information and knowledge. We will explore how children's cognition and literacy can be enhanced by reading such technology-empowered transedited literary works.

## 4 Case Study

### 4.1 Bookworm Bilingual Series

The Bookworm is a series of bilingual literary works for young readers co-published by Oxford University Press from the UK and Foreign Language Teaching and Research Press from China. Each book in the series consists of such sections as preparatory work, adapted story, Chinese translation, comprehension exercises, and grammar points. Therefore, by reading these books readers can not only learn about the content and relevant knowledge of the story but also enhance their language competence in both Chinese, their mother tongue, and English, the first choice of foreign language to learn for most Chinese children. The books in the series are graded in seven levels according to their difficulty in vocabulary and language. Books of the introductory level are in the form of comics, while books of Levels 1 to 6 are arranged in an English-Chinese parallel format with key words annotated on each page and exercises following the main content to help test the readers' comprehension and their command of English. Each book in the set comes with an MP3 CD containing the audio materials of the content, read by native professionals.

This paper takes *The Wizard of Oz* from the Bookworm series as an example for case study. The book was written by L. Frank Baum, a journalist from the Midwest of the U.S., and was rewritten by Rosemary Border from the U.K. The translator of this English-Chinese version for children is Xiao Yue from China.

### 4.2 Transediting of *The Wizard of Oz*

#### 4.2.1 Overall Adjustment

*The Wizard of Oz* talks about the adventure of Dorothy, a young girl from the countryside of Kansas. The book is also commonly regarded as an allegory for the political, economic and social events of America in the late 19th century [21, 22]. At that time, due to major fiscal redistribution, most farmers in the west of the U.S. became debtors while the bankers in the east became creditors. When the price level fell, the true value of the debt rose accordingly, thus enriching the banks at the expense of the farmers' interests. The solution to the problem was to mint silver coins. However, as money supply was actually determined by the amount of gold, the interests of farmers could not be guaranteed. In this regard, the political, economic and social allegory is thus manifested. Meanwhile, many metaphors are employed in the original text. For example, when describing Dorothy's hometown, the writer portrays the landscape of Kansas prairie as gray to indicate the unfortunate life of farmers. The witch's silver shoes and the golden brick road are used to allude to the monetary policy of the time.

Considering that such background information may be unfamiliar to the Chinese young readers, the Bookworm version deleted all the descriptions of the "gray" tone and replaced "silver" shoes with "red" shoes. The later adaption might be influenced by the change from silver shoes to ruby slippers in the 1939 movie as it was believed that out of technical considerations "red showed up more vividly on the film stock of the period than silver" [23]. In addition, the color of red is a more pleasing and typical color in Chinese culture, thus more comprehensible for the target Chinese young readers.

In the transedited version, some subplots and details of the main storyline were removed, resulting in a combination of many chapters into one. This was done with the target reader in mind as complicated plot with too much information might be hard for children especially those from different cultural background. Therefore, extracting the main story and simplifying the storyline can help reduce the reading and comprehension barriers for young readers of the transedited text.

#### 4.2.2  Treatment of the Specific

In this section, examples selected from the first two chapters of the transedited version will be analyzed and discussed in detail.

4.2.2.1 Title

The original book published in 1900 was entitled *The Wonderful Wizard of Oz*. The English title of the Bookworm series is *The Wizard of Oz*, naming after the adapted musical staged in 1902. With the word "wonderful" being left out in later versions, it leaves more space for the readers to form ideas through their own reading rather than telling them right at the very beginning that the wizard is in fact "wonderful". Such adaptation helps in enhancing children's independent cognitive ability.

An early Chinese version for the title is 奥兹国的魔法师, which is a literal translation of "The Wizard of Oz". Later, 绿野仙踪, which literally means "green field fairy trace", gradually dominated the market and received wide acceptance among the Chinese readers. The latter version of the Chinese title takes into account the cultural differences as wizards are rarely mentioned in the Chinese cultural context, thus relatively unfamiliar to the target reader. In this regard, the Chinese version adopts "fairy trace (仙踪)", a more pleasant-yet-mysterious word in connotation, to translate the title. In addition, the adoption of four-Chinese-character-phrase for the title is in line with the preference of Chinese for book titles, pleasing in sound and easy to remember. In transediting the title, the pre-determined commentary word "wonderful" was removed from the English version, and the Chinese title was translated in a way that is more in line with the reading habits of Chinese readers.

4.2.2.2 Setting

In laying the setting of the story, the author described the living conditions of Dorothy as follows.

Eg. 1

The original text:

> Dorothy lived in the midst of the great Kansas prairies, with Uncle Henry, who as a farmer, and Aunt Em, who was the farmer's wife. Their house was small, for the lumber to build it had to be carried by wagon many miles.

The adapted text:

> Dorothy lived in a small house in Kansas, with Uncle Henry, Aunt Em, and a little black dog called Toto.

The transedited text:

> 多萝西和她的舅舅亨利、舅妈埃姆以及小黑狗托托住在堪萨斯州的一幢小房子里。

The phrase "the great Kansas prairies" in the original text might be difficult for Chinese young readers to understand for they do not have sufficient background knowledge nor relevant life experience, so it is left out in the transedited text. In addition, the transedited version omits some details, such as the identity of Uncle Henry and the conditions of the house. The original two complex sentences are combined into one simple sentence with clear subject-verb-object structure after transediting. Such change takes into account the cognitive abilities of the target reader as children might be easily confused by too complicated information. The removal of unnecessary details, therefore, helps children to grasp the main story clues rather than being distracted by unnecessary information.

The cellar is perhaps the most important item in the setting, and the story starts from the cellar.

Eg. 2

The original text:

> There was no garret at all, and no cellar—except a small hole, dug in the ground, called a cyclone cellar, where the family could go in case one of those great whirlwinds arose, mighty enough to crush any building in its path.

The adapted text:

> There were cellars under all the houses. And when a cyclone came, people went down into their cellars and stayed there. And when a cyclone came, people went down into their cellars and stayed there.

The transedited text:

> 有时候会突然刮起风速极大的风，这就是龙卷风，它能将树木和人甚至房屋卷走，因而每幢房屋都有地下室。当龙卷风刮起时，人们就钻进地下室躲起来。

Comparing the different versions, we can find that the logic of the transedited version is clearer. It first introduces what "cyclone (龙卷风)" is, followed by description of its mighty power that it could blow away people, trees, even houses. Therefore, under every house there was a cellar, which was used to protect people against cyclones. The original text, however, seems to assume that the readers already have enough knowledge about the windiness of the Kansas prairies, so it refers to the cellar directly without much introduction. In addition, the adoption of both "cyclone" and "whirlwind" in the original text might bring confusion to children who do not have a large vocabulary. In order to avoid unnecessary reading obstacles, the adapted text and the transedited text avoid the word "whirlwind", or 旋风 in Chinese and chose to use "cyclone (龙卷风)" consistently throughout the whole section.

It is worth noting that despite the distinction between "cellar" and "cyclone cellar" in the original text which denies the existence of the former in the neighborhood, the adapted and the transedited texts make no distinction of the two and directly mention cellars as something commonplace or even a necessity for each household. Such transediting helps in smoothing out the logic of the story and in presenting it in a more friendly way for young readers. In addition, the simplified vocabulary in the transedited text helps in facilitating child readers' reading and comprehension.

The cyclone is the trigger of the story. It was the cyclone that blew Dorothy away to another world. In the original text, the author described the cyclone in great detail.

Eg. 3
The original text:

> The house whirled around two or three times and rose slowly through the air. The north and south winds met where the house stood, and made it the exact center of the cyclone. In the middle of a cyclone the air is generally still, but the great pressure of the wind on every side of the house raised it up higher and higher, until it was at the very top of the cyclone; and there it remained and was carried miles and miles away as easily as you could carry a feather.

The adapted text:

> The house moved, and then it went slowly up, up, up into the sky.

The transedited text:

> 房子开始移动，然后慢慢升高，升高，升高，一直升到了半空中。

The original text describes the process when the house was being blown up by the cyclone in much detail, not only depicting the change of state of the house, explaining in depth the formation of the cyclone, but also giving the reason why the house could be raised up by the cyclone. In contrast, the transedited text does not include any in-depth depiction of the house as it was being hit by the cyclone nor a scientific explanation for how it could be blown up into the sky. It simplifies the whole process into one short sentence and omits all the detailed information to make it easier for children to understand. In addition, the transedited text adopts three repetitive "up (升高)" to mimic the feature of child language. With the combination of audio and visual effects, it helps in arousing children's interest and making them fully immersed in the story.

4.2.2.3 Characters

On the journey to the Emerald City, Dorothy had three friends accompanying her. Scarecrow and Tin Man were two of them. In the original text the author stated how the little girl made friends with them, but in the transedited text changes were made to this section.

Eg. 4
The original text:

"Good day," said the Scarecrow, in a rather husky voice.

"Did you speak?" asked the girl, in wonder.

"Certainly," answered the Scarecrow; "how do you do?"

"I'm pretty well, thank you," replied Dorothy, politely; "how do you do?"

"I'm not feeling well," said the Scarecrow, with a smile, "for it is very tedious being perched up here night and day to scare away crows.

"Can't you get down?" asked Dorothy.

"No, for this pole is stuck up my back. If you will please take away the pole I shall be greatly obliged to you."

Dorothy reached up both arms and lifted the figure off the pole; for, being stuffed with straw, it was quite light.

"Thank you very much," said the Scarecrow, when he had been set down on the ground. "I feel like a new man."

The adapted text:

"Good day," said the Scarecrow.

"Oh!" said Dorothy. "You can speak!"

"Of course I can speak," said the Scarecrow. "But I can't move, up here on this pole... Can you help me?"

Carefully, Dorothy took the Scarecrow off his pole.

"Thank you very much," said the Scarecrow. He moved his arms and legs, and straw went everywhere.

The transedited text:

"你好啊。"稻草人说。

"哦!"多萝西惊叫,"你居然会说话!"

"我当然会说话了,"稻草人回答道,"不过我不会动,只能待在这根杆上……想下来。你能帮我一下吗?"

多萝西小心翼翼地将稻草人从杆上取下来。

"非常感谢。"稻草人说。他动动胳膊,又动动腿,稻草掉了一地。

In the original text, the author adopted quite a number of adverbs such as "politely" and prepositional phrases such as "in wonder" and "with a smile" in the reporting clauses to describe the tones and attitudes of the speakers in the dialogue. Despite the simplification in the adapted English text, its Chinese equivalence, the transedited text, follows the Chinese norm of using a variety of reporting verbs to vividly represent the tone of the speaker (e.g. 惊叫 "astonishedly cry") or the function of the utterance in contributing to the coherence of the dialogue (e.g. 回答道 "answer say").

It is worth noting that as children's books become audio, it largely enhances children's reading experience. By listening to the story, children are not only more immersed in it but also provided with opportunities to imitate the tone of different characters in different contexts and at the same time to learn new words and enhance their overall language competence.

Eg. 5
The original text:

> One of the big trees had been partly chopped through, and standing beside it, with an uplifted axe in his hands, was a man made entirely of tin. His head and arms and legs were jointed upon his body, but he stood perfectly motionless, as if he could not stir at all.

The adapted text:

> They saw a man by a big tree, with an axe in his hand. He was made of tin. He stood very still and shouted "Help!" again and again and again.

The transedited text:

> 他们看见一个锡做的人，手持一把斧头，站在一棵大树边。他一动不动，一遍又一遍地喊"救命"。

In introducing the Tin Man, the original text adopts a first-person narration, which enables readers to cast themselves into the role of the characters. The adapted and the transedited texts, however, shift the point of view to third-person narration, which may unfortunately weaken the reading experience as it has lengthened the distance between the reader and the characters.

Such undermined experience is also reflected in the order of information as discrepancy is found between different versions. In the original text, what Dorothy saw is stated in detail at the beginning with the fact that it was actually a tin man placed at the end. In contrast, the transedited text reveals directly at the beginning that the man was made of tin, which unduly damages the effect of suspense, a key factor in creating surprise in literary works.

4.2.2.4 Events

Dorothy was blown by the cyclone into another world and by accident smashed an evil witch to death when her house fell onto the ground. The Witch of the North, in gratitude, showed Dorothy the way to home and gave her a kiss which could give her protection. This event is a foreshadow of the following story as the kiss indeed protected Dorothy on her way home.

Eg. 6

The original text:

> "No, I cannot do that," she replied; "but I will give you my kiss, and no one will dare injure a person who has been kissed by the Witch of the North."
> She came close to Dorothy and kissed her gently on the forehead. Where her lips touched the girl they left a round, shining mark, as Dorothy found out soon after.

The adapted text:

> "I can't go with you, but I can give you my kiss." She gave Dorothy a little kiss. It looked like a small red flower on Dorothy's face. "Now nothing can hurt you," she said."

The transedited text:

> "我不能陪你去，不过我可以给你一个吻。"她轻轻吻了多萝西一下，那个吻就像贴在多萝西脸颊上的一朵小红花。"从现在起没有什么能伤害你了，"女巫说。

The focus of this section is that the witch's kiss can protect the little girl. The original text chooses to put the focus in the front, while the adapted and transedited texts move it to the back. As it is mentioned above, saving the key information to later revelation contributes to the creation of suspense, thus enhancing the reading experience.

The original text describes the kiss as "a round, shining mark" which is more abstract compared with "a small red flower" in the adapted text or "little red flower (小红花)" in the transedited version. The image of red flowers is very familiar to children, especially to Chinese, as red is an auspicious color in Chinese culture thus commonly used and seen. In this connect, the employment of the red flower simile helps not only in facilitating comprehension but also in conveying the positive connotation of the kiss.

### 4.3   Technology in Bilingual Literary Books for Children

In the age of technology, various technological inventions have been applied to education. As far as children's bilingual books are concerned, technology contributes to the educational significance of children's literature on at least three aspects —language competence, cognitive capability and social skills. Taking the Bookworm bilingual series as an example, the use of talking pens not only facilitates children's vocabulary learning but also adds great fun to book reading. By a simple touch with the pen, readers can get easy access to the pronunciation of the words or expressions they want to learn about. The availability of the audio versions of the books brings more vivid stories with both audio and visual narrations to children. By listening to and imitating the tones of different characters in different contexts, children will have better understanding of emotion and interpersonal communication, thus improving their cognitive capability and social skills. Meanwhile, audiobooks can enhance children's interest in literary works offering them with different and novel reading experiences.

Taking into consideration the features of educational technology in children's bilingual books, transeditors of children's literature may make full use of its advantages to create more enjoyable and instructive books for children. For example, given the accessibility of audiobooks, transeditors may use more dialogues and onomatopoeia in their transediting of children's literature.

## 5   Conclusion

Transediting is a kind of tailored translation for specific purposes or for special target readers. Based on our discussion and case analysis, it can be found that transediting of children's literature in the age of technology mainly involves considerations from three dimensions—narrative, language, and culture.

Considering children's limitations in cognition, language and the world knowledge, transeditors usually make adaptions to literary works to ensure smooth reading and comprehension. Such measures include deleting branching plots and extracting the main storyline, using basic vocabulary and simple sentence structures, and transforming foreign cultural elements into familiar ones. At the same time, some contents that are incomprehensible or unsuitable for children, such as cultural metaphors and violence, might be removed in the transediting process.

In this new era, technology has empowered many works of children's literature. Some transedited children's literary books are presented as audio or even video books. In this regard, the educational significance of these books particularly their contribution to language acquisition turns to be more prominent. Meanwhile, technology-empowered books also add fun to the reading process thus enhancing children's reading experience.

**Acknowledgements.** This work was supported by the Guangdong Philosophy and Social Science Research Programme (GD20XWY10, "A Textual Cognitive Approach to the Transediting of Children's Literature").

## References

1. Zhang, M. F.: Theory and practice of adaption: a case analysis within the Functional Theory of Translation (编译的理论与实践——用功能翻译理论分析编译实例). J. Sichuan Int. Stud. Univ. (2), 95–98+113 (2004)
2. Webb, J.: Text Culture and National Identity in Children's Literature. Nordinfo, Helsinki (2000)
3. Yasuda, H.: Introduction. In: Wakamiya, N., Solarski, M., Sterbenz, J. (eds.) IWAN 2003. LNCS, vol. 2982, pp. 1–2. Springer, Heidelberg (2004). https://doi.org/10.1007/978-3-540-24715-9_1
4. Oittinen, R.: Translating for Children. Garland Publishing, New York (2000)
5. O'Sullivan, E.: Narratology meets translation studies, or, the voice of the translator in children's literature. Meta Transl. J. **48**(1–2), 197–207 (2003)
6. Shih, C.: Corpus-based study of differences in explicitation between literature translations for children and for adults. Transl. J. **12**(3), 1–14 (2008)
7. Coillie, J.V., Verschueren, W.P.: Children's Literature in Translation: Challenges and Strategies. St. Jerome Publishing, Manchester (2006)
8. Lathey, G. (ed.): The Translation of Children's Literature: A Reader. Multilingual matters, Clevedon (2006)

9. Lathey, G.: The Role of Translators in Children's Literature: Invisible Storytellers. Routledge, London (2010)
10. Zhang, J.Q.: Translation of Children's Literature in the Late Qing Dynasty and the Birth of Chinese Children's Literature (《晚清儿童文学翻译与中国儿童文学之诞生》). Fudan University, Shanghai (2008)
11. Zhang, D.Z.: Zhou Zuoren's thoughts on translation of children's literature (论周作人的儿童文学翻译思想). J. Anyang Inst. Technol. 3, 121–123 (2006)
12. Wen, J., Wang, C.S.: Translation of reportages in China during the Sino-Japanese War (外国儿童文学的译介及其影响). Comparative Lit. China 4, 10–20 (2008)
13. Xu, D.R.: Child-Oriented Translation Studies and Literary Criticism (《儿童文学翻译的文体学研究》). Juvenil & Children's Publishing House, Shanghai (2020)
14. Zhao, J.L.: Review of children's literature translation during the past 30 years in China (国内30年间儿童文学翻译研究综述). J Lanzhou Jiaotong Univ. 5, 28–31 (2016)
15. Zhao, J.R.: On translation of Chinese children's literature in Chinese culture "Going Global" (中国儿童文学"走出去":对外译介现状分析). J. Guangdong Univ. Foreign Stud. (2), 128–138+160 (2020)
16. Lin, H.T.: A Companion for Chinese Translators (《中国翻译词典》). Hubei Education Press, Wuhan (2005)
17. Xu, L.: An analysis of news compilation under the guidance of Functional Equivalence Theory (功能对等理论指导下的新闻编译探析). J. News Res. 1, 64–66 (2022)
18. Valdeón, R.A.: Fifteen years of journalistic translation research and more. Perspect. Stud. Translatol. 23(4), 634–662 (2015)
19. Davies, E.E.: Shifting readerships in journalistic translation. Perspect. Stud. Translatol. 14(2), 83–98 (2006)
20. Leonardi, V.: Ideological Manipulation of Children's Literature through Translation and Rewriting: Travelling across Times and Places. Springer Nature (2020)
21. Lai, J.C.: The Wizard of Oz and Modern American Monetary history (《绿野仙踪》与美国近代货币史). View Financial 6, 24–25 (2017)
22. Zhang, Y.: Metaphor analysis of The Wizard of Oz(《绿野仙踪》的隐喻分析). Tangshan Lit. 2, 114–115 (2017)
23. Barbarese, J.T.: The first American children's book. In: Baum, L.F. (ed) The Wonderful Wizard of Oz. Branes & Noble Classics, New York (2005)

# A Study on Knowledge Network Acceptability Facilitated by a Computer-Based Translation Learning Platform

Yuanyuan Mu[1] , Lizhen Du[1]($\boxtimes$) , and Qianyu Li[2]

[1] Chaohu University, Hefei, China
3065180045@qq.com
[2] Hefei University of Technology, Hefei, China

**Abstract.** The research aims to prove knowledge network acceptability in/between Chinese and English translation learning by interviewing 82 junior EFL undergraduates who have used a computer-based platform for one semester. With the assistance of Likert Scale and statistical tools, it reveals that students can widely accept the concept, translation knowledge network, and this computer-based translation learning strategy, and they even consider this strategy more efficient than traditional offline teaching-learning activity. Based upon exploration of translation learning strategy on the platform, experiment design and analysis of experiment data, the study finds how the knowledge network acceptability can enrich students' translation learning strategies, learning resources management strategies.

**Keywords:** Knowledge network · Translation learning · Learning strategy

## 1 Introduction

With the boost of online learning and multi-language communication, advanced technologies are utilized in the language teaching-learning field. Language learners commonly adopt learning resource management strategy, including references and computers, in order to advance the efficiency in the novel learning activity [1]. As a language learning method, translation requires multifaceted activities from the perspectives of lexicon, syntax and text, in which professional knowledge is connected in a systematic network. Textwells, a computer-based translation learning platform, has been designed and developed by our research team, where knowledge nodes in/between Chinese and English translation are

Supported by Chaohu University.

annotated based upon the knowledge network. An intelligent algorithm can automatically recommend related knowledge as learners click to learn, which helps learners form the translation knowledge network and learning strategy.

Interdisciplinary approaches support the research project, which are natural language processing, translation studies, bilingual corpora, EFL (English as a Foreign Language) education, information management, functional linguistics, computer science, etc. Textwells provides a revolutionary and efficient knowledge-network-based learning model for the bilingual learners in classroom or Internet-based courses to alleviate their resource management pressure.

## 2    Translation Knowledge Network

### 2.1    Knowledge Network

Some papers have reviewed the concept of knowledge network in a general manner. This paper aims to introduce the term, knowledge network, in a specific field, namely translation education field. In Web of Science database, the content in the topic was searched as (knowledge network AND (translation teaching OR translator education OR translator training OR translation pedagogy)), 186 pieces of records are retrieved. The term, knowledge network, was firstly used by Hamburg in translation field in 1983, while "knowledge" has many meanings. It is widely applied in different disciplines like computer science, education research, communication and engineering, whose records are representatively 118, 72, 52 and 37 in the whole database [2,3]. And some papers have applied the term into translation education field in recent years [4–6]. The publications has remarkably increased each year since 2010, reaching the peak in 2020. Accordingly, another database, CNKI (China National Knowledge Infrastructure) was also retrieved in order to gain more literature information, where several authors explore knowledge network in translation education field. The published papers, which both discuss knowledge network and translation education, usually lay emphasis on the macro framework in teaching-learning activity, namely how to construct corpus-based systems; however, there are not enough feasible and empirical studies about how knowledge network can influence translation learning activity and how to testify that [7,8]. In the research, a further exploration is made between knowledge network acceptability and learning strategy. The former term comes from one dimension of knowledge network, which means learners can accept the definition, knowledge correlation and understandability of knowledge network. These data and phenomena indicate knowledge network is a novel and meaningful concept in translation education field, where related researches are at its initial stage and further discussions will be beneficial.

### 2.2    Computer-Based Platform Design

The Textwells is mainly designed for translation educators and learners, who interact through annotated bilingual texts, online recorded translation courses and translation practice projects [9,10].

For the learner account, there are six options in the navigation bar area, namely translation learning, translation practice, course interaction, Q&A (Questions & Answers), user data and my favorites (Fig. 1). Translation learning, as the indispensable part, is comprehensively and precisely annotated by scholars in accordance with a systematic knowledge node classification, which is the base of knowledge network [11–13]. There are totally six categories, namely lexicon, syntax, text, information, rhetoric and intertextuality, and fifty-six knowledge nodes, such as semantic matching, sentence component addition and rhetorical device alteration. Scholars extracted adopted knowledge nodes from classic or representative texts as they have a good knowledge of text linguistics, stylistics, functional linguistics, and discourse studies. In the knowledge-network-based translation learning section, learners can click to study according to text themes (eight first-level themes: culture, finance, law, literature, public affair, technology, prose and media; thirty-one second-level themes, such as education, natural scenery and holidays) or genres (five first-level genres: expository, narrative, argumentative, descriptive and applied writings; fourteen second-level genres, such as academic writing, publicity writing and narration of events), where learners form their own knowledge network. In the user data section, the learner's data are automatically monitored by the platform, which helps learner adjust their learning strategy.

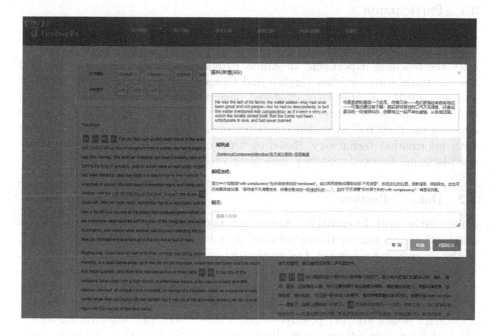

**Fig. 1.** Translation learning of the Textwells platform.

For the teacher account, the platform endeavors to provide a convenient teaching information management system, including teaching management, exercise & homework management, and project management. Teacher can give feedbacks to their students as they study knowledge nodes to form knowledge network.

The innovations of this platform lie not only in its advanced algorithm but also in its scientific and theory-supported translation knowledge annotations. As a technology-driven system, this platform provides favorable interactive experience among students, teachers and these knowledge networks. The advanced algorithm endeavors to support students based-upon knowledge network monitoring. This platform, like a map, provides a translation knowledge learning channel, while the knowledge network forms the road for the learners on the platform.

## 3   Experiment Design

Facilitated by the computer-based translation learning platform, this research aims at proving that students can widely accept translation knowledge network, and computer-based translation learning strategy. Textwells, a knowledge-network-supported platform, helps the experiment testify that knowledge network is feasible to influence translation learning activities.

### 3.1   Participants

The experiment involved 82 junior undergraduates majoring in English-Chinese translation, one experienced English teacher, and two trained teachers to conduct the teaching experiment in Anhui Province, China. These students had studied translation between English and Chinese for three semesters in offline courses, which indicated they mastered basic translation knowledge, including translation methods, strategies and skills. Before they participated in this online experiment, they had attended computer operating courses and were familiar with information technology. Based on this, every student could well operate the platform, Textwells, as they were instructed.

### 3.2   Data Collection

**Diagnostic and Formative Assessments/Tests.** 82 students attended a diagnostic assessment at the initial stage in order to test their translation ability. In the diagnostic assessment, the source text is an English text about 220 words, whose theme is natural scenery (Fig. 2) [14]. During the teaching-learning activity, teacher instructed students to learn translation knowledge nodes, including 9 knowledge nodes which appear in the text of formative assessment. The 9 knowledge nodes are: (1) positive-negative alteration; (2) semantic matching; (3) rank alteration; (4) sequence alteration; (5) voice alteration; (6) perspective alteration; (7) sentence component alteration; (8) rhetorical device alteration; and (9) notional word omission, which belong to four categories, namely lexicon, syntax, text and rhetoric. In the knowledge nodes learning process, students accepted and formed knowledge network through inner correlation among nodes.

**Fig. 2.** Diagnostic assessment.

At the end of the semester, all students participated in a formative assessment to testify their knowledge network acceptability and its influence on translation learning. In the formative assessment, the source text is an English text about 210 words, whose theme is people and events. The source texts in diagnostic assessment and formative assessment both belong to literature, which are similar in language style.

In the whole experiment, teacher and students were allowed to use this platform and English-Chinese paper dictionaries instead of other electronic and paper resources. As they were informed to translate another text in the formative assessment, students could develop their independent learning strategy with this platform after knowledge nodes were explained by their teacher. To ensure the reliability and accuracy of test, students could not turn to other pages on the platform except the translated text page when the paper dictionaries were the available references.

The scores were recorded on the platform as two trained teachers mark scores and provide comments on all translation versions. They mark scores according to the translation scoring standards of TEM-8 (Test for English Majors, Band 8, which is used to test senior undergraduates). When the threshold between two scores was or less than 7 points towards the same translation version, the two scores were averaged as the final score of the tested students. Otherwise, the experienced English teacher scored for the third time and the three scores were averaged as the final score. With the help of SPSS 26.0, one statistical software, the study analyzed these scores to form quantitative results and verify how to improve translation learning by knowledge network learning strategy.

Besides the diagnostic assessment and formative assessment, the research also collected useful data through Likert Scale questionnaire and one-one interview to explore students' acceptability towards translation knowledge network and this translation learning strategy based-on knowledge network in a comprehensive view. The following figure illustrates the methods to collect data in this experiment and detailed description (Fig. 3).

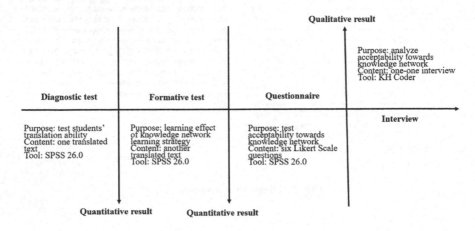

**Fig. 3.** Methods to collect data.

**Questionnaire.** The questionnaire consists of six questions, which were designed according to Likert Scale. In the Likert Scale, there are five answers in each question, where the numbers, 5, 4, 3, 2, and 1, respectively indicate strongly agree, agree, somewhat agree, disagree and strongly disagree [15]. The research verifies the reliability of the questionnaire structure and validity among questions for further factor analysis. The reliability is demonstrated by the value of cronbach's alpha as validity is proved by the value of KMO in the software SPSS 26.0. The details and data analysis will be introduced in the next section.

**Interview.** One-one in-depth interviews were conducted among 82 students. The interviewed question is: How do you evaluate the platform and knowledge network learning strategy and please give a specific evaluation description instead of giving a simple grade evaluation. Before they were interviewed, the above question was sent to the students several days in advance. Their answers were non-structured and non-standard, which cannot be analyzed by software directly. After the answer texts were processed into semi-structured form, the study selected the text processing software, KH Coder, to explore the deep opinion towards knowledge network and this learning strategy. Data analysis will be presented in the next section.

# 4    Analysis of Experiment Data

## 4.1    Score Data

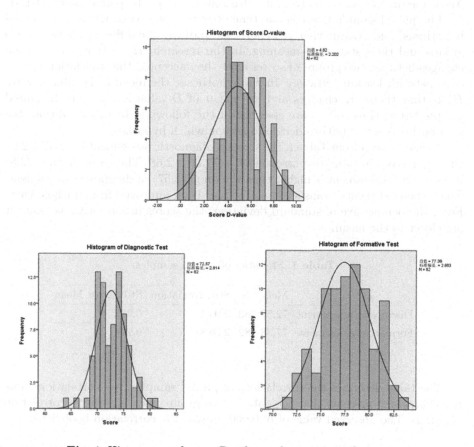

**Fig. 4.** Histograms of score D-value and scores in each group.

The research counted and calculated 164 records of scores of 82 students, which were made by three teachers and collected in the diagnostic assessment and formative assessment. The experiment aims to prove that translation knowledge network improves learners' translation learning by analyzing the two groups of scores and their difference. The relationship among scores was analyzed by paired sample t-test, where scores in each group and D-value (score of formative assessment subtracts one of diagnostic assessment) of two groups need to be in accordance with normal distribution.

At the initial stage to analyze, the scores in each group and score D-value of the same student in two groups are approved to be taken as normally distributed in SPSS 26.0, whose results are respectively illustrated in the following figures (Fig. 4). The histograms of diagnostic and formative assessments demonstrate that the distribution of the scores and student number in each test is symmetrical, which is the typical feature of normal distribution. As observed in the same way, D-value and student number can also be regarded as normally distributed. According to the above analysis, it is feasible to apply the paired sample t-test.

The paired sample t-test is one type of hypothesis tests, where $H_0$ (invalid hypothesis) and $H_1$ (alternative hypothesis) indicate the difference between two groups and their statistical meaning. In the research, $H_0$ is that there are no changes between two groups of scores after they accepted the translation knowledge network learning strategy. In $H_0$ hypothesis, the mean of D-value is zero. $H_1$ is that there are changes and the mean of D-value is not zero. In paired sample t-test, three tables are essential in the following. In this condition, the standard $\alpha$ is set as 0.05 to decide to accept which hypothesis.

As can be seen from Table 1, the score in diagnostic assessment is $72.57 \pm 2.91$ while the score in formative assessment is $77.38 \pm 2.68$. The score mean (77.38) in formative assessment is higher than the one (72.57) in diagnostic assessment, which shows students' translation ability had been improved from a whole view. From the perspective of standard deviation, the scores in formative assessment are closer to the mean.

**Table 1.** Statistics of paired samples.

|                        | Mean  | N  | Std. Deviation | Std. Error Mean |
|------------------------|-------|----|----------------|-----------------|
| Diagnostic assessment  | 72.57 | 82 | 2.914          | 0.322           |
| Formative assessment   | 77.38 | 82 | 2.683          | 0.296           |

The table describes the correlations of paired samples, the correlation value is 0.693, which presents that the data in two groups have a positive correlation (Table 2). The observed value of p, 0.000, means the correlation is obvious.

**Table 2.** Paired samples correlations.

|                                                  | N  | Correlation | Sig. |
|--------------------------------------------------|----|-------------|------|
| Pair 1 diagnostic and formative assessment       | 82 | .693        | .000 |

From the above table, the observed value of p, 0.000, is less than 0.01 (standard $\alpha$ is usually 0.05 or 0.01), indicating a convincing result to reject $H_0$ hypothesis and accept $H_1$ (Table 3). The p value supports the great changes between groups of data. As observed in the above table, mean and t values are negative, which illustrates the data in diagnostic assessment are less than ones in formative assessment in general. It can be known from these values that there are differences or changes between two groups, which are meaningful in statistics. Combined with $H_1$ hypothesis, the conclusions of t-test are: (1) There are

**Table 3.** Paired sample test.

| | Paired differences | | | | | t | df | Sig. (2-tailed) |
|---|---|---|---|---|---|---|---|---|
| | Mean | Std. Deviation | Std. Error Mean | 95% Confidence Interval of the Difference | | | | |
| | | | | Lower | Upper | | | |
| Pair 1 Diagnostic-formative assessment | −4.817 | 2.202 | .243 | −5.301 | −4.333 | −19.809 | 81 | .000 |

obvious changes between two groups of scores after they accepted the translation knowledge network learning strategy; (2) Students can accept knowledge network and this learning strategy to improve their translation ability.

## 4.2 Questionnaire Data

**Table 4.** Questionnaire and Likert Scale results.

| English Question | Likert Scale | | | | |
|---|---|---|---|---|---|
| | 5 | 4 | 3 | 2 | 1 |
| Q1. The linguistic knowledge involved in the definition of the tagged knowledge nodes is acceptable after explanation | 32 | 47 | 3 | 0 | 0 |
| Q2. There may be more than one knowledge node involved in the annotation of the example sentence. There will be other related knowledge nodes combined to explain the translation method. You think the combination of knowledge nodes is acceptable | 42 | 38 | 2 | 0 | 0 |
| Q3. The knowledge network learning method of combining the knowledge nodes mentioned in question 2 is helpful for translation learning | 40 | 39 | 3 | 0 | 0 |
| Q4. Through this platform learning, you agree to conduct translation learning with knowledge nodes and their combination of knowledge network learning | 40 | 38 | 4 | 0 | 0 |
| Q5. As shown in the platform, the translation learning of the knowledge network is more accurate in positioning and more effective in learning and mastering than the explanation of the translation method in the traditional classroom. You agree with this above-mentioned statement | 31 | 42 | 7 | 1 | 1 |
| Q6. In the future study, you are willing to consciously cultivate yourself a translation learning mode that starts from knowledge nodes and forms a knowledge network | 38 | 39 | 4 | 1 | 0 |

82 students finished the online Likert Scale questionnaire after they had attended the formative assessment. In the Likert Scale questionnaire, there are five answers in each question, where the numbers, 5, 4, 3, 2, and 1, respectively indicate strongly agree, agree, somewhat agree, disagree and strongly disagree, which is clearly showed in the following table. These five questions are designed to explore students' acceptability towards knowledge-network-based platform. Knowledge network acceptability is classified into definition acceptability, knowledge correlation acceptability and understandability acceptability towards knowledge network. The definition acceptability towards knowledge network is studied in the first question while understandability acceptability is evaluated in the fifth and sixth questions. Other questions are about knowledge correlation acceptability. According to the collected data, only two students disagree the opinion in the fifth question and one student is against for the sixth question. The student strongly disagreed with the fifth opinion, which indicates this knowledge network learning strategy cannot absolutely replace the traditional classroom learning. Without further analysis, it can be simply concluded that students can accept the translation knowledge network from its above aspects and the knowledge-network-based learning strategy. More evidences are in the following tables and explanation (Table 4).

The scale data are statistically analyzed with the help of these values, mean, standard deviation, Kurtosis and Skewness. As can be observed in the table, the means of six questions are all over 4 points, suggesting a strongly positive attitude toward knowledge network acceptability (Table 5). The listed values of standard deviation are smaller than 1 point, indicating a rather low discrete distribution of students' scale option, which means the scale numbers are very close to the means in each question. In addition, the value of Kurtosis is over 0 point, showing a wide distribution of scale option in each question, while that for negative value vice versa.

**Table 5.** Statistical results of questionnaire.

| English question | Mean | Std. Deviation | Kurtosis | Skewness |
|---|---|---|---|---|
| Q1 | 4.35 | 0.553 | −0.779 | −0.066 |
| Q2 | 4.49 | 0.55 | −0.955 | −0.408 |
| Q3 | 4.45 | 0.57 | −0.776 | −0.42 |
| Q4 | 4.44 | 0.59 | −0.643 | −0.497 |
| Q5 | 4.23 | 0.758 | 3.35 | −1.288 |
| Q6 | 4.39 | 0.643 | 1.06 | −0.861 |

Considering the above analysis, the questionnaire proves that students have a strongly positive knowledge network acceptability of this translation learning strategy, while it is noted that this knowledge-network-based learning strategy cannot absolutely replace the traditional classroom learning.

To ensure the rationality and validity of data, it is indispensable to verify the reliability and validity of the questionnaire, which is proved by the values of cronbach's alpha and KMO. The following tables show the details.

Cronbach's alpha shows the internal consistency and relationship of a group of items or a set of scales, which is considered one of the most universally adopted measures of reliability in science research [16]. As cronbach's alpha is measured in a questionnaire, it measures the reliability or consistency of 6 interviewed items and five scales [17]. The following figure illustrates the cronbach's alpha of questionnaire discussed in the study, where the coefficient of reliability is configured as $\alpha$. $\alpha$ ranges from 0 to 1 in the cronbach's alpha analysis, where high score means high internal consistency in the items. Based on this premise, cronbach's alpha is 0.974 in the result, which shows a very high reliability (Table 6). As a result, the questionnaire design is reliable and consistent in the study.

**Table 6.** Reliability statistics.

| Cronbach's Alpha | Cronbach's Alpha Based on Standardized Items | N of Items |
|---|---|---|
| 0.974 | 0.977 | 6 |

In the following table, KMO value is 0.868, which is over 0.5 when compared with this fixed number (Table 7). It indicates there is a relatively ideal validity in the questionnaire, proving the correctness of collected data assisted with the questionnaire. Factor analysis is not the main topic in the study, thus there is no further exploration about that.

**Table 7.** KMO and Bartlett's test.

| Kaiser-Meyer-Olkin Measure of Sampling Adequacy | | 0.868 |
|---|---|---|
| Bartlett Test of Sphericity | Approx, Chi-Square | 873.129 |
| | df | 15 |
| | Sig. | 0 |

## 4.3 Interview Data

A further exploration about knowledge network is an interview, where the interviewed question is: How do you evaluate the platform and knowledge network learning strategy and please give a specific evaluation description instead of giving a simple grade evaluation. The study adopts KH Coder, one text mining software (developed by Koichi Higuchi), to analyze the inner connection in interviewed text (over 2000 English words), whose co-occurrence result is in the following figure [18].

In KH Coder, the figure is one form of co-occurrence network of interviewed text, suggesting words with similar appearance patterns and high degrees of co-occurrence. Only the words connected with lines or edges have strong co-occurrence. The darker or thicker the line is, the stronger the co-occurrence is, which can be observed by coefficient. The word or node size vividly represents its frequency (larger nodes for higher frequency words), which can be seen by frequency value. The colors indicate how central each word plays the role in its network. Circles representing nodes are colored with colors through light yellow to dark blue, reflecting their ascending degree of centrality. As can be known in the figure, there are two most central and strongest co-occurrence networks except the non-complete meaning networks (Fig. 5). The first network includes nodes, namely "be", "very", "good", "think" and "platform". The second network includes nodes, namely "learn", "knowledge", "network", "improve" and "method". It can be well illustrated from the above networks that students think the platform is very good and knowledge network provides a novel learning method. More evidences can be found in the interview.

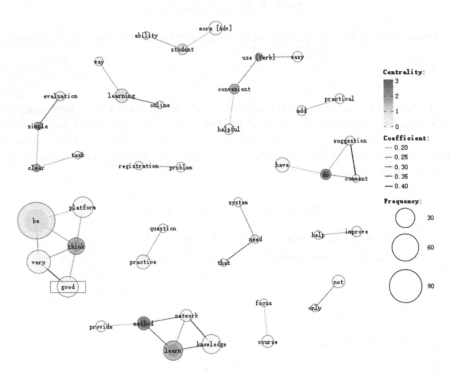

**Fig. 5.** Co-occurrence of interviewed text.

Students commented that "I think this way of learning is very good, and this kind of translation learning based on knowledge network is also more suitable for those who want to do translation. Knowledge nodes are more comprehensive and have wide coverage and strong operability.", indicating comprehensive knowledge nodes help students learn translation. Although some students described this knowledge-network-based learning strategy from different dimensions, they positively supported this learning model and accepted knowledge network. They argued that this novel knowledge network model "provides different knowledge modules to facilitate learning and correction for different problems", "really provides me with a very maneuverable and self-learning translation learning method", "definitely help our translation study" and "make breakthrough for the traditional translation practice method".

It is worth noting that there is one negative scale towards the sixth question in the questionnaire. In the interview, one student argued that "I personally think that the method is a little difficult for basic translators. It would be better if some unfamiliar concepts were explained first.", indicating students' learning habits influence their willingness of forming a novel learning strategy. In general, students held positive attitudes towards translation knowledge-network-based learning strategy. Combined with the detailed interviewed content, it is believed that students give a much positive evaluation concerning the platform and knowledge network learning strategy.

## 5    Findings and Conclusion

The research has drawn on a series of methodologies, Likert Scale and statistical tools, to reveal knowledge network and this translation learning strategy. Based on the results of diagnostic and formative assessments, it can be seen that students can accept knowledge network. There are improvements in students' translation scores after they learn the knowledge nodes to form their knowledge networks. From the data analysis of questionnaire, the students widely accept knowledge network and this translation learning strategy. It is essential to conclude that this knowledge-network-based learning strategy cannot absolutely replace the traditional classroom learning; students' learning habits influence their willingness of forming a novel learning strategy. The interview supports the above findings with more detailed evidences. Students believed that "the platform is very good and knowledge network provides a novel learning method." These finding are found with the help of qualitative and quantitative methodologies. There is no argument about the results of qualitative methodologies, questionnaire and interview. However, disagreement may be found in the finding of scores, where knowledge network and this learning strategy cannot completely determine students' scores. As can be observed in the scores, there are significant improvements after students accept knowledge network. To some extent, it is undeniable that knowledge network has a positive influence on translation learning.

Finally, there are two main limitations in the research. Firstly, only 82 students of the same grade in a certain university attend the experiment, which limits the universality of findings. It is necessary to conduct further experiments in order to testify the validity of the universality. Secondly, because of the distinctive algorithm and platform layout, the knowledge network and this learning strategy differ from traditional translation learning tools, suggesting this training mode may not apply to other teaching platforms. Therefore, the research team needs to explore further in terms of platform design and application.

**Acknowledgements.** The work was substantially supported by The National Social Science Fund of China (Project No. 19BYY125: A Data-Mining Driven Mode of Co-construction of Knowledge Network for Translation Learning and Its Application).

# References

1. Luciano, M.: Learning strategies, teaching strategies and new curricular demands: a critical view. Perspect. J. TESOL-Italy **29**, 45–56 (2002)
2. Gao, J., Ding, K., Pan, Y., Yuan, J.: Analysis of the research status of knowledge network at home and abroad. Inf. Stud. Theor. Appl. **38**(9), 120–125 (2015)
3. Phelps, C., Heidl, R., Wadhwa, A.: Knowledge, networks, and knowledge networks: a review and research agenda. J. Manage. **38**(4), 1115–1166 (2012). https://doi.org/10.1177/0149206311432640
4. Aldahdouh, A., Osório, A., Caires, S.: Understanding knowledge network, learning and Connectivism. Int. J. Instr. Technol. Distance Learn. **12**, 3–21 (2015). https://doi.org/10.5281/zenodo.46186.E
5. Michael, H., Wolff-Michael, R.: Learning by developing knowledge networks. ZDM **36**, 196–205 (2004). https://doi.org/10.1007/BF02655693
6. Zaheer, M.: Role of knowledge networks in distance learning. Pak. J. Distance Online Learn. **6**(1), 221–230 (2020)
7. Bonifacio, M., Bouquet, P., Cuel, R.: The building blocks of a distributed approach to knowledge management, vol. 8, pp. 652–661 (2002)
8. Liu, H., Jiang, Y., Fan, H. et al.: Visualization analysis of knowledge network research based on mapping knowledge. J. Sign. Process. Syst. **93**, 333–344 (2021). https://doi.org/10.1007/s11265-020-01595-2
9. Mu, Y., Tian, L., Yang, W.: Towards a knowledge management model for online translation learning. In: Hao, T., Chen, W., Xie, H., Nadee, W., Lau, R. (eds.) SETE 2018. LNCS, vol. 11284, pp. 198–207. Springer, Cham (2018). https://doi.org/10.1007/978-3-030-03580-8_21
10. Tian, L., Mu, Y., Yang, W.: Designing a platform-facilitated and corpus-assisted translation class. In: Hao, T., Chen, W., Xie, H., Nadee, W., Lau, R. (eds.) SETE 2018. LNCS, vol. 11284, pp. 208–217. Springer, Cham (2018). https://doi.org/10.1007/978-3-030-03580-8_22
11. Zhu, Y., Chen, J.: The theoretical conception and engineering practice of a corpus-based computer-assisted translation. Technol. Enhanced Foreign Lang. Educ. **4**, 52–57 (2015)
12. Zhu, C., Mu, Y.: Towards a textual accountability-driven mode of teaching and (self-) learning for translation and bilingual writing: with special reference to a CityU online teaching platform. Chin. Translators J. **2**, 56–62 (2013)
13. Mu, Y., Yang, W.: A teaching experiment on a knowledge-network-based online translation learning platform. In: Popescu, E., Hao, T., Hsu, T.-C., Xie, H., Temperini, M., Chen, W. (eds.) SETE 2019. LNCS, vol. 11984, pp. 319–328. Springer, Cham (2020). https://doi.org/10.1007/978-3-030-38778-5_35
14. DiBello, L.V., Roussos, L.A., Stout, W.: Review of cognitively diagnostic assessment and a summary of psychometric models. In: Rao, C.R., Sinharay, S. (Eds.), Handbook of statistics, vol. 26, pp. 979–1030 (2007)

15. Joshi, A., Kale, S., Chandel, S., Pal, D.K.: Likert scale: explored and explained. Br. J. Appl. Sci. Technol. **7**(4), 396–403 (2015)
16. Cronbach, L.J.: Coefficient alpha and the interval structure of tests. Psychometrika **16**, 297–334 (1951). https://doi.org/10.1007/BF02310555
17. Bonett, D.G., Wright, T.A.: Cronbach's alpha reliability: interval estimation, hypothesis testing, and sample size planning. J. Organ. Behav. **36**(1), 3–15 (2015)
18. Clauset, A., Newman, M.E., Moore, C.: Finding community structure in very large networks. Phys. Rev. E. **70**(6), 066111 (2004). https://doi.org/10.1103/PhysRevE.70.066111

# On the Design of Computer-Aided Translation Teaching

Beibei Lin[✉]

College of Foreign Languages, Zhejiang University of Technology, Hangzhou, China
linbeibei@zjut.edu.cn

**Abstract.** The current translation teaching turns out to be poor in efficiency. Many students lack practical ability and cannot sufficiently deal with translation tasks in reality. How to motivate their study initiative and improve their translation ability is the question we are interested in. This study tries to make full use of the computer technology and advance the traditional teaching mode with the aid of the ClinkNotes online platform, designed for translation teaching. In accordance with the characteristics of translation course, we, taking the Task-Based Language Teaching approach, apply this platform and design the classroom teaching in a new way. Students are well encouraged to participate in the study and give prompt responses to the translation task with several rounds of discussion. It finds that the design of this teaching model can have a positive impact on students' learning efficiency. We hope this study could be enlightening for the future teaching reform.

**Keywords:** Online Teaching Platform · Translation Teaching · Task-Based Language Teaching (TBLT)

## 1 Introduction

Currently, we adopt a teacher-centered mode in the translation classroom. The teacher explains the key points in the textbook and then assigns the exercise to the students, who are required to apply what they have learned just before. The classroom is the main place for teaching. Problems with such teaching mode have been spotted, and it proves to be inefficient. First, the listening-and-practicing mode can not fully encourage students, who are busy with taking notes, to actively participate in the classroom. This has greatly affected their enthusiasm in learning. Equally important is that the textbook used is of limited content and it cannot include the latest cases in reality because of the long process of editing and publishing. Moreover, due to the constraint of class time, it is almost impossible to allow all students of different levels to effectively master the points taught. They can not get timely help when they encounter difficulties in the learning process. In this regard, many students lack practical ability and fail to sufficiently handle the translation tasks in reality.

How to improve the students' translation ability while interesting them during the whole process of teaching? A new teaching mode is apparently in need. Trying to

C. S. González-González et al. (Eds.): ICWL 2022/SETE 2022, LNCS 13869, pp. 460–470, 2023.
https://doi.org/10.1007/978-3-031-33023-0_43

redesign the translation course and advance the teaching methods to work out the students' potential and get a better teaching outcome, we resort to the computer-aided teaching (hereinafter referred to as CAT).

## 2 Assisting Translation Teaching with the Online Platform

### 2.1 Literature Review on Computer-Aided Teaching

Since 1950's when it was first initiated in the USA, CAT has been gaining more importance. Many researches discuss the integration of computer technology in the process of teaching. Feurzeig, *et al.* (1964) is one of the early attempts, which designs a computer teaching system and applies it to teach medical diagnosis [1]. This century witnesses the emergence of more teaching systems. Anger *et al.* (2001) develops a skill-teaching system and demonstrates the implementation of this system with statistics [2]. Abdou *et al.* (2006) discusses the system applied for Arabic-pronunciations teaching and comes up with a data set to show the accuracy of the speech recognizer [3]. Cavus & Momani (2009) looks into learning management systems and comes up with an evaluation system to choose the most suitable system for different needs and requirements [4]. Cingi (2013) compares computer-assisted education and traditional-mode education, and finds that the teaching system makes education more effective and better [5]. Akhtar, *et al.* (2017) works on a learning system which may monitor the participation of the students [6]. Alghamdi *et al.* (2020) applies an intelligent based examination system, which is more efficient than the paper-based examination system [7]. Gu & Li (2022) designs a computer-aided translation teaching system, and finds that this system proposed can provide students with better English learning experiences [8]. These are just a few of the discussions on the computer-aided teaching system applied in different disciplines in the 21 century; they find that assisting teaching with the designed system could improve the teaching efficiency.

### 2.2 The Translation Teaching Platform

Translation teaching, involving the conversion of two languages and two cultures, embraces the technology-enhanced mode. The application of the teaching system has been a topic of concern. The corpora as the teaching platform is well established and developed. Among them, we take the ClinkNotes Online Platform to facilitate our teaching. It, with a knowledge-network-based system, is designed to improve the efficiency of translation teaching/(self-) learning [9]. There are three modules: corpus module, topic board module, and exercise module, which are designed to help realize the network-based teaching [10, 11]. The corpus module covers different genres of high-quality bilingual texts. The bilingual data are annotated with a system of knowledge nodes ("tagwords"). These Annotations explain cultural background, textual phenomena, stylistic effects, information management, and translation skills in detail, which can be accessed in multiple modes, such as the tagged words, feature-based navigation, and so on [12, 13]. They reflect the translation decision-making process of professional translators. The annotations, with knowledge-based and theoretically-informed relevance, are conducive to the self-study of novice translation students and the classroom explanation of translation teachers. In addition, the topic board provides comprehensive and in-depth explanation of topic knowledge points, and the multiple exercises on a certain knowledge point, both of which allow the students to explore further in their studies [14]. In general, this teaching platform has very obvious advantages in translation teaching. It takes "tagwords", the key words to annotations, as the knowledge-connection nodes to navigate to the inter-related points of knowledge; therefore, it gives full play to the potential teaching value contained, and guides the students to look into translation details to deepen their understanding of translation.

## 3    Teaching Design Based on TBLT

After investing time to understand the ClinkNotes online platform so as to skillfully use it, we try to design a new mode for translation teaching and make an experiment with the course *Advanced Translation*, in the purpose of improving students' theoretical knowledge, and cultivating their practical translation ability.

### 3.1    The Advanced Translation Course

*Advanced Translation* is an elective translation course for senior English-major undergraduates. It requires the students, who have taken several translation courses before, to have a relatively good command of English and Chinese, as well as some basic translation knowledge. In this course, the similarities and differences between Chinese and English languages and cultures are further discussed, and the students' translation ability is expected to be improved with a number of practical training. And the students are encouraged to explore the translation with some translation theories, which may help them raise the translation consciousness.

### 3.2    The Teaching Method

To ensure its reliability and validity, we design the course teaching on the basis of Task-Based Language Teaching (TBLT), first advanced by Prubha in the "Bangalore Project" in 1983 [15], and further investigated by many scholars [16–28]. TBLT targets at cultivating the students' ability of using the foreign language in the reality [29]. A task-based teaching method is in consistent with the study of the students' learning a foreign language [30]. In this approach, the task is most important. David Nunan, after reviewing the relevant literature, tries to clarify this key concept of task and defines it as follows:

> "A task is a piece of classroom work that involves learners in comprehending, manipulating, producing or interacting in the target language while their attention is focused on mobilizing their grammatical knowledge in order to express meaning, and in which the intention is to convey meaning rather than to manipulate form. The task should also have a sense of completeness, being able to stand alone as a communicative act in its own right with a beginning, a middle and an end." [31]

The definition indicates that the task, applied in the classroom teaching, gives the students an opportunity to do with the target language as it is used in the real world, and it also mentions the general criteria of the task. And there are more detailed criteria of a task for a better teaching [32]:

"1. The primary focus should be on "meaning";
2. There should be some kind of "gap";
3. Learners should largely rely on their own resources (linguistic and nonlinguistic)
4. There is a clearly defined outcome other than the use of language."

According to Ellis, the class takes the task as its principle component, which consists of three phrases: (1) Pre-task. It prepares the students to perform the task, including activities before the task, including establishing the outcome of the task. (2) During task. It, the only obligatory phrase of the teaching, focuses on the task itself, giving various instructional options of how to do the task, such as time pressure. (3) Post-task. It concerns with follow-up procedures on the task performance, affording a number of option, such as the learner report [33].

### 3.3  Teaching Design

Here we take the unit "Translation of Sentences" for example to illustrate our design of teaching. This unit aims to explain the syntactic differences between the Chinese and English, and improve the students' translation skills of dealing with sentences, exposing them to the differences between two cultures and thinking patterns, and cultivating them teamwork ability. The aims are expected to be achieved with the following teaching activities, according to the framework of pre-task, during task, and post-task.

(1)  Pre-task activity

To get the students ready for the task at the next phrase, we select the topic boards relevant to our teaching content and ask students to read them, which would help them to reconsolidate their knowledge of translation. For example, the following topic board "Clause Management--Alteration of Rank" explains the definition and application of this translation skill (Fig. 1).

**Fig. 1.** The topic board

And the students could refer to the extended topic boards, such as "Clause Management--Conversion of Voice" to have a better understanding of translation at the sentential level.

(1) During-task activity

First, the students are assigned the following Chinese-English translation task, which is taken from the platform, independently (Fig. 2).

**Fig. 2.** The task

Inevitably, they encounter some problems in translation and therefore they are encouraged to share their own translations with other students, which would help them to come up with the debatable points for further discussion. Then, we tried to solve those problems with the help of the annotations. Clicking the marks before the sentences, we could see a window jump out (Fig. 3).

It gives the target text (TT) for reference and further explains why it is translated as such. The source text (ST), as a passive sentence, includes no subject to indicate the agent. Such sentence structure cannot be reproduced in the translation, so the object of ST "本地传媒" is taken as the subject of TT "the media", and the passive voice is adopted to avoid mentioning the agent. After explaining the translation of this sentence, it also tells the students the situations in which the translation skill of Voice Alternation is used and gives a sample translation. The tagword "VoiceAlteration" links to another page which shows the definition of this translation skill and much more sample translations (Fig. 4).

**Fig. 3.** The annotation

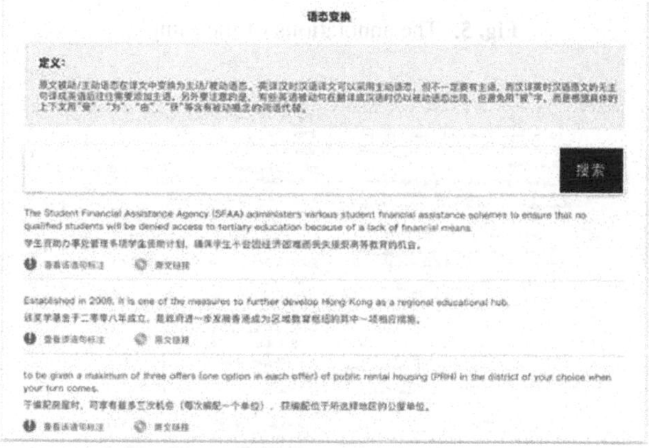

**Fig. 4.** The tagword

Below every sample translation are two links, one for its explanation and the other directing to the whole passage from which the translation is taken.

The annotations of the sample translation well demonstrate the application of this translation skill in the sufficient authentic texts (Fig. 5). And referring to the original passage allows us to see the translation in the context (Fig. 6).

Those plenty resources help us to solve questions related with voice, voice alteration, and the like.

**Fig. 5.** The annotations of the sample

**Fig. 6.** The passage

Of course, there is more to be discussed with the translation of one single sentence. By clicking another mark before it, we could find that this translation is approached in the aspect of "sentence component alteration". The original object "增强教育功能" of the verb "要求" is rendered as the prepositional phrase "for educating the young people" to indicate the purpose at the end of the sentence, and the sentence structure is reorganized. The sample translation shows us the application of this translation skill in another situation.

Similarly, the tagword "Sentence Component Alteration" exposes us to the resources concerning the translation knowledge point (Fig. 7).

With the support of this knowledge network, we examine every details worthy of attention in translation, which help reinforce the brainstorm of the class and encourage the students to summarize the translation principles according to their work at the sentential level and the beyond. This can be very helpful for their work on translation of similar texts.

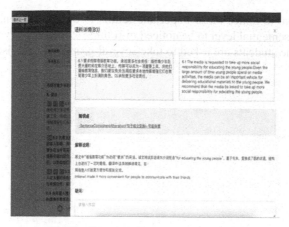

**Fig. 7.** Sentence Component Alteration

On going through those debatable points sentence by sentence, we activate the translation of the given text (Fig. 8).

**Fig. 8.** The translation

The students are asked to further compare their own translations and the one displayed in this teaching system. They could make comments, raise questions and advance a better translation.

(1) Post-task activity

Upon the completion of the translation task, the teacher, according to the students' observations, summarizes the syntactic differences between the Chinese and the English, encouraging them to notice those important details in the translation, and translation strategies at the sentential level to be noticed in future.

Moreover, the students are asked to take several groups of exercise in the exercise board (Fig. 9).

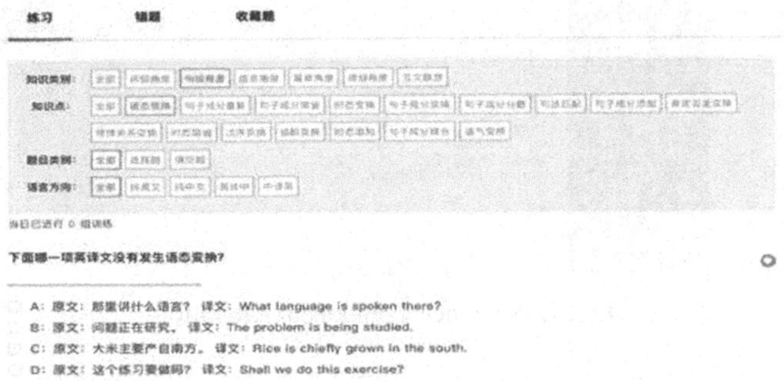

**Fig. 9.** The exercise

The exercise relevant to the tagwords we have discussed in class can help students reinforce their translation knowledge. At this phrase, most exercises are perfectly done. If there is any mistake, we'll ask the students of different opinions to argue with other parties and find the right answer themselves. And the teacher is ready to help during their discussion.

After class, the students are encouraged to log in the platform to explore more with the help of those tagwords mentioned during class in this knowledge-network system, and they may ask questions as well as discuss with teachers and other teachers online whenever and wherever possible.

### 3.4 Assessment

This course *Advanced Translation* adopts a final examination, which includes one EC translation and one CE translation, covering the knowledge points explained in class, to evaluate the students' learning upon the end of the semester. There are two classes, one adopting the above teaching design with the ClinkNotes Online Platform, and the other in the traditional teaching mode, taking the examination. Their examination papers, with the students' information blank covered, are marked by two teachers. And it turns out that the average score of the former is higher and there are more A grades in this class.

## 4   Conclusion

In our experiment, we find such design of teaching on the basis of the ClinkNotesonline platform can help us better achieve the teaching aim. The knowledge-network system, constituted by the different knowledge nodes, allows students to probe into the important and difficult points via tagwords to gain a more systemetic understanding of translation.

They are asked to apply the theoretical knowledge to deal with a translation task taken from the real life, in which the problems they have encountered can be promptly solved by several rounds of discussion. This improves the teaching efficiency. Besides, this teaching mode allows them to share their idea in class, and they are more concentrated in classroom activities, which enhances their leaning enthusiasm and makes them better participate in class. With the online platform optimizing the learning mode, students gain a chance to conduct self-learning whenever and wherever they like. The results of the assessment suggests that the translation quality of students is better than that of students in traditional teaching mode, which suggests the knowledge-network-based teaching mode functions well and, to some extent, we can say it is efficient and effective, though further statics concerning the students' learning performance and their feedback is still to be collected. It could be stated that the knowledge-based online platform is capable of establishing a positive learning environment and further generating an effective mode for translation teaching.

**Acknowledgements.** The work was substantially supported by Zhejiang University of Technology (Project No. z20160152).

# References

1. Feurzeig, W., et al.: Computer-aided teaching in medical diagnosis. Acad. Med. **39**(8), 746–754 (1964)
2. Anger, W.K., et al.: cTRAIN: a computer-aided training system developed in SuperCard for teaching skills using behavioural education principles. Behav. Res. Methods Instrum. Comput. **33**, 277–281 (2001)
3. Abdou, S.M., et al.: Computer aided pronunciation learning system using speech recognition techniques. In: Ninth International Conference on Spoken Language Processing (2006)
4. Cavus, N., Momani, A.M.: Computer aided evaluation of learning management system. Procedia Soc. Behav. Sci. **1**(1), 426–430 (2009)
5. Cingi, C.C.: Computer aided education. Procedia Soc. Behav. Sci. (103), 220–229 (2013)
6. Akhtar, S., Warburton, S., Xu, W.: The use of an online learning and teaching system for monitoring computer aided design student participation and predicting student success. Int. J. Technol. Des. Educ. **27**(2), 251–270 (2015). https://doi.org/10.1007/s10798-015-9346-8
7. Alghamdi, A., et al.: Design and implementation of a computer aided intelligent examination system. Int. J. Emerg. Technol. Learn. (iJET). **15**(1), 30–44 (2020)
8. Gu, S., Li, X.: Optimization of computer-aided English translation teaching based on network teaching platform. Comput. Aided Des. Appl. **19**(S1), 151–160 (2022)
9. Mu, Y., et al.: Towards a knowledge management model for online translation learning. In: Hao, T., Chen, W., Xie, H., Nadee, W., Lau, R. (eds.) Emerging Technologies for Education. SETE 2018. LNCS, vol. 11284, pp. 198–207. Springer, Cham (2018). https://doi.org/10.1007/978-3-030-03580-8_21
10. Zhu, C., Mu, Y.: Towards a textual accountability-driven mode of teaching and (self-) learning for translation and bilingual writing: with special reference to a CityU online teaching platform. Chin. Transl. J. **2**, 56–62 (2013)
11. Wang, H.: Incorporating an in-depth annotated corpus into the translation classroom. Chin. Transl. J. **36**(1), 50–54 (2015)

12. Zhu, C.S., Yip, P.C.: ClinkNotes: towards a corpus-based, machine-aided programme of translator teaching. Meta **5**(2), 387–408 (2010)
13. Tian, L., Mu, Y., Yang, W.: Designing a platform-facilitated and corpus-assisted translation class. In: Hao, T., et al. (eds.) Emerging Technologies for Education. SETE 2018. LNCS, vol. 11284, pp. 208–217. Springer, Cham (2018). https://doi.org/10.1007/978-3-030-03580-8_22
14. Wang, H.: Corpus annotation and its application to translation teaching: introducing an annotated corpus of English financial reports with Chinese translations. Foreign Lang. Teach. Res. **44**(2), 246–255 (2012)
15. Prahbu, N.S.: Second Language Pedagogy. Oxford University Press, Oxford (1987)
16. Nunan, D.: Designing Tasks for the Communicative Classroom. Cambridge University Press, Cambridge (1989)
17. Foley, J.: A phycholinguistic framework for task-based approaches to language teaching. Appl. Linguist. **12**(1), 62–75 (1991)
18. Thomson, C.K.: Learner-centered task in the foreign language classroom. Foreign Lang. Ann. **25**(6), 523–531 (1992)
19. Willis, J.: A Framework for Task-based Learning. Longman, London (1996)
20. Long, M.H., Robinson, P.: Focus on form: theory, research, and practice. Focus on form in classroom. Second Lang. Acquis. **2**, 15–41 (1998)
21. Skehan, P.: Task-based instruction. Annu. Rev. Appl. Linguist. **18**, 268–286 (1998)
22. Carless, D.R.: Factors in the implementation of task-based teaching in primary schools. System **31**(4), 485–500 (2003)
23. Littlewood, W.: The task-based approach: some questions and suggestions. ELT J. **58**(4), 319–326 (2004)
24. Oxford, R.L.: Task-based language teaching and learning: an overview. Asian EFL J. **8**(3), 94–121 (2006)
25. Hismanoglu, M., Hismanoglu, S.: Task-based language teaching: what every EFL teacher should do. Procedia Soc. Behav. Sci. **15**, 46–52 (2011)
26. Van den Branden, K.: Task-based language teaching. In: Graham, H. (eds.), The Routledge Handbook of English Language Teaching, pp. 238–251. Routledge, London (2016)
27. González-Lloret, M.: Technology for task-based language teaching. In: Chapelle, C.A., Shannon, S. (eds.), The Handbook of Technology and Second Language Teaching and Learning, pp. 234–247. John Willey & Sons, New York (2019)
28. Crookes, G.V., Ziegler, N.: Critical language pedagogy and task-based language teaching: reciprocal relationship and mutual benefit. Educ. Sci. **11**(6), 254 (2021)
29. Ellis, R.: Task-based language teaching: sorting out the misunderstandings. Int. J. Appl. Linguist. **19**(3), 221–246 (2009)
30. Erlam, R., Tolosa, C.: Pedagogical Realities of Implementing Task-Based Language Teaching. John Benjamins Publishing Company, Amsterdam/Philadelphia (2022)
31. Nunan, D.: Task-based language teaching in the Asia context: defining task. Asian EFL J. **8**(3), 12–17 (2006)
32. Ellis, R., Shintani, N.: Exploring Language Pedagogy through Second Language Acquisition Research. Routledge, London (2013)
33. Ellis, R.: The methodology of task-based teaching. Asian EFL J. **8**(3), 19–42 (2006)

# Transferring of Communicative Rhetorical Modelling in College English Reading-Writing Teaching Based on Cognitive Apprenticeship Facilitated by Rain Classroom and Pigai.org

Jingjing He[✉]

School of Foreign Studies, Hefei University of Technology, Hefei, China
Sophiahe.good@163.com

**Abstract.** Communicative rhetoric exhibits the attributes of being transferable and generative, which facilitate the methodological elements of cognitive apprenticeship such as modelling and scaffolding, encompassing a transfer of knowledge-transforming skill-set and strategies to sustain the College English reading-writing teaching. This essay is oriented to explore and visualize the feasible communicative rhetorical paradigms of the teacher and the journeyman situated and recycled in the real-life-issued reading contexts, which are sustainable and transferable to be applied in the English advanced writing. Simultaneously based on the communicative rhetorical modelling in the reading teaching facilitated by the platform of Rain Classroom and the empirical analyzing of target students' writings submitted to the online intelligent assessing system on pigai.org, this research aims to investigate the validity and effectiveness of the communicative rhetorical modelling on the improvement of students' advanced writing through interactive reading teaching.

**Keywords:** Cognitive Apprenticeship · Communicative Rhetorical Modelling · Transferring and Outputting · Rain Classroom · Intelligent Assessing on Pigai.org

## 1 Introduction

Targeting the freshman-year non-English major learners in recent years' College English reading-writing teaching, it has been detected in their in-class interactions in reading course and after-class discourse outputting that the test-oriented thinking modes have been overwhelmingly embedded in their preliminary English learning spans, such as the irreversible preferences for the mechanic memorization of the English language domain knowledge(the conceptual and factual knowledge)---lexical collocations and grammatical rules without explorations of further applications in the outputting. These lopsided tendencies of the second language acquisition have deprived the college freshmen learners of the inclination, impulsiveness as well as the initiative to conceive the discourse outputting of critical thinking and have stereotyped them in the mechanic

C. S. González-González et al. (Eds.): ICWL 2022/SETE 2022, LNCS 13869, pp. 471–481, 2023.
https://doi.org/10.1007/978-3-031-33023-0_44

repetition of vocabulary inputting and crammed them in dominant consciousness of multiple-choosing quiz among grammar and structure.

The communicative rhetorical paradigms such as the prioritizing of advanced vocabulary, the diversifying of syntax, the impromptu branching of controversial issues into effective paragraphs, and ultimately the well-knit composing of discourse haven't been synchronously modeled together with the linguistic domain knowledge. Hence the problems such as the misspelling, misinterpreting and inappropriate choice of the advanced vocabulary, the monotony of syntax, as well as the lack of coherence are spotted in the routine writing practices and exam writings. The preliminary test-oriented teaching mode has bored and bewildered the college English learners and will in the long term hinder the modelling of sustainable deep learning systems which will sustain the junior and senior college English self-learning and improve their discourse-composing competence.

To optimize the reading-writing teaching, by assimilating the methodological elements of cognitive apprenticeship such as scaffolding and modeling into rhetorical analyzing and thinking, this research is oriented to visualize the feasible communicative rhetorical modelling of the expert---the teacher and the journeyman in the blended reading-writing teaching facilitated by the digital and technical platforms---Rain Classroom platform and the intelligent writing assessing platform pigai.org (www.pigai.org), and to promote the transferring of the communicative rhetorical modelling from the teacher to the students and accordingly help the students to internalize the communicative rhetorical modelling, which will sustainably improve students' English outputting competence.

## 2   Literature Review on Cognitive Apprenticeship and College English Teaching

### 2.1   Literature Review on Cognitive Apprenticeship

Cognitive apprenticeship, proposed by Collins, Brown, and Newman in 1987, blends the idea of apprenticeship with the traditional reading, writing and mathematical classroom by placing emphasis on the process of tailoring the procedural skills, visualizing the thinking modes as well as transmitting the heuristic strategies through the integration and coordination of six teaching modes---modeling, coaching, scaffolding, articulation, reflection and exploration, oriented to enable students to acquire the cognitive and meta-cognitive strategies for "using, managing, and discovering knowledge" [1, 2] in the real-world contexts and problem-solving situations.

To explore the correlative research between cognitive apprenticeship and college English teaching, the author in this study has conducted an overall survey of the relevant researches with CNKI (China National Knowledge Infrastructure) as theoretical sources and searched for academic journals with the key concepts "cognitive apprenticeship" and "college English". This retrieving process has yielded about 20 essays. Among these relevant research essays in China, one has generally tracked down the theoretical development of cognitive apprenticeship researches in China [3]; some have focused on the explorations of the applications of cognitive apprenticeship in the teaching designing of

English listening course [4] or college English speaking course [5]; one has conducted some questionnaire analysis of the feasibility of application of cognitive apprenticeship in the college English reading teaching [6]; another has centered around using cognitive apprenticeship teaching method in teaching English writing for non-English-major writing course mainly through sorts of in-class training and activities [7]. There are few studies on the integrated application of the specific rhetorical modeling methodology on the basis of cognitive apprenticeship with the digital and technical platforms--- Rain Classroom and pigai.org. in college English reading-writing blended teaching.

### 2.2 Cognitive Apprenticeship and College English Teaching

The application of the modelling methodology of cognitive apprenticeship---the strategy-oriented visualization of the complex skill-set and implicit rhetorical modelling sampled by the teacher and recycled in the teacher-student interactive reading-writing teaching, is "designed, to bring these tacit processes into the open, where students can observe, enact, and practice them with help from the teacher…" [1]. This integrated teaching mode facilitated by digital and technical platforms perfectly compensates the relatively inadequate College English teaching hours (2–4 periods weekly in teaching curriculum in most universities in China) and considerably caters to the freshman-year students' earnest for the references in the transitional phrase from high school English learning to college English learning, sets transferable rhetorical modelling for them to imitate and further extend to their after-class self-learning and self-practicing.

This study will probe into the specific scheming and modelling of the enactment in the interactive reading-writing teaching and will highlight the scaffolding and constructing of the rhetorical paradigms for the students to mimic, imitate and transfer in the advanced phase of self-learning. And more crucially, there will be relevant data analyses on the efficiency of the rhetorical modelling for the pragmatic enhancement of the college English learners in advanced writing. All the perspectives above will constitute the new pivotal issues of discussions in this research.

## 3   Research Design

Learning to read, think and write rhetorically may find overlapping in diverse disciplines of linguistic acquisition. In this interactive reading-writing teaching study, rhetorical modelling incorporates rhetorical analyzing, thinking as well as relevantly designed outputting, which doesn't refer to the aesthetic adornment of the language---the applications of figure of speeches, while is oriented to unveil the layers of expert's communicative rhetorical modelling processes, to deconstruct the underpinnings of the rhetorical schemes and habituate the learners to those rhetorical paradigms in the outputting through interactions and activities.

Simultaneously, this blended interactive reading teaching process facilitated by Rain Classroom differentiates from the traditional reading procedures such as source-target language translation, the multiple choices of comprehending the text or the exemplifying of words and expressions in sentences sampling. It mainly encompasses the inferring and exploring of the implicit connotations of advanced vocabulary, the analyzing and applying of the various syntax, the extending and developing of effective paragraphs and the reiterating of coherent discourses, which will reciprocally contribute to the learners' effective discourse outputting in the advanced writing.

### 3.1  Participants

The participants of this research were the non-English-major freshmen (about 183 students from five classes; about 36 students per class) from Grade 2021 in the author's college English reading-writing course. Most of them have got averagely high scores (120+/150 scores) in English in college entrance examination, who had rightly undergone the concentrated English tests, acquired a considerable scope of English vocabulary (approximately 3000 words) while still confronted with the problem of switching from test orientation to the transferable and generative modelling in reading-writing learning.

### 3.2  Procedures

As illustrated in Fig. 1, the entire scheming and transferring of this communicative modelling in the College English reading-writing teaching briefly consist of three steps: Pre-modelling on the Rain Classroom, four types of rhetorical modelling which are sampled, activated and recycled through reading-writing interactions and activities in class with an aid of Rain Classroom and the after-class advanced writing assigned on pigai.org which is motivated to involve the learners to incorporate, transfer and reinforce the communicative rhetorical paradigms acquired in the previous learning phases.

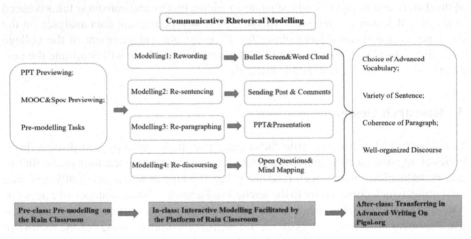

**Fig. 1.**  Communicative Rhetorical Modelling

Specifically, firstly, the pre-class activities and tasks are modelling-oriented and delivered through Rain Classroom. The students are supposed to preview the self-learning video resources and PPT and take on some exercises typified in Fig. 2., which is motivated to prepare for the modelling interactions in class. For instance, the self-learning video resources include Spoc concerning ways of paraphrasing and introductions of concrete words and compound words, the rhetorical classification of sentences and etc. to provide the learners with the fundamental communicative rhetorical concepts and notions that will serve as the theoretical and strategic prerequisites for the in-class modelling interactions and activities.

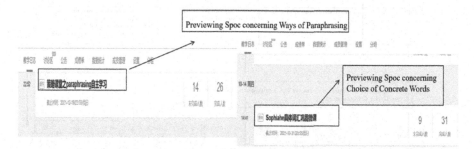

**Fig. 2.** Rain Classroom Pre-modelling Snapshots

Secondly, in-class: depicted in Table 1, in class, the teacher initializes the sampling and visualizing of four rhetorical modelling procedures contextualized in the shared reading environment from the dominant rhetorical vision---the communicative rhetoric [8]. Avoiding the lengthy and repeated practice of isolated sub-skills such as traditional vocabulary, grammar and structure analyses, with the aid and applications of interactive functions of Rain Classroom platform, the four communicative rhetoric modelling(rewording, re-sentencing, re-paragraphing and re-discoursing) in this study provides the interpretive and interactive coaching sessions, which mainly focus on the epistemological perspective---the modelling of communicative rhetorical paradigms---the heuristic, applicable and executive "rules of thumb" to accomplish the reading-writing reciprocal and hierarchical tasks of sequencing complexity and diversity (Figs. 3, 4 and 5).

**Table 1.** Communicative Rhetorical Modelling and Compatible Outputting

| Rhetorical Modelling | Learning Objectives | Specific Schemes | In-class Interactions (See Figure.3.,4.,5.) |
|---|---|---|---|
| Rewording | Distinguish the shades of connotations of advanced vocabulary and prioritize the applications in the outputting | Substitute the synonymous advanced vocabulary such as concrete words, compound words and etc. for the original key expressions | Send bullet screen &comments of the synonymous advanced vocabulary to the Rain Classroom, and formulate word cloud images |
| Re-sentencing | Vary the syntax in outputting, avoiding monotony | Replace the original sentences with variety of synonymous syntax and extend the details | Send posts&comments of variety of synonymous syntax to Rain Classroom, which are subsequently projected |
| Re-paragraphing | Improve the coherence of paragraph | Restate the paragraph in the readings by clarifying the transitions and appreciating the patterns of development | Make presentations of paragraph restatement with PPT to deliver rhetorical analyses |
| Re-discoursing | Improve the layout of discourse | Draw mind maps to display the outline of the whole reading text | Send snapshots of mind maps to the Rain Classroom, which are displayed and shared for co-analyzing and co-appreciating |

Frequency of Bullet Screen &Comments Sending on Rain Classroom

| 2 | 学号 | 所属学院 | 所属行政 | 姓名 | 课堂表现总分 | 线下互动 | 总分(满分 | 观看总页 | 弹幕总次数 | 投稿总次数 | |
|---|---|---|---|---|---|---|---|---|---|---|---|
| 3 | 20202106 | 计算机与 | 信息安21- | 高骞蓉 | 420 | 30 | 390 | 178 | 127 | 4 | |
| 4 | 20212145 | 计算机与 | 信息安21- | 徐进升 | 412 | 10 | 402 | 178 | 34 | 2 | |
| 5 | 20212145 | 计算机与 | 信息安21- | 朱宇泉 | 292 | 10 | 282 | 168 | 9 | 1 | |
| 6 | 20212145 | 计算机与 | 信息安21- | 王超凡 | 260 | 20 | 240 | 117 | 92 | 3 | |
| 7 | 20212145 | 计算机与 | 信息安21- | 陆海拓 | 249 | 60 | 189 | 120 | 234 | 4 | |
| 8 | 20212145 | 计算机与 | 信息安21- | 洪锋 | 253 | 10 | 243 | 178 | 57 | 2 | |
| 9 | 20212145 | 计算机与 | 信息安21- | 赵翔 | 358 | 30 | 328 | 178 | 15 | 2 | |
| 10 | 20212145 | 计算机与 | 信息安21- | 刘日旺 | 278 | 20 | 258 | 149 | 66 | 2 | |
| 11 | 20212145 | 计算机与 | 信息安21- | 戴培明 | 446 | 30 | 416 | 175 | 133 | 3 | |
| 12 | 20212145 | 计算机与 | 信息安21- | 沈炳阳 | 205 | 10 | 195 | 128 | 69 | 3 | |
| 13 | 20212145 | 计算机与 | 信息安21- | 汪易聪 | 301 | 30 | 271 | 163 | 14 | 2 | |
| 14 | 20212145 | 计算机与 | 信息安21- | 郑沐旸 | 456 | 60 | 396 | 153 | 150 | 2 | |
| 15 | 20212145 | 计算机与 | 信息安21- | 王艺博 | 299 | 50 | 249 | 143 | 27 | 3 | |
| 16 | 20212145 | 计算机与 | 智能科技 | 周蔚然 | 158 | 20 | 138 | 57 | 9 | 2 | |
| 17 | 20212145 | 计算机与 | 智能科技 | 岳晓激 | 441 | 60 | 381 | 175 | 87 | 2 | |
| 18 | 20212145 | 计算机与 | 智能科技 | 刘峰麟 | 415 | 30 | 385 | 163 | 12 | 3 | |
| 19 | 20212145 | 计算机与 | 智能科技 | 徐祥 | 126 | 10 | 116 | 55 | 47 | 2 | |
| 20 | 20212145 | 计算机与 | 智能科技 | 王坤 | 127 | 10 | 117 | 171 | 44 | 2 | |
| 21 | 20212145 | 计算机与 | 智能科技 | 胡峰 | 77 | 10 | 67 | 48 | 5 | 2 | |
| 22 | 20212145 | 计算机与 | 智能科技 | 韩孝铜 | 218 | 10 | 208 | 133 | 65 | 3 | |
| 23 | 20212145 | 计算机与 | 智能科技 | 杨岭哲 | 201 | 30 | 171 | 83 | 11 | 3 | |

**Fig. 3.** Statistics about Bullet Screen and Comments on Rain Classroom

**Fig. 4.** Frequency of Interactions and Activities On Rain Classroom

**Fig. 5.** A Snapshot of Word Cloud Image

The above communicative rhetorical modelling, exemplifies and activates the rhetorical distinguishing of the diverse shades of connotations embedded in the advanced vocabulary, the diversifying of various syntax as well as and the simulating of the coherent paragraphs and the visualizing of epitomized layout of discourse situated in real-life-issued reading materials in the textbook, which help to attain a multi-dimensional and in-depth comprehension of the texts and reciprocally to organize and compose effective, precise and affective discourses in the after-class advanced writing.

Thirdly, by probing into the after-class advanced writings of the participant students on pigai.org, the transferring of communicative rhetorical modelling could be traced and tracked in the students' advanced writings. Through close reading and analyzing of their writings and collecting of the relevant assessing data on pigai.org, the author detects the subtle choice of advanced vocabulary such as the high frequency of using the specific words and compound words, the flexible alternating among different rhetorical sentence types---the loose sentence, periodic sentence and the paralleled sentence, the coherent developing of the paragraphs and the well-knit layout of the discourse. Further empirical analyses and relevant findings could be detected in the following part.

# 4 Data Analyses and Conclusion

## 4.1 Data Analyses and Findings

The effectiveness and validity of transferring the communicative rhetorical modelling in the interactive reading-writing teaching explorations based on the applications and regulations of methodological modelling of cognitive apprenticeship could be evidently demonstrated from the following data collection and empirical analyses facilitated by pigai.org.

The relevant data collected and analyzed in this study is based on the two national English writing competitions assigned as after-class advanced writing tasks (writing task No.2505421 and No.2622702) on pigai.org respectively in October-November, 2021(181/183 students delivered their final writings) and in April-May, 2022(175/183 students delivered their final writings). The majority of the target participants of this research (in all 183 non-English-major freshmen of Grade 2021) attended these two national English writing contests. The topic of writing task No.2505421 is "My Views on Double Reduction" and the topic of writing task No.2622702 is "My View on 'Together for a Shared Future'". The basic requirements for these two pieces of advanced writing tasks are similar---300–500 words of expository articles.

Firstly, by comparing and contrasting the average linguistic dimension analyses shown in Table 2, after one-year implementation of modelling-oriented teaching, it is evident that the average writing competence of the research-targeted freshmen have been dramatically improved, illustrated by the employment of more advanced vocabulary (5.921:5.725) such as more specific words and compound words...and the extending and lengthening of sentences (25.065:22.736), the improvement of spelling accuracy of vocabulary(0.994:0.989) and the precision of grammar (0.893:0.872) and most distinctively the quantity of complex sentences of variety applied in the writings (23.667: 2.932). And shown in Fig. 6, by comparing the statistics of high-frequency errors between writing task No.2505421 and No.2622702 on pigai.org, it is evident that the overall writing errors such as punctuation errors, spelling errors, sentence structure problems, and etc. have obviously declined.

**Table 2.** Comparison on Average Linguistic Dimension Analyses of Students' Writings

| Average Linguistic Dimension Data | Writing Task No. 2622702 (April-May, 2022) | Writing Task No. 2505421 (October-November, 2021) |
|---|---|---|
| Lexical Difficulty | 5.921 | 5.725 |
| Sentence Length | 25.065 | 22.736 |
| Spelling Accuracy | 0.994 | 0.989 |
| Grammar Precision | 0.893 | 0.872 |
| Quantity of Complex Sentence | 23.667 | 2.932 |

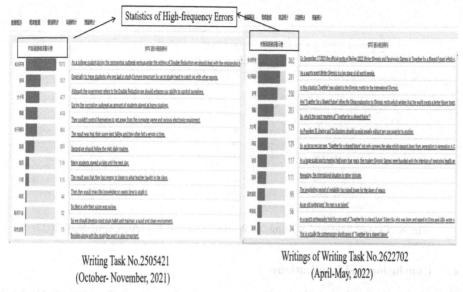

**Fig. 6.** A Comparison of the Statistics of High-frequency Errors between Writing Task No.2505421 and No.2622702

Secondly, as shown in the Figs. 7 and 8, the average scores of the writings automatically assessed by pigai.org platform have been improved from 83 scores to 84.3 scores. More typically, as this study probes into the frequency of students' self-polishing which mainly involves the processes of rewording, re-sentencing and re-paragraphing---the crucial methodological elements of this research, the increasing statistics well demonstrate students' internationalizing and transferring of the communicative rhetorical modelling strategies in their advanced writings.

**Fig. 7.** Data of Students' Writings of Writing Task No.2505421 (October- November, 2021)

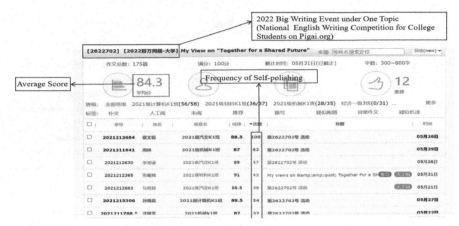

**Fig. 8.** Data of Students' Writings of Writing Task No.2622702 (April-May, 2022)

## 4.2 Conclusion and Implications

The communicative rhetorical modelling process of interactive reading-writing teaching in this research exemplifies many of the theoretical features of cognitive apprenticeship---the scheming and modelling of communicative rhetorical paradigms, the internalizing and transferring. It has proved to be remarkably effective in raising students' performances in advanced writing. The most important part of why we select the perspective of constructing the communicative rhetorical paradigms in the application and exploration of cognitive apprenticeship in this study is that the communicative rhetorical strategic skill-set is transferring and generating, which will ultimately contribute to the innovative and original outputting as the applications are situated and recycled in the dynamic reading contexts. The explorations in this study have provided a set of prompt and procedural facilitation that is designed to reduce students' information-processing burden by allowing them to select from the communicative rhetorical paradigms. Simultaneously the author is still expecting to develop more sophisticated and flexible "knowledge telling" strategies and cognitive analyses to facilitate and sustain English learners' further linguistic self-exploring process.

**Acknowledgements.** The work was substantially supported by the Social Science Fund Project of Hefei University of Technology (Project No. JS2020HGXJ0013) and Anhui Provincial College English Teaching Team of Curriculum Ideology and Politics (Project No. 2020kcszjxtd63).

## References

1. Collins, A., Brown, J.S., Newman, S.E.: Cognitive apprenticeship: teaching the craft of reading, writing and mathematics. Tech. Rep. (403), 4 (1987)
2. Collins, A., Brown, J.S., Newman, S.E.: Cognitive apprenticeship. Thinking. J. Philos. Child. (1), 2–10 (1988)
3. Chen, J.: A review on the studies on cognitive apprenticeship in the past 20 years (认知学徒制二十年研究综述). J. Distance Educ. (5), 97–104 (2010)

4. Song, X.: A study on listening strategies teaching based on information technology and cognitive apprenticeship (基于信息化和认知学徒制的听力策略教学研究). J. Hunan Ind. Polytech. (5), 76–79 (2016)
5. Cai, W.: The research on oral English teaching method of speaking workshop based on cognitive apprenticeship (基于认知学徒制的Speaking Workshop口语教学模式研究). J. Qiqihar Univ. (7), 181–184 (2017)
6. Yang, W.: An empirical study on feasibility of cognitive apprenticeship teaching mode of English reading (认知学徒制英语阅读教学模式的可行性研究). J. Hubei Corresp. Univ. (11), 174–175 (2017)
7. Xing, L., Li, Q.: Using cognitive apprenticeship teaching method in teaching English writing for Non-English Majors (认知学徒制教学法在非英语专业学生写作教学中的应用). J. Lishui Univ. (1), 125–128 (2015)
8. Huang, R.: English Rhetoric: An Introduction. 2nd edn. (英语修辞学概论修订本) Shanghai Foreign Language Education Press, Shanghai (2014)

# An Empirical Study on Knowledge-Network-Based Translation Learning

Yuanyuan Mu[1] (ID), Qianyu Li[2(✉)] (ID), and Lizhen Du[1] (ID)

[1] Chaohu University, Hefei, China
[2] Hefei University of Technology, Hefei, China
2020729956@qq.com

**Abstract.** This research aims to provide an empirical study on the digitalized application of a self-developed knowledge-network-based online translation learning platform by conducting the training to junior undergraduates majoring in translation who have used this online platform for a certain period as explained below. In this research, data mining technology is used to explore the internal relationship among translation knowledge nodes and establish translation learning knowledge network, which is considered to be beneficial to translation learning. To prove this, this paper introduces a knowledge-network-based translation training camp based on Textwells, an online translation learning platform, which contains annotated bilingual texts with theory-informed annotations of translation methods. The training camp used the research methodology with a pretest and a posttest to measure training effects. Compared to the pretest, students' translation performance has been improved substantially in the posttest. Therefore, it is shown that the knowledge-network-based translation learning does help improve students' translation performance.

**Keywords:** Knowledge network · Translation learning · Textwells

## 1 Introduction

Foreign communication in the areas of economics, science and culture is constantly increasing, and translation is an important means of communication. It is very important to further explore and innovate the training mode for English translation talents, so as to cultivate foreign exchange talents with high levels of bilingual capabilities and knowledge construction.

At present, the cultivation of applied translation talents has encountered great challenges. One is the challenge of theoretical innovation and application. Second, translation technology brings challenges and opportunities to translation education; Third, there is a lack of faculty [1]. In the post-epidemic era, it will become a new trend in higher education to use strategic technology innovation such as big data, cloud computing and

Supported by Chaohu University.

artificial intelligence, to improve curriculum design and promote online digital education [2]. Moreover, a large number of new BTI (Bachelor of Translation and Interpreting) and MTI (Master of Translation and Interpreting) programs in China have encountered faculty shortages [3]. Knowledge-network-based online translation learning platform, Textwells, developed by the research team of the authors, makes use of technology to find out the connections between various knowledge nodes in translation theory, and help take full advantage of the faculty resources. In traditional translation learning, teachers teach translation theories in class, lead students to take part in translation learning activities, and then carry out practical training. This is usually a large class teaching activity led by teachers, which to some extent ignores students' learning process. While in translation learning based on knowledge network, data mining technology is used to explore the inner connections among translation knowledge nodes. Teachers guide students to learn these knowledge nodes and initiate self-learning activities based on the connections among knowledge nodes. Moreover, in this case, students' learning trajectory will be recorded by Textwells, which helps students customize personalized learning programs according to their own learning characteristics.

## 2 Literature Review

Big data has reshaped language learning patterns by providing learners with more attractive and easier ways to learn. Learners need to master innovative language learning methods with big data and explore future language learning modes with artificial intelligence [4]. In order to promote the innovation of research methods, current researchers should make full use of AI pattern recognition, data mining, algorithm model and other technologies and methods to understand translation technology in a more comprehensive, objective and dynamic way [5]. So it is very significant to use data mining technology to explore the inner connections among translation knowledge nodes, establishing a translation learning knowledge network and promoting the further integration of technology and traditional translation learning.

"Knowledge network" is a concept proposed by contemporary Swedish economists. Knowledge-intensive industries stand out from the fierce competition. Knowledge network is very significant for knowledge transmission and creation, and it also plays a very important role in the development of economy and society. So more and more people are interested in the knowledge network [6]. A knowledge network is a dynamic framework consisting of three elements: first, the actors; second, the various relationships among the actors; and third, the resources each actor uses in its relationships, as well as institutional attributes, including structural and cultural aspects, such as control mechanisms, communication patterns, etc. These elements are combined to accumulate and use knowledge through the process of knowledge creation and transfer, and ultimately to achieve value creation [7]. Knowledge network is widely used in computer science, business economics, educational research and other fields. With the help of software technology, the construction process of knowledge network system can be analyzed from the perspective of knowledge exchange and sharing inside and outside the enterprise. The construction of knowledge network can help enterprises manage knowledge scientifically and promote knowledge sharing and innovation [8]. The concept of knowledge network can also be introduced in the construction of English grammar learning system using fill-in-the-blank exercises. The knowledge network represents the relationships among exercises depending on the differences in their knowledge. The grammar learning system discussed on 12th International Conference of Knowledge-Based Intelligent Information and Engineering Systems judges learners' grammar learning status according to their answers, and then makes personalized learning plans for learners with the help of knowledge network [9].

Although there are various literature on the application of knowledge network to the field of education, at present, there are little literature on the application of knowledge network to translation learning. There was no relevant article retrieved from CNKI, and only 1 relevant article was retrieved from WOS core collection (the search date is April 24, 2023), in which researchers have proved that the knowledge network is useful for translation learning [10]. The research applies knowledge networks from the field of cognitive psychology to the study of literary translation from an interdisciplinary perspective and the research perspective is innovative. The construction and application of the knowledge network of translation teaching can promote the standardization and methodological innovation of translation teaching and improve the teaching and research level. Furthermore, in view of the achievements of knowledge network in educational research and other fields, translation learning based on knowledge network is of high research value and deserves more empirical studies.

## 3   A Research on the Application of Knowledge Network in English Translation Learning

### 3.1   Research Questions

This translation training camp is based on Textwells, an online platform for translation teaching and learning developed by the research team of the authors, and students need to learn about the operation of Textwells. Students were trained to learn how to use the knowledge-network-based learning approach to learn translation in a short time of about one week. Then the researchers try to investigate the following questions in the experiment.

Will students accept the knowledge-network based translation learning?

Based on the theoretical guidance of a knowledge network, does the students' translation performance change after systematic training in translation training camp? If so, in what ways?

At the end of the training, do students have any comments or suggestions towards Textwells or knowledge-network-based learning approach? How can the researchers explain students' acceptability of the knowledge-network based learning?

### 3.2   Research Subjects

The research subjects include 96 junior English majors from a university in Anhui, China. These students have different levels of translation performance. We choose junior students for the following reasons. After three years of learning, juniors have a deeper understanding of traditional college English teaching methods. What's more, they have better learning abilities than younger students, learning how to operate Textwells faster. Besides, they not only need to prepare for the upcoming TEM-8 exam to improve their translation skills, but also to prepare themselves to become professional translators in the workplace. Therefore, they are more interested in new translation learning methods than other students.

### 3.3  Research Design

The teacher's clear instruction and active guidance of learners' independent exploration are the basis of an effective translation class [11]. The overall research includes three steps. First of all, one translation exercise for pretest is arranged. Secondly, the introduction and operation instruction for Textwells are introduced. Thirdly, the whole process of the experiment is described. In the end, interviews, questionnaire survey and other translation exercise for the posttest are arranged. It is very important that the pretest and the posttest all belong to literary genre, and they are similar in terms of word count and lexical difficulty.

First of all, one translation exercise for pretest is arranged.

Before the beginning of the translation training camp, we distributed a translation exercise to students. They were acquired to finish the exercise before the training started.

Secondly, the introduction and operation instruction for Textwells are introduced.

This translation training is carried out based on Textwells, which is designed according to the inner connection between knowledge nodes. There are five main modules in Textwells as shown in Fig. 1, and they are Learning Module, Practice Module, Classroom Interaction, Data Analysis, Question and Answer, and Favorite. There are also many free video courses hosted by experienced teachers. So students can study independently by watching them whenever and wherever possible. The Learning Module is divided into four sections. And they are Texts as Language Material, Knowledge Nodes, Topical Boards, and Sentences as Language Material. There are 56 different knowledge nodes on the Textwells platform, divided into 6 categories, Word Structure, Sentence Structure, Information Structure, Text Structure, Rhetorical Device and Intertextuality. Most of the texts in the Learning Module are annotated according to the above-mentioned 6 categories of knowledge nodes. The annotations demonstrate the translation theory and explain the reason why to adopt this translation theory. Moreover, students can learn these texts and their annotations in Learning Module based on theme, Chinese-English translation or English-Chinese translation and style. After learning, students can do some exercises in Practice Module to consolidate the key knowledge nodes. Students can operate repeatedly on the computer platform, which helps them understand and remember the knowledge nodes. In the Data Analysis, students' learning behaviours can be monitored and analyzed, so as to help students keep up with their recent study. If there are any problems during the course of self-studying, students can leave a message in Question and Answer to ask for online help. And then the teacher will answer them.

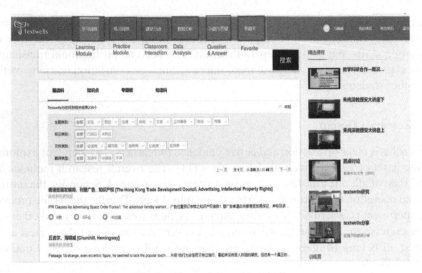

**Fig. 1.** Six modules of textwells

Thirdly, the course of the experiment is described.

The translation training camp, based on Textwells, is an online distance learning program. For a start, the teacher introduces the concepts and characteristics of translation learning based on knowledge network. The size of the node in the translation knowledge network reflects the use frequency of the translation knowledge nodes they stands for. The larger the node is, the higher the use frequency of the knowledge nodes will be. And the density of internal connections depends on the strength of relationship among knowledge nodes. Each knowledge node in the knowledge network is inherently related to each other, so the description and interpretation of specific texts, cultural phenomena or translation methods often involve the association and interaction of multiple knowledge nodes [12]. Then students are guided to understand the interrelationships among knowledge nodes to master translation knowledge points and learn independently on the platform.

In the end, interviews, questionnaire survey and the other translation exercise for the posttest are arranged.

This experiment collects data by means of performance test, questionnaire survey and interview. The performance test consists of two tests, the pretest and the posttest. The pretest and posttest are literary translation exercises, with similar word count and the same lexical difficulty. The grading standard of the pretest and posttest is based on TEM-8. The questionnaire consisted of 12 single-choice questions, and the answer of questionnaire will be designed to utilize five-point Likert Scale ("strongly agree", "relatively agree", "generally agree", "disagree" and "strongly disagree"). Four interview questions aim to know about students' learning feelings and evaluations.

### 3.4 Data Collection and Analysis

#### 3.4.1 The Pretest and Posttest Result Analysis

There are 102 students who participated in this translation training camp, and 96 of them finished pretest and posttest. First of all, the pretest and posttest were scored by two teaching assistants according to the grading standard of TEM-8, and the average score marked by two teaching assistants was a student's final grades. Moreover, for one text with large differences in two grades, another independent grade would be given by an experienced professor as its final score. Table 1 shows that the average score of students increased significantly after the training. Table 2 shows that there are significant differences in the average scores of students after the training camp ($P < 0.05$).

**Table 1.** Paired sample statistics

|  | Average value | Numbers of participants | Standard deviation |
| --- | --- | --- | --- |
| The mean of pretest | 72.266 | 96 | 2.9584 |
| The mean of posttest | 77.161 | 96 | 2.7053 |

**Table 2.** Paired sample test

|  | Average value | t | Sig |
| --- | --- | --- | --- |
| The mean of pretest-The mean of posttest | −4.8958 | −22.152 | 0.000 |

#### 3.4.2 The Questionnaire Result Analysis

102 questionnaires were distributed at the end of the training camp, and 82 copies of effective questionnaire were retrieved. Over ninety percent of students thinks learning the knowledge nodes and annotations on the online platform is helpful for them to finish the post-test. Over ninety-five percent of students believes it is acceptable that the annotations in the example sentence may involve more than one knowledge nodes, with the combination of other related knowledge nodes used to explain the translation method. Last but not least, almost all of students agree with the translation learning method based on knowledge network, and they will keep using that approach in the future study.

#### 3.4.3 The Interview Result Analysis

Based on the above analysis, most of the students approve the knowledge-network-based translation learning method, which really improves students' translation performance. According to the interview, knowledge-network-based translation learning is helpful to translating learning and has been widely approved by students. The interview results of three students are now randomly selected to analyze students' learning feelings and evaluations in detail. The three students are labeled as student A, student B and student C.

When it comes to whether the translation quality has improved after knowledge-network-based translation learning, student A, student B and student C all think it has been improved. Student A thinks he becomes more logical when analyzing passages. Student B thinks that in the translation of long and difficult sentences, many details are better than before. Student C thinks that the specific improvement is reflected in the choice of words, which makes his translation more faithful and elegant.

When it comes to the advantages or disadvantages of knowledge-network-based translation learning compared with traditional translation learning, student A believes that knowledge-network-based translation learning can help him better grasp the context and logic of knowledge. Student B believes that this kind of systematic study can help him learn translation knowledge nodes completely and comprehensively. Student C believes that the translation knowledge network provides more translation knowledge and larger information, which is helpful for students to absorb knowledge more comprehensively.

When referring to the evaluation of knowledge-network-based translation learning, student A indicates this platform is very good, and the web page is also relatively simple and neat. This learning method is of great help to prepare for CATTI. Student B indicates that through Textwells, he can learn anytime, anywhere, and he can review the video courses repeatedly to better understand the knowledge and master the knowledge. Student C indicates the knowledge-network-based translation learning on Textwells is of great help to his translation learning, and it has achieved a lot in the innovative application of knowledge network.

## 4    Discussion

### 4.1    Acceptability of Knowledge-Network-Based Learning Approach

Can students accept knowledge-network-based learning approach to learn translation? According to the comparison of pretest scores and posttest scores, most students' scores have increased. 42% of students improved their grades by 0–5, and 54% of students improved their grades by 5–10 (Table 3). In the questionnaires and interviews, most students also stated that they felt their translation skills had improved and they approved of knowledge-network-based translation learning method. With evidence from this experiment, it is clear that students can accept knowledge-network-based learning approach to learn translation.

**Table 3.** Improvement in student scores

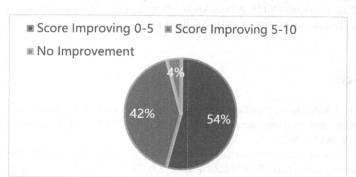

## 4.2 Effects of Knowledge-Network-Based Learning Approach

In what ways does the students' translation performance change after systematic training? Compared to the pretest, students' translation performance have improved a lot. From the perspective of word level, students can translate words more precisely. From the sentence-level perspective, students can do better in syntactic matching and sentence component alternation. Moreover, students has a finer command of rhetorical device alternation.

Most of the students consider Textwells is easy to operate and deserves popularization. Some suggestions are given to Textwells. For example, the platform system should be optimized appropriately. Furthermore, more practice items can be added. These suggestions will be took into consideration to help Textwells get better.

## 5 Conclusion

At present, English is the most common foreign language taught in China. So there is no doubt that the people with a high level of English and good translation skills, particularly non-native English speakers, will be more competitive [13]. The knowledge-network-based translation learning method is different from the traditional education method. With the help of data mining technology, it carries out education and learning activities scientifically based on the inner relationships among knowledge nodes. It is of positive significance to the cultivation of trans-cultural communication talents with comprehensive capabilities. Based on the data analysis, the knowledge-network-based translation learning method does help translation learning. However, the research of the knowledge-network-based translation learning still needs more attention from the academic field. There are a few studies on knowledge-network-based translation learning at home and abroad, so further research should be well developed. In addition, Textwells needs to be further optimized and upgraded, and the research team of the authors, as designers and developers of the platform, will work hard in this regard.

**Acknowledgements.** The work was substantially supported by The National Social Science Fund of China (Project No. 19BYY125: A Data-Mining Driven Mode of Co-construction of Knowledge Network for Translation Learning and Its Application).

# References

1. Zhou, L.: Exploration of applied translation education and teaching with multi-dimensional integration and empowerment (多维融合赋能的应用翻译教育教学探索). Shanghai J. Transl. **6**, 28–33 (2021)
2. Hu, A.: Teaching management and talent training for translation major: new trends, new changes and new ideas (翻译专业教学管理与人才培养:新趋势,新变局与新思路). Chin. Transl. J. **42**(01), 68–74+191 (2021)
3. Mu, Y., Tian, L., Yang, W.: Towards a knowledge management model for online translation learning. In: Hao, T., Chen, W., Xie, H., Nadee, W., Lau, R. (eds.) SETE 2018. LNCS, vol. 11284, pp. 198–207. Springer, Cham (2018). https://doi.org/10.1007/978-3-030-03580-8_21
4. Xie, X., Zhou, L.: Language learning in the era of big data–a case study of Google translation learning (大数据时代的语言学习研究——兼论Google翻译学习案例). Educ. Res. Monthly **11**, 95–103 (2019)
5. Wang, H., Liu, S.: A review of translation technology studies at home and abroad (2000–2021) (国内外翻译技术研究述评(2000—2021)). Technol. Enhanc. Foreign Lang. Educ. **1**, 81–88+92+113 (2022)
6. Broekel, T., Balland, P.-A., Burger, M., van Oort, F.: Modeling knowledge networks in economic geography: a discussion of four methods. Ann. Reg. Sci. **53**(2), 423–452 (2014). https://doi.org/10.1007/s00168-014-0616-2
7. Seufert, A., Von Krogh, G., Bach, A.: Towards knowledge networking. J. Knowl. Manag. **3**, 180–190 (1999)
8. Jing, C., Wan, Z., Kong, Y.: Knowledge Network System Building and Realization, pp. 1–5. IEEE Computer Society (2009)
9. Goto, T., Kojiri, T., Watanabe, T., Yamada, T., Iwata, T.: English grammar learning system based on knowledge network of fill-in-the-blank exercises. In: Lovrek, I., Howlett, R.J., Jain, L.C. (eds.) KES 2008. LNCS (LNAI), vol. 5179, pp. 588–595. Springer, Heidelberg (2008). https://doi.org/10.1007/978-3-540-85567-5_73
10. Mu, Y., Yang, W.: Knowledge-network-based inter-institutional collaborative teaching of translation. In: Pang, C., et al. (eds.) SETE/ICWL -2020. LNCS, vol. 12511, pp. 411–419. Springer, Cham (2021). https://doi.org/10.1007/978-3-030-66906-5_39
11. Tian, L., Mu, Y., Yang, W.: Designing a platform-facilitated and corpus-assisted translation class. In: Hao, T., Chen, W., Xie, H., Nadee, W., Lau, R. (eds.) SETE 2018. LNCS, vol. 11284, pp. 208–217. Springer, Cham (2018). https://doi.org/10.1007/978-3-030-03580-8_22
12. Zhu, C., Mu, Y.: Towards a textual accountability-driven mode of teaching and (self-) learning for translation and bilingual writing: with special reference to a CityU online teaching platform. Chin. Transl. J. **2**, 56–62 (2013)
13. Bao, S., Meng, F.: The design of massive open online course platform for English translation learning based on Moodle. In: Proceedings-2015 5th International Conference on Communication Systems and Network Technologies, CSNT 2015, pp. 1365–1368 (2015)

# Designing Blended Learning Model for Medical English Course Based on POA

Hongli Ji[1(✉)] and Shuangshuang Zheng[2(✉)]

[1] School of Humanistic Medicine, Anhui Medical University, Hefei, China
merry_jili@hotmail.com
[2] School of Foreign Studies, Hefei University of Technology, Hefei, China
335294975@qq.com

**Abstract.** The development of informational technology and the proliferation of electronic gadgets make blended learning (BL) possible. In recent years, BL has been widely employed in language teaching. In this paper, the authors give an explicit elaboration on the application of the integration of online platform (rain classroom) with traditional face-to-face (F2F) classroom to medical English teaching under the guidance of POA, which can solve the problem of separation between learning and using of medical English. The thoughtfully designed BL model demonstrates a new way to help teachers to be informed of students' learning in time, provide materials accordingly for students' autonomous learning, and offer efficient evaluation on the one hand, and ignite students' intrinsic enthusiasm for learning, and increase their active involvement on the other hand.

**Keywords:** Blended learning · Production-oriented Approach (POA) · Medical English

## 1 Introduction

In the past decades, English teaching and learning in higher education has undergone great revolution in mainland of China. Remarkable innovations have been made to enhance EFL (English as a Foreign Language) learners' English proficiency. In the process, numerous language teaching methodologies, such as Text-Centered Instruction, Audiolingual Method, Communicative Approach, Task-Based Language Teaching (TBLT), Content-Based Instruction (CBI) have been introduced in China. Accordingly, English learning has shifted from teacher-centered principles to student-centered principles, with text-oriented method to communication-oriented method. Meanwhile, English teaching also transforms from EGP (English for general purposes) to ESP (English for specific purposes). But most of the above-mentioned methodologies meet restrictions in the context of China's language learning. Chinese language scholars are increasingly aware of the significance of the localization of Second Language Acquisition (SLA) methodologies so as to adapt to China's context [35]. In China, college English teaching is faced with such practical challenges as large class sizes, shortage of advanced pedagogies and proper assessment methods, examination-oriented culture, etc. Production-oriented approach (POA) developed by Wen Qiufang [30] is an indigenous theory with

C. S. González-González et al. (Eds.): ICWL 2022/SETE 2022, LNCS 13869, pp. 491–501, 2023.
https://doi.org/10.1007/978-3-031-33023-0_46

Chinese characteristics, which is a theoretical exploration on how to carry out foreign language teaching in China, with the purpose of handling the problems of "separation of learning and using", "high investment and low effectiveness" [3], and "dumb English" [6].

On the other hand, the high-speed development of Information Technology and the popularization of electronic products such as smart mobile phones and computers have a huge impact on the diversification of language teaching forms. Online technology can be used in language teaching [20, 38]. Traditional F2F classroom teaching has been unable to meet EFL learners' requirements, while online learning has gradually become a trend in higher education [36]. So blended learning, which combines the advantages of online and traditional offline teaching activities [7, 13], is most properly becoming a major teaching method for EFL learners. Actually, it has been widely used in the field of English learning. Front-line language teachers make every attempt to explore how to successfully implement BL in various language learning settings, such as EGP [26, 28], ESP [25], EAP [4, 37], and MIT translation theory [10]. Medical English, as an ESP, also attracts many researchers to construct BL model. Liu Bing explores to design flipped classroom teaching model for medical English [17], and Mu Xiurong does an empirical study of task-based teaching model for medical English listening [19]. However, there is less research carried out from the perspective of POA to construct BL model for medical English. Without an appropriate methodology, a simple mixture of technology and content can definitely fail to ensure effective learning.

Therefore, this research aims to apply POA in the specific teaching setting of medical English to design BL model, in order to improve learning efficiency and achieve best learning outcome.

## 2 Literature Review

### 2.1 Blended Learning

So far, many researchers have sought to define Blended Learning from different perspectives. Garrison and Kanuka hold the opinion that BL is to integrate F2F instruction with online instruction [7]. Book and Graham propose that BL is a combination of F2F teaching and computer-mediated teaching [2]. Smith and Kurthen describe BL as online activities employed in F2F learning no more than 45 percentage [23]. Watson advocates that there are seven categories of BL continuum between fully online and completely F2F courses where few or no Internet-based resources are used [29].

By contrast, Chinese scholars put more focus on influencing elements and impacts of BL on learners. He Kekang is the first person that brought forward the concept of BL in China. He presents that BL is just to combine traditional classroom instructions with digital learning, maximizing teachers' role in guiding, inspiring and monitoring, and fostering learners' initiative, enthusiasm and creativity [8]. Li Kedong and Zhao Jianhua believe that BL is a product of an integration of traditional and online teaching, aiming to enhance learning efficiency [16]. Generally speaking, BL refers to the organic combination of traditional classroom teaching and online teaching, for sake of more challenging courses, with the purpose of increasing learners' participation and improving learning efficiency.

## 2.2 POA Theory

In the middle of 1980s, several principles emerged in SLA theory, such as input hypothesis [14], output hypothesis [27] and interaction hypothesis [18]. The prototype of Production-Oriented Approach (POA) is based on Swain's output hypothesis. POA, blending the curriculum theory with SLA theory, is introduced by Professor Wen Qiufang, which puts an emphasis on the leading role of teachers and attempts to solve the problems of English traditional classroom teaching in higher education.

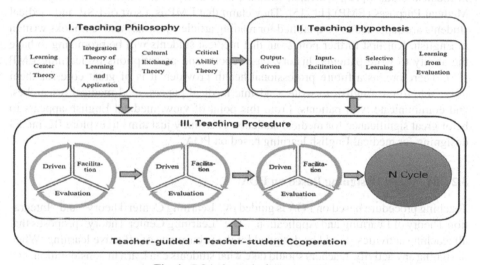

**Fig. 1.** POA theoretical system [33]

The latest revised theoretical system of POA, which is illustrated in Fig. 1, is composed of three parts: teaching philosophy, teaching hypothesis, and teaching procedure. In the whole teaching process, teachers are supposed to play the role of scaffolding. Teaching philosophy is the guiding ideology of teaching procedure designing, teaching content choosing, and training goal determining. Teaching hypothesis should be tested by teaching practice, and it also offers the basis for compiling textbook exercises, designing and arranging activities. The teaching procedure is revised as N cycles of "output-driven, input-facilitation, and evaluation". Here, output-driven refers to teachers' assignment of output tasks, which requires learners to do on their own. Input-facilitation means teachers' assistance in offering certain guidance according to learners' performance of output tasks. And evaluation has something to do with the preset of indicators for output evaluation, and the active introduction of teachers' reviews and learners' mutual evaluation.

# 3  Blended Learning Model for Medical English Course

## 3.1  Medical English Course

Many scholars have tried to define ESP [1, 5, 9, 22, 24, 34]. Generally speaking, ESP is to equip learners of different fields with specific English proficiency required in the related settings of academics, professions and workplaces. English has been widely used in medical field since the later 20th century. Kang highlights the role of English in medical studies [12]; Kurfürst, Joesba and Ardeo put an emphasis on English for Medical Purposes (EMP) [11, 15]. They claim that EMP is a sort of ESP, and medical students are supposed to be qualified for reading articles, journals and textbooks written in English. Kurfürst further points out that medical students will be promising to have the ability to write patients' history, case reports and prescriptions by learning EMP [15]. Therefore, as a future professional health provider, it is of great core for them to be able to use English to write academic medical papers, read medical researches, and communicate with patients. From this point of view, medical English appears to be of great significance for medical students. This study just aims to explore BL model designing for medical English learning based on POA.

## 3.2  BL Model Designing Based on POA

Teaching procedure based on POA is guided by "Learning Center Theory" and "Integration Theory of Learning and Application". The "Learning Center Theory" proposes that all teaching activities should be designed for the occurrence of effective learning. When designing any activity, teachers should take what students can learn in consideration, and play the role of scaffolding in guidance of students' completing output tasks, in order to cultivate students' English communication competence. The "Integration Theory of Learning and Application" is mainly embodied in the process of facilitation, which includes both input "learning", such as listening and reading, and output "application", such as speaking, writing, interpretation and translation. The accomplishment of each output task requires three conditions: content, language and discourse structure. The output tasks should be of accuracy, progressivity and diversity [32]. The diversity refers to information delivery channels, communication patterns and activity forms. Information delivery channels include input and output activities. Communication patterns can be designed as lectures, news reports, dialogues, discussions, debates, interviews, monologues, cosplays, speeches and so on. Activities can be taken out in forms of individuals, partners, teams and classes. The main teaching process can be described as "output-input-output". The first link of "output" refers to teachers' making students do assigned output tasks in line with the teaching objectives before class. The second link of "input" means teachers providing with reasonable suggestions concerning students' output performance and offering related knowledge about English vocabulary, grammar, and expression, and meanwhile students' doing selective learning. The third link of "output" has something to do with students' practicing the output task again based on teachers' guidance.

The BL model shifts the learning of complex and boring knowledge about medical English from monotony F2F lectures to the mixture of online and offline teaching. It enables teachers to select proper language input according to the output task, and students to reasonably allocate their time in input learning and output application, and ultimately overcoming the disadvantage of separation between learning and application.

In order to make research on how to apply POA to medical English teaching, so as to verify the impacts of the teaching model on students' engagement and learning efficiency, the authors apply POA to *Medical English – An Integrated Course* published by Nanjing University Press, taking unit 6 for an example, with the theme of epidemiology, to design BL model. The target students of this course are sophomores majoring in clinical medicine. They are medium in English, with a certain reserve of English knowledge about vocabulary and grammar.

**Teaching Objectives.** Teaching objectives in the unit cover three aspects --- language competence, cultural awareness and vocational ability, which conform to the "Key Ability Cultivation" of POA, shown in Table 1.

**Table 1.** Teaching objectives

| Teaching objective | Cognitive activity | Realization approach |
|---|---|---|
| Language competence | Remembering, understanding, and applying | An e-learning online and a F2F learning offline; A F2F demonstration offline and an e-evaluation online |
| Cultural awareness | Understanding, analyzing, and evaluating | An e-learning online; A F2F discussion and presentation offline |
| Vocational ability | Understanding, criticizing, evaluating, and applying | An e-learning and e-evaluation online |

For language competence, students are expected to develop their competence in using English for communication, taking in vocabulary, useful expressions and sentence structures relevant to epidemiology.

For culture awareness, students are expected to strengthen their nationality identity, the emotion towards their country, and their cultural confidence, and establish their awareness of building a community with a shared future, so as to become a civilized citizen with social responsivity.

For vocational ability, students are expected to be adapted to their future career as a medical practitioner, with the professional spirit of be dedicated and excellent.

**Teaching Procedure.** The teaching process based on POA is composed of three phases: pre-class motivation, in-class facilitation, and post-class evaluation. The BL model is designed adhering to the teaching objectives, as is shown in Fig. 2.

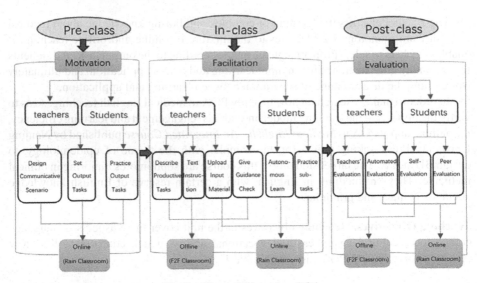

**Fig. 2.** BL model based on POA

Before Class (Motivation): According to POA, in the first stage of motivation, teachers are required to design the communicative scenarios, and set productive tasks before class on the platform. The communicative scenarios must be as authentic as possible. They should be most like what students will encounter in their future endeavors. The productive tasks mainly take the form of oral expression and writing.

In this unit, two scenarios were designed based on the theme of epidemiology and teaching objectives:

Scenario 1: Imagine it is at the time of the beginning of COVID-19 outbreak. People knows little about the highly contagious virus. Being isolated at home, most of them surf both the domestic and foreign Internet to browse the concerning information and download medical advice to relieve their COVID-19-caused anxieties. It's a pity that your family members can't understand the information in English on the foreign websites except you. So, you are expected to interpret or translate the related messages about COVID-19 to help them be informed of the overall situation worldwide.

Scenario 2: While browsing microblog, you read some inaccurate reports on China's COVID-19 and the nation's epidemic prevention measures. You feel obligated to make a clarification.

Relevant productive tasks were set and segmented into several sub-tasks in the next phase. (See Table 2).

**Table 2.** Productive tasks and sub-tasks

| Scenario | Productive task | Sub-task |
|---|---|---|
| Scenario 1 | 1) Read two pieces of information about COVID-19, and translate them into Chinese<br>2) Listen to two pieces of news about COVID-19, and interpret | 1. Individual work: Collect epidemic-related words, expressions and terminologies<br>2. Group activity: Translate the complex sentences in the first Text and compare your version with your teammates |
| Scenario 2 | 3) Write a short paper on the topic *Current COVID-19 Situation in China*<br>4) Make a speech on the topic *China's COVID-19 Prevention Measures* | 3. Class activity: Read the second Text by oneself and make an oral presentation<br>4. Partner activity: Watch and listen to online materials concerning COVID-19, and make a summary of the main idea. Share your version with your partner |

This step is generally realized on the platform of Rain Classroom (a smart mobile teaching tool developed by Tsinghua University in 2016). In tradition F2F classroom teaching, it's impossible for all the students of different levels to fulfil the tasks in a fixed time, which will inevitably affect student's participation. What's more, because of the limited statistical methods, it's difficult for teachers to get an overall knowledge of students' performance in the output tasks. Therefore, they can't meet the requirement of accuracy in the facilitation stage. The online form makes students deal with the productive tasks flexibly. It can also, to some extent, reduce the learning anxiety of students and generate their intrinsic motivation of learning. In addition, teachers can learn about students' real ability and design more pertinent activities accordingly.

In Class (Facilitation): The second stage of facilitation is imperative for the entire teaching process. In this phase, teachers are expected to present the teaching objectives clearly to students, make a specific description of students' productive tasks, disassemble these tasks into sub-tasks, and guide students to accomplish one by one. Students are supposed to do selective learning and complete the productive tasks under the guidance of teachers. Here, one point that facilitation doesn't just means teachers' providing input information deserves being emphasized. Output activities taken out in F2F classroom also function as facilitator [21].

In this unit, the first text *Epidemiology and Its Application* was instructed in the F2F classroom teaching, while the second text *Epidemiological Research on SARS in China* was assigned to students for their autonomous learning. Different from traditional teaching, text instruction based on POA only deals with language knowledge related to the theme of the unit instead of a comprehensive explanation of every language point appearing in the text. In this unit, teachers only make an introduction about the relevant words, expressions and terminologies in the aspect of epidemiology. At the same time, teachers upload more added input materials of relevant topics, including exemplary essays, audio and video materials. Students are encouraged to do selective learning and supervised to accomplish the productive tasks. Finally, teachers are supposed to check up the productive tasks. The output exercises should be carried out step by step under the guidance of teachers. At the end of each micro-activity, immediate assessment is required.

The productive tasks are decomposed into several sub-tasks to enable students to accomplish one after another. Besides, each micro-task is devised for a certain specific learning objective (See Table 3). In the process, teachers play the role of scaffolding.

**Table 3.** Sub-tasks and teaching objectives

| Sub-task | Teaching objective |
|---|---|
| 1. Individual work: Collect epidemic-related words, expressions and terminologies<br>2. Group activity: Translate the complex sentences in the first Text and compare your version with your teammates | Language competence |
| 3. Class activity: Read the second Text by oneself and make an oral presentation | Cultural awareness |
| 4. Partner activity: Watch and listen to online materials concerning COVID-19, and make a summary of the main idea. Share your version with your partner | Vocational ability |

The time for F2F classroom teaching is limited, so it should be reasonably allocated so as to maximize the learning efficiency and stimulate students' learning enthusiasm.

After Class (Evaluation): POA adopts Teacher-Student Collaborative Assessment (TSCA), which is consisted of timely assessment and delayed assessment. TSCA is divided in three stages: TSCA pre-class preparation, TSCA in-class implementation and post-class activities. TSCA involves choosing samples, setting evaluation criteria, students' self-evaluation and revision according to the criteria, teachers' illustration of common problems among students, and peer evaluation or self-evaluation of the rest products after class [31].

In this practice, different assessments are employed to promote learning, involving self-assessment, peer assessment, automated assessment and teacher's assessment. First of all, teachers choose some samples of students' output product anonymously before class. Then teachers make some comment on the output samples, and set up the grading criteria as well. Then in class, students can make self-evaluation towards their own output task respectively according to teachers' criteria. This is a good way to make students have a good understanding of their shortage of knowledge, and stimulate their hunger for relevant information. Automated assessment is quite useful for such output tasks as writing and translation. Students hand in their products on the website www.pigai.org where teachers' scoring formula is uploaded on the website beforehand. Then students' output products can be evaluated automatically. Peer evaluation is favored in oral tasks. In this unit, students are required to make an oral presentation based on the second text. As non-English major students, the English class in higher education is usually carried out in large-scale class teaching. It is impossible for each student to make a presentation in class. So, in class, teachers can issue the output task in courseware in the form of exercises on Rain Classroom platform. Students are required to submit their oral presentation online. And their scripts for the oral presentation must be submitted as well. Last but not least, teacher's assessment always plays an irreplaceable part in the whole assessment system. Teachers' role as a mediator is extremely crucial.

# 4 Conclusion

POA has been developed as a response to such weaknesses of the traditional English classroom instruction in China as students' low participation and time-consuming eval-uation. It is advocated as a resolution of the problems existing in China's EFL context. Blended learning, as a product of the development and proliferation of digital technolo-gies, integrating the advantages of both online and offline learning, has been widely employed in higher education in China. This paper designs a new hybrid teaching model for medical English under the guidance of POA, expounds the application strategies of the online learning platform (Rain Classroom Platform) in terms of before-class moti-vation, in-class facilitation, and after-class evaluation, with the purpose of stimulating students' learning enthusiasm, promoting their participation, and ultimately, optimizing their learning efficiency. In the whole teaching procedure, teachers play a scaffolding role, with students' autonomous learning within their controlled range. The introduction of the online learning platform makes it possible for teachers to be informed of students' learning situation in time, provide support for students' autonomous learning, improve students' curriculum participation, and offer timely evaluation for students' performance of the output tasks.

However, this study is just a preliminary attempt at the application of POA to the blended teaching for medical English, and it only stays in the stage of theoretical design. In the future, empirical studies will be carried out on the specific application effect of this teaching model in the field of medical English learning. Meanwhile, with the continuous advancement of Internet technology, a more reasonable and scientific teaching plan will be formulated for the blended learning, including online and offline allocation of learning time, online supervision and evaluation. The teaching model needs to be gradually improved in the practical teaching in the future, and more researches are expected to be conducted for medical English instruction for undergraduates in medical universities.

**Acknowledgements.** The work was substantially supported by The National Social Science Fund of China (Project No. 19BYY125: A Data-Mining Driven Mode of Co-construction of Knowledge Network for Translation Learning and Its Application) and The Philosophy and Social Science Fund for University Scientific Research of Anhui Province (Project No. 2022AH050617: A Study on the Construction of the Discourse System for the External Communication of Traditional Chinese Medicine Cultural Classics from the Perspective of Eco-translatology.)

# References

1. Aglaua, C.M.: Ethnographic needs analysis as basis for the design of EAP syllabi. Paper presented at the 34th RELC-SEAMEO International Conference, Singapore (1999)
2. Bonk, C.J., Charles, R.G.: The Handbook of Blended Learning: Global Perspectives. Local Designs. John Wiley & Sons, New Jersey (2006)
3. Cai, J.G.: College English Teaching: Reviewing, Reflections and Research. Fudan University Press, Shanghai (2006)
4. Cai, J.G.: Design of a project-based blended instructional model for EAP. J. PLA Univ. Foreign Lang. **3**, 39–47+160 (2019)
5. Celani, M.A.: When myth and reality meet: reflections on ESP in Brazil. ESP J. **27**, 412–423 (2008)
6. Dai, W.D.: Spending enormous time but obtaining poor outcomes in foreign language teaching. Foreign Lang. Foreign Lang. Teach. **7**, 10–14 (2001)
7. Garrison, D.R., Kanuka, H.: Blended learning: uncovering its transformative potential in higher education. Internet High. Educ. **7**, 95–105 (2004)
8. He, K.K.: On new trend of theory for educational technology from blending learning (Part 1). E-educ. Res. **a**(3), 1–6 (2004)
9. Hutchinson, T., Waters, A.: English for Specific Purposes: A Learning Centred Approach. CUP, Cambridge (1987)
10. Jiang, Q., Tao, Y.L.: The application and effect analysis of flipped class in MTI translation theory teaching —taking the introduction to translation as an example. Foreign Lang. Educ. **5**, 70–74 (2018)
11. Joesba, M., Ardeo, G.: Student engineers, ESP courses, and testing with Cloze Tests. ESP World **2**(10) (2005)
12. Kang, S.J.: A Korean medical doctor's experiences in learning and use of English in the United States: Individual and environmental affective factors. Paper presented in 16th Annual Conference in Ethnographic and Qualitative Research in Education, University of Albany, SUNY, New York (2004)
13. Karkour, I.: A blended learning model for teaching reading in English as a foreign language. Teach. Engl. Technol. **14**(4), 17–31 (2014)
14. Krashen, S.: The Input Hypothesis: Issues and Implications. Longman, London (1985)
15. Kurfürst, P.: English? Sure, but how? Paper presented at the International Conference on Lingua Summit, Trencín, Slovakia (2005)
16. Li, K.D., Zhao, J.H.: Principles and application models of blended learning. E-educ. Res. **7**, 1–6 (2004)
17. Liu, B.: Medical English flipped classroom teaching model: construction and practice. Foreign Lang. Educ. **5**, 62–65 (2016)
18. Long, M.H.: Native speaker/non-native speaker conversation and the negotiation of comprehensible input. Appl. Linguist. **4**, 126–141 (1983)
19. Mu, X.R., Xu, H.Q.: Empirical study of the application of task-based language teaching in English listening teaching in medical universities. J. Gansu Univ. Chin. Med. **4**, 110–117 (2018)
20. Mu, Y., Tian, L., Yang, W.: Towards a knowledge management model for online translation learning. In: Hao, T., Chen, W., Xie, H., Nadee, W., Lau, R. (eds.) Emerging Technologies for Education. SETE 2018. LNCS, vol. 11284. Springer, Cham (2018). https://doi.org/10.1007/978-3-030-03580-8_21
21. Qiu, L.: Designing enabling activities in the production-oriented approach: criteria and examples. Foreign Lang. Educ. China **3**(2), 12–19 (2020)

22. Richards, J.C., Schmidt, R.W.: Longman Dictionary of Language Teaching 7 Applied Linguistics. Pearson Education, Harlow (2010)
23. Smith, G.G., Kurthen, H.: Front-stage and back-stage in hybrid e-learning face-to-face courses. Int. J. E-Learn. **6**, 455–474 (2007)
24. Smoak, R.: What is English for specific purposes? Bureau of educational and cultural affairs. Engl. Teach. Forum. **41**(2), 22–30 (1996)
25. Sun, X.H., Zhang, Q., Sun, Z.D.: ESP flipped classroom teaching design: a multiliteracies perspective. Technol. Enhanc. Foreign Lang. Educ. **4**, 38–42+65 (2017)
26. Suo, G.F., Chi, R.B.: Research on blended cross-cultural foreign language teaching based on MOOCs. Foreign Lang. World **3**, 89–96 (2018)
27. Swain, M.: Communicative competence: some roles of comprehensive input and comprehensive output in its development. In: Gass, S., Madden, C. (eds.), Input in Second Language Acquisition, pp. 235–256. Newbury House, Rowley, MA (1985)
28. Wang, N., Chen, J.W., Tai, M., Zhang, J.Y.: Blended learning for Chinese university EFL learners: learning environment and learner perceptions. Comput. Assist. Lang. Learn. **1**, 1–27 (2019)
29. Watson, J.: Blended Learning: The Convergence of Online and Face-to-Face Education. North American Council for Online Learning, Columbia (2008)
30. Wen, Q.F.: Developing a theoretical system of the production-oriented approach in language teaching. Foreign Lang. Teach. Res. **4**, 547–558 (2015)
31. Wen, Q.F.: Teacher-student collaborative assessment: the new evaluation form created by production-oriented approach. Foreign Lang. World **5**, 37–43 (2016)
32. Wen, Q.F.: Chinese features displayed in the production oriented approach. Mod. Foreign Lang. **5**, 348–358 (2017)
33. Wen, Q.F.: Production-oriented approach in teaching Chinese as a second language. Chin. Teach. World **3**, 387–400 (2018)
34. Wright, C.: The Benefits of ESP. Cambridge Language Consultations (1992)
35. Yu, A.Q.: Understanding information technology acceptance and effectiveness in college students' English learning in China. University of Nebraska: doctoral dissertation, Nebraska (2019)
36. Zhang, H.R., Zhang, W.X., Yang, F.: An investigation of the influence of MOOC-based blended learning on learners' English learning strategies — in the case of basic English listening and speaking course. Technol. Enhanc. Foreign Lang. Educ. **5**, 39–44 (2019)
37. Zheng, Y.Y.: A study of the learning effects of a SPOC blended English academic writing course. Technol. Enhanc. Foreign Lang. Educ. **5**, 50–55 (2019)
38. Zhu, C., Mu, Y.: Towards a textual accountability-driven mode of teaching and (self-) learning for translation and bilingual writing: with special reference to a CityU online teaching platform. Chin. Transl. J. **2**, 56–62 (2013)

# Application of Formative Assessment Model in College English Course Assisted by Digital Platforms---Taking HFUT as an Example

Wenhui Zhang[1,2](✉)

[1] School of Foreign Studies, Hefei University of Technology, Hefei, China
1592634228@qq.com
[2] Center for Literature and Translation Studies, Hefei University of Technology, Hefei, China

**Abstract.** With the help of internet and digital technology, online and blended teaching in institutions of higher learning in China are becoming a reality and the original assessment model is out of date. A scientific, diversified and digital assessment model is badly needed. The paper will present a new model aided by digital platforms applied in HFUT, in which summative assessment accounts for 50% and formative assessment another 50%. This paper focuses on the latter which consists of autonomous listening (10%), oral English (20%), assignment (10%) and class performance (10%). The assessment content, assessment method and means and marking criteria of the above four components are displayed in detail and a questionnaire is conducted so as to reveal its implementation effect. Findings show that students have a relatively high satisfaction with the formative assessment model which proved to be more objective and operable. Nevertheless, respondents' suggestions taken into account, a slight adjustment and improvement will be made later.

**Keywords:** Online and Blended Teaching · Formative Assessment · Digital Platforms · Objective and Operable · Adjustment and Improvement

## 1 Introduction

During- and post- COVID 19 epidemic period, online teaching and blended teaching in institutions of higher learning in China are becoming a reality. Changes in means of teaching call for changes in assessment model, formative assessment (FA) one in particular. Assessment, used as tools by teachers for tracking what and how well students have learned, plays a critical role in college English teaching. The overall objective of assessment and testing is to push the reform and development of College English Course forward, to improve the quality of teaching steadily, to cultivate high-quality foreign language talents, and to better serve the overall development of the country. With the rapid development of information technologies in education practice and research, college English is also experiencing tremendous reform and innovation in terms of technology-enhanced teaching modes and assessment ones as well. According to *College English Teaching Guidelines* (2020) issued by the Steering Committee of College

C. S. González-González et al. (Eds.): ICWL 2022/SETE 2022, LNCS 13869, pp. 502–512, 2023.
https://doi.org/10.1007/978-3-031-33023-0_47

Foreign Language Teaching in China, an integration of online and offline teaching should be highlighted and a complete teaching system containing in-class interaction, students' practice, assignment feedback and assessment should be established, keeping a balance between the traditional teaching modes and the modern ones.

A scientific assessment and testing system is of vital importance to ensure teaching quality, and vice versa. Under the circumstances of modern information technology, a fresh assessment mode should be explored, in which each part of the curriculum system is taken into full account by means of various methods and means, so as to keep a balance of "formative assessment for learning" and "summative assessment of learning" [1].

Based on the study of previous research findings and the results of questionnaire survey, this paper presents and analyses the current practices of College English assessment in Hefei University of Technology (HFUT), and proposes suggestions for the adjustment of the FA model.

## 2 Formative Assessment in College English Course

### 2.1 Literature Review on Formative Assessment

There has been a relatively long and extensive study on language teaching and the FA abroad. In 1967, Michael Scriven coined the terms formative and summative assessment and stated two roles that assessment may play [2]. Two years later in 1969, Benjamin Bloom employed the two terms, suggested that the same distinction might be applied to improving the teaching-learning process for students, and presented his ideas on mastery learning [3]. Since then, more and more researchers began to show great interest in the topic. Some focused on the distinction, some highlighted summative assessment. After 1990s, more and more researchers attached importance to formative assessment. Among them, the most representatives were Black and William, who strongly advocated formative assessment and defined it.

In China, College English teaching modes have been constantly reformed and innovated while assessment and testing modes seems to stand still. The summative assessment has long been the only way to evaluate students while the formative assessment which can help teachers obtain feedback and provide students with an effective means to adjust their learning methods and strategics, has not been attached importance to.

The author has conducted an extensive survey of the research literature with CNKI (China National Knowledge Infrastructure) as literature sources by searching for core journals with the key concept "formative assessment" and this process has yielded about 160 papers to study. The retrieving results suggest that the research on FA began from early 2000s, steadily rising year by year. It covers a number of aspects and courses such as review and reflection of formative assessment studies in China [4, 5], validity study of assessment system [6, 7], formative assessment of the course on reading and evaluating research papers [8], formative assessment of academic English [9, 10].

College English formative assessment has achieved tremendously, which can be reflected from the increasing papers published, and most of them fall to the field of review and reflection of domestic research and practice [11], validity study of the college English evaluation system [12], construction and application of assessment system [13, 14], empirical study [15].

However, there are not many researches on the assessment practice, the researches call for further development. With the deepening of the college English teaching reform and popularity of the digital and smart teaching means, teaching contents, means and evaluation standards are all badly needed to improve, to meet the needs of students, universities and society in the new era. That's the very reason why we research on the blended teaching and formative assessment so as to improve the teaching efficiency and effect.

## 2.2 Formative Assessment

A comprehensive, objective, scientific assessment system is of great importance to the realization of the curriculum goal. Leung & Mohan (2004: 336) pointed out that "the evaluation of students' learning consists of summative assessment featuring standardized tests, and formative assessment highlighting learning process and aims" [16]. As a rising evaluative method in recent years formative assessment is parallel to summative assessment. Assessment refers to all those activities undertaken by teachers - and by their students in assessing themselves - that provide information to be used as feedback to modify teaching and learning activities. Because teachers need to know about their pupils' progress and difficulties with learning so that they can adapt their own work to meet pupils' needs [17].

Drawing both on their definitions in 1998 and the definition of the Assessment Reform Group (ARG, 2002), Black & William restate the definition of formative assessment as follows:

Practice in a classroom is formative to the extent that evidence about student achievement is elicited, interpreted, and used by teachers, learners, or their peers, to make decisions about the next steps in instruction that are likely to be better, or better founded, than the decisions they would have taken in the absence of the evidence that was elicited [18].

In 2007, *College English Curriculum Requirements* defined FA as "procedural and developmental assessment conducted in the teaching process i.e., tracking the teaching process, providing feedback and promoting an all-round development of the students, in accordance with the teaching objectives and by means of various evaluative methods" [19]. It facilitates the effective monitoring of students' learning process and promotes the evaluative ideas of teaching and learning. More importantly, various evaluative methods and means used alone or simultaneously, serve as an assessment series to better promote the teaching and learning activities.

# 3   FA Model Applied in HFUT

Considering the existing problems in the undergraduate education such as nonstandard teaching process, unscientific teaching assessment model, etc., the 2015 Teaching Plan of HFUT clarified the importance of teaching process administration, in which a curriculum assessment should cover various evaluative means including assignment, mid-term test, class performance and so on. In view of the facts, the research focuses on the deep integration of college English teaching and digital technology so as to further the reform of teaching model and assessment one.

In HFUT, the college English course as one of the required courses of General Education, comprises the comprehensive course (oral English and intensive reading) and listening course. The former places emphasis on improving students' speaking, reading, translating and writing abilities, which is conducted by a blended teaching with a combination of classroom teaching, Rain-class room and online teaching, while the latter attempts to improve students' listening ability realized by their autonomous learning in computer room or their smart phone.

In accordance with the *Guidelines*, in the light of the university' specific circumstances, students are assessed by means of FA (50%) and summative assessment (50%) for their college English course. And according to the FA criteria, a digital platform-based and diversified FA model has been established in HFUT. This paper will present the practice of FA model in HFUT, hoping to adjust and improve it.

## 3.1   Prerequisite of the FA Model---Blended Teaching

It is of vital necessity to introduce the blended teaching model applied in HFUT so that the FA model will be fully illustrated and understood. The blended teaching model is shown in the following Graph.

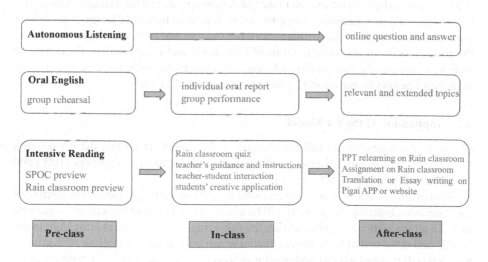

**Graph.** Blended teaching model

First of all, before class students' learning based on several digital platforms is data-oriented. Students are supposed to conduct their autonomous listening in the library, computer rooms or on their smart phone. By means of campus net, they can easily log in the Tsinghua University Press Online English Learning. In terms of oral English, according to the tasks assigned by the teacher in advance, students are divided into groups of four or six. Each one of a group will take on different tasks; they will search for information, make PPT, practice oral presentation, role-play etc. When it comes to intensive reading, students are required to read the new vocabulary and the text aloud, get acquaintance with some background information and related knowledge via words, pictures, audios and videos on our self-made SPOC of our university, and meanwhile detect the difficult points by marking them. In this way, students will have an immersive previewing experience and at the same time be clear about their difficulties. Of course, the platforms will automatically record the results they achieved.

In class, a blended teaching model is carried out in HFUT, which combines the traditional face-to-face teaching and online Rain classroom teaching. Students on campus and students detained at home due to COVID-19 pandemic have an equal opportunity to learn. The specific procedure goes like this: two or three oral groups display their activities followed by peer assessment and teacher's evaluation in 20 min or so; with the help of Rain classroom platform, a time-limit test will be given to the students concerning the vocabulary and reading comprehension about the text they have previewed; according to the results of the test, teachers will focus on the difficult points and explain them in detail; afterward under the guidance of teachers, students will try to paraphrase the long and difficult sentences, work out the structure of a text, acquire the writing strategies used, and conclude the viewpoint of the author. Eventually, students will air their opinions as to the text or extended topic through group discussion or debate.

After class, students will gain an individualized instruction with the aid of Rain class room and other digital platforms. During the process of autonomous listening, students and teachers can have an interaction in the Q&A message area on the Tsinghua University Press Online English Learning; students can review what they have learned and submit their homework such as blank-filling, multiple choices and oral retelling of the text on the Rain class room platform; in terms of translation and essay writing, Pigai APP or website offers an effective way to make use of; what' more, students can communicate with their teachers by means of QQ anywhere anytime if needed.

## 3.2 Application of the FA Model

Changes in teaching model call for changes in FA model. In HFUT, the FA consists of four parts: autonomous listening (10%), oral English (20%), assignment (10%) and class performance (10%), 50% in total.

First of all, autonomous listening accounts for 10% of the FA. At the very beginning of each semester, listening assignment will be given by teachers and students are supposed to finish all the eight units online during the following semester with at least 15 h. In the middle and at the end of the course, a listening test will be released online respectively. Students will be rated with a combination of their total time spent (30%), their progress of all the eight units (15%), their grades of the eight units (15%) and the grade of the listening test (40%). The platform has recorded what students have done and made calculations automatically so that teachers can easily download their students' listening final score and make a detailed analysis. The weight setting is shown in Table 1.

**Table 1.** The weight setting of autonomous listening

| student ID | name | score (total learning time) | score (completion percentage) | score (eight units) | score (listening tests) | final score |
|---|---|---|---|---|---|---|
| | | 30 | 15(100%) | 14.72 | 33.2 | 92.92 |
| | | 13.5 | 12.45(83%) | 13.03 | 29 | 67.98 |
| | | 30 | 15(100%) | 14.66 | 24.8 | 84.46 |
| | | 30 | 15(100%) | 14.78 | 36.4 | 96.18 |
| | | 30 | 15(100%) | 14.83 | 35.2 | 95.03 |

Secondly, oral English accounts for 20% of the FA. 10% comes from oral presentation and group performance of the weekly course, in which peer assessment plays a critical role. Of course, teachers will tell students the standard, rules and methods as to how to evaluate themselves and their peers. The other 10% is based on the end-term oral test, in which students will be scored or evaluated by their teachers according to their pronunciation, fluency and ideas etc.

Thirdly, another 10% of the FA is based on the after-class assignment. Its evaluation is combined the Rain-classroom assignment of each unit with translation or essay-writing on Pigai APP or website. The weight setting will take three factors into consideration: rate of finished assignments, complexity and score of each assignment. Finally, Rain classroom assignments which focus on multiple choices and blank-filling account for 34% while translation or essay-writing on Pigai APP or website is 66%, which is shown in Table 2.

**Table 2.** The components of assignments

| student ID | name | score (essay 1 on Pigai APP) | score (essay 2 on Pigai APP) | score (Rain-class room assignments) | final score |
|---|---|---|---|---|---|
| | | 92.5 | 88.5 | 79 | 86.7 |
| | | 86.5 | 84.5 | 91 | 87.3 |
| | | 85.5 | 88 | 89 | 87.5 |
| | | 82.5 | 78.5 | 83 | 81.3 |
| | | 80 | 77.5 | 62 | 73.2 |

Finally, class performance accounts for the rest 10%, which lies in students' rain-class room attendance rate, teacher-student interaction and in-class quizzes and SPOC preview as well. Rain classroom data is shown in Table 3 and SPOC preview data is shown in Table 4.

**Table 3.** Rain-class room data

| student ID | name | score (Rain-class room performance) | score (Rain-class room quizzes) | final score |
|---|---|---|---|---|
|  |  | 33.19 | 54 | 87.2 |
|  |  | 31.11 | 51 | 82.1 |
|  |  | 32.8 | 45 | 77.8 |
|  |  | 23.78 | 51 | 74.8 |
|  |  | 38.4 | 33 | 71.4 |

**Table 4.** SPOC preview data

| student ID | name | video watching and learning on SPOC | discussion & interaction on SPOC | final score |
|---|---|---|---|---|
|  |  | 51 | 3.08 | 54.08 |
|  |  | 53 | 12.58 | 65.58 |
|  |  | 53 | 23.37 | 76.37 |
|  |  | 53 | 36.75 | 89.75 |
|  |  | 53 | 44.08 | 97.08 |

To optimize students' learning, the marking criteria for each assessment procedure should be transparent and explicit. Therefore, the FA marking criteria are definitely interpreted and informed of all the students during the first period of each semester. Students are expected to be actively involved in the whole learning process and be aware of the importance of the FA in their entire evaluation. The FA score book is shown in Table 5.

**Table 5.** The FA score book

| formative assessment index | | score | index weight | final score |
|---|---|---|---|---|
| autonomous listening | 15 hours | | 30% | |
| | 8 units | | 30% | |
| | 2 tests | | 40% | |
| oral English | weekly oral report& group performance | | 50% | |
| | oral English test | | 50% | |
| assignments | assignments on Rain-class room | | 34% | |
| | assignments on Pigai APP | | 66% | |
| class performance | SPOC preview | | 50% | |
| | class attendance rate teacher-student interaction in-class quizzes | | 50% | |

From the above, we can see clearly that the crucial feature of the FA model employed in HFUT lies in its diversified and holistic approach, which not only touches on every aspect of learning process based on the teaching objectives and tasks: autonomous listening, oral English, assignment and class performance, but integrates teacher assessment, peer assessment with digital platform assessment. In addition, the model takes both students' effort and their achievement into account.

## 4 Questionnaire and Findings

Since 2019/2020 academic year, the FA model has been applied in HFUT. The college English teaching group of late designed the questionnaire so as to learn of its implementation effect and make further adjustment and improvement.

The subjects of the questionnaire are freshmen and sophomores in HFUT who are having college English course. All of them come from different majors or departments except for English major. The questionnaire was devised on the Questionnaire Star Website and issued to students involved through QQ and WeChat at random. Finally, 503 students submitted the questionnaire and 503 was effectively received with effective rate 100%. The questionnaire is partly shown in Table 6.

**Table 6.** The simple list of the questionnaire

| Option statistics / Question items | A | B | C | D | E |
|---|---|---|---|---|---|
| 1. Does your English teacher introduce the evaluation approach to college English course at the beginning of each semester? | Yes, briefly | Yes, comprehensively | No, I got it the other way around. | No, I have no idea. | |
| | 25.05% | 73.36% | 0.99% | 0.6% | |
| 2.Are you clear of the marking criteria of each component in the current FA model? | Yes, quite well. | Yes, well. | Yes, basically. | Yes, a little. | No, not at all. |
| | 21.27% | 17.89% | 54.47% | 4.77% | 1.59% |
| 3.Do you think your teacher has performed an objective FA of students by employing supporting platforms of the teaching textbook, app and other digital ones reasonably? | always | frequently | occasionally | seldom | never |
| | 49.3% | 41.75% | 7.55% | 0.99% | 0.4% |
| 4.Do you think your English teacher has performed each component of the FA carefully? | Yes, all of them. | Yes, most of them. | Just so so. | No, not at all. | |
| | 67.2% | 30.42% | 2.39% | 0% | |
| 5.After receiving the FA feedback, you spend ____ time on English learning. | more | usual | less | unclear | |
| | 54.67% | 37.38% | 1.99% | 5.96% | |
| 6. After receiving the formative assessment feedback, you will improve....? | learning method | learning attitude | learning goals. | nothing | |
| | 81.31% | 69.98% | 57.85% | 7.36% | |
| 7. The FA accounts for 50%, do you think it is reasonable? | No, it's lower. | No, it's higher | Yes, it needs adjustments of certain items. | Yes, it is. | |
| | 3.58% | 10.34% | 52.88% | 33.2% | |
| 8.Are you satisfied with the current FA model? | Yes, very much. | Yes, a lot. | Yes, basically | Yes, a little. | No, not at all. |
| | 44.53% | 28.03% | 25.05% | 1.59% | 0.8% |
| 9.Your any suggestions for the current FA model will be appreciated. | Specify the grouping in oral English class and increase the assessment index. | | | | |
| | The model should be more simplified. | | | | |
| | FA should be a step-by-step practice rather than tasks. | | | | |
| | A comprehensive evaluation of students' English level is expected according to what they have done and how difficult it is regardless of forms of the tasks or performance. | | | | |
| | The FA phase should be shorter instead of a whole semester, which may be more helpful for students to highlight everyday learning and accumulation. | | | | |
| | FA should be able to promote students' autonomous learning interest and ability in English. | | | | |

From Table 6, the survey's findings are obvious. Students have a relatively high satisfaction with the FA model, which has been implemented well. 98.41% (Q1 & Q2) respondents are clear about the FA model and marking criteria; Over 90% (Q3) think their teachers have performed an objective FA of students by means of digital platforms and over 97% (Q4) think their teachers have carried out the FA carefully; 54.67% (Q5) said after receiving the FA feedback, they spend more time on English learning and over 92% (Q6) said after receiving the FA feedback, they will improve their learning attitude, method and goals; 86.08% (Q7) think it is reasonable that FA accounts for 50% of the total evaluation and over 97% (Q8) are satisfied with the current FA model.

The current FA model is far from being perfect. Some suggestions (Q9) were put forward by some respondents, which promotes us to conduct one-to-one interviews among students as well as teachers, collect more useful information, and revise the model for mutual benefit. For one thing, the new model is expected to drive students keen on learning and teachers improving instruction; for another, the new model can be operable and easy to follow.

# 5 Conclusion

Aided by internet and digital technology, online teaching and blended teaching in institutions of higher learning in China are becoming a reality. College English teaching appears more complicated, diversified and colorful. Accordingly, its assessment model is supposed to be shifted and adjusted. It's high time for scholars, college English teachers and administrators to reexamine and reflect on some key issues concerning assessment model: what' the objective? what should be assessed? in what way? how to balance the FA and summative assessment? how to integrate the traditional means and digital ones? how to make use of digital feedback data to help learning and teaching? how to monitor teachers' assessment process? Solution to these questions is definitely beneficial to college English teaching.

*College English Teaching Guidelines* deliberately expounded FA, but how to put it into practice remains unsolved. Therefore, researches on FA practices are urgently needed [5]. No doubt, college English teachers in HFUT have spared no effort to attempt FA in spite that problems still exist one way or another. More attempts from different teachers and different universities are welcomed and mutual learning and joint efforts are certain to profit our college English teaching.

**Acknowledgements.** The work was supported by Teaching and Research Project of Anhui Province (2020jyxm1519), Anhui Philosophy and Social Science Project (JS2018AHZS0013), and Postgraduate Teaching and Research Project of Hefei University of Technology (2021YJG006).

# References

1. The Steering Committee of College Foreign Language Teaching. College English Teaching Guidelines. Chinese Higher Education Press, Beijing, China (2020)

2.  Scriven, M.: The methodology of evaluation. In: Tyler, R.W., Gagné, R.M., Scriven, M. (eds.) Perspectives of Curriculum Evaluation, vol. 1, pp. 39–83. Rand McNally, Chicago, IL (1967)

3.  Bloom, B.S.: Some theoretical issues relating to educational evaluation. In: Tyler, R.W. (Ed.) Educational Evaluation: New Roles, New Means: The 63rd Yearbook of the National Society for the Study of Education (part II) (Vol. 69(2), pp. 26–50). University of Chicago Press, Chicago, IL (1969)

4.  Yang, H., Wen, Q.: Dynamic patterns of goals in real-time formative assessment in foreign language classrooms.(目标在外语课堂即时形成性评估中的动态变化特征及方式). Foreign Language Teaching and Research (bimonthly), (3), 389–400 (2014)

5.  Yuan, S., Shu, D.: Formative assessment studies in foreign language teaching in China: Review and reflection (我国外语教学中的形成性评价研究: 回顾与思考). Foreign Language Learning Theory and Practice. (4), 51–56 (2017)

6.  Li, Q., Kong, W.: A validation framework for formative assessment in EFL teaching (外语形成性评估的效度验证框架). Foreign Language Learning Theory and Practice (1), 24–31 (2015)

7.  Gu, Y., Li, J.: Validity in formative assessment (形成性评估的效度). Foreign Language Education in China. (3), 34–41 (2020)

8.  Wen, Q.: Formative assessment of the course on reading and evaluating research papers: Theory and practice (《文献阅读与评价》课程的形成性评估: 理论与实践). Foreign Language Testing and Teaching (3), 39–49 (2011)

9.  Zhang, L.: Exploring the model and effect of formative evaluation for teaching academic communications in English (学术英语交际课程形成性评估模式及效果研究). Foreign Languages in China (2), 72–80 (2017)

10. Xu, Y., Zhang, Y.: Applying formative assessment to the teaching of English for academic purposes (形成性评估在学术英语教学中的应用). J. Xi' an Int. Stud. Univ. (1), 61–66 (2020)

11. Jin, Y.: College English testing and assessment: current practices and future developments (大学英语评价与测试的现状调查与改革方向). Foreign Language World (5), 2–9 (2020)

12. Wang, D.: Validity study of the college English evaluation system (大学英语评价效度研究). Foreign Languages in China (2), 13–20 (2010)

13. Zhou, P., Qin, X.: The application of formative assessment in multimedia computer-assisted language learning (形成性评估在大学英语网络教学中的应用). Technology Enhanced Foreign Languages (5), 10–14 (2005)

14. Yang, M., Liu, J.: Exploration of college English teaching practice based on formative assessment (基于形成性评价的大学英语教学实践探究). Technology Enhanced Foreign Languages (6), 97–102 (2019)

15. Tao, Q.: A study of the formative evaluation reform for academic performance of college English learning (大学英语学业成绩形成性评估改革调查研究). Technology Enhanced Foreign Languages (8), 81–85 (2019)

16. Wang, H., Fu, C.: The review of research on formative evaluation in foreign language teaching (形成性评估在外语教学中的应用研究综述). Foreign Language World (4), 67–72 (2006)

17. Black, P., William, D.: Inside the black box: raising standards through classroom assessment. In: The Phi Delta Kappan, vol. 80, No. 2, 139–144, 146–148 (1998)

18. Black, P., William, D.: Developing the theory of formative assessment. Educ. Assess. Eval. Account. (2), 1–40 (2009)

19. Wang, S.: On the Revision of "College English Curriculum Requirements" (进一步推进和实施大学英语教学改革—关于《大学英语课程教学要求 (试行) 的修订》). Foreign Languages in China, (1), 4–10 (2008)

# Developing Translation Abilities Through Knowledge-Network-Based Translator Training

Yingyi Zhuang[1]($\boxtimes$) and Shuangshuang Zheng[2]($\boxtimes$)

[1] The Chinese University of Hong Kong, Shenzhen, Shenzhen 518100, China
zhuangyingyi@cuhk.edu.cn
[2] Hefei University of Technology, Hefei 230009, China
335294975@qq.com

**Abstract.** While the popularity of translation technology in professional workflows as well as translation teaching and learning brings translation productivity, it also undermines the development of translators' own translation abilities to some extent, which happens to be the core competency that distinguishes a good translator in the marketplace, even in the age of artificial intelligence. This paper attempts to bring the focus of translator training back to translation abilities development. It carries out a case study at The Chinese University of Hong Kong, Shenzhen among undergraduate translation students using a knowledge-network-based translator training platform called *Textwells* for self-learning, putting the acquirement of knowledge and analytical skills in priority, and then conducts an in-depth analysis of students' work to assess their learning outcomes. The paper may be of interest to translator educators looking to cultivate students' translation skills and enhance their lifelong learning abilities with the assistance of machines rather than produce assembly line workers purely dependent on machines in the technology era.

**Keywords:** Translation Abilities · Self-Learning · Textwells · Knowledge-Network-Based Translator Training

## 1 Trends and Problems in the Current Translation Industry and Translator Training

In the era of big data and artificial intelligence, the use of translation technology, such as computer-aided translation, translation memory and machine translation, etc., is becoming much more common in the translation industry. The rise of translation technology has greatly bolstered the development of the industry through rapidly elevating productivity. However, while a large number of translated texts are entering the big data world and becoming part of translation memory, new risks and challenges also emerge. Studies have shown that although machine translation keeps improving, the quality of machine translation is still far from satisfactory when it comes to complicated texts, such as literary works featuring linguistic and stylistic diversities. The low-quality literary translation may discredit the original author, cause harm to readers, especially considering the negative impact the widespread non-standard language usage might have on

The original version of this chapter was revised: the description for figure 7 needs to be revised and one citation and corresponding reference are missing. This was corrected. The correction to this chapter is available at https://doi.org/10.1007/978-3-031-33023-0_51

© The Author(s), under exclusive license to Springer Nature Switzerland AG 2023, corrected publication 2023
C. S. González-González et al. (Eds.): ICWL 2022/SETE 2022, LNCS 13869, pp. 513–524, 2023.
https://doi.org/10.1007/978-3-031-33023-0_48

children who are still in the early phase of language learning, and hinder the cross-cultural communication of literary ideas [1]. It is also pointed out that the prevalence of translation technology has, to some extent, weakened and marginalized translators' skills while reducing diversity, creativity and even further development of language by suggesting reused and simplified language expressions in order to avoid heterogeneity and contingency [2].

Similarly, influenced by the big data and artificial intelligence fad, teaching and research regarding courses of Computer-Aided Translation, Translation Technology, Terminology Management, and Project Management have become increasingly popular in recent years. The teaching mode mainly adopted in these courses is to introduce different kinds of software and train students on the use of the software [3–12]. This kind of teaching mode is often limited to technical training, and its pairing assessment scheme tests students' proficiency in software use rather than their comprehensive translation knowledge and skills. While project-based translation teaching collaborated with translation companies like YiCAT and Transn allows students to experience in-house translation processes via professional translation software, it does not explain any translation methods or strategies to students. The fundamental pillar of translation—language and knowledge abilities is almost conveniently neglected during the training process. The should-be priority of translation teaching in these courses—promoting students' translation skills with the assistance of machines seems to yield to improving machine translation's accuracy and efficiency, reducing students to assembly line workers who are overly dependent on machines and who are as such unable to produce a quality translation as machine-independent translators.

Compared with mechanically reciting or using "that" or "what" given by either a translation memory or a teacher as if there is only one translation answer, knowing "how" and "why" matters more for a translator. The abilities to understand, analyze and translate texts are basic skills for translation and are still vital to becoming qualified translators even in the technology era. The study aims to help students sharpen language skills and develop independent translation abilities through a knowledge-and skill-centered self-learning project to solve the teaching deficiency of putting technical abilities before translation skills prevalent in today's translation courses. Specifically, we introduce a translator training platform to an undergraduate practical translation course, observe students' self-learning progress and evaluate their learning outcomes.

## 2    Textwells and Its Applications

*Textwells* (see Fig. 1) is a corpus-based translation and bilingual learning platform. The platform consists of six modules: learning space, exercises, course management, data analysis, Q&A, and favorites. The learning space is the core module that features a systematized knowledge network based on six levels of knowledge linked with linguistic characteristics, cultural phenomena and translation methods—word, sentence, information, text, rhetoric and intertextuality. Each level contains key knowledge nodes that describe common translation phenomena and processes and are rigorously defined and systematically classified on the basis of linguistic and translation theories. So far, a total of 56 knowledge nodes have been summarized by the platform (see Fig. 2).

The examples of the knowledge nodes are given and can be linked to texts from which they are retrieved. These annotated parallel texts together form an extensive bilingual corpus covering literature, news, business, public administration, etc. Apart from the knowledge nodes and the corpus, the learning space also has topical boards which share summaries of translation and linguistic knowledge from the six levels. The exercises module helps to measure student users' learning outcomes, and other modules help to enhance interactive learning processes. The platform's data mining and analysis function can automatically track user activity, produce a detailed, individualized picture of each user, and navigate users directly to the knowledge nodes through an intelligent relevance and recommendation system.

**Fig. 1.** Textwells: A Snapshot

Since its launch, *Textwells* has been tried out in several universities in China to aid translation teaching and learning, and relevant pedagogical research has also been conducted to explore teaching models, course designs and learning strategies paired with the platform, test their feasibility and effectiveness, and offer suggestions for improvement. For instance, Mu and Yang experimented with a teaching and learning model for the application of *Textwells* and received positive feedback and learning outcomes from student users [13]. Taking the literary translation course as an example, Tian and Zhu showed how to integrate *Textwells* into the specific course design and teaching procedures, and their exploration has helped to systematize literary teaching while promoting learner initiatives and translation competence [14]. In another study, through a close examination of the collaboration between five universities on the Textwells-based online teaching design during the COVID-19 pandemic, Mu and Yang demonstrated the

| Level | Knowledge Nodes |
|---|---|
| Word | Function Word Addition, Function Word Omission, Function Word Repetition<br>Notional Word Addition, Notional Word Omission, Notional Word Repetition<br>Word Class Alteration, Semantic Matching, Terminology Matching |
| Sentence | Tense Addition, Tense Alteration, Tense Omission<br>Modification Alteration, Mood Alteration, Positive-Negative Alteration<br>Rank Alteration, Sequence Alteration, Voice Alteration<br>Sentence Component Addition, Sentence Component Alteration<br>Sentence Component Distribution, Sentence Component Merging<br>Sentence Component Omission, Sentence Component Repetition<br>Syntactic Matching |
| Information | Information Addition, Information Distribution, Information Merging<br>Information Omission<br>Focus-Topic Alteration |
| Text | Textual Content Addition, Textual Content Distribution<br>Textual Content Merging, Textual Content Omission<br>Cohesive Device Alteration, Left Branching-Right Branching Alteration<br>Logical Relation Alteration, Perspective Alteration<br>Textual Progression Alteration, Viewpoint Alteration<br>Logical Relation Retention |
| Rhetoric | Rhetorical Device Addition, Rhetorical Device Alteration<br>Rhetorical Device Omission, Rhetorical Device Retention |
| Intertextuality | Allusion Addition, Allusion Alteration, Allusion Omission, Allusion Retention<br>Background Knowledge Addition, Background Knowledge Omission<br>Image Alteration, Image Retention<br>Context Matching, Intertextuality Matching, Register Matching |

**Fig. 2.** List of Knowledge Levels and Knowledge Nodes

effectiveness of such inter-institutional collaborative teaching and discussed its prospects in online translation education [15].

Since this comprehensive platform is proved helpful in translator training, the trial version of *Textwells* has been introduced to several undergraduate translation courses at The Chinese University of Hong Kong, Shenzhen. The biggest highlight of the platform is the massive knowledge network encompassing common aspects concerning specific linguistic and cultural features found in either the source text or the target text and concrete transfers between the two texts, applicable to various text types in all fields. Once students master the knowledge network, they can better understand patterns, procedures, methods and strategies involved in the translation process and can, as a result, apply the methods and strategies and navigate the translation process more efficiently in producing their own translations, which are the essential abilities that a good translator should possess.

## 3 Self-learning in News Translation: A Case Study

The case study is centered on students' self-learning outcomes of using *Textwells* in one of the undergraduate practical translation courses—news translation at The Chinese University of Hong Kong, Shenzhen. The course adopts a teaching model that combines classroom teaching with supervised online self-learning to guide students' learning of the knowledge nodes from the six levels. The students' learning outcomes are examined through an assignment that could test their mastery of the knowledge nodes.

## 3.1 Teaching Objectives

The course studied is a major elective course initially developed for undergraduate translation students in their sophomore year or above at The Chinese University of Hong Kong, Shenzhen. It aims to familiarize students with the production and translation of news, and to develop and reinforce students' skills required for news translation between English and Chinese.

Upon completion of the course, students are expected to:

(a) understand the language, structure and style of different news genres;
(b) enrich their vocabulary and relevant knowledge of journalism;
(c) acquire basic skills for analyzing and translating different types of news texts;
(d) perform tasks pertaining to the writing and translation of international news; and
(e) understand the working procedures and norms of newswriting, news transediting and translation in different types of news organizations.

As shown from the expected learning outcomes, it is clear that language, analytical and translation skills are highly valued in the course. Even in the era of artificial intelligence when translation technology has provided relatively mature tools for translation, language is still the basis of translation, and therefore, translation learners, especially undergraduate translation majors, should be able to look into the minute language details and dissect texts with keen observation and a logical, consistent and knowledge-informed approach before they can start to translate and translate well. The knowledge network established by *Textwells* happens to provide students with such an approach.

Based on this pedagogical perspective, in the fall and spring semesters of the academic year of 2019–2020 and the fall semester of the academic year of 2020–2021, a total of 112 students enrolled in the news translation course were invited to the trial use of *Textwells* for after-class self-learning. It is expected that after a semester's learning, the students will be able to master the knowledge nodes, take an analytical and critical view of the translation process and build an acute sensitivity towards texts.

## 3.2 Teaching Model

The present teaching model (see Fig. 3) used in the news translation course is designed to combine classroom teaching with supervised online self-learning, with the latter as the dominant mode. The whole learning process consists of three sequential components: pre-class learning, in-class analysis and discussion, and after-class reading and exercise. First, students are asked to preview key knowledge nodes relevant to each week's lecture topic and content. In class, the teacher weaves the explanation of that week's knowledge nodes into the analysis of specific texts where examples of relevant knowledge nodes can be found. After class, students are required to closely read specified bilingual texts with annotations, which are meant to deepen their understanding of linguistic and cultural specificities as well as translation methods and strategies used in the texts. In the hope that students can consolidate and apply the knowledge they have just learned, they are assigned a translation practice each week, which will be reviewed and discussed later in tutorials.

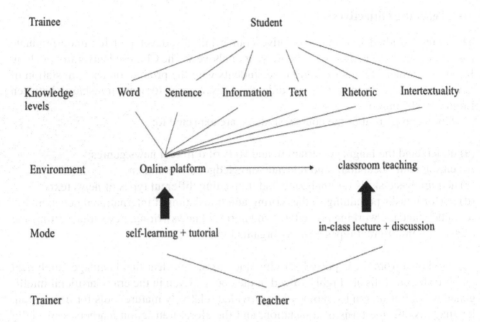

**Fig. 3.** The Teaching Model Used in the News Translation Course

One of the highlights of *Textwells* is its powerful artificial intelligence and data mining (AI & DM) functions. While students are self-learning on the platform, their activities are all automatically recorded and analyzed by the AI & DM system. From the students' side, after a period of study is completed, a series of recommendations of relevant knowledge nodes, knowledge node combinations, exercises and texts will be made to students based on their individual learning history and exercise results. As for teachers, they will be able to track students' learning activities and progress through visual background data generated by *Textwells* (see Fig. 4) and give prompt suggestions based on students' learning traces.

Throughout the news translation course, the teacher arranges the teaching content of each week sequentially according to the six knowledge levels. During the corresponding teaching period for each knowledge level, the teacher gives suggested self-learning tasks targeting knowledge nodes, examples, texts, exercises and topical boards for that knowledge level at the end of the classroom teaching session. By the end of that teaching period, the teacher checks each student's learning activities from backstage to see whether the suggested learning task is accomplished. The learning data is then accumulated, analyzed and summarized to understand students' learning interests and difficulties. Based on these observations and results, the teacher sometimes adjusts the teaching plan by adding further explanations of key knowledge nodes the students fail to understand correctly in the tutorial session. It is guaranteed that even self-learning is not randomly handled but effectively supervised.

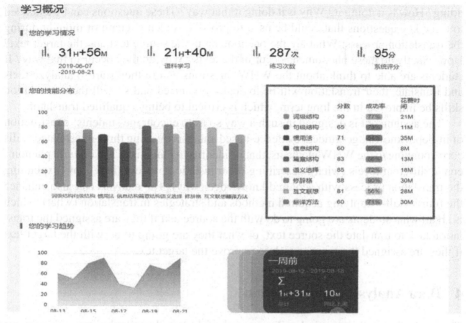

**Fig. 4.** Learning Data of a Student User (Sample)

## 3.3 Assignment Design

For the three semesters, students are all given an assignment about conducting an in-depth analysis of three news examples to examine their self-learning effects. During this process, students are expected to put their emphasis on the analysis of linguistic and cultural details as well as methods and strategies used in the translation process. The instruction for the assignment is as follows:

> Please give three news translation examples (sentences or paragraphs) and analyze them by applying the knowledge node framework from *Textwells*. The target text could be a given translation, your improved version of a given translation, or your own translation. At least three knowledge nodes of three categories should be identified in your examples.

As pointed out earlier, it is more important for students to know "how" and "why" than simply accepting "that" or "what" given by translation memories or teachers so that they can become independent and make good translation choices or decisions on their own. The so-called 6Ws—what, who, when, where, how and why are six basic elements that build up a story, introduce a case or organize an event. In both text analysis and writing, people are usually reminded to take the 6Ws into consideration since these elements tell readers the worthiest information of a text. Among them, the WHW—what, how and why, describes a series of prompts that could be aimed at a single word, a passage, or an entire text and that could be used to scaffold the mechanics of thinking, writing and translation. It effectively seeks to prompt students to answer: What is the text doing? How is it doing it? Why is it doing it that way? These questions can be extended to three key questions that could be used to provoke students' chain of thought during the translation process: What are the phenomena in the source text and the target text? How exactly do these phenomena occur in the texts? Why do they occur in that way? If students are able to think about the WHW questions before they start to analyze texts and translate, their translation will be logically organized and so will their translation skills be improved in the long term, which is critical to being a qualified translator.

The assignment is designed in such a way so as to encourage students' construction of in-depth knowledge-guided, evidence-based analysis by using three interrelated skills corresponding to the WHW elements, that is, identifying linguistic and cultural phenomena at different levels (what), describing the translation process (how), and explaining the translation process with acquired knowledge (why). The analysis can also enhance the fourth skill—applying acquired methods and strategies in translation (what), which is about what students are going to do with the source text if they are assigned the translation task to translate the source text, or what they are going to do with the target text if they are assigned the revision task to improve the target text.

## 4   Data Analysis and Discussion

The study first collects and classifies a total of 112 students' submitted assignments across three semesters, and then analyzes their work through quantitative and qualitative approaches.

### 4.1   Quantitative Analysis of Students' Assignments

In the quantitative analysis, both numbers and corresponding percentages of the knowledge nodes mentioned in the students' assignments are counted. According to the statistical results of the 112 assignments (see Fig. 5), all six knowledge levels were covered in students' analyses. It is found that most students focus more on the knowledge nodes from the word level and the sentence level. The students have identified 569 knowledge nodes in total, among which, 25.83% are from the word level, 27.59% from the sentence level, 15.11% from the information level, 12.48% from the text level, 11.78% from the rhetorical level and the intertextuality level accounts for the lowest, only 7.21%.

It is obvious that the knowledge nodes from the word level and the sentence level are considered easier to understand, assimilate and analyzed, and they are also much more common in texts, which explains why they are favored by students in giving examples. In contrast, knowledge nodes from the intertextuality level are comparatively more abstract and difficult to understand, and examples of such knowledge nodes cannot be as easily found as the knowledge nodes at other levels, which explains its fewest occurrences in students' assignments.

Specifically, Fig. 6 demonstrates the knowledge nodes with the highest and lowest frequencies from each knowledge level. Word class alteration, the most common way of translation transfer, dominates in the students' assignments, with a percentage of nearly 10%. Function word repetition, image alteration, and image retention are not mentioned at all in the 112 assignments. Taking a close look at the definitions of the three

| Knowledge Level | Number | Percentage |
|---|---|---|
| Word level | 147 | 25.83% |
| Sentence level | 157 | 27.59% |
| Information level | 86 | 15.11% |
| Text level | 71 | 12.48% |
| Rhetorical level | 67 | 11.78% |
| Intertextuality level | 41 | 7.21% |
| Total | 569 | 100.00% |

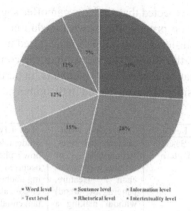

**Fig. 5.** Overview of the Knowledge Nodes Analyzed by Students

**Highest**

| Knowledge Level | Knowledge Node | Number | Percentage |
|---|---|---|---|
| Word level | Word Class Alteration | 54 | 9.49% |
| Sentence level | Sequence Alteration | 33 | 5.80% |
|  | Voice Alteration | 33 | 5.80% |
| Information level | Information Addition | 31 | 5.45% |
| Text level | Logical Relation Alteration | 19 | 3.34% |
| Rhetorical level | Rhetorical Device Omission | 34 | 5.98% |
| Intertextuality level | Background Knowledge Addition | 10 | 1.76% |
|  | Context Matching | 10 | 1.76% |

**Lowest**

| Knowledge Level | Knowledge Node | Number | Percentage |
|---|---|---|---|
| Word level | Function Word Repetition | 0 | 0 |
| Sentence level | Modification Alteration | 1 | 0.18% |
|  | Tense Omission | 1 | 0.18% |
| Information level | Information Merging | 9 | 1.58% |
| Text level | Perspective Alteration | 1 | 0.18% |
|  | Viewpoint Alteration | 1 | 0.18% |
|  | Textual Content Addition | 1 | 0.18% |
| Rhetorical level | Rhetorical Device Alteration | 4 | 0.70% |
| Intertextuality level | Image Alteration | 0 | 0 |
|  | Image Retention | 0 | 0 |

**Fig. 6.** Frequencies of the Knowledge Nodes Analyzed by Students

knowledge nodes, we could find some possible reasons behind their absence in students' examples. Function word repetition is about repeating function words, including articles, prepositions, interjections, conjunctions, grammatical auxiliary words, etc., to create rhythm, parallelism, emphasis, echo, and so on in order to make the expression vivid. Cases of this kind of translation method are more commonly seen in literary texts than in news texts. Similarly, image alteration and image retention, are both associated with the abstract, figurative use of language, often found in literary texts, too.

## 4.2 Qualitative Analysis of Students' Assignments

As discussed in 3.3., when analyzing and translating a text, students should consider the three WHW questions. In answering these questions, they have practiced translation skills at the three levels—identifying linguistic and cultural phenomena (what), describing the translation process (how), and explaining the translation process (why).

It is expected that students can offer suggestions for the improvement of the target text or even propose their own translations, through which they can step further onto the fourth-level skill—applying acquired translation methods and strategies (what). Therefore, the study closely examines the content of students' assignments by looking at the "what-how-why-what" elements, in particular, whether the three WHW questions were considered and answered in their analyses and whether the last W task was also fulfilled.

| Level | Level One: What | Level Two: How | Level Three: Why | Level Four: What |
|---|---|---|---|---|
| Basic Pattern | Student describes, summarizes, or restates a phenomenon (feature, pattern or trend) without making a connection to any unobservable or critical parts. | Student describes how a phenomenon occurred, addressing unobservable or critical parts tangentially. | Student traces a full causal process for why a phenomenon occurred, using ideas with observable and critical parts to explain the phenomenon. | Student figures out a way to deal with a phenomenon after thoughtful consideration based on knowledge and experience. |
| Translation Analysis Pattern | Student identifies a knowledge node without further explaining how the knowledge node is used and why it is used. | Student describes a translation phenomenon or translation process at the surface level. | Student explains a phenomenon or translation process by quoting *Textwells* and other different sources of references. | Student proposes suggestions or his or her own translation version, giving rigorous knowledge-based justification. |

**Fig. 7.** "What-How-Why-What" Elements

The above figure (Fig. 7) outlines the basic patterns of "what-how-why-what" at the four levels (partially based on Thompson et al. 2009 [16]) and summarizes the students' translation analysis patterns from their assignments. It is found that the majority of the 112 students (74.11%) could take the WHW questions into consideration and employ the corresponding three skills. However, a few students (8.93%) stayed at the first level of "what," only identifying the knowledge nodes in the examples. Meanwhile, 16.96% of the students were able to activate the fourth skill by offering their suggestions for the given target text, or offering their own translations and comparing different target texts.

## 5   Findings and Conclusions

Translation abilities are the core competency that makes a translator stand out in the wave of machine translation instead of being drowned by it in the artificial intelligence era. This study showcases in detail the way of applying *Textwells*, a knowledge-network-based translator training platform, in a news translation course, and explores students' learning outcomes. It takes a minimalist view of the translation abilities, defining it in terms of four interrelated skills—identifying linguistic and cultural phenomena at different levels (what), describing the translation process (how), explaining the translation process (why), and applying acquired methods and strategies in translation (what).

Through the analysis of students' assignments, it is found that most knowledge nodes have been covered in the students' examples. To be specific, knowledge nodes that are simple, common, easy to understand and detect were more likely to be included in their analyses, while knowledge nodes that are complex, abstract, and difficult to understand, find or identify occur least frequently in their analyses. Most students can not only identify the knowledge nodes, but also describe and explain the translation process in detail. A number of students can even use the translation methods and strategies they have learned from the platform to improve given translations or propose new translations.

The results show that the knowledge-network-based platform is helpful for students to consolidate their translation knowledge and strengthen their translation skills. It also proves that the present teaching model of self-learning supplemented with supervision and teaching used in the news translation course is a feasible and effective practice for the application of *Textwells*. In the future, this teaching model can be replicated in more translation courses to promote translation teaching and self-learning aiming at developing students' core translation abilities, and more research can be conducted to test its general applicability and bring forward new teaching designs.

**Acknowledgements.** The work was substantially supported by the Teaching Innovation Grant of The Chinese University of Hong Kong, Shenzhen, 2022 (Project No. I10120220284) and the 2022 Guangdong Tertiary Education Teaching Quality & Reform Project (2022 年度广东省本科高校教学质量与教学改革工程项目).

# References

1. Taivalkoski-Shilov, K.: Ethical issues regarding machine(-assisted) translation of literary texts. Perspectives **27**(5), 1–15 (2018)
2. Lan, H.: On the ethicality of translation technology (关于翻译技术伦理性的思考). Shanghai J. Trans. **4**, 8–13 (2019)
3. Alcina, A., Soler, V., Granell, J.: Translation technology skills acquisition. Perspectives **15**(4), 230–244 (2007)
4. Austermuehl, F.: Future (and not-so-future) trends in the teaching of translation technology. Revista Tradumàtica **11**, 326–337 (2013)
5. Declercq, C.: Crowd, cloud and automation in the translation education community. Cultus **7**, 37–56 (2014)
6. Doherty, S., Kenny, D.: The design and evaluation of a statistical machine translation syllabus for translation students. Interpret. Trans. Train. **8**(2), 295–315 (2014)
7. Lu, L., Mu, L.: Computer-aided translation technology and translation teaching (计算机辅助翻译技术与翻译教学). Foreign Lang. World **28**(3), 35–43 (2007)
8. Wang, H.: The practice of translation technology teaching in the information age (信息化时代背景下的翻译技术教学实践). Chin. Trans. J. **33**(3), 57–62 (2012)
9. Wang, H., Li, D., Li, L.: Translation technology teaching in MTI programs in China: problems and suggestions (翻译专业硕士(MTI)翻译技术教学研究: 问题与对策). Technol. Enhanc. Foreign Lang. Educ. **40**(3), 76–82+94 (2018)
10. Xu, B.: Application of CAT in teaching and researching (CAT与翻译研究和教学). Shanghai J. Trans. **21**(4), 59–63 (2006)
11. Xu, B., Guo, H., Guo, X.: Applications of computer-aided translation: an overview (21世纪的计算机辅助翻译工具). Shandong Foreign Lang. Teach. **28**(4), 79–84 (2007)
12. Xu, B.: CAT: teaching and course offering. (计算机辅助翻译教学—设计与实施). Shanghai J. Trans. **25**(4), 45–49 (2010)

13. Mu, Y., Yang, W.: A teaching experiment on a knowledge-network-based online translation learning platform. In: Popescu, E., Hao, T., Hsu, T., Xie H., Temperini, M., Chen, W. (eds.) Emerging Technologies for Education. SETE 2019. LNCS, vol. 11984, pp. 319–328. Springer, Cham (2020). https://doi.org/10.1007/978-3-030-38778-5_35

14. Tian, L., Zhu, C.: Making connections through knowledge nodes in translator training: on a computer-assisted pedagogical approach to literary translation. Int. J. Trans. Interpret. Appl. Linguist. **2**, 15–29 (2020)

15. Mu, Y., Yang, W.: Knowledge-network-based inter-institutional collaborative teaching of translation. In: Pang, C., et al. (eds.) Learning Technologies and Systems. SETE 2020. LNCS, vol. 12511, pp. 414–419. Springer, Cham (2021). https://doi.org/10.1007/978-3-030-66906-5_39

16. Thompson, J., Braaten, M., Windschitl, M., Sjoberg, B., Jones, M., Martinez, K.: Examining student work: evidence-based learning for students and teachers. Sci. Teach. 76(8), 48–52 (2009)

# 1st Workshop on Hardware and Software Systems as Enablers for Lifelong Learning (HASSELL)

# A Theoretical Framework for Computer Vision Learning Environment

Luigi Laura(✉) and Antonio Miloso

Uninettuno University, Corso Vittorio Emanuele II, 39, 00186 Roma, Italy
luigi.iaura@uninettunouniversity.net,
a.miloso1@students.uninettunouniversity.net

**Abstract.** Nowadays, the World Wide Web gives access to most of the world's knowledge, nevertheless, people require competence to interpret and comprehend most of that knowledge. The Lifelong Learning approach introduces a new way of constantly pursuing knowledge consistently. Nevertheless, learners need to test and carry out projects to reinforce the study of theoretical concepts. Mostly in computer science, where they often need to experiment with large amounts of sensitive data to generalize beyond small training samples. However, in the past years, the European government enacted several regulations concerning privacy after catching up with sectors such as AI and Data Mining. The study illustrates a theoretical framework that includes hardware and software characteristics to avoid privacy violations and comply with European privacy regulations. The resulting framework could be applied for learning purposes as well as IoT applications regarding computer vision technologies to ensure correct and compliant communications between different devices.

**Keywords:** Computer Vision · GDPR · Lifelong Learning

## 1 Introduction

Nowadays, the World Wide Web allows access to most of the world's knowledge, nevertheless, people require competence to interpret and comprehend most of that knowledge. During the last years, many people looked to expand their competencies through online services according to Google Trends, probably due to the pandemic period [1].

The Lifelong Learning approach introduces a new way of constantly pursuing knowledge consistently with several new e-learning platforms or other sources of learning that are much more than in the past. Nevertheless, learners, either associated with a formal educational institute or a self-educated individual, need to practice with concepts to better understand them. Thus, they take advantage of a protected environment such as the class, either a physical structure or an online space. However, often those environments do not consider privacy issues. To protect the privacy of individuals, in the past years, the European government enacted several regulations concerning privacy after catching up with the rising speed of innovation in sectors such as AI and Data Mining.

C. S. González-González et al. (Eds.): ICWL 2022/SETE 2022, LNCS 13869, pp. 527–534, 2023.
https://doi.org/10.1007/978-3-031-33023-0_49

Not every educational environment is directed by a tutor. Many learners are self-taught with free available resources that it is possible to find online. Therefore the learning project is designed to take into account more the availability of resources than privacy issues. In computer science, learners often experiment with their sensible data, however, in fields such as computer vision or machine learning, the aim is to be able to generalize beyond the small sample created with personal data.

The study aims to present a theoretical framework that includes hardware and software constraints to avoid privacy violations and comply with European privacy regulations. The resulting framework could be applied for learning purposes as well as IoT applications regarding computer vision technologies to ensure correct and compliant communication between different devices.

The study will deal with the relevant literature regarding computer vision as a field of application of the framework, privacy regulation in Europe as the main issue to consider, and the learning approach the framework depends on to be adopted in education environments. The second part of the study will introduce the theoretical framework describing: hardware suggestions on the suitable technology that we identified as appropriate according to the literature review and software architecture constraints and configuration compliant with privacy restrictions.

## 2  Background

### 2.1  Computer Vision

Over the past 50 years, innovations in the research area of computer vision have been numerous. Progress made on the topics of object recognition and facial recognition are examples of the most diverse application fields such as biometrics, information security, access control, law enforcement and surveillance systems [2, 3].

Thanks to the continuous experimentation in this sector, it is possible to obtain more and more performing results, thanks to the innovations that take place in the field of AI. For example, new models allow more accurate results even with small samples. And improved data collection and data processing techniques improve the data quality used for training, positively affecting the model performance [4–7].

In this way, the field of computer vision benefited from Deep Learning models, new hardware breakthroughs (GPU) and large data availability. Consequently, related areas - such as facial recognition and object recognition - profited, leading to more and more applications in the most diverse fields.

Nowadays, object detection is applied through the smart-city concept to make applications capable of detecting real-time traffic levels, implementing smart schedules for street cleaning, mapping available parking slots and crime activity detection [8–11]. Furthermore, facial recognition technology is widely applied not only for public safety purposes but also for access to restricted areas. For example, in workplaces, by replacing access badges or for passport control. In short, wherever biometric recognition is necessary and also a facial recognition approach since it feels more natural and less intrusive than other identification methods. [2, 11–13].

## 2.2 Privacy Regulation in Europe

The potential applications of surveillance technology poses an ethical problem concerning the privacy of individuals. In democratic countries, politics has worked to create a systemic regulation about data collection to avoid any abuse of these technologies by both the private and public sectors. Following this path, it should be possible to avoid any abuse of new AI techniques to manipulate user behavior, online communication and information exchange. Therefore, in order to realize this vision, the European Community decided that the development of new AI must be carried out using a risk-based framework.

One of the first relevant frameworks was the GDPR (General Data Protection Regulation), approved in 2018. The GDPR represented the concretization of the public concern for the privacy of individuals. After the case of Cambridge Analytica, the awareness regarding those issues grew, so policymakers designed a regulation that could indicate the behaviors to adopt for the data management for companies operating on European territory [14].

The regulatory text begins by giving several definitions of the agents and processes related to the use of data. This step was necessary since the previous European regulations were inadequate in dealing with privacy in a digital context. Nowadays, the privacy discipline operates in a context that is mainly IT and consequently requires a discipline consistent with these new tools.

For example, the "right to erasure" (Art 17) takes up a right already present within the European codes by encoding it in a digital context. Thanks to this right, the data subject can request the cancellation of his data at any time (considering the necessary exceptions). For the data controller, this implies that he must always be aware of where those data are physically located to proceed with the cancellation if requested by the data subject.

Similarly, it is possible to see the application of the "right to restrict processing" (Art. 18–19). Data subjects not only have the right to request the deletion of their data but also to temporarily change the way their data is processed. It is possible to exercise this right if the data subjects believe that the information is inaccurate, is used illegally or is no longer needed by the controller for the purposes claimed. For the Data controller, it means being ready, as in the previous case, to have the data available to proceed with any rectification or erasure of personal data or restriction of the processing.

In addition, with a regulation concerning data management, Europe focuses on the pressing issue of artificial intelligence. During the last few years the advancement in AI is at the center of the evolution of Industry 4.0 [7]. The White Paper on Artificial Intelligence written by the European Commission in 2020 defines the principles that must lead to the following regulations, subsequently inserted in the Artificial intelligence Act in 2021 [15].

Among the themes discussed, there is the intention to promote AI systems that are knowledge-driven and reasoning-based that uphold human principles. Furthermore, characteristics associated with inherently high-risk are identified [16]. It highlights the need to consider the impact of technologies, such as face recognition, on fundamental rights and freedom [17]. In fact, within this text, a position of unconditional rejection is assumed regarding AI-driven biometric recognition for surveillance or to track, assess or categorize human behavior [18–20].

### 2.3 Project Based Learning

Nowadays, there are several possibilities offered to those who intend to learn knowledge in the field of AI. From formal educational institutes, such as schools and universities, to E-learning platforms. Moreover, numerous online resources allow self-taught learning resulting in a lifelong learning process. Lifelong learning is defined as "the constant pursuit of knowledge for reasons that are either professional or personal". In other words, in a reality in which technology evolves rapidly, the learning process never truly stops: it is always necessary to be up to date on new tools or techniques to be competitive within its sector [21].

We are experiencing one of the most relevant periods for development and innovation of AI technology. As mentioned previously, the computer vision sector is experiencing rapid development thanks to the worldwide interest in the use of these new technologies. The consequence is an interest not only resource-oriented (hardware and software) but also competence-oriented. Companies are often looking for figures capable of working with AI technology. However, due to its constantly evolving nature, learning topics such as computer vision or machine learning need lifelong learning.

Practical experimentation must support theoretical knowledge to acquire those skills properly. Thus, prototyping boards are often used in education to teach computer vision. The great advantage of this type of tool lies in a machine dedicated to learning and experimentation to favor Project Based Learning (PBL). Widely applied in engineering, business and medicine, it focuses on carrying out projects during the learning phase. Thus, the learner has to confront problems that stimulate him to seek solutions inside the theory [22, 23].

## 3 Theoretical Framework

After reviewing the relevant literature, in this paragraph, we propose a theoretical framework for didactic purposes about computer vision projects taking into consideration privacy issues.

While experimenting, learners often find themselves with limited regard for privacy regulation since they usually experiment inside a controlled environment. However, when the project reaches a significant dimension, the risk of stumbling upon privacy issues becomes real.

The proposed framework aims to offer a valuable tool to use during projects and experimentation as part of the learning process. To achieve this goal, it is necessary to describe hardware and software characteristics to suit the European privacy regulation.

### 3.1 Hardware

For the hardware configuration, we thought about the Raspberry Pi. It allows practitioners to experiment with hardware configuration thanks to its electronic interface. It is possible to run a machine learning model (according to the resource available). Moreover, recent models have focused on improving the computational capability resulting in a larger model to be executed on this little device [23, 24].

In the academic literature, there are other cases where the Raspberry Pi was used to test computer vision projects inside a didactic environment. That is the case in the didactic experiment of Marot and Bourennane. The researchers investigate the teaching process regarding micro-controllers and digital signal processing applications, using a low-cost single-board computer. They describe a setup for image processing using a Raspberry pi, primarily selected for its low cost but also because it was easy to extract visualizations on the status of both hardware and software components. The results show how learners prefer a practical approach to learning image processing techniques. Furthermore, the tool used in the experimentation results is particularly suitable for new learning techniques [25]. Nevertheless, the experiment does not cover any privacy concerns, probably because it took place in 2017, one year before the GDPR, and perhaps the public wasn't concerned yet with privacy issues.

For computer vision hardware architecture, it is mandatory to consider an optic sensor to capture images. Raspberry Pi Foundation also sells a proprietary camera module often used in prototyping. This solution is widely adopted since exhaustive documentation is provided, just like the prototyping board. Pagnutti et al. extensively reviewed the hardware characteristics of the camera module, finding it appropriate for "scientific applications associated with computer vision, biophotonics, remote sensing, HDR imaging, and astronomy" [26].

Moreover, there are also other valid alternatives if a one-brand solution is not a priority. For example, OpenCV (Open Source Computer Vision Library) launched the OAK-D thanks to a Kickstarter campaign that ended in 2020. It is a spatial AI powerhouse, capable of running models and equipped with two stereo cameras and one 4K camera. This solution provides a state-of-the-art sensor perfect to realize different projects [27, 28].

### 3.2 Software Architecture Constraints

Unfortunately, the software settings of the framework depends whidely by the application and the task that the project aims to accomplish. Thus, we defined only the architecture constraints that should characterize the software setup to avoid any privacy issues.

The AI model must run on the device itself carrying out their tasks autonomously. This concept could seem redundant if dealing with only one device but when several devices are connected through a network, it will be important to know exactly where the information is stored. Since we are dealing with people's images, storing the footage directly on the device allows the user to track where the sensitive information is according to privacy regulation.

Also, the software architecture cannot use any third-party cloud solution since the sensitive data will potentially transit towards unknown servers. Without proper knowledge of the cloud service, privacy concerns are likely to be penalized for the performance of the service itself.

Since the device itself must contain the sensitive data to be stored without moving across the local network, the communication between that device and the network will be handled through API services. Thanks to the API the device will receive inputs which will contain configuration parameters for the model and will return outputs that will share anonymized data.

For example, in the case of a face detection application distributed through a network of devices, each device will perform its own AI model. When one device will have a match it will send an anonymized id to the computer that will associate that id with a profile. In this way the main computer will not have direct access to the footage but in the same way the edge device will not have access to the profile associated with that id.

On the other hand, when it will be necessary to delete sensitive data, because requested by a data subject, the user could send an input through the API to delete specifically the data associated with that data subject id.

The use of artificial intelligence at the edge has been covered extensively in the past few years by academics. The rise of AI models capable of running even on devices with low computing power allowed them to connect different devices deploying the models directly on them [24]. Thus, edge computing was adopted for the different advantages that it could provide to organizations, such as energy cost reduction, great reliability and enhanced security, among other benefits [29, 30].

## 4  Conclusion

The theoretical framework illustrated represents a useful tool to learn and experiment with computer vision applications, providing a suitable hardware configuration compliant with privacy policies.

This study, by its premises, remains a theoretical research and the validity of the framework described will be tested with further studies.

## References

1. Google Trends. https://trends.google.com/trends/explore?date=today%205-y&q=%2Fm%2F01xzx
2. Parmar, D.N., Mehta, B.B.: Face recognition methods & applications. Int. J. Comput. Appl. Technol. (2014)
3. Chen, L.-F., Liao, H.-Y.M., Ko, M.-T., Lin, J.-C., Yu, G.-J.: A new LDA-based face recognition system which can solve the small sample size problem. Pattern Recogn. **33**, 1713–1726 (2000)
4. Heaton, J.: Ian goodfellow, yoshua bengio, and aaron courville: deep learning (2018)
5. Kapoor, A.: Hands-On Artificial Intelligence for IoT: Expert machine learning and deep learning techniques for developing smarter IoT systems. Packt Publishing Ltd., Birmingham (2019)
6. Abadi, M., et al.: TensorFlow: a system for large-scale machine learning. In: Presented at the 12th USENIX Symposium on Operating Systems Design and Implementation (OSDI 2016) (2016)
7. Soni, N., Sharma, E.K., Singh, N., Kapoor, A.: Artificial intelligence in business: from research and innovation to market deployment. Procedia Comput. Sci. **167**, 2200–2210 (2020)

8. Sukel, M., Rudinac, S., Worring, M.: Urban object detection kit: a system for collection and analysis of street-level imagery. In: Proceedings of the 2020 International Conference on Multimedia Retrieval, pp. 509–516 (2020)

9. Xiao, W., Vallet, B., Schindler, K., Paparoditis, N.: Street-side vehicle detection, classification and change detection using mobile laser scanning data. ISPRS J. Photogramm. Remote. Sens. **114**, 166–178 (2016)

10. Balchandani, C., Hatwar, R.K., Makkar, P., Shah, Y., Yelure, P., Eirinaki, M.: A deep learning framework for smart street cleaning. In: 2017 IEEE Third International Conference on Big Data Computing Service and Applications (BigDataService), pp. 112–117. IEEE (2017)

11. Karim, S., Zhang, Y., Laghari, A.A., Asif, M.R.: Image processing based proposed drone for detecting and controlling street crimes. In: 2017 IEEE 17th International Conference on Communication Technology (ICCT), pp. 1725–1730. IEEE (2017)

12. Okumura, A., Komeiji, S., Sakaguchi, M., Tabuchi, M., Hattori, H.: Identity verification using face recognition for artificial-intelligence electronic forms with speech interaction. In: Moallem, A. (ed.) HCII 2019. LNCS, vol. 11594, pp. 52–66. Springer, Cham (2019). https://doi.org/10.1007/978-3-030-22351-9_4

13. Mascio, T.D., Fantozzi, P., Laura, L., Rughetti, V.: Age and gender (face) recognition: a brief survey. In: International Conference in Methodologies and intelligent Systems for Techhnology Enhanced Learning, pp. 105–113. Springer, Cham (2021). https://doi.org/10.1007/978-3-030-86618-1_11

14. Hinds, J., Williams, E.J., Joinson, A.N.: "It wouldn't happen to me": privacy concerns and perspectives following the Cambridge Analytica scandal. Int. J. Hum Comput Stud. **143**, 102498 (2020)

15. Commission E: White paper on artificial intelligence: a European approach to excellence and trust. Com (2020) 65 Final (2020)

16. White Paper on Artificial Intelligence. https://www.eesc.europa.eu/en/our-work/opinions-information-reports/opinions/white-paper-artificial-intelligence

17. FRA: Facial Recognition Technology: Fundamental Rights Considerations in the Context of Law Enforcement (2019)

18. Tiple, V.: Recommendations on the European Commission's WHITE PAPER on Artificial Intelligence-A European approach to excellence and trust, COM (2020) 65 final (the' AI White Paper') (2020)

19. Yeung, K., Howes, A., Pogrebna, G.: AI governance by human rights-centred design, deliberation and oversight: an end to ethics washing. In: The Oxford Handbook of AI Ethics, Oxford University Press, Oxford (2019)

20. Mantelero, A., Esposito, M.S.: An evidence-based methodology for human rights impact assessment (HRIA) in the development of AI data-intensive systems. Comput. Law Secur. Rev. **41**, 105561 (2021)

21. Laal, M., Salamati, P.: Lifelong learning; why do we need it? Procedia Soc. Behav. Sci. **31**, 399–403 (2012)

22. Kokotsaki, D., Menzies, V., Wiggins, A.: Project-based learning: a review of the literature. Improv. Sch. **19**, 267–277 (2016)

23. Jamieson, P., Herdtner, J.: More missing the Boat—Arduino, Raspberry Pi, and small prototyping boards and engineering education needs them. In: 2015 IEEE Frontiers in Education Conference (FIE), pp. 1–6. IEEE (2015)

24. Chen, J., Ran, X.: Deep learning with edge computing: a review. Proc. IEEE **107**, 1655–1674 (2019)

25. Marot, J., Bourennane, S.: Raspberry Pi for image processing education. In: 2017 25th European Signal Processing Conference (EUSIPCO), pp. 2364–2366. IEEE (2017)

26. Pagnutti, M.A., Ryan, R.E., Gold, M.J., Harlan, R., Leggett, E., Pagnutti, J.F.: Laying the foundation to use Raspberry Pi 3 V2 camera module imagery for scientific and engineering purposes. J. Electron. Imaging **26**, 013014 (2017)
27. Rojas-Perez, L.O., Martinez-Carranza, J.: Towards autonomous drone racing without GPU using an OAK-D smart camera. Sensors **21**, 7436 (2021)
28. Perazzo, D., et al.: OAK-D as a platform for human movement analysis: a case study. In: Symposium on Virtual and Augmented Reality, pp. 167–171 (2021)
29. Zhou, Z., Chen, X., Li, E., Zeng, L., Luo, K., Zhang, J.: Edge intelligence: paving the last mile of artificial intelligence with edge computing. Proc. IEEE **107**, 1738–1762 (2019)
30. Giammatteo, P., Valente, G., D'Ortenzio, A.: An intelligent informative totem application based on deep CNN in edge regime. In: Saponara, S., De Gloria, A. (eds.) ApplePies 2019. LNEE, vol. 627, pp. 191–198. Springer, Cham (2020). https://doi.org/10.1007/978-3-030-37277-4_22

# Correction to: Digital Divide, Local and Global? Surveying Augmented Reality Educational Usage in Europe and South America

Matthias Heintz, Effie L.-C. Law, Santawat Thanyadit,
Hernan Nina, and Pamela Andrade

**Correction to:**
**Chapter "Digital Divide, Local and Global? Surveying**
**Augmented Reality Educational Usage in Europe and South**
**America" in: C. S. González-González et al. (Eds.):**
*Learning Technologies and Systems*, **LNCS 13869,**
**https://doi.org/10.1007/978-3-031-33023-0_1**

The original version of this chapter was inadvertently published with an incorrect author name. It has been updated as Hernan Nina.

The updated original version of this chapter can be found at
https://doi.org/10.1007/978-3-031-33023-0_1

# Correction to: Developing Translation Abilities Through Knowledge-Network-Based Translator Training

Yingyi Zhuang and Shuangshuang Zheng

**Correction to:**
**Chapter "Developing Translation Abilities Through**
**Knowledge-Network-Based Translator Training" in:**
**C. S. González-González et al. (Eds.): *Learning Technologies***
***and Systems*, LNCS 13869,**
**https://doi.org/10.1007/978-3-031-33023-0_48**

In the original version of this paper, the description for figure 7 needs to be revised and one citation and corresponding reference are missing. This was corrected.

---

The updated original version of this chapter can be found at
https://doi.org/10.1007/978-3-031-33023-0_48

# Author Index

C. S. González-González et al. (Eds.): ICWL 2022/SETE 2022, LNCS 13869, pp. 535–537, 2023.
https://doi.org/10.1007/978-3-031-33023-0

Printed in the United States
by Baker & Taylor Publisher Services

Printed in the United States
by Baker & Taylor Publisher Services